A HISTORY OF
THE SCOTTISH PEOPLE
1560-1830

A HISTORY OF
THE SCOTTISH
PEOPLE
1560-1830

By
T. C. SMOUT

COLLINS
ST JAMES'S PLACE, LONDON

First published 1969
Second Edition 1970

ISBN 0 00 211326 0
Printed in Great Britain
Collins Clear-Type Press
London and Glasgow

Til Anne-Marie

CONTENTS

7

CONTENTS

CONTENTS

9

CONTENTS

ILLUSTRATIONS

11

ILLUSTRATIONS

PREFACE

When Messrs. Collins first suggested the idea of writing a social history of Scotland since the Reformation, I was filled with feelings of mingled excitement and dismay. The excitement was at the prospect of so challenging a task: the dismay arose from my awareness of the large areas of almost totally unresearched ground lying within the subject, and of the ill-defined character of social history itself.

How far I have succeeded in resolving my problems is open to doubt. My main feeling on completion of the story to 1830 is inadequacy. In some chapters, markedly in the second, my direct debt to other historians will be transparent to all who know the literature, while in other directions so little Scottish secondary work is available to draw upon that I have been able to do little more than to indicate the shape and surface of the problem. Chapter XI on the population increase of the eighteenth century and Chapter XVI on the industrial workforce are typical of these. In some places we may soon know much more than the superficial picture that I have been able to provide —the University of Edinburgh project on Scottish historical demography, for instance, may in time throw new light on this most vital question. In other areas no work of any weight seems to be currently in progress. Perhaps the very inadequacy of what I have written may inspire some in the growing army of Scottish historical scholars to go back to the grass-root records and find out what did happen.

As to the problem of what social history is, I have resolved this in a way unlikely to satisfy the purists. Several chapters of the book are basically about politics, because it seems to me impossible to understand the social development of Scotland without a background of political history. In this respect my interpretation of the Scottish political past before 1600 differs in emphasis from that of some recent distinguished writing: I cannot accept the view that late medieval Scotland was not a disorderly place, or that faction and feud in the sixteenth century were no more significant than party strife in eighteenth-century parliaments. It seems to me that there were very considerable differences between the violence implicit in the sixteenth-century situation and the order implicit in the eighteenth-century situation, and that the change is of some moment in Scottish history. Other chapters of the book are about cultural history: here I have frankly compromised and written mainly on what has interested and impressed me, without any

15

serious effort to be comprehensive. It would have been pleasant to have covered much more ground in this direction, and especially to have discussed all those aspects of culture that belonged to the people rather than to an elite—sport, dancing, folk-music and the like. I have tried to indicate in the suggestions for further reading at the end of each chapter where one might follow up some of these interests.

The remainder of the book is mainly about the social organisation and material conditions of life for the Scottish people between the Reformation and the eve of the Great Reform Bill. It is by no means the first book to be written on the subject. H. G. Graham, *The Social Life of Scotland in the Eighteenth Century* (London 1899) was a classic in its day, and is still remarkable. L. J. Saunders, *Scottish Democracy 1815–1840* (Edinburgh 1950) was probably the best and most original work in Scottish history since the war though it is very little known to the general public. Other works, like Marjorie Plant's *Domestic Life of Scotland in the Eighteenth Century* (Edinburgh 1948) are not insubstantial. This work does not seek to replace or to rival them. What I have tried to do is to give the broadest possible picture of a longer period of Scottish history in a way that has not previously been attempted in the hope that it may show certain perspectives.

The illustrations are drawn from a variety of sources, and the following have kindly consented to their reproduction: the National Library of Scotland, the Scottish National Portrait Gallery, the Scottish National Monuments Record, the Scottish Record Office, the Ministry of Works, the British Museum, Glasgow University Library, Edinburgh University Library, Edinburgh Public Library, Kirkwall Public Library, the Earl of Dalhousie, the Earl of Stair, Sir James Hunter-Blair, and the Earl of Eglinton. The provenance is indicated by each individual illustration.

I am grateful to a large number of people for the help they have given me while I was preparing the book. Professor S. B. Saul read virtually the whole of the first draft and made many penetrating and helpful criticisms. The librarians at the National Library of Scotland, like their colleagues in Register House, are so kind and efficient that academic research in Scotland is made a pleasure indeed. Many people to whom I spoke about this or that problem in my research stimulated and aided me, often without knowing it. I thank them all most sincerely. If the book gives pleasure and interest they and I will be amply repaid.

Edinburgh 1968   *T. C. Smout*

N.B. I have taken the opportunity of this reprint to correct a number of factual errors to which colleagues and correspondents have drawn attention. Their help—often extremely painstaking and generous—should make this a more accurate book, and I thank them most sincerely.

Introduction

THE MIDDLE AGES
1050–1560

CHAPTER I

The Birth of the Scottish Nation

1. THE EARLIEST KINGDOM

In 1066 William the Conqueror won the Battle of Hastings. In 1057 the Gaelic prince Malcolm Canmore killed Macbeth in a fight for the Scottish throne near Lumphanan in Aberdeenshire. William's victory gave him command over the richest, the widest and most governable part of the island of Britain. Malcolm's made him king in a land much poorer, more divided and more isolated than England, a country that the Roman invaders themselves had failed to conquer fully or to hold completely. Neither victory seemed more than an episode in squalid royal ambition: only in the perspective of a thousand years did each appear as a turning point in the social development of the two nations.

Malcolm's kingdom was a wild place. Much more than half the land was barren mountain: the great granite complex of the Highlands occupied more than two-thirds of the country north of the Forth-Clyde line. Only in scale was it more formidable than the high barriers of the Southern Uplands and Galloway fronting onto England. Even today after several centuries of systematic land reclamation, some eighty per cent of Scotland's surface is classified as moor, rough pasture or otherwise uncultivable ground. Some of the valleys had great potential fertility, especially in the Berwickshire merse and in Dumfriesshire, along the broad shores of the Forth and Clyde in the waist of Scotland, in parts of Angus and up in the Moray Firth area between Aberdeen and the Black Isle, but to a much greater degree than today even the best of the lower ground was covered with forest, bisected with unbridged rivers and spoiled by shallow loch and bog—'if one takes the modern map of Scotland and considers the enormous number of names which contain an element denoting marsh or bog the wonder is that any room was found at all for permanent habitation'.[1] This environment sheltered an exotic natural fauna which throughout the middle ages included several animals now extinct, such as beaver, wolves, aurochs and wild boar, as well as the more familiar red-deer, roebuck, wild cat, grouse and salmon that still abound. It also sheltered an uncertain number of human beings; it may be guessed about a quarter of a million, but nobody really knows.[2] Virtually everyone lived by some form of agriculture. Pastoral farming, herding rough-haired cattle, goats, and those small brown sheep of which the Soay breed from St. Kilda represents a survival into modern times, inevitably played a larger part in this activity than primitive tillage for bread grains, though in a few very favoured areas on the east side of Scotland the reverse may have been true even a thousand years ago. Here the relative warmth and dryness of the summers and the fertility of the soil tilted the advantage to the ploughman and the sower. In the steep, rain-sodden, peat-covered mountains of the west, however, hunting and fishing were probably then, as they were much later, just as important as agriculture.

The peoples of Scotland do not in these early times seem to have lived in large nucleated villages, except in parts of Lothian where the pattern of settlement was more like that of eastern England than of Scotland. More typically their houses were grouped in small settlements which in the south would have been called hamlets and in Scotland were, later at least, often called clachans or farmtouns. The buildings themselves were of turf or stone, skin or brushwood, and often partly subterranean in their struggle with the Scottish weather. Town settlements of a kind existed on fortifiable rocks, as at Edinburgh, Stirling and Dumbarton, but with little that we would have identified as urban life—there was no coinage until the twelfth century, few sophisticated crafts and evidently no organised trade to the outside world until Malcolm's reign. The only geographical feature in Scotland's favour was the sea, the long fingers of the firths that poked deep into the body of the country and did not so much hinder communication as make it possible. A sea journey might be as dangerous as a land journey, but it was always more direct and much easier to undertake if goods or people had to be moved over any distance.

The people of the country came from five different ethnic groups who had occupied or invaded northern Britain in the Dark Ages. The oldest were an ancient Celtic people, known to their foes as the Picts, whom the Romans had fought and Tacitus described, noticing those features of red hair and large limbs that cartoonists, not without reason, still regard as characteristically Scottish: by 500 A.D. they were confined north of the Forth-Clyde line, their main settlements apparently lying along the eastern side of the country from Fife to the Moray Firth, and marked today by the distribution of Pictish symbol-stones (like those gathered in the wonderful little museum at Meigle in Perthshire) and by placenames carrying the prefix Pit- (like Pitlochry). In the opposite quarter of Scotland, below them to the south-west, were the Britons, who occupied the land of Cumbria stretching all the way from Dumbarton over to Carlisle, and including also a wide area south of the Solway in what is now Cumberland and Westmorland: they were the northern half of the southern Celtic peoples, the 'Ancient Britons' of popular parlance whom the invading Teutonic Angles had pushed back into Wales and Scotland when the Romans withdrew from England. The Angles themselves had swept up from their base in Northumberland seeking more and more fertile land, and in the seventh century had stabilised their main northern settlements in the Lothians. Some two centuries before that another Celtic people calling themselves the *Scotti* had invaded from Ireland and established themselves in Dalriada, or what is roughly modern Argyll: a second branch of the same people invaded Galloway to the west of British Cumbria, and founded there a society which was to have strongly separatist tendencies for many centuries to come. Finally, at the end of the eighth century, the Norwegians had attacked from Scandinavia and settled all the northern and western islands, the shores of the Pentland Firth and parts of the western seaboard from Wigtown to Sutherland: this onslaught, combined as it was with the invasions of other Norsemen in England and Ireland, virtually encircled the older peoples of Scotland and the modern English border counties and cut them off from their Celtic and Teutonic relations elsewhere in the ninth and tenth centuries. Each of the five peoples spoke a distinct language, each was warlike, each was centred in a distinct geographical area. It is true that there had been a certain degree of cultural contact and interpenetration at an early date, so that Anglian crosses may be found today in south-west Scotland and in Fife, and Celtic placenames mingle with

21

Anglian ones in Lothian. Nevertheless it is remarkable that all except the Scandinavians should have been giving allegiance to the same royal house by the time Malcolm reached the throne.

The union of the kingdom had been mainly the work of the *Scotti* in the centuries when the older peoples had been isolated and threatened by the Scandinavians. In 843 their king, Kenneth MacAlpin, had first overcome the Picts and then united his people with them to form a single kingdom of Alba north of the Forth-Clyde line. In or around 971 Edgar, king of English, had given Lothian to the king of Alba; it was rather doubtful if Edgar had the right to do it over the head of the Anglian Earl of Northumbria, but the king of Alba made good the gift in a battle against the southern Angles in 1016. Cumbria was ceded by the same Edgar in 945 in return for help against the Norse, and once again a paper grant became a reality when the Britons of the northern half of Cumbria, the region of Strathclyde that was centred on Dumbarton, accepted a prince of the *Scotti* as their own king. By 1034 the Picts, the Scots, the Lothian Angles and the Strathclyde Britons owed a common allegiance to an Alban king.

The kingdom had therefore a strong Irish-Celtic emphasis, for it had been the men of Dalriada who proved themselves strongest in arms and subtlest in diplomacy. Yet it would be wrong to think of it in any sense as a state, Celtic or otherwise. There was as yet no notion of a law that could be applied to all peoples in all places—until deep into the Middle Ages we hear of the law of the 'Britons and the Scots' that applied only to the Celtic parts, Alba and Cumbria, and of distinct codes for Anglian Lothian and also for Galloway. The law of the Gallovidians survived until at least 1384. Still less did anyone envisage the inhabitants of Scotland as a united or homogeneous people. 'That wicked army', said the English chronicler of the host advancing to the Battle of the Standard in 1138, 'was composed of Normans, Germans, English, or Northumbrians and Cumbrians, of men of Teviotdale and Lothian, of Picts who are commonly called Galwegians, and of Scots'.[3] It lost the battle mainly because the incompetent Gallovidians insisted on fighting in the vanguard, and in its rout the component parts of the army fought together among themselves all the way home. Scotland, in fact, was much less an identifiable state than a confederacy of peoples with distinct characteristics and traditions, each prone to rebellion and to internecine war, held together only by allegiance to the person of the king. Even this was insecure—most of Malcolm Canmore's predecessors died the same violent death as he meted out to Macbeth.

Nothing shows the isolation of Scotland from England and from Europe as forcibly as the position of the church in the period immediately before Malcolm came to the throne. Scotland had first been converted to Christianity mainly by the efforts of Saint Columba and other missionaries, operating from Ireland and also from Northumberland in the sixth and seventh centuries; it had nominally accepted Roman in place of Celtic usages at the start of the eighth century, following the church in the north of England after the Synod of Whitby in 664. Then came the Norse encirclement, and contact with the outside world virtually ceased. The Scottish church developed characteristics of ritual and discipline that were out of line with those practised in England and on the Continent. The clergy, for example, were by no means all celibate, rather through ignorance of what was expected of them by Roman canon law than through moral laxity. Most endowments were in the hands of laymen. The only forms of ecclesiastical art were the beautiful but, to eleventh-century eyes, archaic and insular forms of the Celt. Until Malcolm's great, formidable and religious English queen, Saint Margaret, began to encourage some tentative changes, the Scottish church had remained uninfluenced by the reforming movements that had been sweeping up from the south of Europe since the turn of the first millennium.

Such was the character of Scotland nine centuries ago. The aim of this introductory chapter to a history that does not purport to begin before 1560 is not to give a detailed description of the social life of the Scots in the middle ages, but to ask certain questions about their development as a nation between the middle of the eleventh century and the middle of the sixteenth century. What turned this isolated medley of different peoples into a nation both Scottish and European, proud of its nationality almost to the point of obsession yet contributing to and drawing from the mainstream of European civilisation, and why when the inhabitants had once ceased to think of themselves in terms of Pict, Scot, Gallovidian, Angle, Briton and Norseman did they form themselves anew into the hardly less formidable divisions of Highlanders and Lowlanders which had not been envisaged before? Until this problem is met it is not very easy to discuss the subsequent social history of the Scots.

2. NORMAN LEADERSHIP, 1100-1286

Until the end of the thirteenth century Scotland was ruled by a succession of unusually able kings, the descendents of Malcolm Canmore and Saint Margaret, all of whom held the values of European civilisation more dear than the traditions of Celtic Alba whence they sprang. Malcolm and Margaret themselves introduced southern foreigners into the court: most of these were either expelled or murdered by resentful Alban Celts after the death of the royal couple, but southern influence grew steadily in the reigns of their sons. The youngest and ablest of these, the great David I (1124-1153) came to the throne after spending the better part of forty years at the Anglo-Norman court in the south of England, where he had acquired both a wife and an earldom, that of Huntingdon with lands attached in fourteen counties. He came north with an enthusiastic and adventurous host of followers drawn mainly from these lands and with a strong personal respect and love for the institutions of the Anglo-Norman state founded by William the Conqueror. His grandson, Malcolm IV, was a dedicated successor both to his energies and his enthusiasm: William the Lyon, Alexander II and Alexander III who completed the dynasty were all equally devoted to the foreign ideal, and two of them also had wives from England. Within a generation or so after Malcolm Canmore's death, therefore, the royal house was Norman in blood and heart, 'French in race and manner of life, in speech and in culture' Walter of Coventry called them in 1212.[4] Since Normans everywhere were inheritors of Rome and the European tradition, it is not surprising that the kings should work to give their polyglot kingdom a structure that would tend both to impose uniformity within and to be in harmony with contemporary ideas without. The tools they used were four—the introduction of feudalism, the reform of the church, the plantation of burghs and effective personal control over the machinery of government.

The introduction of feudalism was the most important of all. We know little about the organisation of the native peoples anywhere in Scotland before David's reign, but Celtic society was clearly tribal, based on a real or fancied kinship between every free man and the head

24

of his tribe. The tribes apparently occupied fairly distinct areas of the country, had reached the stage of individual ownership of land among the tribesmen, were organised in social strata (the law of the Britons and Scots mentioned earls, thanes, freemen and carls) and possessed differing tribal laws that were memorised by hereditary wise men who handed them down unaltered to their sons. It would be wrong to imagine either simplicity or uniformity in such arrangements—a primitive society is usually a complex one, and social muddle may have formed one reason why the Norman kings wished to introduce the strict and tidy forms of feudalism. Theoretically, feudalism is the antithesis of tribalism, since it based itself upon territorial units that had nothing to do with kinship or other personal relationships. In a feudal country, all land was royal land: all authority resided in the king. If the king chose to make his nobles a grant of land, he granted with it a measure of responsibility for those dwelling on the land—in feudal jargon, the 'lord' granted his 'vassals' a 'fief'. This took place at a ceremony of homage that made explicit not only that the vassal was a delegate in certain matters of authority and government, and that he was bound to maintain a castle to help the king keep order, but also that the vassal owed very precise services in exchange—usually the duty of arriving armed on horseback with followers in time of war, and of attending his court and council (later his Parliament) when required. The vassal in turn could 'subinfeudate', or grant part of his fief to a subtenant on similar terms: the process could go on for several stages until the peasant was reached at the base of the pyramid, the recipient of no rights other than that of his lord's protection and of permission to cultivate the land, but owing his lord heavy duties in the form of labour services and payment of agricultural produce. The fiefs themselves were hereditary but if heirs should fail the land reverted directly to the lord: similarly, if the heir was a minor, the rights and profits of administration returned to the lord during his minority. All rebellion or disaffection automatically carried the penalty of forfeiture. The whole feudal edifice rose to support the king at its apex as the ultimate lord of all land and the sole fountainhead of all justice. Provided it was controlled by a strong personality at the top, it was an extremely effective way of ruling a diffuse medieval state.

How thoroughly was Scotland feudalised? The initial grants by David I were all to the Normans or Bretons who followed him from England; they were all confined to Lothian and southern Cumbria and to royal estates where the incomers would not intrude upon the native aristocracy. Not until the reigns of Malcolm IV (1153-1165) and William the Lyon (1165-1214) was the policy of feudalism for all begun in earnest. Malcolm systematically colonised British Strathclyde with Normans and Flemings, while William crossed the Forth-Clyde line to do the same in Angus and Perth. The alien friends of the kings ultimately received fiefs even in such remote and Gaelic areas as Aberdeen and Moray.

Increasingly, moreover, the powerful *mormaers*, the Celtic earls who had been the backbone of the indigenous aristocracy in Alba, were brought into feudal relationship with the king. This happened with an element of compromise between the old order and the new. Many of the earls were not required to render the conventional 'knight-service' for the feudal host because by earlier Celtic tradition they already had the duty of calling out a tribal host of their kin and followers in time of war—a duty based in their case not upon homage for the land they occupied but on traditional respect for the blood of the Alban monarch whom they served. Their survival in areas of traditional influence, exercising some of their old functions in the old way, helped the survival of the old Celtic tie of kinship: and as the native aristocrats quickly began to inter-marry with Norman families, respect for this tie spread to the entire ruling class. As Miss Grant put it—'into the purely feudal relationship had crept something of the greater warmth and fervour of the simpler and more ancient bond of union of the clan'.[5]

The kings were not always unopposed in their innovations though opposition to them was fragmentary and disjointed, based on appeals to various traditions but not upon nationalism since nothing that could be called Scotland yet existed on which to base national feeling. There were however elements among the Celts, especially in Moray and Galloway, who rebelled repeatedly against the outsider and his newfangled ideas, and even after their suppression (often with the help of less conservative Gaelic nobles) the mature forms of Norman feudalism remained largely excluded from the fastnesses of the western Highlands, despite the fact that some later charters, such as those of David II purported to grant land in feudal form to chiefs in the west. The truth of the matter was that even knights and castles, the effective teeth of feudalism, could do no more than grip the fringe of this fierce country for the king. Feudalism, therefore, with the Anglo-Norman families that came with it, helped more than anything to obliterate old distinctions in the low country between Angle, Briton, *Scotti* and Pict but because geography checked its penetration into the high north-western third of Scotland, it also helped to create a distinction between Lowlander and Highlander that had hardly existed before. This distinction as we shall see became more obvious when other factors than the purely feudal one helped to emphasise it.

The reform of the church must rank second only to feudalism for the depth of its social impact. Saint Margaret herself had begun it by convening councils of the native clergy and sitting down with them to argue them out of insular observances like the saying of mass by what she called a 'barbarous' rite and the commencement of Lent five days after everywhere else in the Christian world. She had also founded, at Dunfermline where she lies buried, the first Benedictine monastery in Scotland. She staffed it with monks from Canterbury and it was later rebuilt to resemble the great Norman cathedral at Durham. The organisational strength and spiritual discipline of the Benedictine order stood out in a land where monasticism had always been of the disorganised 'desert hermit' type, typified at its best by the unworldly Culdean community on St. Serfs Island in Loch Leven, but at its worst by the many institutions where laymen had taken the title of abbot, diverted the revenue of the church into their own pockets and maintained a few priests to say the offices.

Even at Saint Margaret's death, however, reform had not progressed far and it was left to David I to carry it nearer fruition. One way in which this was achieved was by establishing church government on the organisational basis of the diocese made up of many parishes. Bishops themselves were not new in Scotland: even before Malcolm Canmore's day there had been a 'Bishop of Scotland' centered on St. Andrews and some others apparently without any very permanent territorial assignments. The novelty was in the completeness of the network and the thoroughness of the organisation. By 1200 there were eleven sees covering the whole kingdom. Every bishop ruled a defined territorial area with the help of an archdeacon and rural deans. Every diocese contained a new or a reconstructed cathedral run by a chapter of canons responsible for electing the bishop. Such ruins as those of the majestic cathedral at St. Andrews and of the still more sumptuous building at Elgin express something of the importance attached in the medieval kingdom to the episcopate. Every centre of population

27

(within the feudalised area) probably possessed a new stone church, with an incumbent responsible for the spiritual welfare of the souls in his parish. The contrast with the formlessness of the earlier church, where even the parish was a unit unknown outside Anglian Lothian, was very marked. The reorganised church was a force for unity, since, being everywhere subject to the same Roman discipline and everywhere saying the same unvarying services and preaching the same doctrines, it gave to the diverse peoples of Scotland identical habits of worship and a common spiritual bond in some ways even more pervasive than the bond of feudal society. Once again, however, the bond was weakest in the western Highlands—none of the cathedrals were within the heart of the Highland area, and the ministrations of priests in the enormous parishes of the far west must often have been haphazard in the extreme.

The other means of church reform was by plantation of abbeys. Before 1100 there were very few monastic foundations, good or bad, south of the Forth-Clyde line: a century later such famous houses as Coldingham, Kelso, Dryburgh and Melrose adorned the Border, with others like Dundrennan and Paisley in the west and others still like New-battle and Holyrood in the east. Beyond this line, in old Alba where monasticism had been slaphappy, the Celtic monks were obliged to accept a European rule, and many more new houses came to join them —such as Scone, Lindores, Coupar and Arbroath in Angus, Perthshire and Fife, or Beauly much further north beyond Inverness. But along the wild western coast and in the isles houses were very thin on the ground: only five monasteries and one friary were founded in this region in the middle ages, and none had much reputation.

David's own admiration for Saint Bernard of Clairvaux brought him to encourage in particular Cistercian, Tironian and Premonstratensian monasticism, which laid emphasis on the virtues of hard work and withdrawal from the world. Many of these houses became economic pioneers in the twelfth and thirteenth centuries: the Border abbeys engaged in sheep-farming on an unprecedented scale, Cistercian Newbattle led the way in coal-mining and lead-mining, and arable farming on the granges of Coupar had no peer in the kingdom. The order of Augustinian canons was greatly favoured for new foundations in the neighbourhood of royal palaces and for refoundations of well-meaning Celtic groups judged to be in need of discipline: the Augustinian reputation rested on scholarship, hospitality and fervent preaching. In the late thirteenth and fourteenth centuries fashion switched to the new orders of friars who went out into the world as preachers and confessors rather than remaining at home in monastic seclusion: Dominican, Franciscan and Carmelite houses were therefore mainly situated in the towns like the Greyfriars kirk in Edinburgh. Each type of religious order made its own separate impact, partly spiritual, partly cultural, partly economic. Each type had been introduced from foreign soil, in the first place with English or French monks as the sole inhabitants of the houses, and with the Tironian and Cistercian foundations in particular always retaining the closest links with the ultimate mother-house in France. Just as the diocesan organisation of the secular clergy had ensured conformity with the full Western ecclesiastical tradition, so the introduction of 'regular' monastic clergy grafted new cells of European civilisation into the social body of the Scots.

There were further profound results of this change. For the first time there was an organised body of literate intellectuals in the country, men of one common purpose to whom the location of their dwelling place, whether in the civilised cathedral town and sea-port of St. Andrews or in the wild backwoods of the Border counties, was almost irrelevant. These intellectuals were the most European of all Scots, and from them would be drawn the first to make an impact beyond the Scottish borders. The Scottish scholar became known to European academics sometimes as a colleague, more often as a pupil who would return in the fullness of time to his country.

It was also the churchmen, no doubt partly because of their strong personal links with the monarchy, who contributed more than anyone else to formulating a conscious notion of 'the Scottish people'. It was set on this path by the need to fight early for its own corporate independence. The church beyond the Tweed, having no archbishop of its own until 1472, had no obvious head and was therefore in an ambiguous position. From 1072 onwards the English archbishops of York tried repeatedly to absorb Scotland into their province, but both Scottish kings and Scottish ecclesiastics doggedly refused to have any truck with them, despite considerable pressure from the Papacy itself to make them submit.

Then, in 1192, the Pope reversed his policy owing to a quarrel that he was having with the English kings: the Scottish church was made his 'special daughter', subject only to Rome, and in 1225 he conferred upon it the right to hold independent councils under the presidency of a

Scottish bishop. Here indeed was unequivocal recognition of the Scottish church's distinctive and separate national existence. In the thirteenth century the church became steadily more assertive of its separateness, prepared to defy on occasion the authority of papal legates and to set aside legatine statutes, until, after the outbreak of the Wars of Independence, it was prepared to resist even a papal excommunication of the king. In or around 1310 it gave Robert Bruce a stirring oath of fealty, describing him as 'solemnly made King of Scots . . . with him the faithful people of the Kingdom will live and die'. From a great abbey ten years later came the Declaration of Arbroath, almost certainly penned by its abbot: its sonorous wording expresses all the fierce nationalism of the fourteenth century.

> As long as there shall but one hundred of us remain alive we will never consent to subject ourselves to the dominion of the English. For it is not glory, it is not riches, neither is it honour, but it is liberty alone that we fight and contend for, which no honest man will lose but with his life.

The third tool for the transformation of Scotland was the foundation of burghs. Towns and some trade had existed before the twelfth century, but burghs, in the sense of communities in which merchants and tradesmen (immigrants as well as natives) were granted specific rights to support their purpose of internal and external trade were quite new. David I copied the idea from England. The earliest of which we have clear knowledge were Berwick and Roxburgh, but Edinburgh and Stirling were also significant at a very early date, and the codified laws of these four ultimately formed the basis for the laws and privileges of all the remainder. Aberdeen, Perth and Dundee (with St. Andrews among the episcopal burghs) rose with them to pre-eminence in foreign trade. All these had such a good geographical position that strong urban communities would probably have grown up there without royal grants of privilege. It is important not to exaggerate their size; Froissart writing of Edinburgh in the later fourteenth century called it the 'Paris of Scotland', but said it had not more than 400 houses, and Stirling about 1550 had only 405 male adults.[6] In a rather different category were the numerous small burghs (none of them in modern eyes bigger than small villages) which David and his successors in the twelfth and thirteenth centuries deliberately planted by the side of new royal castles to help civilise and hold in subjection the remoter parts of the realm—Dingwall and Inverness in the far north were two such examples, Ayr and Renfrew in the west two more. Though burghs proliferated in Scotland after 1130, many founded by the king—the 'royal burghs'—others by the church or sometimes by the barons, it was significant that none were settled in the mountains or up the west coast between the Clyde and the Pentland Firth. This region was judged again to fall outside the sphere of effective royal control.

The founding and multiplication of burghs had many social repercussions. The intensification of trade at all levels which took place at the same period and was no doubt stimulated by rising population as well as by urban foundations, brought peasants to the towns to sell skins or wool-fells and to buy iron or salt; town traded with town exchanging the local surpluses of different regions, and the burghs traded abroad to exchange Cistercian wool for French wine or Flemish cloth. This made them a doorway to the European world and the home of a small commercial class of urban men who supported peace and order because war and violence spelt their economic ruin. Again, the uniformity of burgal constitutions imposed a certain unity on Scotland in the same way as that of the monastic house and the parish church. Royal burghs were held in a particular sense to lie outside the feudal system. Not only did they become individually self-governing, but by the end of the thirteenth century there developed a Court of Four Burghs to adjudicate on matters concerning the most important. From this there ultimately grew a convention of Royal Burghs uniting all such communities in a formal assembly in the sixteenth century. Nor did privilege stop at their own walls. Very soon the burgesses (i.e. those inhabitants of the burgh who were qualified merchants and craftsmen) obtained monopolistic rights over commerce within the areas in which their burghs were situated, and by this they drew together very diverse hinterlands into a common commercial practice. The laws relating to buying and selling, to debt and to credit, would not be very different round Dumfries, Inverness, Edinburgh or Ayr. This was another bond for all the Lowland Scots.

Perhaps most important of all, the people within the burghs were never predominantly Celtic or Gaelic-speaking. 'The fortified places and burghs of the Scottish kingdom are known to be inhabited by English' wrote William of Newburgh just before 1200.[7] By this he probably meant that their main tongue was a dialect of English, for we know from lists of burgesses that Flemings and Normans, Englishmen (or at least Angles) and Scandinavians were all settled in the new burghs, and not merely in the larger southern towns like Berwick or Edinburgh but even in the small northern settlements like Inverness and Dingwall. It is not difficult to see why the king wanted them: in their own slightly more advanced societies they had acquired crafts and commercial skills still lacking among the less experienced Celts. It is harder to understand why they bothered to come. Perhaps like Sweden in the sixteenth century and Africa in the nineteenth century, Scotland in the twelfth and thirteenth centuries appeared to be a country of economic promise, poor maybe, but a place where a man with initiative could make a fair living buying and selling among the natives. If the structure of the older Scottish tongue is any guide, Angles and Scandinavians may have been the predominant elements among the immigrants. Few problems in Scottish cultural history are more baffling than why the Celtic language drew back and disappeared from the whole of Lowland Scotland during the middle ages, but a clue seems to lie in the plantation of these little groups of Teutonic aliens up and down the country, who must have involved the common people in their unfamiliar language for so many of the ordinary economic transactions of life.

Fourthly and finally, the Canmore kings furthered the social change simply by being effective monarchs. The machinery of government was developed to supervise the feudal system. Norman Scotland (excluding again the western third of the Highlands and islands) was split into sheriffdoms for civil purposes just as it had been divided into dioceses for ecclesiastical purposes. Each sheriffdom had as its focal point a royal castle; each was under the control of a royal officer, known as the sheriff, who might be either a Norman incomer or a Celtic earl in a new guise. His office was in any case not now hereditary. His functions were diverse—he held a court in the king's name, which in due course came to hear appeals from the jurisdiction of those vassals who held fiefs within the sheriffdom. He was responsible for defence, both in maintaining the royal castle and in leading the feudal host. He was also responsible for collecting rents due to the crown, and on him the king relied for execution of orders sent from the court. Organisation round the court itself also proceeded apace, and among the various household officials the chamberlain and the justiciars emerged with special functions as co-ordinating agents. Both were itinerant. The chamberlain travelled the country visiting the Royal Burghs, uplifting revenue, ascertaining if justice was being done and whether the towns were being lawfully governed: the justiciars travelled through the sheriffdoms with similar aims, supervising the sheriffs and hearing certain types of lawsuit which the crown reserved to itself and tried before a jury. Without responsible control through the sheriffs and the household officers, the cohesion of the feudal system, of the church and of the burghs would often have collapsed.

The king also had the greatest military force in Scotland, and used it both to keep firm control over rebellious subjects and to extend the area of his rule. Nothing but force impelled the allegiance of, for example, Moray and Galloway which were at different times strongly separatist in political tendency. Only an army saved Malcolm IV from the relentless ambition of the Norse-Celtic leader Somerled in 1164 after that remarkable chief from Argyll had broken the power of the Norwegian king in the southern isles and begun to turn his attention to the Norman dynasty. Royal victory over the Scandinavians came in two stages—Caithness was taken in the reign of William the Lyon, but not until after the Battle of Largs in 1263 were the Western Isles formally ceded by Magnus of Norway to the Scottish crown. Even so victory here was largely an illusion, since for a very long time after that it was the descendents of Somerled and not the feudal officials of the king who controlled both the isles and the bulk of the western mainland. But the only total failure of royal arms was the attempt to retain those parts of Cumbria south of Carlisle in Scottish hands. Malcolm Canmore died fighting William Rufus for the lands beyond the Solway, and by the time David I came to the throne English lordship there was an accomplished fact.

How can we summarise the changes that had overtaken Scottish society before 1286 as a result of the operations of the Norman kings? Firstly, Scotland had become a much more European country: all the new and aggressive cultural forces had entered from the south—feudalism, church reform, the burghs, strong central and local government. Secondly, Scotland had become a more united country—everywhere belonging today to modern Scotland except Orkney and Shetland (acquired from the Danes, 1468-9) held the king to be in some sense their overlord, though in the north-western third this lordship was no more than nominal: in the eastern and southern thirds the powerful leavens of cultural change were slowly working on the diffuse peoples of Anglia, Alba, Cumbria, Galloway and Caithness to produce a nation more uniform in law, custom and nationality. Thirdly, the very success of the Normans in the areas where they governed was already working to produce the ultimate rift of Highlander and Lowlander, distinguishing a region of largely Gaelic culture where the king's writ did not run from the increasingly Europeanised zone where the king ruled effectively.

We must be careful, however, of exaggerating the completeness of any change. Scotland was never merely a cultural extension of Anglo-Norman England—the mingling of Celtic sentiments of kinship and the independency of the church prevented that. Nor was Lowland Scotland in the twelfth and thirteenth centuries inhabited everywhere by a people who thought themselves Scots rather than merely subjects of the Scottish king: William the Lyon still addressed his charters to his 'faithful subjects, French, English, Scots, Welsh and Gallovidian'. The idea that some people were 'Highlanders' and some people 'Lowlanders' had not yet been formulated even by such a man as Somerled. The Canmore kings were still pioneers, pressing forward the effective boundaries of their institutions further in one place than in another, more at one time than another, more completely in some ways than in others: the limits of the effectively governed areas shaded off imperceptibly, and Gaelic was probably still the common tongue of most men north of the Forth.

In a sense, thirteenth century Scotland was tripartite. The centre was the medieval diocese of St. Andrews, roughly the area within a line enclosing the Royal Burghs of Aberdeen, Dundee, Perth, Stirling, Edinburgh and Berwick: here wealth was greatest and government most secure. Beyond this lay a belt of great earldoms running from Galloway, across Carrick, the Central Highlands and Moray to Sutherland and Caithness: here forms were generally more Celtic, the strength of government less certain, rebellions more frequent—though seldom prolonged or successful. Beyond that again, the Western Highlands and the Western Isles were a law unto themselves, though nominally subject both to the church and the king. Scotland governed in this way seemed to be set on the safe road to truer unity and greater internal strength: but the second half of the middle ages began with the traumatic experience of the Wars of Independence which, while making the Scots far more conscious of themselves as a nation undid in other ways much of the work of the Norman kings.

3. THE LOWLANDS IN THE LATER MIDDLE AGES

Scotland's political misfortune after 1286 was a double one—she incurred the enmity of England and she suffered too often and too long from weak or helpless kings. War against England was not in itself novel. Malcolm Canmore had invaded the south five times and perished in the last attempt. David I suffered defeat at the Battle of the Standard. William the Lyon was captured at Alnwick. Alexander II endured an English army despoiling Lothian. Yet between 1100 and 1286 war occupied only ten years: it was otherwise an age of peace and even of cordial friendship between the courts of England and Scotland. There had also been little bitterness among the families on either side of the Border; Anglians and Cumbrians spanned the frontier and still felt themselves more Anglian and Cumbrian than English and Scot. Since most of the wars were rooted in Scottish claims to southern Cumbria, most of the invasions were of Scots into England and not vice versa.

After 1286, the relationship between the two countries became quite different. Following the death of Alexander III and that of his heir, the Maid of Norway, Edward I tried to establish the Scottish king as his vassal, and Scotland as a feudal appendage to England: legal argument was eventually backed by an invasion of unprecedented force and terrifying efficiency which set a pattern for future conflicts. Under Robert Bruce, Scottish resurgence and the famous victory at Bannockburn in 1314 checked English pretensions: after his death the massacre of the Scots at Halidon Hill outside Berwick in 1333 revived them. There followed a hundred years of fluctuating warfare in which the Scots strove to evict the English from the southern counties all the way from Haddington to Dumfries, not ending until 1460 when James II fell regaining the castle of Roxburgh. Berwick-on-Tweed, never was permanently regained. Half a century of peace between monarchs then ensued, though it was no longer observed by their subjects along the Border. In 1513 official warfare erupted again with the tragic campaign of Flodden and the death of James IV. After Flodden came another truce, then the Scottish defeat at Solway Moss in 1542, the 'Rough Wooing' and the further defeat at Pinkie in 1547.

What this hostility could on occasion mean was shown by the reports of the Earl of Hertford to Henry VIII in 1544 that he had plundered and burnt Edinburgh, Leith and Holyrood, with Newbattle Abbey, Haddington, Burntisland and Dunbar, taking 10,000 cattle and 12,000 sheep: in 1545 he came again and reported sacking seven abbeys (including Dryburgh and Melrose), sixteen castles, five 'market towns' and no less than 243 'villages'. Devastation on this scale was certainly exceptional, but the endemic fighters on the Borders who cared little for royal proclamations of peace and war had long been used to 'putting man woman and child to fire and sword without exception where any resistance shall be made against you, . . . and extending like extremities and destructions in all towns and villages whereunto ye may reach.' as Henry had directed Hertford in 1544.[8]

War of this bitterness over so long a period had many side effects on Scottish society, but its first and most lasting result was to fuse the Lowlanders into a single people. The wars of the fourteenth century and later were a crucible in which all lost their old racial loyalties and became part of a coherent Scottish nation, assertive, warlike, resilient, patriotic and freedom-loving. 'Scotland was born fighting' was an old saying and a true one: no one can read the language of official documents in the fourteenth century without realising the extent and depth of the new national pride which the wars had called forth.

The other half of Scotland's hardship was the frequent failure of royal government. In the century after the death of Bruce in 1329, two Scottish kings (David II and James I) were kept prisoner in England for a total of twenty-nine years, and the other two (Robert II and Robert III) reigned for a total of thirty-five years with such desperate incompetence that in the words of one chronicler justice herself seemed an outlaw from the kingdom. James I after he emerged from captivity in 1424 was a strong and reforming monarch who did his best to restore the faded prestige of kingship: his reign ended on an assassin's dagger in 1437 and for nearly two hundred years after that every Scottish monarch came to the throne as a child. James II succeeded at the age of six years, James III at eight years, James IV at fifteen years, James V at one year, Mary Queen of Scots at only one week and James VI at one year. Between 1406 and 1587 there were thus nearly one hundred years of minority rule and regency. This extraordinary misfortune meant that no matter how strong some of these later kings were in their majority, in the regency cliques of the nobility manœuvred for control while

France and England tried their hands at internal intervention and anyone with a strong arm and no principles stood his chance for an hour of power.

The first thing that happened in this situation was that the lords secured such privileges that they themselves approached the status of petty kings. Feudalism collapsed as a vehicle for unity, and became instead the vehicle of faction. The sheriff ceased to be a civil servant removable when he failed in his duty: the office usually became the hereditary property of the greatest baron in the sheriffdom. Justiciars serving the king thereafter made less and less attempt to supervise their administration of the so-called royal sheriff courts or royal castles. The vassal's own duty of keeping order in his fief became transmuted into the right to hold 'baron courts' where more and more offences were tried without genuine appeal to the crown: ultimately these came to include not only all disputes between landlord and tenant (where the lord was naturally happy to act as both plaintiff and judge) but also many cases involving capital punishment, the jurisdiction of 'pit and gallows'. Then many of the greatest lords obtained in the fourteenth century heritable grants of 'regality', which legally recognised them as having all the rights of the king himself over extensive territories; royal servants and royal writs were formally excluded from such an area, and the court of regality was declared competent to hear every case except high treason itself. The surrender of privilege and power on this scale generally did no more than acknowledge a situation that already existed. The king had so often failed to govern that a lord stepped into his shoes and ruled at will to prevent local society collapsing into total anarchy, or to stop a strong neighbour taking his fief from him. But in recognising the *fait accompli* kings made it more difficult for themselves to recover power later. For example, when James I made vigorous efforts to recreate the machinery of central government and royal justice, he was forced to ride rough-shod over his predecessors' extravagant grants of private right: his murderer believed he had slain a tyrant who threatened the liberties of the nobles and his dagger plunged the country back into the anarchic confusion of a long minority when faction fought interminably for possession of a baby king.

It was this recurrent threat of anarchy which increasingly moulded the character of society in the rural Lowlands at the end of the middle ages. People coagulated round the barons for security, the barons coagulated into bands round each other and the bands feuded together whenever they were not restrained by a higher power. From time to time, of course, an adult king was able to impose considerable restraint, though this was never likely to be effective for long outside the diocese of St. Andrews. Even near the centre of royal power the fear of some relapse made men loyal to their lord first and only to their king afterwards. The further the baronies lay from the centre, the stronger would be local allegiance to the barons and the weaker the allegiance to the king. By the time the Borders were reached no allegiance was possible except to the Humes, the Armstrongs, the Scotts, the Chisholms and other great families who ruled in contempt of the central authorities except when it suited their book to give a show of loyalty to the king. So outrageous was their disregard for law and order, and so pressing the need of the population for protection both from the English and other neighbouring barons, that the Borders came to form a zone almost as clearly defined and separate from the rest of the country in the late middle ages as the Highlands themselves.

The first characteristic of Lowland society in the late middle ages, then, was that men were tied to the local magnate, and magnates were its main focal points of society. The nature of the tie in most cases was feudal, based on the lord's ownership of land and on the rights and duties of a sub-vassal towards his superior: the tenants of the nobility formed their fighting force and gave them economic support by rents in kind and money. It was not, however, invariably so. There were also ties of 'voluntary' alliance created by 'bonds of manrent' by which the magnates drew into their spheres of influence the small lairds in the district, occasionally granting them land but more often granting them no more than protection in exchange for their loyalty and armed service. Then there was the tie of kinship. Every nobleman surrounded himself by a net of lesser gentlemen who bore his surname and gave him unquestioning devotion, while he judged their causes and protected them in their feuds with others of a different name—economically speaking such 'gentlemen' might be little more than peasants, but if they were the kin of the lord they had a family right to protection. When a great family rose in power, his surname rose with him: the rise of the Earls of Huntly in the north-east was accompanied by the rise of all the cadet branches of the family and by the proliferation of small tenants named Gordon throughout the counties of Aberdeen and Banff; when the cathedral of Dunblane fell into the hands of successive bishops surnamed Chisholm, its main offices were also held for generations by clerics surnamed Chisholm. 'None durst strive against a Douglas nor yet a Douglas man' was said of the whole of Scotland when the greatest of these Lowland networks of kinship rose to the apex of power in 1526–8. It was this combination of feudal and family loyalties that made the followings of the magnates cohesive and almost indestructible units. Forfeiture of estates by the crown could destroy a feudal tie in its legal sense, but it was quite useless in eradicating a family loyalty.

Respect for kinship was therefore another distinguishing feature of the Lowlander in the late middle ages. Its natural corollary was the pride of the whole kin in their good blood, a pride which could be quite divorced from their own economic position or social rank. It was a joke in sixteenth-century France that any ragged Scot would call himself a nobleman—'that man is the cousin of the king of the Scots' was a popular derisive saying against any boaster. But the poor man did not in fact claim the rank of an earl or a baron: what he claimed was something he valued more, to belong to a family of incomparable nobility and martial valour, and by virtue of that to be as good as any earl, baron or commoner of different family in the land. This did not make Scottish society democratic, as some commentators have suggested, for the kinsman regarded hereditary rank in those of his own name with reverence. He gave earls and barons of his kin all the deep respect due by a son to a father, though he never treated them with the abject deference due from a mere commoner to a remote and mighty lord. The whole atmosphere of kinship was a complex one, compounded both of egalitarian and of patriarchal features, full of respect for birth while being free from humility. It appeared uncouth beyond Scotland mainly because it was a legacy of Celtic influence unfamiliar to the outside world.

Legal servility was also absent from all ranks of late medieval society. This was another important distinction which the Scots did not share with many other countries, but in this case it was one of recent development. Celtic Scotland had been thoroughly familiar with slavery though the extent of its economic importance is never clear. After an invasion of England in 1070 so many prisoners were captured that according to an English chronicler 'there cannot (now) be found a hamlet or even a hut without slaves and handmaids of the English race'.[9] The Normans had also recognised serfdom, and in their charters frequently spoke of the *nativi* who could be bought and sold like any other goods—'Edmund the son of Bonde and Gillemichael his brother, their sons and daughters and the whole brood descended from them' came on the market and were disposed for three marks in the reign of William the Lyon.[10] But the entire institution died a quiet death in the fourteenth century: documentary references to *nativi* simply become more and more infrequent until 1364, when the last one occurred. No contemporary mentions this social revolution: perhaps no one thought it important compared to the fight for national existence and the general collapse of law, though they surely would have done so had farming depended predominantly on servile labour.

The reasons for its decline remain obscure. They may have connected with the national crisis—the lord could hardly risk having men on their land who might be suborned into disloyalty by promises of freedom from his neighbour or the English enemy, and every feudal leader must also have discovered that free men made better warriors than serfs. On the other hand the disappearance of serfdom cannot be disassociated from the wider context of geographic and economic change. In the twelfth and thirteenth centuries population must have been increasing in Scotland as it was elsewhere in Britain and Europe and the rural poor must have been grateful to get land however degrading the conditions attached to it. In the later fourteenth century however, the Black Death struck Scotland on several occasions, first of all in 1349.

> In Scotland the first Pestilence
> Began, of so great violence
> That it was said, of living men
> The third part it destroyed then;
> After that within Scotland
> A year or more it was wedand (raging).
> Before that time was never seen
> A pestilence in our land so keen;
> Both men, and bairnies, and women,
> It spared not for to kill them.[11]

Wyntoun's statement that a third of the population died is probably not mere poetic licence, at least not if one includes the subsequent visitations between that date and 1401: it fits in with what we know of the effects of this first appalling visitation of the bubonic plague in England. This enormous loss coming on top of mortality caused by war must have upset dramatically the previous balance between men and land. Henceforth the bargaining position would all be in the peasants' favour, and lords would be only too anxious to get tenants on their estates even if it meant granting every man his personal freedom and agreeing to other terms less favourable to themselves. For whatever reason, it appears that for nearly three hundred years after the middle of the fourteenth century no Scotsman was a serf.

The notable Scottish churchman and historian John Major, describing the upper grades of the peasantry in 1521, showed how their freedom in law was accompanied by a very remarkable freedom of spirit. He calls the tenantry much more 'elegant' than those of France: it is a strange word to use, for most commentators are at pains to point out how rough and dirty the Scottish peasant was, but he means by it that they attempted to rival the lesser nobles in their style of dress and in their arms: 'and if one of these should strike them they return the blow upon the spot'. At the same time they held their lord in devotion, and looked forward to his feuds, keeping horse and weapons so that they could make his quarrel their own 'be it just or unjust . . . if only they have a liking for him, and with him if need be (they will) fight to the death'. Such men were the substantial peasants who 'rent their land from the lords but cultivate it by means of their servants', and who sent their sons into service as the lord's retainers but held all useful handicrafts as 'contemptible and unfit (training) for war'.[12] Perhaps some of them were among the feuars who at this period of the late middle ages were able to obtain perpetual leases at a fixed rent (see Chapter VI below). Major refers to them as farmers, though since warfare and not tillage was obviously their joy in life it is unlikely that such a class made satisfactory husbandmen. Awareness of the ties of kinship may often have been particularly strong in such a group, and when it was it would have made nonsense of any distinction between them and the lesser gentlemen or small freeholders. The 'servants', subtenants or cotters whom they employed to work the land, probably felt less personal loyalty to the baron, but such small peasants still lived in too close proximity with the larger ones to develop separate conscious social objectives of their own.

Scotland in the late middle ages incidentally escaped the precocious class warfare that had rocked English society in the Peasants' Rebellion of 1381 and caused renewed tremors in Tudor England, or which tore through Germany and Jutland in the 1520s. Scottish rural society was so largely organised to pursue war and feud and was so closely bound in blood and duty to its lords that it had no conception of itself as divided along other lines by economic interest. The English peasants' jingling question, 'when Adam delved and Eve span who was then the gentleman?' had little meaning where degree could be recognised but class was just not identified.

Such a society was largely a product of political instability: this same instability helped to condemn the countryside to continuing penury, not only because of the physical destruction and disruption of markets caused by the periodic inroads of the English or by the feuds of the lords but also because of the attitude of mind such things bred in the population. Few landlords would feel inclined to undertake radical agricultural improvements if the incursions of a powerful neighbour could destroy in a few hours the care and investment of a lifetime. Land tenure itself had to be organised to maximise fighting power rather than productivity; the best warriors rather than the best farmers got the best holdings. There was perhaps a tendency to keep to pastoral farming even on ground that would have done better under the plough, because animals could be quickly driven away in an emergency: corn always had to be left behind to be burnt. Until this basic problem of law and order was solved in the Lowlands there would be no lasting escape for the Scots from their reputation for poverty. On the other hand there were several other factors apart from disorder keeping the Scots poor in the late middle ages. Lack of markets, a bad climate, shortage of fertile and dry land and an international ignorance and disinterest in agricultural technology would have prevented their rural economy from experiencing any immediate basic transformation even under the strongest kings.[13]

4. THE EMERGENCE OF THE HIGHLANDER

In the fourteenth century another development of incalculable importance took place when the Highlanders emerged for the first time as a people with their own conscious identity. John of Fordun, the chronicler from Aberdeen, writing in 1380, was the first to describe the division of Scotland into two cultures.

The manners and customs of the Scots vary with the diversity of their speech. For two languages are spoken amongst them, the Scottish and the Teutonic: the latter of which is the language of those who occupy the seaboard and plains, while the race of Scottish speech inhabits the highlands and outlying islands. The people of the coast are of domestic and civilised habits, trusty, patient and urbane, decent in their attire, affable and peaceful, devout in Divine worship yet always prone to resist a wrong at the hand of their enemies. The highlanders and people of the islands, on the other hand, are a savage and untamed nation, rude and independent, given to rapine, easy-living, of a docile and warm disposition, comely in person but unsightly in dress, hostile to the English people and language and owing to diversity of speech, even to their own nation, and exceedingly cruel.[14]

This passage with its hostility expressed in tones of mingled fear and contempt, is already a mature example of the attitude towards Highland Gaelic society that was to persist in the Lowlands for nearly six centuries. Every medieval writer after Fordun makes the division—to John Major it was the 'wild Scots' and the 'householding Scots', for many of his successors simply the 'Irish' and the 'Scots'. Why did this deep rift become obvious in the late fourteenth century in a way it had never been before?

We have seen how in Norman Scotland the advance of alien forces faded out slowly towards the fastness of the Western Highlands, leaving a gradation between the almost entirely Norman diocese of St. Andrews and the almost entirely Celtic areas of the far north-west, the area between changing so slowly that contemporaries were scarcely aware of tension. Gaelic speech and culture in those days had been on the retreat, hemmed in on one side by the Scandinavians and pressed on the other by the enthusiasm of the Norman kings. In the fourteenth century, the boot was on the other foot: the collapse of Norse power in the Isles in 1263 followed so quickly by the Wars of Independence and then the partial prostration of the Scottish monarchy led to a sudden renaissance of Gaelic power and confidence in its mountainous stronghold. The Scandinavian wedge having been knocked out, strong connections with Gaelic Ireland were revived after four hundred years and fostered by Robert Bruce in his struggle against English aggression. Then, as subsequent monarchs were in no position to assert leadership, a dynasty descended from Somerled arose in the west to fill the power vacuum. The Lords of the Isles (as they called themselves) exercised so much control over the other chiefs on the Western coast at the height of their power in the late middle ages that they approached the status of a second royal house in Scotland. Their eventual destruction and forfeiture by James IV in 1493 abolished that control without making it any more possible for the crown to assert its own. The Highlands in the sixteenth century became more anarchic and more hostile to the Lowlands than they had been before.

Meanwhile on the south-eastern fringe of the mountains, the decline of the fourteenth-century crown had given feudal nobles the chance to go native for their own ends. The Wolf of Badenoch was the supreme example—a son of the king and a royally-appointed Earl of Buchan, he gathered the tribal hosts around him to fight the king's sheriff, destroy his castles, and plunder far into the Lowlands. Thus the chronicler told how in 1390 with his 'wyld wykked helend-men' he: 'Burned the town of Forres, the choir of the church of St. Laurence there, also the manse of the Archdeacon, and in the month of June following . . . he burned down the whole town of Elgin, eighteen noble and beautiful manses of canons and chaplains and what was further still more cursed and lamentable the noble and highly adored church of Moray, with all the books, charters and other valuable things of the country therein kept'.[15] Many a family in the east with a Norman pedigree likewise transformed themselves into Highland chiefs, either to preserve their power in a new environment or to further their banditry. The mountain Gaels, thus encouraged, swept back over the hybrid zone to the very limits of the hills, and met the Normanised people of the diocese of St. Andrews with only a narrow buffer land between them, or with no buffer at all. At the confrontation of two extremes, the clash of culture became explicit. Since by the late fourteenth century the English language seems to have become almost as universal in the Lowlands as Gaelic had always been in the Highlands, it is easy to see how the confrontation assumed an aspect of racial as well as of cultural conflict.

It is an old platitude to state that the Highlanders were organised in clans, but it is more difficult to define the practical differences between their society and that of the late medieval Lowlander. Certainly all the emphasis of the clan was on ties of kinship linking members in an indissoluble relationship that had nothing to do with land. The chief, or supreme head, was linked by close consanguinity to the chieftains of

44

the septs, or main branches of the clan: the dependents of the chieftains, down to the humblest herdsman on the mountain, sometimes were and sometimes only imagined themselves to be blood-relations of each other and of the chief. In cases where the fiction was hard to sustain it was necessary to invent a common ancestor, preferably as distant and heroic as possible—the Macgregors in 1450 traced descent from one Cormac Mac Oirbertaigh, swapped him in 1512 for Kenneth Macalpin, and finally for Pope Gregory the Great, 'a more mysterious and therefore perhaps in their idea a greater hero'.[16] The clan supported its leaders with military service and food and accepted their judgement and protection in a very similar way to the Lowlanders when they obeyed their 'feudal' superiors. But in the Highlands it was not actually necessary for the chief to have any land in order to gain his dependent's allegiance: the chiefs of the Camerons, the Macnabs and the Macgregors were all apparently landless in 1590, though they had clansmen scattered as tenants of other chiefs over half the Highlands. There was an incident on the edge of the Highland area in 1562 when the Gordon Earl of Huntly called out his Mackintosh tenants as their feudal superior to fight Mary Queen of Scots, only to have them successfully intercepted en route by the chief of Clan Mackintosh, who called them out as their clan superior to fight against Huntly. Economic and every other kind of tie was almost invariably cut across by clan loyalty when it came to a clash of this nature.

The clan system, nevertheless, had also become imbued with some feudal characteristics of Norman origin in exactly the same way as feudalism became imbued with clannish characteristics of Celtic origin. The Highland chiefs or chieftains of the late middle ages all held land by feudal charters accepted from the crown or from each other which gave virtually absolute control over their tenants and their territories. In particular it is necessary to stress that there was in the medieval Highlands no known concept of clan lands to which the peasants had immemorial prescriptive rights of ownership, though such rights were very widely believed in by nineteenth-century crofters, who held them to be of great antiquity, and the existence of such a belief can be traced even in the eighteenth century. But there is no sign of this before 1600. Thus in 1599 Macdonald of Islay thought nothing of removing his 'whole clan and dependaries' from his lands in Kintyre if this would help him make peace with the crown, and clansmen generally thought nothing of being removed if this would please the chief, though perhaps they did expect him to find room for them on other stretches of his lands. Naturally, the lands the chief held were mainly occupied by his own clan, though it was likely that some of his tenants would belong to other clans and that not all his clansmen would be settled on his own territory. However, a chief always had strong incentives to persuade these other tenants to transfer their loyalty to his own clan: renegades, outlaws and 'broken men' could always find a place and change their surnames, and on the eastern side of the Highlands thoroughly feudal landlords like Grant or Fraser of Norman or Fleming origin could in a surprisingly short time transform tenants into 'clansmen' prepared to accept an ancient family history as the true link to their 'chief'.

The succession of the chief was an important matter to the clan, who sought a leader of unsullied bravery and sure judgement to command them. Here too, the influence of feudalism can be traced, for old Gaelic law had known nothing of the feudal idea that an eldest son automatically succeeded: the selection of an heir from the most suitable male kin was probably the most usual practice in the old Scottish kingdom of Alba. By the fifteenth century this was rare but not unknown—even in 1513 the Macdonalds of Moidart deposed and murdered the eldest son of a previous chief on account of his cruelties and then chose his uncle as successor. By 1550 the feudal practice of primogeniture was almost universal, and its coming added slightly more stability to clan life by removing one internal bone of contention.

It was very striking that when contemporaries wrote about the Highlands the one thing they did not stress as being different from the Lowlands was the clan system. Fordun called the Highlanders 'unsightly in dress', Gaelic-speaking, lawless and uncivilised: he said nothing of clans. Major made similar points, adding that the 'Wild Scots' were mainly a pastoral people. He did also mention that one part of the Highlands was ruled by 'worthless and savage chiefs . . . full of mutual dissensions, and war rather than peace is their normal condition', but this was not much different from his condemnation of the Lowland nobles among whom if 'of equal rank (and) happen to be very near neighbours, quarrels and even shedding of blood are a common thing . . . their very retainers cannot meet without strife'. Bishop Leslie writing in 1578 also described the Highlanders as Gaelic-speaking, pastoral, different in dress and culture and given to fighting 'if their master command them': but again it is the Lowland nobles whom

he describes as maintaining 'great families . . . partly to defend themselves from their neighbours with whom they have deadly feud,
partly to defend the realm'.[17]

The differences in social structure between agrarian society in the
Highlands and Lowlands were therefore mainly ones of emphasis—
Highland society was based on kinship modified by feudalism, Lowland society on feudalism tempered by kinship. Both systems were
aristocratic, unconscious of class, designed for war. Other distinctions
making a rift between them were deeper because they were racial and
cultural, based on the survival of the Gaelic language and the fact that
the church and the burgh and royal control had had such difficulty in
penetrating the area. Highland life was actually very similar to Border
life in the sixteenth century, and for the same reasons that the land was
hilly and the king remote. Leslie spoke of the family feuding of the
Borders in terms which could have applied to the Highland clans.
James VI legislated against anarchy in the two areas as though they
were an identical problem, and Privy Council referred to both Highlanders and Lowlanders quite indiscriminately as 'clannit'. We must
conclude that the main determinant of social life in all the upland parts
of Scotland was the fact or fear of uncontrolled violence. Change,
whether social or economic, could only come about where and when
that fear was overcome. On the other hand Scotland was not the only
country in the world to be torn by internal and external war. Her
problem was shared in greater or lesser degree by both France and
England in the fifteenth century, and in many other places. It had to be
overcome in each one before there could be much material progress.

From what bases could reform spring? It is worth summarising
quickly the position of the forces of law and order in late medieval
Scotland. There was, firstly, the royal government, which could and
did act effectively when the king was an adult. None of the kings from
James I to James V gave up the fight to control the nobility: several of
them won in the short run, even devising effective new tools to help
maintain their control. Gunpowder for instance, and the huge cast-iron
guns of which Mons Meg is so remarkable a survival, came to Scotland
and remained a monopoly of the crown in the fifteenth century. They
were clumsy to move and dangerous to play with—James II was blown
up by one of them at the siege of Roxburgh—but they could hammer
down an obdurate castle as nothing else could.

The Stewarts also devised new legal machinery, exploiting the notion of a royal 'brief' by which a law suit could be abstracted from baronial courts and brought into their own. James V, by setting up the College of Justice in 1531 started royal jurisdiction on a new and more permanent footing. The institutions of a General Council (where representatives of the baronial and clerical estates gathered round the crown) and of a Parliament (bringing together barons, clerics and burgesses from the towns) were elaborated from the fourteenth century onwards and used to promulgate laws, which at least expressed good intentions even if the machinery to carry them out was generally lacking. It is also very remarkable that through more than two centuries of invasion, faction and royal minority the Stewarts kept their throne. The Scots were as faithful (though not as obedient) to their kings as to their lords: Celtic respect for blood proved their salvation in this direction as it did their bane in others.

Besides the crown, two other institutions bolstered order—the burghs and the church. The burghs remained strangely inviolate from the disorder that so often broke out around them. They were seldom sacked except by the English, or in some parts by the Highlanders and Borderers: Selkirk's charter of 1540, for instance, spoke of it as 'often burned, harried and destroyed' through its proximity to 'England, Liddesdale and other broken parts'.[18] The nobles were generally more concerned about feuding among each other for the sake of rural power and family honour than in plundering the towns. Besides, the burghs kept their own inhabitants in a prickly state of martial readiness: every burgess had normally to show that he could provide armour and weapons before he was admitted to the full community of the town, and to be ready to do his stint of watching and warding on the walls. The local magnates, though they might have town houses and might infiltrate the government of the burghs with their nominees, would hesitate directly to attack or to alienate such a community of well-armed men whose own wish was merely to be allowed to proceed with buying, selling and manufacturing in peace.

For whatever reason, the towns grew slowly but distinctly in wealth and trade in the century before the Reformation, hindered, perhaps, by the backwardness of the countryside but not on that account prevented from all progress. The second half of the fifteenth century, in particular, a time of peace between the kings of England and Scotland, saw a considerable revival in their fortunes. This is the period of the more magnificent town churches like St. Michael's at Linlithgow and

Hermitage Castle, Roxburghshire. A fifteenth-century castle still formidable in the reign of Mary Queen of Scots. A timber gallery or "war-head" ran below the window-openings

A lowland farmstead before the agricultural revolution, at Dunfermline, Fife, c. 1690 from J. Slezer, *Theatrum Scotiæ*

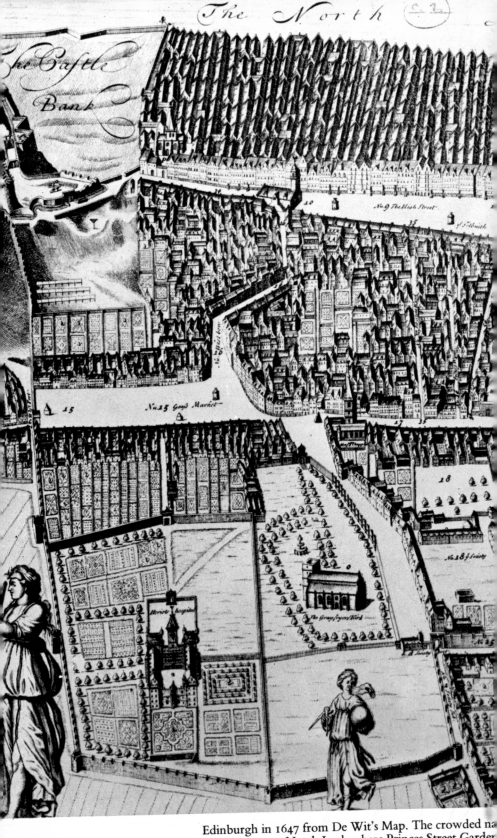

Edinburgh in 1647 from De Wit's Map. The crowded na[...]
North Loch where Princes Street Garden[...]

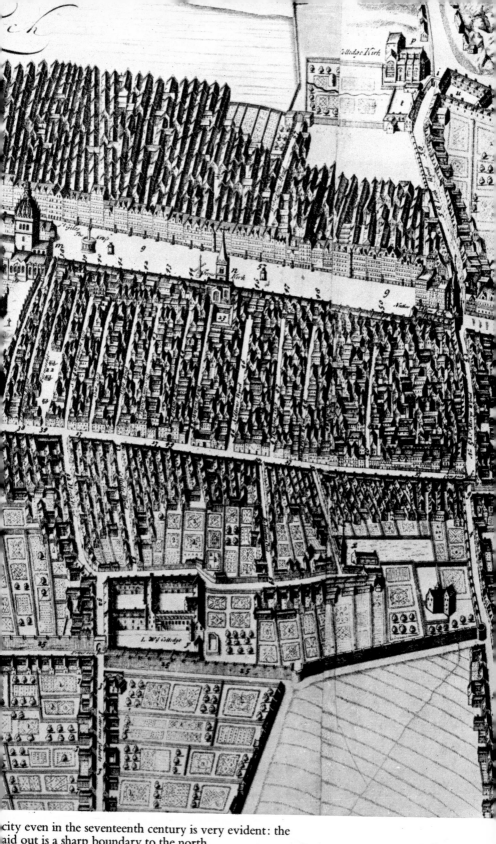

city even in the seventeenth century is very evident: the
aid out is a sharp boundary to the north

John Knox. The picture is by A. Vaensoun,
engraved by Hondius and first published 1586

The devil preaching to the witches at North Berwick. The other scenes
in the plate relate to spells and incidents to which the East Lothian
witches and their warlock "confessed" at the trial

the Holy Rood at Stirling, that were filled with chaplainries and altars endowed by rich merchants and craftsmen. It was also the time when many lords founded their own burghs—some fifty such burghs of barony were erected between 1450 and 1513, though not all of them had much life. But the larger and more successful of the Royal Burghs, with their widespread trading connections ranging from Bergen and Danzig in the north to Bordeaux and Spain in the south kept an open window on the European world through which both goods and cultural ideas were able to enter the kingdom.[19]

The church was differently situated. From the middle of the fourteenth century onwards it suffered from the increasing decay of its corporate spiritual life, as it did everywhere else in Europe. This was greatly accelerated in Scotland by the erosion of its own freedom: kings gained the right to nominate bishops and abbots, and abused it by appointing their own bastards to high clerical office when they were still only children: nobles came to control monasteries and cathedrals and took over church lands as though they were their own. By 1560, as we shall see in the next chapter, the church was very largely at the mercy of the unspiritual laymen, its foundations corrupt and worldly, its parish churches empty and ruined, its bishops a byword for immorality and its congregations often contemptuous of its services. But to this black generalisation there were several bright exceptions. Throughout the fifteenth century there had been great clerics, like Bishop Wardlaw, who founded Scotland's first University at St. Andrews in 1410, Bishop Turnbull who founded Glasgow University in 1451 and Bishop Elphinstone, who founded King's College, Aberdeen in 1496 and was the first patron of printing in Scotland. They did more than any layman for Scotland's cultural life and educational reputation. In the sixteenth century John Major, Hector Boerce and Bishop Leslie, historians and social commentators, were all churchmen who, like Elphinstone, tried to bring to their country the new humanist learning of the Renaissance in Italy, France and Germany. Even the greatest of the pre-Reformation poets, William Dunbar, was apparently a cleric. The corporate church might lie prostrate, but individuals in her kept alive regard for civilised movements that would otherwise have been much weaker.

Court, burgh and church thus formed a triumvirate of half-eclipsed power opposed to the endemic disorder and insecurity that lay sapping so much of the potential strength of Scottish society. As mid-century approached the Scottish scene became no more orderly: the ravages of the English, the factions of the nobles and the outrageous scandal of the church grew worse after the death of James V in 1542. It was the darkness before the dawn. The court, the burgh and the church were about to assert themselves over their country with a new and unsuspected authority.

Part One

_____

THE AGE
OF REFORMATION
1560-1690

CHAPTER II

The Reformation

1. THE BACKGROUND TO THE REVOLUTION

On 11 May 1559 John Knox, a revolutionary priest imbued with the theology of Calvin's Geneva, preached a sermon 'vehement against idolatry' in the ancient and beautiful church of St. John in Perth. As a result of this, a mob of those whom Knox at the time referred to as 'the brethren' and some years later as 'the rascal multitude' damaged the ornaments in the kirk, and then rushed out to sack the houses of the Grey and Black Friars, and the Carthusian monastery. The infuriated Queen Regent, Mary of Guise, ordered government troops to muster at Stirling before marching on Perth to punish the preacher and the burgesses. Knox and his friends in turn called up an army of nobles and lairds from the corners of the Lowlands styling themselves 'the Faithful Congregation of Christ Jesus in Scotland' and they prepared to wield 'the sword of just defence' against the crown. In a country too often bedevilled by faction, rebellion was no novelty; and the Regent could not but notice that all her personal and political enemies were ranged with the heretics. But this time there was much more at stake than the desire of one aristocratic clique to thrust another from power. This was a great popular revolution backed by a large number of articulate men of every class discontented with the political and religious environment in which they lived. And the outcome of the struggle which began at Perth had the most profound effects upon Scottish society. Before it, Scotland had been a Catholic country with peculiarly close links to Rome for five hundred years. After it, the Scottish Parliament declared the country Protestant and independent of Rome—and so it remained in following centuries. Before it, Scotland had been for a decade the pawn of France; but this itself was merely an extreme consequence of the hostility which had prevailed between England and Scotland for 250 years. After it, England became Scotland's firm ally, and the stage was set for the gradual integration of Britain which was to result first in the Unions of 1603 and 1707, and then to grow stronger with every decade until in the twentieth century the survival of national identity itself appeared endangered to Scots of many different political persuasions. In Scotland the medieval world began to die with the Reformation: the modern world began to be born.

Though there was nothing inevitable about the way it came or the form it took, a religious revolution had been expected in Scotland for some time before 1559. There was, for one thing, an abundance of tinder into which a radical incendiary could fling his torch, for the Scottish church had long been remarkable for the depth of its corruption. Even in the late fourteenth century certain Scottish monastic houses were getting an unsavoury reputation, and being reported to Rome as 'in many ways deformed and broken down'. In the fifteenth century James I, disgusted at the laxity of traditional monasticism, had tried to leaven the lump by introducing the extremely strict and ascetic Carthusian order into Scotland: but apart from the one house at Perth founded by the king there was no impact from them. Most laymen therefore stopped endowing monasteries and friaries, and put their money into town churches or collegiate establishments (like the marvellous chapel at Roslin in Midlothian) where ordinary priests said mass for the donor's soul. Even they were evidently not above reproach: the incumbent of a chaplaincy at Linlithgow in 1456 was obliged to find security that he would neither pawn the books, plate and vestments of the town kirk nor maintain for his enjoyment 'a continual concubine'. It does not sound somehow as if his sponsors would have had much objection to his enjoyment of an occasional concubine.

Such is the nature of late medieval sources that we cannot always be sure how much of clerical life was like this; but when we cross from the fifteenth to the sixteenth century all ambiguity vanishes in a flood of documentation. Except in the Carthusian house at Perth, which still bravely kept up the old austerities, the Scottish monasteries had by 1559 long since ceased to be the vehicles for spirituality. They had become nothing more than property-owning corporations. Control over the property was frequently in the hands of laymen, or sometimes of secular clerics who by hook or by crook had secured the title simply of abbot or 'commendator' (literally 'protector') in order to divert the income of the monastic lands into their own pockets. The crown itself had been the worst offender in this respect. James V, for example, in 1532, when he was still only twenty, had wrung permission from the Pope (so involved in his struggle with Henry VIII that he dared not risk offending the Scottish king along with the English by refusing his request) to appoint three baby sons, all illegitimate, to be titular abbots of Kelso and Melrose, priors of St. Andrews and Pittenweem, and abbot of Holyrood respectively: a fourth was later made prior of Coldingham and a fifth abbot of the Charterhouse. The king thus got his bastards beautifully provided with an income at the churches' expense, but the monasteries were lumbered with the farce of a baby master. The ordinary monks, however, were by now entirely absorbed in the material benefits of their life. Their houses being rich, their portions were generous even under a lay abbot. They were few in number—Melrose, for instance, had only sixteen monks in 1555— both because of the declining spiritual appeal of their life and because they did not readily hasten to admit new brethren to share their cake. Their lives were, on the whole, morally respectable: only the abbots were commonly charged with lewdness. But they were incredibly dull intellectually: it seems quite extraordinary that the whole of the Reformation came and went with hardly a word spoken for or against it from the indwellers in any Scottish monastery.

Their brethren in regular orders, the Augustinian canons and the Franciscan, Dominican and Carmelite friars, appear after this as relatively dynamic. Because their establishments were built in the burghs, involved in some parish cures and in preaching to the laity they could hardly help becoming actively caught up in the Reformation struggle. They did in fact provide spokesmen on both sides. The friars were neither particularly rich nor particularly corrupt, though their role as professional beggars was certainly resented by the burgh poor who felt they needed the alms more. The nuns, on the other hand, though few in number, were more scandalous than the monks. They were normally too illiterate even to write their own names. A report to Rome in 1556 gave a colourful account of their unchastities. They were frequently so undisciplined that they no longer even bothered to live within the nunnery precincts. By mid-century a Scotsman could hardly have done worse by his daughter than in sending her to a nunnery, unless, perhaps to the nunnery of Sciennes outside Edinburgh which seems to have been as exceptional in keeping up standards for women as the Carthusians of Perth were for men.

If this was the state of monks, friars and nuns, what was to be expected of the secular clergy in the parishes? They took their tone from a hierarchy where appointments had for many years been made on purely political grounds. The king had, in the course of the fifteenth century, been able to oblige the Pope to appoint whomever he pleased to bishoprics in the Scottish church. Spiritual qualifications for office were in these circumstances seldom considered. The first requisite of a prelate was, from the royal point of view, that he should support the crown: in a poor country, it was also highly convenient if the officers of state or the royal children could themselves be supported by making them bishops. James IV had set the pace by making his illegitimate son Archbishop of St. Andrews at the age of eleven. Another holder of the Primacy, the notorious Cardinal David Beaton who died at the hand of Protestant assassins in 1546, held three rich benefices at the same time and lived a life of flagrant sexual immorality. His successor, Archbishop Hamilton, had a justified reputation as a reformer within the church, yet found nothing incongruous in acting on medical advice that prescribed a ten-week course of 'moderate and carefully regulated incontinence'.[1]

The greed of prelates, abbots and commendators, however, was often of more moment than their private lives. For centuries it had been customary to 'appropriate' the revenue of a parish, and by the sixteenth century in eight or nine parishes out of every ten the funds were being diverted to a cathedral, bishopric, collegiate church, abbey or similar institution. The cure of souls was therefore left in the hands of underpaid vicars who were driven to all kinds of abuses to wring a living wage out of their parishioners—they became pluralists holding several livings at once: they became merchants, trading on the side to supplement their earnings: they exacted the last penny for carrying out the rites of the church, refusing to bury the poor until they had received the customary cow and cloth as mort-dues, or to administer the sacrament until the communicant had disgorged an Easter offering. Meanwhile the church fabric crumbled around them for lack of maintenance funds or for fear that if they were maintained anarchy and war would soon reduce them to ruins. In Berwickshire in 1556, twenty-two churches were derelict, a few without walls, some without roofs, most without windows, fonts, vestments or books so that the mass could not be celebrated. The destruction of parish churches and abbeys which popular legend blames on the followers of John Knox is only partly attributable to the Protestants. More is due to the shameful negligence of the old church, to the savagery of English armies, particularly of the Earl of Hertford's troops in the Rough Wooing, and to the prolonged neglect of landowners whose property the fabric of the abbeys often became.

It is not surprising that the priests attracted to these parish cures should so often be miserably unworthy. Ecclesiastical sources abound with the evidence of priests coming to the altar half drunk, of priests hardly able to read the services either in Latin or in English, and of a 'profane lewdness of life' in general at all levels. It was a Jesuit who in 1562 called the Catholic clergy 'extremely licentious and scandalous': that this was no overstatement is shown by the fact that legitimations of priestly offspring were so numerous that, in mid-century, when perhaps two Scotsmen in six hundred were priests, no less than two legitimised children in seven were the bastards of priests.[2] In these circumstances society at large treated the church and its services with open irreverence. There were many people who as a General Council complained in 1552 had 'fallen into the habit of hearing mass irreverently and impiously, or who jest or behave scurrilously in church in time of sermon, or who presume at such times to make mockery or engage in profane bargainings in church porches or church yards'.[3]

Nevertheless, the old Catholic church in Scotland fell not merely because it was rotten, but because in the sixteenth century a European movement took fire which found the contemporary condition of religion no longer a matter for cynicism or indifference, but a grossly intolerable offence to God and man. By mid-century half of Europe had renounced Papal supremacy and the mass: broadly speaking, parts of Germany and the whole of Scandinavia followed the revolutionary theology of Luther, first enunciated at Wittenberg in 1517, while other parts of Germany, of the Low Countries, of France and of Switzerland followed the still more radical teaching of John Calvin of Geneva. England was caught up in her own variety of Protestant reformation. The other half of Europe, while retaining its allegiances to the Papacy and to conservative theology, was scarcely less reformist in every other way—the Council of Trent which began its meetings in 1545 but did not publish its findings until 1563 announced the intentions of the

international Catholic church to tolerate no longer the abuses of pluralism, immorality and ignorance in the clergy. The problem in Scotland
is not why reform came, but why it followed a Protestant and not a
Catholic model.

The failure of the conservatives in the Scottish church was certainly
not due to lack of royal support, for the crown had a vested interest in
maintaining a church whose revenue could now relatively easily be
diverted to its own pockets by appropriating abbacies, staffing bishoprics with civil servants and imposing heavy taxation. Nor was it due
to complete indifference among the conservatives themselves—the
old church had never been lacking (for all its corruption) in outspoken
members like John Major who criticised the wealth of an institution in
which 'piety the mother was smothered by luxury the wanton daughter'. By 1540 such voices were no longer isolated: the clamour of
European and English revolutions, the pointed criticism in Parliament
of the 'unhonesty and misrule of kirkmen', above all the spread of
heresy within the kingdom, combined to make many intelligent
clergy anxious for a conservative and Catholic reformation before it
was too late. The accession of Archbishop Hamilton in 1546 gave
them an eleventh-hour chance—General Councils of the Scottish
Church held in 1549, 1552 and 1559 sketched out a whole programme
for reform, some of it surprisingly radical. The state of church morals
was unsparingly condemned: the Universities were to be reformed:
clerics holding office were to be examined: bishops were to reform their
own lives, and to inspect parish churches and monastic houses: everyone was to place great emphasis on preaching and on instructing the
laity: derelict churches were to be rebuilt. The Archbishop himself
issued a catechism in 1552 dealing with such questions as the Eucharist
and justification by faith in a manner highly sympathetic to Lutheran
thinking. Nothing was said in this document of Papal headship, and
indeed its doctrinal tone of the catechism would have shocked the
theologians at the Council of Trent as going more than half way to
meet heresy. Yet the programme failed, and the Protestant army of the
Faithful Congregation was in arms in the same year as the last of the
General Councils was conducting its deliberations.

This failure was due to a number of causes. Firstly, the reform for
which the laity were now clamouring above all other was a decent
standard of pastoral care at parish level: the Hamiltonian proposals
might have produced learned dons, respectable nuns and chaste

bishops, but in their failure to deal with the crying scandal of appropriated parochial revenues they would have perpetuated the vicar starved of a living wage and all the abuses that flowed from that poverty. Secondly, the conservatives moved too slowly, and there were justifiable doubts about their sincerity. Had the Council of 1549 achieved a marked improvement it might have been different, but their decrees were largely dead letters; the primate and many of the bishops went on showing in their own lives little of the chastity and zeal expected of reformers, and ten years later it was too late. Thirdly there was a general identification in the popular mind of ecclesiastical corruption with the hierarchy, of the hierarchy with the regent, of the regent with the resented satellite status of Scotland to France, of France with Catholicism and militant Papacy. Few thought it would be possible to tip out the bathwater and save the baby—it would be altogether better to refill the bath and get a new baby—and the Protestants in 1559 had one ready to hand.

Religious radicalism itself evidently had no deep roots of native tradition in Scotland. In the fifteenth century there had been little more than intermittent flickerings of the Lollard heresy following the preaching of Wycliffe in England and a couple of foreigners, infected by Lollardry, burnt at the stake at Perth and St. Andrews. Then in 1525 came an act of the Scottish Parliament against the importation of Lutheran books, showing that the arch-heretic of Wittenberg was beginning to find hearers in the north. Three years later came the burning at the stake of Patrick Hamilton for preaching Luther's doctrine of justification by faith, then in 1530 the large scale illegal importation of Tyndale's English bible, in 1535 further acts against heresy, and in 1546 a second famous martyrdom, of George Wishart for preaching the Swiss Protestant doctrine of rejecting all beliefs and practices for which authority could not be found in Scripture. Thereafter Protestant numbers snowballed, until between 1555 and 1559 a network of organised congregations grew up in the main burghs using the English prayer-book, denouncing the mass as idolatrous and sustained by the ministrations of preachers who, like Knox himself, were mainly priests who had broken with the old church. By 1559 there was already an alternative church existing in many parts of Scotland, awaiting some revolutionary stroke to bring it to power.

The success of Protestantism was not, however, solely due to the fact that it offered a programme more radical, more enthusiastic and less open to suspicion than that of the conservatives. It succeeded also by taking the right strategic bastions in society. First of all it succeeded in the burghs, where, as Knox put it, the work of the preachers was enormously helped by the merchants and mariners 'who, frequenting other countries, heard the true doctrine affirmed and the vanity of the papistical religion openly rebuked'.[4] Once within the gates it was in-eradicable, for not only did the doctrine of a laity equal to the clergy both in the sight of God and in ability to discover divine truth in the bible appeal to self-confident and literate burgesses, but also the traditions of secrecy and co-operation among members of craft guilds and of merchant guilds, and of co-operation between the burgesses of different towns acting in their common interest, made towns the ideal environment to sustain a secret and cellular church organisation. There was another advantage: a sixteenth-century town generally contained a concentration of poor who could be whipped up into a rabble by demagogues dwelling upon the hatefulness of idols and the abundance of salt beef in the friars' kitchens until they were ready to go onto the streets to loot a church or take some other spectacular iconoclastic action which would both advertise the revolution and impel the Government to retaliate without there being much danger that retaliation would be effective. The rising of May 1559 was triggered by just such a riot, when Knox incited the Perth mob to attack the Charterhouse and the friaries. Similar riots occurred within a few weeks at Dundee, Scone, Stirling, Linlithgow and Edinburgh. Something very like it has since become a classic manœuvre, much favoured by revolutionary writers in the twentieth century.

Nevertheless, capturing the towns was only a first step; the burghs were much too small for it to be decisive. It had to be followed by winning a significant number of lairds and magnates who would take the initiative against a hostile crown with a well-armed offensive army —the failure of an attempted coup at St. Andrews in 1546 when a band of Protestants seized the town after the murder of Cardinal Beaton and held out in the castle for a year, showed this only too clearly. The business of winning such men began to be achieved by 1557, when a group of Protestant lords signed a Covenant to 'apply our whole power, substance and our very lives' to establishing the re-formed faith. To do this the preachers tapped several seams of sentiment other than the purely religious one. Firstly, there was economic resent-ment, particularly strong among the lesser lairds, such as those in

Angus or in Ayrshire and other parts of the south-west, who being relatively poor themselves, detested having to pay heavy tithes to churchmen ostentatiously wealthy in a poor country. This was intensified by the fact that unlike the nobility round the court they generally had no chance to recoup their expenses by placing their kin in church offices or appropriating the revenues of monasteries by becoming commendators or lay abbots. Secondly, there was a significant group of the nobility, led by the Earls of Argyll, Morton and Arran, who felt they had been grossly neglected in the affairs of state by the Queen Regent since she had taken over the reins of power in 1554. Thirdly— and most general of all—there was the feeling that the Regent had betrayed Scotland to make it a French province. A French alliance had been necessary (not for the first time) to rescue the realm from the English in 1548, but since 1554 Mary of Guise had gone to extremes, filling high offices with Frenchmen, sending the ancient crown of Scotland to Paris to crown the Dauphin when he married the adolescent Mary Queen of Scots in 1558, and seeming hell-bent on integrating the two countries into one unequal state. The result was a popular equation very helpful to the Reformers. If you were a patriot you were anti-French and therefore pro-English and Protestant: if you were a Protestant and pro-English, you were therefore anti-French and a patriot.

The Lords of the Faithful Congregation, therefore, set out in 1559 with the double slogan of defending the Protestant faith and freeing the country from 'the bondage and tyranny of strangers'. Even so they would have failed without English help: the final ingredient to make the Scottish Reformation successful was added when Elizabeth's fleet sailed into the Forth early in 1560 to cut the lines of supply of the Regent's large French army and to save the hard-pressed Lords from almost certain defeat. The Treaty of Edinburgh in February 1560 excluded the French from Scottish affairs and laid the foundation for a new and portentous alliance between Scotland and England. Parliament in June accepted Knox's Confession of Faith and the Protestant religion in the name (but without the authority) of Mary Queen of Scots. The Protestant Reformation had come: the question still remained, what kind of Protestant Reformation would it be?

2. THE COURSE OF THE PROTESTANT REFORMATION, 1560–1690

The reformed Church of Scotland broke to the surface in 1560, but it did not at that point assume all the characters which we now associate with it. For the next 130 years it went on changing and developing, twisting in its ecclesiastical polity first to one side and then to another to accommodate differing shades of religious opinion until finally, in 1690, it emerged as the classic presbyterian church of the eighteenth and nineteenth centuries, with its elders, deacons and ministers, its kirk-sessions, presbyteries, synods and General Assembly, its frequent but not invariable association with sabbatarianism and puritanism, and its convictions of ecclesiastical parity. Too often the whole scheme is imagined to have existed in the head of John Knox from the start, and only to have been prevented from seeing the light of day by the worldliness of kings and bishops. In fact Knox would have found presbyterianism unfamiliar and perhaps in some ways absurd: the development of the Reformation from 1560 to 1690 was a slow and organic process in which first one feature and then another was introduced and fought over, and in which the ideas and aspirations of Andrew Melville and seventeenth-century divines were at least as important as those of Knox. We must trace this evolution lest when we come to speak of the social impact of the reformed church in the following chapter we fall into the trap of imagining the reforming church always to have been the same.

The earliest Protestant church had only the most tenuous grip on legality. Mary Queen of Scots, who came to Scotland from France in August of 1561, whilst accepting the change as a *fait accompli* never ratified the legislation of her June Parliament or altered her own devotion to the Catholic faith. The position of the Reformers was therefore highly ambiguous until her deposition by another rebel army in favour of the infant James VI in 1567. Perhaps this made the new church tread more softly than it otherwise would have done; at any rate Parliament, to the anger and disillusionment of Knox who wished the revenues of the old church to be immediately placed at the disposal of the new, left the Catholic clergy in possession of two-thirds of

their old incomes for the remainder of their lives and allowed the per-
petuation of the monasteries as property-owning corporations from
which the monks also drew their portions and the lay abbots or commendators (including not a few Lords of the Faithful Congregation)
kept their grip on the lands. There was no vindictiveness, no fanaticism,
no revenge: the clergy of the old church were simply forbidden to
carry out their spiritual functions, especially that of saying mass—very
few tried to do so, and of those that did only one (or perhaps two)
suffered death as Catholic martyrs for their faith. Even among the
bishops only one felt so strongly about the Reformation as to leave the
country, and three of them came over to the Protestants and helped to
carry the programme of the reformed church through in their dioceses.
Perhaps only in Scandinavia was the take-over of the Protestants accompanied by less ill-feeling. England was a blood-bath by comparison:
there was in Scotland 'none of that cold-blooded scaffold and faggot
work which was so conspicuous in the England of Henry VIII, Mary
and Elizabeth Tudor'.[5]

This lack of rancour can be partly explained by the comparatively
low theological content of the earliest stages of the Scottish Reformation. We have already noted how far the old church was ready to go
even in 1552 towards a Protestant position in Archbishop Hamilton's
catechism. The new church was Calvinist, but (apart from its determination to ban completely the Roman mass on the grounds that it was
'idolatrous') it found its most immediate and pressing business in the
first decade after 1560 was not a new ideological teaching but the organisation of some method to bring effective spiritual care to the people
after years in which pastoral attention of any kind had been largely
lacking. Behind this reformist, essentially practical and undoctrinal aim
almost the whole country was united. There were only two guiding
ideas—firstly, the parish must be kept to the fore as the most important unit of church life, and secondly, the laity must be allowed
a large measure of participation and control to prevent the old abuses
of the priests rising up in a new guise. Congregations therefore assumed
the power of electing elders and deacons on an annual basis to form a
kirk-session with the minister. The minister himself was to be chosen
by the congregation and subjected to the kirk-session: his duty was
the priestly one of preaching and administering the sacraments according to a liturgy closely modelled on that of contemporary England,
but because the new church was badly understaffed at the beginning,

untrained readers were appointed to read prayers and lessons and also (after 1572) to officiate at baptisms and marriages. Over the minister were placed superintendents who (as Professor Donaldson has convincingly demonstrated) were bishops in all but name.[6] Finally, the General Assembly came into being not because of any wish on the part of the church to assert theological independence from the state but because the church differed from all the other European reformed churches in not possessing a Protestant prince to be its head: clearly Mary Queen of Scots could not occupy this position, so her place was taken by a council exactly reproducing the composition of the old Scottish Parliament—with lords and barons in one part, burgesses from the towns in another, and superintendents with selected ministers in the third. Nothing in the polity of the church could yet be described as presbyterian: apart from the accident of the General Assembly it parallels at many points the Danish Lutheran arrangements, and has been aptly described in modern terms as 'congregationalism with a dash of episcopacy'.[7] Indeed, in 1572 the Concordat of Leith made the Scottish church quite explicitly episcopalian by arranging to fill the old sees with Protestant bishops as they fell vacant, the Crown nominating the candidates but the General Assembly holding them under its discipline. Knox in his old age gave the Concordat his blessing—qualified, for he feared the bishops by this arrangement would become tools of any unsympathetic crown, but nevertheless a blessing.

It was shortly after his death that a new and rigidly academic theology entered the church, and made a bid to transform the character of the Reformation. Its protagonist was Andrew Melville, who arrived in Scotland in 1574 after six years at Geneva and became principal of the University college at Glasgow. He had been heavily influenced abroad by the novel presbyterian teachings of Theodore Beza which had recently disrupted Calvin's own reformed church in Switzerland. Melville's views were quite incompatible with current Scottish practice. In the first place, episcopacy in any form was held to be unscriptural, since it raised a minister above his fellows and Melville could find no grounds for believing the early church was hierarchical. Secondly, since it was still necessary to oversee the ministers, a system of church courts composed of ministers and life-appointed elders and consisting of kirk-session, presbytery, synod and General Assembly was to be set up: the duty of the new presbyteries was the examination and admittance of ministers: the General Assembly was to lose its

The Tulloch Mazer. Made by James Gray, Canongate, about 1557

A Scottish town in the open countryside; Linlithgow about 1690
from J. Slezer, *Theatrum Scotiæ*

The change from fortified castle to country mansion. Claypotts Castle (above), second half of the sixteenth century. Kinross House (below), late seventeenth century, home of Sir William Bruce

character as representing the three estates like Parliament, and to become instead a gathering of ministers and elders representing the other church courts. Thirdly, the authority of the church was held to be different from the authority of the state, and superior to it in that the latter should bow to the former in matters of conscience and religion as defined by the church. In the whole Melvillian scheme the tendency was to raise the power of the minister and depress that of the laymen. What was more, theocracy was implicit in it (as, indeed, it had been in some of Knox's pronouncements), for 'where lay the need for a king's council when the ministers claimed that they were in counsel with God?'[8]

The story of the next hundred years was one of conflict and compromise between presbyterians and episcopalians in the church. In 1578 the General Assembly after bitter controversy adopted Melville's proposals, persuaded partly by the new theology, partly by the presbyterian programme's practical solution to certain problems at parish level—particularly the financial one, for Melville revived Knox's claim to the complete property of the old church whether in clerical, lay or royal hands. Parliament, however, refused to ratify its decision and in 1584 the Crown came up with its own reply, reaffirming royal authority over the church, declaring the episcopate legal and making the bishops virtually its own tools to govern the church. Two extreme positions were thus in conflict, but forces were also at work to effect a compromise. In 1592 Parliament gave way sufficiently to recognise presbyteries and synods as legal courts of the church, and to suspend the office of bishop from effective power. Then in 1610, the Crown reintroduced the administrative episcopacy by arranging for the bishops to be recognised as permanent presidents of presbyteries and synods, while at the same time arranging for much more generous financial provision for the church in the parishes. This last compromise seems to have been widely acceptable to most politicians and churchmen, but a band of extremist clergy in the Melvillian camp kept the presbyterian cause very much alive even after they had been forbidden to preach in public, by teaching at private meetings, and by circulating books or manuscripts illicitly. By 1630 the number of ministers who were dedicated presbyterians was small, but their enthusiasm and sense of mission had, if anything, grown over the years. They also had some following among ordinary citizens moved by their zeal and bravery. Yet there was no reason why the settlement of 1610 should not have gone on indefinitely had Charles I, king of both Scotland and England, not blundered so hopelessly in his conduct of national affairs.

The fall of the Scottish bishops in 1638 was the first incident in a new revolutionary situation that eventually engulfed the whole of the British Isles in a raging storm of civil war. In Scotland the country had been awash with resentment against the crown ever since Charles's accession in 1625, and the position had gone from bad to worse. The nobility and a great many lesser lairds were terrified by the king's repeated threats to resume possession of all the property in lands and teinds (tithes, in English) that the old church had possessed in 1540: hardly a secular landholder in Scotland would have been unaffected if the king had carried out his threat. The burgesses were feeling hardly less persecuted by the growing weight of taxation and municipal debt that Charles's financial policies laid upon them. Then, in 1636 and 1637 the crown published details of a new ecclesiastical policy which would have gone a long way towards assimilating the practices of the church in Scotland with those of the Church of England. In particular it came close to forbidding extempore prayer, it made no reference to General Assembly, Presbytery or kirk-session, and it obliged the Scots to accept a new prayer book which recalled the mass and the much more Catholic practices of the Anglican church under Archbishop Laud. Only a man totally out of touch with the realities of Scottish feeling could have gone ahead with it, and his decision to do so provided both a cause and a pretext for a general revolt.

In 1638, amid dramatic scenes at the Greyfriars Kirk in Edinburgh the representatives of the Scottish people therefore gathered to sign a national protest, the National Covenant, the nobility and barons signing it on one day and the burgesses and ministers on the next. The document recited the previous struggle of the Scots against 'popery', declared their resistance to any change in worship not previously approved by free assemblies and parliaments, and pledged the signatories to defend their religion against all who came against it. Those who signed it however, included very many who at some later stage came to fight for the king in the civil wars, for the document was neither anti-Royalist nor anti-episcopalian; it affirmed the loyalty of the people to the crown and took care not to attack the institution of church government by bishops. Nevertheless there was a minority among the signatories of convinced presbyterians whose aim from the start had been the downfall of episcopacy. The king played into their hands by treating everyone who signed the National Covenant as a rebel and preparing to move an army into Scotland: then he capitulated at the very moment that presbyterian influence had begun to snowball and agreed to call the first General Assembly for nearly twenty years. To his horror it abolished the bishops: the presbyterians did so out of principle, and the bulk of the nobility who attended did so out of disgust for the bishop's behaviour in backing the crown's unpopular and intransigent policies. Charles declared their proceedings illegal, and again gathered an army. The Scots, now almost completely united behind the presbyterians on account of the king's hostility and apparent untrustworthiness, gathered their own first army of the Covenant and prepared to resist.

To the little band of Melvillian enthusiasts who in 1638 had emerged from the shadows to claim the spiritual leadership of the Covenanting movement this was indeed the wonderful day of the Lord, the second Reformation appointed by heaven for the purging of the Scottish church from prelacy and the glorious establishment of presbyterian rule. Their language took on the extravagant tones of Apocalyptic prophecy. Scotland must be a chosen nation: 'now, O Scotland, God be thanked, thy name is in the Bible'. She was the divine church whom Christ 'made a fair bride to Himself'. She was the new Israel: there was 'a verrie near paralel betwixt Izrael and this churche, the only tuo suorne nations to the Lord'. And if this was the case, then she was called to great things. She had already become the most perfectly reformed church on earth: she must now seek to bring England into conformity with her: that done, what was to stop a glorious crusade of British Covenanted Presbyterians from invading the Continent and routing the forces of Rome? 'Until King Jesus be set doun on his throne, with his scepter in his hand I do not expect God's peace'.[9] If the God of Battles was for Scotland, who could prevail against her? 'Brethren', exclaimed a moderate:

> these times require other meditations and calmer thoughts. Take a view of the mapp of the earth, there ye shall find that the kingdom of Scotland is not all the earth; and that England and it together make but one not immense isle.[10]

But such words had little effect on the climate of public opinion in the years immediately after 1638. In 1640 the Covenanting army marched into northern England and occupied Newcastle. In 1643, in return for a promise to give military help to the English rebels they entered into a Solemn League and Covenant with the English Parliamentarians designed to impose presbyterianism on England and Ireland 'according to the Word of God and the example of the best reformed churches'. In the same year the 'Westminster Confession' was drawn up to provide a basis for complete British uniformity, and adopted for the kirk in Scotland by the Scottish Parliament and General Assembly— though it was never so adopted in England. Thus by a strange accident it was not at the Reformation or in Edinburgh but eighty years later at a conference in London where eight Scots participated among more than one hundred Englishmen that the worship, doctrine and model of government which was to guide the Church of Scotland over hundreds of years was formally drawn up.

Few would have guessed from that promising start to their Apocalyptic programme that seven years later the Covenanting cause would lie in ruins below the sword of an English republican general, who, though uncompromisingly puritan, was also uncompromisingly antipresbyterian. The chain of events between the second descent of the Covenanting army into England in 1644 and Cromwell's devastating victories over the Scots at Dunbar in 1650 and Worcester in 1651 is a highly complex one, encompassing among other things the rebellion of Montrose, the capture of the king by the Scots at Newark, his surrender to the English at Newcastle and subsequent execution, the landing of Charles II in Scotland and his acceptance of the Solemn League and Covenant in a futile effort to win enough support to regain his thrones. The Covenanters did not lose just because of political and military accident, or because their programme was humanly impracticable. They also lost because their leaders tried to impose a religious control over the country more resented by those classes that traditionally held social power in Scotland even than the threatened rule of the king and bishops which had started the original rebellion. They thus alienated a majority of those who had signed the original National Covenant. The mercilessness of their warfare perhaps also contributed to their fall. Theirs was the religion of the Old Testament run amok, and for the first time in Scottish history massive cruelties were inflicted on the population in the name of God. Thus after the Battle of Philiphaugh in 1645, when Montrose's Highland army was defeated by General Leslie's Covenanters, all the prisoners, including women and children, were massacred to the cry of 'Jesus and no quarter', and even the professional soldiers who had seen service as mercenaries in the Thirty Years War in Europe were sometimes sickened by the vengeful zeal of the ministers. Leslie on another similar occasion turned to a Covenanting minister with the words, 'now, Mr John, have you not once gotten your fill of blood'.[11]

Cromwell in 1653 abolished the General Assembly and forced a measure of religious toleration on the Scots, though his military government did not allow either popery or prelacy. Charles II, restored to his father's throne in 1660, however, made a rather more lasting settlement. He did bring back episcopacy, and though he continued to have nothing to do with a General Assembly, he did also integrate the rule of bishops with a presbyterian structure of kirk-session, presbytery and synod, and was tolerant of the puritan forms of worship that had grown up in the 1640s, sometimes so extreme that even the Lord's Prayer was regarded as a dangerous and ungodly liturgy.

Nevertheless, this second period of episcopalian compromise, which endured from 1662 to 1690, was by no means so widely acceptable either to church or country as the one of 1610 had been. Nearly three hundred clergy were ejected from their livings, unwilling to accept the government of bishops. Among them were many who moved to positive opposition, unable to believe that God's Covenant with Scotland could be extinguished by mere political action, regarding king and bishops as the creatures of anti-christ. Furthermore there was fairly widespread support for the Covenanting movement after 1660 among the humble, who had never found the theocratic claims of the General Assembly a threat to themselves in the same sense as the nobles, lairds and burgesses, whose command in the community had been directly threatened. The peasantry over a wide area in the Lowlands seem to have been passively sympathetic—at least if we can judge by the reverence in which the names and works of dissenting Covenanters were held in districts such as the Lothians in the eighteenth century. On the other hand it was only in Ayrshire, Dumfriesshire and Galloway, in the central Borders, in parts of Fife and Easter Ross, and in a few burghs, that the excluded ministers were able to gather a following together significant enough to enable a secret church to be kept going. In the south-west the Covenanters met out of doors at field preachings where hundreds came together to hear their heroes. This was a land where small lairds and owner-occupying peasants could act without the risk of reprisal or eviction by landlords which in other parts might come upon tenants if they defied their social superiors by attending a rebel church.[12]

The Government, in any case, regarded the open-air 'Conventicles' as seditious, and vainly attempted to put them down by force. In 1666 a rising in the south-west and a march on Edinburgh ended in defeat for the Covenanters at Rullion Green, but it did not end their resistance or reduce their bitter hatred for an 'uncovenanted' state and church. In 1679 James Sharp, Archbishop of St. Andrews was assassinated by extremists, and thereafter 'something like open war' broke out in the west marked this time by brutality from the Government's Highland troopers poured into the area to hunt down the rebels and the ministers, and by torture, arbitrary trials, execution and transportation of prisoners and suspects brought to Edinburgh. These proceedings, and the continued failure of the royal army to make an end to the resistance, helped to give the Covenanters enough martyrs to hide some of the stain on their own hands.

It is doubtful, however, whether they would ever have won wide enough sympathy and support from the influential upper classes anywhere in Scotland had not Charles II's brother and successor to the throne been a Roman Catholic. This was the one thing needed to unite the Scots again against the crown. James VII came to the throne in 1685 and almost immediately entangled himself by proposing religious toleration for all creeds including his own, and, for good measure, moving again towards arbitrary government. In 1688 there was another national convulsion both in Scotland and England: the king was toppled from his throne by the nobility, and the Scottish bishops who (unlike the English) had foolishly and sycophantically supported him as 'the darling of Heaven' found themselves once more helplessly floundering in public opprobrium on the losing side.

A new constitution for the Church of Scotland (its last until 1921) was worked out in a national Convention of Estates and ratified by William III in 1690. Like every other settlement since 1560, this one, too, was a compromise. On the one hand it was overtly Presbyterian, for bishops were abolished and the General Assembly restored, the structure below consisting as before of synods, presbyteries and kirk-sessions. Worship and theology retained or regained its intensely puritan character, based on the Westminster Confession. On the other hand, theocracy received short shrift, since the church remained subject to Parliamentary statute and civil penalties for ecclesiastical ex-communication were abolished. The vast majority of Scotsmen of all ranks adhered to the Church of Scotland as thus established; it was the only one to which it was lawful to belong. Nevertheless, five hundred of the old clergy gave up their livings rather than submit to it; from them the Episcopal Church in Scotland had its origins, though it failed to gain any popular support at all except in the conservative north-east. A remnant of the Covenanters also remained outside the establishment, and maintained some following as the Cameronians in the south-west reinforced early in the eighteenth century by another small break away movement in the same area, the Hebronites. Both Episcopalian and Presbyterian dissenters remained as a rule introverted and untroublesome to authority. Warfare in the name of Christ was at an end.

With the constitution of 1690, therefore, it is possible to draw a line under Scottish ecclesiastical history and declare the Church Reformation completed—though completed in a way that neither John Knox nor Andrew Melville would have viewed with complete equanimity. Its course had been complex and at times tumultuous: its bitter history, no less than the character of the church that emerged, had an effect on Scottish life of the most profound kind. It is to these social results of ecclesiastical change that we must turn in a new chapter.

CHAPTER III

The Social Impact
of the Reformed Church

1. THE STRATEGY OF THE KIRK

In January 1561, in the first flush of the Protestant victory, John Knox and a small group of preachers placed before a convention of nobility and lairds a rough draft of a national programme for spiritual reform. Their proposals reached beyond the ecclesiastical formulae for establishing a 'true kirk' to preach the Word and administer the Sacraments: implied in them also was a wider vision of a Godly Commonwealth, the old idea which the Calvinists had borrowed from St. Augustine of a *Civitas Dei*, by which society on earth through submission to the divine will interpreted by the Church would come to be a perfect mirror of the Kingdom of God in Heaven. The Book of Discipline was not a philosophical dissertation, but the stern and visionary social theology behind it is visible in every clause.[1]

First of all, since there was but one state in Scotland, so should there be but one church, the godly reformed kirk of whom all Scots must become living members. Secondly, it was the duty of the State to govern strictly with 'good laws and sharp execution of the same', and in a Godly Commonwealth it is also the duty of the state to listen when the Church interprets the divine moral law: in particular, since the Law of Moses had declared certain crimes capital, murder, blasphemy, adultery, perjury and idolatry (by which the Reformers meant primarily the sacrifice of the mass) should become punishable by death at the hands of the civil authorities.

The power of discipline, however, could not be left solely to the state. The church, too, must have its authority, for without it 'there is no face of ane visible kirk'. The sphere of ecclesiastical discipline was carefully and sharply defined: 'it stands in reproving and correcting of those faults which the civil sword doth either neglect either may not punish . . . drunkenness, excess (be it in apparel or be it in eating and drinking), fornication, oppression of the poor by exactions, deceiving of them in buying and selling by wrong mete or measure, wanton words and licencious living tending to slander do properly appertain to the Church to punish the same as God's word commandeth'.[2] In applying sanctions the church should not only have the backing of the state, but also the same power as its Catholic predecessor to excommunicate the impenitent from all sacraments and human intercourse on earth in order to warn him of the damnation that will be his lot after death. Finally, 'to discipline must all estates within this realm be subject if they offend, as well the rulers as they that are the ruled':[3] the seeds of a theocracy are sown.

The whole system of discipline was to be supplemented by a national scheme for education, for while discipline serves merely to correct the adult after the offence, education by touching the soul of the child may altogether avoid the sin. Children are born, not innocent, but 'ignorant of all godliness', so 'of necessity it is that your Honours be most careful for the virtuous education and godly upbringing of the youth of this Realm, if either ye now thirst unfeignedly (for) the advancement of Christ's Glory, or yet desire the continuance of his benefits to the generation following'.[4] For this end there must be a schoolmaster appointed to every church, that none may escape the teachers' net. For the poor, if need be, education may be given free: for the rich it is only necessary to see that education is given under proper supervision. The Book of Discipline also made detailed provision for the reform of the Universities; on them the responsibility of training a supply of candidates for the ministry and the schools largely rested.

Lastly, Knox and his friends recalled society to a sense of its duty towards the deserving poor who were victims of old age and misfortune, or of man's wicked avarice: 'we are not patrons for stubborn and idle beggars who running from place to place make a craft of their begging . . . but for the widow and fatherless, the aged, impotent or lamed' and for 'your poor brethren, the labourers and manurers of the ground . . . that they may feel some benefit of Christ Jesus now preached to them'.[5] The sick, the elderly, the widow and the fatherless child, those whom the sixteenth century called the impotent poor, should be given 'reasonable provision' by the church in their native parishes and not encouraged to go begging through the kingdom. The able-bodied poor should be obliged to work, but landowners were warned of 'God's heavy and fearful judgements' upon those who, possessing former church lands, were 'as cruel over their tenants as ever were the papists'. Social obligation was a part of the policy of the reformed kirk.

The cost of this socio-religious programme was to be met from the parish teinds of the old church, devoted (the implication was that it should be roughly equally devoted) to the support of the ministers, the erection of schools and succour to the poor. The lands of the former bishoprics and cathedrals were to be devoted to the maintenance of the universities; the lands of the monasteries were, in effect, recognised as having passed irredeemably into lay hands and no attempt was made in the Book of Discipline to regain them. The convention to whom it was submitted accepted the document as a working blue-print, though they expressed reservations about the financial provision. The landed classes were in fact bitterly opposed to any arrangement whereby any of the lands and incomes of the old church that they had already appropriated before the reformation might be resumed by the new church —and they had got their hands on a good deal over and above monastic revenues. Late in 1561 the Privy Council made a quite different financial settlement for the new church from that envisaged in the Book of Discipline: it authorised the annual collection of one third of all the old church benefices and its division between the crown and the new church: the remaining two thirds were to remain in the hands of their old possessors, the holders of Roman benefices. 'I see two parts freely given to the devil and the third must be divided betwixt God and the devil' was how Knox angrily described it. The Book of Discipline never attained the force of statute, and the church never obtained the money to realise its programme. It remained, however, a declaration of intent, the implementation and modification of which formed a vital theme in the social history of the next century and a half.

The first battle of the church was to get itself accepted as the Body of Christ in Scotland. Unambiguous state recognition came effectively in 1567 on the deposition of Mary, and if it was not exactly on the theocratic terms that Knox would have wished, it was at least true that from then until the eighteenth century (with a brief interlude under Cromwell from 1657 to 1660) only a minister of the Church of

Scotland could legally perform ecclesiastical duties. The saying of the mass anywhere in Scotland became, as Knox had wished, a capital crime, but the clerics of the old church were not the stuff of which martyrs are made. One or two paid the supreme penalty; some fled to Europe. Others became reforming ministers: 'until much work is done, statistics will remain so incomplete that it is dangerous even to suggest figures at all, but it seems likely that over the whole country the proportion of those who conformed and continued to minister in their old spheres under the new regime was at least a quarter'.[7] Most of the rest remained in contented possession of their two-thirds of ecclesiastical income, doing nothing to help the new church and nothing to revive the old. Lay adherents of the old faith were discouraged by their example, and at least in the burghs they were subjected by the kirk-sessions and baillies to an 'endless pressure of interference, abuse, preaching, the pillory, the jail, ostracization, homelessness and economic ruin'[8] until they conformed. Roman Catholicism had died out before 1600 except in the households of some great nobles, such as the Earls of Huntly in the north-east and the Maxwells in Dumfriesshire, who, with their kin, were too powerful locally to be driven in any direction in which they did not freely wish to go. But it looked to be only a matter of time before it would be only a memory everywhere.

Such, however, was not quite to be the case. Throughout the North, and especially in the Highlands (always very thinly staffed by clerics), the dismantling of the old church had gone on faster than the plantation of new ministers to fill its place. In many remote parts a religious vacuum developed even greater than that of Catholic times, and persisted until long after 1690. In Badenoch in 1646 all the kirks were empty because no Gaelic-speaking ministers could be found: in Lochaber, an area of 1800 square miles formerly served by three Catholic churches, the people were heathens 'never taught if Christ came in the world, or that there is a Sabbath or a life to come, which cannot be but a nationall sin'.[9] Into such areas after 1600 Jesuit priests from the Scotch College at Douai in France carried the revived Catholic faith with much courage and no little personal suffering. Several districts went Catholic then and have remained in that faith ever since—Barra and South Uist, Glenmoriston, Abertarff and Glen Garry are such examples. The local synod might find out about these, and storm against 'two idols . . . called our Lady and her babe trimed up in their apparrell and ornaments' kept by Macneill of Barra in his private chapel in 1643,[10] but in the circumstances of the seventeenth century there was little they could do about it.

Apart from such remote though persistent pockets of Popery, however, the Church of Scotland was little troubled by Catholicism until the nineteenth century. Nor was it unduly troubled before 1690 by the innate tendency of Protestantism to split within itself. Between 1574 and 1638 the tension between presbyterian and episcopalian views on polity was never allowed to break the unity or continuity of the kirk. The Melvillian clergy after 1610 were neither able nor willing to create a rival church. For a time after 1647 the internal dissensions of the Covenanters threatened to break them in many pieces but still the church kept the face of unity. Cromwell's brief Edict of Toleration of 1657 permitted for three years the growth of a little Congregationalism, Anabaptism and Quakerism in country areas like Aberdeenshire and Roxburgh, but they were numerically insignificant again a decade later. After the Restoration in 1660, the unreconciled Covenanting presbyterians provided the strongest dissent yet, especially in the south-west, but the fugitives never lost hope of reuniting with the church by winning command over it.

In this respect Scotland showed greater cohesiveness than England or most other north European Protestant states. The internal strength of government based on kirk-session and presbytery (with or without a bishop) generally prevented breakaway movements attaining much strength or momentum, and even where they occurred they often took the form (as in the south-west) of being more Calvinist than the church itself. For the overwhelming majority of Scots everywhere, the Church of Scotland as recognised by the state was the only true kirk: thus far, the foundations for a Godly Commonwealth were truly laid.

It is another question as to how far the church inspired true allegiance and respect in the community. When it came to power in 1560 it was faced with a task of superhuman difficulty: in many places throughout the country churches were ruinous, sacraments and services held in ridicule and the population to a great extent indifferent to both the kirk and the kirkmen. Such obstacles could not be overcome in a day. In some places, like Lochaber, they were hardly tackled for two hundred years, and generally throughout the seventeenth-century Highlands progress was extremely halting. There came a persistent trickle of extremely ungodly reports reminiscent of pre-Reformation days in the Lowlands. Thus at Glen Urquhart in 1671 no communion had been held for twenty-five years, at Dunlichity in 1672 two lairds fought a duel in the kirk, in 1674 the minister of Duthel got so drunk in Inverness on a Saturday night that he could not preach on the Sunday.[11] At Boleskin in the same presbytery 'the dogs that followed the people to church fought over the human bones that protruded through the earthen floor'.[12] A great many churches were ruined and empty of furniture except perhaps for a stool of repentance. In many places in the north—in the Lowland plain as well as in the hills—the 'superstitious' habits of Catholicism lingered more persistently than the faith, and presbyteries prosecuted those who made pilgrimages to wells and old chapels or carried images to funerals. As late as 1643, the old statue of St. Finian from Dunlichity was publicly burnt in the market place at Inverness. Nevertheless, it must still have come as a shock to the Presbytery of Dingwall in 1656 when they discovered that the supposedly Protestant inhabitants of a large area of Wester Ross between Applecross and Loch Broom were worshipping the cult of St. Mourie (or Maolrubha: he gave his name to Loch Maree) with rites as foreign to the Roman church as to their own—with sacrifice of bulls, sunwise perambulation of holy places, adoration of stones and libations of milk.[13] The power of the old saint, like that of fairies and trolls, was believed in more deeply than the creed of the new kirk. In vain the minister exhorted the Highlandmen to family worship and pressed the virtues of regular attendance at sermons. Such piety was to come, but not in the fastnesses of the hills and islands much before the nineteenth century.

In the Lowlands, particularly south of the Tay, as also over much of Highland Perthshire and Argyll, success came more swiftly and more completely. Even so it did not come at once—the precarious finances of the church, if nothing else, ensured that until around the beginning of the seventeenth century in many country parts livings went vacant, with the familiar tale of ruinous churches and neglected sacraments. The first victories were in the burghs, where the kirk-sessions, with the whole-hearted help of the town baillies who were in very many cases themselves elders in the session as well as magistrates in the town, quickly enforced universal attendance at sermons both on Sundays and weekdays, together with observance of the sacraments and respect for the elders and the minister. In burghs and country places alike official 'searchers' patrolled on Sundays to make sure everyone was at church, and they fined absentees. It sounds, from the context of the session minutes, as if they were often very successful in compelling something like universal attendance: thus, when in 1650 a Culross man was charged with 'sitting in his owne hous the whole tym' of worship, he confessed his sin on his knees before the kirk-session and was told he would have to stand in the public place of repentance if he did it again. This could not have happened in quite this way if a lot of other absentees were also missing—it sounds exceptional and particular.[14] On the other hand the necessity for kirk-sessions to pass acts against 'sleepers in church' suggests that some people had their own forms of passive resistance.

Outright disorder directed against the kirk authority was also put down with a firm hand. It was easy to punish simple people like the wife of a baillie in Crail who in 1561 shouted to the congregation to pull the minister 'owt of the pulpot be the luggis',[15] but it was altogether harder to discipline a man like Gilbert Keith, son of the Earl Mariscal, who retorted, when charged with an incident of fornication, that if they had asked him sooner he could have told them of fifty more faults. He refused to submit to discipline and remained a thorn in the flesh of the elders for years, staying away from church, lighting fires in the streets at Midsummer eve (regarded as a superstitious custom) and even breaking the windows of the kirk and shooting bullets into its door. But they got him after seven years, and in 1609 made him stand before the congregation and 'in maist humble maner . . . craiff first God, then the ministrie and magistrattis, pardoun and forgiffness'.[16] It took all the authority of a large burgh to make an example of so powerful a man.

The success of the church in the towns, however, already largely achieved before 1580, was widely repeated in the countryside in the next half century. The average Lowland Scot does seem to have become a regular church-goer, reasonably attentive to the sermons and reasonably respectful of the session. If few were as diligent in personal devotion and family worship as the General Assembly would have liked, there was always an important minority who were: in the towns such private piety was common among the burgesses, and in the countryside was perhaps especially common among the smaller lairds and the larger tenants who gave many sons to the ministry.

On two groups, however, the reformed kirk made a somewhat limited impact. The first was the nobility, whose personal power in rural areas made them largely invulnerable to the criticism of the session, even if they ventured to voice it. While some of the magnates certainly became pious and serious Calvinist Christians, like the Marquess of Argyll and the Earl of Cassillis in the 1640s, many remained singularly lukewarm towards the kirk, and readily became hostile when it seemed to erode their own powers of social control. One of the results of the Covenanting movement was that in 1649 the nobility temporarily lost any say in the selection of parish ministers even in country areas: they quickly became hostile then to the presumptions of 'such low and mean persons as the clergy, which consisted now of the sons of their own servants and farmers'.[17]

The second group in question was the wide tribe of vagrants, those able-bodied poor who, having no foothold on the land and being treated as social outcasts by church and state alike set the laws of both at naught. There is some evidence that their numbers increased in the sixteenth century as a consequence of rising population and an inelastic economy, but nobody knows how large a proportion they were of the whole of society. In 1596 the General Assembly spoke of the great number of idle poor 'without lawfull calling;—as pypers, fidlers, songsters, sorners, pleasants, strong beggars' who lived in harlotry and never set foot in a church even to baptise their children,[18] and a century later Andrew Fletcher of Saltoun ascribed to the vagrants who gathered 'in thousands' to roister in the hills, a life of incest, crime and godless pleasure.[19] Yet despite these exceptions, the seventeenth-century church won a deep respect and exercised a profound power over all other classes of men. The first intentions of the Book of Discipline had been substantially fulfilled before 1630 outside the inner Highland zone.

2. GODLY DISCIPLINE

The success of the church was greatly assisted by the strength of its discipline over the morals of its congregations, and this in turn could not have come to fruition without support from the civil authorities. We have already seen how vital it was to the earliest kirk-sessions that the burgh magistrates were ready to use their secular power against Catholics, absentees from church and disrespectful persons: they carried this support further and punished in a variety of ways any whom the kirk found guilty of moral outrages. Furthermore, the state itself, though never prepared to knuckle under completely to the judgement of the ministers, made a whole variety of moral misdemeanours statutory offences against the crown—adultery in 1563, fornication in 1567, sabbath-breaking in 1579, drunkenness in 1617 and so forth. Crucial to the system was recognition that a person excommunicated from the spiritual society of the church for persistent immorality was also an outlaw from the civil society of the state: in 1572 excommunicated persons were held incapable of bearing office or giving witness at law: in 1609 they were declared unable to enjoy lands, rents and revenues. In the days of royal control of the church through bishops excommunication was used sparingly, but after 1640 the theocratic Covenanters in the General Assembly resorted to it again and again for political as well as for moral offences, thus adding immeasurably to the confusion, division and hatred of the civil wars. It was for this reason that, although the civil penalties attached to excommunication were retained in the episcopacy of Charles II, they were finally abandoned in 1690 lest the restored General Assembly should ever again be tempted to misuse its independence. In 1712 the Toleration Act forbade magistrates to enforce kirk censures or summonses. The central claim of the Book of Discipline that the whole kingdom 'as well the rulers as the ruled' be subjected to the church, which had been repeated in still more resounding terms by Melville and his successors, was at last destroyed by these acts. Inevitably the terrors of church discipline thereafter began to wane in the popular eye.

It is extremely interesting to see what offences the church courts regarded as particularly heinous. Right from the start, and right down until after the end of our period irrespective as to whether episcopalians or presbyterians were in command, it was sexual offences that monopolised most of the session's attention. For example, the kirk-session of St. Andrews heard about 1,000 cases of this type between 1560 and 1600, or about one a fortnight: in Edinburgh forty out of sixty cases that came before the Canongate session in 1566 were of this type—St. Cuthbert's heard twenty-seven such cases in 1681, thirty-four in 1691 and eighteen in 1699.[20]

Most of the sexual offences were described as adultery or fornication. The first was much the most serious, and offenders were heavily punished—generally by being forced to stand dressed in sackcloth, bareheaded and bare-footed, first at the kirk door and then on the public

80

stool of repentance in front of the congregation on every Sunday for six months, or occasionally for several years, and sometimes by whipping and fining as well. Few chose to resist, for by statutes of 1563 and 1581 anyone guilty of 'notour and manifest adultery' who refused to submit to ecclesiastical punishment could be put to death by the civil sword.

Fornication was always a less serious matter, though the term covered offences of differing character. 'Harlotrie' was the problem of the towns, especially of Edinburgh where kirk-sessions and baillies alike were concerned by the numbers of brothels they discovered in the swarming closes of the Cannongate and the High Street: the men were usually brought to public penance, and the prostitutes banished after ducking 'in the deepest and foulest pool of the town'. In the country-side and small burghs casual intercourse was more typical. 'Fornication', said Sir Antony Weldon in 1617 (he did not like the Scots and his evidence should not be taken too seriously) 'they hold but a pastime, wherein man's ability is approved, and a woman's fertility is discovered'.[21] Misbehaviour, however, usually went undetected even by the eagle-eyed session until a child was on the way: the church then busied itself discovering the father, compelling a marriage if it could and finally punishing both partners by several weeks penance *in sacco*. Somewhat different was co-habitation after a formal betrothal or 'hand-fasting', a social custom of great antiquity which the Scots shared with the Scandinavians and many other races, but which seemed to the reformers not only to be wicked in itself, but also a threat to the holy sacrament of marriage—as many couples were content to live together all their lives without further religious ceremony. This, too, was punished on the stool of repentance often to the surprise and indignation of the offenders who were unaware they had done anything wrong but who dared not resist for fear their children would not be baptised. All varieties of fornication were punishable by fining according to a statute of 1567 ratified on several occasions down to 1690.

It is not easy to measure the effect of the campaign against sexual irregularities. It certainly did not worry the vagrant poor, nor did it much affect the Highlander. For the rest of the Scots, it is uncertain whether it reduced the total of promiscuity and premarital intercourse or not. The General Assembly often thought not, and a modern commentator has remarked that 'the frequency of the occurrence must have taken from its seriousness and (like a modern police court conviction) the discipline was perhaps more likely to make reformation difficult than to induce it'.[22] Certainly when illegitimacy statistics first became available in the later nineteenth century they lend some support to the view that any change in Scottish sexual *mores* cannot have been both universal and enduring: in many rural areas it was still normal for the labourer's first child to be born, or at least conceived, out of wedlock.

Yet it is really impossible to believe that such a campaign could be sustained enthusiastically for a century and a half and have no impact at all. If nothing else it transformed the outward attitude of society from one of great permissiveness before 1560 ('so that sin is reputed to be no sin') to one of rigorous and inquisitorial disapproval in the seventeenth century. All who offended must now have done so much more furtively and guiltily wherever the kirk-session was functioning normally. And in those groups to whom the kirk had particular appeal—the burgesses, the smaller landowners and the larger tenants—the moral change does seem to have been permanent. Sexual respectability has been the apparent mark of most of the Scottish middle classes ever since, even though in the eighteenth and nineteenth centuries furtive middle class brothel-goers were never very rare.

There may also have been other results. The terror and shame that some girls felt at having to parade before the congregation after giving birth to a bastard child drove them to kill their babies: several commentators believed that infanticide increased as a result of kirk discipline. There is some indication that homosexuality also increased at the time of the most intense and hysterical puritan inquisitions in the middle of the century, though whether more was practised or more was found out is again an open question. It was horribly punished: 'the culprits of all ages, from boys to old men, are heard of every few months as burnt on the Castle Hill of Edinburgh, sometimes two together', writes Robert Chambers under the entry of his *Domestic Annals* for 1657.[23]

It is not at all easy to understand why the reformers concentrated on the prosecution of sexual offenders: it was a quite unscriptural emphasis. Perhaps it was simply because a sexual offence was concrete and identifiable: an offender was caught in bed with a girl, or a fatherless baby was produced in the community, and everyone could see what had happened. The deadly sins of greed, pride, untruthfulness, self-righteousness and hypocrisy, on the other hand, were not so easy to define and to see, and the church could not pursue them in court. But the long term effect was to associate in the popular mind the idea of immorality almost exclusively with that of sexual immorality, to the neglect of other forms of sin. It was a serious burden that most Protestant societies laid upon themselves, and one from which they do not find it easy to escape even at the present day.

In all other directions, the earliest Reformed church was not particularly concerned to impose a puritan morality. It was much more concerned about such matters as idle slanderers in its congregations, about blasphemy (which the state refused to make a capital offence, though in 1581 Parliament passed an act imposing fines for swearing), and about a variety of criminal acts such as murder, manslaughter, assault and perjury which the civil sword neglected to prosecute. It is true that the General Assembly also expressed its disapproval of the observation of Christmas and of holding markets on the Sabbath, but the first does not seem to have worried the sessions much before the 1570s and the second—as session records also show—was part of a wide campaign to avoid distractions in time of preaching rather than Mosaic Sabbatarianism as it was later known. The church was also concerned in a general way about certain forms of indulgence. 'The preachers', said Knox in 1562, 'were wondrous vehement in reprehension of all manner of vice, which then began to abound; and especially avarice, oppression of the poor, excess, riotous cheer, banqueting, immoderate dancing, and whoredom, that thereof ensues'.[24] But this did not mean the church was puritan in the sense that it later became. Knox himself did not utterly condemn dancing, and as late as 1576 the General Assembly gave a surprisingly moderate reply to the question whether a minister might be allowed to keep an alehouse—'ane minister or reader that tapis ale or beir or wyne and keeps ane open taverne sould be exhortit be the Commissioners to keep decorum'.[25]

Puritanism really began to take root simultaneously with Melville's presbyterianism, and from 1574 until about 1612 it showed itself in many different directions. There were renewed and much more sustained attacks on Christmas and on other traditional holidays such as Midsummer Eve. Bonfires, pilgrimages, dancing, carol singing and plays on these occasions were all forbidden though they did not on that account immediately die out. Men were forced to do penance for failing to work on Christmas day. The ministers were commanded by the

General Assembly to keep their hair short and to dress in sober colours as an example to their flock, while Parliament passed an unsuccessful sumptuary law in 1581 to restrict the dress of laymen. The General Assembly spoke of card-playing, excessive drinking and gluttony, 'gorgeous and vaine apparell, filthie and bawdie speeches' in the same breath as adultery and incest, and attacked display and merrymaking at weddings and burials. Above all there was now a much stricter Sabbatarianism. Parliament in 1579 forbade all forms of labour, bodily recreation and drinking on Sundays: the General Assembly added a general condemnation of Sunday dancing and travel. This was enforced through the efficient machinery of the session and presbytery, backed in many cases by the civil courts, and the tide seemed set in the direction of the strictest imposition of puritan morality.

For a time, however, the tide was stemmed. James VI, many laymen and not a few of the ministers themselves set their faces resolutely against the puritans—'cherish no man more than a good pastor, hate no man more than a proud puritan' wrote the king in his advice to his eldest son. As soon as the crown regained firm control of the kirk by reviving the effective episcopate, the more extreme rules began to be relaxed. The Archbishop of St. Andrews, for example, took rather ostentatious pleasure in playing golf on the Sabbath after the time of church was past. The last of the Articles of Perth in 1618 commanded celebration of the five main festivals of the Christian year, and the Archbishop in 1620 also gleefully imprisoned a St. Andrews tailor for not observing Christmas. Though there was popular resistance in some of the kirk-sessions to this withdrawal from puritanism, and though the king took care not to enforce the Articles of Perth too strictly, for the moment a balance was kept between the puritan and anti-puritan sentiments in Scotland.

All this came to an abrupt stop with the Covenanters after 1638, and a second period of compulsory puritanism, more intense than the first, swept the country for a generation. 'Friday the 25 of December, of old called Yool-day, and whereon preachings, and praises, and thanksgiveing was given to God in remembrance of the birth of our blessed Saviour, and therwith friends and neighbours made mirrie with others, and had good cheir: now this day no such preachings nor such meittings with mirrieness, walking up and down; but contrair, this day commanded to be keeped as ane work-day . . . feasting and idlesett forbidden out of pulpitts' wrote Patrick Spalding of Aberdeen in his chronicle for 1641, 'the people wes otherwise inclyned, but durst not dissobey'. Then again in 1642 'Pashe-day 10 Aprile, no fleshe durst be sold in Abirdeene for making good cheir as wes wont to be . . . a mater never befoir hard of in this land'.[26] All the old legislation was re-enacted, usually with more stringent penalties, and a rigid attempt made to enforce it in the sessions—particular attacks were made on festive burials and weddings, 'fruitful seminaries of all lasciviousnesse and debaushtrie', and in 1649 the General Assembly passed an act prohibiting 'promiscuous dancing' on all occasions.

The regime of Oliver Cromwell that followed the rule of the Covenanters was in complete sympathy with these puritan tendencies however much it might abhor their kirk polity, and in 1656 Parliament passed an Act that marked the high-water of Scottish Sabbatarianism, forbidding anyone to frequent taverns, dance, hear profane music, wash, brew ale or bake bread, 'profanely walk' or travel or do any other worldly business on Sundays. The burgh authorities and the kirk-sessions again threw their weight behind the campaign and sometimes, on local initiative, even tried to extend them. Thus, for example, the session at Ceres in Fife punished children for playing on Sundays, and in 1657 gave a public warning against carrying in water, sweeping houses or casting out ashes on the Sabbath. At Glasgow in 1652 the kirk-session appointed paid spies to report on the congregation's lapses: but the same thing had happened in 'episcopal' Aberdeen as far back as 1603.[27]

Inevitably these measures were unpopular among wide sections of the community, though not necessarily with the majority. The rejoicing with which many Scots greeted the Restoration must have been due in large measure to a feeling that the cheerlessness and regimentation of life would now come to an end. Convulsive reaction against the puritans followed in many places so that 'many behaved as if they had been delivered to work abomination: the flood-gates of impiety were opened'.[28] The restored episcopalian establishment was very concerned lest reaction should go too far, and carefully re-enacted the Sabbatarian statute of 1579 in 1661, as well as also attempting to restrict luxury at weddings and burials and promoting a number of puritanical sumptuary laws, which remained on the statute book until the nineteenth century. The presbyterian General Assembly after 1690 made a fresh and very determined attempt to impose them through the kirk-session, and for some years the atmosphere recalled that of the 1640s.

Nevertheless, without state backing for excommunication the tide turned again. The repressive statutes were observed less and less as the eighteenth century progressed. By 1760 the most puritan kirk-sessions were those of the secession churches, which had by then split away from the body of the Church of Scotland and gathered their main support from sections of the peasantry and of the town craftsmen. If it had not been for the remarkable general upsurge of puritan sentiment in the nineteenth century, the whole tradition would in time have died a natural death.

Once again it is hard to judge how far the church succeeded: did Scotland become a puritan country in the seventeenth century? It certainly did not in the northern Highlands, where the ministers themselves ignored the General Assembly and continued to go around gaily dressed in plaids and drinking with their parishioners on Sundays even in Covenanting times. It perhaps made rather little impression in the Lowlands north of the Tay. Enthusiastic ministers might impose it through their sessions for a time, but there was little feeling for it among the congregation and no desire to cling to it once the Restoration had come, though respect for the Sabbath was perhaps more deeply ingrained than other aspects of puritanism.

In southern Scotland its reception was much more mixed. The nobles and vagrants could and did ignore it in their different ways. In many areas of the south observance of the Sabbath was for a long time even into the eighteenth century so scrupulous as to amount almost to a superstition; yet there were always weak souls giving way, however strict the kirk-session—millers unwilling to stop their wheels, salt-masters unwilling to quench their fires, fishermen unwilling to leave their nets, countrymen everywhere unwilling to leave the harvest or the sowing when the Lord sent fine Sabbath weather. As late as 1672 there was still a recognised Sunday market at Elie, and in 1705 still one at Anstruther Wester, both apparently having continued from time immemorial. Puritanism probably had a really firm grip as a way of life in those areas that clung, actively or passively, to the Covenanting tradition after 1660 and among those small lairds, tenants and burgesses who practised family worship and other aspects of Calvinist piety most seriously. This was the influential minority that was most shocked by the falling away after 1660, and which backed the General Assembly in its rearguard action on behalf of godly discipline in the years after 1690. The rest of the population were at least made conscious that they ought to feel guilty if they were not puritan in their hearts, which was not without influence on the general character of the Scottish people in the centuries that followed.

3. EDUCATION AND POOR RELIEF

As we have seen, the reformers' plans to punish the adult for his sin were, from the start, intended to be supplemented by an ambitious scheme for education. They were fortunate in this respect to be able to build on earlier tradition, for Catholic Scotland had been generous in scholastic foundations. Three universities—at St. Andrews, Glasgow and Aberdeen—existed already, though their curricula and teaching methods were narrow and old-fashioned by European standards. Song schools and grammar schools, some intended primarily to teach music and staff the church choirs, others also undertaking elementary instruction in reading, writing and Latin grammar, existed in all the main burghs and in many quite small towns like Kirkwall, Montrose, Brechin and Musselburgh.[29] Private tutors worked in the lairds' castles to good effect, since of the 216 barons who 'signed with their hands at the pen' the Bond of Association in 1567 only sixteen could not write their names.

The reformers did not find it easy to advance beyond this position, or to set up a school in every parish and either a college or a grammar school in every burgh, as was their expressed intention. Some progress was made early in higher education. Melville reformed St. Andrews and Glasgow Universities between 1574 and 1579, Edinburgh University received its charter in 1582, and Marischal College was founded as a new university in Aberdeen in 1593 due to the lethargy of King's in responding to the pressures of the reformers. Primary education on the other hand was hamstrung from the start by lack of finances. Here and there in the countryside schools were set up, the minister as often as not having to fulfil the schoolmaster's function as well as his own. In the burghs the old schools were maintained; both the song schools and a number of new foundations were transformed into reformed grammar schools or into ordinary parish schools. Musical teaching decayed. It is hard to believe there was much advance in educational standards over the country as a whole before 1600, but a child did not necessarily get a negligible schooling. James Melville, for instance, left a fascinating account of the teaching he received in the 1560s at the village school of Logie-Montrose where the parish minister doubled as schoolmaster. He learned his catechism, prayers and scripture, Latin grammar and French language, something of Horace, Virgil and Cicero and even something of Erasmus. He also learned archery, fencing, swimming, wrestling, running, jumping and golf. But probably neither then nor at any other times, were there many village schools that did so much for their lads.[30]

In the seventeenth century there was more activity. It was in 1616 that the state at last backed the kirk by an act in Privy Council commanding every parish to establish a school 'where convenient means may be had', and in 1633 Parliament ratified this with the additional provision that heritors (landowners) should be taxed to provide the necessary endowment—though the phrase in the 1616 act still left them with a loophole through which to escape payment if they were really determined to do so. With the Covenanters, the education programme again received important emphasis. From the start the revived General Assembly expressed concern for schools,[31] and this received legislative form in an act of 1646 which forced the heritors without exception or excuse to pay for the parish school. In the half century before 1660, the plantation of schools therefore made great strides. In Fife, for instance, by the time of the Restoration all the parishes in Dunfermline Presbytery had a school-master, in Kirkcaldy Presbytery thirteen out of fourteen parishes had one, in St. Andrews and Cupar Presbyteries seventeen out of the nineteen parishes in each; in Ayrshire half or more of the parishes in the Presbytery of Ayr had a schoolmaster, and in Ellon Presbytery, Aberdeenshire, six parishes out of eight. Many areas to the north were less well served. The northern and north-western Highlands may have had no parish schools at all, though the foundation of isolated schools in such burghs as Inverary and Dingwall was satisfactorily accomplished and children came even from the Macleod lands in the western isles to attend the grammar school at Rosemarkie.

The pattern was therefore patchy, but making allowance for numerous 'adventure schools' run by private persons outwith church control (but often tolerated by the local session) it is clear that a considerably greater proportion of the Scottish population was literate in 1660 than had been the case a century or even a generation before. Perhaps even more important, the Covenanters and their predecessors had established solid institutional foundations for later achievements. Although in 1661 the legislative position reverted to that of 1633, the network of schools continued to be extended over the next thirty years. Professor Donaldson is prepared to say 'with some confidence' that 'before the Revolution if not indeed before the National Covenant, it was the normal thing for a Lowland parish to have its school'.[32] In 1696 a further act restored the provisions of 1646 with means of enforcement 'more suitable to the age', and this continued to regulate Scottish elementary education until 1872.

School life began for the Scottish child in the seventeenth century at the age of five, though many did not arrive until they were seven and may have attended an unofficial dame-school first. It was meant to continue for five years before the child either departed or went on to a larger burgh school or possibly straight to the University according to his ability, but at this period the parents of poor children could seldom let them stay much beyond the age of eight unless they won a bursary. While he attended, the child was worked hard. There were no official school holidays during the year, though as it was impossible to stop country children being withdrawn at harvest time many masters recognised the facts of peasant life and closed for a month or more in the summer. The school day lasted eight to twelve hours, generally starting at 6.00 a.m. in the summer and allowing two breaks of an hour each for breakfast and lunch. Since small children could not possibly be kept at their books for that length of time for six days a week, two or three 'play-days' were instituted each week to allow for bodily exercise—'let the master see that they play not at any unlawful or obscene pastime or such as may readily defile or rent their clothing or hurt their bodies' ran the rules drawn up for Dundonald school in Ayrshire in 1640.[33]

The curriculum varied according to the knowledge of the master, but everywhere religious instruction and good behaviour—'godliness and gud manners' as they were called at Pittenweem—took pride of place. 'The fear of the Lord is the beginning of wisdom' was what a child scribbled on the first volume of Ellon kirk-session minutes.[34] Everyone learned reading and writing. Many schools also taught Latin to the older and more able children: arithmetic was taught in the burghs. Other subjects were unusual. The main emphasis was on piety, whatever the subject in hand—the Bible was the only English reading text. Corporal punishment was very frequently regarded as part of the system. Although excessive use of the tawse was deplored by the kirk-session, insufficient use was also generally noted with disapproval. Thus in 1675 the Synod of Aberdeen asked its presbyteries only to ask three questions of the schoolmasters: whether he makes them learn the catechism, whether he teaches them prayers for morning and evening and a grace for meals, and whether 'he chastise them for cursing, swearing, lying, speakeing profanietie; for disobedience to parents and what vices that appeares in them'.[35]

The best teachers, however, regarded education not merely as a mechanical or a punitive process, but also as an intellectual one. The catechism must be learnt: could it not also be explained to the child? The Bible must be read: could it not be used as a basis for elementary theological exposition? At some schools—for example, Dundonald— the children's attendance at Sunday sermons was compulsory in order that the class could be examined on their content on Monday mornings. The church authorities, assisted by the baillies in the towns, kept strict supervision over the schoolmaster to ensure that he was orthodox, and as long as the kirk-session remained itself enthusiastic and strictly Calvinist, it was likely enough that the parish children would be brought up good supporters of the Godly Commonwealth. If the session was to lose any of its fervour it was always possible that the training of children to think, without making it absolutely clear what they must not think, could have social consequences quite different from those the reformers intended.

The other major social institution which the Reformers bequeathed to succeeding centuries was the Scottish Poor Law. Here again they were not building without foundations—the medieval church and state alike had recognised, since the fifteenth century, that paupers fell into two categories, the able-bodied vagrant poor who should be severely punished for their idleness, and the helpless impotent poor, victims of old age, disease or disability, who had a genuine claim on the charity of society and might be licensed as 'King's Beggars' or 'Bluegowns'. The principle that every parish should be responsible for its own poor had been laid down by a statute of 1535, and all these features became embodied in poor law legislation after the Reformation.

The earliest reformers, however, though hostile enough to the idle vagrant, tried to appear in a special sense as the champions both of the impotent poor and of the peasant and labourer. One of the opening shots of the Reformation campaign had been a 'Beggars Summonds', nailed to the doors of the friaries in all the main towns calling on the friars to surrender their possessions to the poor 'to whom it rightfully belongs'. The Book of Discipline of 1560 had proposed using part of the patrimony of the kirk as a fund for the relief of the poor, and had called on landlords to cease from oppressing their tenants. In this first statement of intentions, the sphere of ecclesiastical discipline had been defined as including many offences against the poor. So prominent a part of Knox's programme did social justice appear that a foreign Catholic in 1565 was moved to exclaim 'even Mohammed never had such arms as the heretics have now with their freedom in printing, licence in promising, their abuse of taxes and imposts as unendurable and the hopes they hold out of dividing the goods of the church among the poor'.[36]

The complete failure of Knox's followers and successors to carry out any part of this programme makes the most depressing reading of anything in the history of the Godly Commonwealth. In the first place, since the reformers failed to appropriate the patrimony of the old church they were unable to carry out their expressed intention of basing poor relief upon income from tithes, a proposal which, had it been carried out, would have been unique in European history. By the time the finances of the church had been set in order Knox's idea had been forgotten and other, more traditional, methods of financing relief, mainly from voluntary church collections, had become institutionalised. Secondly, the church after a time forgot its duty of protesting against the economic oppression of landlords—the last time the General Assembly seems to have attempted to interfere in these matters was in 1596 when they listed among the 'common corruptions of all estates within this realm' the 'cruell oppression of the poore tennents quhairby the haill commons in this countrie are utterly wrackit'.[37] Thereafter nothing more was heard, either from the episcopalian establishment or from the Covenanters or from the presbyterians after 1690, though there were plenty of occasions for protest. The enserfment of the colliers took place in the seventeenth century, for example, without a murmur from the church (see page 180 below). A similar fate befell the intentions to protect the poor through ecclesiastical discipline—a quite insignificant number of cases of unfair exploitation came before the earliest sessions in the burghs, most were referred at once to the baillies and very few offenders ever reached the stool of repentance: at St. Andrews, for instance, one usurer was indicted between 1560 and 1600 compared to the thousand or so sexual offenders.[38] Indictment for economic offences was virtually unknown in the seventeenth century. Both in the countryside and in the towns the explanation is probably the same—the lairds, merchants and tradesmen formed so important a part of the kirk's supporters both in the session and outside that the church became blind and silent before the prospect that the economic self-interest of landlords and the middle classes could be sinful. The older tradition of strict punishment of the idle and sparing charity to the impotent came to the fore again in the practice of both church and state.

The formal Scottish poor law as it developed after the Reformation rested primarily on the statute of 1579, which decreed that all sturdy beggars should be arrested and scourged, that all impotent poor should be placed in alms houses or given badges to beg within their own parishes, and that the parish indwellers could be assessed to provide a poor rate for the support of their own paupers. It owed much to the example of an English act of 1572. Another act of 1597 transferred to the kirk-session the duty of supervising relief, and one of 1617 gave the local justices and constables the duty of punishing the vagrant and assessing the parish. There were several further acts especially after the Restoration, aimed primarily at forcing the idle into useful employment, but few of them were enforced. In practice, very little of the whole corpus of legislation was workable. Scotland remained as full of idle vagrants as ever, since, as the Edinburgh justices once remarked, there were not enough jails to house one-tenth of the beggars. The impotent poor seldom received the benefit of a poor rate because local communities resisted the efforts of central authority to make them submit to any rating assessment. There was a surprising instance of this in 1623, when the crops failed and many peasants abandoned their empty holdings and wandered begging through the countryside in search of alms to ward off starvation. Privy Council, sensing the dangers from a national famine, commanded justices to raise a temporary poor-rate from everyone else: there was no question of trying to raise one on a permanent basis, as the council seem to have appreciated that that task had already become impossible. Even so they received a remarkably dusty answer from several counties, and especially from the justices of East Lothian who threatened to go on strike if they were obliged to levy the rate. 'Every contribution is odious and smellis of ane taxatioun', they said 'we think it ane hard matter to be employit in ane service toylsome and trublesome unto us, importing nathair credeit ner benefeit bot ane schadowing appeirance of ane commoun weill'.[39]

In England, despite some initial resentment to compulsory assessment, it had become virtually universal practice by the second half of the seventeenth century and the income from it was dispensed at the hand of the parish overseers, who were secular officials. In Scotland, however, the resistance to compulsory assessment was completely successful throughout the century (not more than two or three parishes seem to have adopted a poor rate even as late as 1700) and such poor relief as was distributed remained in the hands of the kirk-sessions. The funds they had available consisted of collections raised for the poor at the church services, of income from lands or money bequeathed to the poor, of the sessions fines levied for moral offences and of the cash raised by hiring out a parish hearse or mort cloth at burials. It generally amounted to a very modest sum even in the wealthiest parishes.

This was distributed to the impotent poor by the minister or his deputy after careful investigation into the material and moral condition of the recipients. At Aberdeen in 1621 paupers were given indoor relief only on condition that they attended church daily and the catechising every Monday, and that they received no guests in their homes and never swore. Such extreme strictness however was probably unusual.[40] Most relief took place in the pauper's own house, though the large burghs always had alms-houses. These were never adequate—Aberdeen, for example, with a total population of some 9,000 in the 1640s, had five 'hospitals' which could house about fifty paupers.[41] Large burghs also often set up a 'house of correction' where vagrants were set to work at some supposedly useful task: these were very small (that at Aberdeen had room for ten paupers) and not very efficient, but it was only by entering one that any able-bodied pauper became entitled to any relief at all.

In the countryside it is possible that as long as harvests were good the amount of relief dribbled out in this way may have been just sufficient to keep starvation from the doors of those whom their own families could not support. The elders in a small community would know exactly who was most in need, though to have any recourse at all to the charity of the session was for a long time held in Scotland to be a personal disgrace. If the harvests failed, however, the church became helpless to relieve the suffering of the masses from its own small pittance. In the eighteenth century the landowners often came to the rescue in such a crisis by buying corn from outside and selling it at or below cost price: we do not yet know if this was the case earlier. In any case it proved impossible to relieve the famine of the 1690s, of which some account is given in chapter VI below, by any means at all. There were inevitably some terrible occasions in rural life—and this was one —in which even the most elaborate schemes to finance poor relief on an adequate and generous basis would not have sufficed.

But there is no disguising the fact that the Scottish poor law in the seventeenth century was weak and mean, and the very opposite from what had been intended by the reformers in that first flush of excitement and idealism when they nailed the 'Beggars Summonds' to the door.

4. THE AFTERMATH OF THE REFORMATION

The Godly Commonwealth, as outlined in the Book of Discipline of 1560, had plainly failed by 1690. Scotland had not become a theocracy; ecclesiastical discipline had been fatally weakened by the withdrawal of state support for excommunication; the General Assembly was on the defensive fighting a rearguard action for certain moral values, some of which were alien to the intentions of Knox; the original policy of the kirk towards the poor had been twisted out of all recognition; the Highlanders and the vagrant poor had neither been won to the Calvinist ideal; the nobility and other social 'rulers' had not been made to submit to the kirk along with the 'ruled'. On the other hand, the exertions of the kirk to change society had made an indelible mark upon it; many had become pious and enthusiastic Protestants; the social attitude to sex had been profoundly affected; a strain of puritanism had taken root in some sections of southern Lowland society and the educational system had been developed to a point considerably in advance of anything known before, and considerably in advance of anything known in England or in most other European countries. What relevance had these facts to the long term development of the Scottish nation, and in particular to the remarkable flowering of national achievement on both the economic and cultural level in the later eighteenth century?

Max Weber's classic thesis suggested a close link between the rise of Calvinism and the rise of a capitalist economy in European societies.[42] The Calvinist ethic, with its stress upon a man's 'calling' and on the virtues of hard work and frugality, in its destruction of medieval taboos against money-lending and in its belief that the successful acquisition of wealth is a sign of God's blessing, is said to provide the ideal soil for the rooting of economic individualism. Few countries were more completely Calvinist than Scotland, yet it is hard to see how any support can be found for Weber's thesis from the situation in this country between 1560 and 1690. Within this period the Reformation cannot be shown in any way to have favoured the rise of economic individualism. On the contrary, the medieval restrictions on free competition imposed by the privileges of the Royal Burghs, by the regulations directing Scottish trade to the Netherlands to one staple port, and by the rights of the merchant guilds and of the craft guilds in the towns survived intact for a full century after 1560 with their strength in those communities and among those classes which had from the start been most attracted to the Reformation. The restrictions only gave way slowly in the forty years after 1660 for reasons which appear to be unconnected with religion: their life was therefore considerably more prolonged in Calvinist Scotland than in most other European societies.

Nor is this altogether strange. The ethic of the kirk-session, with its strong group discipline over moral behaviour, fitted in so perfectly with the tradition of the guild and burgh with their group discipline over civic and economic behaviour that the former may have strengthened the communal framework in which the latter thrived. It is certainly not always easy to know whether it is the guild or the church speaking on certain topics. For instance, in the sixteenth century the General Assembly speaks of the evils of forestalling and regrating at the markets as though it were a guild; and in the seventeenth century the merchant guild of Stirling denounces opening shops on Sundays and wearing bonnets in church as though it were a session; a merchant's indentures threatens an extra two years' service for an apprentice if he commits the 'filthie sins of fornication or adulturie'.[43]

Furthermore, in the public writings of divines and in the private letters of merchants alike it is impossible to discover any emphasis upon the idea that God rewards virtue with riches: what does appear is the quite differently emphasised proposition that God punishes sin by an economic calamity. This may be national calamity: all the famines of the late sixteenth and seventeenth centuries were attributed to the sins of the nation. It may be individual calamity: when a Scottish merchant in Rotterdam was caught smuggling yarn in 1688 he wrote to his friend explaining his chagrin and his feelings: 'This is a grivous cross to me, for I stayed here partly because I was afraid of sinfull snairs at home, and I thought I had got some hop from the Lord that I might get myselft cleared of som debt (but) I have wofully involved myselft in that which utterly defeats any hop I can ever extricat myself. I deseyer submission and to be humbled under the Almighty Hand that is justly against me. For there was an very immediate Hand: for if the boat had come on either trak above or below I had missed that fellow . . . a watcher'.[44] Alternatively an unsuccessful business venture was seen as the will of an inscrutable Providence: 'You seem to be most uneasy about the misfortune of a bad market and do not submit your-self to the providence of a Divine hand which orders all things as he seeth meet'.[45] Such a philosophy, by setting the businessman to ex-amine his soul rather than his account books might prove positively discouraging to economic progress.

Nevertheless, if we take the long view of Scottish history it does become difficult not to believe that Calvinism contributed certain things which could hardly help but favour the expansion of economic activity and the enrichment of cultural life. The Knoxian idea of education as an indispensable necessity for all was certainly one bequest of the utmost importance to posterity. As we shall see in chapter XVIII below, the eighteenth century carried the work of planting schools even further than the seventeenth: new experiments were made in education for the middle-class and the lower middle-class in the towns: the universities were reformed (by churchmen) and made much larger in intake and more comprehensive in curriculum than they had been in the seventeenth century. All this was done by building upon the foundations that had been laid years before, but it was carried through without quite the same emphasis on religious orthodoxy. By 1780 the Lowland Scot could boast with some justice of having a more ex-tensive and liberal educational system than any in Europe. The pro-vision of elementary education that would teach everyone in the rural Lowlands and many in the towns and the Highlands to read and write, and the accessibility of secondary education and even of university

Craigievar Castle, Aberdeenshire, c. 1620. Perhaps the apotheosis of
Scottish baronial architecture. Note that it has only one door, which
could be defended by an iron yett or grille

Dr. Webster preaching to a congregation in Edinburgh, about 1750

education to an exceptionally wide spectrum of the middle classes, must have had very great cultural implications. It enabled the country to develop and maximise its talents in a way that had not been possible in the past and might not always be possible in the future.

Another factor, operating on the psychological rather than the institutional plane, picks up again the themes associated with Weber. It concerns the growth of what we might call the serious-minded strain in the Scottish character. To the question as to what the true purpose of life was, both the Catholic church and the reformers would have replied that it was to prepare the soul for entry into Heaven: 'to glorify God and enjoy Him for ever' as the Scottish catechism says. Most Scottish laymen of the later middle ages, however, if they thought about the subject at all, generally assumed that a man would enter Heaven irrespective of the quality of his life provided he paid the church taxes and was absolved from his sins at an opportune moment— theologians taught somewhat differently, but few went to sermons or were prepared to take moral lessons from a blatantly immoral secular clergy. After the Reformation, the reformers not only got the Lowland population into the churches to listen to their ethical teaching but also taught that those predestined to the Kingdom of Heaven were distinguished by the consistent quality of their lives on earth—by their personal piety above all, but also by their sober carriage, their frugality, their industriousness and their conscientious fulfilment of the duties of their social position. Children were taught from the beginning that their life was a serious pilgrimage from the wicked ignorance in which they had been born to the perfect knowledge of God in which they ought to die, and as the hall-mark of Grace was living a godly life, this was the practical objective to which they ought to be striving. 'The God of Calvinism' says Weber 'demanded of his believers not single good works but a life of good works combined into a unified system . . . the moral conduct of the average man was thus deprived of its planless and unsystematic character and subjected to a consistent method of conduct'.[46]

For the first century after 1560 the achievement of a godly life remained the satisfying objective to which this 'method of conduct' was directed. The kirk-session, the town baillies, even to some degree the landed classes and the state itself—all these ruling institutions in Scottish society paid great respect to the man who devoted his existence to ordered personal piety by scrupulously observing the sabbath,

97

attending church, carrying out family worship at home and avoiding those external sins which were the prey of the session. Then came the partial revulsion from the puritanism which had resulted from the rule of the pious between 1638 and 1660, followed by the rearguard action of the General Assembly to defend the old ideals in the years after 1690, and finally, the long, slow decline of enthusiasm in the eighteenth century as puritanism went on the defensive. In accounting for the decline of puritanism we need look no further than the general exhaustion of society with religious controversy which, though it remained a satisfying occupation to some groups even in the eighteenth century, by then no longer held the interest of most of the influential middle classes or of the lairds. In the national context intense religious emotion led not to the attainment of the City of God but to sterile squabbles between episcopalians and presbyterians, and then between presbyterian factions themselves. In the international context Scotland was affected by the whole European movement towards greater religious toleration, and towards a much more secular outlook among the intellectuals of England, Holland and France to whom she looked for a lead.

For many people brought up to believe that life was a pilgrimage towards an objective, therefore, extreme personal piety no longer sufficed as the ultimate goal. The world might even treat it with derision. Yet the teaching of their childhood had been strong, and the teaching that they gave to their children was likely to remain strong. Once the threshold has been crossed from an unmethodical to a methodical view of moral conduct it appears to be remarkably difficult for society to revert quickly to the *status quo ante*. They therefore handed on an ingrained respect for sobriety, industriousness and the fulfilment of a social role, and above all they felt the need within themselves to work compulsively and systematically to some positive purpose.

If intense piety was becoming unsatisfactory, what could replace it as a purpose? Scotland towards the second half of the eighteenth century began to be presented with a series of economic opportunities which she grasped with extraordinary verve. All the 'Calvinist' qualities could now be switched to a purely materialistic end. She also embarked upon a cultural golden age the like of which had never been seen before or since. The singleminded drive that is seen so often in business, farming and trade in the eighteenth century, and which appeared in cultural matters in men as diverse as Adam Smith, James Watt and Sir Walter Scott, is strangely reminiscent of the energy of the seventeenth-century elders in the kirk when they set about imposing discipline on the congregation. Calvinism thus seems to be released as a psychological force for secular change just at the moment when it is losing its power as a religion: indeed, it could not be released any earlier because a systematic Calvinist religion is itself so all-consuming in its demands.

Other writers have suggested different links between religion and the kind of psychological changes which are most favourable to the maximisation of economic talent. McClelland, in particular, has demonstrated how children subjected between the ages of four and ten to 'conscious training for self-reliance and mastery which kept clear of the extremes of leaving the child to make its own way (arising from sheer neglect or indifference) on the one hand and excessive restrictiveness and authoritarianism on the other' developed what he called a high 'need for achievement'—a quality that includes the desire to innovate and the desire to accept responsibility and make decisions.[47] Flinn has shown how the child-rearing practices of certain non-conformist English sects in the early eighteenth century, especially the congregationalists and the unitarians, did correspond very closely to the training envisaged by McClelland, and that these sects also contributed a disproportionate number of entrepreneurs and inventors to the British industrial revolution.[48] Whether a parallel situation existed in Scotland is not altogether clear, but it seems at least possible that when the traditional Calvinist teaching of 'godliness and gud manners' became slightly less obsessed with orthodoxy and discipline it might begin in some respects to approach McClelland's golden mean. Marjorie Plant has produced a certain amount of evidence to show that child-rearing in the upper classes became less authoritarian in the course of the eighteenth century, but she believes it was still stricter in the first half of the century in Scotland than in England.[49]

In conclusion we dare to assert that both the large part played by Lowland Scots as pioneers in the industrial revolution and even the peculiar richness in the flowering of the Scottish cultural enlightenment after 1740 can be partly explained by a process of action and reaction from the reformation—the first making a section of the Scots feel a deep need to treat life as a serious pilgrimage towards an objective,

99

the second making sure that that objective would not always be a purely religious one. We are not claiming that Calvinism 'caused' economic growth: all it did was to ensure that when the opportunity came for that growth, after many other preconditions had been fulfilled, the Scots would be a nation psychologically well equipped to exploit the situation to the full.

CHAPTER IV

The Revolution in Government

I. A FACTIOUS SOCIETY

The second half of the sixteenth century was a great age for building among the European nobility. In England the Elizabethan manor-house was essentially an undefended home with thin walls, plenty of glass and pleasant gardens. In Scotland the equivalent buildings were still castles, not so grim now as they had been in the middle ages, but nevertheless defensible with armories, magazines, grilles over the windows, gun-ports, iron yetts and other military features. A century later this distinction had been lost. In the 1680s Sir William Bruce was designing Scotland's first series of classical mansions with long frontages and regular fenestration in the manner of the European renaissance. The thin walls of Hopetoun or Kinross enclosed accommodation for servants and guests. The thick walls of Glamis and Crathes had been made for armed men and retainers. This change was an outward and still visible sign of an event almost as important in Scottish social history as the reformation of the church; the law and order of a modern state was coming at last to replace the faction and violence of a late medieval aristocracy.

To say this is not to imply that the late medieval kings had been neglectful of the problem of government. In one sense, reconstruction began as early as 1424, when James I returned from captivity in England with a purposeful programme to end the disorder that had been en-demic since the death of David II in 1371. It gained some stimulus in 1493 with the forfeiture of the Lord of the Isles (although this led in the short term to increased disorder in the Highlands) and again in 1532 with the foundation of the College of Justice to strengthen the powers of royal law. Step by step Stuart kings in their majorities had tried to strengthen central institutions against the forces of the periphery. Unhappily none of these advances made a permanent basis for stability: again and again their work was unravelled in the chaotic minorities of their children.

> Sum time the realme was reulit be Regentis
> Sum time lufetenantis, ledaris of the law
> Than rang sa mony inobedientis
> That few or nane stude of ane other aw,
> Oppression did so lowd hys bugle blaw
> That nane durst ride bot into feir of weir
> Jok-upon-land that time did mis his meir.[1]

Sir David Lyndsay of the Mount wrote this in the reign of James V. On the death of that monarch in 1542 the power of government sank once more to a deplorable level, and at this ebb it remained for nearly half a century. Little progress was possible in the 1540s and 1550s, dominated by Scotland's position as a pawn between France and England. The 1560s began with the Reformation forced on an unwilling crown by rebellious lords and people, followed by Queen Mary's residence in Scotland—one sorry tale of royal indignities and civil broils, culminating in her imprisonment by the Confederate Lords and subsequent escape into England. In the intense confusion of 1570–2 noble regents followed one another with startling speed, though the last of them, the Earl of Morton, ruled until his execution in 1581. The following year the young James VI, then sixteen years old, was kidnapped by a band of presbyterian earls and held in Ruthven Castle for a year. After he had escaped, royal government at last became more positive. But the danger of it being twisted again into an instrument of faction through the capture of the king's person by another band of magnates only began to fade in 1595 after the defeat of two rebellious Catholic earls, Huntly and Errol. It did not totally vanish until 1603 when James removed himself out of temptation's way by succeeding also to the English crown and departing to rule from London. It was at this point that progress in government really began to surpass all efforts by his predecessors. Before this time the crown's weakness meant the nobles' strength, and with strength came the abuse of power. James, who had no chivalrous illusions, summed up the 'fectlesse arrogant conceit' of the noble estate in *Basilikon Doron* in 1597. The nobility drank in 'with their very nouis-milke' the notion that their honour depended on them committing three iniquities:

(First) to thrall by oppression the meaner sort that dwelleth neere them to their service and following although they hold nothing of them.

(Second) to maintaine their servants and dependers in any wrong although they be not answerable to the laws . . .

(Third) for any displeasure that they apprehend to be done against them by their neighbour, to take up a plaine feide against him and without respect to God, King or Commonweale to bang it out bravelie, he and all his kinne against him and all his.[2]

'Banging it out bravely' was altogether characteristic of the six-teenth-century Scot. We tend first, perhaps, to think of feuding in a Highland context since the history of the north provides so many stories of clan fighting handed down in Gaelic tradition and recounted in the relatively sober annals of the Privy Council register. The blood-curdling story of the suffocation in a cave of the Macdonalds of Eigg by a band of Macleods (possibly in 1577), the treacherous attack on the Macleans enjoying the hospitality of the Macdonalds of Islay in 1586, the burning to death in a church of a congregation of Mackenzies by Glengarry Macdonalds at Kilchrist in 1603 and the ambush and massacre of a band of Colquhouns by the outlawed Macgregors whom they had been sent to punish at Glenfruin in the same year may suffice as examples. The last instance was regarded as particularly shocking, since a number of Lowland students who had come along with the Colquhouns to see the fun were unsportingly killed by the Macgregors during the battle. Most of these feuds were of local significance only, but sometimes the webs of alliance and kindred spread the flames of a small private war over a much wider area. In 1590 such a bushfire swept through the clans of Gordon, Grant, Mackintosh, Cameron, Campbell of Cawdor and the Lowland Dunbars at the same time. Five years later a political quarrel between the Earl of Huntly, head of the Gordons, and the Earl of Argyll, head of the Campbells, involved almost the whole of the northern mainland and assumed the pro-portions of a civil war until the Campbell followers were defeated by Huntly at Glenlivet and Huntly himself forced to retreat again before his sovereign's army.

Feud, however, was no monopoly of the north. The wild country of the Borders can provide almost as many stories of terror, particularly in the middle marches where the Kers and the Scotts were at feud and in the west where the Maxwells and the Johnstones carried on incessant private war. One case illustrates the way in which ill-judged grants of office by the crown could exacerbate the local situation. In 1579 John Johnstone of Johnstone was made Warden of the Western March and Lord Maxwell took exception to the grant. In 1582 and 1583 he sent three or four hundred men against the Warden, 'riding on him, burning his house, spoiling his friends, slaying his relations and taking them prisoners. Almost eighty houses were burnt at one time and three hundred at another.'[3] Ten years later it was Maxwell's turn to be made Warden and Johnstone's to take offence: in 1593 the two sides met at Dryfe Sands where the Warden was killed in a ferocious battle between the followers and kin of the two families. With men of this type in office on either side of the Border, it is hardly surprising that raids across it went on in spite of the peace treaty signed between the two countries in 1560. As late as 1596 the Kers of Cessford struck into England as far as Alnwick on the east side, and Walter Scott of Buccleuch, the Keeper of Liddesdale, carried out his astonishingly daring attack on Carlisle castle to release Kinmont Willie Armstrong from the clutches of the English warden. The English, for their part, raided into Scotland from time to time. On the other hand Border families from both sides were quite happy to gang up to help in each other's feuds, an English surname joining a Scottish surname against another Scottish or English family as occasion required. As Borderers they all had more in common with one another than with the tiresome governments in Edinburgh and London who inexplicably required them to be obedient and peaceful subjects.

The lowland plains of central Scotland were naturally more governable, but the fact that stories of feud and disorder in this region are generally less familiar should not mislead us into assuming that such things were very rare. One well-known instance relates to the Ayrshire vendetta that lasted for more than a century between the Cunninghames, the Montgomeries, and different branches of the divided Kennedy family, a particularly ugly and merciless feud.[4] Another illuminating example is that told by Sir James Fergusson of the Forresters of Garden, 'not by any means uncharacteristic of their generation.'[5] Alexander Forrester was a laird of middling estate, holder of minor crown offices as 'heritable forester and keeper of the Torwood' and several times Provost of Stirling. He was accustomed to intimidating his neighbours, and in 1592 when one of them complained to Privy Council about a disputed boundary Forrester simply called out his retainers—'ane thowsand men on horse and fute, bodin in feir of weir'—and forcibly barred the Lords from making a personal inspection of the site. Such high-handed private action successfully defying the most solemn tribunal in the land created just the sort of situation where resentment would ripen into violent feud as the aggrieved parties all took the law into their own hands. Soon the local Bruces and Livingstones allied against the Forresters, who in turn invoked the support of the Earl of Mar, the most powerful Stirlingshire noble to whom they normally adhered: a leading Forrester was waylaid and murdered by 'clannit men', and given a provocative funeral procession through Livingstone lands by Mar. Something like open war broke out in the county, and when a royal pursuivant tried to declare Forrester an outlaw from Stirling Cross on the grounds of his general lawlessness, the wretched man was beaten up by two of the laird's sons. After this the feud had to be quickly mended: Mar feared his friends had gone too far in assaulting a pursuivant. The fact that it could break out at all, so violently, in so central a county and in a decade when the king was reckoned to be making more impression on the country than for some time, may serve to measure the extent of the problem that royal government had to face throughout Scotland.

Such feuding was not picturesque, though the lairds might consider it virile: 'he was a verie active man, he burnt and harried Sleat for his pleasure' wrote a contemporary of the chief of the Mackenzies of Kintail.[6] For those on the receiving end it was often hideously brutal and destructive. 'Neither man, wife, bairn, house, cover nor bigging had been spared', ran the summons after a Macleod raid on Coigeach in Wester Ross, 'but all barbarously slain, burnt and destroyed.'[7] Much further south, in Kintyre, eighty-one merklands of agricultural land out of a total of 344 were reported as lying waste as a result of similar depredations in 1596, and 113—a third of the whole—in 1605. In the Borders the situation was much the same, though the eastern Borderers at least were said to spare human life on their raids if they could. On the other hand, in the most ordered parts of the realm—the Lothians, Fife —physical destruction was probably slight, though it was often anticipated. A building like Johnscleuch, an unusual survival of a small laird's house near Garvald in East Lothian, where the ground floor has no original windows and was evidently given over to accommodation for cattle between its thick walls, was not built in this comfortless way for fun.

Faction influenced in many ways the nature of contemporary social and economic rural life. It determined, for example, the complicated webs of kinship and alliance that bound together both the Lowland and the Highland families in elaborate offensive and defensive alliances, giving rise to such peculiarly Scottish institutions as the 'bond of manrent' by which a lesser baron or knight not in any way related by blood to a greater lord placed himself under the latter's protection and promised to assist him in all his actions, causes and 'deadly feuds'. A lord's standing was reckoned in terms of followers. 'The Scots, living then in factions, used to keepe many followers and so consumed their revenew of victuals, living in some want of money' was Fynes Morrison's summary: he used the past tense because he was writing in 1617 about a visit in 1598, and twenty years later things were already a little different.[8] This in turn meant that agriculture was inefficient and relatively little food reached the market to sustain the development of towns or to permit the rise of industrial communities, though abundant grain would not of itself have cured economic backwardness. Finally disorder meant that there was ample room for those who operated on the fringes of the feudal system—the 'broken men' without lands or lords who sold themselves to the highest bidder wishing dirty work done expeditiously, or who alternatively enjoyed a life of piracy and banditry in the wilder parts where neither the king's nor the lord's justice could easily reach them. It is perhaps not too much to say that any significant advance of the whole of Scotland towards what the modern world would regard as 'progress' depended on the prior extinction of the disorder and instability to which the country was prey.

2. THE VICTORY OF ROYAL POWER

James VI saw what had to be done with perfect clarity: 'rest not untill ye roote out these barbarous feides', he wrote for his son in 1597, 'their barbarous name is unknowne to any other nation. For if this

treatise were written in either Frenche or Latine I could not get them
named unto you but by circumlocution'.[9] Even before this was written
he had begun to make progress to this end: twenty-eight years later
when his successor finally ascended the throne, the work was largely
done. Scotland, though still turbulent in parts compared to some of the
more settled and flatter states of Europe, had become by its own
standards tamed and orderly. In several ways circumstances made his
task easier than for his predecessors. It was an advantage to rule Scotland from England because the person of the king was secure from the
threats and importunities it had been hard to resist in the informal
atmosphere of Holyrood on the doorstep of a turbulent and easily
roused city whose mob had more than once been made the tool of
faction. As king of Great Britain he also had greater power to punish
and reward his subjects than had been available to him as monarch of
Scotland alone. Although feuding was primarily caused by the naked
ambition of nobles wishing to get as much power as they could over
their neighbours there is some reason to believe that in the sixteenth
century the situation, particularly in the Highlands, had been made
worse by land-hunger caused by rising population. James VI was perhaps lucky in so far as the rate of increase of population appears to
have begun to slacken in his reign due to a recurrence of famine and
disease between 1590 and 1610 (see page 164 below).

Furthermore, the king was able to get help from certain sections of
the population who were potentially hostile or indifferent to the self-
interest of the nobles and who had been gaining in numbers since the
start of the sixteenth century. His policy with these groups was to
associate them with royal initiative and then to keep them in royal
leading strings to ensure that they did not wander away to become the
tools of any other interested party. The burgesses of the Royal Burghs
had always been interested in peace—tumult was bad for trade. James
encouraged regular meetings of the Convention of Royal Burghs
under strict royal surveillance. The barons or smaller lairds were
another such group: the feuing of church and crown lands in the late
fifteenth and sixteenth centuries (for which see chapter VI below) had
provided many with middling estates on perpetual heritable tenure;
these men often had no kinship ties with the nobility and only wished
for security. Traditionally they were supporters of the government, and
if the king could show he was better able to provide order than the
lords they would certainly come over to his side. In 1587 the king

initiated the county franchise act (a revival of the obsolete statute of 1428) to organise the representation of small barons in Parliament so that they could offset the predominant influence of the nobles there. Then he developed that Parliamentary steering committee of proven friends to the crown known as the Lords of the Articles to the point where it took over virtually all legislative power under the guidance of Privy Council.

The lawyers, too, were instinctively behind the king. Their living depended on a reasonable respect for the law. Perhaps paradoxically, their profession was already a large and important one, for society was conscious of the security implied in a charter or an instrument of sasine safely hidden in a great chest to give hope for the eventual recovery of property in cases of usurpation. James VI did all he could to encourage the formal organisation of the profession—the Faculty of Advocates emerged as a definite body with entrance examination requirements in 1619, the Society of Writers to the Signet appeared in 1594, and the qualifications and training necessary for a Notary Public were regulated by statute in 1587. The Court of Session was the cornerstone of law and James professed great respect for it: it was, however, characteristic of his approach to state affairs that appointment of all its judges remained his own prerogative, that Privy Council remained as a superior court with particular interest in cases of riot, and that royal fingers seldom hesitated from tampering with the course of justice when he felt that royal interests demanded it.

There was also the Reformed Church, whose growing success was creating another set of allegiances altogether irrelevant both to earthly kinship and to temporal monarchy. On the one hand, it was explicitly opposed to lawlessness, oppression and promiscuous feuding— the utterances of the General Assembly on these matters are every bit as severe as those of the monarch, and Knox himself had suggested a role for the church to initiate proceedings against lawless men whom the civil sword neglected to punish. On the other, it was always liable to add to the danger of civil strife by throwing its weight heavily behind factions that seemed to be Protestant and godly: James never forgave it for supporting the Ruthven raiders when they forcibly removed him from the influence of the Duke of Lennox, who was suspected of favouring Catholics, when he was sixteen. He finally solved the ecclesiastical problem by his revival of the office and powers of bishops, coupled in 1606 with the exile of that troublesome presbyterian Andrew

Melville. Henceforth the General Assembly and the episcopate, like the Convention of Royal Burghs, Parliament and the Court of Session, would be obliged to take its lead from Privy Council and be turned in the general direction of backing the central government against faction and abuse of private power.

It was, however, in dealing with the nobility that James showed to best effect that cunning, patience and deep knowledge of the Scots which he called his 'kingcraft'. A rasher man would have launched a frontal attack on the aristocracy and provoked a revolution he could hardly have controlled. James' policy depended on offending no one who could conceivably form a focal point for disaffection. Only one of the great Lowland families—the Ruthvens, Earls of Gowrie—was extirpated for the numerous treasons that had marked the early part of his reign. The other great lines—the various branches of the House of Stewart, the Hamiltons, Campbells, Gordons, Douglases, Erskines and so forth—remained entrenched in their lands and welcome at court as they had been for centuries. James treated them all with courtesy and was careful to avoid the appearance of undue favouritism towards any one of the big networks: the experience of his minority had taught him just how easily faction arose from the simple causes of jealousy and fear when the balance between them was abruptly disturbed. Similarly James made no serious attempt to destroy the feudal jurisdiction that added so much to their local power—his one tentative move in this direction, the appointment of Justices of the Peace on the English model, was allowed to lose most of its force when it was seen how impossible it was for them to exert their authority independently of that of the lords.

Lastly, the king chose for his Privy Council men of whom he could be absolutely sure. The great nobles had to be included, for it was traditional they should have a close position to the fountain of power, but increasingly the real work was done by a handful of devoted and skilful officials who were there by virtue of their ability and not of their birth. Such were the Octavians, councillors to the Queen whom James put in charge of the treasury in 1596—a group of eight professional men, mostly the sons of minor landowners many of whom had long and distinguished careers in different parts of the royal service. 'This I must say for Scotland', said the king in London in 1607, 'here I sit and govern with my pen, I write and it is done, and by a clerk of the council I govern Scotland now, which others could not do by the sword'.[10] Yet in the last resort his success rested more on his knowledge of personalities and of national susceptibilities than on his use of institutions.

In the Lowlands, the benefits of the King's peace began to be felt with some sureness from the first decade of the seventeenth century: even earlier they had begun to make their mark. Admittedly, the consequent social and economic change was not all that rapid: it could not be as long as the old-style lords thought in the traditional ways about men and land. Such conservatism could not die in a generation, and who would disband his retainers and pull down his castle on the assumption that the peace would last for ever? When Sir Robert Kerr wrote to his son about renovating the old family tower in 1632 he warned him to leave the inconvenient windows as they were 'strong on the out syde because the world may change agayn'.[11] Nevertheless, the general level of food supply seems to have improved as a direct consequence of more settled conditions, and some of the new men on the land—especially the lawyers and court families—built themselves houses without accommodation for followers or the slightest hint of fortification, like Alexander Seton's house at Pinkie and the Earl of Winton's house at Pencaitland, both a few miles east of Edinburgh. They were also among the first to use lime to increase the productivity of the land in East and Midlothian, and to drive down coal mines or build salt pans in large numbers along both shores of the Forth. Little towns like Culross and Prestonpans sprang up where they had been busy, with some claim to be considered as Scotland's first industrial communities.

To the Royal Burghs, too, order seems to have brought prosperity. All the most important ones and many of the little ones grew in population and affluence as internal and external trade began to expand. Anyone who walks with his eyes open today through the old trading towns of the East of Scotland will become aware of the numbers of stone houses built for merchants and craftsmen bearing a date from the last two or three decades of the sixteenth century and the first two or three of the seventeenth. Generally it is engraved over the lintel with a godly injunction such as 'Thank Ye God for all His Giftes'. For Edinburgh the withdrawal of the court from Holyrood in 1603 was more than compensated for in material terms by the increased activity of the lawyers in the Court of Session and Privy Council. Generally more ships than ever before were going from Scotland to London with

Scottish linen and skins and coming home with English consumer goods: more were sailing to the Baltic and Norway to bring back corn, wood and iron for the swollen urban populations: Scotland's ability to import French and Dutch wares was significantly improved by the addition to her export list of increased quantities of coal and Scottish salt.

On the Borders, too, pacification was followed by certain economic benefits. The king found the problem of management infinitely easier when both halves were under the same government, and by 1620 he had quenched disorderly feuds so effectively that many had emigrated to fight for the King of Sweden rather than stay at home in inactivity. An envoy in Copenhagen explained to the Danish king that 'the country was full for want of employment now that the general peace between England and Scotland had been restored and that at the same time great distress had arisen from the excess of population'.[12] Trading began to take the place of raiding as a serious Border pastime: the cattle drovers could make their way unmolested from Galloway towards the London market, the first fortunes of Glasgow burgesses were made by peddling linen along the same path, and wool production rose throughout the southern shires. This last Sir William Seyton in 1623 attributed entirely to the 'solid government' which had prevailed 'since his sacred majesty's happie arryvall to the commandement of both kingdomes'.[13]

In the Highlands the situation was rather different, since feuding was more intense and more difficult to prevent owing to the nature of the countryside and the rudimentary communications. The king's programme, inflamed by racial prejudice as well as by a wish for order, was outlined in *Basilikon Doron*:

> As for the Hie-lands, I shortly comprehend them al into two sorts of people: the one, that dwelleth in our maine land, that are barbarous for the most parte yet mixed with some shewe of civilitie: the other that dwelleth in the Iles and are alluterlie barbares . . . reforme and civilize the best inclined among them, rooting out or transporting the barbarous and stubborne sort and planting civilitie in their roomes.[14]

The king firstly made it plain that he expected from the whole of the Highland zone the same regard for the legal system as he was getting from the rest of Scotland. In 1597 all Highland landowners were ordered to produce their titles to land and also to find sureties for their general good behaviour: any who failed to do so were declared to have forfeited their lands. In 1608 the government succeeded by trickery in enticing on board a ship a troublesome clique of leading West Highland chiefs who had been intriguing with their kinsfolk in Ireland. There was not much difference between a Macdonald of the Isles and a Macdonell of Antrim. Before they were released they and some other chiefs were obliged to come to Iona for a conference at which they subscribed to the Statutes of Icolmkill. Herein they undertook to obey the law, to live in peace with one another, to plant churches on their lands, to reduce feudal burdens on their tenants and to send their children to be educated in the Lowlands: none of the chiefs carried out these undertakings to the letter once they had got home again, but they certainly treated the central government with more respect afterwards.

Secondly, James had a policy of colonisation. In order to drive a wedge between the Celts of Ireland and the Celts of the Isles whose intricate family alliances and feuds had made the government of each part difficult both for the English and the Scots in the sixteenth century, James confiscated land in Ulster from the native aristocracy and systematically planted Lowland Scots and Englishmen upon it. In this he was entirely successful, but his efforts to carry the policy further by planting Lowlanders in Kintyre, Lochaber and Lewis were more patchy. Lochaber was not attempted. The Lewis scheme was abortive. Here the colony of Fifers who on three occasions between 1598 and 1610 tried to gain a foothold were driven out by the 'barbarous bludie and wicket Hielandmen' who attacked them on land and cut their communications by sea. The settlement of Kintyre was partly, but not entirely, successful: many of the colonists moved on to Antrim when conditions got difficult in Argyll.

The king made greater gains by his third method, which was to work through, rather than against, the indigenous society of the chieftains. He enlisted the aid of those nobles, especially the Campbell Earl of Argyll, the Gordon Earls of Huntly and Sutherland and the Mackenzie Earl of Seaforth, whose lands formed bastions on the southern, eastern and northern sides of the hills and who were themselves half-Lowland in outlook. All three clans were greatly strengthened and given tasks of government which fitted both their dynastic ambitions and the aims of royal order. The Campbells, for example, were encouraged to grow at the expense of the Macleans and tacitly allowed to destroy the power of the turbulent Macdonalds of Islay in a private war; they were also given the agreeable duty of extirpating the Macgregors who, it will be recalled, had blotted their copy-book again by winning the Battle of Glenfruin. 'They were hunted like vermin, under pain of death they were prohibited from carrying weapons (except pointless knives for their food); from meeting together more than four at a time, and (a crowning infamy from their standpoint) they were compelled to renounce their very name.'[15] One Campbell chieftain granted land free of all rent and service other than that of carrying fire and slaughter against Clan Gregor: another gave the same reward for the head of a Macgregor as for the head of a wolf.

All this was very far from bringing peace to the Highlands, though it drove home the lesson that those chiefs who were to prosper were those who were also prepared to back their king, and to keep good lawyers in Edinburgh as well as sharp swords at home. The strengthening of the families on the Highland edge helped to save the Lowlands from promiscuous raids, though these did not disappear. It is instructive to read the cheerful letter of Cameron of Lochiel to the laird of Grant about a raid that the latter believed had damaged one of his dependants: 'Praised be God I am inocent of the same, and my friends, in respect that they were not in your bounds, but to Murray lands where all men taken their prey'.[16] The shores of the Moray Firth were potentially among the most productive lands in all Scotland, but they lay in a dangerous situation, and it was to be many years before their inhabitants were left to farm them in peace.

3. REACTION AND RESTORATION, 1625–1690

When Charles I succeeded to the throne in 1625, Scotland was thus, within limits, quiet and prosperous; for a dozen years afterwards it continued so, directed by the administrative machine and the careful constitutional balance created by his father. Charles, however, was without either the guile of kingcraft or the instinct for compromise which James had possessed in so large a measure. He was neither interested in nor informed about the society he had left behind at the age of four. This made him a dangerous monarch for Scotland, and when he finally blundered into the north with an innovating and alien church policy he was like a man with a burning torch tripping into a carefully stacked powder magazine. To most in the Reformed Church the aggrandisement of bishops above the modest role assigned to them by James VI smelt of popery, and the pseudo-Anglican form of worship announced in the new prayer book simply was popery. The burgesses and lairds rather than the nobility formed the principal lay support of the kirk, but all classes of landowners were thoroughly alarmed by the proposal to endow the bishops with church lands and teinds that the laity had enjoyed since the Reformation or before. The nobility themselves were also smarting under innumerable small slights inflicted by the tactlessness of an absent king, and to them the reliance of their monarch on episcopal advice was 'unkingly and unnatural', far more offensive than the earlier reshaping of Privy Council because it relegated them to the position of a remote provincial aristocracy without hope or influence at the fountain of power. The National Covenant was therefore a conservative protest by the leaders of society against unseeing misrule from a London king. It was primarily Charles who turned it into a revolutionary document by treating the signatories as rebels: thereby he played into the hands of fanatics who were then able to use it as a lever to overturn episcopacy.

In the fighting of the next decade one can see in many ways the return to an older Scotland. The nobles rode out once more with their tenants in battle array. The Marquess of Argyll aspired as the servant of the army of the Covenant to a position of viceregal power: his rise involved the aggrandisement of his family, and the triumph of the Campbells produced its own counterweight in the Highland army of Montrose. Old scores were then paid off—Campbell tenants were harried and slaughtered in Perthshire, Clackmannan and Argyll by men from the north; Macdonalds in turn were massacred or transported after Campbell victories in Kintyre. True banditti reappeared, like Lord Kenmure in Kirkcudbrightshire, who raised as his standard a barrel of brandy on a staff, gathered together all the vagabonds and broken men he could find and marched about the country harrying and looting in the king's name.

Disorder brought its own reckoning as the tale of destruction lengthened and levels of production sank. The plaiding drying on the tentering frames in peaceful Aberdeenshire valleys was burnt along with the houses of the weavers by the Highlanders hurrying south; two generations of fisher captains and their boys from the prosperous little burghs of east Fife perished at the battle of Kilsyth; in 1651 Dundee, the second burgh to the capital in population and wealth, was brutally sacked by English troops; by then there were scarcely a dozen Scottish boats paying dues at the Danish Sound—before the wars started a hundred or more had paused there every year on their way to and from the Baltic markets. Famine and plague stalked in the footsteps of war: faction, chaos and poverty seemed again to be the order of things.

Yet, in the last analysis, the reappearance of feudal disorder was itself temporary and unreal. For the lairds, the burgesses and the lawyers as well as for the ministers the wars were about religion rather than about which families should have the pick of the spoils of state. No party could hope for success without the support of these classes; no party would get their allegiance without putting an acceptable religious programme before the appeal to kinship. This became explicit as it had been never before, and after the wars were over the central plank of government was seen to be religious compromise: Charles II practised it on an episcopalian frame; James VII failed to practise it at all, and lost his throne; William III practised it on a Presbyterian frame; Anne had to see that this frame was kept intact as a prerequisite for Union with England. It was still important to placate the nobles, but it was no longer so important as placating the other classes through an acceptable church polity.

Secondly, the feudal host was found in the course of the civil wars to be a weak weapon in modern conflict. General Leslie defeated Montrose at Philiphaugh because he was a professional using an army stiffened by mercenaries home from service in the Thirty Years' War. After Dunbar, Cromwell kept the country down by garrisons of professionals in all the main burghs. Charles II learnt by his example, and retained in his service men like General Dalyell, a wicked old mercenary who had seen service with the Czar and was the terror of Covenanting rebels after the Restoration: he was backed by a small core of trained soldiers for use in an emergency. When the nobles intrigued in the future it would have to be by manipulating political, legal and religious forces rather than by the crude use of a force of followers.

On the conclusion of the wars in 1651 Cromwell's military government was so effective that even hostile commentators admitted that the country had never been so free from disorder. Nevertheless the destruction of the previous years, the heavy taxation imposed to pay for the occupation and the effects of the temporary Incorporating Union with England that fell upon an exhausted country and exposed her to unfamiliar competition precluded prosperity, except in a few sectors such as the salt and linen trades which were able at once to respond to the opportunities of an open market in England.

After 1660, Charles II broke the Union, returned to the constitution of his grandfather and ruled again through Privy Council, a tame Convention of Royal Burghs, Parliament controlled by the Lords of the Articles and an episcopal Church. His government was thus a matter of balance and control like James', but since the forces of active feudalism were everywhere so gravely weakened it did not need to be so subtle and personally-directed a balance as before. Provided he maintained a High Commissioner as viceroy and knew when to dismiss him for arousing too much animosity among his fellow aristocrats, the country could be governed at a high level of respect for forms of law. It was therefore altogether appropriate that the greatest intellectual achievements of his reign should be those of Fountainhall, Mackenzie and Stair, the Lords of the Court of Session. The *Institutes* of Stair, published in 1681, presented Scottish law for the first time as a complete and coherent system. As a recent historian has remarked, 'it was to his synthesis of philosophical jurisprudence and of the civilian commentators that most of the characteristics of our modern system are due'.[17]

With the Restoration, too, the economic scene began to look cheerful again, especially to the townsmen. Food had become, and stayed, remarkably cheap, though this may be partly due to epidemics in the 1640s reducing the number of consumers. Traders re-entered their old markets in force, though as tariffs were rising abroad they did not find it so easy to export as before: Glasgow men prospered perhaps above all others, and founded a new trade, though an illegal and small-scale one, with the English colonies in America. There were losses in the Dutch Wars of 1665–7 and 1672–4, but equally there were gains in the period 1674–80 when Britain reaped the fruits of neutrality while the whole of northern Europe was at war. Merchants set up small new industries encouraged by a Privy Council policy that had found fresh tenderness towards the burgesses—sugar refining, paper manufacture and the weaving of finer quality woollens around Edinburgh and Glasgow were the most important examples. The older industries revived and grew: the coal and salt masters built several new harbours (like Wemyss in Fife and Saltcoats in Ayrshire), while Aberdeenshire was to regard the 1670s as the golden age for her plaiding trade. There were slumps and setbacks certainly, but the general commercial situation did not seem anything other than satisfactory.

On the land, the trend towards manor houses rather than castles appeared irreversible with the attractive buildings of Sir William Bruce, and those that could not afford a new home revamped the old. 'There is no man more against these old fashion of tours and castles than I am' wrote the Earl of Strathmore, 'for who can delight to live in his house as in a prisone? . . . Such houses truly are worn quyt out of fashione, as feuds are, which is a great happiness, the cuntrie being generally more civilized than it was'.[18] Admittedly even in this age the Bishop of Aberdeen was horrified to learn that Highlanders were still coming down to the Lowland edge to carry away by force unmarried girls as well as fat cattle,[19] but in the difficult terrain of the north raid and lawlessness would still take the better part of a century to die. Elsewhere there was a surprising mushrooming of public markets, partly stimulated, no doubt, by the decline of those followings whom Fynes Morrison had described as staying behind to consume the victual rents. 'The fact that the modern dining-room was at this time taking the place of a baronial hall represents a vital change in the manners and customs of the nobility'.[20] Only one grant of a market or fair outside a burgh had been made between 1517 and 1570, and only ten were made between 1571 and 1660: but there were no fewer than 246 such grants between 1660 and 1707.

In these circumstances we might have expected change to go further, and the expansion of a market economy to bring about the creation of a farming system based on enclosure, on a revolution in tenure and on the maximisation of agricultural productivity. The examples of contemporary England and Holland were enough to show to the Scots that farming need not be unchanging. The reasons why larger changes did not occur at this point are not altogether clear, but they seem to be connected with low levels of demand relative to the new abundance of supply. Export opportunities were limited. Corn went from the carse-lands of the East of Scotland to Norway and Rotterdam, and cattle went from many areas over the Border to England, but foreign governments imposed restrictions that gravely hampered sales. Internal demand was limited both by the slow growth of population—(it may not have completely recovered even in 1690 from the falls in mid-century)—and by the continuing absence of a large or broadly based industrial sector to provide income and stimulate employment. Prices for agricultural produce were therefore low, rents were not buoyant and capital accumulation was difficult for the land-owner. There seemed to be no large economic incentive to persuade him to abandon a system which was, after all, hallowed by centuries of social tradition: to have done so in these circumstances would have been to break completely new ground, to incur odium in local society that still looked upon him in some senses as their protector, and to embark upon capital expenditure with a very uncertain chance of eventual profit.

In sum, therefore, the revolution in government had produced order out of factious confusion in the Lowlands. It had had important repercussions on the household habits of the landed classes, while not being in itself sufficient to produce economic reorganisation on the land. On the other hand it did permit economic advance in other directions which, while strictly limited, pushed the Scottish economy several steps in front of anything it had known in the middle ages. Finally, without it the much more sweeping changes in agriculture and manufacture that came about in different circumstances during the eighteenth century would not have been possible at all. In any state a reasonable stability of government, and reasonable immunity from foreign invasion and civil war, is a necessary prerequisite for fast economic growth. Though it does not of itself create such growth, it permits it to occur.

CHAPTER V

The Countryside
I. Settlement and Agriculture

---

1. THE FARMTOUN

Around 1690, the population of Scotland numbered about a million—one fifth of the present numbers, and distributed much more evenly than is the case today. As late as 1750 one half of the Scots lived beyond the Tay, and fully a quarter of them in five counties of the Highlands which now hold only seven per cent of the whole. Furthermore, although there were certainly more living in urban settlements in 1690 than there had been in 1560, even at the most generous estimate these can only have accounted for ten or fifteen per cent of the total. Eight or nine out of every ten Scotsmen dwelt on the land, and depended for their living on the productivity of its farms. They were, overwhelmingly, a rural people.

To imagine what their world looked like requires an effort of the historical imagination. To begin with, one must efface from the map almost all traces of the existing road system, and substitute for it a network of tracks meandering between settlements—routes pockmarked with the hooves of animals, fit for cattle, suitable for a tough pony with panniers or bags slung over its back, or drawing a sledge over the slimey mud, but normally impassable to four-wheeled carts. There were, of course, some long distance routes between large burghs —carts could often be taken in the seventeenth century from Glasgow to Edinburgh via Stirling and Bo'ness, from Glasgow to Paisley and Newark, from Leith to the Lanarkshire leadmines via Biggar, and from Edinburgh to Haddington or even to Dunbar. A lot depended on the weather. A noble could use even a coach in Fife and some other areas in a dry summer. North of the Tay, however, even the main routes, like the one rather grandly described on Edward's map of Angus in 1678 as 'the King's Way betwixt Dondei and Brechin', were not passable to wheeled vehicles. The state of land communications was both a reflection and a cause of peasant subsistence. Had there been more goods to move, there would have been an incentive to improve the roads. Had the roads been better, farmers would more readily have attended market to sell their grain. It was not until the eighteenth century that the vicious circle was broken.

The whole appearance of the farmland, too, was quite different from what it is today. In place of a chequer-board of separate fields one must imagine the ground everywhere lying as open as moorland, studded with thickets of broom and gorse but unprotected from the sweeping winds by woods or planted rows of trees and seldom divided in any way by hedge, wall or dyke, apart from the broad earthen 'head dyke' which marked the perimeter of the cultivated area round a settlement. The pastoral land beyond the head dyke was all more or less rough brown waste: there was no question of grass being cultivated as a crop. The ploughed land within was a series of undulating strips or rigs, divided into blocks by weedy baulks, studded with large boulders (which have mostly been cleared today) and running higher up the hillside than is customary now. A slope was a drain. Except where knolls presented a chance for island cultivation the narrower valleys had to be neglected except as a source for a little rough and rushy hay: their bogs presented a problem that no one had felt equipped to tackle since isolated and small-scale efforts undertaken by some monastic houses early in the middle ages. The contemporary English travellerswho wrote about this countryside, squelching through it on a wet horse from one dirty inn to another, found it all intensely depressing and greatly inferior to the neat, prosperous enclosed farms of much of their own country. Even the mountains which were to move later visitors to transports of romantic appreciation appeared to them only grim. Admiration of scenery starts from a certain base of comfort.

Outsiders also noted the absence of villages as they were known in England. Only the south-east, which had once been part of Anglian Northumbria, contained many nucleated settlements with a great house or castle, a church, an inn and a large number of peasants' houses focussing on a central street or green, as at Dirleton and Stenton in East Lothian or at Ceres in Fife. It is difficult to say precisely why this should be so. On the one hand there was no need to crowd houses round a spring, as in chalk or limestone country: water was everywhere. On the other hand broad stretches of ploughable land were hard to come by: good arable land was scattered, and settlement followed it. Much of the agriculture except in the Lothians was originally mainly pastoral (although it always had to have some arable base): pastoral agriculture seems generally to give rise to more dispersed farms than arable agriculture.

In Scotland, therefore, the common unit of settlement was a hamlet centering on a notional 'farm', the size of which was determined (initially at least) by the area that one or sometimes two or three plough teams of horses or oxen could keep under cultivation. In the Highlands this was often called a baile, in the Lowlands a farmtoun, or a kirktoun if it happened to contain the parish church, a milltoun if it embodied the mill and a cot-toun if poor cottars but no husbandmen occupied the site. There could easily be a dozen of these in a single parish, as well as some isolated settler's houses which had sprung up at a later date when additions had been made to the cultivated area. With the passage of time the pattern of settlement might appear to become diffuse and haphazard, yet careful investigation generally reveals an underlying unit based on the plough team, the 'ploughgate'.

The 'farm' could be divided and cultivated in any one of a number of different ways. A single husbandman might enjoy tenancy of the whole, and cultivate it independently with the help of lesser men, his subtenants and servants. 'In this corner, where the chief dependence was upon corn, each tenant had commonly a ploughgate', said Ramsay of Ochtertyre of the straths of eastern Stirlingshire and south Perthshire.[1] It was frequent for two or four husbandmen, and sometimes as many as eight, sixteen or twenty (each with a number of subtenants) to share the farm between them as 'joint tenants'. This too could involve diverse arrangements. At its most primitive the husbandmen held in common, cultivating the land in common, sharing the crop communally and paying the rent as a lump sum. Such 'mass tenure' was practised in Ross and Cromarty and in parts of the Hebrides as late as the early nineteenth century, but there is no evidence that it was practised elsewhere even in the sixteenth and seventeenth centuries. Slightly more sophisticated was 'runrig' division, with separate ownership of several scattered strips of arable, each one of which lay between those of different joint tenants to ensure a fair distribution of good and indifferent lands. Under 'periodic runrig' the strips were reallocated at intervals among the husbandmen: under 'fixed runrig' they were permanently associated with a single holding. A modification was division by 'rundale', where some of the strips were consolidated into blocks which themselves lay intermingled with those of other joint-tenants. Finally, the stage was reached where it became possible to divide the arable into completely separate and consolidated holdings like small modern farms. No one can yet say which forms were most prevalent in the seventeenth century, but it is likely that periodic runrig, like mass tenure was already restricted mainly to the Highlands. Fixed runrig, and more often rundale, was common enough but not universal throughout the Lowlands. It is usually supposed that consolidated holdings were very rare. This is probably an exaggeration. On the Panmure estates in Angus, for example, some farms were split in the rentals into north, east, south and west quarters, each occupied by a single tenant for a period of years, after which they moved to a different quarter.[2] This looks like four consolidated holdings exchanged at the end of a short lease in deference to the old traditions of reallocation. But the evidence of rentals is seldom completely unequivocal.

To cultivate a farm by any method of joint-tenancy inevitably made for communal work. Peasants holding runrig or rundale had to decide on a common crop, a common rotation and common dates for sowing, reaping and cultivating their scattered and intermingled strips: they had also to contribute animals to draw the community's plough, and to do much else by general agreement. In England the cultivation of the open fields seems often to have allowed some variation in choice of what to grow in the strips, even turnips being included by enterprising tenants in the seventeenth century. In Scotland there is no evidence of such variation. Perhaps because the range of crops chosen from was so much smaller—often only oats or bear (a primitive form of barley). The holders of consolidated land could hardly be exempt from communal work either, unless the individual husbandmen were rich enough to possess a full plough team and could push the bounds of cultivation far enough out to make it worth their while to do so. Even then, as the animals of the settlement were pastured on a common and undivided moor they would still have to agree together over herding.

Co-operation, however, was socially difficult to achieve. Rural communities were always in danger of being hamstrung by the bickering between the peasants—someone threw stones into his neighbour's rig when he was clearing his own; a second using his sickle carelessly at harvest swept a few handfuls of oats from one rig to another; a third let his cows stray into the arable stubbles before the last corn had been cleared in the autumn. To keep discord within bounds it was essential to devise institutional means of controlling it, and the simplest and most effective was to appeal to tradition. It was sensible to fix an unvarying date for sowing the oats or taking the cows to the hill pasture because four or sixteen farmers could never have agreed on precisely when to do it if the choice had been left flexible. Nor did it do much harm to agree that one third of the best land should always be reserved for the bear-crop when this proportion was related to the subsistence needs of the community for ale. The trouble was that in the course of time tradition became a god, and when better agricultural practices became known or farming for the market became increasingly important the peasants' blind worship of custom often proved a stumbling block even to changes that might benefit the community as a whole. A commentator on Peeblesshire writing in the reign of Charles II already appreciated this. He said of the Tweeddale peasantry:

> They are an industrious careful people, yet something wilfull, stubborn and tenacious of old customs. There are amongst them that will not suffer the wrack (old weeds) to be taken off their land because they say it keeps the corn warm, nor plant trees for wronging the undergrowth nor take pains upon their hay to make it well-smelled and coloured because they allege musty hay brings cows a-bulling, nor ditch and trench a piece of boggie ground for fear of the loss of five or six foot of grass for a far greater increase. And this humour with a custome they have of overburdening their ground, which they call full plenishing, makes their cattel general small, lean and give a mean price in a market. But otherwise they are a provident laborious people.[3]

Obedience to tradition was supplemented as a means of achieving co-operation by the institution of the Baron Court. This had two functions. On the one hand, it served as a place where the tenants of a laird's estate, often comprising many farmtouns, could come together and interpret custom. On the other, it acted as the laird's private court of jurisdiction through which he could exert his control over society, compel payment of rents and services due to himself and punish crimes committed by the peasants against himself or against the community.

Some of the little court houses have still survived, like the one at Ceres in Fife with its motto carved over the door: "God Bless the Just".

The character of these courts varied from place to place and from time to time depending on the vigour and interest of the lairds, but they had an underlying unity of purpose which a few examples may illustrate. The Baron Courts of the Campbells of Glenorchy, Highland lairds in Perthshire in the early seventeenth century, were like small replicas of Parliament, legislating with 'the advice and consent of the whole commons and tenants' in the same way as the king did with the 'consent of his estates'. Much of what was 'statute and ordanit' by Campbell's court was concerned with the operations of husbandry. Burning on the moors was restricted to the month of March; head dykes were to be repaired every year; peat was not to be cut in corn-lands, or cut with any other implement than a 'lawland peit spaud'; tenants were to plant trees and to kill vermin; more inexplicably they were ordered to cut no briar or thorn except 'in the waxing of the moone'. Many acts were concerned with social order. No one was to give shelter to a poacher or a vagabond. No wife was to drink without her husband being in the premises; no weaver was to ask more than a firlot of meal for making a plaid. In 1622 the miller was ordered not to play dice or cards with the gardener. In 1625 an aleseller was fined for selling drink to the commons while they were already drunk, and in 1629 a man was fined for being sick on someone's floor: he 'confessis he drank by dyet'. In 1623 one tenant was prosecuted for allowing the children of a dead man to die of starvation; apparently he had taken the family's cattle in payment for a debt. In the same year at a solemn and important trial before a jury of fifteen the laird accused a couple of stealing cattle, sheep and other goods from within the barony; the woman, who was a MacGregor, was ordered to be scourged and banished, and the man was hanged.[4] Campbell was here the patriarchal Highland chieftain taking a deep interest in and exercising a strong control over the minutiae of the lives of his tenants and clansmen. Hanging a man for misdemeanours of which he had been found guilty before the baron court would scarcely have been possible in the Lowlands in the early seventeenth century.

Some of the Lowland baron courts, however, show a spirit which is not far removed from that of the Campbells of Glenorchy. In the Roxburghshire barony of Stitchill the records of the court held by Robert Pringle and his successors from 1655 shows a seventeenth-century Lowland laird in action in a manner hardly less personal and painstaking. His moral attitude was that of the godly magistrate backing the kirk-session: in 1660 and again in 1664 'taking into his serious consideration how great necessity church discipline has of the assistance and concurrence of the civil magistrate' he ordered his baillie to 'put into execution all acts and decrees of the kirk-session against all persons whomsoever'. Five years earlier he had commanded (there was no question with him of the 'consent of the commons and tenants') that none within the barony 'drink excessively, nor be sensibly drunk, nor use filthy nor scurrilous speeches and that none mock at piety . . . curse, swear or blaspheme'. Parents were put under a ten-pound penalty if they failed to send their children to school. Rioters and sabbath-breakers were put in the stocks at the kirk door. Otherwise the court was mainly concerned with the usual round of small rural offences—non-payment of rents and services to the laird, questions of debt, of trespass of tenants' cattle and fowls in each others' corn, and disputes about boundaries. It also made rules for the cutting of peats, planting of peas, erection of dykes and many other particulars of orderly husbandry.[5]

At a third court, that of the Barclays of Urie in Kincardineshire, the laird was a Quaker. He therefore had nothing to do with the kirk-session and one looks in vain for cases relating to excessive indulgence or neglect of moral principles. The laird was even ready to place himself at the bar in 1669 to answer an accusation which he had heard murmured behind his back that he was an unjust oppressor of the tenantry; the embarrassed peasants refused to prosecute 'in regard they confessed they had no reason to do so'. Like Pringle, however, Barclay was nevertheless strict in exacting the payment of rents and services due to himself, in ordering the planting of trees, arranging the settlement of debts within the community, punishing misdemeanours that ranged from poaching the laird's game to striking another tenant on the nose, and generally legislating for neighbourly farming.[6] A little further to the north at the barony of Forbes in Aberdeenshire there was a similar indifference to backing kirk discipline, accompanied if anything by a still greater zeal to exact the rights of the laird in rents and services, to punish violence and to settle debts.[7]

The baron court was presided over by the laird, or, more usually, by his baillie. This generally meant, of course, that the laird's cause went unopposed, but it was not invariably the case: Campbell of Glenorchy was sued by a tenant in 1627 for a crop of straw and was awarded half of what he asked for. The court also normally embodied a jury of tenants, between four and fourteen in number, often described in the Lowlands as birlaymen. In Lowlands and Highlands alike we also sometimes hear of the settlement or the barony possessing a court of birlaymen or constables which is differentiated from the larger and more formal baron court, and had more to do with purely agricultural affairs and less to do with petty 'police court' jurisdiction. Thus at Stitchill an 'inquest' of fifteen men was appointed to help the baron in his decisions, while a separate panel of nine 'bourlawmen' were chosen to decide 'with advice and consent' of the laird's factor 'all matters questionable and debateable among neybors and to impose stent and public impositions and to desyde the samyn equally'. At Yester in East Lothian, the boorlaw court was institutionally quite distinct from the baron court, though both consisted of the landowner's Baron Baillie and two other baillies chosen by the feuars: it met three times a year, had in 1760 a code of thirty-seven acts described then as having been 'from time immemorial the Boorlaw of Yester', and was exclusively concerned with such matters as the maintenance of head-dykes, the straying of animals, the overstocking of the common by an individual grazing more cattle than the number allowed to him by the court, and so on.[8] It clearly had a large part to play in keeping husbandry running with the minimum of friction.

In the Highlands the birlaymen were possibly elected from the tenants on a more or less democratic principle. In the Lowlands they seem normally to have been imposed from above by a laird nominating experienced tenants to serve upon it. In either case there was some appearance of consultation accompanied, no doubt, with a great deal of attachment to blind tradition. It was no doubt for the latter reason that in the eighteenth century birlaymen and their courts died out of common usage, and were replaced by a brisk factor who, being abreast of the new systems of husbandry borrowed from England, told the tenants what they should do without asking their opinion. This often aroused hostility: cases of petty and wilful damage to the laird's property—not unknown in the seventeenth century and common by the eighteenth—usually appear where peasant husbandry is being dictated with no account of the old channels of custom and communication by one who is not himself a peasant farmer.

2. THE FARM

The traditional farming that was regulated and controlled in these ways appears bizarre and inefficient to modern eyes: it is not easy to describe in a short space, because regional variations undermine almost every generalisation we can make.

It is probably true that everywhere the arable land was divided into two types, 'infield' and 'outfield', the terms being descriptive not of separate field areas but of types of ground that often lay in intermingled blocks. Infield, perhaps normally only a quarter or less of the total tillable area, was fertile enough to bear grain crops year after year without ever enjoying a fallow break. Outfield was poorer land that could only be farmed by alternating several years of fallow with several years of oats.

Infield was the division that carried the drink-crop of the community, bear, or four-rowed barley, that was sown in the spring (in April in the south of Scotland) some three weeks after the ground had been ploughed. This normally occupied a third or a quarter of the total infield land, except in Galloway where it monopolised the whole and was therefore grown on the same ground year after year. Elsewhere it rotated with other crops and usually received a dressing of manure, giving an average return over the whole country of something like four or five grains to every one sown. After harvesting—for all crops the slower sickle was generally preferred to the scythe, possibly because it wasted less grain—the bear was generally malted and brewed by husbandmen at home and consumed in the household: some peasants, however, served as brewers and retailers of ale to cottars and others who did not grow enough for themselves. Bear, though eaten as meal in an emergency, was reckoned a very inferior food except as a pot-grain to put in the broth.

In East Lothian, Fife, the Berwickshire Merse and some parts of Angus a further quarter of infield was often given over to wheat with here and there another division for peas and beans. Flax and hemp too was an infield crop, very often grown only on a single, heavily-dunged rig that sufficed to meet each household's requirements, every family spinning its own ropes and making its own linen according to necessity. In some places, however, especially round the shores of the

Firth of Clyde and along the lower Tay linen manufacture was the specialised occupation of tenants who combined it with husbandry, and either bought flax from importing merchants or grew it themselves. This kind of cottage product fed a wide market elsewhere in Scotland and England even in the seventeenth century, and represented an industrial intrusion into an agrarian economy which was to become of greater social and economic significance after the Union of 1707.

Oats was the other, and more usual, crop on infield. As it was also the only crop grown on outfield land it predominated throughout the country as the main product—the food crop—of Scottish husbandry. Ground intended for oats was generally ploughed in the autumn and sown before the bear in the early spring, often as early as February. On infield it was seldom manured: here two or three years of oats might follow the bear in rotation so that the ground on which it was sown got dung one year in three, but there was never a break in cereal production. On outfield practice varied: it might be thrust into the ground without preparation and grown on the same plot until the land was temporarily exhausted, but it might (as in Galloway, Aberdeenshire and East Lothian) be planted on land which had been divided into eight or ten 'brakes' or 'shotts' that were cultivated in logical rotation, with animals folded between temporary fences on one division every year before the fallow was broken up. The average return for oats does not seem to have exceeded three to one, 'ane to graw, ane to gnaw and ane to pay the laird withaw' ' as the bitter old proverb had it. The grains were more like wild oats than the fat seed of modern husbandry.

After the harvest, most Lowland peasants were obliged to take their grain to the water-mill to which they were 'thirled' by their tenure, and then obliged to pay a heavy 'multure' to have it ground into meal. Throughout Scotland this servitude was resented and evaded if possible and its imposition gave the baron courts one of their main tasks. It made the miller both an important and an unpopular figure in the community, as indeed, he seems to have been throughout Europe: 'I care for nobody, no not I, if nobody care for me'. The mill had further to be supported by peasant labour conscripted by the baron court to repair the leets and weirs, and to carry a new mill stone from the nearest quarry when the old one broke. This last was one of the occasions that united the community in effort and enjoyment. The stone had to be trundled over the bad roads on its circular edge with a young tree thrust through the centre like an axle, an operation needing a great

The Angus countryside, c.1677 from Edwards Map of Angus. Notice the large number of "mosses", the scarcity of woodlands, enclosures restricted to the parks of great houses and the shortage of roads

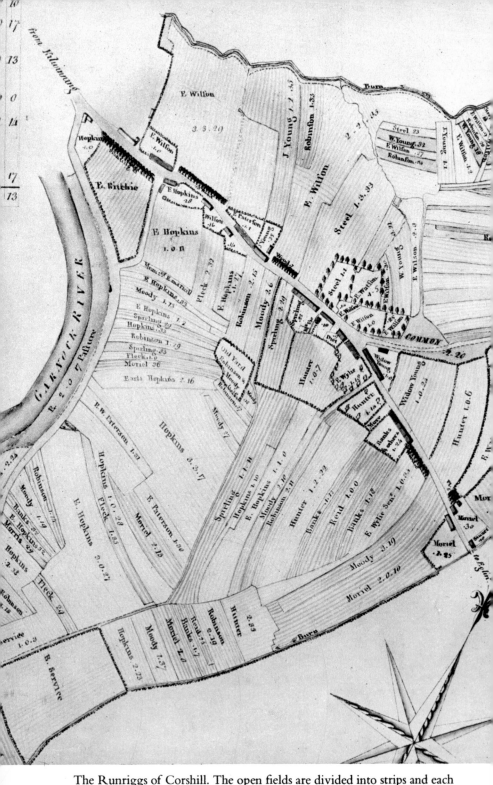

The Runriggs of Corshill. The open fields are divided into strips and each owner holds several blocks intermingled among those of his neighbours. This was characteristic landholding before the days of consolidation and enclosure

deal of labour and ale to carry to a successful conclusion. In the Highlands, where water-mills were scarce, grinding was normally done at
home by hand-querns. Many housewives elsewhere also kept querns
on the quiet to grind a little meal without taking it to the miller.

Of the animals of the farm, the plough team were the most essential
in all Lowland districts. The beasts might be horses or oxen. Their
numbers varied according to the weight of the plough in local use,
which was partly determined by the nature of the soil, and this in turn
had a bearing on the number of joint-tenants in a farmtoun. In some
parts with flat land unencumbered by many stones as many as twelve
oxen were needed to drag the cumbrous implement (all wood save for
an iron coulter) through the stiff, wet, winter ground. Then there
might be as many as twelve tenants, each contributing an ox to the
plough. On other soils, particularly in rocky parts like Kintyre, a
lighter plough drawn by four horses would be more useful, and then
there might be only four tenants. But the number of tenants was not
always the same as the number of plough animals: in Kintyre we hear
of a share called a Horse's Foot, which was apparently a quarter of a
Horsegang and a sixteenth of a Four-Horse Ploughgang—presumably
four of those who held a horse's foot would combine in some way to
provide an animal. In Galloway some districts ploughed with eight to
ten oxen and some with horses, but although ox-ploughing was slower
and less efficient the peasants preferred to use it where the land allowed.
Oxen gave more dung, were cheaper to feed and could, according to
the commentator, be sold for a 'good price' to local drovers when their
working life was over.

Horses or ponies were also kept as carrier animals and in the vicinity
of towns and coal-mines a specialised class of carrier tenants sometimes
arose, devoting most of their time to the transport of coals, cloth, peat
or farm produce between the farmtoun and the market. There were
some at Alloa in the middle of the eighteenth century, carrying the
Erskines' coal from the mine to the quayside: they were described as
having carts 'no better than wheelbarrows', and being so occupied with
carriage services that their small farms became totally neglected and
covered with gorse.

The remainder of the stock were important to the peasants as
direct providers of food and clothing. Every rural family kept at least
one dairy cow to provide milk, cheese and butter. The herds of black
beef-cattle in which the south-west and the Highlands particularly

specialised provided meat, leather and tallow. They also provided animals to pay over to the landlord as rent in kind. Goats were an important dairy and meat animal, particularly in the Highlands where they existed in astonishing numbers: 100,000 goat and kid skins were sent to London in a single year at the end of the seventeenth century. Sheep were ubiquitous in all hilly districts, small, brown and hairy ones in the Highlands, larger and woollier ones in the Borders: they also provided, as well as wool, meat and tallow. The peasants themselves were often quite skilled at processing the products of their own animals. The men were often passable tanners and shoemakers for their own families, and could render tallow into candle-grease at home; their wives spun the wool, and coloured it, but professional weavers in the villages usually made it up into cloth.

The main day-to-day problems of animal husbandry among the peasants were deciding how many animals might be kept by each man and arranging for their proper herding on the settlement's common lands. The birlaymen had an important part to play in both questions. The number of animals that might be kept—the souming—was generally fixed by tradition according to the size of the holding, but any problem of interpretation or ambiguity arising was referred to them. The allotment was reckoned in terms of cattle or their equivalent. Thus near Inverness 'a soume is as much grass as will maintain four sheep: eight sheep are equal to a cow and a half, or forty goats . . . the reason of this disproportion between the goats and sheep is that after the sheep have eat the pasture bare the herbs, as thyme, etc. that are left are of little or no value except for the brouzing of goats'.[9] Most later observers considered that this system permitted the land to be grossly overstocked with grazing animals, and one can see, at least, why if forty goats were reckoned the equivalent of a cow and a half, Scotland became a relatively tree-less country.

The birlaymen also regulated herding. Enclosures of any sort were rare—at best a field for horses, or a temporary fold between earthen dykes on a section of the outfield destined to go under the plough the following autumn. Most animals therefore wandered on the grounds round the settlement under the surveillance of herdsmen. Beef animals and sheep spent the summer on the rough pasture and moorland outwith the head dyke and were admitted to the stubbles after the harvest. Milk cows and horses were generally kept closer at hand, either tethered to the weedy baulks between the rigs or confined to the slightly better pastures near the settlement known as 'laigh lands' or 'burnt lands', which flooded in the winter but were not subjected to any form of controlled management. Any careless or selfish farmer was quickly punished. It was not allowed at Yester, for instance, to have an animal lying outside the house at night between May 3rd and the end of harvest in case it broke into the crops, nor was it permitted to keep a frisky horse unhobbled in case it dashed away through the corn, or to allow beasts to be herded separately from the rest of the community's flock in case they were allowed to do damage to a neighbour's property that no one else could see.

In the Highlands the grazing area was so extensive, and human settlements with their small arable core were so scattered that it paid to practise a form of transhumance. About midsummer every tenant took his 'souming' of milk-cows, calves and steers to 'shielings' in the mountains where summer grass grew thickly round the hill springs. Here the women and children spent a month or six weeks tending the herd, making butter and cheese, and living in temporary huts until the harvest came and recalled them to labour in the fields. In Highland and Lowland alike, herdsmen had to guard the animals from vermin and human predators. As late as 1621 each tenant on the Perthshire estates of Campbell of Glenorchy had to provide 'four croscats of iron' annually for slaying wolves. The wolf became extinct about 1690: the cattle thief took longer to extirpate.

The other difficult problems of keeping stock came in the bleak months from December to April, when the stubble had been eaten and the shielings, the moors and the pastures were a useless brown desolation. Root-crops were unknown: straw was used as winter-keep and a few sheaves of oats might be spared for the horses: the only approximation to hay was usually the coarse marsh grass, bents and broom which peasants cut in the summer. Many animals were therefore sold to market or slaughtered at home before the cold weather began, and the survivors had to live on anything they could find round the steadings, supplemented with the coarse fodder fed to them when the land was under snow. By the time there was bite on the pastures again they were often too emaciated to reach the moor, so in the Highlands 'Lifting Day' became an established date when the peasants carried the cattle out of their homes and byres and deposited them on the grass to recover their strength. Pigs and poultry that lived on household offal, scraps and scratchings of corn were not liable to the same disadvantages. In the Highlands, however, there was a universal superstitious prejudice against pigmeat, and even in the Lowlands pigs were kept sparingly. Poultry, however, was universal.

To what extent was peasant farming in the seventeenth century subsistence farming? Much of what we have said has indicated the degree to which peasants produced for themselves, but the dramatic geography of the country was enough in itself to compel a certain regional variety in the balance of husbandry and a consequent exchange of goods. In the Highlands, for instance, the peasant was, as we have implied, primarily a herdsman among the mountains reckoning his wealth in terms of cattle, sheep and goats. Though oats were grown wherever the soil could be scratched the region as a whole was an importer of grain and an exporter of cattle, exchanging produce at little frontier towns (like Dunkeld, Dunblane, Kirriemuir, Inverness and Dingwall) on the fringes of the Highland line. By contrast, the carse-lands of the east, around the Moray Firth, in Angus, Fife and the Lothians, formed a great sickle of fertile land where men were primarily tillers and thought of their wealth in terms of the bolls of grain their land would yield. They, too, marketed a surplus to the burghs and uplands, and even sent grain over the North Sea. In the upland parts of Aberdeenshire and Stirlingshire, the Borders and over much of the west pastoral husbandry again predominated, with sheep runs in the east and over in Wigtownshire producing wool that again might find a European sale either in raw form or as cloth: in Galloway and South Ayrshire it was black-cattle country with surplus beasts sold as far afield as Smithfield market in London even in the seventeenth century. But interspersed with these uplands were the fertile straths of the Berwickshire Merse, Annandale and Clydesdale all producing excess corn to exchange with their neighbours.

There were thus plenty of areas of which, like the merses of Galloway, it was said 'except in years of great scarcity (they) abundantly satisfy themselves and furnish the moorlands plentifully with victual'. There were also plenty of little markets like that at Minigaff, where the 'moormen' bought 'great quantities of meal and malt' from the men of the carse, and at Wigton, where there were two horsefairs a year frequented by the borderers from Annandale, a cattle fair frequented by the Dumfries butchers, and a cloth fair frequented by merchants from Edinburgh, Glasgow and Ayr.[10] Then there were other fairs less mercantile:

In the Kirkyard of Kirkanders upon the ninth day of August there is a fair kept called Saint Lawrence Fair where all sort of merchant wares are to be sold, but the fair lasts only three or four houres and then the people who flock hither in great companies drink and debauch and commonly great lewdness is committed here at this fair.[11]

In this way it is true to think of Scotland as a land of regional specialisation accompanied by internal and external trade in foodstuffs, which (as we have seen in the last chapter) was tending to grow in volume throughout the second half of the seventeenth century. On the other hand it is important to realise that there was a kind of basic uniformity in Scottish farming settlements despite their outward differences. The balance between arable and pasture might differ, but all farms were essentially mixed, holding one type of land to produce bread, ale and linen yarn for the community against another to produce milk, meat, leather, wool and draught animals. Geography determined which type was dominant: it could not determine that one would completely replace the other.

Furthermore careful investigation shows that marketing, and even the use of money, was more limited than we might suppose from a simple count of the number of markets and fairs authorised to be held. Buchan, the hinterland of Aberdeen, was a fairly settled and civilised part of Scotland selling grain to the Firth of Forth and to Norway in the second half of the seventeenth century. This was what one reporter had to say of it in the reign of Charles II:

This countrey is well peopled, for all things necessary to life are easily had here. The occupation of the men, whether gentry or commons, is labouring and husbandry: other trades, except what is simply necessary are scarce plyed. And generally all are accustomed to learn and practise so much of these as serves their own term, that there is little encouragement for arts and trades here.

In other words the district is still at a stage where the division of labour is at a primitive level and the emergence of village craftsmen is retarded. We know, however, from poll tax returns, that there were some village craftsmen practising their own trades in Aberdeenshire in the 1690s. He goes on:

Victual then is all the product of this countrey and when it giveth a

133

good price then it goeth well with the masters and heritours, but when it is otherwise they are ordinarily much straitened for money. The women of this countrey are mostly employed in spinning and working of stockings and making of plaiden-webs, which the Aberdeen merchants carry over sea. And it is this which bringeth money to the commons, other ways of getting it they have not.[12]

When the commentator said that the common people had no money except from their wives' earnings he was not necessarily using a figure of speech. The earliest full account of the conditions under which cottars and farm servants were given employment is an assessment of wages made by the justices of Midlothian in 1656. All the superior grades listed—the 'whole hinds' (a ploughman employing his own servant to help him), the 'half hinds', the herds and the taskers (or threshers) got no money at all for their wages. Instead they were given payment in food, and by having a free cottage with a kail-yard, some ground on the infield to sow with oats, bear and peas, and a souming for a few animals. Only the inferior servants, unskilled hands, juveniles and women, got any cash.[13] Thus, even on the very outskirts of the capital of Scotland it was reckoned an inferior and less desirable thing to receive a money wage for work than a fragment of ground in the farming community. In the Aberdeenshire Poll Tax returns of 1696 a very similar position is recorded: subtenants and herds appear to get no money at all, and the only wage payments are to the landless.[14]

It is facts like this that remind the historian of the depth of the gulf between a society of this kind and one like our own. In many ways there are much greater similarities between the peasant culture of seventeenth-century Scotland and those of the more backward tribes of Asia and Africa than between that culture and that of the modern rural Scotsmen who were their direct descendants.

CHAPTER VI

The Countryside
II. Tenure and Living Standards

1. THE LANDOWNERS

Land farmed in the way we have described had to provide two types of income; one for the peasants to keep themselves and their families alive, one paid as rent to support the landowners in their privileged position as the leaders of Scottish society under the king. The landowners were not numerous—outside the south-west where very small estates were common there were probably less than 5,000 men who possessed the right to inherit or to sell the ground they held. Nor were they homogeneous—the bonnet-laird and the nobleman differed enormously in their economic power, in their social prestige and in their relationships to other men. To understand the stratification of the class it is necessary to grasp something of the complexities of the living Scottish tradition of feudal law which treated all landowners as vassals or sub-vassals, holding by heritable tenure from a king in whom was vested the ultimate ownership of all land.

At the apex of the pyramid stood fewer than a hundred great families, those of the nobility and principal Highland chiefs, distinguished both by their aristocratic rank and by the fact that most of them acknowledged the king as their immediate feudal lord to whom they rendered the casualties and duties incidental to their tenures. Some of these were very mighty indeed. The Marquess of Huntly, who with Argyll, Hamilton and Angus was the head of one of the four greatest houses outside the royal kin of Stewart, held the 'eight and forty davochs of Huntly', an area of perhaps 20,000 acres in the fertile north-east. Others, particularly those of lords of seventeenth-century

135

creation like the Earls of Haddington or Hopetoun, might hold less than a tenth of this. The remaining landowners—the vast majority—were not of noble rank: they were comprehended under the general title of lairds, some holding directly of the crown but most as sub-vassals of the nobility. For noble and laird alike the two commonest forms of tenure by which they held their land were 'wardholding' and 'feuferme'. They differed widely in character.

Wardholding was the older of the two—'the most proper feudal holding we have' Stair described it, since it originated from the knight's tenures of the high Middle Ages, and still contained those essential elements of personal obligation which marked the Norman world of David I and Malcolm IV. Every wardholder was still obliged to give his lord military service, to provide free hospitality and to attend his superior's court when called upon to do so. It was this that gave the nobility their continuing grip and power to call out great feudal hosts in private or public war, and consequently led to the abolition of wardholding tenures after the 1745 rebellion. Though the wardholder could securely inherit or alienate his land much like an English land-owner his estates were subject to the casualties of relief, ward and mar-riage which originated in the theory that the land did in fact revert to the superior on the death of the holder. 'Relief' arose if an heir was of age on the death of his father: he then had to pay a sum normally equal to one year's produce of the estate to obtain entry. 'Wardship' arose if he was a minor: the superior then administered the lands and creamed off the rents until his majority. 'Marriage' arose if the heir was a minor or a woman: he or she could then be married off without his or her consent to anyone whom the superior regarded as profitable to choose. Finally, if there was no heir the land 'escheated' (reverted) to the super-ior. All these archaic and onerous customs which could destroy years of careful estate management overnight were still in use in the late sixteenth and seventeenth century, though by 1690 wardholding was the characteristic tenure only of the Highlands.

Feuferme was more recent in origin and much less pristinely feudal in character, since it rested on a basis of cash rather than of personal obligation. It was obtained by paying a superior a large sum as down-payment known as the 'grassum', followed by a rent known as the 'feu-duty' that came to be regarded as fixed in perpetuity. Feuferme like wardholding normally conferred perpetual heritable occupation, but it differed from the older form in carrying with it no trace of military or judicial obligation or payment of any arbitrary casualty. It first became popular in the course of the late fifteenth and early sixteenth centuries when the crown and the church alike felt the need for large money incomes in a hurry—a need that obviously could not be met by alienating to wardholders. Later the nobility in the more settled regions also appreciated the cash advantage of feuing, and before the close of the seventeenth century it had almost completely ousted wardholding throughout the south and east.

The expense of purchasing a feuferme charter was not small. The land was often feued in large blocks (the whole of Strathearn in one case), grassums were heavy and feu duties intended to be geniune economic rents when first fixed. These considerations often put the lands beyond the reach of the peasants who farmed them when they came on to the market, but for the old nobility, the lairds and for rich urban incomers from trade, the law or court office this presented a golden opportunity of adding to their estates or of buying one for the first time. As inflation snowballed—there was heavy monetary depreciation throughout the sixteenth century—the original purchasers found their economic position greatly improved by the fall in the real value of the fixed duty. Lairds who held in this way might become powerful to support the crown in its efforts to restrict the faction of the nobles, although lords were often able to maintain their control over the feuar's loyalty either by involving them in bonds of manrent (by which they undertook to come to one another's support in times of trouble) or by feuing only to their own kin.

In a few areas, however, especially in those remote from Edinburgh or any other major burgh that could contain a nucleus of buyers ambitious for land, the church and crown appear to have alienated at lower rates and in smaller parcels, so that the larger peasants (perhaps generally the kindly tenants, for which see below page 147) had a better chance to buy their holdings. This was quite possibly the origin of the bonnet-lairds, small independent owners who tilled the ground with their own and their servants' labour, who were numerous in Galloway and some other counties south and west of the Clyde, but occur elsewhere only occasionally and in small numbers. The owner-occupier, the equivalent of the English yeoman, was otherwise a relative rarity in Scottish society.

These three groups, the noble, the laird and the bonnet-laird, were the only ones who enjoyed heritable tenure and can properly be described as landowners. The first two were also rentiers, existing without labouring with their hands: the last came close in economic status to the larger peasants. There were, however, two further groups, the wadsetter and the tacksman. Being sometimes rentiers, sometimes farmers, and sometimes both rentiers and farmers, they cannot exactly be described as peasants. However, since they failed to establish heritable right to their tenure they cannot properly be called landowners either. Their characters were quite different. The wadsetter was merely a creditor of the landowner enjoying use and free tenure of part of his estate as long as the debt remained unpaid. Such mortgages were often held by fellow lairds, but sometimes by cadet members of a landed family or by legal or commercial families who worked towards a permanent foothold on the land by starting as wadsetters. They were also sometimes held by large tenants who had succeeded in accumulating enough capital to lend some to the laird. The tacksmen were tenants in a more orthodox sense, but they were restricted to the Highlands and parts of the adjacent areas where they first appeared in the early seventeenth century. Frequently they were close relatives (often brothers, cousins or younger sons) of the chief, leasing a large block of land for several years or for the duration of one or two lives, and acting as viceroy over this portion of the estate, if necessary training and organising the clan peasants for war and appearing with armed followers at his bidding. The tacksmen also paid rent in money or kind to the chief and obtained a larger rent in money or kind from the peasants, living on the difference between the two. Sometimes, however, they farmed on their own account. It is not always clear how often this was the case, since in some parts of the country (such as Kintyre) the situation is confused by the fact that the expression 'tacksman' was also used to denote any farming tenant who had been given a lease (a 'tack') for a term of years, rather than to describe a viceroy or kinsman who had a purely passive role as middleman between the landlord and the man who cultivated the ground. Normally there was no justification for the middleman type of tenure except in a para-military society. It was destined to perish in the later eighteenth century when law and order finally made it archaic.

From the chief and the nobleman to the tacksman and the wadsetter, then, the landed classes lived primarily off rents. Relative to the low productivity of the land these were heavy, commonly reckoned at one third of total output, and since in arable husbandry another third of the oats and another quarter of the bear were required for seed, the peasant enjoyed only a small margin of subsistence between the upper and nether millstones.

Rents were paid either in money or in kind, depending partly on the type of farming and partly on the geographical location of the farm. Wherever arable husbandry predominated the main rent was reckoned in terms of a fixed number of bolls of grain and probably still paid over in kind in most areas, though in some parts (such as East Lothian and Fife) the institution around 1620 of county 'fiars', by which the money equivalent of a grain rent was fixed according to the price of corn in that year, suggests that commutation was spreading. In areas of pastoral husbandry there was general use of money rents in place of rents of living animals though the rent was frequently paid partly in silver and partly in kind. Here commutation probably developed as rural marketing increased and the need to feed retainers in the castle declined. Thus in Angus by the middle of the seventeenth century it is easy to see which are the upland estates and which the low-lying ones by a glance at the rentals—in 1636 the lands of Glenesk paid 4026 merks, those of Menmuir 'above eighty chalders of victual' and those of Lethnot, lying between, nine chalders of victual and 1273 merks.[1] On the other hand in the great pastoral zone of the centre and west of the Highlands peasants still in the seventeenth century often paid a substantial proportion of their rents in live bestial: silver was scarce, markets were few, and the needs of the chief's household were still so great that it made sense to do so. Thus in 1728 a daughter of Ewen Cameron of Lochiel expressed the difference between Lowland and Highland landed incomes: 'its not land-rents that maintaine me and my family but the real product of cattle and land-labouring'.[2]

Apart from the main rent, and the teinds (tithes) where the landowner possessed them, the laird received various other payments in kind or in service from the peasants—these again varied from place to place, but they usually included an annual payment of so many chickens, perhaps of pigs or lambs, often of cheese, or of ells of linen in flax-growing counties. Trusses of straw were paid to help with the laird's thatching and fodder requirements, and the obligation to carry peats for the castle fires was widely imposed. Where the laird had a home farm there might also be harvest and ploughing services, but by the seventeenth century these seem to be rare. The plethora of varied payments in kind and money made the rentals complex documents: that of the Barony of Panmure in 1671 comprised the following typical assortment—110 bolls of wheat, 553 bolls of bear, 597 bolls of meal and two bolls of malt, being the main rent of the lands; then 31 dozen capons, 17 dozen hens, 23 dozen 'poultry' and 15 dozen chickens, with 14 dozen ells of linen, 30 dozen pigeons, three firlots of beans, 80 straw 'threaves' and 22 'huikis', probably reaping sickles; finally there were money payments described as 'silver duties and wiccaradge silver' amounting to £798 Scots.[3]

The collection and disposal of such a miscellany could only be done with the help of paid grieves or factors in the Lowlands and through the tacksmen in the Highlands. Throughout the north-east the lairds kept their payment of meal, oats and bear in great 'girnals' or barns, selling some back retail to the country people, disposing of some in the markets of the local burghs, and very often in the seventeenth century selling the grain straight from the girnals to a merchant of one of the royal burghs who exported the crop to Norway, to the Firth of Forth or to other places along the coast where a market was available. Sometimes the landowner himself chartered or owned vessels to export his victual on his own account—the Earl of Seafield, for instance, had several ships on this trade and suffered severely when French and Jacobite privateers cut the coastal line of communication between Buchan and the Forth after 1690. Highland chiefs with cattle rent were faced with similar problems: Campbell of Glenorchy in 1640 had to find pasture and herdsmen for nearly a thousand black cattle and sheep, and to sell those his household could not consume within the year. It was not, perhaps, a great problem for a Perthshire laird but it was certainly hard for those of the interior whose droves had to run the gauntlet of hostile clans on their way south.

The relationship of the landowner to the peasant was not all taking and control on the one side and giving and obedience on the other. Until 1600 landowners everywhere had a socially important duty as the protectors and war-leaders of their tenants. By 1650 this function was extinct in the Lowlands: in the Highlands (though the estate and the clan was not necessarily conterminous) it lasted for a hundred years after that. For several generations after the military justification for it had passed away landowners tended to cling to the old feeling that the number of men on the estate was more important than the levels of rent: this sentiment softened the economic relationship, prevented change in the agricultural system and encouraged the splitting of peasant holdings to accommodate as many tenants as possible. Nor must it be forgotten that the judicial privileges of the baron court, though valuable to the laird, had a real function in rural society by providing the tenants with quick and probably fairly impartial justice in their disputes with one another. Finally even the taking of rent was not always one-sided. Many peasants, especially in the Highlands and the west held by 'steelbow' tenure, by which the landlord himself provided stock and seed with the land in the same way as the 'metayer' system of France. This was not necessarily more benevolent or advantageous to the tenant than other tenures, but it did provide an incoming peasant with the working capital to start husbandry. Even where this was not practised, rent was often remitted in years of poor harvest, and when serious shortage struck, the landowners (at least in the eighteenth century) would frequently distribute from their own girnals at less than market rate. The whole relationship was essentially paternal—a very personal and often very warm paternalism in the clan where the members felt themselves to belong to the same family whatever their rank, a more remote and chilly paternalism in the Lowlands where the ties of kinship were weaker. On the other hand the warmth of paternalism was also influenced by the abundance or scarcity of population. Any landlord would be happy to remit a peasant's rent if the alternative to not evicting him was a barren holding and no chance of further rent for some years: his generous feelings would be much harder to touch if he knew that other tenants were queuing up to take the holding.

The state in which a landlord lived varied, of course, according to the size of his rental and whether or not he was expected to entertain a military retinue. In James VI's time a powerful Highland chief of the Western Isles like Sir Rory Mor Macleod kept uproarious hospitality at Dunvegan, surrounded by retainers, relatives, pipers, fiddlers and poets in the full traditions of Ireland and Scandinavia. One of the Gaelic poets of the time, Neil Mor MacMhuirich, celebrated his visit in the following verses:

The merriment of the harp and of the full bowls,
With which hatred and treachery are not usually accompanied,
The laughter of the fairhaired youngsters,
We had inebriating ale and a blazing fire . . .

We were twenty times drunk every day,
To which we had no more objection than he had,
Even our food was in abundance . . .[4]

Dunvegan was indeed amply supplied with food and drink—in the 1680s the chief was receiving 9000 hens a year from his lands, and from Skye alone 400 stones of butter. In another Highland castle in the early seventeenth century Lord Lovat, chief of the Frasers, was said to consume with his household and guests ten stone of malt and meal a day with seventy cows in a year and a large amount of poultry, mutton, venison and game. Wine, sugar and spices he imported from France in exchange for the salmon from his estates. When he died in 1631 five thousand armed men attended the sumptuous funeral celebrations.[5]

John Taylor, Ben Jonson's friend who had a hilarious holiday in Scotland in 1618, said the nobles keep 'thirty, forty, fifty servants or perhaps more . . . and can give noble entertainment for four or five days together to five or six earls and lords besides knights, gentlemen and their followers, if they be three or four hundred men and horse of them, where they shall not only feed but feast, and not feast but banquet'. He, too, went to a great Highland party, and gives an account of the Earl of Mar's *al fresco* catering arrangements at a hunt in Braemar.

The kitchin being alwayes on the side of banke many kettles and pots boyling and many spits turning and winding, with great variety of cheere; as venison bak't; sodden, roast and stew'de beefe; mutton, goates, kid, hares, fresh salmon, pidgeons, hens, capons, chickens, partridge, moorecoots, heathcocks, caperkellies and termagants (ptarmigan); good ale, sacke, white, and claret, tent and alleant (Alicante wine), with most potent *Aquavitae*.[6]

Plainly this was a society devoted to conspicuous consumption, and that form of consumption most admired and emulated was the offering of hospitality on a prodigious scale.

Of the interior furnishings of the seventeenth-century baron's house less is generally said by outside visitors, and it appears that in the early days they were often somewhat sparse: the long trestle tables and a 'high board' for the lord (often raised on a dais), with chests, cupboards, forms, a few chairs or stools and the box-beds would be the main items: there might be wainscot panelling (but relatively seldom tapestries) painted deal ceilings (but relatively seldom plaster); straw would take the place of carpets on the floor, wooden platters and spoons (sometimes pewter) the place of china and cutlery on the tables, while each man in the Highlands kept a dirk in his sock to serve equally as a dagger and table knife.[7] But some nobles could do better than this. Castle Campbell in Clackmannanshire, the dower-house of the Earls of Argyll, had a very full inventory made of its contents in 1595. These included several four-poster beds, eighteen pieces of tapestry, 'ane cheir coverit wit reid crammasie velvet' and various folding chairs covered with white damask or leather.[8] Forty years later when times were kinder (and even lairds had curtains) the Earl of Haddington in his Lowland home had several great velvet chairs, a set of twenty red-leather ones, oil paintings, many tapestries depicting Biblical scenes, state beds including 'ane grein French cloath bed with rich lace and fringe, with chairis, stoolis, covering and table cloath', mirrors, rugs, curtains and forty silver plates.[9] Jewels, plate and heirlooms were favourite possessions in an aristocratic household. The Campbells of Glenorchy at Balloch in 1632 thus had a set of silver cups, a stone 'the quantity of half a hen's egg' worn by the first laird when he fought at Rhodes against the Turks, a targe of gold set with diamonds and enamel given to the family by James V and a modern golden jewel given by James VI's queen. The Earl of Eglinton at the same date had two musical boxes, an enamelled striking clock and even a pair of spectacles bound with silver.[10]

As the century proceeded and military needs lessened there was a progressive revolution in manners which did not leave even the Highland nobility unaffected. Rory Mor's successors at Dunvegan were roundly attacked by the poets for the degenerate quality and quantity of their hospitality; what honest man would eat in private? All over Scotland the Restoration nobles got drunk in their dining-rooms, in front of their friends but not in front of their tenants and followers. They still ate prodigious quantities of food, but their household consumption was much smaller. The paintings, fine silver tableware and cutlery, good quality Dutch linen, imported beds and English chairs which had been coming into the houses in the reign of Charles I now became increasingly common. Perhaps because money incomes were so largely replacing rents in kind, they were buying with the magpie instinct of modern householders instead of merely giving way to intermittent bouts of gluttony.

Not many landowners of either period lived as well as the chiefs and nobles, though no doubt all would have done if their pockets had been deep enough. It would be fitting to end this section with two examples from seventeenth-century Ross-shire lairds which are perhaps more typical of the standards the majority of landowners enjoyed. The first deals with the food the Laird of Balnagoun had set before him in the course of one week in 1663—it included at least one meat dish a day, together with broth, peas, whiting, herring and poultry, beer and bread, and a little sugar. The second is the inventory of the contents of Easter Fearn, a small laird's house, in 1638—it comprised one high board with trestles and forms, one side table, one 'fair cupboard with two drawers', two standard beds, three chests full of clothes, pots, pans, stoups and cups and three vats for salting salmon.[11] On a much smaller scale, the same general pattern is visible here as we noted in the great houses—ample to eat and drink, and a certain amount to possess and hand on. The habit of acquisition would spread down the social scale from the great lairds and the nobility in time, but as yet money incomes were too small to make an impact on the poorer members of the class. Indeed, the very poorest, the bonnet-lairds of the south-west, were no better off in material standards than the peasants themselves.

2. THE PEASANTS

Most Scotsmen, of course, were peasants. Perhaps three out of four came under this general description. Like the lairds, they were organised in social strata determined by their tenure and by their economic position in the farmtoun community.

At the top of the ladder were the tenants, who held the tenancy or joint-tenancy of a farm directly from the landowner or tacksman much as a noble held directly from the king. In the Highlands the term tenant might not cover anyone very prosperous—in a farm held by a dozen joint-tenants on some upland glen there were only small shares to go round, and perhaps no-one employed servants or cottars to help in the business of husbandry. In parts of the Lowlands however, the tenant (often there called the husbandman or gudeman) was the aristocrat of peasant life and often an employer, usually with a much larger holding of land than the tenant in the Highlands. Indeed, some of them claimed the style of gentleman even though they were legally no more than tenants-at-will and use of this empty title involved them in heavier taxes. As one local historian has explained apropos of the poll tax: 'he could, however, escape the imposition by renouncing any pretence to be a gentleman, which renunciation was to be recorded in the Herald Register gratis. It would appear, however, that few availed themselves of this privilege in Aberdeenshire'. Wherever feudalism or clanship was a military force, the tenant was expected to fight if the lord or tacksman required. The grades below were probably expected to do no more than defend themselves when attacked.

Inferior to the husbandman, and usually his own subtenants, employed by him as ploughmen (hinds), herds and threshers, were the crofters, cottars and grassmen. There seems to be little difference between the three descriptions: all had a hut and a kailyard, a small amount of fertile land on the infield and the right to graze a few animals on the moor. All paid their rents primarily by labour on the husband-man's farm, with perhaps a fowl or two to the lairds. The nuances of the different terms vary from place to place, but 'crofter' was generally applied to a man a little better off than someone described as a 'cottar'—the former might have a number of animals and an acre of infield land, the latter sometimes no more than a single cow and a narrow strip. The 'grassman' might be no more than a poor cottar with herding duties: in Aberdeenshire the presence of numerous 'grasswomen' suggests that widows were sometimes provided for by a tenure of this sort. Generally, country shoemakers, weavers and tailors (where these existed as a separate occupation) were also cottars with a holding of infield land.

Lastly there were the landless labourers and indoor farm servants, both men and women, who received some wages in money and some in kind. Many of these boarded in the husbandman's house, others were 'out-servants'. Most were probably junior members of a crofter's or cottar's family, or of the families of a poor tenant. Other members of the cottar's family worked for the cottar himself. We have seen from the Midlothian assessment of 1656 that the 'whole hind' was obliged to maintain a labourer in his own employment to work the plough and help at other tasks—wherever possible it would presumably be his own son. The shepherd was under the same obligation. Cottars' wives had to work very hard indeed: the whole hind's wife in 1656 had to help daily in the harvest as long as needed, to help her husband at haytime

and at winning the peats, at tending the limekiln, at carting and mucking, at tending the byre, at carrying the stacks from the barnyards to the
barns for threshing and at winnowing. Hard female labour was an
essential part of agriculture.[12]

We may be fairly sure that crofters, cottars and servants together
outnumbered the tenants, at least in the Lowlands, but we cannot know
in what proportion the classes existed over Scotland as a whole. Only
for Aberdeenshire in 1696 is there any clear evidence, and even here
there is very great variation from parish to parish.[13] In the Highland
parish of Glenmuick, for instance there were 103 tenants, but only nine
subtenants. There were sixty-two people described as servants (of
whom a third worked for the resident heritors, not the peasant farmers),
a majority of them men. In the Lowland parish of Migvie, by contrast,
there were seventeen tenants, thirty-one subtenants and only eleven
servants (seven in the homes of lairds), but in adjacent Tarland there
were thirty-four tenants, thirty-two subtenants but sixty-five servants
(only twelve were in heritors' houses, and two-thirds of the total were
men). Some of the differences may have been more apparent than real,
for not all the servants in a place like Tarland may have been completely
landless—some are described as working for 'no fee'.

Throughout the country, in terms of married males the landless
servant class was probably rather small, but its size would vary both
according to population pressure and to the local custom about sub-
tenures. Thus in the Highlands in the eighteenth century, and no doubt
earlier, it seems to have been the practice to provide every son with a
fragment of land either as a tenant or a subtenant so far as possible. In
East Lothian, however, the Boorlaw Court of Gifford and Yester
placed a 'stent' on the number of cottars a husbandman might have in
exactly the same way as there was a stent on his holding of cattle,
depending on the size of the farm he had to cultivate, and no-one was
allowed more than three. Every cottar must be able to plough, must
come with a testimonial of their good character and be formally
approved by the baron-baillie.[14] In an area where such rules prevailed,
therefore, population pressure among the peasantry would lead not to
fractionised holdings but to an increase in the number of adult landless
males, who would either have to emigrate to the towns (or overseas)
or find jobs without land attached within the rural community.

None of the peasants had a legal or prescriptive right to the ground
they occupied, whether they were husbandmen or cottars, or whether

they dwelt in the Lowlands or in the Highlands. Husbandmen were either tenants-at-will or held on short leases generally of one to six years. Crofters, cottars and grassmen were invariably tenants-at-will. In this respect the position of the peasantry deteriorated over large areas in the course of the sixteenth century, and a class known as 'kindly tenants' roughly analogous to the copyholders in England lost what amounted to customary (but unwritten) rights of heritable tenure.

In the fifteenth century such kindly tenants had been numerous on church lands, and to a lesser extent also on the estates of the crown and of some lay landowners. Their farms were held at moderate rents, often (on lay estates) tied to the performance of military services, and their holdings had descended undisturbed from father to son over long periods. In the sixteenth century, as church and crown lands were feued out, a few were able to buy their holdings and become bonnet-lairds. More discovered that the ground had passed into the hands of new owners who had little regard for tenures unsupported by charter and who were anxious to recover the heavy expense of the grassum as fast as possible. In a situation in which population appears to have been quite rapidly on the increase as the plagues of later medieval Europe were losing their pristine virulence, rents were raised, holdings reduced in size, new families intruded and old ones expelled or obliged to accept less favourable terms. The area of cultivated land was pushed out as far as possible, and in some places by 1620 liming was used to increase the fertility of the corn ground, but the increase in productivity was apparently not commensurate in the short run with the increase in population.

Even on estates that were not feued the kindly tenants found themselves excluded towards the end of the sixteenth century. Thus in the north-east 'James, Earl of Moray cast them out of their kindly possessions which past memory of man their predecessors and they had enjoyed for small duty but for faithful service, and planted in their place for payment of a greater duty a number of strangers'.[15] In this case the kindly tenants were members of Clan Chattan as well as tenants of the Earl of Moray, and involved their chief in armed retaliation against their landlord. Such a resort to force was no doubt exceptional, but Scottish law in any case would not help kindly tenants. In England the courts showed a respect for custom that beyond question cushioned the blow to the copyholders, many of whom became in time freehold-ing yeoman: but in Scotland law rested on a Roman basis that took no account of unwritten tradition. The kindly tenants appear to have been almost extinct by 1600 in all but a few localities.

Due mainly, no doubt, to the growth in population the lot of the remainder of the peasantry seems also to have grown worse in the sixteenth century. From about the start of the reign of James V in 1513 there began a mounting volume of social complaint directed particularly against rack renting, the crown passing a handful of ineffective statutes in an attempt to stabilise rents, intellectuals exclaiming in verse and prose against the hard materialism of the age. It is unquestionable that the landowners took advantage of economic forces to wring better terms out of their tenants. On the other hand, the deterioration was not merely a manifestation of human greed, as many thought. In a country where agricultural efficiency was low and industrial employment limited, where in addition all peasants wanted use of a foot of land and all lairds valued a high population on their estates for their own protection, even a small increase in numbers would lead either to splintered holdings and thereby to a cut in the margins of subsistence for each family or to an increase in the number of the landless. In the sixteenth century the growth of population seems at times to have exceeded the capacity of the land to support it even on fractionalised holdings, and equally persistent contemporary complaints about the numbers of 'broken men', wandering beggars and thieves, represented the other end of the same problem as the complaints against landed materialism.

Had it been possible to increase markedly the productivity of the land, or to absorb the surplus in non-agricultural employment, hardship might have been avoided. As it was, neither the Scottish economy nor Scottish society was constructed to take the strain of population growth without the peasant suffering even if lairds had been models of virtue instead of ordinary selfish men. On the other hand in the seventeenth century the increase of population was again severely checked by outbreaks of disease and famine, especially virulent in the 1640s and 1690s respectively and by the early eighteenth century, whatever their legal status, peasants again appear often to have enjoyed a measure of *de facto* security in the occupation of their farms.

In portraying the peasants' world of poverty we are heavily dependent on seventeenth-century material. The husbandman's house may set the first scene. Though no actual dwellings have survived, Christopher Lowther in 1629 visited a home at Langholm which sounds similar to the black houses which were inhabited in Lewis until very recent times: 'we laid in a poor thatched house, the wall of it being one course of stones, another of sods of earth, it had a door of wicker rods, and the spiders webs hung over our heads as thick as might be'. It was apparently the same as he describes on an earlier page, 'John a Foorde's at my Lord Maxfield's gate where the fire is in the midst of the house'—that is to say, burning in a circular hearth on an earthern floor with the peat smoke going straight up to the rafters and finding its way out through a hole in the roof.[16]

Sixty years later, Thomas Morer gave the first detailed generalised account of Scottish peasants' houses in the Lowlands which shows how typical the house at Langholm was.

> The vulgar houses and what are seen in the villages are low and feeble. Their walls are made of a few stones jumbled together without mortar to cement 'em, on which they set up pieces of wood meeting at the top, ridge-fashion, but so order'd that there is neither sightliness nor strength . . . they cover these houses with turff of an inch thick and in the shape of larger tiles which they fasten with wooden pins and renew as often as there is occasion; and that is very frequently done. 'Tis rare to find chimneys in these places, a small vent in the roof sufficing to convey the smoake away.[17]

Choice of building materials and techniques of construction varied with locality, but everywhere in a countryside where trees were few it was the timber beams of the roof that were the most valuable part of the structure. Baron courts laid special penalties on those who took their roof tree with them when they removed from their dwellings. Walls were of turf or stone, sometimes of cob or wattle—they were seldom as high as a standing man. Thatching materials were turf or heather, straw being regarded as an animal fodder too precious to be squandered on buildings. We have seen that chimneys were rare: wood or stone floors and any form of ceiling apparently did not exist, and windows, if there were any, formed small square openings without glass.

The husbandman's house had to be large enough for his own family, for the servants who boarded with them, and for the cattle. They all lived under one roof though possibly not all in one room— the cattle at least would be in a byre divided by boards from the living space. If we can follow somewhat later descriptions of traditional houses (see Chapter XIII below) it would be fair to picture the head of the family and his wife sleeping at night in a box-bed, with their children and servants curled up in their plaids on straw pallets around the fire, though sometimes there would be more division of the house, more box-beds and more privacy.

Apart from the bed, the meal kists and a stool or two, the husbandman had little furniture. A Perthshire tenant in 1596, a man with forty sheep, twenty goats, fifteen cattle and four horses had as household possessions just one chest, one pot, one kettle, one brass pot, one chair, two dishes, two cups and four wooden plates: another with twelve sheep, twelve goats, twelve cattle and two horses had a pot, a sack, a sheet, a pan, a spade, a stool, a chair and four cups.[18] A tenant who died in the Lowland parts of Ross-shire in 1649 leaving six great cattle and an ox together with quantities of corn was a little better off in household goods—he had four large tables with forms, six chairs and two backed stools, a press with a folding bed, four great chests and two little ones, and six wooden plates. Another in the same area who died in 1697 leaving four horses and twenty cattle with grain and meal was as wealthy as a small laird—he had nine chests, a standing bed, three chairs, two stools, two little tables, various wooden plates, cups and spoons and—new and unfamiliar items for his class—a brass candlestick, linen towels, bed-clothes, tablecloths and napkins.[19] Not enough inventories and testaments have been studied to justify any general conclusions about trends in the standard of living during the seventeenth century, but it is likely enough that the husbandman was less desperately poor in corn counties by the end of the century than he had been at the beginning.

The homes of the cottars and crofters fell below the humble standards of the husbandmen's dwelling. Thomas Kirke left this description in 1679:

> The houses of the commonalty are very mean, mud-wall and thatch the best: but the poorer sort lives in such miserable hutts as never eye beheld; men, women and children pig together in a poor mouse-hole of mud, heath and some such like matter; in some parts where turf is plentiful they build up little cabbins thereof with arched roofs of turf without a stick of timber in it; when their houses are dry enough to burn it serves them for fuel and they remove to another.[20]

The historian might suspect Kirke of exaggerating if there were not also accounts from the early eighteenth century of lairds depositing their cottars' houses on the dunghill after they had evicted their occupants and illustrations from the same period of Highland homes that were simple tents of wattle with no opening than a hole at ground level through which a man would have had to crawl on hands and knees to gain entry.

In this context, it is interesting to consider the earliest architectural drawings of any rural housing in Scotland. They date from 1701, and are designs for a pair of stone cottages flanking the entrance to the laird's home farm, believed to be at Brechin.[21] One is described as the henwife's house, the other as the foremans' hall: each consisting of a single room thirteen foot by nine, lit by an unglazed window two foot by three, with a chimney-hearth in one corner and what appears to be a box bed in the other. Adjacent to each house is a separate raised privy with three seats, from which the excrement fell into an open midden yard to accumulate until cleared away for use on the farm. Apart from the curious and insanitary toilet arrangements there can be no doubt that this represented something a little superior to the standards of cottar housing described by Kirke. At least the external appearance did the architect credit.

Of the possessions of the cottars within their homes we know little—such men made no wills and had little a bailiff would wish to seize. Presumably they had some sort of meal kist, cup, plate, spoon and cooking pot; they may or may not have had beds, and it seems most improbable they could boast of anything else except the odd stool. Such an almost complete absence of material goods may be found today in the peasant societies of underdeveloped countries: we might guess that nearly half the Scots lived in such a world.

The clothing of the Scottish peasant was described by several travellers. In the Highlands the main garment was not the kilt (unknown until the eighteenth century) but the belted plaid, a long woollen blanket that served as a cloak by day and wrapped round the wearer as a coverlet by night—an admirable garment for a pastoral people who often had to sleep out of doors with their flocks. It was worn by peasant, tacksman and chief alike, its quality varying with the affluence of the wearer: those who could afford it had slashed doublet and long stockings as well—all had a bonnet and thin soled shoes. Morer described the Highland fashion as follows:

The pladds are about seven or eight yards long . . . they cover the whole body with 'em from the neck to the knees excepting the right arm which they mostly keep at liberty. Many of 'em have nothing under these garments besides wastcoats and shirts which descend no lower than the knees, and they so gird 'em about the middle as to give 'em the same length as the linen under 'em and thereby supply the defect of drawers and breeches.[22]

The Lowland peasant had a plaid too, but it was not so ample, and was usually worn with trousers: here there was a bigger class difference in dress, for the lairds dressed like Englishmen, except, as Morer put it, 'when some hasty business calls them forth or when the weather disheartens them to trick themselves better'. The peasant women wore linen skirts, with a plaid draped over their heads, pinned across their bosom and falling to their knees. They were not allowed by the sessions to wear plaids over their heads in church as this was too conducive to sleep. They went barefooted like the children, 'yet the husbands have shoes', said Morer 'and therein seem unkind in letting their wives bear those hardships'.

None of this suggests anything but low standards of clothing, a basic minimum to protect the wearer against the worst of a bad climate. Yet behind the poverty there was undoubtedly a wish to dress as well as possible, comparable to that in modern African or West Indian societies where incomes are likewise at subsistence level and housing squalid. 'They lay out most they are worth in cloathes', said John Ray in 1662 'and a fellow that hath scarce ten goats besides to help himself with, you shall see come out of his smoaky cottage clad like a gentleman'.[22] In the eighteenth century this pride in appearance was to have economic importance in creating an immediate consumer demand for the cheap and colourful textiles on which the industrial revolution was initially based.

The standard of peasant diet, at least by the second half of the seventeenth century when grain prices had fallen from previous high levels, seems to have been rather above that of most very primitive economies at the present time. None of the travellers in Scotland speak of endemic starvation or acute emaciation among the population. The food was certainly monotonous enough. For husbandman and cottar alike oatmeal was the stuff of life, and very often a substantial proportion of the wage by which servants were paid: it could be mixed with milk to make porridge, with water to make gruel, or made into a paste and baked into oatbread or bannocks. Those with ewes, goats or cows—and this included almost everyone in the rural population—drank quantities of milk in summer and could make a certain amount of butter and cheese for their consumption in the late winter when meal reserves had run low, and before spring grass revived the liquid supplies. The Highlanders exchanged their excess dairy produce for the Lowlanders' meal. Kail was grown universally in the Lowlands in the cottars' 'kailyards', and seems at this period to have begun to penetrate the Highlands: it was made into a broth with bear grains or oatmeal. Poultry provided eggs, and the flesh again was usually turned into soup. Herring and other types of fish and shellfish were also widely eaten among the country people but the regular consumption of fresh animal meat, on the other hand, was probably restricted to the husband-man and some Highland crofters, and even then can hardly have figured in his daily fare: for the cottar, meat would be a luxury he might scarcely taste except on occasions of festivity. For all classes the normal drink was ale, with aqua-vite or whisky for celebrations and wine the monopoly of the lairds. One additional thing was added to the peasant's needs in the late seventeenth century; from Shetland to Galloway the craving for tobacco leaf to chew, snuff and spit had taken firm hold by 1690. None of this adds up to a picture of luxury or superfluity, and the food would not be enough to satisfy a modern dietician. Nevertheless there was sufficient food to avoid obvious malnutrition, and enough to spare to make weddings and funerals occasions of considerable gluttony. The common people, said Andrew Symson of the population of Galloway 'except in years of great scarcitie, abundantly satisfy themselves'.[24] It seems clear that, according to their limited opportunities, this was true.

'Except in years of great scarcitie'—Symson qualified his statement, and the qualification was important. In this society which relied so heavily on a single grain, failure of the oatcrop even on a local scale could lead to a situation in which the peasants dropped from their normal plateau of rough plenty into a deep trough of deprivation, even of famine. How serious a dearth would be, depended not only on the weather at the critical periods of seed time and harvest but also on the level of population relative to the amount of food to go round. The second half of the sixteenth century was a terrible time: twenty four years out of fifty were marked by abnormally high food prices. Though not every one of these amounted to a famine, there were many seasons in the 1570s and 1590s that saw men dying of starvation. The first half of the seventeenth century was rather better—there were seventeen dearth years before 1660, many of them concentrated in the period between 1630 and 1650. Then, apparently quite suddenly, there was an improvement. Between 1660 and 1695 only four seasons were marked by high prices, and the rest were distinguished by remarkably low grain prices. The record was spoiled between 1695 and 1699 by four successive years of serious scarcity followed by a murrain among the cattle causing perhaps the heaviest famine mortality for a century.[25] 'King William's Ill Years' they were called in folk memory.

There could be various explanations for this pattern of dearth, but perhaps the most plausible is to be sought in the easing of population pressure brought about in particular by the epidemics of the 1640s coupled with improved marketing and greater output from the land in the second half of the seventeenth century. The catastrophe of the 1690s was presumably an accident of the climate (particularly in the early spring) with its effects accentuated, perhaps, by increases of population in the three good decades that preceded it. Corn prices reverted to a low level immediately afterwards, no doubt partly as a result of the high mortality in those years.

The peasants in time of scarcity attempted first to fall back on other goods. The Highlanders tried to live off cheese, and the Lowlanders off herring; excessive consumption of either could lead to serious and unpleasant bowel diseases. Highlanders (again like some African tribes today) mixed blood with their oatmeal by tapping the vein of a living animal when other food was scarce: there were prosecutions in the famine of 1623–4 at the baron court of Glenorchy for 'blooding the laird's ky'.[26] Then there were various weeds, nettles and draff, which served as emergency provisions. Finally in the last extremity the peasants began to eat the seed corn which was intended to provide their food for the following year—this was the explanation for so many double seasons of dearth (1623 and 1624, 1650 and 1651, 1673 and 1674) which marked the tracks of true famine. When everything the peasant had was devoured, he had no choice but to leave his holding and go begging with his family: the army of vagabonds which always existed in Scottish society was enormously swollen in times of bad harvest, and emigration to Ireland and Scandinavia always ran highest in these years.

Of all the famines which afflicted Scottish society at different times that of the 1690s is the best documented, and it was also the one that burnt itself into the memory of the people much as the Great Hunger of the 1840s did in Ireland. A hundred years afterwards, when the ministers of Scotland were compiling the Statistical Account, vivid stories could still be told about it in parishes as far apart as Mull, Aberdeenshire, Inverness-shire and Fife, and it was also very serious in the south west. The minister of Torryburn said that the number of burials in the parish rose from an average of about 21 a year to 114 in 1697 and 81 in 1699.[27] Elsewhere it was said that a third or even a half of the population died or emigrated, and if the overall mortality for the whole country was nothing like as bad as that it was still very serious. Robert Sibbald in 1699 described the suffering he saw all around him:

> For want some die in the wayside, some drop down in the streets, the poor sucking babs are starving for want of milk, which the empty breasts of their mothers cannot furnish them. Everyone may see Death in the face of the poor that abound everywhere; the thinness of their visage, their ghostly looks, their feebleness, their agues and their fluxes threaten them with sudden death if care be not taken of them. And it is not only common wandering beggars that are in this case, but many householders who lived well by their labour and their industry are now by want forced to abandon their dwellings. And they and their little ones must beg, and in their necessity they take what they can get, spoiled victual, yea, some eat these beasts which have died of some disease which may occasion a plague among them.[28]

None of this was rhetoric. There are many other descriptions of the horrors of these years, of the bodies lying at the roadsides with grass in their mouths, and people dragging themselves towards the graveyards to be sure of a Christian burial. At Monquhitter in Aberdeenshire they remembered a century later the story of a respectable wadsetter driven from his home by want and found dead on the shore with raw flesh between his teeth, and another of an exhausted peasant carrying the corpse of his father towards the church giving up when he reached a farmhouse and crying out 'For God's sake bury his body. But if you chuse not to take that trouble you may place it if you please on the dyke of your kail-yard as a guard against the sheep'.[29]

It is fitting to end our chapters on rural life with the memories of these things. It was the cyclical recurrence of apparently inevitable catastrophe which determined so much of the fatalism and hopelessness of peasant existence in the centuries before 1690. It was the deliverance from these conditions that was the most important work of the economic revolution in the centuries afterwards. Those who are tempted to romanticise the Scottish past would do well to meditate on the 1690s.

CHAPTER VII

The Burghs

1. THE ORGANISATION OF THE BURGH

In the rural world of sixteenth- and seventeenth-century Scotland there were many burghs, but comparatively few populous towns. It is true that Edinburgh at the end of the seventeenth century held upwards of 30,000 inhabitants and therefore vied with Bristol, the second city of England: even so it was no more populous than modern Dumfries or Airdrie, and so compact in its tall crowded tenements and narrow wynds as to cover an area no more than one mile long and a quarter of a mile wide. At the time of the civil wars Glasgow, Dundee and Aberdeen competed for the distinction of second place and probably housed up to 10,000 people apiece—each town a little smaller than modern Prestwick or Galashiels. Aberdeen and Dundee sank in size thereafter, but Glasgow grew to 12–14,000 about 1700. Perth was the only other town whose population seems at all likely to have exceeded 5000 in this period, and the remaining burghs varied in size and standing from ancient regional centres like Inverness, Ayr, Stirling, Dumfries and Jedburgh (all of which must have had a thousand or two indwellers) to tiny places like Inveraray in Argyll, Cullen in Banff, Inverbervie in Kincardineshire and North Berwick in East Lothian, where population was perhaps to be numbered in tens or scores rather than in hundreds or thousands.

All these burghs, great and small alike, belonged to a privileged group known as the royal burghs, of which there were between sixty and seventy in the seventeenth century. There were in addition the burghs of barony, of which no fewer than 210 came into existence before 1707: the vast majority of them were extremely small—

typified, perhaps, by Langholm in Dumfriesshire or Kilmaurs in Ayrshire—with less than a hundred indwellers: a handful were relatively populous and rich, and like Kilmarnock in Ayrshire could overtop their nearest rivals among the royal burghs of the district. There is no doubt that between 1560 and 1690 burghs were becoming more numerous—nineteen new royal burghs and seventy-five new burghs of barony were created in the century after the Reformation. They were also becoming more populous—it seems likely that the great royal burghs of Edinburgh, Glasgow, Aberdeen and Dundee all doubled or tripled in size over the same century until the epidemics of the 1640s checked their rate of growth, and among the burghs of barony proliferating in the Forth basin Sir Robert Sibbald was able to pick out Bo'ness as one where within the memory of a man dying in 1660 there had been but a single house where there were now 'two large and populous parishes'.[1] Limited growth of towns was thus one consequence of the general increase in Scottish population combined with the new opportunities for commerce and industry that characterised the late sixteenth and seventeenth centuries.

Burghs, essentially, were privileged communities granted rights by the king to enable them to develop internal and external trade. The royal burghs were mainly distinguished from the burghs of barony by the greater scope of their commercial privileges. Initially only royal burghs could trade overseas, or retail foreign commodities. Around every royal burgh was an area known as the 'liberty', which in the case of the earliest and most important foundations might be as large as a sheriffdom or county. Within this only the burgesses of the royal burgh might carry on any kind of retail trade even in native commodities. Burghs of barony and small royal burghs of later creation were granted enclaves in the original liberties over which they held similar rights in a very much smaller area. All burghs had some rights of self-government—for instance to elect baillies, to make byelaws, to organise themselves into a merchant guild and craft guilds—but only royal burghs had the right of separate constitutional representation, sending representatives to Parliament and commissioners to a Convention of Royal Burghs which legislated on economic and financial matters of common interest.

These privileges gave the royal burghs a sense of belonging to a state within a state, a feeling which found vivid expression in their contemptuous description of the burghs of barony as 'unfree touns' and in calling their rural hinterlands the 'landward pairts'. It was reinforced by their daily contacts with the ports of North Europe that introduced them to cultures unknown to the toiling peasants of farmtouns. Perhaps something of this exclusiveness waned after 1660, when fairs and markets began to proliferate where there were no burghs at all, and after 1672 when the royal burghs lost practically the whole of their monopoly of foreign commerce. Nevertheless such legal innovations suggest a bigger break with the past than in fact took place: external trade in practice stayed almost wholly in the hands of royal burgh merchants, and the character of the larger burghs as cells of cosmopolitan commerce embodied in a comparatively uncommercial and inward-looking society was only just beginning to change.

The institutional structure of these cells, determined as it was by their similar economic functions and by charters copied from one another, remained as alike as that of a group of scattered beehives. In each burgh there was one basic division into burgesses and non-burgesses, and another within the burgess groups between merchants and craftsmen organised into a merchant guild and craft guild respectively. To the burgesses alone belonged the privileges of being members of a burgh: the rest of the inhabitants were mere indwellers, with no more right to elect the magistrates, to trade or to belong to a craft than a country bumpkin from the landward pairts.

A man could become a burgess in several ways: normally he had to pay some money to the corporation, and to prove that his name was upon the apprenticeship books of the town. In the sixteenth and seventeenth centuries most new burgesses were either the sons or the sons-in-law of existing burgesses. Sons could follow their fathers paying a smaller entry fine and serving a shorter apprenticeship than strangers. Those who married the daughter of a burgess (provided in Edinburgh that she was a 'clene virgine swa repute and haldin') gained the same concession: it was a way of making certain that the daughters of merchants and craftsmen were at a premium in the marriage market. Others, not so lucky in birth or love, had to pay a slightly higher entry-fine and to wait for a period after they had finished their apprenticeship—in Glasgow an extra two years. Strangers and 'outland men', however, no matter how well qualified they might already be as merchants or craftsmen in other burghs, had to pay quite heavily for admission. Rates in Edinburgh for unapprenticed strangers' entry rose from £5 Scots in 1550 to £20 in 1564, £67 in 1600 to £170 in 1647, though they fell again to £67 in 1654. Admission to the merchant guild or any of the craft guilds cost a substantial additional sum and might entail a further period of waiting for those who were not kindred to existing burgesses. Moreover town councils exercised a general supervision over the moral and financial qualifications of the entrants—by an act of the Edinburgh council in 1585, for instance, none were to be admitted to the merchant guild 'except they be of honest, discreitt and gud conversatioun' and possessed 'movabill guids worth ane thousand merkis of frie geir': for the 'handie lawborer using his craft' the qualification was five hundred merks.[2] Such controls effectively excluded mere journeymen, servants and common labourers from the highest echelons of town citizenship in the largest burghs, though in the smallest towns this was not necessarily the case.

Among the burgesses, the merchants provided the socially and politically dominant inner group, exalting themselves above the mere craftsmen in a variety of different ways. Thus the Edinburgh merchant guild admitting a skinner in 1588 compelled him not only to renounce his craft but also to promise that his wife and servants would use 'no point of common cookery outwith his house', would not carry 'meat dishes or courses through the town' and would not appear in the streets with their aprons on.[3] Evidently his wife had been doing a little outside catering on the side, and though this might be socially acceptable in a skinner's family it was definitely not acceptable in a merchant's.

The first purpose of the merchant guild was to maintain a monopoly within a monopoly, to preserve from ambitious craftsmen and unfreemen both within and without the burgh the community's right of foreign trade that only a free merchant burgess could enjoy. Much of their time was taken up by prosecuting unprivileged men who had been caught retailing foreign wares or sneaking on board a ship with a bribe for the skipper and a parcel of petty goods to be sold overseas.

The second purpose of the guild was to provide the organisation by which the merchants could dominate the town council: against such merchant monopoly in burgh affairs the craftsmen fought repeatedly and often riotously from the mid-fifteenth century to the early seventeenth. In this they were partially successful, though they never managed to dislodge their enemies from the fountainhead of influence. The Edinburgh constitution of 1584 provided an ostensible compromise that was widely imitated in other towns, yet here the commanding offices of provost, the four baillies, dean of guild and treasurer were all

Haddington area from Roy's Map about 1750. The contrast between the rectangular farms recently enclosed, and the broad, open rigs of the rest of the countryside is very distinct

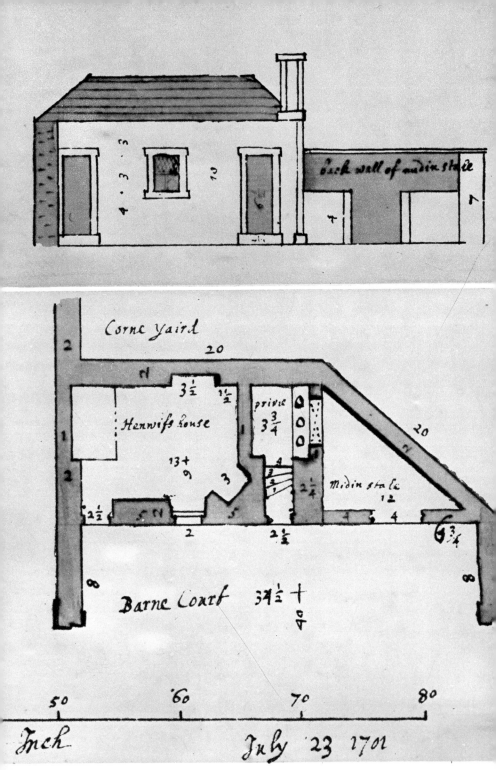

The Henwife's House, probably at Brechin, 1701. The drawing of this tiny cottage, 13 foot by 9, is the earliest for any farmworker's house in Scotland. Note in the house the space for the box bed and the hearth; next to it, the toilet for the farmworkers. The house was planned to be one of two flanking the entrance to the farm reserved for merchants, while of the other eighteen seats on the council ten were always to be reserved for merchants and only eight for craftsmen. In Glasgow, on the other hand, the town constitution of 1605 gave the merchants and craftsmen almost equal representation on the council; but Glasgow was also peculiar in that it readily allowed craftsmen to transfer into the merchant guild instead of placing elaborate obstacles in the way of mobility as for example Aberdeen and Ayr did. This may partly account for her success among Scottish urban trading communities even before the Union of 1707.[4]

When, as happened in many burghs, the old council gained the right of electing the new one an even smaller elite was able to emerge from within the merchant guild and consolidate themselves in positions of power. Thus Dundee in the early seventeenth century was dominated by the Wedderburnes, the Goodmans, the Haliburtons, the Clayhills and half a dozen other families united by bonds of marriage and mutual interest. At Aberdeen at the end of the sixteenth century it was alleged that the main offices had been held by a small clique of interconnected families for eighty years. Inevitably corruption followed in the wake of untrammelled privilege: the town contracts went to the provost's friends, the property of the burgh was let at derisory rents to relatives, and burgess rights were sold for private gain. Long after 1690 the Scottish town councils remained notorious for their graft.

The rule of the town councils was dismally self-interested in other ways. It was, for example, normal for a council to fix the price at which certain commodities could be sold in the markets: characteristically, the commodities which received regular attention were wine and white bread, the staple of rich burgesses—oatmeal, the food of the poor, was not controlled in most towns except in the very worst scarcities. Again, the baillies spent much energy helping the kirk-sessions to enforce ecclesiastical discipline: but their efforts were concentrated on bringing the people to kirk on the sabbath and on punishing beggars and prostitutes. Of the Knoxian injunctions against oppressing the poor by gross usury and other forms of economic exploitation there is scarcely an echo.

Councils were also inept at enforcing their own regulations, even when these were excellent in themselves. As most towns were congested and close built, with a majority of houses either constructed entirely of timber or faced with Norwegian board, the danger of fire was one of the great hazards of communal life. Conscious of this, burghs passed numerous byelaws restricting builders from building too close or using too high a proportion of combustible materials, and ordering such dangerous trades as sugar-boiling, soap-boiling and candle-making to be practised only on more open and isolated sites. Unfortunately since the machinery to compel obedience was often either not used or was unusable frightful conflagrations repeatedly swept the towns. Edinburgh suffered in this way on innumerable occasions, and in 1701 lost all the fine new buildings constructed in the city centre in the previous quarter of a century. Dunfermline in 1624 and Kelso in 1684 were two burghs that seem to have been totally razed by accidental fires in the course of the seventeenth century. These catastrophes were often followed by collections in churches throughout the country in aid of the homeless and bereaved.

In sanitary matters the feebleness of municipal government was still more serious. It was normal for the population of Edinburgh to dispose of their sewage by throwing it out of the window to the cry of 'gardy loo'. A more sophisticated method was to build a closet jutting over one of the wynds, so that the excrement would fall directly on to the heads of pedestrians and not foul the walls. At best, the sewage was piled in heaps at the edge of the road. Councils again passed regulations to discourage people from behaving in this way, but the community was lucky if the burgh employed a man with a horse and cart to shift the middens.

The consequences of neglect were felt with tragic effect when plague struck: it might be typhoid, typhus, bubonic plague or some other killer, but contemporaries usually called it either the plague or the pest. It flourished best where piles of human ordure lay rotting through the town, seeping into the drinking water of the burgh wells and attracting the summer flies to carry infestation far and wide. Deaths came in what Gilbert Skeyne, in a treatise on plague in Scottish towns written in 1568, called the 'stinkand corruptioun and filth quhilkis occupeis the commune streittis and gaittis . . . corruptioun of herbis, moist hevie saver of lint, hemp and ledder steipit in water . . . stinkand closettis or corrupte carioun thairin'.[5] He drew particular attention to the danger from unburied human bodies. As soon as the danger of plague appeared councils imposed very strict quarantine regulations—ships coming from infected towns were obliged to lie offshore, or to land their crews and cargoes on one of the Forth islands such as Inchcolm or Inchkeith, and visitors by land from infected parts were not allowed to trade within the gates. This may well have had some effect in limiting the spread of epidemic disease, but once it got inside the towns there was very little that could be done to control it. The council then attempted to import doctors and 'clensers', commanded children to be kept indoors, punished by banishment any who attempted to conceal a death from plague within their homes, and burnt infected goods: but as a rule the plague ran its course, unchecked, sometimes with frightful mortality.

It is worth pausing at this stage to give an outline of the history of epidemics in Scotland, since they are of considerable importance not only to the towns but also to the demographic history of the whole country. The fourteenth century, it will be recalled, had been marked by the unprecedented outbreak of bubonic plague known as the Black Death which ravaged the whole country in 1349 and subsequent years: between then and 1401 there were three subsequent outbreaks of the same disease, scarcely less general and destructive than the first. These may have driven the population down to levels thirty per cent or more below that of the early fourteenth century. A generation of respite followed, then there were several further outbreaks in the 1430s. In 1450, there was again 'a great pestilential mortality of men through the whole kingdom',[6] with a much more limited outbreak in 1475. A plague of 1499–1500 seems to have been widespread but not comparable to the worst of the earlier ones. The outbreaks of 1514, 1530 and 1539 were probably also quite limited in importance in comparison to those of a hundred years before.

More complex is the general situation in the second half of the sixteenth century. There were certainly some bad outbreaks, such as those of 1545 and 1546, that of 1568 (which was very severe in Edinburgh), that of 1574 (chiefly along the shores of the Firth of Forth) and, especially that of 1584–1588 which, said contemporaries, killed 1400 people in Edinburgh, 1400 in Perth, over 400 in St. Andrews and 300 in Kirkcaldy. In each of these towns this must have amounted to a considerable proportion of the total inhabitants. Nevertheless, the area affected seems to have been restricted entirely to the south-east quarter of the country, and probably to the towns alone. Calderwood, for example, said that the disease 'rageth to the utter vastatioun almost of the principall towns, Edinburgh, Sanct Andrewes, Sanct Johnstoun, etc.',[7] but there is no mention at all of it hitting the villages, and we know that towns outside the south-eastern quarter, such as Ayr and

Aberdeen, had no epidemics at all between 1546 and the end of the century. It seems, therefore, likely that for a majority of Scots the sixteenth century was relatively free of the danger of plague.

Late in the 1590s this pattern appeared to change: a pestilence appeared in Dumfries in 1598, spread to Dundee and to the countryside of Morayshire: soon it was appearing in Edinburgh, in Fife and near Glasgow, and by 1606 had 'spread through manie parts of the countrie and raged in some parts, speciallie in the town of Air, Stirling, Dundie and St. Johnstoun'[8]: in 1608 it returned again to Dundee and to Perth, dying out the following year. For a pestilence thus to rage for a decade, to infect the countryside and to return several times to the same burgh suggests that it may have been of a different kind to the short, sharp epidemics of earlier years, and though less dramatic in any one place at any one time, it may even have killed more people. It was also accompanied in several places by deaths from famine.

From 1609 to 1644, apart from a limited outbreak in 1624, Scotland appears to have been free from great waves of infectious disease. In 1644, however, a pestilence began that lasted for four years and was carried to all parts of the country by the marching and counter-marching armies of the Covenant and Montrose and by refugees fleeing from them. No-one knows for certain what the disease was. The usual statement that it was the bubonic plague appears to be unproven; it is perhaps more likely that it was typhus, an epidemic of which appeared in Denmark a few years later under rather similar circumstances and there killed some twenty per cent of the total population. No-one knows either what the mortality was in Scotland, though Aberdeen apparently suffered 1600 deaths (about one fifth of its population) and Leith 2421 deaths (about half its population). A feature of the plague was the frightful devastation it caused in the countryside, being recalled in some areas hundreds of years after the event. Thus in Kintyre in the nineteenth century 'the old people used to say that the plague came from Ayr to Dunaverty in a white cloud, and spread over most of (the district)'; tradition related that only three chimneys were left smoking in the whole of Southend parish. While this may be an exaggeration, examination of the rentals of Kilcolmkill and Kilblaan parishes in Kintyre in 1651, three years after the epidemic, shows that twenty-nine out of fifty-five holdings were entered as wholely waste and thirteen as partly waste.[10] This, with the famine of the 1690s (also accompanied by an epidemic), was surely one of the two great Killing Times of the seventeenth century.

After this holocaust there seem to be few further outbreaks of serious epidemic disease in seventeenth-century Scotland. (But see also chapter XI below for discussion of smallpox.) The bubonic plague, which struck London again in 1665 and 1666 was kept out of Scotland —perhaps by the strict quarantine regulations enforced by town council and Privy Council alike. Though the middens and the polluted water supplies continued to take their toll of human health and life, it showed not in great sweeping intermittent waves of mortality but in a high urban death rate, year in and year out, particularly among children. But people were used to this, accepted it as one of the hazards of town life, and did not attempt to change it until after the towns became much larger, more dangerous and more crowded in the late eighteenth and nineteenth centuries.

2. THE MERCHANT CLASS

Though a reading of municipal records might lead one to suppose it, the Scottish merchants did not devote their whole lives to prosecuting their social inferiors, peculating the public funds and misgoverning the town. They were above all traders, who spent more days in their counting houses than in the council chambers, and they swam or sank by the success of their trade.

A man entered the mercantile profession as an apprentice, perhaps normally in his early teens. The indentures of Thomas Mitchell, son of an indweller in the unfree burgh of Alloa who became apprenticed to Andrew Russell of the merchant guild of Stirling in 1668 may serve as an example of what this involved. Thomas was to serve his master for five years, adding two days to that period for every day he should be away without permission and another two years if he should ever be foolish enough ('which God forbid') to commit the 'filthie sins of fornication or adulterie'. In return his master provided him with bed and board, undertook to instruct him in all the arts of commerce 'as weel without as within the country', to send him overseas with a cargo of goods for sale on at least three occasions, and to put him in a Dutch school to learn Dutch and arithmetic for as long as Russell thought expedient. As payment for Thomas's training, his father undertook to deliver 'one hundreth and fiftie chalders good and sufficient sea coale's of the heuch of Alloway' whenever the merchant should ask for it.[11] With the exception of the clause about learning Dutch, this agreement was probably fairly typical—a boy at a comparatively early age got not only a thorough mercantile education but also the opportunity to taste the hazards and excitement of travel to those ports across the North Sea where so much of his business in later life would be done.

Having completed his training, the apprentice was qualified both to become a burgess and to enter the guild: this was easy enough if he was himself the son of a merchant, as a great many candidates were. Otherwise he would be obliged either to wait a further period or to pay a heavy entry fine or to marry the daughter of a merchant, preferably that of his own master. Everyone preferred the last course: it gave the apprentice cheap entry, a little capital by way of dowry and the seal of complete respectability; it provided the merchant with easy disposal of a daughter and some guarantee that he would be cared for in his old age by a well set-up mercantile family. The possession of a wife was indeed indispensable to a merchant, for on her devolved the management of the business when the husband was away trading: many widows, too, proved quite capable of carrying on their late husbands' business until such time as they were snapped up by new husbands, who also could enter the guild by marrying them. Finally, if all these methods failed it was always open to the newly fledged apprentice to emigrate. In the sixteenth and seventeenth centuries North Europe, and the Baltic countries in particular, were full of young Scottish merchants tired of poverty or impatient of restriction at home who had gone to seek their fortunes abroad. Some lost virtually all contact with Scotland and became naturalised Swedes or Germans, sometimes very poor peddling 'skottars', occasionally very rich burgesses of Stockholm, Warsaw or Ratisbon involved in high finance and royal purveyance. Others stayed in the ports which Scottish merchants frequented most often, like Rotterdam, Veere, Bordeaux, Elsinore, London and Danzig, providing their fellow countrymen with factorial assistance when they wished to trade with people of an unfamiliar tongue or customs. Some eventually came home, like Andrew Russell, who returned to live in Scotland after twenty-five years as Scottish factor in Rotterdam: they brought with them both their material fortunes and their knowledge of European societies to enrich the Scottish burgh.

The commercial horizons of the royal burgh merchants, though not yet as wide as those of their colleagues in England or Holland, embraced an area impressively large in comparison to that of the peasants of their hinterlands. Edinburgh (using the dependent port of Leith) Dundee and Aberdeen sent their ships every year along the trade routes from Trondheim in Northern Norway and Danzig in the inner Baltic, to Rotterdam and Veere, to Normandy and La Rochelle and Bordeaux in Biscay and sometimes as far as Spain: ships even from quite small towns like Crail or Pittenweem in Fife, Dunbar in East Lothian and Montrose in Angus appeared with the greatest regularity in the delta of the Scheldt, in the Norwegian fjords or the Danish Sound. Some of the last West European ships to come home through the Sound before it was closed for the winter were often herring boats from Crail returning with Swedish iron after selling their catch at Stockholm or Danzig. On the West coast the merchant guilds of Glasgow, Ayr and Dumfries thought primarily in terms of trading to Ireland and to France, though in the later seventeenth century they developed a regular direct connection with the West Indies and the English plantations on the mainland of North America, and also to the Canary Islands: they also began to send boats through the uncharted waters of the Minch to reach Norway and the Baltic, and to use the road to Bo'ness as a lifeline for trade through that unfree burgh to the Netherlands. Though few individual merchants specialised on any route, there were many points of particular concentration that were frequently revisited. Veere in the Dutch province of Zealand, where Scottish merchants since the middle ages had had special privileges to set up a 'staple' for landing their goods under the general supervision of a Conservator appointed by the Convention of Royal Burghs, was obviously one, though increasingly in the seventeenth century it was losing ground to Rotterdam: Bordeaux where the Scots again were for many years given special privileges above other foreigners in the wine trade was another: Stockholm (for Swedish iron after 1590) and London were two more. Generally speaking, however, apart from North America and Eastern Sweden, the places the Scots were familiar with as traders in 1690 were not very different from those they had already known in 1290: it was one of the disappointing things about the merchants in the period after the Reformation that, whether on account of their relative poverty or because of some failure of enterprise in the class, they ignored almost completely the implications of the great voyages of discovery that drew English and Dutch merchants to new horizons from the Arctic to the East Indies. For the seventeenth-century Scots a voyage even as far as Russia or Italy was a rare adventure, and when in 1698 a Dundee boat arrived back from Spitzbergen the town official who entered its particulars in the burgh shipping lists was so ignorant of commercial geography that he added the comment that Spitzbergen was apparently somewhere in the Shetland Islands.[12]

Just as few merchants were specialists in particular trade routes, so still fewer were specialists in particular commodities: the term 'corn merchant', 'wine merchant' or 'tobacco merchant' has no meaning at this period. The exports of the average merchant comprised anything t at he could find in Scotland suitable for a foreign market—an Edinburgh man, for instance, might in one year buy wool from the Quaker dealers of Kelso for shipment for Sweden, linen from Perth fair for the London market, woollen goods from Aberdeenshire for France, Forth herring for the Polish Catholics of the hinterland of Danzig, corn from the Moray Firth for Norway, and coal from Alloa or Port Seton for Rotterdam. In return he would import Swedish iron, Norwegian wood, Polish flax or rye, the delicious clarets of Bordeaux, and a selection of the manufactured goods and colonial luxuries offered by the sophisticated economies of Holland and London—wares that ranged in variety from church bells to needles, from sugar candy and prunes to apothecaries' drugs and weavers' dyestuffs. Some of these he sold in the markets of his own burgh: other items were imported to fill some direct order of a client: still others were redistributed from the large burghs on the coast to the smaller ones or to those that lay far inland. Thus William Lambe in 1696 sent from Edinburgh a parcel of Dutch goods (brass pans, griddle irons, raisins and paper) by packhorse to Jedburgh, and distributed a cargo of Baltic hemp to merchants as far apart as Orkney, Dunfermline, Galashiels and Dumfries.[13] It was characteristic of the latter half of our period that the activities of merchants in the great burghs, especially Edinburgh and Glasgow, were growing at the expense of those in small or middling ones, who were becoming more and more content to receive their foreign imports indirectly from the Forth and Clyde.

Trade, however, was notoriously a risky business and few cared to carry the risk alone. Almost everything the merchant did was done in association with his equals. If he owned a ship he did so in shares with other merchants—better by far to have one eighth of eight boats than sole ownership of one boat that might founder in the storm. If a merchant bought goods at home, chartered another man's vessel or imported foreign wares the arrangements were much the same—he ventured a half or a quarter with his friends. Such arrangements did not normally result in formal or permanent alliances, for merchant partnerships generally subsisted only as long as the venture lasted. True, a man might trade repeatedly with his relations and friends, but he was always free to break the link or to trade with others, and the rise of a consolidated merchant firm involved in a competitive war with its rivals lay far off in the future.

Indeed, thrusting competition was looked at askance by the merchant guild, which still punished members for such medieval crimes as forestalling, or buying up goods before they had been exposed to common view in an authorised market, and still occasionally functioned as a corporate trading body itself, freighting a ship for all its members or buying a cargo brought to the town by a foreign trader. Among the merchants the webs of family relationships, the sense of being the common guardians of valuable privilege and the intimacy of social contact in a small ruling elite were additional forces working against the individualist notion that ruthless material ambition had its own virtues. In this respect there is something saddening and instructive in the story of Sir William Dick, provost of Edinburgh and incomparably the richest merchant Scotland ever saw before the age of the Glasgow tobacco lords, who was quixotic enough to lend the whole of his immense fortune of over half a million pounds Scots to the Covenanting army in 1639 and as a consequence died in deep poverty. Sir Walter Scott in a vivid passage recounts the folk memory of the Edinburgh citizens who watched with wonder as the sacks of silver dollars were emptied into carts from his counting house to pay the troops encamped at Duns. His piety won Puritan approval even as it cost him every penny he had; in the words of a contemporary rhymester:

> 'Such traffic sure non can too highly prize,
> When gain itself is made a sacrifice'.[14]

Few merchants could ever have boasted a tithe of the fortune of Sir William Dick; like George Heriot, the goldsmith, who preceded him as the richest burgess of Edinburgh, he appears to have made some at least of his money by handling financial affairs for the crown; Dick farmed the Scottish customs. It was more usual to be involved only in trade and industry, like Patrick Wood who died in 1638. On paper he was a rich man too: he 'had hemp in his rope works worth £30,000; tackle etc. worth £21,000; "made salt" at Cockenzie, Prestonpans, Kirkcaldy, Wemyss, Bo'ness, Tulliallan and Burntisland valued at £14,000; coal (£3,864), herring, butter, wool cards, a coach, and potash; in venture to Bordeaux, £8,000; to Spain, £1,700; to the Canaries, £783; to Königsberg and Danzig, £10,000; and shares in the *William*, the *Gift of God*, the *Issobell*, and the *Dolphing*. The total value was just over £100,000 . . . creditors were ready to account for nearly all . . .'[15]

The class as a whole was certainly better off in material comforts than anyone else in Scotland except the richest of the nobility. As much as anything else, it was their commercial contact with the European world which gave them the taste and opportunity to live well. It was no problem to a merchant to have red wine and prunes on his table when his boat lay in harbour with a couple of thousand pints of claret waiting to be unloaded: his wife could dress in English cloth and order Dutch hangings for the bed simply by taking her pick of her husband's imports. It cost him something, but everything he obtained was at wholesale prices. The journeys the merchant made to France, London, Holland and the Baltic all provided the chance and the motive for picking up a picture or a piece of silver-plate, perhaps accumulating a small library of pious books or investing in a clock or a mirror. Even merchants in small provincial towns lived in a manner no peasant and few lairds could have afforded. Thus when John Denune died in the little town of Tain in Easter Ross in 1641 he left household plenishings worth £322 Scots: these included beds, tables, cupboards, chests, forms, stools, five chairs, six feather beds and five pairs of sheets and blankets, bolsters, cushions, curtains, four dozen serviettes, fourteen pewter plates and trenchers, a brass basin, four branched candlesticks and an 'aquavitae cellar with five glasses'.[16]

Despite this edge of comfort to their lives, the merchant class was nothing like as ostentatious or as extravagant as the landowners. Their houses, generally speaking, were small: a three or four roomed dwelling in one of the Edinburgh tenements around the Cowgate or the West Bow, with the other floors occupied by craftsmen or lawyers and the attics by common labourers was far more characteristic than the great house (still standing) which the merchant Andrew Lambe built for himself at Leith or the house (now demolished) that Sir William Bruce built for Provost Walter Gibson in Glasgow. The services of one or two maids were essential, but possession of a great household of servants was superfluous. Decent hospitality must be provided for the fellow members of the guild, but there was no attempt to make a fetish of consumption like the hunting earls. There was, indeed, no motive for extravagance, since there was no possibility of impressing a wide area of the countryside and the Calvinist teaching which took root so quickly among the merchant guilds deplored excessive show, long before it turned in the mid-seventeenth century to extreme Puritanism. Besides, who would know better than a merchant that ostentation and debt was the fast road to ruin?

This relative thriftiness meant that Scottish merchants more than any other class in the community had liquid assets—money to leave to charity by endowing an almshouse or a school for the sons and daughters of poor merchants, money to invest in a new industry, such as the establishment in the seventeenth century of a paper work or a sugar manufactory, money to set out on loan at interest. This money gave them the ability to move very readily into the landed classes if they were successful and desired the social power and prestige that came from being a laird. Some reached land by purchase or foreclosure on a mortgage; others reached it through the marriage bed, for no merchant was likely to scorn a girl with an estate in the offing. Likewise few lairds would scorn a merchant's daughter with a fat purse in her dowry. Consequently round the main burghs there was a ring of estates whose owners were both lairds and merchants, becoming in some generations more prominent as landowners, in other generations more prominent as lairds, laird's sons becoming pure merchants, merchant's sons becoming pure lairds, and their daughters intermarrying with each other's sons so freely that the distinction between the two groups becomes quite blurred. Though this was particularly marked round Glasgow there is no reason to believe that it was not generally true round Edinburgh, Dundee and Aberdeen as well.

All in all, considering their material assets, their relatively high propensity to save, their ability to move upwards in society, their ability (at least in Glasgow) to refresh their ranks from those below them in society, and their awareness of the great European horizons beyond their own front doorstep, the merchants of Scotland appear in many ways as potentially the most dynamic class in the community even if they were not as dynamic as those of England or Holland. Both society and the economy would have been much more resistant to change in the seventeenth and in the eighteenth centuries if it had not been for the bourgeois leavening which such men provided.

3. CRAFTSMEN AND UNFREEMEN

The town craftsmen, who formed the second and socially inferior half of the burgess class, had existed from the earliest days of the Scottish burgh. They only began to organise themselves in formal guilds, however, after 1450. Throughout the sixteenth century their organisations were still proliferating in all the main towns. By 1600 Edinburgh and Glasgow both had fourteen 'incorporated trades' each under an elected deacon, Dundee had nine, Perth eight, Stirling and Aberdeen seven, though there were still some relatively small and unimportant places like Renfrew which had only one and others like Brechin in which the craftsmen do not appear to have attempted to organise at all until the seventeenth century.

The purpose of the craft guild, like that of the merchant guild, was primarily to uphold the rights of a small group of privileged citizens from the dangerous pretensions of unfreemen. Characteristically, when the blacksmiths, goldsmiths, lorimers, saddlers, bucklemakers, armourers and other metal workers of Glasgow petitioned in 1536 for permission to set up an 'Incorporation of Hammermen' they grounded their application on the 'great hurt and damage' suffered by other honest burgesses from the work of unqualified men, and made their first rule that no-one should be allowed to set up a metalware booth in the town unless he was an admitted member of the craft 'examined and found qualified to work by three of the best masters'. Subsequently they spent much of their time searching out 'dishonest work', preventing hammermen from neighbouring Gorbals from flooding their market and stopping merchants from employing unfree smiths on private business.[17]

Such activity could be dressed up as being in the interests of consumers and as ensuring high quality in the goods exposed for sale.

In practice it worked mainly in favour of the producers, who were thereby enabled to avoid any competition they could not meet. At first sight it is a damning reflection on the inefficiency of the guilds to perform the services for which they were ostensibly created that in the hey-day of their power Scottish manufactures were known through half Europe for their bad quality and that merchants found a ready market for quite humble foreign consumer goods like iron cooking pots and horse bits which they were allowed to import and sell in competition with the burgh crafts. Yet guild-work was not in itself necessarily bad work, as the records of several medieval crafts abroad show, and indeed as the records of Scottish silver work shows (see page 198 below). Perhaps the fault lay as much in the nature of the Scottish home market as in the bad training of the guilds: the only affluent classes in Scotland, the merchants and the nobility, were supplied with what they wanted in the way of high quality goods from overseas, leaving the Scottish craftsmen to serve a community of low earning power for whom the first requisite in any piece of goods was that it should be cheap. Before the days of factory organisation and mass-production cheap meant bad: there was practically no way of cutting costs in craft industry except by skimping on time and materials.

On the other hand it must also be admitted that the Scottish craftsman seems to have been very reluctant to learn from abroad. When, for example, Parliament in 1661 passed an act to encourage 'skilful artizans' to come from abroad to serve as instructors in textile manufacture, and proposed to give them special privileges to persuade them to settle, the burghs complained bitterly. When foreign workmen did come—for instance to the sugar manufactories in Glasgow—the local guilds did what they could to make life difficult for them by frivolous prosecutions in the burgh court.

The guilds were as small in membership as they were restrictive in policy. In 1604 the fourteen crafts in Glasgow could together muster no more than 361 members (compared to 213 in the merchant guild) to serve a population of 7–8000. The largest guild was the tailors, with sixty-five members, followed by the maltsters and cordiners (or shoe-makers) with fifty-five and fifty respectively: the weavers, the hammer-men, the bakers, the coopers, the skinners and the wrights had between twenty and thirty members each, the fleshers had seventeen, the masons eleven, the bonnet makers seven, the dyers five and the surgeons only two. The list, both in numbers and composition was typical of most large burghs and was itself a comment on the simple nature of guild activities, able to serve only 'the staple day to day requirements of the poorer classes, their bread, clothing, footwear and houses'.[18] Even when enough workers in a luxury trade existed to justify the existence of a separate craft, as among the goldsmiths of Edinburgh, the subsequent organisation seems generally to have been among the smallest in the town.

Normally entry to a craft guild, as to the merchant guild, was through apprenticeship. The Glasgow hammermen again provide an example of what was involved. In this guild the apprentice was usually expected to serve for seven years in return for food and clothing, followed by two more when he received his food alone together with a small wage. At the end of this time he made his 'essay', or sample of workmanship (it might be a highlander's sword-hilt for an armourer or a horse-shoe and eight nails for a black-smith) which had to be tested and approved by three 'essay masters'. Upon payment of burgesses fees he could then become a freeman, with permission to work as an independent master—but to attain the full dignity of 'guild brother' qualified to vote and stand for the deacons office he had to work for another four years, of which the first two must be without assistance from apprentice or servant: then he could pay further fees and enter the full body of the guild. This thirteen-year period of training and probation, combined with the provision that no hammerman could have more than one apprentice at a time, limited recruitment to the guild more effectively than high entry fees. As with merchants, fees were in fact lower for the sons and sons-in-law of guild brothers than for outland men.[19]

The Edinburgh apprentice registers, which have been printed[20], give an indication of the degree to which a trade recruited from the countryside around the burgh (they probably do not, however, give a full record of all the craftsmen who followed their own fathers within the city). Many of the recruits were the sons of 'fermorers', tenants, in the Lothians—especially from the nearby parishes like Cramond, Costorphine, Gilmerton and Pilton, but also from places slightly further away like Humbie and Alloa. Many came from small burghs within a radius of thirty or forty miles, from places like Dalkeith and Mussel-burgh in the immediate vicinity, from the towns of the south Fife coast like Crail, Culross, Anstruther and Kinghorn, or from places in the nearer Borders, like Biggar and Innerleithen. A few came from slightly larger burghs within this area, a slater from St. Andrews, a pewterer from Dunfermline, or an indweller from Linlithgow and Haddington. On the other hand the pull of the capital weakened rapidly beyond that radius—it is possible to find records of men coming from Glasgow, Kirkwall, Aberdeen, Perth, Elgin, Dumfries and Sanquhar, but they have to be sought out: their own local large burgh obviously had a pull that was not over-ruled by Edinburgh's. Most craftsmen apprentices in the Edinburgh area also came from a distinctly lower social origin than the merchant apprentices. The latter were often the sons of lairds or of merchants in other burghs. The former were almost never the sons of lairds and were not often the sons of merchants, except those in the smallest burghs: they were the children of peasants, of other craftsmen, of sailors, even of 'workmen'.

Once having reached the dignity of guild brother, it was, however, possible for a craftsman to become a person of a certain stature in the community—the deacon of his guild, perhaps a town councillor, and in some instances especially in those inland burghs where merchants were weakly organised even a town magistrate. Haddington thus elected a craftsman-provost in 1575 and at Banff in 1600 the officials were said to be all poor men, fishers and craftsmen—horrible irregularities that appalled the Convention of Royal Burghs. The craftsmen also improved their economic position in the sixteenth century by asserting their right to sell what they made direct to the customer instead of through the merchant guild, and also to traffic in some inland wares. They had a bitter fight to get these privileges, and the ensuing settlement varied in different towns. In Aberdeen it was agreed from 1587 that craftsmen could buy and sell butter, sheep and undyed cloth, but not imported wares or 'staple goods' such as fish, hides, skins or wool. It was perhaps an overfine distinction that let a man trade in sheep and cloth and prevented him from trading in skins and wool.

Despite these little gains few craftsmen, apart from the Edinburgh goldsmiths and certain apothecaries, ever died rich, or could afford in their lives the standard of comfort the merchants had come to enjoy. Few, for example, possessed in Edinburgh at the end of the period more than one maid-servant, though the merchants often had two or three. It also was very rare to find a skinner or a tailor whose craftsmanship ever proved so profitable that he could buy himself a small estate, put money out at loan to the lairds or invest in a new manufactory in the burgh. To many the main benefit of the guild must have been not the opportunity it gave for gain but the defence it gave against the horrors of pauperism: every craft collected regularly for the families of poor distressed members, many ran an almshouse like the trades hospital in Glasgow and all hired out a mortcloth under which to give the deceased member a respectable burial. To be a member of a craft guild was to belong to an essentially unadventurous fraternity dedicated to keep both competition and destitution from the door: you could not rise very high as a hammerman or a cordiner, but neither could you fall too low.

Merchants and craftsmen were alone the burgesses. All other inhabitants were 'unfreemen', with no say in how the town was to be governed and no privileges accruing to themselves from living in it. Sometimes unfreemen included substantial numbers of affluent householders such as the chamberlains who administered the town houses of the nobility, and the advocates, writers and notaries of the legal profession. Many of these, however, were honoured by the town by being made burgesses *gratis*, a status which conferred citizenship upon them but usually no substantial rights to assist in the town council or carry on a trade. Lawyers with business at the Court of Session, for instance, in the Edinburgh poll tax returns of 1694 outnumbered the merchants in the central parish of the town by ninety-seven families to seventy-seven. Respectable widows, too, come into this group. They often kept lodging houses. Twenty per cent of the householders in the central area of Edinburgh in 1694 were women; the great majority of these must have been widows, though it does not follow that the majority were also respectable.

Generally speaking, though, the term unfreeman is synonymous with the unprivileged poor, a class which comprised the bulk of the population of any large town but of whom, because they had no rights and left no records, we know relatively little. Some were journeymen who worked for wages for the masters of the craft guilds, and who might (if they had previously served an apprenticeship) benefit at least from the charity of the guild. We do not know how many journeymen had prospects of becoming, ultimately, fully fledged craftsmen in their own right: many obviously ended their days as poor employees, like George Brewer, weaver, servant to Hugh Crystal, weaver in the Canongate, who in 1694 described himself as 'a poor weak infirm man not able to work by reason of a rupture' and James Service, a married journeyman wright, who said 'we have nothing ataill and skarchlie can get breid

The interior of a Highlander's house on Islay 1772. The man was a weaver, and can be seen at his loom on the left-hand side

Fishermen and their wives near Inverness, c.1725. "The women tuck up their garments to an indecent height and wade to the vessels . . . they take the fishermen upon their backs and bring them on shore in the same manner"

Highland Chief, old style. Colen Campbell, sixth laird of Glenorchy: "He was ane great justiciar all his tyme, throch the quhilk he sustenit thee diedlie feid of the Clangregour ane lang space . . . he beheiddit the laird of McGregour himselff". – Black Book of Taymouth

Highland Chief, new style. Sir James Grant of Grant and the Strathspey fencibles: "On the declaration of war in 1793 Sir James was among the first . . . to step forward in the service of the country with a regiment of Fencibles raised almost exclusively among his own tenantry"

Highland women at work. The couple on the left are grinding at a quern, others are "waulking" (fulling) cloth with their feet. They are singing as they work

Harvesting in Orkney 1766. The farmer has come out to see the reapers at work

for our bairns'. Others in the unfreeman class were servants of burgesses, working either in their homes or in the businesses. A great many of these were maids—in central Edinburgh in 1694, for instance, there were 492 maidservants distributed among 548 households, compared with 115 men servants and 144 apprentices: it was 'a mark of a certain social position' to employ a maid, and some noble or legal households had as many as seven or eight working for them.[22]

The rest of the unfreemen were usually little better than casual unskilled labourers, very frequently self employed. There were market porters of all kinds, sometimes a few hawkers (allowed to sell trifles below the dignity of the burgesses) drovers, carters and coalmen—whom the Dundee council attempted to organise under a 'deacon' to have the means of controlling their charges. By the late seventeenth century there were also sedan-chairmen who carried the middle-classes in safety through the slippery streets of the capital. On the coast there were fishermen and seamen: the skippers were often burgesses in small towns like Queensferry and Montrose; and even Glasgow had fisher burgesses in the early seventeenth century. There was a large class of petty ale-sellers (often the poorest widows who had no other way of living), water carriers and milk vendors, who kept cows in the city. Lastly there were the prostitutes, vagabonds and thieves—Edinburgh and its suburban burghs of barony Leith and the Canongate were a notorious haven for criminals, able to hide from all but the bravest and nosiest of kirk-session officers in the warren of tall tenements and wynds.

For all such people, respectable and reprobate alike, life was lived close to the bone of destitution. It was their elderly and crippled who sat on the forestairs, displayed their sores and begged for alms. It was their children who were first found dying in the vennels when the harvest failed and merchants were selling Polish or Irish grain at enhanced prices in the mealmarket. Thus in 1600: 'A scheaff of oat straw was sold for fourtie shillings in Edinburgh. There was also a great death of little childrein: six or seven buried in one day'.[23]

Sometimes it behoved a burgess to have stout shutters. From the sixteenth century onwards Scotland was experienced in the phenomenon of an urban mob, of uncertain and anonymous composition but clearly including many both of the craftsmen and of the poor, whom religious leaders and politicians could whip into a frenzy—as Knox did in Perth at the Reformation and others did in Edinburgh and Glasgow on the eve of the Union of Parliaments. The mob could, however, arise spontaneously for ends of its own. Chambers recounts such an occasion in 1682:

> A riot took place in the streets of Edinburgh in consequence of an attempt to carry away, as soldiers to serve the Prince of Orange, some young men who had been imprisoned for a trivial offence. As the lads were marched down the street under a guard to be put on board a ship in Leith Road, some women called out to them: 'Pressed or not pressed?' They answered 'Pressed' and so caused an excitement in the multitude. A woman who sat on the street selling pottery threw a few sherds at the guard, and some other people, finding a supply of missiles at a house that was building followed her example.

The soldiers turned and fired on the mob, killing nine. 'Three of the most active individuals in this mob were seized and tried, but the assize would not find them guilty. The magistrates were severely blamed for their negligence and cowardice'.[24]

The urban proletariat was not large when set against the total population of Scotland, but sometimes, especially in Edinburgh, its total defencelessness against a life cycle of poverty and its occasional outbursts of violent communal protest make it seem as precocious a class as the douce merchants who sat in the council chamber.

4. PEASANT BURGESSES AND COLLIERS

To move from consideration of these large burghs with several thousand indwellers to the small country communities with a few hundred or less is to move more than half way back to the world of lairds and peasants we were considering in the previous chapters. It is true that even the smallest rural burghs, whether formally royal burghs or burghs of barony, still possessed constitutions that were normally very close copies of the big towns, and when they chose to use them to the full they had many of the characters of the latter. Thus the burgh of barony of Hawick in the borders, never a large place, had a long list of crafts (cordiners, fleshers, litsters, lorimers, maltmen, masons, skinners, smiths, tailors, waulkers, websters and wrights) and a council that worried itself over the quality of craftsmen's work and the regulation of markets as well as about such purely agricultural business as the pasturing of horses and the trespass of hens.[25]

Nevertheless, there were generally two aspects of small burgh life that marked it as being less than fully urban. The first was the dominating presence of the lord. Admittedly, even big burghs often found it hard to keep their government from the machinations of powerful men but even when, as sometimes happened, a noble or his chamberlain had himself elected provost he could hardly hope to exercise the same kind of minute social control as he did in his own estates. In the small rural burghs, however, the lord could, if he chose, dominate it completely. A great many of the burghs of barony actually owed their existence to a landowner who deliberately planned a community and obtained for it market rights so that he could profit from tolls and augmented rents: the Maxwells created Langholm by feuing twelve lots to members of their surname in 1621, and the Stewarts made Newton Stewart in a similar way in 1677. Once they had planned a burgh they were unlikely to permit it such freedom that the burgesses could elect their provost, baillies and council without some kind of direction from above. The lot of many of the small royal burghs was not very different: the freemen of Inveraray could only elect a magistrate who had been formally approved by the Duke of Argyll, and at Cromarty the lord was able to overawe the town so thoroughly that it actually withdrew from the Convention of Royal Burghs and submitted to the humiliation of accepting a new charter as burgh of barony.

The second distinction of the small burgh was its close association with agriculture. In the big town, there might be some citizens who farmed and many who went as casual labourers to the open fields at hay-time and harvest: in the small town, the burgesses themselves were peasants first and only petty merchants or craftsmen as subsidiary occupations. Kilmaurs in Ayrshire is an excellent example: here burgess rights were obtained by feuing a seven-acre holding from the Earl of Glencairn who had created a burgh by laying out forty contiguous lots and obtaining a charter; although the freemen had also all the machinery for urban government, right of market and the exclusive monopoly of trade and carrying on crafts within the barony their living rested upon growing kale plants for sale in the country round. At Newton-on-Ayr in the same county the community included seamen, fishermen and weavers: nevertheless the laws of the burgh were primarily concerned with organising farming, allotting 200 acres of grass and 150 acres of arable among forty-eight freemen, regulating the cutting of turf and the gathering of wrack, and employing a town herd who at the sound of a horn took the burgesses' cows to pasture in the morning and returned them to shelter at night. The picture in burghs like this, comments Professor Pryde, 'is one of tight little communities closely tied to the soil and primarily concerned with land use'.[26] It was a social environment more likely to perpetuate peasant virtues than to breed an affluent or enterprising merchant class.

One group of small burghs was of a quite different character— the coal-and-salt towns that had sprung up on the Firth of Forth wherever landowners began to exploit the coal measures, to build salt pans and to construct little harbours to facilitate export. Alloa and Bo'ness at the head of the Forth, Prestonpans and Cockenzie in East Lothian, Wemyss and Methil in Fife were all of this type: so was Culross, the only royal burgh among them and today the best pre-served example of a sixteenth century industrial town in Britain. These communities were not, it is true, quite divorced from the land or without merchants and craftsmen; Culross still retains a handful of comfortable traders' homes. Its local incorporation of smiths had a national reputation for the manufacture of griddle irons. But the characteristic inhabitants of all of them were the workmen in the coal mines and salt pans: and they, in the course of our period, suffered a degradation without parallel in the history of labour in Scotland.

The first significant step on the downward path was an act of the Scottish Parliament of 1606 which forbade anyone to employ a collier, coal-bearer or salter unless he could produce a testimonial releasing him from employment to his previous master: if workers allowed themselves to be hired without a certificate they could be reclaimed within a year and a day and brutally punished as thieves. This act was extended to cover surface workers at the mines by another of 1641, and both were ratified in 1660. Subsequent legal decisions interpreted the statutes to mean that a man accepting employment in a colliery or saltpans thereby made himself a serf for life: he became a piece of mining equipment that could be bought, sold and inherited by his master, with the sole proviso that he might not be separated from the works at which he started his bondage.

Serfdom, once established, was extended in two directions. A second clause of the act of 1606, also ratified subsequently, authorised masters to arrest vagabonds and force them to work in the mines or pans. Certainly some miserable people were captured and condemned to a lifetime's serfdom in the pits, though they were probably not very numerous. As late as 1701 four men were condemned by the courts to servitude in the mines. One was given away in an iron collar bearing the inscription: 'Alexander Steuart found guilty of death for theft at Perth, the 5th of December 1701, and gifted by the justiciars as a perpetual servant to Sir John Areskine of Alva'.[27] Secondly, the custom of 'arling' was used to bind the children of colliers to follow their parents in the mines: the 'arles' consisted of a present given to the collier and his wife at the time of their baby's christening in return for a promise on the child's behalf that he would be brought up a miner. The promise was not legally binding, and the child might in theory have left the mine within a year and a day of his majority. In practice it made serfdom hereditary, for no miner would suppose that a vow taken in the face of the kirk was legally fraudulent.

The institution of serfdom probably did not become common in the mines until the second half of the century, and perhaps never became universal: there are certainly indications as late as the 1640s that a large number of miners still moved freely from mine to mine on yearly contracts. Nevertheless, as it spread it resulted in incredible degradation for the miner's whole family, who were all regarded as the property of master—'in inventories their value was included, just as was the value of the gin horses or the stock of punch wood at the pit-head'.[28] The man himself, the 'hewer', was helped underground by his wife, acting as 'bearer' and carrying the baskets of coal up the steep turnpike stair of the mine to the pit-head. Their children, boys and girls, entered the mine at the age of six or seven, and worked either for their own parents or as 'fremd' bearers for childless hewers—thus at Bo'ness in 1681 thirteen hewers were assisted by twenty-six house-bearers, of which five were males, and eleven fremd bearers, of whom only one was a male. So low was the social reputation of the serfs that in parts of Fife the rest of the population would not allow them to be buried beside the free in consecrated ground.

The successful attempt to impose serfdom on the colliers and salters does not stand altogether in isolation. The lead-miners (virtually only one community, at Leadhills in Lanarkshire) were enserfed in exactly the same way between 1607 and 1698. Then their employer released them from bondage, possibly because it was difficult to persuade the

English immigrants whose skill was indispensable to the work to accept the terms. Some north-eastern lairds were claiming their fishermen as serfs in the late seventeenth century: the attempt to degrade them was evaded when the men sailed off and disappeared into the blue. Then Parliament, obsessed by the need to 'put the poor on work', passed a whole series of statutes between 1579 and 1672 allowing employers to seize beggars, orphans and poor children and to put them to work either in private concerns or in municipal 'manufactories' for a term of years—often until they were eighteen for girls and twenty-four for boys, but sometimes for a lifetime. The tone of the acts was typified by that of 1605 allowing a master to seize 'all maisterful and strong beggars' that he 'may set his burning iron upon them and retain them as slaves and if any of them thereafter escape the owner may have repetition of them as of other goods'. In fact only a handful of unhappy people seem to have suffered under any of this legislation, partly because it was so severe that magistrates must have hesitated to use it, and partly because it would have been very difficult to employ slave labour in towns where it was easy for a man to escape and vanish into the wynds.

The colliers and salters, in fact, suffered mainly because their occupation was the only one where it was practicable to impose serfdom with a good chance of success. Their communities were small, set in the countryside under the eagle eye of the nobleman's grieves and their work was largely subterranean—all factors that made escape difficult. Their trade (at this stage in its development) was unskilled and therefore possible to organise along serf lines. The coalowners, moreover, included many recently ennobled families who had found a place on Privy Council from which they could promulgate legislation in their own interest while dressing it up as legislation for the public good of furthering the useful employment of the poor and the expansion of the Scottish economy.

On the other hand, it does not follow that just because the opportunities existed to impose serfdom they would be seized. In England, after all, colliers retained their liberty even though the industry was situated in similar places and otherwise organised on similar lines. Perhaps the best explanation of the difference between the two countries is to be sought in their medieval experience. In England, mining of all kinds had existed for centuries as an occupation that peasants carried on in the lands they leased, very often establishing customary rights as 'free miners' digging and selling independently of the lord: this meant that when the great expansion came after 1540 there were large numbers of families familiar with the work and willing to offer themselves for a job even in landlord-run mines. In Scotland, though mining had been carried on since the twelfth century on monastic land, it had always been on a much smaller scale: it also seems to have been organised directly by the landowners and not delegated to the peasants, who under Scottish law would in any case have been unable to establish a customary right to the workings. Consequently when the expansion of the Scottish industry began after about 1580 it grew from a much smaller base than the English but at an equally rapid rate, and found itself unable to attract the same kind of recruit. The peasants of Fife and the Lothians regarded the work as grotesque, unnatural and totally alien to their purely agricultural traditions.

Serfdom thus fell about the necks of the colliers when a group of their employers in a privileged position in the state saw it as a possible means of securing sufficient cheap labour. Seventeenth-century society did not protest either in 1606, in 1641, in 1660 or in 1690: church and state alike saw it as a simple and admirable way out of an economic dilemma. The lot of the inarticulate industrial serfs should give the political historians of Scotland pause for reflection. In what senses can the civil wars, the covenants, and the revolutions of the seventeenth century be held to be about the basic liberties of man when all the contenders paused in the struggle to confirm, as a matter of automatic common-sense, the serfdom of the least privileged?

CHAPTER VIII

Culture and Superstition

1. CULTURAL ACHIEVEMENT

The sixteenth and seventeenth centuries were a time of immense intellectual and artistic achievement—the names of Galileo, Kepler and Newton, of Descartes and Locke, of Rubens and Rembrandt, of Shakespeare and Molière, of Bernini and Wren may serve to remind us of the range and depth of the European mind. From all this, Scotland, poor, small and geographically remote though she might be, was certainly not isolated. Her young men attended universities in France and Holland—even in Italy. Her nobles were visitors to France (especially to the Huguenot areas before 1640), to London and to the Low Countries. Her merchants imported all manner of foreign books and works of sophisticated craftsmanship from England and Europe. By many routes there thus came to Scotland new impulses to enrich and inspire, though seldom to overwhelm or to obliterate, the strong medieval traditions of her vernacular culture. Scotland was a borrower who could repay relatively little of the intellectual debt she owed to Europe but in the century and a half after 1560 there were at least two men, George Buchanan the latinist and John Napier the mathematician, whom the outside world considered as contributing much to the general fund of western culture.

George Buchanan (1506–1582) had much the greater reputation. The son of a small Stirlingshire laird, educated at the parish school of Killearn until he was fourteen, his university training took place at St. Andrews and Paris under John Major. As the greatest latinist of his day at a time when latin was in universal use as a scholarly tongue, and as a man equally at home in the academic circles of Scotland, France, Portugal and England, he was in many ways the epitome of the cosmopolitan Renaissance *savant*. Before 1560 he spent most of his adult life in France; only after the Reformation did he return permanently to his native land to support the Protestant cause, moving first in the court clique around Mary, and then attaining the influential post of tutor to James VI over whom, as a boy, he exercised a compelling influence. Though the king never shared or sympathised with Buchanan's severe Genevan Calvinism, his pedagogue imbued him with a respect for learning and a distinctive Latin accent. 'All the world knows', he said in a speech to Edinburgh University after the Union of the Crowns, 'that my master George Buchanan was a great master in that faculty. I follow his pronunciation both of his Latin and Greek, and am sorry that my people of England do not the like; for certainly their pronunciation utterly fails the grace of these two learned languages'.[1]

Buchanan's contemporary fame rested on the astonishing facility of his latin composition. His varied poems, his dramatic tragedies, his political tract *De Jure Regni Apud Scotos* (in which he defended tyrannicide: but the king only said of it 'Buchanan I reckon and rank among poets') and finally his *History of Scotland* all in turn aroused contemporary amazement in the perfection of their means of expression. One contemporary called him 'by far the greatest poet of his day', and even Dryden a century after his death described him as 'a writer comparable to any of the moderns and excelled by few of the ancients'. Perhaps no Scots before except Duns Scotus in the thirteenth century, (and he may not have been a Scot) and few since, had ever won this kind of unanimous intellectual acclaim.

Today, sadly, it is hard to see Buchanan any longer as a towering genius. Modern classicists regard his poetry as good of its kind but still much inferior to that of the Romans. His drama, history and political thought all reveal in translation an intellectual mediocrity which the virtuosity of the original Latin must have hidden. He had many imitators and successors in the seventeenth century who attempted to surpass him and failed, though the 'Aberdeen doctors' successfully continued a Scottish tradition of supremacy as the finest school of Latin poets in Europe. Nevertheless, this most medieval branch of Renaissance attainment proved an intellectual cul-de-sac as Latin declined from being a literary language to becoming a dead one, and

Buchanan's reputation has shrunk with it. It is ironic to think that he who was once much better known as a poet and dramatist than William Shakespeare is now almost totally forgotten both within and without his native country.

The case of John Napier of Merchiston (1550–1617) is quite different. Like Buchanan he was the son of a laird: his father was only fifteen when he was born, outside Edinburgh in a tower-house now the centrepiece of the Napier College of Technology. Like Buchanan he was sent first to St. Andrews and then abroad for his higher education—'send John to the schools either to France or Flanders for he can learn no good at home' wrote his uncle, the bishop of Orkney. But whereas Buchanan won instant international fame for his work, few of Napier's contemporaries recognised him as a mathematician at all. At home his academic reputation rested on a book in which he demonstrated to the general satisfaction that the Roman Church was the Scarlet Woman of the Book of Revelations. Otherwise he was known as a litigious laird and an eccentric inventor: he had a royal monopoly for a new type of screw-drainage for coal mines, he experimented in the use of salt as an agricultural fertiliser, and had visionary schemes for military burning-glasses and self-propelled armoured chariots like tanks. His serious work was appreciated only by a small international band of mathematicians, who included the two great astronomers Tycho Brahe and Kepler. Kepler was among those who greeted with the greatest enthusiasm Napier's revelation of logarithms in 1614. This epoch-making discovery, coming like an illuminating mathematical flash over European science, provided for the seventeenth century a tool of the same kind of importance as the invention of computers did for the twentieth century: an incalculable aid to rapid computation. Napier even went further: 'Napiers bones', made out of rods of ivory, represent the first attempt to construct a calculating machine. No-one today would deny his greatness. History has been kinder to him than to Buchanan in so far that his branch of learning, instead of withering, has grown into one of the most fruitful trees in the garden of science.

There were, however, few Scots besides Napier who in the sixteenth or seventeenth centuries devoted their lives to science. His only notable contemporary was Timothy Pont (1560?–1614?), the cartographer who had been inspired by the work of that great English Elizabethan topographer Camden to attempt the fantastic task of producing detailed maps of all the Scottish counties. His work, which included detailed and interesting work in the Highlands made at some risk to his own life, was continued after his death by Robert Gordon of Straloch and his son, John Gordon of Rothiemay, and the results partly published in Blaeu's great Amsterdam Atlas of 1654. Somewhat scandalously for the reputation of Scottish scholarship, the full surviving manuscript maps have not been published yet.

In the second half of the seventeenth century there were among the early members of Charles II's Royal Society of London a small number of Scots, mostly elegant amateurs of science: the most important was James Gregory (1638–1675), an Aberdonian educated at Marischal College and Padua who became an astronomer and mathematician of international standing. Among other things he invented the world's first reflecting telescope. Together with his brother and his nephew (both called David Gregory: the family went on producing distinguished mathematicians or doctors for centuries, and have nine members in the *Dictionary of National Biography* all descended from a Rev. John Gregory of Drumoak in Aberdeenshire, the father of James), James Gregory was the main link between Scotland and the work of Isaac Newton, whose mathematics was therefore being taught in Scottish universities in the early eighteenth century before it was in Oxford or Cambridge. It is striking how often, in the seventeenth century, work of really worthwhile academic stature came out of Aberdeen. The universities there proved a good deal more resistant to the theocratic pretensions of the kirk than those of Edinburgh, Glasgow and St. Andrews. The colleges in the South of Scotland tended to fall, from the days of Andrew Melville onwards, into the hands of the most crushingly Calvinist ecclesiastics, such as Robert Baillie, the regent of Glasgow University and minister of Kilwinning at the time of the Covenants who wrote that he would 'gladly consent to the burning of many thousand volumes of unprofitable writers', including those of John Selden, Hugo Grotius and the works of that 'very ignorant atheist' and 'fatuous heretic', Descartes.[2]

The closing decades of the seventeenth century were also brightened by the remarkable versatility of Sir Robert Sibbald (1641–1722), the son of a Fife laird, educated at Cupar burgh school and the universities of Edinburgh and Leyden. It was he who, with Archibald Pitcairne (another Aberdonian) founded in 1681 the Royal College of Physicians in Edinburgh: this was the first small germ of Scotland's later reputation for great medical education. He later became the first professor of medicine in the university, though he was unable, because of religious persecution against him as a Catholic, to teach for very long. He also began the first Scottish investigations into archaeology, and into the natural history of fish, birds, plants and whales, founding the botanical gardens at Edinburgh as a herbarium about 1667, and being commemorated today in the names of Sibbald's rorqual, the blue whale, the largest of all animals, and of *Sibbaldia procumbens*, one of the smallest and rarest of British alpine flowers. He also carried Timothy Pont's geographical work a stage further by initiating the first survey of the coasts, carried out by John Adair, and by collecting the first detailed topographical descriptions of different Scottish regions later published in Macfarlane's *Geographical Collections* and the inspiration and the model for Sir John Sinclair's eighteenth century *Statistical Account of Scotland*. It was from his wide curiosity that there developed the first living traditions of study in many natural sciences. Sibbald, like the Gregories, the lawyers Stair and Mackenzie and the architect Bruce who lived in the same period, was one of the fathers of the Scottish enlightenment of the post-Union age.

Nevertheless, the main native cultural achievements of Scotland in the years between 1560 and 1690 cannot be said to lie either in the traditions of Buchanan's latinity nor in those of Napier's science. If we discount the very considerable intellectual achievements of the lawyers and of at least two theologians, the episcopalian John Forbes of Corse, at Aberdeen and the Quaker Robert Barclay (perhaps unfairly, as falling outside a narrow definition of culture) the best achievements of the Scots lay in the vernacular arts of poetry, architecture and the making of silver. In all, the national performance was outstanding.

In poetry, the Scots entered the period with a magnificent double heritage. On the one hand, there was the tradition of the ballad makers stretching back to a distant medieval origin and now about to produce its finest flowering: on the other, there was the tradition of the 'makaris' of the court circle, especially Dunbar, Lindsay and Douglas who within the last fifty years had given the Scottish tongue a literary force and sweetness which their post-Reformation successors might exploit, even if they did not, in this case, surpass the masters of the late medieval golden age.

The ballads were the anonymous popular poetry of a nation quick

188

to sing, eager to celebrate the heroic, and credulous of the supernatural. While never consciously literary or contrived, the power of the
best of them is immense—born of economy of narration and the con-
joined images of beauty, violence and eerieness: 'memorable speech',
in Auden's definition of poetry. It is, in fact, extremely difficult to
quote extracts of any verse that will give a fair proof of its quality, but
the following stanzas from this ballad (probably of Aberdonian origin,
and early seventeenth-century) may serve. The song has already told of
a sailor returning to his old love and persuading her to leave her husband
and children and come back to the sea with him: after they have
embarked, she realises that neither the ship nor the sailor are any longer
earthly.

> 'O hald your tongue of your weeping', he said
> 'Of your weeping now let me be
> I will show you how lilies grow
> On the banks of Italy'
>
> And aye when she turn'd her round about
> Aye taller he seem'd for to be
> Until the tops o' that gallant ship
> Nae taller were than he.
>
> The clouds grew dark and the wind grew loud
> And the levin fill'd her ee
> And waesum wail'd the snaw-white sprites
> Upon the gurlie sea
>
> He strak the tap-mast wi' his hand
> The foremast wi' his knee
> And he brak that gallant ship in twain
> And sank her in the sea.

It is fascinating to contrast poetry of this kind, so remote from the
Renaissance that Italy is still part of faeryland, with what was being
produced at the same time in the mellifluous and jewelled language
of the court poets. In this sonnet Alexander Montgomerie (1545–1610)
combined Renaissance conventions of form with an older Scottish joy
in alliteration to produce an extremely sensuous and sophisticated
effect—

So suete a kis yistrene fra thee I reft
In bouing down thy body on the bed
That evin my lyfe within thy lippis I left;
Sensyne from thee my spirit wald neuer shed
To folou thee it from my body fled
And left my corps as cold as ony kie;
Bot vhen the danger of my death I dred
To seik my spreit I sent my harte to thee;
Bot it was so inamored with thyn ee,
With thee it myndit lykuyse to remane.
So thou has keepit captive all the thrie,
More glaid to byde than to returne agane.
    Except thy breath thare places had suppleit
    Even in thyn armes thair doutles had I deit.

Another court poet, Alexander Hume (1560?–1609) wrote what Geoffrey Grigson has called the 'delightfully windless poem "Of the Day Estival" . . . a day—or so it seems—partly of the Lowlands, of Berwickshire and Polwarth, where he was born, partly of France, where he spent four years as a law student'. It begins with mist on the moor, the noise of larks, lapwing and snipe, and continues through 'a still Tennysonian morning . . . and through a blistering noon'.

Calm is the deep and purpour sea,
Yea smoother nor the sand;
The wavis that woltring wont to be
Are stable like the land . . .
Back from the blue paymented whin,
And from ilk plaister wall,
The hot reflexing of the sunne
Inflams the aire and alle—

It ends in 'a cooling evening with the smoke straight in the air'.[3]

Here we can do no more than quote fragments at random. As with the ballads, nothing but a good anthology of the courtly verse of the period can reveal to the reader its true riches and surprising range— from the lyrical and amorous to the didactic and frankly abusive. It more than repays the trouble of persisting with what may seem at first sight to modern and Anglicised eyes an involved and difficult language.

What effect did the Reformation have on the writing of poetry in

Scotland? Some have supposed that it instantaneously blighted it, just as it has been supposed that the Reformation at once killed the less well-rooted arts of music (by dissolving the musical teaching at the song-schools where the Catholic clergy had trained boys for their liturgy) and drama (by discouraging dramatic performances on the grounds that they fostered licence and superstition). In fact, for several decades after the Reformation performances of plays and music continued. Knox attended dramatic performances and may even have helped to write a play.[4] The kirk did not turn against drama until the Melvillian period after 1574, and even then plays were possible for another quarter of a century under royal protection. Music in religious services was certainly actively encouraged by the church down to the Covenanting period, and was played in private homes throughout the seventeenth century. Andrew Russell the merchant even when living in Holland thought it best to send his daughter to Aberdeen in 1689 to learn the virginals.[5] So too in poetry. Among the ballads, very many of the finest dated from between 1560 and 1620—'Sir Patrick Spens', 'The Queen's Marie', 'Chevy Chase', and 'Kinmont Willie', for instance. Nor did the triumph of the reformers end the skilful verse of the court—besides Montgomerie and Hume, Sir Richard Maitland and Alexander Scott with many lesser men wrote in the way of the 'makaris' for half a century after 1560. Indeed, far from blighting the poetic tradition, the Reformation at first added its own distinctive contribution to it. Many think of Scottish Reformation verse only in terms of political doggerel and ludicrous adaptations of profane songs to sacred purposes, but it could do better than this. There was, for example, the Scottish Psalter, and a few fine pieces that only gradually became left out of the hymn-books as the kirk turned its face to seventeenth-century puritanism. One is this beautiful carol, more Lutheran than Calvinist in its feeling.

> For us that blissit bairne was borne
> For us he was baith rent and torne
> For us he was crounit with thorne
> Christ has my hart ay
> > For us he sched his precious blude
> > For us he was naillit on the rude
> > For us he in mony battell stude
> > Christ has my hart ay

Nixt him to lufe his Mother fair
With steid fast hart for ever mair
Scho bure the byrth, fred us from cair
Christ has my hart ay.

The first serious break in the Scottish poetic tradition came not at the Reformation but two generations later, and its cause was not religious but political. The Union of the Crowns in 1603 destroyed the court at Holyrood, and with it the environment that had nurtured all the polished and literary verse of the nation from Dunbar to Montgomerie; at the same time, the brilliance of English verse in the age of Shakespeare, Jonson and Donne provided Scottish intellectuals with an ideal to which they were attracted as moths to a candle. A new generation of poets abandoned craftsmanship in their own tongue, versatile and brilliant though it was, in favour of the poetry of standard English:

I know that all beneath the moon decays
And what by mortals in this world is brought
In times great periods shall return to nought,
That fairest states have fatal nights and days.

Verses like this, of William Drummond of Hawthornden, could well, like the poems of Sir William Alexander, be confused with those of the English metaphysical poets: but because the idiom is fundamentally still an alien one to them neither Drummond nor any other Scot of the early seventeenth century became comparable to the best English poets.

The second and perhaps greater blow to poetry came with the victory of the Covenanting puritans in the years after 1638. Puritanism is not inevitably inimical to art—England in the same period nurtured a Milton and a Bunyan. Scottish puritanism, however, proved to be narrowly dogmatic and inquisitorial, and the triumph of the General Assembly coincided with a trauma in the imaginative literature of Scotland. For nearly a century after the death of the anti-puritan Marquis of Montrose, a considerable poet himself, hardly a line of good verse passed from the pen of a Lowland Scot. The court tradition was, of course, dead, but even Drummond of Hawthornden had no successors. The ballads faded out in weak doggerels about the sufferings of Restoration Covenanters in the south-west and a handful of bucolic verses written by Robert and Francis Sempill. The only poets who wrote tolerably well were the 'Aberdeen doctors', who composed in Latin, and the Highland bards, especially those around the court of the Macleods at Dunvegan, like the great Mary Macleod, who wrote in Gaelic. Even in translation her songs are beautiful, like this with its echo of the Song of Solomon:

> Roderick, Roderick,
> Roderick of yonder dun,
> Thou art my mirth
> and my merry music,
> Thou art my rosary
> and the comb of my hair
> Thou art my fruit-garden
> wherein are apples. . . .

The Highlanders, in fact, reached other heights in the seventeenth century. At Dunvegan the great pipers Donald Mor and Patrick Mor MacCrimmon transformed the rigid patterns of the Piobaireachd, and in a composition like the 'Lament for the children' raised it to a classic peak of beauty and power. Meanwhile on the other side of the Highlands Sir Thomas Urquhart of Cromarty in 1653 celebrated the Puritan repression by publishing an apt and riotous translation of the first book of Rabelais. Bureaucracy was never able to get properly to grips with a man who sent to Cromwell a fragment of his own genealogy traced back to the 'Ourqhartos fifth in descent from Noah', and ultimately to the 'red earth from which God framed Adam, surnamed the protoplast'.

It is impossible to know, however, how far the failure in Scottish imaginative literature in the Lowlands can be blamed on the puritans, since if any individual escaped the weight of inhibition and social repression that the kirk session and the sermon sought to lay upon him, it was likely enough that his inspiration would be hampered by finding the Scottish tongue (in which he thought and spoke) was now regarded as an uncouth dialect of an English language that was still only half familiar to him. Perhaps it is not surprising that the late seventeenth-century Scots were so much more eloquent in the unemotional and silent language of building than they were in the dangerous and explicit world of words.

Architecture, indeed, had a golden age for almost the whole of the period between 1560 and 1690, with the exception of the years of civil war themselves: and it is possible to say this despite a long tradition of earlier excellence, illustrated by the medieval abbeys and the earlier sixteenth-century royal palaces in the style of the Renaissance at Falkland, Stirling, and Linlithgow. Post-Reformation building was almost entirely secular, and undertaken either for the nobles and lairds, who had benefited by the transference of ecclesiastical wealth to their own pockets, or on a more modest scale for the merchants in the towns who benefited from the increasing opportunities for commercial profit in a more settled land. For church architecture it was a lean time: the Reformers were far too poor to do more than adapt existing parish churches for Protestant worship, often by destroying the high-altar and building a new aisle at right angles to the nave to make a T-shaped preaching hall. Occasionally, when they had funds, they built simply and well. Burntisland has a square church dated 1592 of original and satisfying design, its stark walls set off by sumptuous carved and gilded furniture. In Edinburgh the Tron Kirk was a good essay in Dutch style from 1637, its deserted remnants visible today over a forecourt of municipal toilets that make it hard to appreciate what it was once like. Gifford has a post-Restoration church of very seemly proportions and attractive appearance built by a laird: it would look marvellous now if its harled walls were painted white.

The style which dominated building for the nobles and lairds from 1560 to 1660 is generally referred to as 'Scottish baronial': the building of the same date in the towns—familiar for instance in the Royal Mile of Edinburgh and in the little burghs of Fife—has no popular name. Superficially, both the baronial and the bourgeois houses appear to be heavily influenced by Continental example. The trimmings of the doorways and the chimney pieces, for instance, are European in feeling: sometimes the records tell us they were actually imported as carved stones from the Low Countries. The painted ceilings of many castles and some town houses also have a European look: on close inspection they are found to have been copied by Scottish decorators using imported foreign pattern-books. There is everywhere an obvious patina of international Renaissance decoration. Did it go further, and influence the basic shape and design of the buildings? It is often easy to fancy in a turretted roofline the echo of a French chateau, or in a crowstepped gable the resemblance to a Dutch town house. Such likenesses, however, almost always appear to be fortuitous, and on close inspection to be extremely slight.[6] The style is basically a Scottish one, evolved by native masons from the model of the fifteenth-century vertical Scottish tower-houses: in the countryside, the new castles were more elaborate and decorative than the old, but still essentially defensive; in the towns they mirror the country house, but without the need to emphasise defence.

Some of the characteristics of the country houses can be illustrated from the two fine examples of Claypotts and Craigievar. They could equally well have been drawn from Amisfield in Dumfriesshire, Glamis in Angus, Crathes in Kincardineshire or from Elcho and Castle Menzies in Perthshire. Many of the same features on an urban scale can be seen in the larger town houses, such as the Study at Culross, Argyll's Lodging at Stirling and Lambe's House at Leith. Scotland is rich in buildings of this period—so rich that the worst of local authorities still think they can afford to let it be destroyed. Claypotts, built outside Dundee in 1569 is very much a defensible fortress. The plan consists of a square keep with two circular towers placed at opposite diagonals: the walls are thick and grim and rise for three stories without ornament, with small windows and an abundance of shot holes to cover the flanks of the castle with a raking fire. All this is very medieval, but just where a fifteenth-century castle would have been crowned with battlements, Claypotts is crowned with a suite of elegant square rooms, corbelled off into the round towers. It is, in fact, a castle with a country house built on top of it, the perfect symbol of the ambitious lairds who wished to enjoy their comforts and of the difficulties of doing so in a land given over to periodic anarchy.

Craigievar, built outside Aberdeen between 1610 and 1626, is a much more sophisticated building. Its basic plan rests on a device, commonplace enough at the time, placing two tower-blocks together to form an L shape, hinged by the turnpike stair that gives access to the apartments in both halves. Here, again, the lower walls are stark and unornamental, though covered by painted harling instead of being left as raw stone: they rise towards upper stories emphasised by a corbelled string-course, and a delicate balance of turrets and pinnacles. 'As a work of art it claims a Scottish place in the front rank of European architecture . . . The whole achieves a slenderness by well-considered proportions, converging vertical lines and rounded corners . . . no infelicity of mass or exaggeration of detail suggests room for improvement Quite perfect, lightly poised upon the ground, it is the apotheosis of its type:' Stewart Cruden gives a verdict that all who have seen it will endorse. Craigievar appears to belong to a less obviously warlike society than Claypotts: but even in 1626 the builder ventured no windows at ground level and provided only one narrow entrance that could easily be barred by a stout yett, or iron grill, against attackers.

The vertical style of the tower-house dominated the first half of the seventeenth century, and yielded only slowly before the influence of more settled conditions and English architectural styles. In the peaceful Lothians, courtiers and civil servants to James VI built Pinkie House and Winton House in an undefended Scottish-Tudor style. The architect of the last, William Wallace, began Heriot's Hospital in Edinburgh in 1627: he constructed four tower blocks in the Scottish tradition and uneasily joined them by four horizontal ranges in the English manner. The external effect is clumsy: but the interior courtyard is quite splendid, and though the resemblance is probably fortuitous recalls on a small scale that of Kronborg Castle at Elsinore in Denmark. Drumlanrig Castle, built between 1675 and 1689 for the Duke of Queensberry in Dumfriesshire, was a later and even more sumptuous essay on the same hybrid plan. All these buildings moved the national taste away from its castellated traditions, but it was not until the defeat of the private armies in the civil wars and the vigorous imposition of order by Cromwell and Charles II that many lairds began to favour houses that had lost all trace of their martial functions.

The Scottish architecture of the post-Restoration period was dominated by the genius of Sir William Bruce (c. 1630–1710) the son of a small Fife laird who entered the royal service as a courtier and prospered sufficiently to become, for a time, 'King's Surveyor and Master of the Works'. Where he was educated, and where he gained his interest in building is not known. It was he above all who made the break from the castle to a country house stylistically possible. He introduced to Scotland the European classicism of Palladio and Inigo Jones, developed it in his own idiom, and became the forerunner of the eighteenth-century Scottish school that was to carry this architecture in new directions and to new heights. Bruce throughout his life remained an amateur: he worked on a variety of buildings in different manners—Holyroodhouse Palace and Prestonfield House in Edinburgh, for instance, display an eclectic knowledge of buildings in England, France and Holland, though the attribution of Prestonfield to Sir

William Bruce has been challenged by some historians.[8] At the same time he was much more than a copyist—his own home, Kinross House, was a more advanced classical design than anything that had been attempted for a country mansion in England at that date. All his buildings have an individual quality which once recognised is not forgotten. Firstly, they are built of fine materials—Kinross of a honey-and-brown stone. Secondly, they are extremely carefully positioned in their landscape, with an eye both for their appearance and for the vistas that open from their windows. It is a marvellous moment when, at Kinross, a small connecting door is opened and it is possible to see, by turning round, a vista from the front of the house reaching down an avenue of trees to the lodges at the edge of the town, and a vista at the back reaching through a formal garden and a water gate over Loch Leven to focus on the island castle in which Queen Mary was imprisoned. At Balcaskie the view focuses on the Bass Rock. Thirdly they show a fine sense internally of the decorative possibilities of contrasting materials, exemplified by a brilliant use of leather hangings at Prestonfield and of pine and oil paintings at Hopetoun. Finally, although the houses all have an undeniable sense of grandeur, their living apartments (where he was able to design the whole house himself) are on a scale carefully related to human enjoyment and comfort. It is impossible to feel an overawed stranger in a Bruce house. All in all he was an artist of large qualities and original mind, and, because he was so much admired by contemporaries and because he trained beneath him the next generation of leading architects, including William Adam, he had a great and altogether beneficial influence on the succeeding century.

To the furnishings of their buildings the Scots contributed little of the first rank. The tapestries that covered the walls of the greatest houses in the reign of James VI were imported from Arras or elsewhere. The art of portraiture was still very primitive—the first man to gain a serious reputation, George Jameson of Aberdeen (?1588–1644) was competent enough, but to refer to him as 'the Scottish Van Dyck' is only misplaced flattery. After the Restoration there seem to be more Dutch or English pictures than Scottish ones in Scottish houses. As furniture makers, too, the Scottish craftsman worked with little distinction—most of the best pieces were again imported. It is therefore very remarkable that in the single art of making fine silver the Scots excelled to an exceptional degree. There were three directions in which they did so. In the second half of the sixteenth century the goldsmiths of Edinburgh created a series of magnificent standing mazers—silver-gilt communal drinking cups with wooden bowls—of which the three finest, the Tulloch Mazer, the Galloway Mazer and the Craigievar Mazer by James Gray and James Craufuird of Edinburgh have won the highest admiration from connoisseurs:

> These standing mazers are not undeserving of Commander How's praise of them as 'the most beautiful objects ever produced by the goldsmiths of this or any other country'. They are elegant and impressive enough to satisfy the most sophisticated taste, and there is nothing in them of the extravagance or misplaced ingenuity, which mars so much of the finest Continental work and even some English plate of Tudor times.[9]

In the seventeenth century, particularly after an Act of 1617 ordering all parish kirks to provide themselves with baptismal basins and communion cups, there was a boom in the production of church plate, of which the delicately balanced cups of Gilbert Kirkwoode of Edinburgh were the most numerous and beautiful. Finally in the second half of the century the silversmiths produced the silver quaich, a two-handed drinking vessel of simple form which had originally been fashioned in horn or wood and was now imitated in durable metal to considerable effect. In all their best achievements, the mazers, the communion cups and the quaich, as well as in many other objects such as ewers and ceremonial maces, the Scottish smiths showed a feeling for unencumbered line and fine proportions which also went on in an unbroken tradition into the eighteenth century. This, like good building, was one thing at least that puritanism never killed.

2. THE PERSECUTION OF WITCHCRAFT

The seventeenth century, it has been said, was Janus-faced. In many ways the artistic achievements of Scotland between 1560 and 1690 formed the culmination of an independent medieval tradition of earlier centuries: the scientific achievements, such as they were, began a tradition that would only flower in the later centuries. But the third phenomenon we are considering in this chapter, the persecution of witchcraft, belonged neither to the past nor the future. It is an extraordinary fact that in the centuries before the Reformation, and again in those since the Union of Parliaments, the number of recorded executions for witchcraft in Scotland could be counted on one man's fingers: but in the years between 1560 and 1707 considerably more than 3000 people, and perhaps as many as 4500, perished horribly because their contemporaries thought they were witches. In England, with a population five times as large, only about one thousand were killed as witches. This unique wave of judicial murder deserves a historian's serious attention.

It was, of course, the murder and not the superstition that was novel. Medieval Scotland believed in saints, whose favour could be procured by sacrifice and pilgrimage: it believed in devils and fairies, whose quiescence at least could be procured by libation of milk on the hillside, or by leaving a little grain in the ground for the 'Old Gudeman'. It believed in the power of priests, who served the saints, and likewise in the power of witches, who were in communication with the devil and could control some of his supernatural powers either to do good by healing or to do evil by cursing and destruction. A medieval Scot, however, rarely thought of persecuting a witch: it was like trying to persecute a saint, or a fairy—an act of foolhardiness that could hardly hope to succeed. The good and evil spirits of the world were invulnerable, and the best you could do with a witch was to bribe her with oatmeal and milk. There must have been many an old woman with a small knowledge of herbal cures and a good line in invective who in her widowhood found it profitable to be thought a witch. It might be a sinister and lonely profession, but it was not very dangerous.

About the time of the Reformation, this attitude underwent a profound modification. Initially it was the leaders of society who for purely intellectual reasons began to find witchcraft intolerable. The most important single influence probably came from the Continent, initially from Germany where in the late fifteenth century two priests Jacob Sprenger and Heinrich Krämmer had published what purported to be a compendium of witchcraft, the *Malleus Maleficarum*: this systematised the diverse rural superstitions of Europe so that they appeared to form a vast organised conspiracy by the devil and his witches to work against man and the Holy Church. The Pope had published a bill in 1484 enjoining the extirpation of sorcerers, and entrusting the task to the authors: their book ran to twenty-five editions. Germany, France, Switzerland, Lorraine, Scandinavia, the Basque country and many other parts of Europe both Catholic and Protestant were thereafter swept for a century and a half by wave after wave of persecution as religious leaders and princes strove to stamp out the devil's fires. One of the more conservative reckonings has put the number of executions in Germany alone at over 100,000.

There is no doubt that intellectual Scots travelling in Europe and reading European literature (not only the *Malleus Maleficarum* but also the works of Lutheran, Calvinist and Catholic authorities) were impressed by the seriousness with which foreign authorities treated the threat from the witches—just as they were impressed by other aspects of European statecraft, political and religious thought. Calvin himself declared 'the Bible teaches us that there are witches and that they must be slain . . . God expressly commands that all witches and enchantresses shall be put to death and this law of God is a universal law'.[10] James VI published in 1597 his own frightening and learned treatise, the *Daemonologie*, to confound an impious Englishman who had denied that witches existed or could be a danger to the state. Knox, influenced especially by Calvin, played a personal and vigorous part in at least one witchcraft trial at St. Andrews, and Scottish lawyers were enthusiastic in supporting the church in its literal interpretation of the Mosaic text 'thou shalt not suffer a witch to live'. It is not too much to say that in the later sixteenth century the need to extirpate witchcraft was becoming as clear to thinking Scots of all shades of religious and political opinion as the need to extirpate tuberculosis or polio is clear to thinking men today. It was looked upon as a disease of the body politic.

The persecution of witches was no Protestant monopoly: but it is probably true that in Scotland the Reformation made the attack on witchcraft a powerful and popular crusade, as opposed to a movement of intellectuals and rulers alone. Protestantism had, in the first place, destroyed the medieval world of good and evil spirits that a man might placate impartially: to worship saints now was not a virtue but a superstition; but to put out milk for the fairies or give oatmeal to a witch was not superstition but a sin, a positive act of sustenance for the agents of Satan. The old neutrality became a moral impossibility, and a sincere minister or a fervent congregation became impelled to denounce the local witches: having tasted blood, denunciation became not an act of conscience (as it was at first) but a compulsive pleasure, the deep psychological grounds of which contemporaries were quite incapable of recognising either in themselves or in others.

At first sight it is strange that the kirk never set about a bloody search for Catholics in the same way as it did for witches, especially since in Europe the association between a witchcraft hunt and a heresy hunt was normal. It may be connected with another peculiarity of Scottish witch-hunting: the landed classes and the wealthiest burgesses were seldom or never accused of witchcraft, whereas in Europe no class was exempt. Scottish victims were mainly women, the wives of farmers, country and town craftsmen and cottars, or poor old widows: the minority of men 'warlocks' were drawn from the same classes, together with a certain number of pipers and tinkers who were almost vagabonds. Any hunt for Catholics must, logically, have involved a head-on clash between the local kirk-session and the Catholic notables who formed the focal point of popery where it survived in Scotland, as in parts of Dumfriesshire or Aberdeenshire. No-one was going to risk a head-on collision with a Lord Maxwell or a Marquis of Huntly, particularly since, in David Mathew's words, every Calvinist knew that Catholics were the followers of anti-Christ: 'God was not mocked, and this led them to the conviction that each papist would go in time to his own place'.[11]

Witches, however, could be smelt out without logically having to include the lairds at all, although the upper classes were in fact sometimes also suspected of dark practices. The Countess of Stair who died in 1692, for instance, was rumoured to be able to fly around the room, and Sir Robert Gordon, the fourth Baronet of Gordonstoun, was said to have no shadow (the devil had taken it in mistake for Sir Robert one day when he was learning the Black Arts in Rome).[12] Nevertheless, it was possible to identify the stronghold of witchcraft as lying among the lower classes, who certainly provided the herbal remedies, spoke the traditional charms and would sometimes administer something stronger. In Ross-shire in 1576 Lady Foulis wishing to get rid of her step-son and his wife, employed a humble wizard called Lasky Loncart who, having failed to dispose of them by throwing magic arrows at images of butter, used rat-poison to greater effect.[13] In fact the new theology taught very clearly that there could be no distinction in the eyes of the law between a good witch, who tried to cure illness, and a bad one, who used poison, since both must have made a pact with the devil. 'It was the calling-down of Satan to sit in the but-and-ben on a

Scottish hillside that cried out for exemplary punishment'.[14] In other words, if a humble person was called a witch, there was no reason for an upper-class person to come to her rescue: if a humble person was called a papist, an upper-class person might well identify himself with her and defend her. As for the occasional upper-class necromancers, the local population could always console itself with the thought that, in their case Satan too was ultimately not mocked: everyone in Gordonstoun heard the devil's coach dashing up to the castle the night Sir Robert died.

It is likely that the tenets of the new religion themselves affected the character of witchcraft, making its devotees more numerous and more morbid, so that in addition to a class of witches who were no more than herbalists, there arose a class of deluded Satanists who really believed they had sold themselves to the devil. The power of the preachers on a simple rural population should not be underestimated—Sunday by Sunday they poured their fierce and eloquent sermons into the souls of their hearers—dreadful warnings and vivid descriptions of hellfire and the personal devil, a piercing insistence on predestination, and on the hopelessness of a man ever attempting to earn redemption by his own efforts and spiritual strivings. It is not surprising that some in the congregation came to believe they were irretrievably damned, and being damned were the devil's own servants, and as servants should become witches and learn to imitate the rites which were so widely publicised by confessions at witchcraft trials. Most witch's confessions were extorted after revolting torture, but some came from women who surrendered themselves voluntarily and poured out a rigmarole which sounded like the hallucinations of a mind that had cracked under Calvinist bombardment. Their private hell was a long way from the gently racketeering witch who played on rural credulity to get a little oatmeal.

In Scotland, as in Europe, the persecution of witches was a social disease that ebbed and flowed, rather than one that claimed a constant number of victims annually. There were three or four terrible epidemics in which the majority of the 4000-odd people died: in 1590-1597, in the late 1620s, in the 1640s and in 1660-1663. The persecutions began after 1563, when Parliament decreed death for anyone practising witchcraft or consulting a witch, but until 1590 trials were intermittent and by no means always ended in conviction, or if in conviction, by no means always in execution. In 1590, however, the first great witch-hunting epidemic broke out following the nation-wide publicity touched off by the trial of a coven of witches at North Berwick whose various members confessed after torture to having attempted to encompass the king's death by raising a storm to wreck the vessel on which he was returning from Denmark with his royal bride. James VI himself heard the witnesses describe how Satan had preached to them a midnight sermon from North Berwick church—'he did greatly inveigh against the King of Scotland . . . the king is the greatest enemie hee hath in the world'. This spine-chilling testimonial flattered the credulous and intellectual king, who with the enthusiastic collaboration of his subjects unleashed a great wave of persecution against the devil's fancied agents. In 1598, when it began to die down, the church threatened to 'proceid . . . with the highest censures' against magistrates who set witches free after they had been convicted.[15]

Thereafter there was a sudden stop, with relatively few cases for fifteen years, and then a slow gathering of momentum again, with far more cases in the 1620s than in the 1610s and another wave approaching an epidemic from 1628 to 1630. It has been said that 'whenever Presbytery was dominant witches became prominent'[16], but this persecution took place at a period of strong episcopal command in the church. What brought it about at this time remains obscure, but some people evidently found it highly convenient. The second Earl of Lothian was found dead in circumstances that suggested he had taken his own life. His family, to refute such a disgraceful notion, petitioned Privy Council to keep two suspected witches in prison to await trial for killing the Earl by witchcraft, 'that God may be glorified, justice ministrat opoun the offendouris and the honnour and reputatioun of that nobleman vindicated and relieved'.[17]

The next waves came in the very different circumstances of the triumphant Covenanters of the 1640s when the General Assembly was calling for a general new reformation of the whole country and a crusade against immorality in many forms. That body passed acts in 1640, 1644, 1645 and 1649 calling on presbyteries and sessions to take the lead in searching out witches and destroying them: consequently, there was a burst of cases brought to trial in 1643 and 1644, and again in 1649 and 1650. The final wave came after the Restoration, and was partly a result of the near-prohibition of witchcraft trials which the English government had imposed in the Scottish courts when they ruled the country in the 1650s: in 1661 the floodgate of restraint burst, and cases that had been festering in local communities for a decade were brought to justice. By 1663, however, the Scottish authorities were beginning to experience a revulsion themselves: after 1680 successful trials were increasingly unusual, and after 1700 hardly known at all.

Persecution was an epidemic in area as it was in time, and some places were always immune. Over the whole of the Hebrides and most of the mainland Highlands (except Perthshire) witchcraft trials were unheard of even in the worst years of the seventeenth century, though these were among the most superstitious parts of the country in which belief in sorcery has persisted until very recent times.[18] They held, however, to the older medieval view, that some witches did good, some did harm, and all should be tolerated for fear of stirring up a hornets' nest of the supernatural. The most notorious prosecution in the Highlands was the trial and torture of twelve Maclean kindly-tenants by their Chisholm landlord in 1662, but this was recognised even by contemporaries as a case not of true witchcraft but of brutal eviction—the cynical Chisholm was apparently avenging himself on his tenants in the most horrible way he knew. Some Lowland areas also suffered witchcraft trials for only a short period. Aberdeen was wracked by terror in the 1590s, yet thereafter remained surprisingly quiet even when the rest of the country was in uproar. Orkney was troubled in 1594, in 1616 and intermittently till 1650, but seldom thereafter. By contrast, persecution in Dumfriesshire and Ross-shire was quite unusual before 1625, but then went on for nearly a century—the last witch to die in Scotland was condemned by the sheriff-depute of Dornoch in 1727. Other regions, the Lothians (Dalkeith was a black spot), the south of Fife, the Clyde valley, and parts of Perthshire seemed to experience successive waves of persecution whenever there was any feeling against witches in Scotland at all: perhaps this was because they were close to the court and the General Assembly from which the first impulses to persecute might go out. Ayrshire and Galloway, though the head-quarters of the popular Covenanting movement in its later stages, were never badly touched even when Dumfries was inflamed. This is hard to explain, but the main social alliance here seems to have been between the excluded ministers and the independent peasants against the great landlords and the magistrates. Perhaps, if the potential witnesses and the judges were thus at loggerheads a climate for a witch-craze could never occur.

The spasmodic character of the witchhunts must have been largely due to their revolting character, and the mass hysteria that went with it. The normal pattern was for a woman suspected of being a witch to be denounced in her local community (often by the minister in the kirk-session) and then brought to trial. Unless she had already made a voluntary confession, it was necessary to extort proof of her guilt before the trial began: this might be done by the most severe tortures, such as use of the thumbscrew and breaking irons, or by keeping the victim from sleeping ('the choicest means they use in Scotland for discoveries of witches') or by witch-pricking: in the last case a man 'skilled in the art' would prick the woman all over her body until he found a so-called 'witch-mark' (often a mole or a birth-mark) that was insensitive to pain and supposed to indicate that the victim was marked by the devil for his own use: this alone was enough to prove guilt. Once a 'confession' had been elicited—and the victim had virtually no option but to confess in the end—the 'witch' was encouraged to denounce her 'confederates', because it was always believed that sorcery was practised in covens of thirteen. The woman, by now often half crazy with pain and terror, might name a dozen local wives at random, all of whom would be brought to the torture chamber and required to name yet more. From one trifling case a convulsive wave of witch persecution could follow that might wrack a county for years on end.

The confessions seldom make pleasant reading: very often they began with the admission of some harmless cure, and then ran on into insane fantasies. In 1662, for instance, Isobel Gowdie from Nairn confessed to having been baptised by the devil in the parish church and joined a coven of thirteen who met at night for feasting and cursing: she had been by magic down into the earth to feast with the King and Queen of the fairies; she could fly, or become a hare, a cat or a crow at will; she could inflict fever or sciatica; she had taken the milk from her neighbours' cows and weakened her neighbours' ale; she had made the minister very ill by swinging a bag with boiled toads and nail parings over his bed; she had killed a ploughman with elf-arrows the devil gave her; she had killed the laird's child by sticking pins in a wax image: sometimes the devil beat her and raped her; 'he would be beating us all up and down with cords and other sharp scourges, like naked ghaists': he was a stag or a bull, or 'a very mickle, black rough man'.[19]

The effect of this terrible crazy story, and of the public spectacle of the witch being strangled at the stake and then burnt in pitch, can be imagined: the mingled fright and sadism of the population grew to hysterical levels until no old woman was safe. There must have been many like the wretch awaiting execution who told her story to Sir George Mackenzie about 1660:

(she) told me under secresie that she had not confest because she was guilty, but being a poor creature who wrought for her meat and being defamed for a witch, she knew she would starve, for no person thereafter would either give her meat or lodging, and that all men would beat her, and hound dogs at her, therefore she desired to be out of the world. Whereupon she wept bitterly and upon her knees call'd God to witness to what she said.[20]

The first slackening of the persecution in Scotland came when lawyers like Mackenzie began to doubt, not the existence of witcher, but the validity of the means used to bring them to justice. There are some signs of this as early as the 1620s, when the accused were first allowed defence lawyers and Privy Council required bishops to see that malicious or frivolous cases were not brought, as much evidence seemed 'to be very obscure and dark'. However the events of 1638 and subsequent years reversed all this: it became once more almost impossible to escape alive from the charge of witchcraft. It was not until 1662, when the Privy Council had been restored and the conscience of its lawyers aroused by some particularly atrocious example of miscarriage of justice in witchcraft trials, that important reforms were made: it became illegal to practise witch-pricking without licence from the Council; it became illegal to torture in any way to extort a confession; when voluntary confessions were made, magistrates were under the obligation to see that the accused appeared fully in their right mind. With such restraints placed upon the witchfinders, it was really the end of the age of mass confession, mass conviction and mass execution: fewer and fewer cases were brought, and fewer of them ended in the death of the accused.

Nevertheless, it was many years after 1662 before even the intellectuals of Scotland were prepared to admit that they did not believe witches existed as malevolent and potent agents of the devil: and very many years again after that before the common people gave up a general belief in witchcraft. In 1736, very belatedly, the statutes against witchcraft in Great Britain were repealed by the Westminster Parliament: for a long time afterwards this Act was still regarded by some Seceders as 'contrary to the express law of God'. It was, after all even then only nine years since the sheriff-depute of Dornoch had had an old woman strangled for turning her daughter into a pony.

Part Two

THE AGE
OF TRANSFORMATION
1690-1830

Introduction

The period covered by the second part of our volume begins with a revolution and ends with an invention. The revolution was the deposition of James VII—to many Scots a shattering break with their national history, for it was the deposition of a dynasty that had ruled since 1371. There had been opportunities to dethrone the line before: the crowned medieval infants, for instance, had been tempting prey to their regents, but their hands were held by the certainty that no usurper would be tolerated by a people to whom feudal loyalty and kinship meant so much. Charles I had perished, beheaded and discrowned, after a Scottish army had handed him over to the English— but no Scot had sat among the regicides or raised a voice to support them, and his death had shocked the people into a sudden and unquestioning unity behind Charles II and the Stewart cause. Now, forty years later, a Convention of Estates and a General Assembly of the Church were endorsing with relish the deposition of a Stewart and his replacement by a Dutch stranger. The country at large was not everywhere so happy as its representatives in Edinburgh for there had to be a further small civil war ending in the death of the loyalist leader, Claverhouse, Viscount of Dundee, at Killiecrankie and the defeat of his Highland troops at Dunkeld before William III could feel secure, but never again, despite the Jacobite risings in 1715 and 1745 would a king of the native dynasty stand a chance of occupying the throne of Scotland. More truly than the Act of Union, it was 'the end of an auld sang'.

The deposition of James VII may also serve as a symbol summing up the changes of the seventeenth century and pointing forward to the conditions of the eighteenth. It could not have come about without

211

the Union of the Crowns: the Scottish rebels in 1688–1690 relied on prior English initiative, on the assistance of English arms against the Highlanders and on the unanimity of English public opinion which made the Stewart loyalists a tiny northern minority on the British island. It thus foreshadowed the conditions of the eighteenth century when England absorbed Scotland's parliamentary identity. Likewise, the revolution could not have come about without a prior change in the character of the Lowland landowner from that of a military magnate with strong feudal loyalties and antipathies to that of a peaceful member of the British landed classes, anxious only to secure his estate from the arbitrary predation of an impersonal crown. The Whigs in England and Scotland, because they had come to have much the same outlook, thus worked against James for similar reasons. This again foreshadowed the eighteenth century, when respect for established law, respect for property, and respect for the rule of the landlord in the state went unquestioned until the final decade, and were even then only ineffectively challenged by the radicals. Lastly, the revolution of 1688–1690 was a frenzied popular rejection of the King's attempt to reintroduce or even to allow the practice of Roman Catholicism: the strength of public reaction revealed a state where the passions of religious feeling were strong enough to eclipse the older feeling of dynastic loyalty. The settlement that followed 1688 once more set the scene for the eighteenth century: it established the Church of Scotland with a Presbyterian government which survived all subsequent threats and schisms to prove itself to be, as far as the state was concerned, the final ecclesiastical solution. In all these ways, therefore, the passing of the last Stewart king puts a full stop to the past, and points forward to the future. It makes a fair point of departure for our story.

The invention which concludes our period is J. B. Neilson's discovery of the hot-blast smelting process, patented in 1828, which for the first time enabled the Scots to use the immense resources of black-band ironstone which had lain untouched since David Mushet first discovered them in 1801. There are various dates at which 'The Industrial Revolution in Scotland' may be said to have begun. An earlier generation of historians often chose 1759, when Carron Iron Works, the first of the great industrial concerns on a modern pattern, was begun on a virgin site near Falkirk: but one swallow does not make a summer, and there was little else in the 1760s to mark a major departure from the economic structure of the past. 1783 is a better choice: the end of the American War of Independence coincided with the astounding expansion of the cotton industry based on applications in several different parts of Scotland of the new factory technology of Lancashire. From the 1780s onwards the industrial sector in the Scottish economy grew very fast, yet contemporaries were at least as impressed by the concomitant changes in the structure of farming, in the improvements in transport (with the completion of the Forth-Clyde and Monkland canals and many new roads) and in the changing distribution and numbers of population which were starting to rend the traditional fabric of Scottish society in several directions. Radical technical change in manufacturing industry before 1830 had in Scotland been restricted almost entirely to textiles: the rise of the heavy industries, iron, steel and shipbuilding, along with a great new expansion in coal mining, depended on the use of ores which Neilson's process alone made possible. In this volume we therefore take leave of Scotland at a point when she had undergone about half a century of rapid economic change, yet while she was still a country in many ways dominated by the rural and agricultural character of her economy and institutions.

The plan of this section is to devote the first three chapters to the formal environment of social stability and change, 1690–1830—first with the institutions and changing character of the state and the church, then with the economic and demographic changes that accompanied the first stage of Scotland's 'take-off' towards sustained economic growth', to use W. W. Rostow's useful phrase. In a social history we must be content with offering a description rather than an analysis of the causes of economic change, though some of the catalysts which assisted change will be discussed in later chapters. The following six chapters are concerned with different social groups—the landowners, who in the Lowlands stood at the head of society when the great agrarian changes were made, and the farmers and peasants who followed or assisted them when these changes came about; the Highlanders, whose world was shattered and changed by political as well as by economic factors; the middle classes of the towns, who provided so many of the merchants, entrepreneurs and inventors of the first phase of the industrial revolution; and finally with the emergent class of industrial workers who formed the first true industrial proletariat in society. The two last chapters concentrate on intellectual matters. The eighteenth and early nineteenth centuries are commonly regarded as a golden age of Scottish education, so the truth of this claim and the relationship between education and social and economic change must be examined. In particular, it is certainly regarded as the golden age of Scottish cultural achievement: in what respects and for what reasons was this so?

Since the years 1780–1830 in particular are years of transition between a traditional society and an industrial one we must beg the reader's indulgence if all the topics intimately connected with emergent industrialism are not fully discussed in this volume. Although there are many references, for instance, to the rapid growth of towns, there is no chapter here on the problems of public health and housing in early nineteenth-century Glasgow or Edinburgh. We cannot deal with everything at once, and these topics, like a number of others, must await another book which will deal more properly and fully with the problems of industrial society in Scotland since the 1820s. For the moment, the emphasis of our attention in the second half of this volume must lie where the emphasis of Scottish society itself lay before 1830— on the problems and turmoils of a changing but still predominantly rural society.

CHAPTER IX

The State and the Church

1. SCOTLAND AND WESTMINSTER

In many respects the whole history of Scotland since the end of the seventeenth century appears overshadowed by one event, the Union of Parliaments, which erased the formal Parliamentary independence of Scotland, reduced her to the status of a 'region' in the new hybrid kingdom of Great Britain, created an Anglo-Scottish common market that was the biggest customs-free zone in Europe, and provided access to one of the largest empires of the world. 1707 is a watershed that seems to split our view of the past into two distinct halves.

Nevertheless, Union did not fall like a bolt from the blue. It marked only a stage, though certainly an important one, in the long story of Scotland's absorption into a wider Britain, a process that began in the middle of the eleventh century when Malcolm Canmore married an English wife, and in many ways is not complete even today, when people still worship in a Church of Scotland and stand trial before the High Court of Justiciary. In a seventeenth-century context the treaty of 1707 was also only the second half of the Union of 1603, the capstone to a process of constitutional amalgamation that James VI and every monarch after him had earnestly desired. In another sense it was the logical conclusion of 1689, when the nobles of England and Scotland, by deposing the Catholic James VII and accepting the Protestant William III, had shown how a British identity of interests could exist outside the personal interests of the monarch. Even when the treaty was under discussion in 1705 and 1706, amid much talk from its opponents of Scotland's ancient traditions of independence and many boasts of her ability to thrive again as a separate state, it became clear to most Scots how hard it would be to refuse the Union which England was pressing upon them without bringing down on themselves another era of chaos in the shape of internal division, dynastic war and commercial blockade. England wished for a full union primarily in order to avoid dangerous disputes over the succession to the throne when Queen Anne died. Among those in the Scottish Parliament a majority would have preferred some looser form of federal union to the three choices of staying as they were in the Union of Crowns, of setting up a completely separate state or of a Parliamentary Union. When it became clear, however, that England would settle for no Union less complete than an Incorporating Union of Parliaments, the Scottish Parliament decided for incorporation rather than separation. Some modern historians have asserted that the Union only came about because leading Scottish politicians were bribed by English gold and the promise of office in the British state. This point, even if it were satisfactorily proved (it never has been), would not invalidate the common argument that in the circumstances which faced Scotland in the opening decade of the eighteenth century it was wiser for the country to unite with England than to cast off on her own.[1]

Constitutional lawyers rightly insist that Scotland did not surrender her sovereignty to England in 1707: she surrendered it with England's, and the two kingdoms amalgamated to form a new state. The letter of the law, however, was not altogether the same as the spirit, for the partnership was a grossly unequal one. Scotland had only about one-fifth the population of England: her wealth (as contemporaries measured it in terms of the yield from the land tax and from customs and excise revenue) was hardly one-fortieth: on these grounds, therefore, she was given representation in the Westminster Parliament of only sixteen seats among 206 in the House of Lords, and forty-five among 568 in the House of Commons. In all but a few details, Scottish political and economic government had to conform to England's established practice, and there was little question of the treaty creating institutions that would compromise to make a genuine new British government. For these reasons there was little to stop England from totally absorbing Scotland, except those parts of the treaty guaranteeing the separate existence of the Church of Scotland and the Scottish law courts. These, though not immune from erosion, remain one obvious source of the surviving distinctions between the two halves of the same island, and rallying point for national consciousness today.

The most important political consequence of Union might seem to be the extinction of Scottish Parliamentary independence. But what in fact was lost? Scotland never had had the bold tradition of Parliamentary initiative which, in England, had been so richly developed from the reign of Elizabeth onwards. James VI and Charles I kept Parliament caged behind the Lords of the Articles, so that it never dared to promulgate anything offensive to the Crown. On the signature of the National Covenant in 1638 it escaped for a time, but Cromwell's victory nipped that venture in the bud. After 1660, the Parliaments of Charles II and James VII proved capable of moments of restive and even strenuous criticism, but they never actually seized initiative from the Crown on any important point. Down to 1689, therefore, Parliament was only a little more than a solemn rubber stamp.

The accession of William created a new situation, in so far as the subsequent constitutional settlement abolished the Lords of the Articles and restricted the power of Privy Council, while the new assembly showed itself anxious for independence by exerting control over its own disputed elections and standing up for its rights to initiate novel legislation even if the Crown did not like it. The sort of conflict this might lead to was shown in 1695 when the Scottish Parliament conferred a charter on a new national trading corporation, the Company of Scotland, which promptly invaded territory claimed by the neutral King of Spain on the Isthmus of Panama when William III and his English ministers were desperately trying to keep Spain out of a military alliance with France. Not unnaturally, London thereafter attempted by a judicious mixture of threats and bribery to exert precisely the kind of control over the Scottish Parliament that the Lords of the Articles had had in the past. They were not always successful. For two years, in 1703 and 1704, when the Scottish Parliament responded to the oratory of Andrew Fletcher of Saltoun and went so far as to threaten to untie the links with the south to save Scotland from 'English or any foreign influence', Scottish Parliamentary independence perhaps really did exist; but in 1705 and 1706, when the Scots were trying to weigh up the pros and cons of Incorporating Union and the English were straining every nerve to reassert control over the members, it was under attack again. Thus its apparently irrevocable loss in 1707 was not nearly so important an event to contemporaries as it seems in retrospect to us.

After the Union of 1707, Scottish Parliamentary life as reflected in the careers of Scottish members at Westminster became for a long time so moribund as to be scarcely relevant any longer to a general history of Scottish society. British Parliamentary life itself in the eighteenth century was not in any case very dynamic, glamorous or inspiring. The English Government ruled from the basis of a solid block of sycophantic votes organised by experienced managers dispensing safe seats with the one hand and lucrative positions of government office with the other. Their eye picked out the Scottish newcomers to the Westminster assembly as promising recruits: they organised them under one of their own number until, with a little training, they became almost as bovine in their passivity to the English administration as their forefathers had been to the Scottish Lords of the Articles.

Perhaps predictably, it was two great Campbell grandees, the Duke of Argyll and his brother the Earl of Ilay, who became in 1725 the first to attain to the powerful, quite unofficial but universally recognised position of Scottish Parliamentary managers. Before that time the Scottish members had not been so highly organised and had, indeed, even been able to show flashes of genuine independence—as in 1713, when the Scottish members combined in an attempt to prevent the levying of a tax of sixpence a bushel on Scottish malt. The Campbell brothers shared power between them for a generation though much of the effective day-to-day work of management was done by able deputies in the Edinburgh legal profession, such as Lord Milton and Duncan Forbes of Culloden. After 1761, however (apart from an interval from then until 1765 when Argyll's nephew Lord Bute managed Scotland and was himself for a time prime-minister of Great Britain), effective government passed into the hands of a succession of Lord Advocates, whose own office was a government appointment from among the ranks of Edinburgh lawyers. Of these the most accomplished and powerful was Henry Dundas, whose term spanned the years from 1775 until his impeachment by political enemies in 1805. He was the past-master of gentlemanly management, and in the 1790s kept the Scottish politicians mutely obsequious behind the Government of William Pitt while it suppressed the campaign of the first Scottish radicals inflamed by the principles of Tom Paine and the French Revolution. While he ruled Scotland, even church preferment became a political matter—'I can warrent his good principles towards the present Government and he will be a useful minister of the Gospel', wrote one gentleman to Dundas in pursuit of preferment for his children's tutor: 'in every case where matters of Government have been spoken of in the parish, large and populous as it is, there never appeared any seditious or improper tendency but I checked it' wrote another minister, not afraid to blow his own trumpet in pursuit of a similar aim.[3] The fall of Dundas, so unexpected and from such a height that 'people could scarcely believe their senses', changed the man but not the system. Though no other manager was able to repress criticism of the Government so effectively, it was not until after the Reform Bill of 1832 that the country was able to tear itself out of the managerial leading strings.

Corruption at General Elections was, of course, the obverse side of the coin of sycophancy at Westminster, and for this, the narrowly-based Scottish franchises (which originated not from the Union settlement but from an Act of the Scottish Parliament of 1681) gave exceptionally large openings, though there is no reason to believe they were widely used for corruption before 1707. In 1820 the voters' roll for the county constituencies of Scotland held only 2,889 names, or one voter to every 625 members of the population. In Cromarty the member was returned by nine freeholders. Ayrshire had the biggest electorate in the country with 240 voters. Even so, not all the voters were necessarily landowners, and indeed relatively few of the landowners were voters. From the 1770s onwards it became the practice to create votes by disposing of the title deeds or superiorities of nominal portions of land to so-called 'parchment barons', who had bound themselves to support the donor of the superiority. Thus in Lanarkshire the sixty-six voters who really did hold land of their own were outnumbered by ninety-five parchment barons, who were creatures of the Duke of Hamilton or the Lord Advocate: the Hamiltons explained in the House of Commons that they had been forced to create so many because the Lord Advocate had tried to unseat Lord Archibald Hamilton (who held mild reforming opinions) by suborning voters in traditional Hamilton territory. In the burghs the situation was worse: the member for Edinburgh, for instance, was returned by thirty-three voters, who were all town councillors with the right of choosing their own successors to city office and the voting roll: the population of the capital of Scotland in 1821 was 138,000. Glasgow, with a population of 147,000, shared a single member of Parliament with Rutherglen, Renfrew and Dumbarton: he was elected indirectly by four delegates from the four councils, and Glasgow's delegate was chosen by the votes of thirty-two members of her town council.

Bribery took many forms—an open gift of cash was not too coarse for a baillie, whose own council would certainly be even more corrupt than the London Parliament of which it was a near microcosm: the half-veiled promise of a regimental commission for a second son or an East India post for a nephew was likely to prove more efficacious with a brother laird. Once elected, a successful candidate departed to London eager to recoup his heavy election expenses and further his career: what he said and did there were not usually of the first importance to the constituents whose palms he had so thoroughly greased on his way.

The system, with all its explicit subservience to the ministry and to England, did not survive without protest, though for a long time after 1725 it was very hard indeed to detect any squeak of non-compliance. Before 1790 the only hints that things might not be perfect came from a handful of conservative men who were disturbed not by corruption or influence *per se* but by the extension of management in new directions. The creation of votes by making 'parchment barons', did not begin until about the time that Henry Dundas reached the saddle in the 1770s. This met with some ineffectual disapproval over the next two decades. Similarly, dragging the church into the business of state patronage began on a large scale in the 1780s, and met with sharp criticism from men deeply attached to the establishment as it had worked in the earlier eighteenth century. The other main lines of reform were directed not so much at Parliament as at the corrupt corporations of the burghs: this was more of an innovation, and the champions of change were here the middle classes. But burgh reform, too, had not made much headway as a cause before 1789.

The impact of Tom Paine's publication of *The Rights of Man* in 1791 and *The Age of Reason* in 1794, allied to the outbreak of the French Revolution in 1789 and the war against the French democracy which followed in 1793, however, was to alter completely the structure of opposition. For nearly a generation, both the conservative upper class and the majority of middle-class critics alike were silent and frightened before the spectre of unleashing a revolution which threatened to sweep away all established order. The initiative of protest passed to a new and revolutionary radical element, that drew the bulk of its membership from the ranks of the urban artisans and lower middle class and some of its best leadership from eccentric elements in the upper middle class.

The story of the challenge of the radicals to the established order must wait until a later chapter: it is sufficient to say here that the failure of the attempt to hold a popular National Convention with delegates from all over Britain in Edinburgh was followed by a series of trials before the Court of Session and the subsequent transportation of the leaders. Thereafter, the radical movement was both less united in its aims and less open in its methods. One section reached its climax and defeat in the pathetic risings in 'the Radical War' of 1820. Another section advocated alliance with the moderate or tepid middle and upper-class reformers who after a time once more began to raise their heads. The founding of the *Edinburgh Review* in 1802 by three young, middle-class Whigs, the advocate Francis Jeffrey, the politician Henry Brougham and the economist Francis Horner, marked a departure here: the *Scotsman*, too, was founded in 1817 with the express intent of harnessing radicals to the common peaceful cause of moderate Parliamentary reform.

There were by 1825 at least three significant types of critic of the established order—there were the radicals, partly working class people, working towards a democracy; there were the middle-class reformers who wanted a constitution in the burghs and in Parliament that made the country safe for property of all kinds and representative of all honest men of means; lastly, there were a number of aristocratic Whigs, including the Hamiltons and the Breadalbane Campbells who were both impatient of municipal corruption, and wanted a county franchise in Scotland that would represent landed property and power as accurately as the county franchise did in England. In England the reforming movement was certainly no less popular and varied. It is a testimony to the power of the British government over the obsequious bulk of the English members as well as the Scottish members that it was able to ignore the whole of this criticism, and to refuse even the smallest concessions to the opposition. It still felt able in the reign of George IV to rule in much the same way as its predecessors had ruled in the reign of William III—by the arts of parliamentary management that took no account of the wishes of the bulk of the people. All this would change in 1832, mainly in the direction of enfranchising at least some of the middle class whose power and prestige had grown so remarkably in the course of the eighteenth century (see chapter XV below).

2. LAW AND DISORDER

A trend towards effective central government had been one of the main characteristics of change in Scottish society since the 1590s. Nevertheless, even a century later, standards of order were in many respects well below those south of the Border. In 1680 the last major pitched battle between two clan armies had been fought at Altimarlich in Caithness between the Sinclairs and the Breadalbane Campbells; but nine years later, Morer could still write of the Highlanders:

> Once or twice a year, great numbers of 'em get together and make a descent into the Low-lands, where they plunder the inhabitants and so return back and disperse themselves. And this they are apt to do in the profoundest peace, it being not only natural to 'em to delight in rapine, but they do it on a kind of principle and in conformity to the prejudice they continually have to the Lowlanders, whom they generally take for so many enemies.[4]

The Lowlands themselves were more law abiding, but the burghs had their own traditions of urban riot (which could certainly be parallelled in England) and the countryside had its bands of vagrants whom many observers in the seventeenth century had accused of extorting alms by force. Andrew Fletcher of Saltoun (who proposed sending all able-bodied beggars into slavery) was thoroughly alarmist about the problem.

> This country has always swarmed with such numbers of idle vaga-bonds as no laws could ever restrain . . . they are not only a most unspeakable oppression to poor tenants (who if they give not bread or some kind of provision to perhaps forty such villains in a day are sure to be insulted by them) but they rob many poor people who live in houses distant from any neighbourhood.[5]

If Fletcher was exaggerating, his statement was not entirely without foundation. For example, in 1700 a band of thirty 'gipsies' under the leadership of James Macpherson, and apparently protected by the goodwill of the Laird of Grant, terrorised the markets of Banff, Elgin and Forres which, though on the Highland borders were certainly not Highland towns. They came marching in with a piper playing at their head, their matchlocks slung behind them and their broad swords or dirks by their sides to mingle in the crowd, inspect the cattle shown for sale and watch for bargains passing among individuals in order to learn who was in the way of receiving money.[6] Then they took appropriate action. Macpherson was in fact hanged, but only after a long career in depredation of the countryside.

The Union of 1707 handed over ultimate responsibility for the proper observation of law and order to an English government, which had both higher expectations of civil obedience than the old Scottish Privy Council ever harboured, and larger resources for dealing with trouble than the Stewart kings had been able to deploy. This combination of higher aims and greater force was to accentuate the trend towards stronger government. Violent popular disturbances which marked the French Revolutionary period in the south were less common north of the Tweed; contemporaries were inclined to say, smugly, that this was because the Scottish worker was better educated. It is also possible that the Scots were quieter because they had learned over the previous century a certain caution in resisting the powers of a well-armed and ruthless modern state.

From the point of view of London, the main problem after the Union was the Jacobites, whose strongholds in the hills beyond the Tay might yet have proved the Achilles heel of the whole British Protestant Establishment. The civil war of 1689, the two major Highland risings in 1715 and 1745, and two other abortive attempts in 1708 and 1719, seemed to show their fears were justified. On the other hand, neither the English ministry nor the Pretenders ever understood the extent to which the rebellions were provoked not by loyalty to the Stewart cause but by hatred of the great clan Campbell, whose steady aggrandisement at the expense of smaller, weaker and less politically minded clans was a cardinal objective of Government policy: after all, the political managers of Scotland from 1725 to 1761 were successive Dukes of Argyll, and the idea of using this clan to hold down and civilise its neighbours had been part of royal policy since the days of James VI. This was largely the reason why the rebellions in 1715 and 1745 produced so brilliant an explosion in the north and so little effect in the south: Lowlanders had no special reason to hate the Campbells or to love the Stewarts, and they were certainly not inclined to rise spontaneously against the Westminster government at the beck of a Catholic prince.

Government policy towards the Highlands was composed of several inter-related themes, of which the aggrandisement of the Campbells was one, and the attempt to alter the Highland character by making the clansmen industrious and godly another. In this direction, the work of the S.S.P.C.K. and allied bodies must be left for consideration to a later chapter. The third and most straight-forward way was to keep a standing army in the north, centred on garrison forts like Fort William, Fort Augustus, and Inverness (a policy begun by Cromwell and extended under William III and his successors) and capable of fast movement along the roads which General Wade and his successors began to build in the glens after 1715. The presence of these troops, stationed to contain the Jacobites, was more effective than anything else in limiting and eventually extirpating the lawlessness which was native to the hills.

On the other hand, old habits took a while to extirpate. General Wade in a report to the government nine years after the suppression of the rebellion of 1715 could still write in much the same terms as Morer:

> The clans in the Highlands most addicted to rapine and plunder are the Camerons in the west of the shire of Inverness, the Mackenzies and others in the shire of Ross who were vassals to the late Earl of Seaforth, the Macdonalds of Keppoch, the Broadalbin men and the Macgregors on the borders of Argyllshire. They go out in parties from ten to thirty men, traverse large tracts of mountains till they arrive at the Lowlands . . . they drive the stolen cattle in the night time and in the day remain in the tops of the mountains or in the woods with which the Highlands abound, and take the first occasion to sell them at the fairs and markets that are annually held in many parts of the country.[7]

Wade's answer, apart from building the famous network of roads and bridges between Fort William, Inverness and Perth, completed mainly between 1726 and 1733, was to enlist the loyal clans into a vigilantes patrol—the 'Black Watch'—which would look out for disaffected Jacobites and cattle thieves alike. The guard was surprisingly effective, though it could not altogether stop blackmailers like Colin Macdonell of Barrisdale, who had a steady £500 per annum from protection money levied on the cattle droves passing to Glen Garry out of Skye. The withdrawal of the Black Watch to fight in Europe in 1739 as a regular regiment of the British Army was an ill-advised move on the part of the Government. There was an immediate resurgence of cattle-raiding, including large scale depredations on Moray by the men of Badenoch, and a return to the atmosphere of endemic disorder that the Jacobites found so congenial. In May 1745 the Black Watch were fighting a bloody and brave battle at Fontenoy in Europe: three months later Prince Charles Stewart, slipping round the back, raised his standard at Glenfinnan in the western glens. To his chagrin and surprise the whole of the Highlands did not immediately leap to arms. Some of the most powerful families, like the Macdonalds of Sleat and MacLeods of Dunvegan who had been out in the 1715 declined to join him because he had not brought with him the promised support from France. Their caution was fully justified by events. Despite initial successes by the prince at Prestonpans and his advance down to Derby, there was insufficient backing for the Jacobites from the rest of British society for him to march on London.

The subsequent inglorious retreat culminating in the rout of the Jacobite clans and their prince at Culloden in 1746 was followed by a campaign of attrition against the rebels. The battle itself was followed by atrocities against the Highland prisoners intended to make an example to discourage future rebels. A series of statutes deprived the rebel chiefs of their lands, and handed their administration over to a Committee of Forfeited Estates dominated by Edinburgh lawyers: the clansmen were forbidden to carry arms (except for cattle drovers, whose need of self-defence was still recognised); they were also forbidden to wear the kilt or to play the bagpipes, both the dress and the music being considered too barbarous and martial for good citizenship. As further precautions, the road system was extended and a new fort built at Fort George. Settlements of loyal soldiers were planted in villages like Callendar and Kinloch Rannoch on the pattern of the old Roman *colonia* of soldier-peasants to hold down and civilise the glens. It was a pity the soldiers had venereal disease.[8] Through the S.S.P.C.K., the Board of Trustees of Manufactures, and the Committee of Forfeited Estates, new and more strenuous efforts were made to convert the Highland population to Lowland values.

The result, ultimately, was the extirpation of disorder. Deprived of their leaders, their minds benumbed by the defeat at Culloden and their will to resist eroded by the ideological campaign against them, the wilder and more traditional clans succumbed at last to the rule of law. When, in 1773, Dr. Johnson and James Boswell wandered through the glens in search of a vanishing patriarchal society, they regarded themselves as a great deal more secure than if they had been alone and un-armed on Hampstead Heath: the only clan feuds they found were commercial ones, as on Coll where the local Macleans were prepared to pay excessive rent to keep a Campbell tacksman from exercising supervision over them. By 1784 it was even considered safe and politic to hand the forfeited estates back on generous terms to the families of their original owners: the Government never had reason to regret this stroke of magnanimity.

The conquest of the Highlands is the best known, but not the only instance of the growing effectiveness of the central government in the eighteenth century. In the Lowlands too, and not least in the towns, the state expected and exacted greater obedience. Riots in the burghs had been common in the sixteenth and seventeenth centuries, stirred sometimes by national events, like the Reformation or the Union negotiations, sometimes by purely local grievances, like the unwanted curiosity of a customs man when a wine boat arrived at an outport, and occasionally by straightforward economic pressure, such as by the greed of baxters and mealmen in time of scarcity. There are too many instances of riot to cite more than a few. There was the famous Refor-mation riot at Perth when the 'rabble', stirred up by Knox and appar-ently led by respectable citizens burst into the friaries and tore out their images and treasures: there was a scarcely less famous riot at Glasgow, in the same period, when the tradesmen and apprentices turned out to defend their cathedral from the menace of over-zealous Protestant despoilers. In 1678, the Provost of Glasgow was beaten up in his own streets by a mob of 'mean' women whom he disturbed at worship in an illegal Conventicle. In 1705 an Edinburgh mob with a broad base of popular support prevented the release of the crew of an English East Indiaman, the *Worcester*, who had been wrongfully convicted of piracy against a ship of the Company of Scotland: the sailors were executed on the sands of Leith while the government characteristically wrung its hands and deplored the scandal.

In the first half-century after Union there were two famous instances of urban riot. The first was the Glasgow Malt Tax riots of 1725, when the houses and property of those who supported Walpole's new excise were razed to the ground by a very large crowd that included many more elements than that of the 'canaille' alone. This would not have got out of hand in the way it did had there not been hesitation and uncertainty on the part of the executive as to who it was that was supposed to restore order in a case like this now that the Scottish Privy Council was no more. The second instance was the grim Porteous Riot in Edinburgh in 1736 when a government officer on whose orders a volley of fatal shots had been fired into a jeering and hostile crowd watching a Grassmarket execution, was himself taken from the tolbooth by a mob apparently mainly composed of craftsmen, apprentices and labourers and lynched at the place of public execution. They planned the operation with a military precision, shutting the gates of the city, and avoiding disturbances in the immediate vicinity of the castle which might have alerted the garrison while they carried their victim to his death. Their discipline, and their sense of being the instruments of justice, were underlined by leaving a guinea in payment to the ropemaker into whose shop they broke to get a rope with which to hang Porteous.[9]

These events, which would surely have been deplored but taken for granted in Queen Anne's Scotland, seemed to Walpole's Britain to be a disgraceful challenge to the authority of the King's government, the more serious since the rioters were obviously not a simple rabble of paupers and jail-birds. The two burghs were forced by the government to pay heavy corporate fines for their failure to bring the ringleaders of either riot to justice. Magistrates seem thereafter to have taken their duties of controlling and preventing mobs somewhat more seriously, though in the absence of an effective police force they were still some-times reduced to timely capitulation rather than suppression (see page 368 below).

From 1736 until near the end of the century there does appear to be some decline in the frequency of riot, and a complete absence of riots with a marked political inspiration. Disturbances did not totally die away—in the dearth of 1740, for example, mobs in Edinburgh raided the granaries in the Dean village, in Leith and at Gilmerton, and forced the leading grain merchant to fly from the city in fear of his life. There were also various riots with a religious basis, of which much the most serious was that of 1779 when Edinburgh, Glasgow and other towns (even as small as Jedburgh) were torn by 'no-popery' mobs demon-strating against the repeal of penal laws which debarred Roman Catho-lics from inheriting property. Nevertheless the general record of Scotland was probably quieter than that of England in these middle decades of the century: the equivalent of the 'no-popery' riots of 1779 in Scotland were the Gordon Riots of 1780 in London, when the civic authorities lost all control over the mob for seven days: 285 rioters lost their lives in the resultant military intervention in London, but no fatal casualties are reported at all in Scotland.

The outbreak of the French Revolution in 1789 demonstrated the enormous potential of the mob as an instrument of popular action on the Continent: the history of the years 1790 to 1820 in Britain is in some ways dominated by the fear that the mob might be used to effect a similar revolution for radical democracy in this country. England, in these years, had many anxious moments, especially after 1812—the Spa Field riots in London, the march of the 'Blanketeers' from Manchester, the 'Pentridge revolution', the Huddersfield 'rising', and the attack on peaceful demonstrators by an armed yeomanry at 'Peterloo' in Manchester in 1819. Above all, England had the Luddites, the organised or semi-organised proletarian machine-wreckers, who, at the height of the disturbances in 1812 tied up 12,000 troops between Leicester and York—more than the Duke of Wellington had with him on his famous expedition to Portugal in 1808. Scotland in this period, though not without some street demonstrations, was remarkably unviolent. There was virtually nothing known here of Luddism or machine breaking, though there were by 1812 plenty of machines to break: the manifestations of the radical movement, like the calling of National Convention in 1793 and the organisation of the great strike of the Glasgow cotton weavers in 1812 were marked by a careful avoidance of violence. There were admittedly some disturbances in which lives were lost—eleven men were shot by the military at Tranent in 1797 resisting recruitment to the Militia; in 1819 and 1820 there were mass meetings, rioting and violence used by both sides in several parts of the west of Scotland, culminating in the so-called Radical War of 1820 which has more of the characteristics of the proletarian disturbances of contemporary England. The story of the radicals and of their failure in the short term to gain any of the objectives, however, is one we must tell at a later point (see page 440 below). It is sufficient to point out here that there is a contrast between Scotland and England and to suggest that one of the reasons for it may possibly have been the degree of control which the British government succeeded in impressing upon Scotland in the first half of the eighteenth century.

The imposition, after the Union, of stronger central government resulted in another change of which James VI would have greatly approved, for he had once tried to do it himself—the abolition in 1747 of landowners' private jurisdictions (along with the forcible conversion in 1746 of all military tenures into a form of feuferme). As long as the government had depended, as it did for most of the seventeenth century, on the help of a native semi-feudal nobility, the system which gave the inheritors of sheriffdoms, stewartries, regalities and baronies power to punish their own tenants and humble neighbours for a host of ordinary offences survived. After 1707, however, the stability of Scotland obviously depended on English troops. England regarded the feudal power of the Scottish nobles as archaic, appertaining to 'a corrupt aristocracie . . . opressing their tenants beyond all measure', as Charles Davenant said in 1705.[10] The nobles, as they became more British and less Scottish, became themselves more sensitive to this view. Scottish lawyers saw the private courts as obstructive to good law, as they quite clearly were. The abolition of the jurisdictions (after financial compensation to their owners) was carried out as part of the general revision of Scottish affairs after '45. Regality courts, heritable stewartries and sheriffdoms were scrapped outright and the competence of baron courts was reduced to such a petty level that they died of inertia before the end of the century. As the old edifice collapsed, a properly con-stituted system of sheriff courts, with the sheriff appointed by the crown, rose to take its place: this began to place the standards of public justice on an equal footing with those of England. A further step in the right direction, no less important, was the reform of the Court of Session by a series of statutes from 1808 onwards. This had the effect of dividing the court into two divisions (thereby simplifying and ex-pediting what had become chaotic procedure) and of instituting trial by jury in civil causes from 1815. The courts thus became the first Scottish institution to depart in any important respect from the con-stitution they had received from pre-Union times: before Parliament, before the municipal corporations, before the church, they had begun in some sense to reform.

3. CHANGE AND DIVISION IN THE KIRK

It was only to be expected that in politics and government England and Scotland would grow more alike after 1707. The same phenomenon in their churches is much more surprising. The settlement of 1690, by abolishing episcopal rule, and the Union of 1707, by confirming Presbyterianism as the established polity for Scotland even in a United Kingdom, seemed to open and to fix in perpetuity the gulf between the Church of Scotland and the Church of England. Indeed, in matters of church government, order and theology the churches remained ossified at opposite poles of thought. The drawing together came in the subtler (but nonetheless real and vital) spheres of social outlook and position, in which the Scottish church came to occupy a very similar standpoint to the English church. By 1790 neither Presbyterian nor Anglican leaders had any time for puritanism, both believed that the social order was already organised in a way highly satisfactory to God and both assumed the Lord to be as moderate in His religious views as they were themselves. Both were also plagued by an Evangelical party within their own church, and by popular Dissenting or Seceding groups outside it that challenged their complacent assumptions.

The change in the Scottish church is the more surprising because in 1690 it appeared to be the puritans who had the initiative and the upper hand. Admittedly, things were not so favourable to them as they had been in the 1640s. The state refused to back excommunication with civil penalties, and virtually the whole of Scotland beyond the Tay would have little truck with the deliberations of the restored General Assembly. It was nearly half a century before the last of the episcopal ministers were excluded from Church of Scotland livings in the former diocese of Aberdeen. A few of the old Covenanters of the south-west, too, walked out of the Established Church to form die-hard 'Cameronian' congregations of their ow   devoted to a still more severe and private Calvinism of their own.

Nevertheless it was plain that the General Assembly meant to use its power to lead Scotland back to a narrower path of morality than the one in which the puritans thought she had walked since 1660. In 1694, they recited the sins of the nation:

> God is dishonoured by the impiety and profaneness that aboundeth . . . in profane and idle swearing, cursing, Sabbath-breaking, neglect and contempt of Gospel ordinances, mocking of piety and religious exercises, fornication, adultery, drunkenness, blasphemy and other gross and abominable sins and vices.

Then they announced their comprehensive remedies. Ministers were to 'denounce the threatened judgements of God against such evil doers, to bring them to a conviction of their sin and danger'. Kirk-sessions were to 'faithfully exercise church discipline against all such scandalous offenders'. Clergy and elders alike were instructed to visit every home to see that family worship was everywhere practised in a decent and regular manner, and children brought up in knowledge of the scriptures at their own fireside. Even servants were not to change their jobs or their parish of residence without bringing with them testimonials of 'their honest and Christian behaviour'. It was a programme for ecclesiastical supervision recalling in many ways the aims of the Book of Discipline.[11]

In this manner, without visible weariness, the General Assembly continued for a generation, calling almost annually for fasts to avert the 'heavy displeasure and just indignation of the Holy One', re-enacting the old edicts against Sabbath-breaking, forbidding merriment at weddings and funerals, denouncing dancing, and of course never allowing itself the credit for the smallest success. Thus in 1705 they lamented the profanation of the Sabbath day by people 'walking idly upon the streets of the city of Edinburgh, pier and shore of Leith, in St. Ann's Yards and the Queen's Park': in 1710 they bewailed again 'immoralities of all kinds come to a great height', committed, as they said almost incredulously, 'by a professing people in a reformed land against the clearest light of the Glorious Gospel'.[12] It was baffling that man could be so obdurate.

Although this austere face of the established kirk ultimately cracked, the change did not come about quickly, uniformly, or universally. Some time in the 1720s puritanism seems to start to lose some of its impetus. By 1750 it was obviously declining even in the south of Scotland relative to the position fifty years before. Many ministers began to drop their primitive character of preachers and eager re-provers, and to adopt the *personae* of polite and unenthusiastic gentlemen, able to embellish God's word in an elegant address indicating to the poor the prime virtues of obedience and industry, and able to catch up the standard of Scottish culture to bear it proudly in the European Enlightenment. The heyday of the polite church lay between 1762 and 1780 when Principal William Robertson of Edinburgh University led the victorious Moderate party in the Assembly. Perhaps the most perfect expression of the values it stood for was Alexander Carlyle's eulogy of the Scottish clergy when Robertson held undisputed command:

There are few subjects of fine writing in which they do not stand foremost . . . Who have written the best histories, ancient and modern? It has been a clergyman of this church. Who has written the clearest delineation of the human understanding and all its powers? A clergyman of this church. Who has written the best system of rhetoric, and exemplified it by his own orations? A clergyman of this church. Who wrote a tragedy that has been deemed perfect? A clergyman of this church. Who was the most profound mathematician of the age he lived in? A clergyman of this church. Who is his successor in reputation as in office? Who wrote the best treatise on agriculture? Let us not complain of poverty for it is a splendid poverty indeed![13]

It was splendid poverty, but was it splendid ministry?

Several factors lay behind the change in the character of the church. The chances of the puritans making a deep and lasting impression on society were lessened by the fact that excommunication was not now accompanied by civil penalties: in the last resort an obdurate offender could laugh at the session and get away with it. 'What care I?' said a man threatened with excommunication at Fetteresso, Kincardineshire, in 1748, 'the Pope of Rome excommunicates you every year, and what the waur are ye o' that?'[14]

More important as a solvent of puritan ideals even than the change in the attitude of the state was the transformation of the character of the ministers. This was brought about partly by European intellectual currents, and partly by a change in the methods of appointment. Scottish ministers were taught in Scottish universities; from Knox's day onwards the Church of Scotland had prized herself on an educated ministry. Scottish universities, which had traditionally enjoyed close links with the Continent, could not remain always untouched by rational and liberal ideas that were stirring the intelligentsia abroad. Led in the first instance mainly by Francis Hutcheson, professor of Moral Philosophy in Glasgow 1730–46, the Scottish Universities quickly developed their own distinctive and important philosophical contribution to the European Enlightenment, associated with such men as David Hume (though he was never given a chair), Adam Smith, Adam Ferguson and Thomas Reid (see chapter XIX below). While this would have been impossible without some liberty having already been won from theological restrictions, it acted as a strong solvent on

Shieling huts on Jura: the summer huts of those who tended the cattle on hill pastures

A Cottage on Islay: the family's permanent house. "A set of people worn down with poverty; their habitations scenes of misery"

Woodhead farm, the home of the Bairds of Gartsherrie in the early eighteenth century, and High Cross farm to which they moved in 1808. The rising standard of comfort is obvious, but for small tenants the houses even at the latter date left much to be desired: "Mr. John Baird and his brothers . . . slept in the garret (and) frequently awoke in winter with the coverlet of their bed sprinkled with snow blown in through openings in the tiles"

the rigidity of the church's own intellectual horizons. None of the great philosophers were theologians in the narrow sense of the word, but their distinctive concern for moral problems, and for the inter-relationship of different branches of knowledge relevant to the study of human society, split the old husks of Calvinism. The appointment of Hutcheson and his friend William Leechman to chairs at the University of Glasgow, wrote Alexander Carlyle, meant that:

a new school was formed in the western provinces of Scotland where the clergy till that period were narrow and bigoted ... though neither of these professors taught any heresy, yet they opened and enlarged the minds of the students which soon gave them a turn for free enquiry, the result of which was candour and liberality of sentiment.[15]

Another important influence on the personnel of the ministry was the Patronage Act of 1712, by which the rights of lay patrons to appoint ministers to charges was reasserted for the first time since 1690. It is certainly true that in the first half of the seventeenth century lay patrons had exercised these powers to the advantage of the sons and friends of lairds who dominated the ministry without seeming to affect the currents to and from puritanism very strongly. We do not know enough about the period after 1690 to say whether ministers were drawn from a different social class when lay patrons temporarily laid aside their powers of presentation. The revival of patronage after 1712, however, came about in altered circumstances. For one thing, the landowners were as a class increasingly looking to England for their cultural models, and therefore wanting to see someone in the manse as polite and friendly to the laird as the average Anglican parson was to the squire. For another, the controversy as to whether the congregation or the laird should appoint the minister had become so explicit that the minister was bound to see himself as the laird's creature when in fact he was appointed in this way, and to share the landowner's general outlook and social aims. Lastly, the church got drawn into the system of political patronage operated by the Lord Advocates, which was not likely to produce either doctrinaire puritans or dedicated men.

The established church was also able to change because many of those who would have opposed the backslide from puritanism had left it to found their own churches. The sectarian position in Scotland in the eighteenth century is complicated. Neither Episcopalians nor

Roman Catholics made much headway or enjoyed much popular support, except among immigrant Englishmen and Irishmen to whom they were the link with home. The English Methodist preachers had some superficial success. George Whitefield in particular aroused great popular enthusiasm which culminated in 1742 in the 'Cambuslang wark', a hysterical but ephemeral religious 'revival' in the west of Scotland. Methodist organisation, however, never put down deep roots in Scotland. Most native groups who rebelled from Calvinist theology, like the Glasites (founded in 1730 by John Glas, minister of Tealing near Dundee) with their stress on Christian love and their belief in the voluntary nature of religion, and the followers of Robert Haldane (a retired sea-captain who in 1797 effectively began Congregationalism in Scotland), failed to gain any large measure of popular support. In this sense, therefore, the non-Presbyterian churches were unimportant.

On the other hand, the Church of Scotland itself split badly in the eighteenth century. In 1740 the General Assembly expelled four ministers led by Ebenezer Erskine, the minister of Stirling, who had formed the most implacable opposition to the Patronage Act. Erskine and his friends represented in most ways the stern traditions of the old Covenanters, leavened but not mollified by the theology of an eighteenth-century divine, Thomas Boston, whose republication of an old English pious book, Edward Fisher's *Marrow of Modern Divinity* in 1718, had caused acute controversy by playing down the doctrine of predestination without slackening any insistence on the need for grace or on the duty of diligent performance of personal Christian piety. The secession of 1740 ultimately resulted in the emergence not of one but of four new dissenting Presbyterian churches, the Old Licht Burghers and the New Licht Burghers, the Old Licht Anti-Burghers and the New Licht Anti-Burghers. Their names described stubbornly held differences about the lawfulness of taking oaths to the civil authorities and about whether the historic covenants were literally binding or whether some departure from them might in time be appropriate. The two New Licht groups, who represented the less ossified view that the seventeenth-century covenants were not binding for ever, did come together in 1820 to form the United Secession Church. A second secession from the Church of Scotland in 1752 produced yet another body, the Relief Church, led by Thomas Gillespie of Dunfermline. It had little in common with the churches of the first secession, being much more liberal in outlook and influenced by

English non-conformists. None of these churches made any attempt to join the Cameronians of 1690, who in the eighteenth century were reorganised to form the Reformed Presbyterian Church.

Various points need to be made from this complex story. Firstly, the total of dissenting Presbyterians in time became substantial: by 1820 the United Secession Church itself had 280 congregations, and its headquarters lay on the western side of the Central Belt of Scotland, perhaps especially in Glasgow where forty per cent of the population by 1819 were dissenters. Most of the dissenters were much more puritan and more earnest than the established church, deploring such lapses from grace as the statute prohibiting prosecutions for witchcraft, and continuing to practise a stern form of kirk-stool discipline after it had lapsed elsewhere. They appealed in particular to the lower middle class, the peasants and the artisans: indeed it could be argued that the real reason why the first secession was so successful was not because of the theological aspects of the patronage question but because patronage exercised by heritors produced ministers who had nothing in common with the bulk of their parishioners. How the humble man in the pew must have warmed to the sermons of Ebenezer Erskine: 'I can find no warrant from the word of God to confer the spiritual privileges of His house upon the rich beyond the poor; whereas by this Act the man with the gold ring and the gay clothing is preferred unto the man with the vile raiment and poor attire'.[16] Lastly, the departure from the Church of Scotland of so many earnest puritan leaders with a wide popular appeal, and their subsequent failure to make common cause either with one another or with sympathetic elements inside the established church, made the position of the Moderates' opponents within the church very weak.

The Moderates had always had opponents, known as the 'evangelicals' or the 'high flyers', whose tenets were not very dissimilar to those of Ebenezer Erskine but who were not willing to join him in secession. From about 1762 until after 1780 they were almost completely powerless. Then, when command over the Moderate party in the General Assembly passed from Principal William Robertson of Edinburgh University to Principal George Hill of St. Andrews University, their prestige rose by contrast to that of the party in power: 'under Hill Moderatism took on ugly features, becoming little more than the Dundas interest at prayer, with nepotism and pluralism the main order of service'.[17] Their revival was enormously helped by the adherence to the evangelical cause of Thomas Chalmers in 1811, the most intellectually gifted and dedicated of the young ministers of the early nineteenth century whose first major impact on Scottish affairs was caused by the success of his ministry in the poor working-class district of St. Johns in Glasgow during the destitution of 1815–23. Although the Evangelicals did not gain a majority in the General Assembly until 1833, it could certainly be said that with the increase of their influence at this time, and the formation of the United Secession Church in 1820, the last decade of our period was experiencing a resurgence of the forces that would favour puritan attitudes. The significant fact, however, is that for three-quarters of a century such forces had been too weak and too disunited to prevent an important change towards permissiveness over a very wide sector of society.

In the Established Church, the erosion of puritanism can be traced in a variety of different directions. In the second quarter of the eighteenth century it was already becoming unusual for the General Assembly to call for a fast; such exercises in national repentance were henceforth reserved for harvest failures and military defeats. Then it became less usual for the minister and elders to visit the congregation in their own homes to see whether they were practising family worship and to examine them on their beliefs. 'Catechetical and scriptural examinations of sections of the parish in succession were by degrees greatly, if not wholly discontinued', wrote an Ayrshire secession minister speaking with deep disapproval of his brethren in the Church of Scotland about 1780.[18] Again, it became rarer to use the kirk stool as an instrument of punishment by public example. As early as the seventeenth century it had been possible under some circumstances to compound public appearances with a fine paid to the session on behalf of the poor. As the eighteenth century progressed this became general, and there was a sharp decline in the practice of public rebuke, particularly between 1760 and 1790: in some places, such as Alyth near Dundee in 1761, the change is brought about by a session decision that 'such as decline going to the ordinary place of repentance shall pay twelve lib. of penalty', or by the habit at Carluke (Lanarkshire) of requiring at most a single public appearance, and more generally a private rebuke administered by the session combined with a fine.[19] Burns's success with the Kilmarnock edition of his poetry satirising the kirk-session for the public humiliation of his friend Gavin Hamilton was so great because educated and articulate opinion in the kirk had come to view the kirk stool, not as a symbol of godly discipline, but as a symbol of pettymindedness and tyranny. Even fines, at the end of the eighteenth century, were getting rarer, and were exacted almost entirely for sexual offences, drunkenness or breaches of sabbath observances. Many Moderate clergy forbore even to exact these, though there was some resurgence of older disciplinary ideas as the evangelical party revived, and they had never been abandoned by the dissenters.

Puritanism, of course, did not die without a fight. One of the most celebrated contests, which may help to establish something of the chronology of the decline of puritanism, was over the question of the theatre. Scottish Presbyterians since 1574 had always set their face sternly against the temptations and worldly horrors of the playhouse, which according to some, was 'the actual temple of the Devil where he frequently appeared clothed in a corporeal substance and possessed the spectators whom he held as his worshippers'.[20] In 1715 a band of English players visited the capital: at intervals in the 1720s and 1730s they returned again. Continually pursued by the magistrates and denounced by the presbytery they lived on the very edges of the law, but in the 1740s the theatre gained a permanent building in Edinburgh (disguised as a concert hall) and a considerable popular following. Then, just before Christmas 1756, the capital was electrified by the production of the 'Tragedy of Douglas', a sensationally popular play made doubly sensational by the fact that it had been written by one minister, John Home of Athelstaneford, and presented in the very obvious presence of another, the redoubtable and flamboyant Alexander Carlyle of Inveresk, who for good measure got himself publicly involved in a scuffle with a drunk in the audience. Both men were notable members of the Moderate party and had powerful friends in the General Assembly; the attack upon them by the outraged high flyers had therefore to move circumspectly. It was commenced by the Edinburgh Presbytery suspending the humble minister of Liberton for attending the play in January 1757: 'he owned the charge but pleaded by way of alleviation that he had gone to the playhouse only once and endeavoured to conceal himself in a corner to avoid giving offence'. From this they moved to bigger prey—Home 'spontaneously' resigned his charge, and Carlyle was rebuked by the General Assembly, who, however, acquitted him of the charge of having broken church law, while enacting that in future no minister of the Church of Scotland 'do, upon any occasion, attend the theatre'.[21] Time, however, crumbled even this new bastion: in 1784, when Mrs. Siddons appeared on the Edinburgh stage, the General Assembly altered its timetable to allow the clerical delegates the opportunity of attending the matinee performances of that great actress. The first theatre to be publicly licensed in Edinburgh without having to resort to the subterfuge of putting on 'a concert of musick with a play between the acts' was erected in 1764. In the same year, a mob in Glasgow burnt down the first permanent theatre there on its opening night. Even in the west, the populace gradually became accustomed to dramatic art, however, and by the nineteenth century were confirmed and enthusiastic theatre-goers.

The ministers who went to see Mrs Siddons were also the ministers upon whom Sir John Sinclair prevailed to send in descriptions of their parishes for the *Statistical Account*. One has only to turn the pages of that remarkable compilation to see them come to life, not as pastors, but as intelligent gentlemen sowing clover, speculating on ornithology, applauding a new linen work or a new road, agitated over the expense of poor relief, nervous of the effect of rising wages on rural virtue and watchful for any signs of idleness among the labouring classes. While it could well be argued that the weight of the established church thrown behind the cause of economic growth was not a small contribution to the welfare of Scottish society, there were others who saw the ministers as betrayers of a great charge.

Declining the active and energetic discharge of the duties of their spiritual and evangelical functions, too many of the pledged servants of the Lord betook themselves to literary study, or the culture of their glebes, perhaps farms, or to other secular concerns. They cultivated connection with the upper classes of society in their parishes, declining intercourse with those of low degree to whom the Gospel is preached, and set themselves earnestly so to arrange matters connected with the poor as to save expense to the heritors.[22]

This was a very fair comment. It comes from the pen of a secession minister, whose own church represented older and more conservative values which were still held to among the Presbyterian dissenters and among some Church of Scotland congregations with Evangelical ministers. As we have seen, the dissenting ministers were always a good deal more puritan, a good deal slower to abolish public appearances on the stool of repentance, and much more insistent upon the need for family worship and instruction. They also drew their main support from lower down the social scale than the ministers of the establishment. They had the character of stern, pious and perhaps melancholy men, but never of flatterers or of trimmers to the winds of moderation and favour.

It is not impossible that there was a peculiar value for Scottish society in the contrast between the traditionalists in the church, both dissenters and Evangelicals, and the Moderates, the one representing a relatively lower-class milieu in which traditional values were instilled into the child by religious instruction in family worship and in church, the other a relatively upper-class milieu in which the church no longer taught a repressive creed, but invited intellectual enquiry over a very wide spectrum of human activity. People moving up the social scale from one environment to the other may have found a remarkable momentum from the contrast: the traditionalists equipping them from childhood with the ability and wish to seek a definite objective in society through disciplined effort, and the Moderates opening up to them an enormous range of possible objectives of which their society approved other than the purely religious one—especially in the spheres of intellectual, artistic and economic achievement, in which so many Scots excelled at the turn of the eighteenth and nineteenth centuries. Robert Burns and Thomas Carlyle, for example, had poor, infinitely pious fathers who carefully and gently instructed them as children in a traditionalist religious environment, and then, when launched as adults into a world of middle- and upper-class approbation, these children were able to maximise their enormous literary potential in a purely secular way. It is hard to believe there could have been such a cultural flowering as there was in Scotland in the reign of George III had all the church been as stern as it was immediately after 1690. It is equally hard to feel that those who sprang from solid Calvinist backgrounds had not gained some special benefit from the earnest character of their upbringing which could be utilised in a freer atmosphere. Such ideas are easy to formulate but hard to prove. The reader must judge for himself whether they receive any support from the following chapters of this history.

CHAPTER X

The Transformation
of the Economy

I. THE PRELUDE TO THE TAKE-OFF, 1690–1780

Modern economists, struggling as they are in a world of underutilised natural resources and rapidly growing populations, are obsessed by the problems of how to produce fast growth in underdeveloped countries. Economic historians, trying to examine parallel phenomena in the past, are similarly obsessed by what they refer to as the industrial revolution or the 'take-off'—that unique point in the history of each advanced modern society in the world at which the national economy changed gear from a 'traditional' situation of sluggish change to a 'modern' situation of growth and continuous expansion. Before this point is reached, a traditional economy shows, to a greater or lesser extent, all the main characteristics of the underdeveloped world today: most people get their living from the land, they are poor, generally under-nourished and badly housed, and own little in the way of material possessions; the rate of innovation is so slow that decades and even centuries may go by without appreciable material progress being made by the bulk of society, or by anyone at all.

The 'take-off', by contrast, inaugurates a more or less inevitable and self-sustaining progression towards a modern economy, although it may be very many years before the 'modern' features in society are sufficiently well-established to overshadow those of the traditional situation. The take-off's most obvious feature is fast industrialisation, though it is also frequently characterised by a previous, or a near-simultaneous, transformation in agriculture. Nevertheless, farming and rural life inevitably decline in importance before the explosive vitality

240

of the urban and industrial sectors, and the force of this rupture may produce social confusion so great that many intelligent observers in all ranks of society will deplore the fact that it ever happened. In the long run, however, as self-sustained growth becomes the norm, very great benefits accrue from the industrial revolution. It becomes possible, for example, for a new kind of level of personal consumption to be reached as the bulk of the population acquires an enormous variety of material goods: it becomes possible, for the first time, to finance a programme of social justice through a welfare state that will redistribute resources to the needy and poor. We have not, in modern Britain, yet attained either universal affluence or perfect social justice: but the gains from two centuries of self-sustained growth since the take-off have brought us within reach of a material Utopia of which our ancestors even in their wildest dreams would not have ventured to imagine.

Most historians today would regard the take-off in Scotland and in England as part of the same phenomenon, beginning around 1780, associated in Scotland mainly with the advent of the cotton textile industry and the dramatic acceleration of agricultural change that began towards the close of the American War. Most would also agree that for half a century before there had been significant changes in the Scottish economy which helped to make a breakthrough possible in the 1780s. They would agree that even by 1825 Scotland was still predominantly a rural country, with almost as many features of the old economy remaining as of the new one emerging. It is not our place here to usurp the role of the economic historian and account for the pace and timing of the Scottish take-off: we must content ourselves with the simpler role of giving a chronological account of the main developments in the Scottish economy up to and after the turning point, and within the period 1690 to 1825, as background to the social changes with which the remainder of the book will deal.

In 1690, and for half a century after that, Scotland showed in a peculiarly acute form all the evils of a traditional underdeveloped economy. Indeed, she was underdeveloped not only in the sense that all nations were before the first industrial revolution took place in Britain at the end of the eighteenth century, but also in the sense that she was poorer and more backward even in her pre-industrial economy than the states to which she most frequently compared herself— England, to which she was linked by a common king, and Holland and France with which she had close cultural ties. Then again, the limited and jerky, but nevertheless perceptible, upward progress that had characterised the economy for a hundred years before 1690 seemed to be grinding to a halt. War broke out against France, bringing a string of commercial troubles in its train: this partly masked and partly exacerbated the trouble in which many Scottish merchants and producers found themselves due to their growing inability to meet competition in the traditional export markets of Europe. And what they lost on the European swings they could not, thanks to tariffs and restrictions imposed by the English on the Border, make up on the British roundabouts.

The difficulties and depressions of the commercial sector, however, were soon overshadowed by the universal calamity of famine. Grain was short in some counties in 1695; the harvest failed badly and universally in 1696, bringing death to many the following spring; recovery from this was very incomplete when the crops failed again in 1698, and again the next year in many areas in 1699. We shall never know how many people died: contemporaries spoke of a fifth, or a quarter, or a third or even more of the inhabitants having died or fled in some areas, and from what we know of similar disasters in other north European countries in the seventeenth century, they could have been right. Jacobites regarded the famine as evidence of God's wrath against Presbyterians: Presbyterians as evidence of God's wrath against the sins of a stiff-necked people. It was a terrible instance of the vulnerability of a primitive economy to bad weather, but although it stimulated the first two or three printed tracts on agricultural improvement no-one at all regarded the possibility of building an economy that would reduce and ultimately avert calamity on this scale.

Yet, paradoxically, it was at about this point in history that the Scots first began to consider economic growth as an objective at which society should aim. They did not express it like this—they merely saw themselves as a poorer nation than their neighbours, and they came to believe they could end this state of affairs by a mixture of planning and patriotic effort. Their first determined effort in this direction was the attempt to emulate England and Holland by seizing part of the colonial trade which had contributed so much to the affluence of those countries: it collapsed, as is well known, in the failure of the Darien scheme and the virtual bankruptcy of the 'Company of Scotland' to which the Scottish people had committed so much both in money and in hopes in the years after 1695. The eighteenth century began in an atmosphere of gloom and despondency, in a trade depression, the shadow of famine and the crushing news of the loss of the colony: Scotland was resigned at this point, wrote Sir John Clerk of Penicuik years later, 'to sit down under all these losses and misfortunes and in a kind of glade poverty live on what remain'd'.[1]

Within five years of the final denouement at Darien, however, events had taken a new turn with the achievement of the Union of Parliaments. Its causes were highly complex: economic interest was one strand among many, but not the least important. Many Scots saw as a panacea for Scotland's poverty the creation of a British common market: the brilliant and biting pen of Daniel Defoe, England's visiting propagandist in Edinburgh, dwelt upon the opportunities in such a common market for Scottish cattle and linen cloth sold in London with the tariff barriers down—there would be such a flow of money and capital north that Scotland's balance of payments problem would vanish like the dew, and finance would be available at last for the exploitation of Scotland's own natural resources, such as her fisheries, her forests and her lead mines.[2] It was an argument that went down very well, since for nearly twenty years Scottish trade to Europe had been in decay while Scotland's exports to England had gained in importance throughout the seventeenth century. If most Scots regretted the passing of their parliament, they sweetened the pill with the expectation that the economy would quickly show a big improvement.

For a generation and more they were utterly disappointed and Union proved as useless a panacea as Darien. Linen consignments to England probably rose, but failed to develop their potential before 1740 because the quality of what the Scots had to sell was too low to match continental competition in London. Cattle exports rose, but supply proved disappointingly inelastic as long as they were limited by hide-bound stockrearing practices in the north. The tobacco trade with America developed, but Glasgow found it had to push hard (and smuggle hard) to muscle in on a market occupied for a century by English merchants in near-monopoly conditions.[3] There was no quick break-through anywhere along the line. On the other hand, the harm that Union did to the Scottish economy is usually greatly exaggerated. Native Scottish industries were not much disturbed, let alone ruined, by English competition: the trading burghs of the east coast did not all decay on the morrow of Union: the country was certainly not 'bled white' by heavy taxes imposed on the Scots and sent south to swell the

English exchequer, though all these allegations are frequently made. The biggest loss was probably brought about by the heavy expenditure of rents raised in Scotland by noblemen and lairds travelling and living in England.

The decade before the middle of the century does, however, mark an important new beginning in Scottish economic history. The ice began to break. Slow and unspectacular at first, the process of change then began to accelerate in the 1760s, until by the outbreak of the American War in 1775 practically all classes in Scottish society were conscious of a momentum which was carrying them towards a richer society. With the wisdom of historical hindsight we can see that Scotland was beginning to move with England towards the watershed of the industrial revolution: we can see that the movement depended partly on the Union, and that Defoe's optimism no longer looked facile—it was above all the response of the linen trade, the cattle trade and the tobacco trade to stimuli that originated in England that carried the economy forward, and the close connection between the two countries allowed the immediate transmission of technological advances from the one to the other. What mattered more to contemporaries was that both national income and income per head were rising in a way no-one had had any experience of in the past. In the place of passive resignation to poverty, there was a lightening of the spirit that showed through every aspect of Scottish life and culture.

Some of the material progress in this first prelude to the take-off can be partially illuminated by the primitive production and trade statistics that are available to us for the period. Linen cloth, Scotland's premier industry given Government help by export subsidies and by funds disbursed through the Board of Trustees for Manufactures had markets at home, in England and in the plantations. Output rose three-fold in volume and four-fold in value between the years 1736–40 and 1768–72—nearly thirteen million yards were woven yearly at the latter date. Imports of tobacco from Chesapeake Bay in America increased still more—from eight million pounds in 1741 to forty-seven million pounds in 1771: the Scottish share of the British tobacco trade similarly rose from ten per cent in 1738 to fifty-two per cent in 1769 largely because Scottish enterprise proved better fitted than English to meet the rising tide of demand for tobacco from the French. Nearly all tobacco that came in was re-exported, thereby providing Scotland with something to sell to the Continent and rejuvenating her old European commercial connections. A new branch of this was the trade from Russia to import flax for the linen industry. In seeking out this new market at the far end of the Baltic, East Coast merchants to some degree matched the enterprise of their West Coast brethren who were founding stores, lending credit and organising the trade in tobacco on the other side of the Atlantic. Sailings to Russia increased from twelve ships a year in the early 1730s to 120 ships in the early 1770s. There are no general statistics of Scottish foreign commerce until 1755, but between then and 1771 the official value of imports rose by two and a half times, and of exports (including re-exports) by three and a half times: at the same time the share of Scotland in British foreign trade rose from less than five per cent to about ten per cent of the total. On the other hand, since in 1762 for example eighty-five per cent of imports and fifty-two per cent of exports consisted of tobacco, these commercial statistics can give a misleading impression of Scottish economic growth as a whole. Glasgow's entrepot trade, important though it was, brought prosperity mainly to a group of merchants and financiers in that city. Of course, some of that prosperity spilled over from the enclave when orders were placed in the Borders for shoes, or in Dunfermline for linen and in Musselburgh for woollens, all to be exported to America to help buy more tobacco: but the Glasgow traders also often placed orders for such goods in Liverpool or Belfast. All in all the repercussions from a trade of this kind tend to be very much less important than from one in which the main commodity is (as it became later) a Scottish manufacture.

Simultaneously with the rise in overseas trade there was the growth of a strong banking system consisting of the Bank of Scotland (from 1695), the Royal Bank of Scotland (from 1727), the British Linen Company (from 1746, but still in this period entirely concerned in financing the linen trade) and a number of unchartered joint-stock banks and partnerships. These were both a sign of and an assistance to economic development: it has been calculated that the total assets of Scottish banks rose from around £600,000 in 1750 to around £3,700,000 in 1770.

Developments in other sectors of the economy, particularly in the vital sector of agriculture, cannot be so quickly illustrated. It does, however, seem clear that by 1775 important changes were in the air throughout the length and breadth of the country. In at least a few places in every county farmers and landowners were trying their hand at new techniques and introducing new crops, like clover and turnips, that enabled them to send more beasts to the Falkirk tryst for sale to the English drovers. They were using improved implements, like the handy iron plough invented by the Berwickshire farmer James Small, and enclosing and dividing the landscape into its modern pattern of compact fields, windbreaks, woods and individual stone-built farms. Only in a very few areas had this process gone far enough to create a real 'revolution' in rural life. It had probably gone furthest in the Lothians, on some estates of the north-east and on black-cattle lands in Ayrshire and Dumfriesshire; but even in these regions it is unlikely that as much as a third of the total land surface was yet enclosed. In other and remoter areas there seemed to have been hardly any stirring at all except, perhaps, a new awareness of the possibilities of the cattle trade encouraged by the probing of the drovers who were now reaching even to the furthest islands in search of supplies for London. Despite the example of noted improvers, therefore, the great age of agricultural change still lay in the future on the eve of the American War.

The same was even more true of industrial change despite the striking success of linen textiles. Although (compared to 1740) there were by 1775 more and deeper coal and lead mines, and a good many more minor manufacturing concerns such as paper-mills, snuff-mills, linen works, soap works, dye works, glass works, distilleries, breweries and small foundries, there were not yet so many more as to make the sort of dramatic impression on contemporaries of a surging industrial sector that one sees thirty years later. Scotland still seemed backward compared to the South. The typical industrial unit was still a single master working with an apprentice and a journeyman within the framework of craft regulations on premises no bigger than a backyard. The one or two large capital-intensive concerns, like Prestonpans Vitriol Works (begun in 1749) and Carron Iron Works (founded in 1759) and the lead mines at Leadhills and Wanlockhead (greatly enlarged in this period) stood out mainly because of their novelty, though it was true that in their field they could stand comparison with most in England, and even in England the large concern was still the rare exception. But like the slowly growing New Town of Edinburgh (begun in 1767) and the newly projected Forth and Clyde Canal (of which the first sod was cut in 1768 and the last dug out in 1790) they were important mainly as symbols that Scotland was a country on the move.

To this prosperity events in the 1770s offered a temporary and unforeseen check. In 1772, the generous giant among the Scottish unchartered joint-stock banks, the Ayr Bank, collapsed amid the ruins of its over-liberal lending policy. The reverberations of its fall were hardly over when in 1775 the American War broke out. The tobacco merchants, however, had foreseen the breach, and for the most part pulled out their money in time: they were remarkably successful in finding new openings in the West Indies. If none of the available statistics of the period 1775–1783 show much advance, it is no less significant that they show little loss compared to the level of the 1760s. The outward events of the decade recalled the 1690s: there was war, there was collapse of a great company, there was even a bad failure of the harvest (only the second of the eighteenth century) in 1782–3. In 1772 the London press was not far out when, in reporting the consequences of the Ayr Bank crash, it said 'all the buildings and agricultural improvements in that country have stopped . . . the new town between Edinburgh and Leith is suddenly stopped. In short the same shock has now been given to Scotland as in King William's reign when the Darien Company was broke and the massacre of Glenco happened'.[5] But the fact that the economic results of these onslaughts were relatively transient and insubstantial was itself a measure of the progress of the economy since the late seventeenth century. And it stood now on the brink of great things.

2. THE INDUSTRIAL REVOLUTION, 1780–1820

The Industrial Revolution may be compared with the Reformation as an event that stopped and turned the current of man's social life into new and unfamiliar channels; it must not be imagined on that account that Scotland broke out of one, rural, traditional world and stumbled into a new, industrial, technological one overnight. From 1780 onwards her swelling towns and expanding industries gave a new and dynamic rhythm to her economic life: but, within those towns, more people lived even in 1830 by traditional craft methods than by the technology of steam and factory. And even by 1830 a great many more people lived in a rural environment, as they always had done, than in a town: but on the other hand, even in the remotest extremities and the farthest islands, rural life in many essential respects was radically different from what it had been even half a century before. These forty-five years were a muddled age of transition, and the historian finds himself torn between emphasising the way in which the new and dramatic was carrying all before it, and the ways in which tradition survived, in harmony or in conflict with innovation, to dominate great areas of social existence.

The crucial decades were the 1780s and 1790s. It was then that cotton grew with unparallelled speed from virtually nothing to become by far the greatest industry; it was then the pace of change in agriculture quickened so suddenly as to leave the laggard, and not the improver, as the exception who was laughed at by those who followed the rule. All that came after, in the first quarter of the nineteenth century, though impressive in aggregate, was no more than a logical extension of the changes set off in cotton and farming. It was not until Neilson's invention, and the subsequent development of Scottish heavy industry after 1828, that any important new ingredient was added to the process of economic growth and change.

Why the 1780s? The question of the origins of the industrial revolution is one for British economic history, not for Scottish alone: and even so, the closest analysis has found the 'causes' of the industrial revolution elusive. Clearly it would not have occurred unless British social and economic development had already reached a certain high plateau. British society had become within the previous century politically stable and orderly; social mobility from class to class was possible in a way that was unusual by European standards, and economic success by an individual could prove the stepping stone to social success in a higher group through the general respect accorded to 'property'. Again, England in particular had for centuries enjoyed traditions of industrial activity in textile manufacture, the mining of coal and the working of metals that even in a pre-industrial society affected a larger proportion of the population and a wider area of the countryside than anywhere else in Europe. Industrial and commercial success had bred in England an unusually substantial middle-class. Then the eighteenth-century market was a peculiarly buoyant one for the British. At home, not only was population rising, but it was (at least in the south of England) regarded by many foreigners as a population much more able and accustomed to spend money on industrial goods than the European peasants who spent their income mainly on food: abroad, the British foreign market was vastly enlarged by imperial expansion in North

Plan of the upper Floor

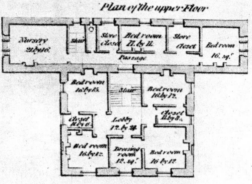

Plan of the First Floor

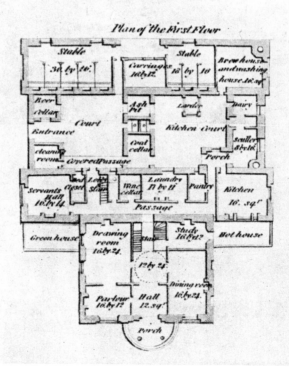

Design for a gentleman farmer. "A House for proprietors of moderate fortune who reside on and cultivate their own estates". This would have cost just over £3,000 to build about 1814

Cockfighting at an Edinburgh pit, 1785. The first book on the sport in
Scotland was published in 1705, and thereafter it became popular throughout many parts of the country. The crowd in this illustration is drawn from
many social levels: contrast it with the crowd in church facing page 97

America, India and the Caribbean, into which manufactured articles could be poured and from which imports could be drawn under conditions of virtual monopoly. On the supply side, the natural resources of Britain, in coal and ore and fertile land, had always been rich: transport improvements in roads, rivers and canal navigation undertaken since 1650 were making them accessible as never before. Above all there were the triumphs of technology systematically applied for the first time to the problems of production—Watt's steam-engine, Arkwright's water-frame, Crompton's spinning-mule, Cort's iron-puddling process: these were the key inventions that gave the 1780s their special spurt and drive. These, in a very brief summary, were the main ingredients of the take-off in Britain—but in what proportions they were mixed, and just how their mixing created the chain reaction that led to self-sustained economic growth is a question economic historians may argue about to the end of time.

It would still hardly be an adequate explanation of the take-off in Scotland to say that it occurred here in the 1780s because it occurred in the south of Britain at the same time. Scottish ability to take immediate advantage of the advance in the south rested on the new strength of her own economy, built up before 1780, and on the fact of Union. The prosperity of the cattle trade had provided new money and new horizons to many who would be in the van of Scottish agrarian change in the next decades. The prosperity of linen had provided capital and experience to many small men who would later switch over to the cotton trade: it had also forged a business link between Scotland and Lancashire through which the new textile technology would be transmitted north. The prosperity of foreign trade, especially of Glasgow's tobacco trade, gave backbone to an economy that had to export to grow, and, as Rostow puts it, it was fruitful in the production of

> men devoted to commerce: men concerned with fine calculations of profit and loss, men of wide horizons whose attitudes communicated themselves in various ways throughout their societies.[6]

We need not stop here: it is notable that, for whatever reason, throughout later eighteenth-century Scottish society there were many, not in the ranks of merchants alone, but among those born to be landowners and farmers, to be university professors, lawyers and clergymen, even to be craftsmen and small retailers, who were no less truly men of wide horizons—'devoted to commerce and concerned with fine calculations of profit and loss'—destined to overturn the conservative traditions of Scottish economic behaviour and to direct her energies in a new and dynamic way. Men like these were in many ways the prime economic asset of their country. The sweeping excitement of the years after 1780 would certainly have been impossible without them, and their emergence had, to a degree, preceded the crucial decades of change.

What actually happened in the 1780s, the 1790s and the succeeding years? It would be very convenient to present a statistical series to illustrate the scale of change: in some directions we have figures that throw light on it, but often those sectors we most want to illustrate in this way remain the most obscure. One of the two great areas of advance was in agriculture: we have no figures of agricultural productivity, but we do know in broad terms that between 1770 and 1820 Scottish population rose by about one half, that contemporaries regarded it as much better fed at the latter date, that exports of meat had risen and imports of grain probably not altered at all in proportion to the increase of population. On these grounds it is logical to estimate that over the whole country Scottish farms produced well over fifty per cent more food than they had done before. This is a low minimum figure. Contemporaries like George Robertson (a careful and shrewd observer not given to overstatement) put the increase well above that. Writing of the period from 1740 until 1829, but commenting that most of improvement took place after 1774, he said: 'There is now brought to market more than double the quantity of provisions that was formerly produced on the land altogether. It would perhaps be nearer the mark to say that the quantity of corn and other vegetables has been doubled, whilst that of animal food has been increased to six times the former extent'.[7]

For the vital parts of manufacturing industry, the statistics appear a little more direct and helpful. We can measure the impact of the industrial revolution on the export trade by the fact that shipments of British-produced goods from Scottish ports rose more than two-and-a-half times from the early 1770s to the late 1790s: from £0.5 million per annum, 1770–1774, to £1.35 million, 1796–1800. By 1810–1814 the figure was over £5 million. Most of the increase was cotton: its growth is partly measured by the leaping imports of raw cotton wool into the Clyde: 0.15 million pounds per annum, 1770–1774; 2.0 million pounds in 1789—then great leaps to 2.8 million in 1798, 3.2

million in 1799, 4.8 million in 1800, 7.5 million in 1801. There was certainly further growth between 1801 and 1825, but the series gives out at this point. Only a proportion of the cotton made up in Scotland was directly imported into the Clyde. A large amount appears to have come in after 1800 as fine yarn sent from the great Manchester cotton-spinning firms of McConnell and Kennedy and A. and G. Murray to the weavers of fine cloths in Glasgow and Paisley. Some of the buoyancy here is perhaps indicated by the growth of capital in the former concern, from just over £9,000 in 1797 to almost £90,000 by 1810.[8]

Cotton is often thought of as displacing the linen industry; it did indeed do so in the west, but the linen industry's output continued to grow—it rose from thirteen million yards a year in the early 1770s, to twenty-two million yards by the late 1790s, and then to thirty-one million yards by 1818–1822. Textiles as a whole were undoubtedly the dominant sector: Sir John Sinclair thought they employed about nine out of ten workers in 'manufacturing industry' (in the ratio of six workers in cotton to three in linen to one in woollens), and gave the nearest outsider, the 'iron manufacture' only half as many workers as those employed in woollens. It is always hard to know how much weight to give his statistical generalisations, but if this is a guess it is probably as well-informed as any contemporary could make.[9]

One of the most interesting (and trustworthy) fragments of statistical information, however, relates to the buoyant little industry of paper-making: rising output of paper relates not only to the efficiency of the manufacturers but also to the thirst of business consumers (who wanted it in large quantities for packaging goods) and of the general literary public (for whose use it is made into newspapers, books and stationery). Between 1740 and 1744 Scottish mills produced a mere 80 tons a year—the 'prelude to the take-off' is measured by the fact that this had risen to 390 tons by 1770–1774: there is then a three-fold leap in the next twenty years (to 1,140 tons by 1796–1800) and a further doubling in the first generation of the nineteenth century (2,400 tons by 1820–1824). The last figure is thirty times as great as the first—it is a vivid shaft of light on three-quarters of a century of cultural and economic change.[10]

Statistics alone, however, are too arid to convey the sense of wonder and excitement with which contemporaries viewed the changes in the world about them. For this, in its full flavour, one must turn the pages of the *Statistical Account*, compiled in the 1790s, and pause at a passage like this one, where the minister of Meigle in lowland Perthshire considers the changes in local agriculture since 1745:

> At that time the state of the country was rude beyond conception. The most fertile tracts were waste, or indifferently cultivated, and the bulk of the inhabitants were uncivilized. The education, manners, dress, furniture and table of the gentry were not so liberal, decent and sumptuous as those of ordinary farmers at present. The common people clothed in the coarsest garb, and starving on the meanest fare, lived in despicable huts with their cattle . . . To emancipate the inhabitants of this country from such a state of barbarism and to rouse a spirit of industry was a bold and arduous enterprise. A gentleman distinguished for his rank, fortune and public spirit undertook and accomplished the task . . . in a few years improvements were diffused through the whole country. The tenant, as if awakened out of a profound sleep, looked around, beheld his fields clothed with the richest harvests, his herds fattening in luxuriant pastures, his family decked in gay attire, his table loaded with solid fare, and wondered at his former ignorance and stupidity. The landlord rejoiced . . .The manufacturer, mechanic and tradesman redoubled their efforts to supply the increasing demand for the conveniences and elegancies of life.[11]

In the minister's prose it has the quality of a fairy story, at once simple and miraculous. It is almost impossible to believe that everyone did not live happily ever afterwards, or that poverty, resentment and bitterness could survive the busy transformation of enclosing and marling, of sowing turnips and selling cattle, building farms and clearing 'yirdfast' boulders from the earth. Writers of a generation later than this were more conscious of the tensions that the rapid disintegration of traditional society had given rise to, and of the disappointments and frustrations that so often followed the first attempts to transform life in an area like the Highlands. But in the 1790s it still was the first golden dawn of the new farming, and only a Jeremiah raised doubts.

One of the interesting contrasts between the earlier and later writers is the extent to which those of the 1790s were aware that the transformation taking place about them on the land was based almost completely on an alien technology. Almost everything was borrowed from the south: methods of enclosure, ideas of rotation, the new crops like clover, rye-grass, turnips and potatoes. The writers of the 1820s dwell much more on the very important contributions the Scots themselves had made in the interim to the common fund of agricultural knowledge—they had not merely joined in the take-off, they had added so much to its impetus that 'Lothian husbandry' came to be held up for admiration in nineteenth-century England in much the same way as the 'Norfolk system' had been copied and admired in eighteenth-century Scotland. In two respects in particular the Scots led the way—they were brilliant in the design of agricultural implements, exemplified with Small's plough in 1763 but continued with the much more important inventions of Andrew Meikle's power-driven threshing-machine in 1786 and Patrick Bell's horse-drawn reaper in 1826: secondly, they pioneered modern field drainage, which in the later nineteenth century enabled the heavy and wet lands of Britain to undergo the kind of revolution hitherto restricted to lighter soils with natural drainage. Here the major breakthrough came with James Smith of Deanston's subsoil plough of 1823, but it had followed half a century of pioneering by a multitude of forgotten and half-forgotten farmers, men like James Anderson of Hermiston. Already by 1829 George Robertson could write of the

thousands and tens of thousands of ells of covered drains that have been made even in single farms of moderate extent, all the country over, in the course of the last sixty years . . . of all improvements in modern husbandry, none has given greater returns for the expenses incurred than this.[12]

And none, he would have added had he known it, had greater potential for raising the productivity of agriculture all over Europe in the following century.

The same story of an English technology, enthusiastically borrowed in the first instance and then still more enthusiastically adapted and advanced by native ingenuity, can be found in the cotton industry. Its genesis in the West of Scotland was, in two directions, a result of Lancashire activity. On the one hand, English manufacturers of yarn, finding their new jennies, waterframes and mules producing a surplus greater than they could sell locally looked north to the West of Scotland, where the skilled linen weavers had been underemployed and hungering for a fine yarn since the early 1770s. The result was a switch of Paisley and Glasgow men, weavers and merchants alike, from linens to cottons: their new skills and wide international contacts gave them an edge in competition that established English firms in the field soon felt—as the great Samuel Oldknow exclaimed from Lancashire in 1786: 'Scotch impudence and perseverance is beyond all'.[13] The genie seemed to be crawling out of its bottle.

Spinning came by a similar route—by the wish of Lancashire men and their friends to cut costs by settling in an area of abundant water-power and low wages. Here, said Arkwright after a visit to Glasgow in 1784 is 'a razor which would shave them all'—a good metaphor for an inventor who began life as a barber.[14] His contacts in the north were men in the textile trade already—Archibald Buchanan, from a family of 'English merchants' in Glasgow, who had served an apprenticeship in the master's mill at Cromford in Derbyshire; and David Dale, who climbed from a weaver to be a linen yarn dealer and importer and then founded the first of the great Scottish cotton-spinning factories at New Lanark in 1786 (as well as half-a-dozen more, from Spinningdale in Sutherland to Newton Stewart on the Solway). Soon there was a crescent of successful water-frame factories, lying in their own villages and using Arkwright's technology—places like New Lanark, Ballindalloch, Deanston, Catrine and Blantyre, situated so as to tap the cheap labour of the agricultural communities and to sell yarn to the weaving areas nearby. They were quickly joined by numbers of very small spinning concerns using hand-powered or water-powered jennies on the Hargreaves pattern in the weaving towns themselves. And everyone in the industry, whether they were weaving or spinning, using waterframes, jennies or mules, was aware of the debt to English experience and ingenuity.

It did not, however, take the Scots long before they began to make their own indigenous contributions to the technology of the cotton industry. It was Neil Snodgrass of Glasgow, for instance, who invented the scutching machine in 1797, the first satisfactory device for processing the wool before spinning, copied after a decade all over Lancashire. It was William Kelly, manager of Dale's mill at New Lanark, who first applied power to Crompton's mule in 1790. It was Archibald Buchanan of Deanston mills who in 1807 built the first integrated cotton mill in Britain where washing, scutching, spinning and weaving were all carried on by power. James Smith, his manager (the same who invented the subsoil plough) contributed a great deal to the improvement of the self-acting mule, the throstle and the carding engine between 1815 and 1836. These men and others like them were not content merely to follow Lancashire's lead, as the previous generation had had to be.[15]

It was, however, always one of the features of the Scottish cotton industry that handloom weaving remained for long the mainstay of the weaving side. In 1820 there were only about 2000 powerlooms in Scotland, compared to perhaps 50,000 handlooms. The explanation is not that Scotland was technically ignorant: it was partly a sign that she had a superfluity of cheap labour (see page 428 below) and partly that she specialised in the production of fine goods which the machines could not weave. The great Glasgow cotton merchant Kirkman Finlay put it like this in 1833:

> A great mistake exists in supposing that powerlooms supplant the handloom weaver . . . the latter can make a great many things which it would not be in the interest of any powerloom manufacturer to make, especially all the finest goods.[16]

In technical performance and entrepreneurial alertness the cotton industry in Scotland did not concede many points to its rivals in the first quarter of the nineteenth century.

The enormous upheavals in agriculture and in the cotton industry led to all kinds of ripples and repercussions extending far and wide through the body of the Scottish economy. It is impossible to trace them all. The demands on the cloth finishing industry led to a boom in bleaching, dyeing and printing: the sudden prosperity of the Vale of Leven, and the foundation of the St. Rollox chemical works to make bleaching powder (it became the biggest chemical works in the world), were two of the consequences. Then the technology of cotton proved applicable, after many teething troubles, to the fibres of flax and wool—the factory system spread out of the west to Dunfermline, Dundee and Arbroath (the great capitals of the linen trade) and ultimately to the hosiery and woollen towns of the Borders.

Factories ultimately learned to use steam rather than waterpower as their motive force: an even greater stimulus to the increased consumption of coal before 1825, however, probably came from the farmers, who needed enormous quantities with which to burn limestone to use as fertiliser on their acid fields. From this sprang another chain reaction. More coal meant more canals to carry it to the consumer. The Monkland Canal and the Forth-Clyde Canal were both finished in 1790, the Union canal in 1822: when that was done, the fine splint-coal of Lanarkshire was available to both Glasgow and Edinburgh, and (by the coasting trade) to all the main centres of population. More coal and lime carried by water demanded more and better roads to act as the capillary veins in the transport system: turnpike trusts and individual proprietors did much in the Lowlands, and the Government provided help to carry through Telford's programme of road and bridge building in the Highlands. More lime raised more barley: the abundance of barley went to feed the prosperity of breweries and distilleries; the fortunes of the great legal distilleries in the Lowlands, however, oscillated violently with changing levels of duty on ardent spirits—as the latter rose the former fell, for they were then heavily undercut by the little illicit stills operating throughout the country from the braes of Glenlivet to the cellars of Hutchesonstown (there was one in the crypt of the Tron Kirk in Edinburgh). It would be pointless to multiply examples: the pattern of economic consequences is infinite once the take-off is set in motion.

It is difficult to summarise the contemporary changes as they appeared to Scottish writers by the 1820s. They did not feel they had become a nation of town dwellers: there were still only seven towns of more than 10,000 inhabitants in 1801, and thirteen in 1821. Nor did they feel they had become machine-minders: agriculture, for all its changes, was as dependent as ever on heavy manual labour, and such basic activities as building, mining, baking, tanning, making shoes or clothes, were quite untouched by change; even in cotton, the most advanced and most 'mechanical' of all industries, probably only one weaver in twenty operated on a powerloom in 1820. What they did feel was the wonder that society had enlarged so immensely the scale and profitability of economic activity. Thus Sir John Sinclair on the steam engine:

It has increased indefinitely the mass of human comforts and enjoyments: and rendered the material of wealth and prosperity, every where cheap and accessible. It has armed the feeble hand of man with a power to which no limits can be assigned; completed the dominion of mind over the most refractory qualities of matter; and laid a sure foundation for all those future miracles of mechanic power which are to aid and reward the labours of after generations.[17]

To this extent they attributed material success to the technological innovations: it is this aspect of the industrial revolution that posterity, too, has dwelt upon. But Sinclair and his friends also saw the industrial revolution as a kind of moral triumph, the victory of industriousness over idleness, of sense over frivolity, of energy over waste:

> ... the spectacle ... of a people naturally possessed but of few territorial resources, and living in a bleak and unpropitious climate, employing their activity, their constancy, and their genius in triumphing over a sterile soil—directing their attention to the riches of the mind ... and making agriculture, manufacture and commerce, instruction, morality and liberty flourish together.[18]

This aspect of the industrial revolution may baffle the historian because he cannot measure 'industriousness' like imports of cotton wool or describe the downfall of 'indolence' like that of hand spinning: he may indeed be repelled by the whole censorious terminology of the middle-class moralists. But he ought to persist. If so many contemporaries spoke of a real and revolutionary change in the common outlook of society which equipped it to undertake the technical and economic revolution at the end of the eighteenth century, it is surely one job of the social historian to try and discover what they meant.

CHAPTER XI

The Population Problem

1. THE SCALE OF CHANGE AND THE PROBLEM OF GROWTH

In demographic history, the eighteenth and early nineteenth centuries saw a revolution in several ways comparable to the take-off in economic history. Population, which had hitherto grown only in fits and starts, with generations of stagnation and sudden, if short, catastrophic declines due to famine and disease, began in this period a dramatic increase, unprecedented in its continuity and size. At the same time, population was redistributed: though every country area in Scotland registered growth, it was the town population, hitherto very insignificant in the total, which grew at the greatest pace. Not every nuance in the relationship between the total increase of population and the economic revolution is yet very clear: but it must be obvious that the growing urbanisation was a direct result of industrial change. And it posed new problems because, as the *Guardian* put it in 1832, 'the manufacturing system as it exists in Great Britain, and the inconceivably rapid increase of immense towns under it, are without parallel in the history of the world'.

Before attempting to explain the revolution, we must first endeavour to show the scale of change between 1690 and 1828. This is not altogether straightforward. Since there were no earlier censuses or enumerations, it remains very uncertain what the population of Scotland was at any point before 1750. We must make do with a figure, bandied about at the time of the Union of 1707, which was probably no more than a plausible guess by an intelligent but unknown Scotsman, that the population was just over one million souls.[1] It must in any case have been rather lower at that point than early in the previous decade; the effects of the famine of 1696–1699, and the heavy mortality that accompanied and followed it, are unlikely to have been obliterated in seven years.

Our first clear picture is for the middle of the eighteenth century, and we owe it to the work of Dr. Alexander Webster, who, partly in order to satisfy his own intellectual curiosity, partly to fulfil a commission from the Government and partly to provide the basis of an annuity scheme for the widows and children of the clergy, used the ministers of the Church of Scotland (of which he himself was a leading and influential member) to enumerate the inhabitants of every parish in the country. Webster himself made carefully calculated adjustments to any returns that were incomplete. The result, it is generally agreed by those scholars who have examined it, can be treated as reasonably reliable, and in a different class from those other eighteenth-century investigations that merely embarked on 'the perilous seas of guess-work'.[2] External evidence suggests some of the preliminary work was done in the 1740s: on the other hand virtually all the returns relate to 1755 and it does now look as though it was the survey of a single year. It is in any case among the very earliest estimates of its kind in Europe.

Webster put the population at rather over 1,265,000. It seems likely both from comparison with the Union guess and from what we know of the growth of Edinburgh, Glasgow and one or two other towns, that already by 1755 population had begun its continuous expansion. Webster's population probably already exceeded the pre-famine figure in most rural areas.

Thereafter, figures exist for greater precision. The next satisfactory count was the census of 1801, giving a population of 1,608,000: ignoring an undoubted loss of some proportion of the natural increase by emigration, this gives a rise of just over one quarter in fifty years, or 0.6 per cent per annum since 1755. In the early nineteenth century the pace was quicker than that. A new census in 1811 put the population at 1,806,000, and in 1821 at 2,091,000, a rate of increase of 1.2 per cent per annum in the first decade and almost 1.6 per cent in the second— the latter is a velocity of population growth that has never been equalled again in Scottish history. In sum, the retained population of Scotland between 1755 and 1820 increased by roughly two-thirds in sixty-five years. That was the scale of growth.

The character of the redistribution can perhaps best be judged from a glance at the two tables on the facing page. Table I shows how population grew in every region of Scotland, as it grew, too, in every individual county: but the increase (after redistribution) was very much greater in the central belt than either to the north or the south. In 1755 just over half the people had lived north of a line from the Firth of Tay to the Firth of Clyde: by 1820 this proportion had dropped to two-fifths, and almost half the Scots now occupied the central belt where only thirty-seven per cent had lived before.

Table II deepens this picture by carrying it to the towns. There are several points to notice. Firstly, the main growth in the central belt is seen to have been in the western burghs. None of the first eight towns on the list was around the Clyde: six of them doubled their populations, but none—not even Edinburgh with her New Town—trebled it. Of the last five towns all except Falkirk were in the Clyde basin; all trebled their populations, Glasgow increased by more than four times (with an immense aggregate increase of more than 115,000 souls in seventy years), Greenock by more than five times and Paisley by more than six. Secondly, far more Scots lived in towns in 1820 than had been the case in 1750. At the first date there had been four towns of over 10,000 inhabitants, containing nine per cent of the population: by 1820 there were thirteen such towns, containing twenty-five per cent of the population. If one considers communities of over 4,000 inhabitants to be large enough to be called urban, then, in 1750, at most one Scot in eight was a townsman: by 1820 it was more like one Scot in three. Thirdly, the converse of this must be that even as late as 1820 seven Scots out of ten still lived in rural communities: the farm and the village were still not replaced as the typical social environment in which a man spent his life.

The causes of the population increase in eighteenth-century Britain have produced much debate among historians in recent decades, but we are as far from an agreed verdict as ever. Some light on the Scottish situation may be cast by considering the age-structure of the population as it was estimated by Webster for 1755 with that assessed by the compilers of the census returns in 1821. The histograms on page 265 (to be read with tables III and IV) may make this easier.

The 1755 picture seems to be one in which both the birth-rate and the death-rate in infants and small children was extremely high. As to the birth-rate, Webster believed there were no fewer than 49,000

TABLE I
Regional Distribution of the Population in 1755 and 1821

REGION	Percentage of land surface	1755 population ('000s)	Percentage of total population	1821 population ('000s)	Percentage of total population
North Scotland	72%	652	51%	873	41%
Central Belt	14%	464	37%	984	47%
South Scotland	14%	149	11%	234	11%

Note: Central belt comprises here the counties of Ayr, Dumbarton, Lanark, Renfrew, Clackmannan, Stirling, Fife, the Lothians and the city of Dundee. North Scotland is the area north of that block, and South Scotland the rest.

TABLE II
Population (in thousands) of the Largest Towns in early nineteenth-century Scotland

	1755	1801	1821
Edinburgh	57.0	81.6	138.0
Aberdeen	15.6	27.4	44.6
Inverness	9.7	8.7	12.2
Perth	9.0	14.8	19.1
Dundee	12.4	26.8	30.5
Montrose	4.1	7.9	10.3
Dunfermline	8.5	9.9	13.7
Dumfries	4.5	7.2	11.0
Glasgow	31.7	83.7	147.0
Greenock	3.8	17.4	22.1
Paisley	6.8	31.2	47.0
Kilmarnock	4.4	8.0	12.7
Falkirk	3.9	8.8	11.5

Notes: Edinburgh includes throughout, Leith, the Canongate and St. Cuthberts.
Glasgow includes throughout, Barony parish, with Govan and Gorbals.
Aberdeen includes Old Aberdeen.
Paisley consists of both the Abbey and town parishes.
Since no attempt has been made to distinguish the landward parts of a town parish from the burgh itself, these figures overstate the urban population: this is particularly the case at Inverness, which included a large rural area. The 13 largest towns in Scotland in the mid-eighteenth century would have been an identical list, except that St. Andrews and probably Elgin would have been rather larger than Falkirk and Greenock.

TABLE III

Age Structure of Scottish Population

Percentage in each age group

	1755	1821
0–4	13.4	13.9
5–9	10.0	12.7
10–14	9.6	11.5
15–19	9.2	10.1
	42.2	48.2
20–29	17.0	16.1
30–39	14.2	11.5
40–49	11.0	9.2
50–59	7.8	6.8
60–69	5.0	4.8
70–79	2.2	2.1
80–	0.5	0.6
	57.7	51.1

Note: Webster's estimate of age-structure was not based on a questionnaire to all who undertook the enumeration, as was the case with the census of 1821. He used a combination of computation, 'according to the most approved tables' of life expectancy (he was attracted to Halley's table of expectancy at Breslau in particular), and of sampling—'in many parts of Scotland the ministers . . . not only numbered the parishioners but distinguished their respective ages'. Had he used the first method alone, his results could be dismissed as the unrealistic application of foreign data to a native situation: because he used the second method as a check, and felt compelled in consequence to construct a different table for Scotland that disagreed in several respects with the Breslau table, his results must be taken seriously. The data of 1821 cannot be broken down in the way Webster had done in 1755, or used to attempt to estimate the contemporary birth-rate. The differences between the histograms of the two dates may be exaggerated by the different methods by which they were compiled. They will not on that account be invalidated. Webster's returns are printed by J. G. Kyd in *Scottish Population Statistics* (Scottish History Society 1952) and the 1821 census returns in *Parliamentary Papers* 1822 Vol. XV.

TABLE IV

Age Structure of Population under 10 in 1755 (in 000s)

Under 1	48.9
Aged 1	34.6
Aged 2	30.3
Aged 3	28.2
Aged 4	27.1
Aged 5	26.5
Aged 6	26.0
Aged 7	25.6
Aged 8	25.2
Aged 9	24.9
Aged 10	24.6

From Webster's returns.

children under one year old in a population of 1,265,000 souls. Almost certainly he was counting as a living member of the population every child that had come from its mother's womb in the previous twelve months, whether it had survived or not: it is equivalent to a calculation of the crude birth-rate of approximately 39 per 1,000. (By comparison it may be noted that the birth-rate in Scotland from 1855 until 1880 varied from 34 to 35 per thousand, and in 1950 was about 18 per thousand: in some underdeveloped countries like Brazil and Egypt it is currently between 43 and 45.) As for child mortality, according to Webster this cohort of 49,000 children under one had been reduced by almost exactly one half by the age of ten, and it was overwhelmingly the first three years of life that were the most dangerous: to judge from Webster's returns, three quarters of those who were alive at the age of three would still be living at the age of twenty-five, and their expectation of life as young adults was a good one. In 1755 forty-two per cent of the total population was under twenty.

Seventy years later the histogram looks different, and the biggest changes have been in the composition of the lowest age groups. One way in which the changes may have come about is through a large saving in the deaths of children under ten: but on the other hand there may be proportionately greater losses among children in their teens, and probably among young adults also. Of a total population now swollen by two-thirds, forty-eight per cent was under twenty years old, so that even more than in the mid-eighteenth century, it was a young world.

Any growth of population can be accounted for only by changes in the birth-rate or the death-rate, or by an excess of immigrants over emigrants: a comparison of our histograms cannot be a proper substitute for precise statistics on these matters, which were not collected before the middle of the nineteenth century. Nevertheless, taken in conjunction with other types of evidence, they might help to suggest some of the likeliest explanations of growth.

In the first place, there is no reason to believe that the pattern of migration in and out of Scotland is of more than marginal importance in explaining the increase. Around 1750 there was apparently very little emigration—a mere dribble to England and America is all that can be detected. Immigration, too, was insignificant—the Irish were the only likely immigrants, and Webster's ministers, asked to count papists, could find a mere 700 in the Central Belt of Scotland (it seems scarcely credible that they only unearthed two in the whole of Lanarkshire). After 1760 there was more movement and its timing may tend to exaggerate very slightly the apparent differences in the rate of population growth between the late eighteenth and early nineteenth centuries. Before 1780 there were clearly more emigrants than immigrants: an American historian has carefully estimated that in the peak period (1768–1775) rather over 20,000 left for the colonies, about two-thirds of them Highlanders.[3] Other Lowlanders were going to England to find work in workshops and offices where their relatively high standards of education often put them at a premium amongst Lancashire and London employers.

After 1780 the balance began to shift towards net immigration. The ministers who wrote in the Statistical Account of the 1790s were already nervous about the flood of poor Irish, with a 'superstitious' religion and alien customs, into the textile parishes of the west of Scotland. In 1819, Cleland made a census of Glasgow and discovered 15,000 Irishmen, though even this was only one in ten in all the city.[4] There were others in Paisley and Greenock, and throughout the industrial towns of the east; but the greatest invasions of the Irish did not come until Victorian times. Meanwhile there was still emigration of Scotsmen going on steadily—unobtrusively into England from the southern counties, dramatically, towards America, from the north, where as many as 10,000 may have left in another emigration boom in

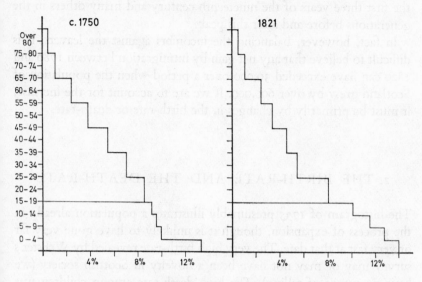

Age Structure of Scottish Population

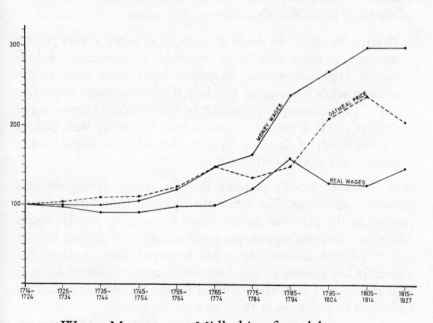

Wages Movements, Midlothian farm-labourers

the first three years of the nineteenth century and many others in the generations before and after this peak.

In fact, however, balancing the incomers against the leavers, it is difficult to believe that any net gain by immigration between 1780 and 1820 can have exceeded 30,000 over a period when the population of Scotland grew by over 600,000. If we are to account for the increase, it must be primarily by changes in the birth-rate or death-rate.

2. THE BIRTH-RATE AND THE DEATH-RATE

The histogram of 1755 presumably illustrates a population already in the process of expansion, though it is unlikely to have gone very far or very fast at that date. The very high birth-rate revealed by Webster's survey may or may not have been a novelty in Scottish society (we have no means of telling). The high death-rate among children was certainly nothing new. The whole picture is similar to that painted in broad, impressionistic colours by Adam Smith in 1774 when he spoke of the home life of the Highlanders in these terms:

> Poverty, though it no doubt discourages, does not always prevent marriage. It seems even to be favourable to generation. A half-starved Highland woman frequently bears more than twenty children while a pampered fine lady is often incapable of bearing any ... But poverty ... is extremely unfavourable to the rearing of children ... It is not uncommon, I have frequently been told, in the Highlands of Scotland for a mother who has borne twenty children not to have two alive.[5]

It need not be literally supposed that the average family size was anything like twenty. The information gleaned from eighteen rural parishes in the *Statistical Account* which bothered to provide details relating to the 1790s suggests the average number of children born in each marriage varied only from five to seven.[6] Some evidence that cotton factory women averaged between seven and eight children in their childbearing span was produced for the Royal Commission on Children's Employment in 1834 (see page 414 below).

The demographic revolution between 1750 and 1820 was an accelerating one. Can it have been accounted for by an unusually high birth-rate being maintained or even increased over a period of years? There are some theoretical reasons why this might occur. In any under-developed society fear of pregnancy may arise when land is short or jobs are few: if land is short the holding may be too small to support a large family or to provide children with land of their own at an early age; if jobs are few there may again be difficulty in supporting a family or in finding employment for the children as young juveniles. In eighteenth-century Scotland, however, the reverse propositions may have held. Early in the century the relative abundance of land as a result of the number of holdings left vacant after the famine might have been an encouragement to breed: later, the introduction of potatoes in the Highlands (see page 269) and the increased productivity of farming in the Lowlands enabled a larger population to be supported off a given acreage, though no longer in the Lowlands invariably upon the peasants' own holdings. The spread of industrial employment, especially in linen and cotton, where so much of it was best performed by women and young adolescents, provided a plethora of jobs at first in country-side villages, later increasingly in the towns.

If for these reasons fear of pregnancy in Scottish society did in fact decline it might well have been possible for the average family to respond by procreating more children. This could come about for example either through girls marrying younger and thus extending the length of the period in which they were most likely to bear children or by married couples ceasing to practise birth control. The only control likely to have been practised in an eighteenth-century peasant society is *coitus interruptus*, to which there are several Biblical references that would hardly have escaped a Scottish congregation. It was said that the abnormally low birth rate at times in eighteenth-century France was brought about by the practice of this form of family limitation.

Unfortunately, however, as far as Scotland is concerned, we are entirely in the realm of speculation. At the moment we know nothing at all as to whether or not the age of marriage fell, or if there was a diminished use of *coitus interruptus*, or, indeed, if *coitus interruptus* was ever practised. Instead of hard evidence we are left with an insubstantial mass of conflicting contemporary opinions, some supporting the view that the birth-rate was rising, others saying that certain contemporary social changes actually discouraged early marriage. Thus the minister of the Small Isles in the *Statistical Account* explains the emigration from Eigg between 1788 and 1790 in these terms:

> The country was overstocked with people, arising from frequent early marriages; of course, the lands were able to supply them but scantily with the necessaries of life. It is not unfrequent upon these occasions for a parent to divide with his newly married son, the pittance of land (sometimes a very small portion of a farm) possessed by him ...[7]

Eigg was one of the islands subsisting largely off potatoes. At Elgin on the other side of the north of Scotland, on the other hand, farms were being thrown together and cottars converted to well-paid day-labourers. But, said the minister,

> Luxury ... most materially affects population. It discourages marriage until persons acquire an income adequate in their estimation to that state, or in other words until they are advanced in years ... How many young women of every rank are never married who in the beginning of this century and even so late as 1745 would have been the parents of a numerous and healthy progeny?[8]

We cannot answer the minister of Elgin's rhetorical question (any more than he could himself). But we may have honest doubts as to whether in any case an explanation of a sustained rise in population of this magnitude could be based on changes in the birth-rate alone, important though a high birth-rate may have been for initiating an increase of population in the early stages. One of the most striking features of Webster's survey is the very large mortality of very young children. Now, most demographic experience suggests that in poor societies the larger a family grows the greater the risk is likely to become of the youngest children dying, since the standard of parental care cannot be so good for a large family as for a small one. A high birth-rate might, therefore, not become very effective in bringing about a sustained increase in the population unless there was, at the same time, a fall in the death-rate among babies and young children.

Was there, then, anything in eighteenth-century society that was saving life, particularly child life, on an unprecedented scale? There seem to be only three factors which might possibly have made a difference. These are improvements in diet, the elimination of smallpox, and (much more difficult to trace and almost certainly less universal) changes in child-rearing practices. The first began to be widely effective after the middle of the eighteenth century, the second and third several decades later. All of them might therefore have played a part in sustaining and accelerating the growth of population, although none of them can have initiated it if, as we believe, the 1750 survey shows a population already beginning to expand.

There were several changes in feeding habits among the Scots in the eighteenth century. There was a growing choice of green vegetables, turnips, carrots, herbs and fresh fruit as the new-found enthusiasm of the upper-classes for gardening began to be copied on a small scale in the kailyards of the peasantry, and a few of these crops—especially turnips and carrots—were utilised for field cultivation. The arrival of tea and sugar as cheap articles of consumption affected quite a wide and low circle of society in the last decades of the century, and as more meat was raised for external sale more found its way into the stomachs of producers at home. All these factors would improve nutrition and raise resistance to disease in proportion to the number able to take advantage of them. But exceeding them in importance, because more widespread geographically and socially, was the arrival of the potato as a common field crop. William Marshall called it 'the greatest blessing that modern times have bestowed on the country'[9]—a remark that rings oddly in the generation of Watt, Arkwright and Telford, but which has more sense behind it than is immediately apparent.

The significance of the potato was three-fold. Firstly, it helped to balance the national diet and to eliminate chronic and debilitating scurvy in communities such as Highland townships and large Lowland burghs where kail, the only traditional vegetable of the common people, was normally unobtainable. Secondly, it provided for the first time an alternative staple to the ubiquitous oatmeal that in previous centuries had supported the Scots through thick and thin: a peasant now had a second string to his bow, and could hope to raise more children if he could supplement the family's ordinary meal allowance with quantities of potatoes grown on his own rig or in his own yard. 'This mild article of food and wholesome root is a prime article of food to the industrious peasant and his children in particular', noted Sir John Sinclair in 1812, 'it is difficult to conceive how the people of this country could have subsisted had it not been for the fortunate introduction and extensive cultivation of this most valuable plant'.[10] Thirdly (and this was partly Sir John's point), the potato could be used as a lifeline when there was a bad failure of the oat crop. From 1700 to 1750 grain prices rose only slightly and slowly, with one year (1740) when dearth approached a famine: the absence of mortality arising from periodic visitations of dearth may well have been one cause of the earliest population growth in the first half of the century. But from 1750 to 1816 the price of grain rose fast, if unevenly over the decades. Crop failures again became common—1756, 1762, 1771, 1782, 1795, 1799, 1800, 1812 and 1816, for instance, were all bad years, though not all of them were catastrophic. Had there been no potatoes to cram into empty stomachs there must surely have been renewed demographic disaster following some of them, such as had occurred so often in the past when a run of good harvest had given way to a run of poor ones.

It is interesting to see how closely the spread of the potato from the garden of the great house (where it had been known since the end of the seventeenth century) followed the tracks of rising grain prices. John Ramsay of Ochtertyre noted how in the Lowlands the effect of high corn prices in 1757 had been 'alleviated by the plenty of potatoes, a root which twenty years before had been confined to gentlemen's gardens',[11] while in the Highlands the same scarcity brought it immediately afterwards to Lewis and to Sutherland (it had been known in Uist and Benbecula since 1743). It is probably true to say that by 1770 the potato was a common crop on the holdings of the poor throughout most of the Lowlands, and fifteen years later universal with one or two exceptions in all the parishes of the Highlands. Already in the scarcity of 1771 Thomas Pennant noted it had proved the 'saviour of the people' in Skye.[12] In the much more serious failure of 1782 the worst catastrophe was said to have occurred in those parishes like Ardersier in Inverness-shire which had not yet introduced the root. One of the reasons for the severity of the famine that year, however, was that potatoes themselves were 'dwarfish from the severity of the weather' and 'also much injured by the frost'.[13] In the Highlands, of course, the potato became the principal food, and tended to displace the older staple. In the Lowlands it was much more often only a useful subsidiary, perhaps alongside turnips or carrots; yet it was a writer on Fife in 1800 who, having described how every tenant and cottager had a potato plot for his own use, went on: 'since this root came into such general repute the nation has never been exposed to such scarcity as was experienced before this time and which sometimes bordered upon famine.'[14]

Most contemporary writers, indeed, stressed above the other two advantages of the potato this third quality, that it saved the people from famine. In this respect it is worth noting that modern research on Scandinavia in the eighteenth century has stressed that the main victims of scarcity were normally children over the age of one: 'the mortality rate for them', writes Gille, 'was one-fourth or one-third higher in years after a bad harvest than after a good harvest'.[15] Thus, not only because it raised the standard of nutrition and provided a greater quantity of food for a large and poor family in normal times, but also because it averted the spectre of death when the oat crop failed, the potato was in a special sense the preserver of children. To prefer it to the factory and the steam engine as the 'greatest blessing of modern times' was not altogether an idle system of priorities.

To some extent eighteenth-century Scotland was fortunate in her epidemiological history. That scourge of earlier periods since 1349, bubonic plague, had now completely (and inexplicably) withdrawn from western Europe. Typhus, which had possibly been the great killer of the 1640s, apparently accounted again for many victims weakened by hunger in the famine years of the late seventeenth century, and then declined in virulence for a time. Malaria had been prevalent in Scotland, and suddenly died out between 1780 and 1800, again for no known reason. Though seldom a fatal disease in itself, it was a very debilitating one and contributed to a high death rate from other causes, especially among children. The demographic benefits of these changes, however, may have been partially offset by the rise of smallpox, a disease which first occurred in Scotland at Aberdeen in 1610, with serious epidemics over a wide area of Scotland in 1635, at Aberdeen again in 1641 and at Glasgow in 1672 (when no fewer than 800 deaths occurred).[17]

By the eighteenth century, therefore, smallpox was by far the worst epidemic killer. So common and repeated were its visitations that, as with the relatively innocuous mumps or measles today, it was over-whelmingly a disease of small children. For them, it was often fatal:

It is computed when the smallpox is favourable, one in seven dies, when moderate one of six or one of five, but when its of a bad kind it makes a cruel havoc. One of four or one of three is carried off: to avoid extremes I shall reckon one of six pays the general tribute ... there may be born annually in Scotland about fifty thousand souls of which two thousand may escape the disease: of the remaining forty-eight thousand by reckoning one of six to die the nation looses eight thousand lives yearly and their posterity . . .[18]

Detailed investigations in eighteenth-century Scotland do not suggest this was a great exaggeration. At Kilmarnock between 1728 and 1764, smallpox was responsible for one in six of all deaths. Dr. Monro, examining mortality records in Edinburgh between 1744 and 1763 found that at least one-tenth of all deaths had been caused by it—as half of the deaths in society were of children under ten years old, the proportion of child mortalities caused by smallpox must have been nearer twenty per cent. Dr. Watt, analysing the records in Glasgow at the end of the century found an even worse picture: between 1783 and 1800 nineteen per cent of all deaths were attributable to smallpox, and more than a third of the deaths of children under ten were caused by it.[19] Even among those who recovered there were some permanently disabled by its ravages.

The conquest of the disease was attempted in two stages; by inoculation, first tried on a wide scale in Dumfriesshire in 1733 (though it was not until after 1765 that it became at all common) and by vaccination, devised by Jenner in England in 1796 and almost immediately taken up by Scottish doctors. Inoculation consisted in giving the child a mild dose of the disease in a controlled environment, thereby giving immunity to 'natural' attacks (though as the child was a carrier during the inoculation attack, it was normally kept in bed and isolated). As early as 1715 there was a reference to a practice in the Highlands of deliberately infecting the children 'by rubbing them with a kindly pock as they term it'.[20] Vaccination gave the child an attack of cowpox, an allied but harmless disease which also conferred immunity to smallpox. Either method, if used on a wide enough scale in society could have extirpated the disease.

The clearest picture of the consequences of inoculation comes from the reports of the ministers of the *Statistical Account* of the 1790s and shows variations from region to region which were very great. In Dumfriesshire and Galloway on the one hand, and in Shetland and Orkney on the other, inoculation had within the previous twenty or thirty years become a more or less universal habit, and was regarded as having saved many thousands of lives. In the vast majority of Highland parishes it had also made great strides, apparently more recently than in the islands. It was also reported everywhere it was introduced as very beneficial—the minister of Fortingal in Perthshire, for instance, commented that 'fewer children die in the Highlands than almost anywhere, particularly since inoculation has been so universally practised'.[21] That was only one man's opinion: but it was an interesting contrast to what Adam Smith had written twenty years before.

With the Highland line and the Solway hinterland, however, the zone where inoculation was practised on a wide scale virtually ended. Throughout the Lowlands there was a deep and persistent suspicion of inoculation although in parts of the eastern side some success was still reported. In Fife, for instance, Cupar had had few fatalities for several years, St. Monance found the disease 'to some degree mitigated' and Leuchars had just been converted to the idea: but more typically in the parish of Poatmoak 'to inoculate is regarded as criminal', and in the great burgh of Dundee the deaths of children under five rose by 250 per cent in years when a smallpox epidemic was raging. On the western side, in the Clyde valley, there had been no progress at all. The dreadful record of Glasgow, where half the children died before they were ten and a third of the deaths were due to smallpox, we have already referred to. It was by no means exceptional: to give instances at random, at Largs, Renfrew, East Kilbride, Cathcart, Eaglesham and Kilsyth, smallpox was still the main killer of children, and all attempts to introduce inoculation had fallen to the ground. In other words, even though in remote country districts its use had become widespread and its effects beneficial, in those urban areas and industrial villages to which population was migrating in the greatest numbers it had no effect at all. The effect of inoculation on population growth outside the Highlands, the south-west, Orkney and Shetland was probably therefore negligible.

At the root of the trouble was the fact that popular attitudes towards inoculation in the north and in the central belt differed profoundly. In the northern isles the habit had bitten into folk traditions: on Yell, in Shetland, there was a man called Johnny Notions, part tailor, joiner, watch-mender, blacksmith and amateur doctor who inoculated everyone on the island:

Unassisted by education and unfettered by the rules of art, he stands unrivalled in this business. Several thousands have been inoculated by him, and he has not lost a single patient . . . he uses no lancet in performing the operation but by a small knife made by his own hands he gently raises a very little of the outer skin of the arm . . . the only plaister he uses for healing the wound is a bit of cabbage leaf.[22]

There was a world of difference between the social outlook that made Johnny Notions possible and the prejudice which Dr. Monro had met in Edinburgh in 1765 where inoculation was 'deemed a tempting of God's providence and therefore a heinous crime: for it was creating a disease by which children's lives might be in danger'.[23] It is this latter attitude that the ministers and doctors were fighting in the Clyde valley in the 1790s. Because of it, exclaimed the minister of East Kilbride, the common people 'sit still in sullen contentment and see their children cut off in multitudes'.[24] There are reports of the same attitude in Kinross-shire, in Aberdeenshire, even in Caithness, and on many occasions Highland ministers speak of a traditional prejudice only recently overcome.

Almost certainly the hostile attitude proved easier to overcome in remote rural areas because in such places smallpox had been more of an adult's disease—the isolation of the communities meant that epidemics struck less often, but when they struck they were no less fatal, slaying the breadwinner or the mother as well as the children. It was therefore socially more important to extirpate it than it was in the towns, where the very frequent visitations meant that it only culled the children. Secondly, in the Highlands and in country areas generally, the minister and the landlord had more social control over the community as a whole. If they believed inoculation was a good thing they could virtually force it on the lower classes, even though the fatalities among the children of the poor (who could not so easily be kept in their beds in warm rooms) were perhaps of the order of one or two in every hundred. In the towns and in the weaving villages of the west of Scotland the population was more independent of their leaders: if they knew of a case where a parent had inoculated a child and the child died, they regarded it as murder—but the death of a child by 'natural smallpox' was a familiar Act of Providence that could be blamed on no-one.

The bad reception of inoculation is in great contrast to the remarkable speed with which the common people accepted the benefits of Jenner's vaccination, which was perfectly safe. The statistics in Glasgow are most striking. Whereas between 1793 and 1802 thirty-six per cent of deaths in children under ten were due to smallpox, between 1803 and 1812, after the introduction of vaccination, the percentage fell to nine. Whereas between 1783 and 1800 nineteen per cent of all deaths in the city were due to this disease, between 1807 and 1812 the percentage was only four. From 1813 to 1819 it was less than two per cent, but due to the immigration of unvaccinated children, it rose again to as high as six per cent in the 1830s.[25] The city had, in fact adopted a policy of free vaccination for poor children as early as 1801, and in the next twenty-one years 25,000 children were immunised through the local authority. In other cities the story seems to have been similar. The overall picture by 1825 was that the disease, though by no means beaten, was becoming relatively unimportant as a killer compared to what it had been. But the big turning point must be dated after 1800. Indeed it would not be surprising if a high proportion of the acceleration of population growth between 1801 and 1821 was due solely to the decline of the smallpox menace.

The importance of other medical advances was probably limited. It is true that the Universities of Edinburgh and Glasgow were the principal seminaries of doctors in the British isles and among the most respected institutions of medical teaching in the world. Their output of degrees, however, was small: Edinburgh conferred about twenty a year in the 1770s and about forty in the 1790s, and perhaps most of those who qualified immediately went to England or abroad to practise.[26] The work of some individual medical pioneers, too, was often limited by the inadequate number of practitioners. William Smellie of Lanark, in treatises published between 1752 and 1763, went far towards developing the science of midwifery: good as they were, as long as there were few doctors or trained midwives in the parishes, and as long as the nature of puerperal fever (the great slayer of women in childbirth) was misunderstood, the saving of life would be restricted to a narrow and mainly upper-class section of society.

Slightly more effective might have been the movement to found hospitals and create dispensaries where the poor could get cheap medical aid. The Edinburgh Royal Infirmary founded in 1741 had 228 beds: the first infirmary of 1729 had had only six. There were also three dispensaries in the capital by 1816. Following Edinburgh's lead, Aberdeen Infirmary was founded in 1742, the Glasgow Royal Infirmary in 1794 (replacing a Town's Hospital of 1733) and further infirmaries or dispensaries at, for instance, Dumfries, Kelso, Greenock, Paisley,

Stirling, Dundee, Montrose, Elgin and Inverness between 1776 and 1807. Some of them had, by the standards of the day, excellent records of medical care. Edinburgh Royal Infirmary, for instance, between 1762 and 1775 admitted 15,600 patients of whom 11,700 (seventy-five per cent) were cured, 1,500 were 'relieved' and only about 750 died. Most of the remaining 1,500 left of their own accord. At the city's public dispensary between 1776 and 1778, 730 patients were given medicine of whom 300 were cured, 170 relieved, 180 were 'no better' as the result of treatment, and eight died. At Glasgow between 1794 and 1814, 16,400 patients were received in the Royal Infirmary of whom 11,100 (sixty-seven per cent) were cured 'and a large number of the residue relieved'. We do not know how many died, but in the one year 1815 there were ninety-six deaths among 1,340 patients. In the associated dispensaries in Glasgow 'during the period of twenty one years, more than 40,000 outdoor patients have received gratuitous advice'.[27]

The main disadvantages of these institutions were that they were restricted entirely to the burghs, their facilities were too small even to cover the towns' needs adequately, and knowledge of hygiene and of the nature of infection was so rudimentary that the operating table, in particular, often proved fatal to those upon it no matter how brilliant the surgeons.

One man's work, however, may have had a much wider and more immediate impact, since it was independent both of hospitals and of the number or expertise of other medical practitioners. This was the advice given to parents in the writings of Dr. William Buchan. Before his time, the most popular Scottish book on family medicine was John Moncrief's *Poor Man's Physician* (1712). Its cure for falling-sickness in children gives an indication of its calibre:

Take a little black sucking puppy (but for a girl take a bitch-whelp), choke it, open it, and take out the gall which hath not above three or four drops of pure choler; Give it all to the Child in the time of the fit, with a little tiletree flower water, and you shall see him cured, as it were by a Miracle . . .[28]

To turn from this to Buchan's *Domestic Medicine* (which ran to twenty-two editions between 1769 and 1826, and eventually earned for its author a resting place in the cloisters of Westminster Abbey) is to turn from the world of witchcraft to the world of Dr. Spock. Buchan's starting point was with his own Edinburgh thesis, 'De Infantum Vita

Conservanda', and his prime concern is the deplorable fact that 'it appears . . . that about one half of the children born in Great Britain die under twelve years of age'.[29]

Domestic Medicine is a monument of common sense and good advice simply expressed. Do not, he says, give babies wine or whisky as soon as they are born: they much prefer milk, and it is much better for them. Do not drop them straight into a basin of cold water: it is better to bathe them in warm water. If you possibly can, suckle your own child rather than putting it out to wet-nurses who will not look after it. Keep it clean—'the importance of general cleanliness does by no means seem to be sufficiently understood'.[30] For all children he recommends warm, clean, loose clothing (frequently changed) and dry accommodation. He gives a list of simple and effective remedies for the commoner illnesses, with the reminder that 'colds kill more than plagues'.

Everything that he had to say was so sensible that it is impossible to believe that it would not have resulted in a considerable saving of infant and child life had its precepts been universally read and universally followed. The numerous editions certainly testify to a large following by upper and middle-class wives to whom, from its tone, it is primarily addressed. What following did it have below those strata? Clearly Buchan meant it to affect the poor as well, for he frequently refers to them: 'the lives of the poor are of the greatest importance to the state'; 'even houses that are built for the poor ought to be dry'. He deals explicitly with the problem of hygiene in families 'where the cattle and their masters lodge under the same roof', and devotes space to the industrial diseases of soap-boilers and miners. He wrote consciously for a patriarchal society in which the minister or the laird might be able to exercise some influence over the medical practices of poor families, in which upper-class health-visiting was popular, and in which servants were often closely imitative of their mistresses in dress, and might well have been no less imitative in matters of child-rearing since they were themselves often closely involved in helping to rear upper-class children. Apart from the attack on smallpox, Buchan's book would certainly seem to be the medical advance most likely to have had a wide impact on the death-rate.

Finally, we must consider the possibility that, despite all the good that was being done in saving the lives of small children by improved nutrition, by the attack on smallpox and by Buchan's propaganda, they were surviving the first few years of life only to fall a prey to other diseases which cut them off between the age of five and twenty. It seems indisputable that many people were saved from smallpox only to die of one of the diseases that were increasing—measles, for instance, accounted for less than one per cent of fatalities in Glasgow between 1783 and 1788, but for more than ten per cent between 1807 and 1812; diphtheria, or croup, had become in parts of the west 'the most fatal disorder to which children are liable'; tuberculosis, above all, was the killer of youths in their teens and twenties, especially in the industrial areas—'old people affirm that in their forefathers' day the disease was extremely rare'.[31] In Glasgow it was clearly demonstrated by Dr. Watt that at least as high a proportion of the population died under the age of ten in the six years before 1813 as had died in the six years after 1783, and it was still one half, according to James Cleland, in 1821.[32]

Was any progress, then, made at all? All the really black evidence comes from the towns, predominantly from Glasgow, which was growing at an enormous and uncontrolled rate with appalling sanitary and housing conditions: if anywhere had a high child death-rate it would be here. Glasgow, and the whole of the textile complex of the west, added to its population far more from immigrants born in the countryside and coming in as young adults than from children born and brought up in its own wynds. The distribution of the population was such that it must have been the success or failure of child-rearing in country parishes that, over the whole period down to 1821, still mainly determined the overall growth of the population. Rural areas would seem to have many advantages that the towns did not enjoy: country children had easier access to fresh vegetables and potatoes, they were more likely to have been inoculated, and to have had parents influenced by the medical teaching of Dr. Buchan. They were also much more sanitary. It is obviously so much better for the public good to deposit human excrement at the bottom of a country hedge than to throw it out of the window in a city wynd. Rural housing was certainly not very wonderful, but it improved in the eighteenth-century Lowlands with the advent of more stone and slate buildings, and more coal fires burning in the grate.

The *Statistical Account* leaves an impression which would support this conclusion: not only are country areas consistently reported as healthier than towns (which we would expect), but country areas are reported as having become much healthier than they had been two or three generations earlier. On the other hand, because all over Scotland rural areas were better at rearing children than at finding employment for them as adults, the population not only grew but also migrated from their birthplaces to urban areas where they could find jobs. To make the towns as safe for population as they were magnetic to it would be the heroic but herculean task of the public health movement in the decades after 1840.

CHAPTER XII

The Lowland Landowners

1. SOCIAL LEADERSHIP AND THE LEADERS

In every age before the middle of the nineteenth century, Scottish society was dominated by landowners. Although at the highest level their leadership might be guided and deflected by the overriding power of the crown, or influenced and occasionally challenged by the high claims of the church, on the local scene down in the countryside where most Scots lived the power of the lord who gave the lease and took the rent was as little to be questioned as the power of God who brought the seedtime in spring and the harvest at the end of the summer.

At the start of the eighteenth century the claims of landed leadership seemed rather strengthened than diminished by recent events. The Revolution of 1688–1690 had been a political victory by the British nobility; the terms of the Union of 1707 were accepted 'mainly because the nobles wanted them'[1]; the Patronage Act of 1712 confirmed the ministers of the Church of Scotland as creatures of the heritor. It was true that the wind later blew more and more straws in the other direction. The loss of most heritable jurisdictions in 1747 was an erosion of ancient right. The great growth of towns between 1750 and 1820 and the multiplication of fortunes based on industry enlarged a sector of society that might become impatient of landed rights. The French revolution and the spread of radicalism after 1789 seemed a still larger and more explicit threat to the old order. Nevertheless the constitution of church and state alike was still unchanged at the end of the 1820s. Thus far the landed leaders had been completely successful in their policy of using the middle-class dread of anarchy to detach the urban rich from the working classes and thereby to maintain their own privileges untouched by concessions to either group. There might be some slight signs of a changing attitude even among those who were not active agitators for parliamentary reform or any other radical programme: 'not many years ago in walking along the high road every bonnet and hat was lifted to the gentry whom the common people met', wrote John Ramsay of Ochtertyre at the start of the nineteenth century, 'the first who would not bow the knee to Baal were the antiburghers when going to church on Sunday. No such thing now takes place . . . it is connected with the spirit of the times'.[2] But these were mere irritants. In every formal sense, landed leadership went riding high right up to the Great Reform Bill of 1832.

To the landed classes the outward manifestations of this social leadership were numerous and gratifying. Firstly, there were political rights on the national scene. The Peers, if their titles were of post-Union creation, had the privilege of sitting in the House of Lords (this was finally established in 1782). In any case they had the right to vote for the sixteen representatives of the Scottish peerage to go to Westminster. Lesser landowners were represented in the House of Commons by thirty county members, though the peculiarities of the Scottish electoral system were such that by 1815 only about one laird in three actually enjoyed a vote himself.[3] Then there were plums in the county pie. The peers could slip into their heritable stewartries, sheriffdoms and regalities before the legislation of 1747; they became Lords Lieutenant after the Militia Act of 1797. Some were also Commissioners of Supply, a post created in 1667 to give the greater heritors in each shire the responsibility for apportioning the land-tax: from 1686 onwards they had, with the justices of the peace (who were usually gentry) additional duties of supervising roads, bridges and ferries and after 1696 of obliging the other heritors to provide a school in each parish. As for the justices, their duty of commandeering country labour for the upkeep of the roads often made them even more feared and respected than their judicial powers, but the latter were effectively increased as the heritable jurisdictions declined.

Every landowner also enjoyed rights as a heritor within his own parish: these perhaps, were the most treasured of all, for they conveyed that sense of immediate paternal lordship which they so much enjoyed. They were able to nominate the minister of the established church and to assist in the examination of the schoolmaster, the two ideological teachers of the parish who could henceforth be relied upon to say the safe thing. With the kirk-session they had enough control over the distribution of parochial relief to ensure that the disrespectful would not find themselves numbered among the blessed objects of Christian charity. As landlords they had the reputation of being the most absolute in Britain. In 1700 most of their tenants held at will, with no rights of compensation for any improvements they might have undertaken on their holdings. Their lord sat in judgment over them in the baron court even after the middle of the eighteenth century; in 1747 the Lord President had advised against outright abolition of this heritable jurisdiction on the grounds that without it rent enforcement would be impossible.[4] The baron courts gradually fell into disuse, but only when the landlord discovered he could be sure of collecting his rents by invoking the state's legal authority. It was a landowners' world, and the possibilities of oppression were enormous.

Although such opportunities existed, however, it would be mere parody to suggest that landowners relished their power only for the chance to abuse it. Certainly they did not neglect their economic self-interest, still less their collective class-interest, but in public statements and private papers alike eighteenth-century landowners reveal themselves as glorying above all else in the paternal quality of their rule. 'The relationship of master and tenant, like prince and people, implies a reciprocal duty and mutual affection', said Lord Gardenstone to his tenants at Laurencekirk in Kincardineshire in 1779, 'beneficence to tenants is the best privilege of landed property'. John Cockburn of Ormiston in East Lothian said in 1726; 'no father can have more satisfaction in the prosperity of his children than I have in the welfare of those on my estate.' John Ramsay of Ochtertyre in Stirlingshire was to echo the sentiment again in 1800: 'without a portion of self-denial and benevolence neither public nor private virtue can be very pure or attractive. What a miserable state of society would it be, were it creditable for every man to make as hard a bargain as he could with his inferiors and dependents.'[5] This is what the Professor of Law at Edinburgh asked his first year students in 1726:

What more agreeable personage can one form for himself than that of a country gentleman living decently and frugally upon his fortune and composing all the differences within the sphere of his activity, giving the law to a whole neighbourhood and they gratefully submitting to it?[6]

Such a life and such fatherly prestige were so desirable that everyone of lower rank bought land if they could, even if by doing so they made an economic sacrifice for themselves or their families. There was nothing new in the eighteenth century in this: the merchants of Glasgow, for example, like those of many other towns, had been deeply involved in the land-market around the burgh throughout the seventeenth century, and by 1700 were so mixed up by marriage, mortgage and purchase that it was almost impossible to tell who in the vicinity was by origin a laird and who was by origin a merchant. Lawyers, too, had always tried to end up on the land: the seventeenth century had provided such successful examples as the Hopes of Hopetoun, the Dalrymples of Stair and the Mackenzies of Rosehaugh and Cromarty: the eighteenth century displayed men like Lord Kames, Lord Gardenstone, Lord Monboddo, Lord Auchinleck and others often no less famous in the annals of improving agriculture than in the annals of law. It is as hard to distinguish the legal class from the landed class round Edinburgh as it is to tell merchants from lairds round Glasgow.

There is also no doubt, however, that more people were ambitious for estates after the middle of the eighteenth century in Scotland than there had ever been before. Several observers noticed it: John Ramsay said the incomers in Stirlingshire were mainly of three kinds—adventurers returned with colonial money from the East Indies, profiteers who had done well out of Government contracts and prize money in the war, and Glasgow tobacco merchants looking for new estates beyond the crowded shores of the Clyde. Thomas Somerville in Roxburghshire identified them as predominantly men from the colonies; from Jamaica, 'the grave of Scotland', but above all from the East Indies. He could identify eight estates near Jedburgh alone that had been bought by East India adventurers, and he believed that two-thirds of the land in the county changed hands between 1750 and 1815.[7] Towards the end of the period the ambitious manufacturer who had made his pile in the cotton trade joined the ranks of those eager for land especially in Ayrshire, Renfrewshire and the west generally.

The economic effort of this was to enliven the land-market and enhance the price of land. In time, a high price of land tended also to raise the level of rents, since newcomers, anxious to recoup the expenses to which they had been put, sought ways of attempting to screw more out of the tenants than their predecessors. Where they proved successful, their example opened the eyes of the rest of the landed class as to how they, too, might enhance their incomes. Rising rents, as we shall see, probably acted as an effective goad to the peasant to increase the efficiency of his farming, but in order to do this successfully he needed other favourable conditions in the shape of a buoyant market for agricultural produce and models of better farming practice to copy. There is no sign, however, that any of the new landowners except the lawyers were particularly effective in directly searching out or propagating such new farming techniques. (This point is also discussed below; see pp. 308ff.)

The social impact of this invasion on the structure of the landed classes was also complicated. On the one hand, it prevented the Scottish landed class from becoming an oligarchy of birth. There were now many men among the class who had had much experience of life outside it, and who by no means despised the values and social aims of the bourgeoisie from which they had risen. They formed an effective bridge between the middle and upper classes from which both benefited. On the other hand, thanks partly to the policy of the House of Lords and partly to the grip of the Scottish laws of perpetual entail from 1684, the newcomers were unable to collect the necessary quantity of land and influence that would have raised them to the peerage. Consequently a marked dichotomy arose between the nobility and the small or middling gentry—the former of old family, owning large estates, usually involved in politics in London and therefore necessarily largely absentees, the latter including all the newcomers and typified by those of the West of Scotland who usually lived most of the year either on or close to their estates.

How many landowners were there? Sir John Sinclair gave his usual confident answer in 1814: there were 7654 landed proprietors of whom 396 owned 'large properties', 1077 'middling properties' and 6181 owned 'small properties'.[8] Sinclair defined large estates as those with land exceeding 2000 lib Scots of the valuation of 1670, middling estates of 500–2000 lib Scots valuation, small estates of under 500 lib Scots valuation. What this meant in real terms in 1814 is more difficult to ascertain since land values had utterly changed, but the first group probably contained almost all the peers (of whom there were less than 100 families) and the last group included numbers of bonnet-lairds in Lanarkshire, Ayrshire, Renfrew, Kirkcudbright and Dumfries whose status was probably little better than that of any English owner-occupier: he was a landowner but not usually a landlord. About forty per cent of the small properties by Sinclair's definition were in the five western counties. We can be sure that a high proportion of the total proprietors had only become landowners since 1750: we cannot know how high, nor can we be quite sure whether there was a much greater number of landowners altogether than there had been a century before, for many older families had apparently gone to the wall in the fifty years before 1815. Such families perished under a burden of debt incurred partly because they were expected to keep up much higher personal standards of comfort than had been the case in the past, and creditors, knowing the potentiality of good land neglected for lack of capital or initiative were probably less inclined than formerly to be merciful to the extravagant.

2. THE REVOLUTION OF MANNERS

In 1729, William Mackintosh of Borlum concluded his *Essay on the Ways and Means for Inclosing*, which had been largely devoted to pointing out how stagnant and backward Scottish agricultural practice was compared to farming in Europe and England, by an acid attack on his own class. He was always hearing, he said, how much the country had been 'improved' in the last twenty years: when he inquired in what way, the answer was always the same: 'how much more handsomely the gentry live now than before the Union, both in dress, table and house furniture'. What does it all amount to, he asks? The gentry were once satisfied with neat homespuns of their 'own sheep's growth and women's spinning'. Now the laird's wife must trick herself out in French and Italian silks, and her husband goes in English broadcloth. At table the family is no longer satisfied with good plain meat courses and honest gravy: 'I see now served up several services of little expensive ashets with *English* pickles, yea *Indian* mangoes and catchup or anchovy sauces.' Morning visiting has ceased to be a pleasure, and become an ordeal: 'I used to be ask'd if I had had my morning draught yet? I am now ask'd if I have yet had my tea? And in lieu of the big quaigh with strong ale and toast and after a dram of good wholesome Scots spirits, there is now the tea-kettle put on the fire, the tea-table, and silver and china equipage brought in with the marmalet, cream and cold tea . . . God forbid,' he ends up, 'we should expect no better improvement from the Union' than these apish and extravagant tricks.[9]

Mackintosh, while he belongs among the enduring legion of those who in all ages believe new fashions in clothes and new standards in comfort to be intrinsically wrong, is not merely a puritan moaning about change. He is also reporting on the early stages of the revolution in the way of life of the eighteenth-century lairds which was to be far-reaching in itself and to have far-reaching consequences for other people. The revolution went much further than substituting tea for ale or chutney for gravy. On the one hand most of the gentry came to enjoy the material standards which had previously been the privilege of the peers and the greater landowners: on the other, they also became a more intellectual and a more 'polite' class. To that extent they also found themselves further removed from the lives, experience and sympathies of the peasants on whom they depended for a living.

The life of a Scottish gentleman at the beginning of the eighteenth century seemed almost unbearably uncouth in the recollection of his successors at the end. Their houses were witnesses to this. Some early improvers, like Sir Archibald Grant of Monymusk found themselves saddled with an old castle:

> with battlements and six different roofs of various heights and directions confusedly and inconveniently combined, and all rotten, with two wings more modern, of two stories only, the half of windowes of the higher riseing above the roofs, with granaries, stables and houses for all cattle and of the vermine attending them, close by.

He was advised in 1719 to pull it all down and build a new 'little comodius house . . . what I call a five hundred pound house' in its place.[10] Even this looked pokey by the end of the century. George Robertson in 1829 recalled the lairds' houses in the Lothians as 'dismal ghostly-looking mansions': dark and gloomy within, devoid of ornament and with very scanty accommodation.[11] By then, of course, the careers of the Adam family and the growing affluence of taste of their patrons had transformed ideas about how comfortable a simple country house might be. The *General Report* of 1814 contained a model sketch for such a house, suited to a landed proprietor of moderate fortune (earning from £1000 to £3000 per annum). It was a design informed by 'simplicity and elegance' for a two-storey, six bedroom house, with a drawing-room, dining-room, parlour, study and nursery, extensive kitchen and servants quarters, stabling for eight horses and their carriages, a brew-house, a hot-house and a green-house. Externally it was pleasantly colonnaded and tipped with urns in regency style, with generous airy windows, and placed in commodious grounds among carefully positioned plantations, so that it may 'embellish the landscape of which it forms a part'. Its estimated cost, leaving aside site values, was just over £3000.[12] We need only to cast a casual eye around the Lowland countryside today to see that many such houses were actually built by the Scottish gentry at the turn of the eighteenth and nineteenth centuries. Almost all of them would have been the envy of the peerage a hundred years before.

As with the building so with the plenishings. In the early eighteenth century there was scarcely any furniture within a laird's house except country-carpentered oak, and often little enough of that. The beds seem to have been the most conspicuous items even in the best rooms, and they were generally box-beds, built like cupboards into the walls, where one or two guests could be shut away for the night if they stayed too long over their drink. A bed 'with hangings', a fourposter, was still a novelty and a prized possession for all but the richest proprietors until well on into the century. It often occupied one of the downstairs rooms where a laird could receive his visitors and show it off: there is a particularly fine example of such a room with the bed still *in situ* off the dining room at Hopetoun House, but this of course, was a nobleman's palace, not a laird's house. A hundred years later lairds enjoyed the choice of an abundance of well-designed furniture, mainly executed in mahogany to designs based on those of the great London cabinet makers, Hepplewhite, Sheraton and Chippendale. With carpets (instead of rushes), wallpaper (instead of bare plaster or wainscotting) and plaster ceilings (instead of bare boards) rooms had become warmer and more soundproof. At the table, china, porcelain and then glass first supplemented and then replaced altogether pewter plates and drinking cups. The big wooden trenchers from which couples formerly shared their meals went quite out of fashion. Knives, forks and spoons gradually became common enough for guests to be provided with a fresh one for each course.

The food served changed no less than the home. Early in the century it had been customary to eat enormous meat meals without vegetables throughout the summer and winter, and to subsist in the winter on salt beef, chickens, broth, eggs and fish, with, of course, quantities of oatmeal prepared in different ways. By 1800 meals were less gargantuan but diet was much better balanced, with a big choice of vegetables (especially turnips, potatoes and greens), more fruit, much more wheat-bread used, and fresh meat available in every month. Tea, as Mackintosh had observed before 1730, was replacing ale and whisky as the polite drink of the day: at about the same period claret was joined and then surpassed by rum punch as the gentleman's drink of the evening. The clergy were split on the problem as to whether drinking tea or spirits was the more depraved, though they usually kept their censures on these matters to the poor. 'One minister in a Stirlingshire village had the problem settled for him very nicely by his parishioners: their last cup of tea was always "qualified by a little whisky, which is supposed to correct all the bad effects of the tea" '.[13]

Changes in consumption habits, of course, are always affected by the whims of fashion, no less than by new levels of income and of expectation. This is obviously truest of clothing, where the 'tie-wigs, jack-boots, enormous sleeves, skirts bolstered out with buckram and buttoned to the heel' of the early eighteenth century looked ridiculous to the eye of the regency critic, less stiffly but no less smartly dressed. Nevertheless, all the evidence points to the fact that the real revolution in the wardrobe was not in fashion but in quantities of clothes. Early in the century the wives of many lairds possessed only three or four fine dresses in the whole of their lifetime, and spent the less formal parts of the day in caps, linen frocks and plaids of 'disgusting slovenliness'. They thought it no disgrace to be waited on by maids without shoes or stockings. Until the middle of the century even upper-class girls did not always wear them. Lord George Murray in 1745 had to write to his daughter recommending her 'to be always neat, especially about the feet, for nothing is more becoming for a young person like you than to wear shoes and stockings'.[14] By the early nineteenth century both sexes thought themselves very poorly off if they could not have several sets of clothes hanging in the wardrobe at the same time, and they obeyed the dictates of fashion so promptly that there was a stream of cast-offs for the servants to wear. Indeed, the strange visitor to the house, unless he was very *au fait* with the fashions, was sometimes hard put to it to discover who was the lady and who was the maid.

All these things are straightforward indications that the gentry as a class enjoyed much more comfortable lives in 1800 than they had in

1700, surrounded as they were by nicer and more abundant material possessions. This, however, was not the whole of the story, for they also reckoned themselves much nicer and politer people than their forefathers. It was no longer, for example, the right thing to get hopelessly drunk at a friend's funeral as the mark of respect for the deceased. It was hardly acceptable to be drunk at all, even at a wedding, though the legal profession and great eccentrics could still afford to flout convention. It became impossible to spit on the floor (one of the consequences, no doubt, of having carpets) and gross housekeeping to leave the family midden by the front gate. It became polite to admire pictures, read secular books and perform or listen to music on the spinet and the piano. The second part of Sir John Clerk of Penicuik's rueful admission about 1700 that he 'understood pictures better than became his purse, and as to music I performed rather better than became a gentleman' would have sounded strange in the second half of the century.[15] Adam Petrie in his *Rules of Good Deportment* of 1720 had shown the absurd fixation of members of his class with learning all the heavy *finesse* of English good manners. The rage for 'elocution' and 'correct pronunciation and elegant reading' as 'indispensable acquirements for people of fashion' was given further encouragement from a visit of Richard Brindley Sheridan's father to Edinburgh in 1761, when he gave a course of lectures on the subject: it took an Irishman to teach English.

It was perhaps something of a paradox that even as polite behaviour became more necessary there was a relaxation in the internal formality of the family and in the strictness with which a child of the upper classes was treated by its parents. On such things it is always hard to generalise, but people later on often referred with wonder to instances of domestic sternness in the early part of the century, when, for example children had not been allowed to speak to or sit down in the presence of their parents, and girls wrote to their mothers as 'Dear Madam', signing themselves 'Your affectionate daughter and humble servant'. Even by 1760 there was more familiarity between parents and children, much less stiffness, and less fear of the father in particular. Old Mrs. Elizabeth Mure reminiscing in the 1790s thought the change had come after 1745 at the same time as the East and West India adventurers began to buy estates: 'Fathers would use the sons with such freedom that they should be their first friend, and the mothers would allow of no intimasies but with themselves . . . Nurses were turned off who would tell the young of witches and ghosts. The old ministers were ridiculed who preched up hell and damnation. The mind was to be influenced by gentle and generous motives only'.[16]

Changes in education were less pronounced on the surface, though the quality and aims of schooling changed quite a lot. At the beginning of the century, though scions of the nobility were often educated at home by tutors, 'by far the greater part' of the Scottish gentry sent their sons to the neighbouring schools with the tenantry, 'every morning, foul day and fair day, carrying their little dinner with them'. By 1800 the balance had perhaps changed, and more had tutors (or went to private boarding-schools in Scotland or England) but there was still a tradition in some places that the laird's son should start his schooling with the common people in the local school. Throughout the century boys commonly went from school to the Universities, and were sometimes also sent to study abroad: more, perhaps, undertook a cultural tour in Europe (if they could afford it) or in England. It had always been common to give younger sons an opening in the army, in trade or in the legal profession, and to equip the heir for estate management by some study of the law and practice with his father's administration of the land, and this broad pattern was not obviously changed within the period. On the other hand, since the children of the landed classes were invariably among the most highly educated in the country (their parents having the means to allow them to spend so long at school and college) they got the full impact of the changing nature and purposes of Scottish education in the eighteenth century which affected its character from the parish school to the university. This is discussed further in chapters XVIII and XIX below. The overall effect must have been to break down narrow formality in learning and to broaden the intellectual horizon of the pupil.

How are we to account for this revolution in manners which began to be obvious from about the third decade of the eighteenth century and gathered momentum after 1760? Obviously, it could not have been sustained (at least in its purely material aspects) unless the gentry as a whole had enjoyed larger real incomes in the late eighteenth century than they did at the beginning. On the other hand there seems to be more to the change than an automatic response to rising rents since they did not begin to lift on a wide scale until some decades after 1720. We must also take account of the desire to copy England. This was the aspect of social change that had impressed Mackintosh so forcibly twenty years after the Union, and which spurred on Petrie and Sheridan. There was no doubt that even highly educated Scots felt themselves backward, boorish and uncouth in the company of the wealthier squirearchy of England with whom they came increasingly in contact. Few landed Scots doubted that England began with a more polite and more desirable civilisation than their own, or that it was a duty of patriotism to match and even to outshine the southerners' model whether it was in teacups, in good tone or (as we shall see) in farming. Again, there was the challenge and the influence of the new-comers to the landed classes: colonial adventurers, war profiteers and merchants who not only had a wide experience of the polite world abroad but also capital (accumulated from other sources than rents) which they could splash in ostentatious display. It was painful for an older laird to see this without making at least an effort to match it.

The effect of these two stimuli was thus to jack up a laird's expec-tations of what his own standard of comfort should be. He could meet the problem either by increasing his rents (which often meant a new approach altogether to the problems of farming on his land) or by borrowing. The first was the long-term solution, but not always a possible one if local economic conditions were unfavourable, as they often were between 1720 and 1780. The latter was a short-term answer which, if followed by nothing more, ultimately led to foreclosure and the sale of his estate to one of the status-hungry incomers from the professions. Thus the revolution in manners was one reason why Scottish land became more efficiently managed and why so much of it changed hands in the course of the eighteenth century.

3. THE IMPROVERS

In 1690, Scotland was a country of peasants who, though by no means equal in status and income, almost all shared in the occupation of some land, and who lived by a traditional system of husbandry in which change was scarcely perceptible even over generations. In 1830, Scotland had an agrarian society broken into sharply defined classes of capitalist farmers and landless labourers, carrying on a sophisticated agricultural system with a flexible and empirical attitude towards new techniques which was the envy of Europe. This was the agricultural revolution, the great divide which meant the end of rural life as it had been lived since time immemorial, and the beginning of rural life as it has been lived ever since. In the full perspective of history, therefore, the most important question about the eighteenth-century landowner must be his relationship to this tremendous change. He was the leader of rural society. His land was being farmed, his demands for rent were being met. Where did he stand? What happened to the peasants will concern us later.

The answer depends to some extent on what part of the eighteenth century we are discussing. It is wrong to imagine the agricultural revolution as something that hit a district in a given decade, and in an intense storm of enthusiasm and upheaval left it all transformed in a few years. It was always slower and more patchy than that: change which had been revolutionary in 1730 might seem to be a very feeble half-measure by 1790; alterations made on one estate did not always spread even to the closest neighbours for half a century. It is useful, however, to make a rough-and-ready division of the period at around 1780; though 1760 might be a better date for some areas like the Lothians in the van of change and in close touch with the market. Before this date the rate of increase of population, food prices, land prices and rents were all comparatively slow: before 1740, indeed, most of the changes were very slow indeed. Economic circumstances generally did not then markedly favour the farmer who went over to modern methods of production, but in that period those exceptional landowners who tried to alter agricultural methods played a vigorous role as innovators and improvers. After 1780, prices and rents rose merrily until the end of the Napoleonic wars, and change in the countryside became much more general and far-reaching. Every landowner now patronised the new husbandry, but their participation in the process of change (though still important) was much more passive.

Practically all the earliest improvers were landowners: there was, indeed, no other class on the land with either the capital, the power or the mental horizons to attempt the transformation of local farming from a backward Scottish peasant model to an advanced English commercial one. It is impossible not to be impressed by the energy and vision with which a man like John Cockburn of Ormiston burst open the high walls of tradition on his estate. In many ways he was not untypical of the first generation of improvers. He was a gentleman and the son of a judge. He was an Anglophile: his father had been one of the commissioners for Union in 1706, he himself was a member of the British parliament from 1707 until 1741 and a holder of minor crown office as a Lord of the Admiralty. His interest in agriculture was a cultural one rather than an economic one. This was his bit for Scotland, his way of dragging her into the Britain of the eighteenth century. He succeeded to his lands in 1714 and immediately set about enclosing with ditches and hedges a farm in his own possession: four years later he began a system of giving nineteen-year leases renewable on payment of an entry fine in perpetuity providing the tenants undertook enclosure on the model of the home farm (but they had to find the capital for themselves). All the steadings on his estate were rebuilt. The sons of his tenants were sent at his expense to the best cultivated counties in England to learn the new husbandry. A stream of correspondence was directed to his gardener and to his best tenants when Cockburn was on business in London, telling them how to plant turnips, sending up saplings and seeds by boat, upbraiding them for their laziness and incompetence: 'our people proceed as half asleep, without any lively spirit in contriving or executing'. He could be offensively frank: 'I suppose you design little poor windows and doors that no-one can go in or out without breaking their head except they remember to duck like a goose. It is a common wise practice which proceeds from their wise heads and noble way of thinking that if any thing is made to look ugly, or if neat is spoiled in dressing, it is thrift'.[17]

The second step in the programme was to rebuild the local farm-toun into a modern English-style village, to serve as a market for the surplus the new farmers were producing. He feued out the 'new town' of Ormiston under strict controls about the accommodation and appearance of the houses, built a brewery and distillery, laid out a bleachfield and introduced workers from Ireland and from Holland to teach the best methods of flax preparation. Fellow landowners waxed enthusiastic over the whole scheme. Sir James Hall of Dunglass wrote to his friend the Earl of Marchmont, saying he had sent three of his best tenants to Ormiston where they had learned more about good farming in two days than in all the rest of their life. He went on in these glowing terms:

His town is riseing exceedingly . . . thers not a boy or girel of seven years old but has something to doe, that ye will not see ane in the

town except in ane hour of play. Blacksmiths, shoemarkers, candle-
makers and baikers, maltsters etc., make throng doeing . . . Ther is
boths building for all their merchandise, and to be market days, and
ther is sixteen houses contracted for nixt season . . . I shall, Dear
Marchmont, in a little time be beter able to let you know more
about it. I have sent for a duble of his tacks and fews.[18]

Cockburn in 1747 unfortunately overreached himself in his expenditure, went bankrupt and sold out to the Earl of Hopetoun. But his
work was not lost. His best tenants, especially the Wight family,
became in their turn the protagonists of the new farming both in the
Lothians and beyond.

Cockburn's programme was altogether typical of the first improvers. It was closely parallelled in the work of Archibald Grant of
Monymusk, another laird whose papers have survived in detail.[19] Most
improving lairds started first on a 'home farm' with enclosure, new
crops and the habits of English husbandry, working on land directly
under their own management or with a trusted bailiff with whom they
kept in close contact. Few (Barclay of Urie in Kincardineshire was an
exception) tried to farm the whole estate themselves—George Robertson in 1829 did not think that more than two per cent of the land was
worked by landowners. In order to persuade the peasants to follow
their own example, they used a mixture of carrot and stick—eviction
for those who could not or would not undertake the new husbandry
within a certain time, long and secure leases at reasonable rents for the
co-operative and willing remainder. Some were more generous than
Cockburn, and financed the division of the runrig, the running up of
enclosure walls and hedges and the building of new steadings from
their own pocket: others financed them indirectly by reductions of
rent for a period of five or ten years after enclosure. Nor did landowners
leave the tenants once the layout of the farms had been changed: a
trickle of skilled Englishmen arrived throughout the century at the
invitation of the nobility and gentry to manage their own farms and
to teach the sons of local farmers better ways; the landowner himself
continued to pour out upon his dependents a stream of gratuitous
advice. This could sometimes be both ill-informed and exasperating
to the recipient. John Hunter, a highly successful tenant who died with
lands of his own and a fortune of £8000 once told Lord Kames, the
author on agricultural subjects most widely read by his fellow land-

owners before Sinclair, 'My Lord, to hear you talk of farming one would think you had been born yestreen.'[20]

Many landowners also followed Cockburn in the construction of a new village, partly to act as a point of consumption for the produce of the estate (an important consideration when land communications were still so bad), partly to provide jobs for small tenants who found themselves squeezed out in the re-organisation of the runrig farms. Joseph Cumine of Auchry in Aberdeenshire, for instance, on succeeding to his estate in 1739 began to enclose land and to lay out new farms, then observing that his tenants lacked a market, he planned a village on a 'moorish part of a farm' which yielded him only £11 a year in rent:

> For a while he felt in silence the sneers of his neighbours, who reprobated the scheme as wild and impracticable; but these temporary sneers soon gave way to lasting esteem. He prevailed upon a few to take feus; he assisted the industrious with money; obtained premiums for the manufacturer; decided every difference by his arbitration, and animated all to their utmost exertion by his countenance and counsel. Settlers annually flocked to Cuminestown . . . and instead of £11 sterling, the original rent, produced him annually from £120 to £150 a year.[21]

In order for these new settlements to function properly, it was necessary to have a nucleus of non-agricultural employment introduced into the town. Fishing was one answer, not much favoured outside the Highlands or the north-east. Alternatively there could be a variety of country trades encouraged—brewing, distilling, sawmilling, sack-making, saddlery and so on—but the scope offered by these was strictly limited. The most obvious and most promising new openings were in the textile industry, and lairds showed themselves most anxious to promote the growth of the linen trade and the woollen industry in their villages (both new and old) in the first three quarters of the eighteenth century. There were two important results. Land-owners found themselves from the start enthusiastic supporters of industrialisation in Scotland, which they often assisted at its embryonic village level by the provision of fixed capital and loans, and which they never obstructed from any suspicion or foresight that it would raise up a power in society to match and ultimately to overtop their own. Secondly, the Scottish countryside was provided with many delightful villages of stone-built, two-storied houses placed in a planned community to replace the insanitary confusion of the old farmtouns. There is no doubt they were intended to look like the villages of southern England, but they were more functional than the new English model villages of the eighteenth century which like Milton Abbas in Dorset were meant to be ornamental rather than useful. Lord Gardenstone's Laurencekirk in Kincardineshire, the Duke of Gordon's Fochabers and the Earl of Findlater's New Keith in Moray and Banff, the Duke of Perth's Crieff and Callander in Perthshire and the Duke of Buccleuch's Newcastleton on the Borders are all outstanding examples of lowland communities which began on green fields in the half century from 1730. There are others in the Highlands, and still more, like Cromarty, which are old towns rebuilt to the landlord's purpose in these years. If a full century from 1730 is taken, probably somewhere between 120 and 150 new planned villages were laid down.

Prior to 1780 the improver was still an exception among landlords, though certainly at that date there were many more than there had been even twenty years before. But who were the exceptions? And what made them turn improver? They were drawn from a wide spectrum of rank. The aristocracy were well represented by such figures as the Duke of Perth, the Duke of Gordon and the Duke of Argyll, or by the Earl of Stair, the Earl of Haddington, and the Earl of Hopetoun, all of whom took an active personal interest in farming, and did not merely leave it to a clever factor, as the Duke of Queensberry appears to have done. The law lords were particularly strongly represented in proportion to their numbers—Lord Kames, Lord Gardenstone, Lord Monboddo, Lord Nisbet and Lord Hailes are examples, and of the most famous first improvers, Cockburn of Ormiston and Grant of Monymusk, were both children of lawyers. There were many gentry like William Mackintosh of Borlum or Thomas Hope of Rankeillor, and Robert Maxwell of Arkland, who carried the main burden of running the Honourable Society of Improvers started at Edinburgh in 1720 as a great propaganda effort to spread knowledge of the new farming. The people who are not at first represented at all among the improvers are the smallest gentry, and those who had no occasion for social contact with London or Edinburgh, or, one might add a little later, with Aberdeen, for the northern capital came to have a vigorous farming club of its own in which professional men and academics played a large part.[22] Peers always had business in one capital or the other. Lawyers were the intellectual linch pin of Edinburgh society after 1707. Cockburn and Grant were members of Parliament in London, coming in daily contact with the great English farmer politicians such as Walpole and Townshend. Hope travelled Europe in search of new ideas, and drained the stinking South Loch of Edinburgh to make the Meadows, as a demonstration of modern reclamation for his friends. Improvers, in other words, were not country bumpkins who shut themselves away on their estates to contemplate their fields. They were, rather, the most alert of their class who belonged to a coherent metropolitan society in which ideas and fashion were transmitted quickly and enthusiastically. This was how they knew enough to become improvers.

Why did they become improvers? It was not because they were good business men. Cockburn lost his estate to the Earl of Hopetoun. Maxwell of Arkland, so lavish with advice as secretary of the Society of Improvers, undermined its propaganda by becoming bankrupt. Lord Gardenstone, transforming Laurencekirk, 'contracted great debts' which 'soured his temper', and was only saved by a fortunate legacy. Grant of Monymusk was an exception; having been expelled from the House of Commons for a disgraceful fraud involving the funds of a charitable society, he began to take the respectable operations of husbandry much more seriously. There was, in his view, no business in life that 'affords profit with greater certainty and less risk'. He certainly succeeded in redeeming both his fortune and his historical reputation by his farming.

The reason for so many of the first improvers' failure to make farming pay was not only that they were pioneers, or that they were operating in a country where incomes were low and demand for agricultural produce generally slack, though these things certainly mattered. It was also that at the deepest level they were not (apart from Grant of Monymusk) impelled by economic necessity to farm as they did. Their spurs were primarily those of fashion, patriotism and the admiration felt by Scots of all political persuasions for a farming system that made the English so much more affluent than themselves. They learnt their farming from manuals liberally spiced with quotations from Ovid and Virgil: they were so contemptuous of the ways of their neighbours and tenants that they even overlooked the traditional dates of sowing and reaping, though the blind imitation of every detail of Norfolk or Berkshire husbandry in a Scottish climate and soil was absurd. They went in for farming, in fact, as another form of conspicuous consumption, just as some of their neighbours might fall into a rage for building, or landscape gardening or the Grand Tour of Italy. Ramsay of Ochtertyre had a shrewder knowledge of his class than most; he described the first Stirlingshire improvers as:

> full of money and of course under no obligation of attending to immediate gain (yet) if their expenses sometimes far exceeded their returns, they were morally certain in the long-run they would be well paid for their improvements. Amusement and the reputation of being good farmers were in truth the great motives.[23]

As a result, most tenants were deeply contemptuous of the dilettante ways of 'gentlemen farmers' and avoided imitating the practice of the home farm unless change was positively pushed down their throat: many landowners also regarded their improving fellows as hare-brained, especially if they themselves did not have spare cash to indulge in the hobby.

On the other hand, in the long run, the contribution of all these vigorous amateurs was of incalculable importance. They broke the crust of custom by riddling it with holes of experiment and endeavour: there were few counties without a number of landowners practising 'English husbandry' even in 1760: there were considerably more by 1780, even though at that date the general structure of agriculture among the tenantry was yet little changed. When in the last twenty years of the eighteenth century rents and prices began to move ahead fast as market opportunities expanded, the scattered improved farms suddenly began to show greatly enhanced profits compared to those of their traditionalist neighbours. When all landowners came to insist on enclosure, and above all when tenants began to copy and to improve the techniques of the gentleman farmers by empirical experiment and adaptations of their own, the effect on Scottish husbandry was electrifying. The main function of the first improvers had thus been to provide the only possible models on which the transformation could be based, but thanks partly to their own characters and partly to the economic situation before 1780, they were generally unable to perfect the models or bring about the transformation themselves.

After 1780 when with sharply rising prices the agricultural revolution was effectively carried out in all corners of the land, the landowners role was usually more passive. That is not to say there was no continuity: the best English farming continued to be held up for admiration and a landowner like Sir John Sinclair, instigator of the great rural investigation whose first fruits were the *Statistical Accounts*, improver of Caithness and builder of Thurso, followed the path of the first improvers even to bankruptcy. There was, however, a sharper division of function between landowner and tenant than had been usual in the past. All landowners raced to become improvers only in the sense that they made the policy decision that now the fields must be enclosed, the waste reclaimed, the farmtouns broken up and new steadings built, and turnips or some equivalent crop that would alter and enrich the traditional rotations grown throughout the estate. But then, instead of laying down the law about precisely what to do, they trusted the tenants with the job of adapting and altering English husbandry so that it fitted the Scottish situation.

There were, of course, regional variations. In the backward parts the landowner was still often unable to find tenants who were willing or able to take initiative upon themselves. Then he might act in the old heroic way like Sinclair in Caithness. More often now, however, the landlord employed a factor who had himself been an experienced tenant farmer. In more central counties like Stirlingshire the tenants learnt fast and edged their masters out of the old role, which they were happy enough to give up: 'the exertions of (two improving tenants) did more to give tenants a taste for improvements than fifty gentlemen farmers opulent in their circumstances but rash or unsteady in their conduct'.[24] Above all it was in the Lothians that it became well established that tenants were the most effective innovators and that landowners should leave them to it with the minimum of disturbance— and Lothian husbandry became the exemplar of Europe. George Robertson explained the situation in this region in 1829.

Agriculture, to be well conducted, is a science, or rather an occupation that requires such unceasing attention and so much laborious industry that few men who are in the independent circumstances of an opulent landholder can bring themselves to dedicate to it their whole talents and time ... should they remain at home on their paternal estates their attentions are commonly directed to the embellishments of their property rather than to its cultivation: they enclose—they plant—they build—they construct highways, erect bridges or plan canals or railroads, they lay out gardens or they erect gateways or other rural decorations. But the labours of cultivation they more generally, perhaps more wisely, leave to the common husbandman of the country, whose toils, stimulated by necessity, and whose schemes, resulting from experience, if not in all cases more rationally formed, seldom fail at least to be conducted with more economy . . . the great mass of improvements which the country has undergone has originated chiefly and been brought to its present comparatively perfect state by the tenantry themselves without being either much prompted to it by the proprietors or led on by their example.[25]

It was a far cry from almost exactly one hundred years before when Cockburn had been upbraiding his tenants for their stupidity, and at the same time excusing them with the thought that perhaps they did not get enough to eat ('and our malt drink is the most stupifying stuff ever contrived'). In the next chapter we shall be examining some of the reasons for the remarkable change in the character and circumstances of the peasantry.

Many people towards the end of the eighteenth century also asserted that landowners were becoming obsessed by the wish for more and more money, to the exclusion of other, older, gentler and more patriarchal values. A tenant, they said, was no longer asked if he had been born on the estate, or even if he was an industrious and sober man: he was simply presented with a demand for as high a rent as the market would bear, and if he could not meet it a stranger was invited to the farm his predecessors had enjoyed perhaps for generations. A village was no longer laid out as a model community, the accommodation of its houses and the constitution of its government controlled by the landlord: the land was feued at the best price perhaps to the owner of a cotton mill, who was allowed to do as he wished with the houses and hands he implanted on the site. Ramsay of Ochtertyre had this kind of behaviour in mind when he wrote in 1800:

I have lived in times when all ranks of men have been changing their modes and manners and sentiments, some for the better and others for the worse. During my course there have been new maxims laid down by proprietors and men of business which sounded to me harsh, precipitate and unpolitic. Indeed for nearly twenty years after I commenced a country gentleman in about 1750 no character was in lower repute than that of a harsh and avaricious landlord . . . it could not be foreseen that the time would come when the raising of rents should occupy the attention of proprietors great and small.[26]

It is always difficult to assess this kind of historical evidence. In every age there are grasping landlords and generous, even quixotic ones. The former existed before 1780: Grant of Monymusk was certainly harsh and avaricious, and there were no doubt excellent reasons why the tenants of the Duke of Perth gave up praying for him at grace when he raised the Callander estate rent. The latter did not disappear in 1780, as the careers of Sir John Sinclair, the Earl of Eglinton and a host of others would testify. On the other hand it would really have been surprising if there had not been a growth of commercialisation in the landed classes. They had to raise the money to live up to the high new standards of comfort they set themselves. They were, in many cases, landowners of first generation themselves, coming in after a fight in hard-headed professions, and not likely to regard the ancient tenants of the outgoing laird with any particular sentiment or consideration. The chances of profit were in any case greater with a temporary sellers' market for leases after 1780, following on a long period before 1760 when tenants seemed hard to replace. Nobody, of course, remembered the sixteenth and early seventeenth centuries or even the years immediately before the famine of the 1690s, when the outcries against oppressive money-minded landlords had been even greater: those had been the last great periods of landhunger and competition among tenants for leases.

This feeling that landowners (even in the Lowlands) had somehow deserted a historic role and were now just out for what they could get was a cause of bitterness at the time and of recrimination later. It matched too well the factory owner's contemporary logic of laissez-faire and the devil take the hindermost. The idea of father-figures who sell up their children is never a very attractive one. On the other hand it was certainly business sense, and writers like Robertson believed that high rents squeezed the most efficient husbandry from the tenant, the highest productivity from the worker and the biggest surplus of food-stuffs for the towns, and doubted whether without realistic pressure exerted in this way by landlords the agricultural revolution in the Lowlands would have come so quickly or so thoroughly. It may not always be by benevolent paternalism that economic good is maximised for the community.

CHAPTER XIII

The Peasant in the Agricultural Revolution

1. PEASANT SOCIETY ON THE EVE OF CHANGE

The Agricultural Revolution of the generations after 1760 enclosed the Scottish fields, broke down the rigs, consolidated the strips, drained the stagnant mosses, took in the common, changed the crops and the rotations, and destroyed for ever the traditions of a husbandry which hallowed and inefficient as it was, had dictated the framework of life for most Scots for as long as our knowledge of agrarian history goes back. In doing so it sundered for ever a peasant economy that had been mainly dedicated to producing enough for itself in a largely rural world where most people were themselves producers: there arose instead a society in which capitalist farmers and landless labourers worked mainly to produce food for great towns filled with consumers, and who did their task so well that the farming system in many parts of Scotland became the envy of Europe.

We have in a previous chapter described both the structure of the old peasant society and its methods of husbandry. Eighteenth-century writers left a number of vivid and detailed accounts of how the peasants lived in the last generations before the great change. Few, apart from those captured in the verse of Burns, are so well known as they deserve: one of the best is George Robertson's account in *Rural Recollections* of the Lothian peasants of the middle decades of the eighteenth century.

The 'gudeman' of Robertson's description was a substantial tenant by the standards of his day, holding about one hundred acres of arable in the most fertile counties of Scotland. He was not, therefore, as poor as most peasants, nor was his husbandry utterly primitive. There is nothing, for instance, in the book which suggests that Lothian gudemen were still farming co-operatively let alone with annual exchange of strips: they probably had relatively consolidated, though unenclosed, farms, and operated as separate units except that all their animals were herded together on the common. This relative sophistication of their economic position makes the following account of their primitive standards of living all the more telling. It represents about the peak of peasant affluence around 1760.

The gudeman's house was the centre of a row of undetached farm-buildings flanked on the one side by barns and on the other by cattle houses. They all looked much alike—low in the walls and thatched with straw interlaid with thin turf sods to bind the roof, and overlooking the great dunghill in which all manner of excrement, human as well as animal, was kept in readiness for the annual manuring of the bear-land. The dwelling-house itself, perhaps thirty foot long and fourteen foot wide, consisted of two rooms only, the 'but' and the 'ben'. These had quite different social functions.

The but was the social focus of the farm. It was used as the kitchen and as the servants' quarters, as the dining room for the whole house-hold and as the sleeping apartment for the maid-servants and the gudeman's own daughters. The floor of the room was earth, the walls were unplastered, and there was, as a rule, no ceiling below the rafters although there might be a few planks nailed between the beams to serve as shelves for storing food. The only window was a foot-and-a-half wide, and a little higher, filled with lozenge glass. The main feature of the room was the enormous 'lum', or chimney, built over the cradle-grate and projecting five or six feet into the room: benches were arranged comfortably around it in a semi-circle 'yont-the-ingle' where the boys and menservants would sit in the evenings together with any hangers-on the family might acquire. Beggars might reckon on hospitality and a seat by the fire in exchange for a story, a ballad or simply for news from the neighbours they had visited before. Tenants were much more tolerant than landlords or kirk of the 'idle sorners that went from place to place begging'. Apart from the benches there would be box-beds in the room, a great table bearing earthenware plates and tankards as well as spoons, also a number of cupboards or chests, spinning wheels and other household implements. The but was a crowded, warm, smokey, busy place where everyone connected with the farm was equally welcome, and where discipline and order was kept by the gudewife.

The ben was the private apartment of the gudeman, floored in deal and plastered on the walls, with a recessed fire and frequently a wooden ceiling, but otherwise of similar appearance and dimensions to the but. This was where the gudeman and his wife, with their younger children, had their sleeping quarters and where they entertained any visitors whom they regarded as social equals or superiors. The furniture reflected the social pretensions of the ben: it was carved, polished, and more varied with chairs and a small table, an easy chair for the gudewife at 'bairntime', a napery chest with the best linen in it, the finest box-beds, and even a mirror and a clock in many homes. Sometimes there would be a writing desk and a chest for papers. Always there would be somewhere to keep the Bible, and the other books belonging to the family, for the Lothian gudemen were both literate and pious.

> In their religious sentiments as they were nearly all the descendants of the more ancient covenanters, so were they actuated by similar principles, and with a veneration for their practices. Hence their books were all of that cast: such as the works of Sir David Lindsay, of Buchanan, of Knox, of Rutherford, of Bunyan and of Boston; and of Woodrow too . . . they also had a taste for ancient histories connected with their country: as Abercrombie's *Lives* and Blind Harry's *Wallace*; and stories about Bruce and Bannockburn; and of Chevy-Chase, and the Douglas; and of Roslin-Muir, and Pentland-Hills, and Drumclog, and Bothwell-Brig, and Sherrif-Muir; and of Culloden, and Duc William, and the Pretender. But no book was so familiar to them as the scriptures . . .[1]

In material food and clothing the Lothian gudemen enjoyed rough plenty: the eighteenth century lacked that dreadful sense of famine stalking from behind which dogged the sixteenth century and much of the seventeenth. After King William's Years in the 1690s there was a long period until 1782 when food prices remained steady and reasonably low, disturbed by higher prices in 1756 and 1762 but broken only by a season of dearth in 1740 when the gentry imported quantities of grain and distributed it free, or at cut prices, to those in need. In all normal times, therefore, food was to be had in abundance, if not in great variety. The gudewife's table in the but was laid for master and man alike: the staple of life was porridge, for breakfast and supper:

dinner was out of the kail-pot, consisting of barley broth with greens and bannocks of barley or pease-meal. Meat was served twice a week, mutton in summer, salt-beef in winter: but in the ben the gudeman might eat lamb or chicken with his guests more regularly. All the food, of course, was produced on the farm: only the salt was extraneous to the domestic economy.

The same was true of the clothing: almost everything was made from home-produced wool or flax, 'except the gudeman's black bonnet and the gudewife's velvet hood', says Robertson, perhaps with some exaggeration. The yarn was spun by the farm maids, woven, fulled and dyed by craftsmen from the nearest town, and made up into clothes by the local country tailor 'on the top of the kitchen table under the gudewife's own eye'. Shoes, too, were made in a similar fashion, from the hide that had once covered the salt-beef they ate all winter, made up by a jobbing cobbler who came round to the farms to fit the families. Most women and children, however, normally went bare-foot.

Apart from the gudemen, peasant society of the Lothians included the unmarried farm servants who lived in the tenant's house, and the married cottars who also generally found some employment on the tenant's farm. Robertson relates that a holding of one hundred acres would generally employ as unmarried servants two young men as assistant ploughmen, a boy for a cow-herd, a thresher (at least in winter) and two or three maid-servants—all living permanently with the gudeman's family. The men and the grown sons of the tenant slept in a loft above the ben (if there happened to be one) or more often with the horses in the stable. The girls slept in the kitchen with the tenant's daughters, though if a strong wind made the lum smoke all the women would go to spend the night with the cows. The principal married servants were the 'hinds', or skilled ploughmen, who had their own cottages and worked on the land with their wives and families. Other cottars had less regular employment, but they would certainly be needed at haytime and harvest, to rush in the crops while the pre-carious Scottish weather lasted: otherwise they would live off their small-holdings, some of as much as five, ten or even fifteen acres, and perhaps have a secondary occupation such as weaving or shoemaking to supplement their earnings from the land.

The standards of living of the whole of this dependent class were obviously inferior to those of the gudeman. A cottar's house, for instance, could be run up in a single day if the materials had been gathered beforehand. It was a stone-walled hut, with walls five foot high and twelve foot long on each side, an earth floor and a timber roof thatched with straw. Not all had chimneys—in many cottages the smoke still rose from the hearth towards a hole left in the roof, or found its way out through the door or the unglazed window. The main piece of furniture in such a hovel was the box-bed, fully enclosed on all sides and accessible only by a sliding door in the front—'Such a form was almost indispensable: it was like a house within a house, for the sake of shelter, whether in the dwelling of the master or of the servant'.[2] Otherwise there might be a couple of chests, two stools, a cooking pot, a wash tub, some wooden mugs and horn spoons to complete the inventory of a cottar's worldly goods. Two pecks of oatmeal weekly and adequate milk formed a major part of the hind's wages, paid in kind, and their own kail-yard kept them in vegetables: the unmarried servants lived off similar fare within the farm house. Perhaps they tasted meat, at the farmer's table, a little more often.

In this society, servants and cottars are poorer than gudemen—yet the distance between them is one of degree rather than kind, even in material things. The gudeman produced food for the market to provide himself with the money income needed to pay the rent to the laird and to meet such wages as were not in kind: but plainly he consumed much of what was produced either in his own family or as wages to his employees. The cottars and servants had only a little cash. The hind payed the rent to the farmer through his wife's work on the land, and raised food in his own kailyard or infield holding mainly for his own consumption. At the social level there were very close bonds. Gudeman and servant ate at the same table, shared the same fireside in the evenings, worked side by side at the same jobs in the fields during the day: their children, as adolescents, slept in the same primitive quarters with the animals or the household smoke. Lastly, they shared the same literary and religious tastes. Where the gudeman bought pious books, the hind bought the cheaper pamphlets, *Christian Ker*, Peden's *Prophecies*, *The Holy War*, which they obtained from travelling chapmen and made their children read to them on Sabbath afternoons after a family catechising. Their minute knowledge of the Bible they also shared with the gudeman, together with the habit of regular household worship. There is something very astonishing in the prospect of a peasant society of very low average material standards in which everyone owns books or tracts, and is in the habit of discussing the scriptures with some knowledge and authority.

One must ask, of course, how far the Lothians can be regarded as typical. Certainly, throughout Scotland, one would find the basic division between tenant and cottar groups, though in very many places a farm as large as the gudeman's one hundred acres of arable would be quite unknown. In some areas the tenant would be replaced by an owner-occupier or bonnet-laird—these were common in parts of the south-west and in patches elsewhere—but the material standards of these men were much like those of the ordinary tenant. Certainly one would also find roughly the same kind of houses, the same kind of food, the same kind of objects of furniture and apparel within tenants' and cottars' houses up and down the country, though probably none would be quite so well off as the Lothian peasants. Eighteenth-century tenants' houses in Wigtownshire, for instance, were also of but-and-ben construction, built out of stone and bog-oak and thatched with straw, but they had neither plaster nor deal in the ben, nor a loft for the young males to sleep in: cottar housing in the same county was also but-and-ben, but the peasant's cow lived in the ben and was only prevented from coming up to the fire-place by the box-bed that divided the house in two. One writer describes how his mother always knew it was time to put the porridge on the fire when she heard the family cow standing behind her pass water for the second time.[3] It is obvious why Sir Archibald Grant of Monymusk in Aberdeenshire instructed his factor to dump cottars' houses on the farm dunghill when he had evicted their occupants.[4]

What is not completely clear from the regional comparisons is how far peasants outside the Lothians were as pious or well instructed as the gudeman and his hinds. Certainly there was a high level of religious interest and active literacy among people like the bonnet-lairds of Ayrshire, and Burns's poem, *The Cottar's Saturday-night*, testified to the same kind of piety and interest among the poorest peasants in that county:

> The chearfu' supper done, wi' serious face,
> They, round the ingle form a circle wide,
> The Sire turns o'er, with patriarchal grace
> The big ha' Bible, ance his Father's pride.

Much of the southern lowlands were no doubt like this. Beyond the Tay there was probably still formal literacy among the Lowlanders but less obvious enthusiasm for reading or popular religious feeling of a radical character. This may be simply because historians have not yet been able to unravel a sufficiently detailed picture, but it is a fair guess that Lothian society saw not only peasant material standards at their highest, but peasant standards of literacy and knowledge of religion also at their best. Some of these matters are considered again in Chapter XVIII below. It is interesting to speculate how far the course of the agricultural revolution in Scotland was affected by the peculiar intellectual character of the counties round the capital.

2. THE MAKING OF THE FARMING CLASS

The nineteenth-century farmer who emerged at the end of the agricultural revolution cut a vastly different figure from the eighteenth-century tenant who stood on its threshold. The gudeman had been a peasant with little capital of his own, living from hand to mouth, dwelling with his farm servants, farming in obedience to unwritten and almost unchanging tradition. The farmer who replaced him was a capitalist of resources and a man of middle-class affluence and expectations, who built his tall stone house to stress his self-identification with the 'landed interest' and to separate himself sharply and obviously from the labourers whose work he controlled. The height of the social climb was therefore matched by the width of the social gulf that now yawned between master and man.

The new men also farmed with an ingenuity, enterprise and vigour that contemporaries soon began to regard as the sole springs of agricultural change. Thus the great English demographer Malthus noted in his travel diary in 1810, 'the improvement of Scotch husbandry has arisen principally from the improving capitals and skills of the tenantry and not from the capitals of the landlords',[5] and George Robertson a generation later made almost the same comment—'the great mass of improvements arising from a better mode of tillage and system of rotation in cropping has been owing almost entirely to the farmers themselves with very little example set them by the proprietors'.[6] Such statements, true in their limited context, ignore the fact that the new farmers themselves were as deliberate and artificial a creation as the quick-set hedge and the Cheviot sheep. The eighteenth-century laird who set about improving his estate also set about improving his tenants.

There were many ways in which he might try to do this, and much advice to which he might listen. Everyone in authority thought that, as a general rule, the traditional tenant class was idle and hide-bound, and that as far as possible only exceptional tenants marked by their own personal qualities should be encouraged by favourable leases. They also agreed that when the land was reorganised it should also be reallocated in larger shares:

> It would be endless to state what is so often repeated in the surveys, that the small farm is found to be attended with an insufficient capital, with puny enclosures down to two acres and with wretched husbandry; that the poor farmer is always a bad one, the lower the rent the poorer the tenant, and with husbandry worse; that idleness and laziness prevail; that a small farm is not worth the attention of any man of ingenuity and property.[7]

While these two ideas held general sway, it was clear that not by any means every tenant of the unenclosed fields could hope to become a farmer of the new enclosures. To some extent the expanding boundaries of cultivation did help to mitigate the ruthless logic of the situation, but many would nevertheless fall to the ranks of the landless labourer. Those who remained as occupiers became increasingly unlike peasants. In 1796 Thomas Robertson was recommending landowners to stock their farms with tenants under the following conditions: each farmer should hold sufficient land to keep him occupied in its management throughout the year; he should perform no manual work on the farm himself; he should see to all management without an intermediary or bailiff; he should have the security of a regular lease; he should pay what was described as an 'adequate rent'.[8] He should be, in fact, an expert at farming and labour management, and be milked of a generous portion of resulting profits without being deprived of the opportunity to accumulate capital or increase his own standard of living. Anything less like the old gudeman is hard to imagine.

There was no stereotype for the pattern of change. Where the Agricultural Revolution began early, the rise of the farmers was often relatively gradual and extended over several generations. Tenants who were readiest to listen with a sympathetic ear to the laird's new fads for turnips and stone dykes in the years before 1760 were likely to put their families at a distinct advantage for the future, since the landowner would regard them as the most 'industrious' and 'intelligent' of his dependents and reward them accordingly with generous leases. If they adopted the new husbandry with a certain initial caution and good sense it would not ruin them (if they took everything the laird said as Gospel the story might be different); and the pay-off would come when prices and rents rose in the succeeding half-century. Contemporaries said the general level of rent was stationary from 1700 to 1750, began to lift markedly from 1763, doubled from 1783 to 1793 and doubled again from 1794 to 1815.[9] Families with prior experience of superior cultivation and secure leases were in a position to increase profits and accumulate capital more effectively than beginners. Thus if any local laird decided to put his rents to public auction or roup (an increasingly common practice from 1760 despite the agricultural writers' insistence that good farmers needed a measure of security), such a tenant had the resources to outbid his neighbours and add to his farm. If on the other hand a laird decided merely to enlarge the average size of his holding, the farmer with capital and experience would be favoured again as the man best able to make use of his opportunities. This principle accelerated the rise of the early starters, and providing the family retained its technical sense and business acumen in an increasingly competitive environment, its rise would be so fast, so steady and so natural from generation to generation that the sense of any sudden break with the past was likely to be blurred. The average Lothian farming family would be aware not so much of a crisis met and overcome as of a series of opportunities which presented themselves and had been grasped and turned to their advantage in order to make rungs for the next stage on their ascent of the social ladder. This partly accounts for the enormous pride and self-confidence of the Lothian farming class in the early decades of the nineteenth century.

Elsewhere the impact of the agricultural revolution might come as a single cathartic shock. Samuel Robinson gave a vivid account of what happened in Wigtownshire, a county at the opposite end of the agricultural spectrum from the Lothians, where until almost the end of the century indigenous peasant society went on almost unaffected by change, paying traditional rents to traditional lairds for lands that they held at will but seldom risked losing by dispossession, and that consisted of open, ridged stoney fields, wide pools of boggy water and

tall thickets of whins. The crisis that 'produced a magical change', came
with the sale of the old estate of Baldoon to the Earls of Galloway in
1787: the new owners at once offered the leases to the highest bidders
at a public roup in the courthouse at Wigton, which brought farmers
from all parts of Scotland:

> Rents were offered then that never had been dreamed of by a
> Galloway farmer ... men of energy and capital came on to the
> field, and a great change passed over the spirit of peoples' dreams
> generally. The old clumsy wooden plough became a thing of the
> past, iron ones were substituted with machinery 'of a' dimensions,
> shapes, and metals' for clearing and pulverising the soil; draining
> and fencing went on with an energy truly surprising.[10]

This was the point of no return for the Wigtownshire peasant
families: either they found a way of raising the enhanced rent, or they
went to the wall and watched a stranger from East Lothian or Ayrshire
take up the land. In this case, as no doubt in many others, the local
population threw up men of real ability almost overnight: Robinson
relates that nineteen years after the fateful Baldoon sale the only three
tenants left in possession of the leases rouped on that occasion were all
Galloway men, and the strangers, for all their push and new ideas, had
not succeeded against local climatic and geographical conditions of
which they had been ignorant when they took the farms. What we do
not know, of course, is the proportion of the old tenants on the Baldoon
farms who never made the transition to modern farmer. Nor for that
matter do we know who apart from the three remaining Galloway
men actually were farming the Baldoon estate after nineteen years.

The farming class was not, even in 1830, a uniform group over the
Lowland counties with everywhere the same set of values, the same
level of affluence, the same size of farm and the same ideas of management. The *General Report* of 1814 demonstrated how there could be
wide differences within a narrow compass: in Peebleshire there was a
world of difference between the 'opulent and the best informed', the
storemasters running thousand-acre sheepfarms on the Moorfoots, and
the poor arable farmer in the valleys, 'possessed of less capital and
generally obliged not merely to oversee but to work upon their own
farms'. Then there were striking differences between one wider
district and another: the arable farms of the south-east between Angus,
South Perthshire and Berwickshire, averaged about 200 acres each but

ranged up to 2000 acres and even more; those in the western counties of Ayrshire, Lanark, Renfrew and Dunbarton seldom reached 200 acres and in Dunbartonshire averaged only about seventy. In the north-east, the stock-and-corn farms of Aberdeen and Banff fell between these two extremes.[11]

The smaller the farm, the nearer the farmers even in the early nineteenth century would be to their peasant forebears. 'Where the farms are in general so small it cannot be expected that the farmers should be remarkable for their improvement and spirit', wrote Dr. George Skene Keith, 'Dumbartonshire farmers are tenants of the old school, men of limited education, following implicitly the practice of their fathers'. How different they were to the great tenants of the Merse of Berwickshire, who 'have almost universally risen above the rank of peasantry in knowledge, education and manners, assimilating in many respects to the character of country gentlemen', or of course to those of East Lothian, 'entitled to rank with those of any other district in the kingdom'. It is interesting to read what Keith has to say about the last:

> This is ascribed chiefly to the example of a perfect cultivation set by many of their ancestors, joined to the capital possessed by most of them, and to the good education they receive: which in many instances is perfected at the University and which, by giving them liberal views early in life, fits them for that intercourse with their brethren on both sides of the Tweed by which they are enabled to acquire the most correct ideas of every useful improvement.[12]

Since these Lothian farmers represent in so many ways the quintessence of the new class on the land, and since they are also the direct descendants of the gudemen with whom we began, it is worth returning to them here in order to see how in the most favourable economic circumstances the agricultural revolution could raise and change the standards of living of the tenant class as the class itself was raised and changed within the social framework.

George Robertson again vividly describes the first steps of change as they were reflected in the furnishings of a farmer's house: the great oaken common dining table was replaced by a more refined article of imported mahogany, and the closed box-beds (the 'house within the house') by stupendous four-posters with damask hangings. Much *trivia* followed—fenders, feather-beds, looking glasses, a barometer:

the farmers were able to take advantage of the cheap productions of the industrial revolution, such as the 'elegant cream-coloured stone-ware invented in 1763 by Josias Wedgwood in Staffordshire' which 'in the course of a few years spread over the whole country'. China tea-equipages and punch-bowls followed, bobbing in the wake of the laird's genteel tastes a decade or two behind, and Lancashire and Lanarkshire cottons began to challenge the hegemony of thick coarse woollens and linen producing a revolution in fashion comparable to that brought about in recent times by synthetic fibres. In these ways standards rose until:

> in the end the simple establishment of the rustic husbandman came to emulate that of the more polished citizen of the capital; insomuch that the gorgeous sideboard, the wine-cooler, the sofa or settee, and above all the elegant piano-forte, not forgetting the carpets of the finest fabric, were now component parts of the furnishings of the farmer's mains.[13]

To accommodate these splendid contents the farmer's house was altered out of all recognition. 'Modern farm-houses', said Sir John Sinclair in the *General Report* 'mark the progress of agricultural improvement and the amelioration in the condition of the farmers more than almost any other single circumstances.' He published the plans of four such houses, which he particularly recommended for his readers. Three of them would have done a middle-sized laird proud a generation earlier. One was actually being constructed at a cost of £847 for a farmer near Tynninghame in East Lothian: it was a well-proportioned, Georgian-style building of two storeys, stone-built with a slate roof; downstairs were three large reception rooms for the family, and a separate kitchen, wash-house and milk-house where the servants worked and ate; upstairs were three bedrooms, one for the married couple, one for the daughters, one for the sons, and also a large nursery with a tiny room off for a maid-servant. The principle of social division explicit in this plan was carried further in two of the others: one, for a large corn farm, embodied a farm-servants' kitchen separate from an ordinary kitchen and a back kitchen, and upstairs had four family bedrooms approached by a different staircase from the one reaching the 'garrats for servants beds' in another part of the house. Only the last of the designs, for a small tenant cultivating less than a hundred acres, had anything in common with the old gudeman's but-and-ben.

Even here the basic design for a kitchen and parlour was supplemented by store-room, pantry, scullery and milk-house, with three bedrooms upstairs.[14] Hundreds of houses approximating to Sinclair's plans survive in Scotland today, yet so brisk was change in sweeping away the old that very few buildings remain in the Lowlands now that give any hint how farmers lived before 1780.

As the furniture grew finer and the house changed shape, so the mental and literary attitudes of the farmer began to alter as well. George Robertson noted with regret a decline in family worship and in intimate knowledge of the Bible: he saw the pious books of the past being replaced by 'the fictitious story, of which the tendency is not always innocuous'. Above all, however, he saw the technical works on agriculture consumed with a greed for knowledge that surprised everyone who knew of it. Thus Henry Brougham wrote to James Loch in 1803:

> Of the *Farmers Magazine* 4200 are sold: of these 300 in Ireland, and about 1000 in England . . . Meanwhile it is singular to remark the different circulation of it in the two parts of this island—not as to the numbers sold but the description of the purchasers. In England the gentlemen alone take it. In Scotland it is circulated amongst the farmers fully as much as the landlords.[15]

Thus we may leave the Lothian gudeman's grandson, sending his son to University and his daughter to Edinburgh boarding-school, driving his wife in a carriage, and reading his way to prosperity. Robertson puts it as aptly as ever: 'with perhaps less bodily labour they outdid their immediate progenitors in assiduity and enterprise . . . their minds became more expanded as the country became more fertile under their hands'.[16]

3. THE LANDLESS LABOURERS

We have seen that many of the old tenants came to be successful capitalist farmers: occasionally, too, one of the cottars rose to this high status. Ramsay of Ochtertyre told the story of John Hunter, the Berwickshire hind who first became overseer of the Earl of Home's 'great operations at the Hirsel' and after several adventures arrived as an opulent tenant in Stirlingshire, holding effects worth £8000 sterling on his death: 'One of the very few made rich by extensive improvement he took just as much and no more of the new husbandry as was sufficient to correct the errors of the old'.[17]

For every man as lucky and enterprising as him, however, there was a multitude of humble farm-servants who stayed firmly in the class of their fathers, and a further host of small tenants who found themselves reduced to the status of labourer. The story of James Somerville, whose son Alexander wrote one of the classic working-class autobiographies of the nineteenth century, is typical enough of the latter. Somerville began as a small independent farmer in the Ochils, lost his holding in the landlord's programme of amalgamations, and went to Alloa to try to support himself as a carter. When his only horse died there he had been too poor to buy another, and took work as a docker at Limekilns in Fife: he abandoned this when his brother who worked at the same job died in a horrible accident under the limedust in a ship's hold. He ended as an agricultural labourer, ploughman and quarryman, sometimes in very straitened circumstances, on the improved farms of the Berwickshire Merse from which Hunter had once made his way. There were far more people whose fate was to be like Somerville rather than like Hunter.

Thus most people who got their living from the land either were or came to be simple wage-earners, and the nearer one approaches 1830 the greater the proportion of the rural population that falls into this category. Therefore the question as to whether the wage-earner was better off or worse off as the period progressed is the same as asking whether the agricultural revolution came as a blessing or a curse to the majority of the rural Scots. The general drift of the answer is clear: there was no steep or prolonged decline in living standards at any point in this period; the average wage-earner was better off in material terms in the 1820s than his predecessor had been up to 1760 (though not much better off unless he was highly skilled) and in all probability he was no worse off than the small tenant had been up to the middle of the eighteenth century. Beyond that, however, the answer differs widely according to the exact decades that are being compared and the precise standing of the farm-servants in question.

One complication is that many workers were traditionally paid in kind. We have described elsewhere (see page 134 above) the assessment of wages by the Justices of the Peace of Midlothian of 1656, the earliest full account of the conditions of farm-service anywhere in Scotland, which does not envisage paying any money at all to skilled and married workers who had their own huts in the farmtoun: the hind and the half-hind, the shepherd and the barnman were paid in bolls of oats or pease, with allowances of ground to sow their own grain and grazing for a cow or two. The only servants in this assessment who received cash even as a minor part of their total payment were those who lived in their masters' houses.

In the course of time this system became modified, but it did not disappear. Even in the 1820s the Lothian hind was still paid partly in grain: every year he received 'a conventional quantity of oatmeal, barley and pease, possibly ten, three and two bolls of each' together with grazing for a cow, harvest victuals and possession of a garden of one sixteenth of an acre. Unless he had a large family he sold some of the meat to village tradesmen or farm servants who were not paid in kind. The hind would now, however, also get a money wage amounting to a half or a third of the value of his total income. To a highly skilled ploughman this might by 1815 be as much as £15 or £20 a year in cash.[18] The unskilled farm worker of the same period, the 'day labourer' who now lived either in a bothy or in his own hut apart from the farm buildings, was almost completely dependent on a money wage. Should he graze a cow and keep meal in bulk like the hind he had to pay the farmer the market price for grazing and corn out of his cash earnings.

This distinction makes it difficult for the historian trying to calculate the level of real wages. It also meant that while the hind and other favoured skilled men receiving food as money were relatively immune from sudden upward shifts in the price of corn, such as occurred in the late 1690s, in 1740, in 1783 and several times between 1794 and 1818, the growing number of unskilled workers divorced from payment in kind stood to suffer very severe deprivation at such times unless they belonged to the household of a hind. In cheap years the traditions of wage payment would narrow the effective differential between the skilled and the unskilled man: in dear years, especially if there was widespread unemployment, they would greatly widen it.

From the statements of contemporaries, and from such figures about wages and prices that we can collect, it is possible to draw a rough and ready outline of changing fortunes of the farm worker. Before the middle of the eighteenth century—before the true start of the agricultural revolution, that is—there are few clear signs of change in any direction. The main improvement is a negative one: after the scourging famine of the late 1690s the price of oatmeal and beer fell back and remained remarkably steady, though inclined slightly upwards over a long period. People no longer died of hunger, but there is no evidence that they were better dressed, better housed, better clothed or better paid in 1750 than they had been a hundred years before.

The next forty years saw significant changes for the better: at the close of it we have the First Statistical Account of the 1790s to draw upon, and the evidence of the ministers is all in the same direction—money wages had started to rise significantly, sometimes in the 1750s and sometimes in the 1760s; prices had also risen, but not in the same proportion; real wages and the standards of living evidenced by what people bought and ate and put in their homes had everywhere improved. At this period the degree of improvement seems to have been almost as marked for unskilled farm workers as for the ploughman: for both, money wages roughly doubled while grain prices rose by about a third. The best period was from the mid-1770s to the late 1780s, when the price of labour accelerated well above the price of meal. The ministers in the following decade reported numerous items which the cottars in the previous twenty years had begun to consume either for the first time—like potatoes, tea, sugar and rice—or were consuming now in larger quantities—like butter, butcher's meat and fresh vegetables. There was a consequent decline in the consumption of such items as warm animal blood mixed with milk, of wild herbs and of the coarsest pease meal and bear meal. Nevertheless, the additions were still trimmings to the basic diet of oatmeal: nothing shook the primacy of 'everlasting oatcake' (as a Wigtownshire labourer ruefully and aptly called it) until well on into the second half of the nineteenth century.

Clothing also improved at the end of the eighteenth century—the domestic consumption of coarse linens rose, and from the 1780s cotton came to rival the older fabric as its price was reduced by successive technical innovations. The sales of cheap coarse Scottish woollens also rose from the 1760s onwards, which would be hard to explain unless the poor were buying more. Shoes show the same trend: though the poorest women and children still went bare-foot, many were now buying shoes who would formerly have gone without. By the 1790s some parts of Scotland had nine shoemakers to a thousand people. More of the poor also had a coal fire, as improved transport

317

and more extensive mining brought down the cost of fuel. 'I travelled' said one writer of Perthshire 'through some places where not many years ago the people were wretchedly poor, want sat upon every brow and hunger was painted on every face; neither their tattered clothes nor their miserable cottages were a sufficient shelter from the cold; now the labourers have put off the long clothing, the tardy pace, the lethargic look of their fathers for the short doublet, the linen trousers, the quick pace of men who are labouring for their own behoof'.[19] Lothian hinds—the best paid rural workers of their day—were appearing at church in velvet waistcoats, corduroy breeches, calf-skin shoes, cravats and hats worth half a guinea. Some were even buying watches.

In many ways, therefore, the picture painted at the time of the *Statistical Account* is a cheerful one. Though the gains were modest enough, and though the country still abounded with paupers suffering real destitution, there was an unmistakable feeling abroad that the material condition of the great majority of the Scottish people was steadily improving. In the next twenty years, however, contemporary writers were much less confident whether things were still improving for the poor. The wars against France, which broke out in 1793 and lasted until 1815, were associated with steep inflation, rising grain prices and several catastrophically short harvests. They were not bad years for farmers: profits rose as well as rents, and there was fast change in enclosure and farming techniques to take advantage of the buoyant market for food. Wages certainly rose, too: the question is whether they kept pace with inflation. The skilled man, whose expertise was at a premium and whose allowances of fixed quantities of meat and milk gave him a cushion against inflation, may well have kept ahead of the price rise throughout the wars. The unskilled (the majority, though many were junior members of the hind's household) were less well placed: their wages did not now rise so fast as prices, or so fast as the ploughman's wage: to a greater extent they were paid in money, and so suffered in dear years like 1799, 1800, 1812, and 1816, when the price of corn was more than double the level of the 1790s. One who lived through it told what it was like:

To be generally pinched of all matters in the consistence of human food for the space of two or three years—to be bleached skeleton thin by a kind of protracted famine wasting by daily degrees the blood from the young heart—was a sad concern, producing a feeling none can thoroughly comprehend from a mere description and few I wish may ever understand from sad experience, to go hungry to bed on a winter night . . . to dream of food—of boiled potatoes . . . to wake again and find 'the soul is empty'.[20]

Yet no-one died of famine: they were hard times, but they were not like the 1690s, a time of national calamity.

Within a year or two of the end of the Napoleonic Wars price levels began to drop, by 1830 grain prices in many areas were falling back to what they had been in the 1790s, but the level of wages for most agricultural workers had hardly been reduced at all. Comparing a series of wage quotations in the first *Statistical Account* with those of the *New Statistical Account* forty years later, A. J. Youngson has suggested that money wages for the skilled agricultural worker rose by fifty or sixty per cent between 1790 and 1830, and for the unskilled by about a third. This would, as he has said, indicate a 'substantial improvement' for ploughmen and standards 'a little above what they had been about 1790' for the mass of rural workers.[21] A similar position is suggested by the figures that George Robertson worked out for unskilled Mid-lothian farm labourers in 1828, and which are expressed in graphic form on page 265. On the other hand some of the gilt is knocked off the gingerbread by considering the employment position: the return of the army after Waterloo, combined with the depression in farming profits that followed deflation, produced a labour surplus which appears to have been mopped up only slowly. The spread of threshing machines on east-coast farms, which had begun as far back as the 1780s and now came close to being universal, added to the problem by making winter employment more difficult to get. It is perhaps significant that Bowley and Wood, the only historians who have attempted to calculate the level of Scottish agricultural *earnings*, as opposed to mere wages, believed that while they had doubled between 1770 and 1795, they were no greater by 1830 than they had been forty years earlier.[22] Stagnation or slight advance since 1790 is thus the best interpretation we can put on the evidence whatever way we look at it.

Apart from the level of earnings, there are other aspects of the life of the agricultural workers to consider. One was the position of women in farm work. At least in the south-east, it had been customary as far back as the mid-seventeenth century for the rent of the labourer's one-room hut to be paid for by the work of their wives—the assessment of 1656 shows that Midlothian women were obliged to work at shearing and carrying for the thresher, as well as mucking out, muck-spreading, carting and winnowing, for no payment in money or kind at all. In the eighteenth century this custom was slightly modified. A demand for much more regular female labour in the fields came in with the introduction of turnips, which had to be hoed and tended for at least six months in the year. This work was paid at day rates; a ploughman's dependent could not refuse to take it but the additional family income that came from this source must have made a considerable difference to the prosperity of the household. By 1800 terms of employment for a typical Lothian cottar included the obligation to provide a woman 'bondager' from his family to shear at harvest time and carry at threshing time for no wages at all (this involved twenty, thirty or forty days unpaid hard labour in a year) and a further obligation to provide a female day-labourer who would work a ten-hour day at rates of up to one penny an hour.

The bondage system, and the fact that the young boys of the household could also be impressed into doing herd duty for sixpence a day or less, meant that the whole of the ploughman's family could be put to labour in the fields at the will of the farmer. It is impossible to believe that this servile dependence would not be resented by small independent tenants who had lost their holdings and taken jobs as hinds, even though in material terms they probably had a higher family income as wage-earners. Hinds at this period also became a notoriously mobile group, frequently taking advantage of the annual hiring-fairs to change their masters on pretexts that often seemed to the latter to be purely capricious: yet it is obvious enough that the search for a slightly better employer—a man more generous or more considerate than the average—could yield in this situation quite disproportionate gains in household comfort.

The cottar's house held under these conditions was only marginally better even in the early nineteenth century than its equivalent had been in 1650, though it was likely to be constructed of more permanent materials and to have a built-in chimney which would at least keep it warmer and dryer. In these words Alexander Somerville describes the dwelling, 'one of a row of sheds' in Berwickshire in which his parents lived for a time with their eight children. It was:

About twelve feet by fourteen, and not so high in the walls as will

The stool of repentance. David Allan's picture belongs to the later eighteenth century. The child, its mother and indignant grandmother are in the foreground

A wedding celebration at Elgin, about 1836. The dance is a foursome reel

The Shoemaker. Shoemakers were sturdy and notorious radicals in the period after 1789. This picture, from the sketchbook of C. Smith, seems to have been made in 1810

allow a man to get in without stooping. That place without ceiling or anything beneath the bare tiles of roof; with no floor save the common clay; without a cupboard or recess of any kind; with no grate but the iron bars which the tenants carried to it, built up and took away when they left it; with no partition of any kind save what the beds made: with no window save four small panes at one side—it was this house, still a hind's house at Springfield, for which, to obtain leave to live in, my mother sheared the harvest and carried the stacks.[23]

Even the windows were not necessarily part of the fittings provided—Somerville explains how his parents 'had a window consisting of one small pane of glass, and when they moved from one house to another in different parts of Berwickshire in different years they carried this window with them'.

The nadir of housing and employment conditions on Scottish farms was reached, however, not with the ploughman's hut, but with the development of the bothy system to house bachelor farm-hands and casual migrant labour. This again was something more characteristic of the highly capitalised farms of the eastern counties than of elsewhere, and arose from the necessity of a relatively large labour force to cope with grain, turnip and potato crops on a big farm, and from the determination not to have the workers living with the farmers' families, as they would have done in less pretentious times. Bands of itinerant workers—usually harvesters from the Highlands or the nearest burgh—had been known before, but now they became much more numerous. Many were Irish, like the band from Antrim that Somerville knew as a boy 'six of whom were named Michael—old Michael, young Michael, big Michael, wee Michael, singing Michael and Michael the laird'.[24] The genteel farmers of the Merse were not equipped to deal with all these Michaels at their fireside.

A bothy was simply a shed that housed men. Hugh Miller, the Cromarty stonemason, had a wide experience of them when as an adolescent he tramped round with his master doing maintenance work on farm-buildings in the north-east. He lived sometimes in large and crowded ones, like this at Conon-side, which was his introduction to bothy life as a young apprentice.

We found twenty-four workmen crowded in a rusty corn-kiln, open from gable to gable, and not above thirty feet in length. A row of rude beds, formed of undressed slabs, ran along the sides; and against one of the gables there blazed a line of fires . . . A few of the soberer workmen were engaged in 'baking and firing' oaten cakes, and a few more were occupied with equal sobriety in cooking their evening porridge: but in front of the building there was a wild party of apprentices.[25]

In a short time he had settled down to the life of a bothy:

We constructed for ourselves a bed-frame of rough slabs and filled it with hay; placed our chests in front of it, and as the rats mustered by thousands in the place, suspended our sack of oatmeal by a rope from one of the naked rafters . . . the rats were somewhat troublesome. A comrade who slept in the bed immediately beside ours had one of his ears bitten through one night as he lay asleep.[26]

Other bothies were smaller, designed to accommodate half a dozen hands or less. William Cobbett visited one in 1830 when he rode up through Fife towards Dunfermline:

I found the boothie to be a shed, with a fireplace in it to burn coals in, with one doorway and one little window. The floor was the ground. There were three wooden bedsteds nailed together like berths in a barrack-room with boards for the bottom of them. The bedding seemed to be very coarse sheeting with coarse woollen things at the top; and all seemed to be such as similar things must be when there is nobody but men to look after them. There were six men, all at home . . . there were ten or twelve bushels of coals lying in a heap in one corner of the place which was, as nearly as I could guess, about 16 or 18 feet square. There was no backdoor to the place, and no privy. There were some loose potatoes lying under one of the berths.[27]

Where a big gang lived in a bothy there was at least a certain *esprit de corps*, and usually enough individuals for one of them to be designated cook for the week, and to provide hot food. Where there were only three or four men the demoralisation was worse: often all food was eaten cold and a high proportion of earnings went on whisky. Miller spoke of the hatred he found under these conditions towards the employer, a thing hardly imaginable to an earlier generation—'bad enough certainly, and yet natural enough, and in a sense proper enough'. Both he and Cobbett, though at opposite ends of the political spectrum, utterly condemned the bothy system as demoralising, 'brute-making' and wicked, threatening the Scottish people in the countryside with sinking 'from being one of the most provident, intelligent and moral in Europe to be one of the most licentious, reckless and ignorant'.[28]

Though none would deny that the bothy system was a blight, the moralists had an innate tendency to exaggerate the extent of the danger. Although it had been spreading fast between 1810 and 1830, it affected only a limited area of Scotland and only a minority of agricultural labourers within that area even in 1830 and the worst Millar could say of it was that, in 'some counties', 'several hundred' had gone into the bothies.

All these changes seem to have left more or less intact the literate character of the Scottish farm-workers as a whole—not least in East Lothian, where the bothies were possibly thickest on the ground. It is easy to overdraw the picture, and no doubt a great many men on the farms had not the smallest interest in or opportunity to acquire reading matter of any kind. A man like Hugh Miller, who drove himself on by reading philosophy and geology by the light of a guttering candle in a Cromarty bothy, was exceptional, but he was by no means isolated. Alexander Somerville, for instance, at the other end of Scotland described how his father, an anti-burgher with strict old-fashioned literary tastes, keeping the *Marrow of Modern Divinity* and Erskine's *Gospel Sonnets* in the house, worked at a quarry with a man who had read 'eighteen different authors on astronomy besides many other subjects'. Alexander himself borrowed a copy of Burns' poems from the stacker 'often read, well read and well-worn', and a copy of Anson's *Voyage round the World* from the smith: he saved up the very large sum of half a guinea to buy George Miller's *Book of Nature* from a Dunbar bookshop. There was a local parish library at Innerwick, which made inadequate provision for serious readers—'the larger part of them were silly stories of that silliest kind of literature, religious novels': more satisfactory were the cheap tracts and magazines published by George Miller at fourpence a month and the circulating library that Samuel Brown had started at Haddington in 1817. Most of the books made available by Miller and Brown were pious; some were secular; almost all were moral in their intent, aiming to drive out 'the vulgar and lewd chapbooks that circulated from "that copious source of mischief, the

Hawker's basket" ' the mere existence of which hints at an alternative level of popular taste.[29] In these south-eastern parts of Scotland men read in the 1820s as they had read in the 1750s; and they probably read more widely as there was more to read. We cannot be so sure about the west and the north, but the difference, if there was one, is likely to be one of degree rather than one of kind.

4. THE PEASANT REACTION TO RURAL CHANGE

When William Cobbett, the great radical enthusiast of rural England, came north in 1830 to inspect Lothian husbandry he was struck by three glaring contrasts between life on these 'factories for making corn and meat carried on principally by means of horses and machinery' as he called them[30] and life on the farms of the South of England which he knew best: farming in eastern Scotland was often technically much more sophisticated; the plight of the workers was to his eyes even more miserable; and no-one, least of all the workers themselves, was making any sustained protest about their lot. He had left the southern English counties in that year smouldering on the edge of social war, with ricks being burnt, new machinery destroyed, men transported and in a few cases executed for their part in the destruction of property. This marked the culmination of a generation of intermittent turbulence in the south that had had no parallel beyond the Tweed, even though the farm-workers in the same period were being subjected to the introduction of the same kind of highly capitalised farming with mechanical threshing which stimulated the maximum uproar in the south. Scotch bailiffs in command of English estates were boasting, to Cobbett's great wrath, of the obedience and orderliness of the rural workers in their native counties, even though industrial workers in Scotland had long been inclined to radical sympathies of a kind. Cobbett came to find out why the Scots were quiet while the English burnt the ricks.

The question he raised is a real one. The answers he provided were at best partial. He explained Scottish quiescence partly in terms of the Scottish poor law, in which the chance of relief was dependent on the minister's approval of the recipient's character, and partly by employment customs. It was difficult for a Scottish farm worker to leave his employment at any time other than that of the May hiring-fair due both to the heavy penalties exacted by Scottish law on servants who broke the annual contract of service, and to the need to carry to new employers references from the old employer and from the minister. In fact, few rural Scots can have worried much about the poor law: a hind's family, at least, would have regarded going to the parish for charity as such a disgrace that they would not have contemplated the possibility in the normal calculations of life. As for changing employment, whatever the actual legal position the chances of a new job depended primarily on conditions of supply and demand in the labour market. There is no sign that the need for references stopped the hinds in their restless shifting from farm to farm in search of slightly better conditions.

A hundred years earlier, when the agricultural revolution was still in its earliest infancy, there had in fact been a rising against it, the so-called Levellers Revolt that kept Dumfriesshire and Galloway in turmoil in the summer of 1724. Though local and short-lived, it was the first instance in Scottish history of a popular rural movement with the character of class war. Fighting in the past had been political, personal or religious but never, till now, determined by an economic grievance with the combatants clearly split along class lines. It was also the last instance of a major organised protest against rural change before the middle decades of the nineteenth century: apart from disturbances of a minor and isolated character in the 1790s (see page 444 below), not until the Crofters' War in Skye in 1882 was there anything else quite like it. It is worth looking at carefully, because some of the answers to Cobbett's question may be rooted in the unique circumstances of this revolt.

It sprang from eviction. Lairds and large tenants who already had specialised farms had been doing well from the sale of cattle to English consumers in the twenty years since the Union, while small tenants, who were much more numerous and depended on inefficient subsistence arable farming rather than on stock, had been hit by a run of poor harvests and fallen badly into arrears with rent payments. Several lairds therefore evicted the small tenants and enlarged their stock-farms by laying the farmtoun lands and commons down to grass, and enclosing the lot with dykes. This might have been the end of it (in similar circumstances before and afterwards it usually was), but the peasants temporarily found leaders and the inspiration of common purpose. One or two of the larger tenants lent their support, and the Edinburgh *Caledonian Mercury* reported that 'a certain mountain preacher' had bitterly inveighed against the heritors' for '(as he term'd it) making commonty property'.[31] Several hundred armed men rose up and over-threw the dykes, broke into the laird of Baldoon's park and killed fifty-three Irish cattle. This was embarrassing to those in authority, since the importation and keeping of Irish cattle was prohibited by law, and such beasts when found were supposed to be killed and their bodies given to the poor. But no-one envisaged the poor taking the law into their own hands in this way.

The peasants banded themselves beneath the ancient Scottish device of a covenant, nowhere more hallowed than in the south-west: they met in well-organised groups on Tuesdays and worked for three days pulling down enclosures before dispersing for the week-end; they even issued a 'manifesto' (the word was used at the time) demanding justice for the poor and return of their holdings. The gentry caught one, described as the 'tax-gatherer' of the levellers, and sent him under escort to Edinburgh tolbooth. The presbytery of the Church of Scotland (clearly no friend of the 'mountain preacher') denounced them as ungodly rebels. The magistrates of Kirkcudbright attempted to dis-perse a gathering in the town by reading the Riot Act: the levellers retorted by reading to the magistrates the text of the Solemn League and Covenant of 1643, with its clear implication that the magistrates and clergy of an uncovenanted king were usurpers of civic and spiritual authority. It is easy to see the hand of the shadowy preacher in the way affairs were conducted.

Alarmed both by the last development, and by the increasing demands and violence of the peasants who were now calling for rents to be levelled and were mutilating more cattle, the government sent in six troops of dragoons in June. There was a skirmish, half-a-dozen levellers taken prisoner, and some semblance of order restored. Night attacks on enclosures went on for about six months: as late as the end of October there were reports of a thousand people banding together near Sanquhar, and pinning their manifesto on the door of Sorbie Church. Thereafter the attacks faded out. The prisoners were gradually released: one or two were sent to the plantations, but there were no executions. The army avoided provocation, and the Government supported moderates among the gentry in over-ruling the firebrands who called for revenge. Authority wanted no new recruits to the mythology of Galloway martyrdom, and that appeared to be the end of it.

The levellers seemed to have achieved nothing, yet they did make at least a temporary impression on public opinion throughout the length and breadth of Scotland. In Edinburgh, a number of pamphlets circulated in support of the levellers' claims. In Aberdeenshire, Sir Archibald Grant of Monymusk filed a copy of the presbytery's denunciation in case he needed anything similar.[32] Many were shocked at least as much by the original ruthlessness of the Galloway landowners as by the subsequent violence of the peasants: the clemency shown to the rioters was one sign of this. Mackintosh of Borlum, a Highland laird and an influential writer on improvement, took a sympathetic attitude in his *Essay* of 1729. 'Justice and gratitude fixes an indelible obligation upon us to use our commons well', he wrote, but he reported that the Galloway evictions had turned peasants throughout the country against enclosure, and that there were widespread (though sporadic and unco-ordinated) instances of dykes being thrown down and young trees pulled up. It was no use relying on intimidation: 'continually hunting such criminals is but living in a state of war; their numbers will prevail over your industry and tire you out of inclosing, as I have known happen more than once'.[33] He believed the peasantry had to be won to see that increases in the productivity of land would ultimately benefit themselves as well as the laird, and he also seems to have been the only landowner before the Highland agitation to make an unqualified assertion that tenants had a prescriptive right to security of tenure:

The commons of Scotland have as much right to live in Scotland and pay rent as any landlord has to live there and receive it: and as God Almighty has destin'd them to earn their bread with the sweat of their brow, he gave them Scotland for their theatre to act their toilsome part on. They are certainly as heritable tenants as we are landlords.[34]

Even if it had sought it, the Levellers' Revolt did not obtain widespread public acknowledgement of this right, though it was probably frightening enough to make the more high-handed improver pause in his tracks, and show a little more tenderness to peasant susceptibilities than he would otherwise have done. It may even have slowed the agricultural revolution itself for a time: certainly in Galloway little more seems to have been done until late in the century, and reporters in Sinclair's day found the area still relatively backward.

Nevertheless, the levellers remained an isolated movement and even the spontaneous isolated acts of sabotage that William Mackintosh refers to became rare by 1750. Opposition to the extinction of the traditional ways of rural life faltered and died. The history of the levellers themselves suggests perhaps two explanations. One reason is probably that little of the agrarian change in the Lowlands had the same 'depopulating' and impoverishing character of that first phase in Galloway. Enclosure was normally accompanied by an expansion of arable and mixed farming, not by the laying down of plough to grass and of houses to cattlesheds: land was also reclaimed in many areas from the waste and the moor. Even with the growth of the average size of farms, therefore, many of those peasants who had formerly held a main share in the lands of the farmtoun directly from the laird retained substantial holdings. For those who had been small tenants, subtenants or cottars, and lost their holdings in the reorganisation, the enclosed farms still offered jobs: an area of land that had been enclosed usually offered as many people a living and as much employment as the equivalent area under runrig divided between many more landholders. Although there were examples cited in the *Statistical Account* to show that this rule was not universally true, the experience of South Perthshire was probably typical:

> Where the farms are enlarged and the country inclosed there is no doubt that the usual population has decreased: but wherever married servants are kept on arable farms and the farms are of moderate size the most knowing farmers in many parts of this district are of opinion that there is very little decrease.[35]

Furthermore, as we have seen, the agricultural revolution was far from impoverishing the peasants. Those lucky ones who became the favoured tenants of farms and made a success of it moved up to the status and affluence of the middle-class. Those who became landless labourers, though they might resent the loss of their small holdings and the status represented by a strip of land in the open fields, were better off in 1790 and 1830 than they had been in 1720 or 1770. Life might be grim in Cobbett's day for a man living in a hut with an earthen floor and a box bed and subsisting off oatmeal and potatoes, but life had always been grim, and often been worse. There was not enough material suffering attributable to the agricultural revolution to make sustained social protest against it inevitable.

Moreover, the peasants lacked both leaders and an ideology. The larger peasants, whom we know to have given some support in Galloway where the lairds had enclosed common land for their own private ranches, were detached from the smaller peasants later in the century by the complete success of the lairds in showing them that agricultural change would lead to their own enrichment as farmers. There had always been a clear division in peasant society between tenant and subtenant or cottar. Now peasant society ceased to exist as such, when the former became capitalist farmers, with their sympathies broadly those of 'the landed interest', and the latter became landless labourers. It was unreasonable to expect farmers to provide the leaders.

The alternative source of leadership could have been found among the ministers as it was in Galloway in 1724, though in exceptional circumstances. The 'mountain preacher', whose name is not known, was a 'Hebronite', a follower of John Hepburn, the minister of Urr, who had seceded from the established Church of Scotland partly on the grounds that it was polluted by the patronage arrangements and partly because it was ruled by the same unrighteous elders and ungodly magistrates who, unpunished, had persecuted the old Covenanters before 1689. The preaching of Hepburn was violent and popular, lashing the 'dumb dogs' of the established church and the gross life of the lairds:

Great persons, who as they generally love to have their heads clapped, their faults connived at and themselves spared and favoured (but a cruel favour it is) so meet with what they desire . . . What f milies are more corrupt and ungodly than those of many noblemen and gentlemen.[36]

Hepburn himself had died before the rising, but Hebronite preaching in this vein must have deeply corroded the bonds of social deference. As the Hebronites also organised themselves into cells to help one another live the Godly life, and met on weekdays in sessions where they were sworn to secrecy, it is easy to see how well they were placed to emerge as leaders of the Levellers, and how their prayer-groups meeting on weekdays might transform themselves into levelling groups meeting on Tuesdays.

No other church in eighteenth- or early nineteenth-century

Scotland could possibly have provided the leaders and inspiration for a peasant movement. The Church of Scotland was the mouthpiece of the lairds: it was a comfort to John Ramsay of Ochtertyre that tenants respected their political opinions, because 'when they wanted information upon that head they had recourse to the clergy'.[37] Eighteenth-century seceders, though less respectful than the Church of Scotland (Ramsay also noticed it was the antiburghers who started the fashion of keeping their hats on when they met a gentleman) regarded submission to the civil authority as a necessary discipline. Their sentiments were aptly summed up in the *Gospel Sonnets* of Ralph Erskine, one of the leaders of the original secession:

> The precept reaches all the human clan,
> Submit to ev'ry ordinance of man.

Erskine and Thomas Boston were among the writers most widely read by the eighteenth-century peasant, and they spoke not merely of submission, but most deeply and movingly of the brevity of life, of the vanity of the world, and of the need to place God before Mammon. Thus Thomas Boston:

Man's life is a swift thing; not only a passing but a flying vanity. Have you not observed how swiftly a shadow hath run along the ground in a cloudy and windy day, suddenly darkening the places beautiful before with the beams of the sun, but as suddenly disappearing? Such is the life of man . . .[38]

Erskine wrote in a similar vein:

If a man desires to be religious, God must have his whole heart: and he through grace must give it, and make a continual trade of religion; if a man desire to be rich, the world will oblige him to rise early and sit up late and eat the bread of carefulness; yea and employ his head and his heart, and all about the world. And therefore God and the world cannot be served by one and the same man.[39]

In another passage he drew his thoughts together in a terse and explicit sentence, 'if you are weaned from the vanity of the world then you will bear the *want* of the world with profound submission'.[40]

It is impossible to argue that the compellingly expressed passivity of this view hindered many peasants from bettering their worldly lot. We have already noticed how fast the larger tenants in fact responded to the opportunities of material gain presented to them by the lairds, and how they also gave up reading Boston and Erskine when they had attained wealth. On the other hand, for those who did not make it in the rat-race these sentiments had enormous strength and comfort to help a man keep his self-respect. All wealth was spurious; rich and poor were equally sinful; earthly life was a brief spasm in existence; ever-lasting rewards came later to the patient, the humble and the penitent elect. In this way rural Calvinism worked against Radicalism. How could there conceivably be any point in protest or revolt? If there were to be rewards they would come in God's good time, and if there was to be vengeance that would come in God's good time too. God was not mocked.

Did it matter that the process of agricultural change was accepted by the peasantry so uncritically? It would only have been obscurantist and stupid to resist the production of more food by fewer people, since in the long run the agricultural revolution raised everyone's standard of living. On the other hand within this period Scotland lost, as England did, but as the Scandinavian kingdoms (for example) did not, that sense and tradition of rural life as a co-operative action. The old farmtoun may have been a society of the poverty-stricken split into at least two distinct social tiers, but it was also based on co-operative, though inefficient and traditional, methods of work, undertaken for the common good of a community in which fellowship was very real. The new and isolated farms were occupied by men in competition, employing at a social distance labour paid by competitive rates. Yet it ill behoves the historian to be sentimental about the vanished Scottish peasantry. The nineteenth-century agricultural labourer himself showed little nostalgia for the past, perhaps because he was better aware than we can ever be just how nasty, brutish and short life had been for his predecessors in the primitive countryside: there is no sign that he found any quality in it, least of all that of co-operative life, the passing of which he in any way regretted.

CHAPTER XIV

The Highlands
1690-1830

1. HIGHLAND SOCIETY BEFORE THE '45

Very few men who were both literate and perceptive wrote at any
length about the Highlands before the middle of the eighteenth century.
The blanket of contempt towards those whom James VI had once
termed 'utterly barbarous' stifled too effectively Lowland curiosity about
their Gaelic-speaking countrymen. Lowlanders usually called them the
'Irish', being unwilling even to admit them as Scots.

Two writers, however, were notable exceptions. One was Martin
Martin, himself a Highlander and steward to the Macleods, whose
Description of the Western Islands of Scotland appeared in 1703 with a
dedication to the Queen's Danish husband and a wish expressed in the
preface that the wide world would soon come to know his country
better, and learn to treat its men with less scorn. The other was Captain
Edward Burt, an English officer on road-survey duty with General
Wade's army around 1730, who sent long descriptions of life in the
central Highlands to a friend in England: they were eventually published in 1754 apparently by the recipient's creditors under the title of
Letters from a Gentleman in the North of Scotland. The contrast in style
between the two men could hardly have been greater. Martin, the
insider, was chatty, discursive and credulous, fascinated with folk
medicine and with stories about local worthies: 'John Fake . . . is
constantly troubled with a great sneezing a day or two before rain;
and if the sneezing be more than usual, the rain is said to be the greater:
therefore he is called the Rain Almanac.'[1] Burt, the outsider, the
Englishman on the frontier of an empire, wrote at first mainly to amuse

his London friend with accounts of the primitive life and wild customs of the natives, later with increasing seriousness and affection for the land he was describing. Taken together, their picture is vivid and compelling. It is of a society which, while already changing in the direction of Lowland norms, belongs still to another cultural milieu altogether. Half the drama of Highland history in the next century is caused by the clash and tangle of these two cultures, and by resolving the differences between them.

The differences existed at many levels. Language, for instance, was one distinction, for people still spoke Gaelic from end to end of the Highland line: the merchants of Inverness would have done little trade unless they had been bi-lingual, and even when Dorothy Wordsworth visited Loch Lomondside within twenty-five miles of Glasgow in 1803, the normal language of conversation among the peasants was still Gaelic. Before 1750 comparatively few natives besides the chiefs and their relations had more than a smattering of English: one of Burt's friends was nearly killed by a bodyguard who shot at him in the belief he had insulted a chief in an unknown tongue.

There were also very wide differences in religion. Few parts of the Highlands, except the heartlands of Clan Campbell in Argyll and Perthshire, enjoyed in the early eighteenth century the ministrations of a properly inducted Presbyterian minister. Some parts, like Barra, Lochaber and parts of Aberdeenshire, were Roman Catholic, converted by missionaries operating secretly in the seventeenth century. In Lowland eyes to be a Highlander and a papist was to be doubly corrupt. When the Earl of Stair devised the destruction of the Macdonalds of Glencoe in 1692 he dwelt upon the fact that they were believed to be Catholics: whether they were or not is still somewhat unclear but it 'plainly gave him added reason to believe he was carrying out a "great work of charity" '.[2] Many more areas were Episcopalian, often with Jacobite ministers who had stayed on in the glens after 1690 undisturbed in their livings for years, and succeeded, perhaps, by others installed by fugitive bishops.

Most Highlanders, however, saw priest and minister but seldom: churches were few and parishes immense. They practised their own startling ceremonies of taboo and propitiation, which owed nothing whatsoever to the teaching of Christian pastors. Martin Martin described some of those of the Lewismen: each May Day a man was sent to cross the Barvas River at dawn, since it was believed that if a woman crossed first no salmon would ascend that year; fowlers who sailed to the Flannans must never name the islands before they arrived, and as soon as they landed they must take off their hats and turn sunways about; within living memory they had even been accustomed on Lewis to pour ale on the sea at Halloween, and call on a god called Shoney to send them seaware to manure their fields, but ministers at Stornoway had recently persuaded them that this was going too far. Skye had a sacred wood, a sacred well and a sacred trout. Fladda had a magic stone which, if washed by a stranger, procured a favourable wind for the sailor; others got the same effect by hanging a he-goat to the boat's mast. St. Kilda had a man called Roderick who said that he received messages from John the Baptist: the saint had evidently told him that if any sheep strayed on to a certain hill they were to be killed and eaten at once by the owners and by Roderick. The last story shocked the Lowlanders so much that it appears to have been one of the inspirations for the foundation in Scotland of the Society for the Propagation of Christian Knowledge whose work in educating and evangelising the north was a major vehicle of social change in the eighteenth century (see pages 463-4 below).

From the standpoint of social organisation, however, the greatest distinction between the Highlands and the Lowlands was the existence of the clan. The Highlands were tribal, in the exact sense that nineteenth-century Africa was tribal. Great Lowland families were certainly rather more tender towards the obligations of family and proven kinship than the English were, and in previous centuries families like the Humes, the Hamiltons and the Douglases had not differed much in the degree of loyalty they could call upon in a crisis than, say, the Campbells or Clan Chattan: but by the eighteenth century the Lowlanders would rightly have rejected as slanderous the imputation that they were clannish.

At the root of Highland clanship lay the myth that all in a given clan were descended from a common ancestor who had, in some incredibly misty period of the past, founded the tribe. From this followed two main consequences. Firstly, the head of the clan, the chief, was deserving of enormous respect and affection as the senior member of the senior branch, and the heads of the septs (the main cadet branches), the chieftains, were worthy of almost as much. Secondly, since all the clansmen from the chief downwards were blood-relations of each other, it followed that the chiefs were expected to feel fatherly obligations even towards the poorest and weakest, and all the clansmen were expected to give unstinted help to each other in time of crisis. It was a creed suited in many ways to a savage society. The proprietors of land, caught in a situation always liable to slip into internecine feud, wished to call upon the strongest of all ties from their dependents; the tenants, threatened not only by violence but also by starvation from the periodic failures of crops, needed the strongest mutual bonds and the protection of powerful men feeling an unlimited moral obligation to come to their aid. Perhaps the state of religion also helped. In a world where the supernatural powers were malevolently waiting for the unwary to break a taboo and omit a sacrifice, it was no doubt comforting to attribute benevolent and heroic qualities to earthly leaders, however undeserving they might be in reality. In Edward Burt's eyes, this attribution of virtue to the chiefs reached the levels of superstitious frenzy: 'he is their idol; and as they profess to know no king but him (I was going farther) so will they say, they ought to do whatever he commands without inquiry'.[3]

Not all chiefs and chieftains were in fact landed proprietors. There were always a few who, because of military defeat by another clan or forfeiture of their lands by the government were owed allegiance by men of their clan yet had no territory of their own: but being deprived of an economic basis for their power they hung tenuously on to the fringes of Highland society. Conversely, there were many proprietors who were not chiefs or chieftains to all their tenants, some of whom owed tribal loyalties outside: this was especially true of the expanding and imperialist clans like the Campbells and Gordons, on the fringes of whose territories were many who loathed their name. These were far from weak, but they stood to be diminished in a military crisis by being unable to reinforce the obligations of tenure by those of clanship.

Nevertheless, the typical chief was a man most of whose clan lived upon his own lands or upon those of his chieftains. He was thus an extremely powerful social figure in war and peace alike. For one thing, he was able as landlord to call upon his vassals to render feudal service in a way that was unthinkable in the Lowlands or in England after the early seventeenth century though it would not have been at all hard to find parallels in some contemporary societies in mainland Europe. Martin Martin explained how the Macneills held Barra as vassals of Sir Donald Macdonald of Sleat, 'to whom he pays £40 a year and a hawk if required, and is obliged to furnish him a certain number of men upon extraordinary occasions'.[4] Then he was able as chief to rely on the devotion of all his clan followers in battle. The stories of their heroism were innumerable, and though the bards would carefully embroider them for convivial retelling in the castle, the reality behind them was undeniable. It was this iron combination of duty and devotion that made the Government so watchful of Highland discontents, and which led in the 1745 to a situation, in which, as Thomas Pennant later reflected, 'the power and interest of poor twelve thousand per annum terrified and nearly subverted the constitution of these powerful kingdoms'.[5]

Like the Lowland landowners, chiefs and chieftains of the early eighteenth century could hold a private court in which they were effectively judge and jury in their own cause, but the rights of this jurisdiction, though still considerable, did not extend any longer to executing the guilty. Burt, however, was convinced that in the remoter parts of the Highlands chiefs still occasionally hanged offenders with whom they were particularly enraged, and there is no reason to suppose he was wrong. Tradition asserts that the last time the Macleods hanged a man was in 1728: right on the other side of the hills, at Gordonstoun in Morayshire, an area surely more Lowland than Highland, Sir Robert Gordon in the years immediately before 1740 was imprisoning men and women in a private bottle-dungeon for the most trivial offences, such as taking a cod's head out of a midden 'which the woman thought was good for curing the gout'. Several of the prisoners died as a result of their experiences.[6] In more innocent directions the authority of chiefs was unquestionably extended to cover things no Lowlander would have meddled with. Martin Martin described how in the southern Hebrides the Macneill chief personally arranged all marriages among his tenants in which a widow or a widower was involved: the latter 'the woman's name being told him, immediately goes to her carrying with him a bottle of strong-waters for their entertainment at marriage, which is then consummated'.[7] Conversely, the chief was ready to saddle himself with patriarchal responsibilities. The Macneills replaced milk cows which their tenants lost in a severe winter, and accepted as life-long guests in their own household tenants too old or too feeble to cultivate the ground any longer. To find parallels to this one must again look outside the British Isles, particularly to the societies of central and eastern Europe where the tradition of strong mutual obligation between lord and peasant persisted (often in conjunction with a legal serfdom lacking in the Highlands) long after it was dead in Britain.

The pleasures and responsibilities of the chiefly life were reflected in the state with which they surrounded themselves in their stone castles. By 1700 it was, admittedly, less than it had been in the days when Rory Mor had lived in barbaric splendour at Dunvegan, and gone to visit James VI with the air of one king calling upon another. In 1693 his successor was accused by the bard of abandoning his Highland home, of dismissing his poets and musicians, of ceasing to entertain his friends and dependents in the manner to which they were accustomed and of squandering his patrimony on French and English clothes.[8] Martin Martin, too, noted with regret the abolition of the heroic contests when the 'Chief Men of the Isles . . . continued drinking sometimes twenty-four, sometimes forty-eight hours . . . there were two men with a barrow attending punctually at such occasions'.[9] Nevertheless, it was a poor chief who could not at least occasionally celebrate the deeds of his clan with a piper and a bard in his retinue, a sword bearer and an armour bearer in attendance, and lavish hospitality of food and drink. The payment of many rents in kind, and the absence of any brisk commodity market led most to excesses of gluttony, and made the maintenance of retainers and the provision of charity to decayed clansmen a relatively inexpensive obligation. By the standards of the outside world however the conspicuous consumption of the chiefs was crude. Edward Burt's English stomach was turned by 'all this inelegant and ostentatious plenty', and there is something disagreeably realistic in his description one night of 'the number of Highlanders that attended at table, whose feet and foul linen or woollen, I don't know which, were more than a match for the odour of the dishes'.[10]

Below the ranks of the chiefs and chieftains stretched a hierarchy of tenants that differed in several significant respects from the equivalent in the Lowlands. Most chiefs, for example, leased a high proportion of their estates at low rents to tacksmen, who v re often the close kin of proprietors, and who acted as their viceroys ᴠ ver the land they held. Some tacksmen were themselves farmers: most were also rentiers like the chiefs themselves and lived primarily off the difference between what they could get by subletting the land they occupied and what they had to pay in rent to the proprietor. Tacksmen were high in social status, and basked warmly in their chief's reflected glory. Burt found them shabby and dignified gentlemen, and described one of them in words that might have come from a Victorian explorer of darkest Africa:

> He met me at some distance from his dwelling with his Arcadian offering of milk and cream, as usual, carried before him by his servants. He afterwards invited me to his hut, which was built like the others, only very long; but without any partition; where the family was at one end and some cattle at the other . . . He was without shoes, stockings, or breeches, in a short coat, with a shirt not much longer, which hung between his thighs and just hid his nakedness from two daughters about seventeen or eighteen years who sat over-against him.[11]

Proprietors and tacksmen alike leased their land to a class known simply as tenants, who were also the principal clan warriors when the need arose. All settlements had some arable land, and in small patches of the Hebrides where it could be constantly refreshed by applications of white shell sand and kelp-manure the return of grain from the quantity sown was probably higher than anywhere else in Scotland before the agricultural revolution. Nevertheless, Highland tenants lived mainly as pastoral farmers, keeping goats and sheep for household subsistence and black cattle primarily to pay the rent. Since the rent was often reckoned in units of cattle, and since possession of many cows was itself a mark of wealth, their pastures suffered from chronic overstocking with many weak beasts. The arable was divided runrig, and the organisation of the whole joint-farm was a co-operative one between eight or a dozen tenants who contributed something to the common plough and obeyed communal rules for the grazing. They were everywhere assisted in husbandry by a large class of subtenants, called in different regions cottars, mailers or crofters, the significance or each term differing in different parts of the Highlands. Normally these men held no more than a diminutive strip of arable and the right to graze a cow or a couple of goats on the pastures. They paid the tenant rent by working without wages upon his land for a certain time each week: the rest of the time they devoted to winning their own subsistence from the ground.

Life for the tenants and subtenants was primitive and grim: nothing could be more misplaced than the glamour with which the fanciful have sometimes invested these strata of Highland society before the '45.

Large families lived in small huts with chickens and sometimes other livestock wandering in and out, and at the best of times a typical Highland house with a turf roof and a central fire in the middle of the floor pouring out peat smoke was no place for cleanliness. 'The young children of the ordinary Highlanders are miserable objects indeed', wrote Captain Burt, 'and are mostly overrun with that distemper which some of the old men are hardly ever freed of from their infancy. I have often seen them come out from the huts early in a cold morning stark naked, and squat themselves down (if I might decently use the comparison) like dogs on a dunghill'.[12]

Burt reckoned the worst time for everyone was the winter, when the farms were cut off by blizzards, the nights were long, dark and boring, and the rain came through the roof mixed with the soot on the encrusted sticks of the ceiling and splashed on the floor like great drops of ink. The spring, however, brought the greatest danger from hunger: 'for then their provision of oatmeal begins to fail, and for a supply they bleed their cattle, and boil their blood into cakes, which, together with a little milk and a short allowance of oatmeal is their food'.[13] Martin Martin found similar conditions on the islands, though more use was made at this season of herbs, and of shellfish gathered in great quantities from the shore. The inhabitants of Tiree, always one of the most fertile of the Inner Hebrides, he described as living 'for the most part on barley-bread, butter, milk, cheese, fish and some eat the roots of silver-weed; there are but few that eat any flesh and the servants use water-gruel with their bread. In plentiful years the natives drink ale'.[14] In this region isolated communities occasionally perished of hunger. In North Rona, about 1685, the chief's steward came ashore one spring and found the last woman lying dead on the rocks with her child at her breast: rats had come ashore from a wrecked ship, eaten all the meal stored in the sheep-skins, and the human population had starved to death.

Highlanders were everywhere necessarily ingenious at fashioning the essentials of life from local materials. Candles, for instance, were made from the pitchy core of living pines or from animal fat cooled in moulds, ropes were woven out of wood-roots, clothing spun and woven from animal hair, and brogues cut from skins. Much of this was done in the summer when the community moved up to the hill shielings and lived in temporary huts, tending their cattle and sheep, churning butter, and taking life with its temporary bounty of abundant food and a modicum of sunshine, in a holiday spirit. An estate might have an occasional specialised weaver and a smith, living partly from their own calling and partly from a holding of land and some animals. It might support a handful of itinerant tinkers (who made spoons from melted horn), a few professional drovers and a very few pedlars. Martin Martin noticed pedlars on Skye, and said they were Lowlanders from Morayshire. A few Lowland merchants, generally of Glasgow or of Inverness (like John Steuart whose letters have been published by the Scottish History Society[15]) sent their boats round to the isles and sea lochs, mainly to barter with the chiefs and tacksmen. Otherwise there was no-one to fill the niche of craftsman, manufacturer or merchant because at this level such a niche hardly existed to fill.

It is tempting to say of such a society, tribal, inefficient and in material terms unrewarding to the great majority of its members, that it must also have had a timeless and unchanging character. By 1700 or 1730 this was not in fact true: several things were manifestly different from what they had been within the living memory of most men's fathers. The decline of the grandest courts and the most arbitrary power of the chiefs we have already noted. Martin Martin added that it was sixty years since any of the island clans had put a young chieftain to the test by making him lead a raid on his neighbours before they would accept him. Edward Burt noted that it had recently become possible to get Highlanders to work on the military roads even when the land-owners did not wish them to do so simply by offering higher wages.[16] Such things showed a slow assimilation of the Lowland norms of behaviour, brought about by the increasing strength of the forces of law and order in the hills, and by the penetration into the Highlands of some of the market forces that regulated the rest of Britain.

Nevertheless, the pace of change was undeniably sluggish, and it did not go very far in any direction. It was partly determined by economic factors. Many writers in the second half of the eighteenth century were to comment on the twin features of Highland life before 1745 of income from rent being low and of landlords preferring to have as many tenants on their land as they could crowd upon it. Some attributed this simply to the need for chiefs to have numerous tribesmen round themselves for their own defence. Others argued that there was no possibility of charging a higher rent because there was no external market for any surplus the Highlanders might produce, and so there was therefore no need to forego the advantages and prestige that a numerous tenantry brought to a chief.[17]

There was something in both arguments, but undoubtedly social factors impeded the penetration into the Highlands of the economic forces that could have changed them. The surplus the Highlanders tried to sell outside was black cattle, but the widespread social institution of stealing cattle from a neighbouring clan was so prevalent that it seriously reduced the profitability of ranching within the hills, and thus limited the impact that market forces could have upon the Highlands until they were completely reduced to obedience to law and order. Captain Burt explained all about it:

The stealing of cows they call lifting, a softening word for theft, as if it were only collecting their dues . . . When a party is formed for this purpose they go out, in parties from ten to thirty men, and traverse large tracts of mountains till they arrive at a place where they intend to commit their depredations . . . the principal time for this wicked practice is the Michaelmas moon when the cattle are in condition fit for markets . . . if the pursuers overtake the robbers and find them inferior in number and happen to seize any of them, they are seldom prosecuted, there being few who are in circumstances fit to support the expense of a prosecution; or if they were, they would be liable to have their houses burnt, their cattle hocked and their lives put in danger for some of the clan to which the banditti belonged.[18]

Eighteenth-century chiefs, it was true, hardly ever played any active part in these disreputable activities in person, though they might organise them from the sidelines, like the celebrated MacDonell of Barrisdale of whom Thomas Pennant said 'he carried the art of plunder to the highest pitch of perfection . . . he raised an income of five hundred a year by black-mail and behaved with genuine honour in restoring on proper consideration the stolen cattle of his friends'.[19] But many chiefs were aware of the lawless sport of their tenants, ready to receive rents in stolen bestial or their money equivalent, and prepared to come to the rustlers' help with bribes for judges and fees for lawyers if things looked like getting out of control. They colluded in the cattle raids partly because it was expected of them, partly because their own lands were also exposed to raid from other clans, and partly to keep the tenants' claymores shining. They felt the need for the clansmen to keep up some military practice in case of emergency. The average Highlander

could move his droves and himself through the hills with the skill of a
Red Indian.

The clan, in fact, was still a martial society. Not only did it have a
military justification for many of its characteristic features but its very
existence made the dangers of a resort to violence more likely. Outright
clan wars were admittedly declining. The last full-scale private battle
between two clans had been fought between the Campbells and the
Sinclairs at Altimarlich outside Wick in 1680. The last spectacular deed
of treachery was the massacre of the Macdonalds of Glencoe in 1692.
Even this was much more the responsibility of the Lowland Earl of
Stair than of the Campbells, who are usually blamed for what
occurred.[19] Danger was kept alive, however, partly by raiding, partly
by the Pretenders who fished in troubled waters for their own ends,
and partly by the general fear that no-one could afford to disarm while
their neighbours were still armed and war still possible. War in fact
came in 1745, to the utter disaster of those who took up arms against
the king. After it had shown the final futility of the Highland appeal to
force, there was very little to stop the clan disintegrating entirely. Many
pressures that had been weighing upon it from the outside now broke
through: new factors appeared after 1750 that had not been dreamt
of at all in Martin and Burt's day. The old Highlands receded in a mist
of romance they had done little to deserve, and within thirty years Dr.
Johnson could pronounce their epitaph:

> There was perhaps never any change of national manners so quick,
> so great, and so general, as that which has operated in the Highlands
> by the last conquest and the subsequent laws. We came hither too
> late to see what we expected—a people of peculiar appearance, and
> a system of antiquated life. The clans retain little now of their original
> character: their ferocity of temper is softened, their military ardour
> is extinguished, their dignity of independence is depressed, their
> contempt of government subdued, and their reverence for their chiefs
> abated. Of what they had before the late conquest of their country
> there remains only their language and their poverty.[20]

2. OPTIMISM AND CHANGE, 1750–1800

The victory of the Duke of Cumberland at Culloden in 1746 was bloody, bitter and complete. Some five thousand men had risen under their chiefs for the Pretender: they were physically smashed as fighting units by the battle and by the atrocities which followed it. Legislation then consolidated the work of the army throughout the Highlands. No-one anywhere in the Highlands was allowed to carry firearms (a significant exemption was made for cattle drovers), or to wear Highland dress or to play the pipes which were associated by the Government with barbarous habits and martial deeds. The hereditary judicial powers of landowners sitting in their courts was largely taken from them in the wider subsequent reform of Scottish law. Military tenures were abolished outright. A committee of Edinburgh lawyers was constituted to administer the estates forfeited from rebel leaders in all parts of the Highlands. Though not in any way vindictive, they worked on the assumption that Highland peasants were ignorant, idle and culturally savage, and they therefore strove to do all they could to eliminate the *mores* of the clan.

These things did not, however, merely create a political and cultural vacuum. Rather, they provided a great opportunity for leadership by men who were convinced of the rightness of their cause and were in a position to act immediately upon their beliefs. Long before 1745 there had been tension in the governing circles of the Highlands between Jacobite clans and Government clans, between Episcopalians and Presbyterians, between proprietors who looked back with affection to the older tradition of the great following and landowners of a new type who were actively responsive to the enthusiasm for 'improvement' and hopeful of the prospects of getting more cattle out to the English market. Not that by any means all the forward-looking landlords were Hanoverian in political sympathy—Mackintosh of Borlum, for instance, was a Jacobite hero. For many decades the forces of change had been gathering momentum. The Campbells under the Dukes of Argyll and the Earls of Breadalbane were aggressive and successful, the S.P.C.K. and its missionary schools carried the orthodox doctrines of the Church of Scotland into the glens, and the character of the landed classes themselves began to change, largely at the same time as their own upbringing changed.

The last point was perhaps the most important, though not the most often appreciated. Before 1700 (and in some parts until 1750) the children of chiefs and chieftains had generally been reared by putting them out to foster-parents, who would be some inferior kinsmen of the clan. This not only gave the chief a special tie in adult life to the foster-brother with whom he had been brought up and who became a close and privileged member of the chief's court but also ensured that the chief sucked in at his childhood nothing but the pure milk of Highland tradition, fed to him by foster-parents who were conscious of their role in handing down to their future leader the purity of the old unsullied ways. After 1700 wherever Lowland and Presbyterian pressure had any weight at all fosterage was abandoned. Boys were brought up anp educated at home, and sent to the Lowlands for college and polish: they were encouraged deliberately to unlearn their 'uncouth' ways and to mix as equals with the Lowland lairds and their children. In this way, an important proportion of the chiefs and chieftains of the Highlands came themselves to imbibe the Lowland view of clan society as being barbarian. Like many converts, they made the most zealous evangelists in attempting to convert their social inferiors to what they now regarded as civilisation.

What Culloden and its aftermath did, therefore, was firstly to remove the last of those in authority who were dedicated to upholding the old values and to leave those who were devoted to promulgating the new ones. Secondly, those who had new ideas were more easily able to carry them out because the threat of disorder was removed. It was now practicable to sit down to plan how to develop a cattle ranch in the hills because the rustlers who in the past had plundered the drovers were suppressed with complete success within a dozen years of 1745. There is a story in the *Statistical Account* of one MacIan, who had sheltered Prince Charles after Culloden when he could have gained £30,000 by betraying him, and several years later was hanged at Inverness for stealing a cow. 'A little before his execution he took off his bonnet and thanked God that he had never betrayed his trust, never injured the poor, and never refused a share of what he had to the stranger and needy'.[21] The new moral world could admire his loyalty, but they would not tolerate this lawlessness. 'I'm resolved to keep no tenants but such as will be peaceable and apply to industry', wrote the

Duke of Argyll to the Chamberlain of Tiree in 1756, 'You'll cause intimate this some sabbath after sermon'.[22] A MacIan could not survive the triumph of order and of Lowland ethics that made the Highlands change so quickly in the second half of the century.

At least as important as the immediate outcome of the battle, however, were the changing economic circumstances of the rest of the country, transmitted to the north as rising demand for Highland products within two decades of the rebellion, and bringing the promise of material rewards for the exploiter of Highland resources on a scale quite without parallel in previous history. Indeed, so persistent and unprecedented was this pressure that it is hard to believe that it would not have made much the same impact on the country even if the '45 had never occurred. The change might have come more slowly, but the profits of bringing it about must have eroded the wild ways of even the most conservative chiefs in the end.

Cattle was the traditional staple exported to the plain, and oatmeal was the traditional import. The price of cattle rose by three hundred per cent between the 1740s and the 1790s while the price of oats did not quite double: besides, with the introduction of potatoes, fewer oats per head of population were now needed. The effective terms of trade between the Highlands and the Lowlands moved sharply in the former's favour. The peasants and lairds who produced cattle therefore began to enjoy the prospect of a much greater money income, though how it was to be shared between profits and rents remained to be resolved. The price of wool, too, began to rise, and from 1760 it was appreciated more and more that the Highlands could become new grazing territory for the Cheviot and Blackface sheep of the south of Scotland. The organisation of sheep-farming, however, unlike that of raising cattle, was incompatible with peasant husbandry (see page 350 below) and any response to rising demand for wool would therefore entail a basic social change in land tenure. Along the indented coast from Sutherland to Kintyre the prospects for the fishery were reviving, and beyond that the remote Hebrides were affected from 1790 by demand for kelp, the ashes of seaweed used in glass-manufacture and soap-boiling in Clydeside, Lancashire and elsewhere. Fishing and kelp manufacture were labour intensive, demanding a larger population than the immemorial habits of peasant farming: where they took root, social change was also inevitable. Timber prices rose wherever wood was accessible to water transport: oak bark was needed for tanning, charcoal for smelting and deal planks for building. Controlled exploitation of the old forests and the planting of new also demanded changes in the traditional patterns of husbandry, especially the extirpation of the goat. Finally, optimism outran reality: great things were also expected of the manufacture of linen and woollen cloth in villages designed for the purpose, and even David Dale, the doyen of the early Scottish cotton manufacturers, thought it worth the risk to erect a large mill at Spinningdale on the Dornoch Firth to utilise Highland labour on the new Lancashire jennies.

Optimism, indeed, was the keynote of those in command of Highland society in the last three or four decades of the eighteenth century: there was an atmosphere of expectation of beneficent change about to take place, a hopefulness without parallel in Highland experience, contrasting with the dark stagnation of the past and the darker disillusion that was to come in the future. Landowners regarded the prospects for the Highlands and the Lowlands in an identical light, and at first made plans for improvement that differed only in emphasis as to the relative balance of animals and grain in the new rural economy they were constructing.

Highland landowners like Lowlanders planned to rest the new husbandry of their estates upon enclosure. Runrig must be abolished, the moor should be divided; the old co-operative methods of husbandry were wasteful and would have to be superseded by advanced systems adapted to Highland conditions. In 1784 the Highland and Agricultural Society was created in order to further this adaptation from the Lowlands, publishing essays and giving gold medals to those who wrote on such subjects as the management of cattle, enclosures, the cultivation of grass and green crops, and the improvement of waste and heath ground. By these and similar methods the landowners expected to raise agricultural productivity. They expected to have to dispossess some small tenants, just as they had had to do in the Scottish lowlands, but they also expected to build new villages up and down the countryside to house the displaced and to provide them with employment of a non-agricultural kind, just as Lowland improvers had built Ormiston in East Lothian and Cuminestown in Aberdeenshire. Many Highland villages remain as monuments to the hopes of this generation: Ullapool in Wester Ross, built by the British Fisheries Society with a pier and storehouses at a cost of over £10,000 for settlers who never came in sufficient numbers to occupy all the feus; Beauly in Inverness-shire, reconstructed by the Committee of Forfeited Estates after their agent had reported that, though 'the common people are generally lazy, ignorant and addicted to drinking' with 'many perverse, obstinate fellows of bad characters', the site itself 'could not miss to attract strangers of different professions from many corners, and would consequently soon diffuse a spirit of trade and industry, as well as promote agriculture through all this extensive country'; then there was Grantown in Inverness-shire, Oban in Argyll, and Tomintoul in Banffshire and many more all designed by Highland landowners in the same spirit of economic zeal and moral reformation that characterises their Lowland counterparts.[23]

It would have been reasonable to expect to find, when this programme had been carried through, that the social structure of rural society in the Highlands would come to resemble that of the Lowlands. One would expect the emergence of a class of indigenous and wealthy capitalist farmers side by side with a class of landless labourers who lived by working for them. In parts of the Highlands (for instance in parts of Perthshire and Angus, western Aberdeenshire, Banffshire and in Cromarty) this is roughly what did happen, though farms tended to be a good deal smaller and farmers to be less well-off than in Lowland areas. Some of the most successful were Lowlanders to whom landlords gave preferential leases in the hope they would be good examples to the natives. Elsewhere, however, particularly in the north and west, Highland society developed along quite different lines. It became overwhelmingly dominated by very large numbers of tenants holding very small pieces of land in very crowded conditions, with few among them who could be regarded either as capitalists or as proletarians. Here, instead of peasant society disappearing as the result of agrarian change, it simply became a different kind of peasant society, based on the smallholding instead of on the joint-farm. Since neither the peasants nor, ultimately, the landowners were better off than they had been before, it must be judged to be the one instance in Scotland of the improvers' failure to improve. What happened in this region is more akin to contemporary developments in Ireland and in certain parts of Europe effected by the same demographic factors and, like the Highlands, lying at a geographical disadvantage.

The reasons for the failure are four. Firstly, the coming of the potato as a common field crop in the decades after 1760 provided the means to support a large population on a small area, even on land torn from the edge of the waste and previously regarded as beyond the margins of cultivation. Secondly, the peasants objected either to moving or to becoming landless. To move was very difficult: in remote regions little was known of the outside world, and the common bond of a Gaelic tongue among the Highlanders also proved a common barrier in getting a job outside the Highlands. To become landless was to be a staring reproach among the neighbours in a society of conservative outlook; the peasants had probably always thought of themselves as having a prescriptive right to some holding on the clan territory, though not necessarily a hereditary right to any given piece of land. The peasants therefore divided and divided again the holdings that the landowners had given them in order to get for their children a potato rig that would enable them to stay, to marry and to raise families of their own. Thirdly, the landowners, who alone had it in their power to check this subdivision, had a very ambivalent attitude towards it. They needed, on many estates, a heavy population to gather the kelp: they enjoyed, such were their own sentiments towards the recent past, the grand emotional feeling of being surrounded by a numerous tenantry. If they could not get the population to stay in any other way than as crofters cultivating potatoes in very small holdings they were not going to object, and they would not be averse to helping the process on by granting them leases (at very easy terms in the first instance) to dig out rocky ground and make themselves a plot on the edge of the moor.

Lastly, the limited initial success of agrarian change in the northwest seemed to provide its own justification. The tacksmen (see page 138 above) who in the old system had been intermediate rentiers between the proprietor and the peasants, now appeared to have no function in the new system and were dispossessed by the landlords. Some anticipating what would happen, had already left and taken local peasants with them to found new clan societies in America. The joint-farms that had been the basis of the previous husbandry were broken down, usually into many smaller units than was the case in the Lowlands or even in the south-east Highlands: the peasants themselves subdivided them into still smaller units, until the land-holding pattern began to resemble the nineteenth-century maze of crofts, each with its own individual patch where a family grew potatoes and oats and with its rights on the moor where they could pasture one or two cows or three or four sheep. Where possible the kelp industry was introduced, or fishing begun as an ancillary occupation to agriculture. The price of cattle and of kelp rose, especially rapidly in the decades hinging on 1800. In material terms the peasants did not seem to be any worse off than they had been when they lived under the subsistence economy of the old Highlands. If people perished of hunger in Highland dearths like that of 1782-3, it was most often in those parishes where the potato had not yet been introduced, and where oatmeal was still the staff of life. The landlords were certainly better off with the increase of rents and the profits of kelping. In 1805 the Earl of Selkirk estimated that the value of the estates forfeited in 1745 had risen from £12,000 per annum to £80,000 per annum in sixty years. Macdonald of Clan-ranald, who owned South Uist, was drawing £17,000 in 1809 from rents and kelping income: early in the eighteenth century his lands had not yielded £1,000 per annum. The Highland landowners were often both greedy and short-sighted in these circumstances. They seem to have creamed off a larger proportion of the total profits into their own hands than did the Lowland lairds with the Lothian or Ayrshire farmers. Clanranald never ploughed anything back into the Uists in the form, for instance, of new harbours or roads or of encouragement for new industry or a more diversified farming. He was content to spend the kelp money on conspicuous consumption and in adding to and servicing the heavy debt charge on his estate.[24]

Altogether around 1800 there were many improvers ready to argue that encouragement of small farms was the correct way to promote economic change in the remoter parts of the Highlands, since it pro-duced results without being completely hostile to the traditional preference of the peasant to keep his feet on land. They might have been right if population had not itself begun to increase, slowly at first, and then in numbers vastly above what the old Highland economy had been able to support. The population of the Outer Hebrides, for in-stance, rose from 13,000 around 1755 to 24,500 in 1811, that of Skye and the mainland parishes opposite from 17,000 in 1755 to 27,000 in 1811, that of Mull and the southern Inner Hebrides from 10,000 in 1755 to 18,000 in 1811. This meant that what had been small farms now became tiny farms: what had been generous permission to allow a father to give his son a patch of his own holding now became a licence for fragmentation: what had been a rural economy based on oats, cattle, and potatoes, became of necessity an economy based more and more on potatoes alone.

Slow deterioration quickened into crisis in the second decade of the nineteenth century. Cattle prices fell at the end of the Napoleonic Wars, and it began to be obvious that Lowland producers, who had land to grow turnips for winter keep, held all the winning cards when it came to competition on reduced profit margins. Kelp prices fell, initially when it became possible to import barilla as a substitute from Spain: kelp had fetched £20 a ton in 1808 and dropped to £10 a ton by the early 1820s. Then in 1825 the manufacture of Leblanc alkali was initiated in Glasgow, and within five years kelp was fetching £3 a ton and was not worth gathering. Fishing, too, proved itself a broken reed all over the west: prices dropped, and the herring moved away from the inshore lochs where the Highlanders had been able to capture them in small boats to deeper waters where only the larger and more expensive boats of the east-coast fishermen were able to operate.

Thus of the four main staples on which the Highlanders had relied for sale outwith the region only one, wool, still remained profitable. The introduction of sheep-farming, however, was incompatible with peasant husbandry in the same area. Those who carried it on were almost always outsiders, since Highland peasants had no reserves of capital themselves and no landowners who were willing to put their hands in their pockets to provide it. Sheep-farmers were normally wealthy Lowland tenants who could offer the laird a high rent in return for a wide concession. Again the new sheep husbandry demanded virtually all the land in areas into which it was introduced. The incomers said they needed, in particular, those hill shielings where the Highlanders took their beasts in June: in fact within a few decades after the introduction of sheep the overcropping of these green summer pastures in the hills made them largely valueless. They also said that they could not tolerate the peasant's hairy brown sheep grazing in the same district as their fine Cheviot and Blackface ewes because of the danger of cross-breeding. Wherever the sheep came the peasant was obliged to move out to the periphery of the fertile area and to limit his own husbandry still more narrowly to the potato rig.

The economic situation of the Highlands after 1815, therefore, suddenly began to look grim. Either the region reverted to subsistence husbandry and increasing numbers of people lived in a vast rural slum, existing off potatoes grown on tiny holdings like their fellows in Ireland or Finland, or the region switched over in a big way to sheep, with the best ground engrossed by a handful of outsiders and the natives existing by digging plots on the edges. The alternatives were squalid enough. A moment's reflection would show the landowner that the second had the advantage from his point of view of averting his own ruin along with that of his dependents. But it demanded a ruthlessness to replace men with sheep that not every landlord immediately found in his own heart.

3. CONGESTION AND CLEARANCE

The crisis was experienced differently in different parts. If one was to consider only the Hebrides, the Highland problem of this period would appear to be created entirely by the pressure of population on resources, and to be one to which clearances and sheep farming were largely irrelevant. The area suffered from the middle of the eighteenth century until the middle of the nineteenth century from the poverty of all its inhabitants who pressed perpetually against the edge of subsistence whether the economy was able to support only relatively few inhabitants or a great many. Thomas Pennant, for instance, coming to Skye in 1772, said this:

The poor are left to Providence's care. They prowl like other animals along the shore to pick up limpets and other shell fish, the casual repasts of hundreds during part of the year in these unhappy islands. Hundreds thus annually drag through the season a wretched life, and numbers unknown, in all parts of the Western Highlands, fall beneath the pressure, some of hunger, more of the putrid fever, the epidemic of the coasts, originating from unwholesome food, the dire effects of necessity.[25]

Twenty years later John Buchanan, Church of Scotland missionary to the isles, described the 'scallags' of Harris, perhaps the most depressed class of agricultural labourer ever to have existed in Scotland in recent centuries. Unfortunately we do not know whether the extremes of their condition represented a traditional situation or a recent deterioration:

The scallag, whether male or female, is a poor being who for mere subsistence becomes a predial slave to another, whether a sub-tenant, a tacksman or a laird. The scallag builds his own hut, with sods and boughs of trees: and if he is sent from one part of the country to another he moves off his sticks, and by means of these forms a new hut in another place ... Five days a week he works for his master, the sixth he is allowed to himself for the cultivation of some scrap of land on the edge of some moss or moor on which he raises a little kail, or coleworts, barley and potatoes. These articles, boiled up together in one mash, and often without salt, are his only food, except in those seasons and days when he can catch some fish, ... The only bread he tastes is a cake made of the flour of barley. He is allowed coarse shoes, with tartan hose, and a coarse coat, with a blanket or two for clothing.[26]

Another writer in 1794 said that 'some time ago' the wages of male scallags had been fixed at £2 a year and four pairs of shoes, and of a female scallag at 6/8d. a year and two pairs of shoes: but now the men would not engage for more than nine months of the year as scallags, and spent three months kelping, 'so that (now) their annual earnings, besides feeding themselves may be rated at something more than £3 at an average'. This commentator, however, thought they were better off than the poorest subtenants because they had no rent to pay.[27]

The gap between this kind of poverty and that continuing to exist in the islands after 1815 is not really very large. Some of the best descriptions of the latter come from the evidence before the Royal Commission on Emigration in 1826 and 1827, when, for example, it was stated that Macdonald of Clanranald in the Uists, was left with a third of the population landless, helpless and dependent on his charity: he had had to spend £4,500 on buying meal for them in 1817, and £1,100 in 1818. Of Tiree, too, it was said that half the families were squatters existing on the bounty of the other half. Maclean of Coll alone of the lairds in the region could claim there was no overpopulation on his island, and he ensured this by a high-handed method familiar to the Macneills of Barra in an earlier time:

He used every means in his power to keep the population down, the means he used were, that he would not allow a young man, a son of one of the crofters, to be married without his consent; he said, if you marry without my consent, you must leave the island.[28]

How effective this was may be seen from the figures: the population of Coll rose only from 1,200 to 1,300 between 1755 and 1831, while

The School at New Lanark mills c.1825. "The superintendant took us upstairs to the large dancing-hall, which opens precisely at seven o'clock every morning. Here we found some eighty or a hundred children of both sexes, at an average of about ten, paraded on the floor . . . moving in measured steps to the music of an orchestra"

Glasgow roughs creating a disturbance at the departure of a London coach

A view of New Lanark cotton mills early nineteenth century. The figures in the right foreground are the village band

The Broomielaw, Glasgow, c. 1820. The tall spire is that of Gorbals church, later wrecked by lightning

the population of neighbouring Tiree rose in the same period from 1,500 to 4,450.

Thus one can only say of the Hebrides that the peasant endured extreme poverty all the time, and the main change after 1815 was not so much in their condition as in that of the landowners, whose income, having risen all the time from about 1750 until after 1815 as they diverted the whole profits of an expanding economy into their own pockets, now began to slide away, and the debt charges on their estates began steadily to mount.

The other change of importance was that the experience of the emigrant boats calling at the islands to take crofters away to a new life in America became more and more frequent as the years passed, for the natural rate of increase on the estates remained high even after the economy had ceased to be able to expand to accommodate it. Organised emigration had in fact taken place from the islands since around 1740, generally on the initiative of tacksmen, but for the whole of the eighteenth century it had been opposed by most proprietors. After 1800, and especially after 1820 it began to be actively encouraged, and even to be arranged and paid for by them, as the only solution they could see for the relief of over-crowding. There is little hint (except on Rhum and Jura in 1826 and on Arran in 1828) of men at this date being turned out to make room for sheep. The misery of the Hebrides is primarily the misery of the congested, not of the dispossessed.

Sutherland, of course, appears to provide the classic instance of the opposite. It was here that, between 1807 and 1821, the factors of the Countess of Sutherland and her husband Lord Stafford who owned more than two-thirds of the land in the county expelled from their homes somewhere between five and ten thousand people to make room for sheep. The violence and the speed with which these evictions were accomplished has made them a *cause célèbre* in Highland history. The most notorious single episode was the clearance of Strathnaver in 1814. In January Patrick Sellar, a Morayshire farmer who was both principal factor to the Sutherland family and incoming tenant on the estate had given the Highland peasants six months notice to quit. By mid-June most of them were still there, and he moved in with men, dogs and fire to clear the valley. Some houses were apparently destroyed while old people were still inside them; others were burnt before the families could get all their animals and possessions out; in most cases the roof timbers, which were the most valuable part of an old house in a treeless county and were always saved to form the basis of a new home on removing, were heaped into a pile and wantonly reduced to ashes. Sellar was made to stand trial for arson, and for the culpable homicide of two elderly people who were alleged to have died as a result of eviction. The defence counsel claimed that 'the question at issue involves the future fate and progress and even moral improvement in the county of Sutherland . . . it is in substance and in fact a trial of strength between the abettors of anarchy and misrule and the magistracy as well as the laws of this country'.[29] Sellar was acquitted, and the Sheriff-substitute of Sutherland who had brought the charge at the request of the tenants was dismissed from office and reduced to grovelling apology.

In time, however, the verdict in Sellar's favour has been reversed, not in law, but in popular opinion. This was brought about partly by the power of the Highlanders to enshrine ancient wrong in oral tradition, which was revived at the hearing of the Napier Commission of 1884, and partly by the literary skill of Donald Macleod, the Strathnaver stonemason who emigrated to Canada and kept up a searing polemic against the Sutherland family thirty or forty years after the event.[30] Strathnaver has become a peculiar symbol for all the resentment of the nineteenth-century Highlanders, and it remains very difficult to consider the Sutherland clearances without the associations of deep emotion that hang around this trial.

It is necessary nevertheless to see all the events in the Sutherland clearances in a deeper perspective. Sutherland had never been as Donald Macleod painted it, a peasant Arcadia of rosy prosperity, plump girls and happy bakers. On the contrary, it had for long been a county of poverty and emigration. Thomas Pennant in 1772, forty years before Sellar's day, described the people as:

Almost torpid with idleness, and most wretched; their hovels most miserable, made of poles wattled and covered with thin sods. There is not corn raised sufficient to supply half the wants of the inhabitants . . . yet there is much improvable land here in a state of nature: but till famine pinches they will not bestir themselves . . . Numbers of the miserables of this country were now migrating: they wandered in a state of desperation; too poor to pay, they madly sell themselves for their passage, preferring a temporary bondage in a strange land to starving for life in their native soil.[31]

Sir John Sinclair, too, twenty years later, found the peasantry struggling in deep poverty and distress, and felt that the only way to help them was to institute reclamation schemes on waste land ('there is scarcely any farm in Sutherland that has not some ground adjacent to it fit for improvement'), and to promote non-agricultural activity like fishing and weaving which would incite them to help themselves. He thought that cotton or linen manufacture would be the occupation most likely to give the Highlanders 'the opportunity of tasting the sweets and advantages of labour', and he wanted a joint stock company established for 'preventing emigrations and establishing manufactures and industry in the Highlands of Scotland'.[32] Most people thinking about the economic problem of the Highlands at this time were writing along these lines.

The plan formulated by the chief land-agents to the Countess of Sutherland after 1807 was a serious and largely conventional attempt to recast the economy of an immense estate to the benefit (it was genuinely if hopefully assumed) of all parties involved. It was clear that the land had been badly managed in the past. Runrig had not been abolished, there was no outside employment, and there had hitherto been little clearance of marginal land. To increase income from the estate the inland straths were to be rented to sheep farmers: to give the peasants displaced a fair chance to revive their fortunes, they were to be resettled near the coast to fish and to weave. This was how the factors answered a question from the Board of Agriculture in 1811:

> Sheep-farms are paying well on the Sutherland estates. The number of Cheviots are now about 15,000. More ground will be laid off for the same mode of husbandry, without decreasing the population. Situations in various ways will be fixed on for the people. Fishing stations, in which mechanics will be settled; inland villages, with carding machines; moors and detached spots calculated for the purpose will be found, but the people must work. The industrious will be encouraged and protected, but the slothful must remove or starve, as man was not born to be idle, but to gain his bread by the sweat of his brow.[33]

Nor was this all mere talk. Large sums were in fact spent in the next ten years by the Sutherland estate on roads, bridges, fishing harbours, inns and steadings. The new village of Helmsdale was one such improvement. Here the family, approached by a Morayshire firm in

1814, first built a complete curing installation at a cost of £1,200 and rented it to them; similar arrangements were made to attract a Berwick firm at a further capital cost of £2,100, and then other firms were persuaded to settle from Leven, Leith and Golspie. An inn and nine large houses were built by the estate, and John Rennie, one of the great civil engineers of the day, was brought in to design a harbour. Within five years the estate had invested £14,000 in creating a modern fishing port and trying to make it a growth-point for the hinterland, in much the same way as private and public economic planners have tried to do in similar schemes for the Highlands on many subsequent occasions over the years.[34]

Unfortunately the investment programme coincided with a time when fishing was becoming less prosperous and the volume of employment hoped for never materialised. At the same time the proposals to set the peasants to work on textiles fell to the ground, and throughout Sutherland it was found that there was in the end practically nothing for the dispossessed peasants to do except dig in their potato rig. Many who had been turned off the fertile straths and been dumped on small plots of shallow, acid land moved out to Caithness and other counties. The population did not fall between the censuses of 1811 and 1821 but unlike that of every other Highland county it did not rise either. It is likely enough that if the agents' plans had worked the Highlanders' distress at their dispossession would have been at least mitigated by the easing of their poverty. But the plans failed, and what was remembered was only the brutality of eviction.

Sutherland was neither the first nor the last county where clearances broke the established pattern of life, but in most instances the landowners made no attempt to help the displaced tenants either directly or by releasing capital to create new employment. Walker, writing in 1812, found seventeen parishes in Dunbartonshire, Perthshire and Argyll where population had fallen since 1750 mainly because of the introduction of large cattle farms.[35] The usual cause of clearance, however, were the Lowland sheep, which spread like a tide over the central southern Highlands after 1764. Generally speaking, the further north it went the larger became the sheepfarms and the greater the degree of social dislocation followed in its wake. In 1785 Macdonell of Glengarry, head of one of the most ancient families in the north, carried out some of the first clearances north of the Great Glen. With him there was no question of investment; he spent most of the proceeds on conspicuous consumption, particularly in devising fantastic Highland games of bogus antiquity, such as that in which paid retainers tried to pull off the legs of dead cows with their bare hands. On one recorded occasion it took five hours to get one limb off. In 1792 a group of proprietors introduced sheepfarms into Ross-shire: this created an ephemeral outburst of rioting on a scale to alarm the Government, who believed that French Jacobin agitators had got loose in the north.

Not all landowners, of course, submitted immediately to the temptation. The Duke of Argyll, for example, on his immense estates was no friend to the wealthy Lowland farmers touting a tempting offer of high rent for empty grazings—but with his wealth he could afford to stand aloof. Other chiefs having resisted the urge to put their lands to the most profitable uses were compelled by the remorseless logic of debt or bankruptcy to sell out to others with less fine feelings, as Lord Reay was forced to sell to the Duke of Sutherland in 1829. Sometimes the great family switched with the generations from a policy of allowing the peasants to subdivide their farms to a policy of clearances. The first Marquis of Breadalbane had loved a numerous population about him in the tradition of his fathers so that, like many other chiefs, he could recruit as many as he wished into his pet Highland regiment. His generosity so imperilled the finances of the estate that when the second Marquis succeeded he set about expelling as many as he could of those whom his father had tempted to stay.

However they came about the clearances shattered at a blow the Highlander's faith in his chief. Their grievance was not that their poverty had been increased: it had not. It was that they had been evicted from land occupied from time immemorial. It passed their comprehension that the landowner could turn off men to make room for animals. The Gaelic poets vented their feelings in a froth of impotent abuse. Thus Duncan Chisholm, whose chief, the twenty-fifth of his line, was one of the great clearers of the north:

Destruction to the sheep from all corners of Europe! Scab, wasting, pining, tumours on the stomach and on the hide! Foxes and eagles for the lambs! Nothing more to be seen of them but fleshless hides and grey shepherds leaving the country without laces in their shoes. I have overlooked someone, the Factor! May he be bound by tight thongs, wearing nothing but his trousers, and be beaten with rods from head to foot. May he be placed on a bed of brambles and covered with thistles. Thus may this stray cur be driven to Atholl.[36]

Rage, however, was totally unavailing. More found comfort in religion. The zeal with which crofters throughout the Highlands embraced the more authoritarian forms of Presbyterianism was perhaps rooted in a wish to replace their reverence for earthly father-figures who had betrayed them by reverence for a heavenly Father whose properties were unchanging and merciful to the weak, but implacably vengeful to the oppressor. Few aspects of social change in the Highlands are more striking than the conversion of almost all the peasantry (except the Catholics) from a state verging on semi-paganism at the start of the eighteenth century to strict religious observance in the nineteenth century. This, which is also connected with the work of the S.P.C.K., is discussed at greater length in Chapter XVIII below.

By 1830, therefore, the Highlanders had become a society of small-holders living in great poverty on congested holdings either on crowded islands or next to extensive sheepfarms: their existence hung above all else upon the condition of the potato crop, and if this failed (as it did so tragically in the 1840s) nothing could prevent the collapse of their economy and a subsequent exodus on a scale that would eclipse by far the Sutherland clearances.

Could anything possibly have been done by the landowners which would have had any other consequence than this? Given the high fertility of the Highlanders and their very conservative outlook, combined with the low fertility of their country, as barren of ores and fuel as it was of rich land, and considering the failure of many well-intentioned schemes to bring fresh employment in new villages and seaside industry, it is tempting to say that nothing in the end could have been done that was not done to avert the collapse of the Highland economy.

Some nagging doubts, however, remain. The eighteenth-century landowner made what was possibly one fatal miscalculation in driving away the Highland tacksman as though he were nothing more than a parasite interposed between a proprietor and his working tenants to suck up the rents. The tacksmen were the only people in the hierarchy who approximated at all to a middle-class position: they were also initially amenable to doing what the landlords told them, and could be expected to exert some direct pressure on the clansmen below. To have kept the tacksmen would certainly have meant a smaller income from rents for the lairds (at least initially) and would therefore have deprived the latter of the immediate chance to shine as brightly as their Lowland fellows in the social occasions at which they all mixed in Edinburgh and London: and it is clear that Highland landlords did desire this advantage even if they had to mortgage their estates to get it. To have kept the tacksmen would also have involved giving them discretion in promoting their own self-interest with the capital that was allowed to accumulate in their hands, and it would have involved consciously re-educating them from habits of the clan to the ethics of the improvers. The dividend that might have been paid would have been the creation of a native entrepreneurial class in the Highlands, the absence of which has hamstrung the economy ever since.

As it was, tacksmen emigrated in scores in the decades after 1750, either directly forced out by the landlord or going of their own accord believing that the new Highlands had no place for their values. Many proprietors were rightly alarmed to see them go, especially when, as often happened, they persuaded substantial tenants who already had some capital (in the form of cattle they could sell) to come with them, leaving only the subtenants and the poor behind. Many of the emigrants who left before 1800 were thus very different from the ragged host that followed after 1815. Had opportunity for the earlier group been found in Scotland in time there might not have been so many of the latter. The criticism that the landowners were too hungry for rent applies also after 1815, when the failure to reduce rents soon enough after the fall in the prices of Highland products forced many peasants to sell their remaining stock on a bad market to pay arrears, and thus, by squandering the resources of those who still had a little capital, all were reduced to the flat level of the crofter.

Finally, it was a tragedy that no-one in authority ever made a serious attempt to harness the co-operative traditions of the joint-farm to the improving ideal, and to create with assistance from the landlords sheepfarms run by groups of Highland tenants who each contributed something to the capital and labour required, and gained mutually from the rewards. The proposal was seriously made by Sir John Sinclair in 1795[37], but it fell on deaf ears. Even he made no attempt to implement it on his own estate. The habit of assuming that the Highlanders were congenitally incapable of any effort or self-help had been ingrained in upper-class Scottish thinking since the days of James VI:

the belief was not to be shaken now. Yet it was madness to assume that any lasting agrarian prosperity could be built except on the basis of carrying the local population with the landowners. The positive response of the tenantry was the whole key to the success in the Lowlands.

In the last resort, however, it is possible that nothing could have been done that would have provided the Highlands with an alternative to congestion or clearance. The grim facts of economic geography have, time and time again, defeated the good intentions of planners. It could not pay to make textiles in the north because the mills of the central belt, and of Lancashire and Yorkshire were so much better located for the market. It was hard to make substantial investments in fishing pay for the same reason. The marketing of cattle, and even of wool itself, was hampered by bad transport when competition sharpened. An area so high, so wet and so remote is at a perpetual disadvantage in a modern economy, and no amount of wishful thinking can make it otherwise. There were men in the eighteenth century who expected to build cities the size of Liverpool in the Western Highlands[38] : there have been men ever since with one version or another of this dream. But perhaps it is all to the good that they do not allow themselves to be diverted from their vision by the study of so dismaying a subject as history.

CHAPTER XV

The Urban Middle Class

1. THE MIDDLE CLASS

The Scottish middle class of the eighteenth century was vigorous and various. It contained many who were on the edge of the landed class, like those judges of the Court of Session who bought estates and played the gentleman (see page 296 above), and like those sons of lairds and noblemen who were put into the professions but who meant to return to the land when they had made their pile. There were many families with a saga like that which Elizabeth Grant (b. 1797) told of her grandfather. The laird of 'the beautiful plain of Rothiemurchus, with its lakes and rivers and forests' had:

> felt some difficulty in maintaining his sons; the result in the generation to which my grandfather Dr. William Grant belonged was that he with a younger brother and a set of half uncles much about their own age were all shoved off about the world to scramble through it as best they could.[1]

William studied medicine at Aberdeen, finished his education at Leyden, practised in London, married an English heiress, and returned to Rothiemurchus to live on his capital as 'the laird's brother', educating in his turn his eldest son as an advocate. Men like William Grant were aware of no tensions between 'the land' and 'the professions': it is partly because there were so many of them that there was, for much of the period, so little sense of conflict between the middle class and those above it in the hierarchy.

At the other end of the social spectrum the middle class also contained a great many who were on the edge of what we would now call the working class, especially those described in contemporary directories as 'mechanics'—the artisans and craftsmen who were partly employers of journeymen and apprentices and partly workers dependent on the skill of their own hands and eyes. Take, for example, the calling of shoemaker. About 1790 there were in Dumfries 110 shoemakers in the incorporated guild, employing eighty-four journeymen and forty-two apprentices: the ratio of master to men is so low that both obviously had a near-working-class character, but with many of the journeymen and apprentices still hoping to become masters one day. In Kilmarnock at the same date, however, there were fifty-six 'master shoemakers' employing 408 journeymen: the calling of shoemaker was here that of the small middle-class employer, but few of the journeymen could here hope to reach the status of master.[2] From this it was only a step to a position like that of William Christie, Deacon of the Cordiners of Glasgow, who rose from a country cobbler to become the greatest shoemaker the city had hitherto known, employing before 1735 upwards of forty journeymen and becoming the first to deal 'in a wholesale way' by exporting 'very large cargoes of goods, shoes and pontoons for the use of the West Indies . . . and also for His Majesty's regiments'.[3] It is because a term like shoemaker could conceal many rungs on the ladder (and because a man like William Christie could climb them relatively easily) that there was also in the eighteenth century little tension between employer and employed. When it did occur it was where it was difficult for a workman to reach the status of employer: a factory worker or a miner was infinitely less likely to become a factory owner or a coalowner than a clockmaker's journeyman was to become a clockmaker. Such conditions were naturally commoner after 1780 than before.

Within the middle class itself there were, moreover, great differences of status and wealth which themselves prevented the formation of any obvious middle-class front. A lawyer like Duncan Forbes or Lord Milton, who moved easily in the circles of dukes, had nothing in common with a master tailor in Dundee, whose apprentice lived in his own household: neither of them had much in common with a dancing master in Montrose, trying to polish the manners and steps of provincial youth. Perhaps it was this variety that inhibited the emergence of any commonly accepted expression to denote what we now mean by the middle class. Already before 1800 it was commonplace to speak of the 'landed classes', meaning the mutual interest of landowners and tenant farmers: the terms 'labouring classes' and even 'the working class' had been used (since 1780 at least) to denote the wage earners; there was as yet nothing commonly used to describe those who lived in towns and lived by employing their brains and their capital. At the beginning of the century contemporaries could speak of lawyers, ministers, merchants, schoolmasters and tradesmen: at the end of the century they could add the categories of office-holder and manufacturer. When we use the expression 'middle class', it is as well to remember that it is only a convenient shorthand to describe a large number of these groups in urban society who were not often seen by contemporaries to have anything very significant in common with one another.

One thing, nevertheless, which almost all groups in the middle class shared was the dizzy sense of opportunity which pervaded the towns from 1760 onwards. Lawyers prospered when farmers and landowners flourished, mainly because a high proportion of their profits came from conveyancing and from disputes about land. Merchants grew wealthy with the opening of new trades to North America, the West Indies and Russia, then to the export markets of France and Germany, and finally (as the Glasgow pioneers broke the monopoly of the East India Company) with the trade to India and China. Businessmen multiplied in old occupations, and appeared in many new ones that had not existed a century before—as bankers, as owners of cotton factories and chemical works, of ironworks, sugar-refineries, distilleries, papermills, glassworks and powdermills. Younger sons found new openings in the English colonies and some returned to live in the towns as bourgeois citizens, describing themselves in the street directories as so-and-so 'late of Jamaica', or 'of the East India Company'. Others battened upon the augmented funds of patronage at home, and became excisemen or other minor office-holders in the Scottish establishment.

All this created a second wave of benefits to those professions that attended to the needs of middle class and landed class alike. Doctors and ministers, for instance, found their incomes rising. There were many more openings (not all well paid) for schoolmasters in the parish schools, the grammar schools, the new academies and English schools, and plenty of scope for free-lance teachers of extra-mural subjects of all descriptions. Printers and booksellers flourished as never before.

and paid their authors sums of exemplary magnitude. Who would not wish to have been a historian in the days when Principal William Robertson received £4,500 for his second book, and David Hume £5,000 for one volume of his history of Britain? Tradesmen and mechanics of all descriptions shared in the general bonanza, for there was a readier sale for everything they made and sold from cakes and wigs to shoes and carriages. Clockmakers, for instance, were found in practically every town and in a great many villages at the time of the *Statistical Account* in the 1790s: theirs had been an unusual occupation a century before. It is difficult to think of any middle-class calling that was not expanding in numbers and affluence in the half century after 1760.

Despite this, there occurred a regular and large export of middle-class Scots taking their professional and commercial talents to England, and to other parts of the world outside Great Britain. Partly this was due to the ease with which a man could obtain a sound primary education and a fair secondary education or university training, so that there were always more educated men than there were openings for them. Partly it was due to the Scotsman's innate clannishness, so that one Scot settled in a profitable niche on the Continent or in the colonies advertised its merit to his kinsmen and his countrymen, and encouraged them to come out and join him. Many of the emigrants, however, ultimately returned to live in Scotland so that bourgeois society was leavened with men of wide experience of other societies and cultures. Its atmosphere might have been provincial, but it was never merely parochial.

Edinburgh and Glasgow represented in their different ways the quintessence of two streams of middle-class life, Edinburgh dominated by the professional classes, and Glasgow by the triumph of the commercial and manufacturing interests. But before we speak of these cities, it should be emphasised that all the towns in Scotland had something of their distinctive qualities. Edinburgh's New Town, for instance, was shadowed in the quarters laid out in Aberdeen and Perth: even a small place like Cupar in Fife had a scheme of fine Regency housing for affluent middle-class citizens. Edinburgh attracted the gentry and the nobility for the winter season: so, on a humbler scale, did Montrose, Dumfries and Ayr and many smaller towns built fashionable assembly-rooms like those in Peebles attached to the Tontine Hotel. Edinburgh had a famous reputation for her educational facilities, which drew families ambitious for their children's future to live in the town (see pages 378 and 474 below). The academies at Perth, Elgin and Dundee were also magnetic in their immediate areas. Dumfries too had a clear idea of the municipal benefits of good schools in a country thirsty for education at all levels:

There are schools for Latin and Greek; for writing, French and drawing, for arithmetic and the various branches of mathematics; for English, reading and for dancing. These are almost all public establishments under the protection and patronage of the magistrates who on every vacancy are at great pains to fill the schools with teachers of character and ability. There are also two or three boarding schools for the education of young ladies ... Its establishments for education hold out considerable inducements to persons of moderate fortune who may wish their children to enjoy the advantages of a well-conducted public education without being removed from under their own immediate inspection.[4]

Many towns like this were little images of Edinburgh, 'most distinguished' as the minister of Montrose said grandiloquently, 'by the residence of persons of opulence and fashion than of commerce and industry'.[5] Even tiny Crieff had something of the same character. Those who habitually disparaged the Highlanders as incapable of any action to help themselves would have been surprised to hear the factor of the forfeited estates report to his superiors that the main reason for the growth of the village was the desire of parents to settle in the vicinity so that their children could attend the grammar school.[6]

There were other communities that were closer models of Glasgow. Greenock and Paisley, Kilmarnock and Renfrew, for instance, were mushrooming with their neighbour on the Clyde and full of thrusting business and ambitious merchants. Dundee and Dunfermline on the east side of the country were equally industrial towns; so were little places like Arbroath, Galashiels and Langholm, though their growth was based on linen and wool rather than on west-country cottons. Perth was perhaps one of the most interesting of all provincial towns at the end of the eighteenth century, for it borrowed almost equally from the characteristics of Edinburgh and Glasgow: it was renowned on the one hand for its academy, its assemblies, its genteel society and its literate interests, and on the other for its linen industry, its cotton work at Stanley, its boot and shoe manufactories, its paper mills, its printing works and its exports of fresh salmon refrigerated on blocks of ice for the London market.

In short, just as all middle-class occupations seemed to flourish in late eighteenth-century Scotland, so all centres of middle-class life appeared to flourish with them. Regional centres thus had a vitality of their own which mirrored but was not yet overshadowed by that of the two great cities. In this sense, it was the golden age of small town life.

2. EDINBURGH AND THE PROFESSIONAL CLASSES

By 1830 Edinburgh was two towns: the Old Town, haphazard, dirty and disorderly sprawled along the spine of volcanic rock between Holyrood House and the Castle—and the New Town, symmetrical, clean and classical, laid out on the lower ridge to the north, and connected to its neighbour by two master-works of engineering, the Mound and the North Bridge, which spanned the gulf between them. The New Town, however, was not born until the Town Council adopted James Craig's plan in 1767: the middle classes had not completed their movement into it until some time after 1800. It was therefore the Old Town that served as the first cradle for the blossoming of Edinburgh's middle-class prosperity.

The Old Town was an extraordinary place. It probably contained, for one thing, more people at the time of the Union of Parliaments than any other city in Britain except London and perhaps Bristol: the figure usually accepted for Edinburgh at about the time of Union is 30,000, exclusive of another 5,500 in Leith.[7] Yet it gave to incoming visitors no overwhelming impression of size: it seemed tall, high-built, narrow and crowded, rather than spacious or sprawling. The century from 1730 onwards was to see a greatly increased population cramming itself into the original centre, mainly by subdividing fine old houses into many one-roomed flats, and by building over former gardens in suburbs like the Canongate. Webster, circa 1750, gave the population of the central core of the old town (exclusive of the parish of St. Cuthbert's and of Leith but inclusive of the Canongate) at 36,000. In 1831 the census gave the population of the same area as 59,000. By the latter date the New Town (which covered a larger acreage) contained about 40,000 inhabitants, while Leith held 26,000 and the population of the whole city inclusive of all suburbs amounted to 162,000. The multiplication of inhabitants in the Old Town even before the end of the eighteenth century made it difficult for the middle class there to maintain standards of environmental comfort, let alone to achieve a new level in their living conditions to which their ambitions aspired.

Visitors usually observed first that Edinburgh was built high. Even in 1700 some of the tenements built on a slope reached fourteen storeys on one side of the building; one such monster, nicknamed Babylon and described as 'ane immense heap of combustible material' appropriately crashed to the ground in flames in a great fire that year.[8] Next they were almost certain to observe that it was very dirty. The Scots were reckoned to be a filthy people even in their rural environment, but what they did in Edinburgh's human rabbit-warren shook the fastidious to the core. Joseph Taylor had this to say about the city in 1705; it is as well to remember that he is talking about the sanitary habits of middle-class citizens, not merely of the poorest in the town:

> Every street shows the nastiness of the inhabitants: the excrements lie in heaps . . . In a morning the scent was so offensive that we were forc't to hold our noses as we past the streets and take care where we trod for fear of disobliging our shoes, and to walk in the middle at night for fear of an accident on our heads. The lodgings are as nasty as the streets, and wash't so seldom that the dirt is thick eno' to be par'd off with a shovel; every room is well-scented with a close-stool, and the master, mistress and servants lye all on a flour, like so many swine in a hogsty. This, with the rest of their sluttishness, is no doubt the occasion of the itch which is so common among them. We have the best lodgings . . . and yet we went thro' the master's bed-chamber, and the kitchen and dark entry to our room, which look't into a place they call the close, full of nastinesse. 'Tis a common thing for a man or woman to go into these closes at all times of the day to ease nature.[9]

So unanimous were visitors on this matter that the Town Council came to feel that the squalor was a reproach to its good name. In the second half of the century there was a temporary improvement. Captain Topham, who visited the city in 1774–5, declared boldly that the Scots now loved cleanliness, and that the old custom of throwing sewage out of the windows had quite ceased in 'the open street':

however, he was obliged to admit that the council had not made them alter their habits in the closes and that human dung still lay in all the wynds for days on end.[10] The New Town never became squalid like that. Perhaps what was really happening was that a new respect for sanitary cleanliness was beginning to spread among the middle classes, who took care to ensure that facilities in the main thoroughfares and in their own new living quarters should be adequate but they did not feel it was yet necessary to preach cleanliness to the poor, much less to make it possible for them to live in the poorest sections of the old town with adequate facilities for sewerage.

The enforcement of law and order in the old town was nominally the responsibility of the Town Guard, a body whose qualifications to keep the peace were more like those of the Chelsea pensioners than a modern police force: the guard was small, elderly, weakly armed and not very ready to withstand violence, though it could tackle a helpless drunk and frighten a pickpocket. Nevertheless most observers agreed that until the last two or three decades of the eighteenth century Edinburgh was without much violent crime, despite the absence of street lighting and the presence of a large number of very poor people to whom so many middle-class citizens with fat purses might have been thought to be a temptation. Contemporaries attributed this partly to the efficiency of Edinburgh's 'caddies', a brotherhood of unofficial guides who carried messages and letters, who helped strangers find their way or find suitable lodgings, and who knew every address in town: 'wretches that in rags lie upon the stairs and in the streets at night, yet they are often considerably trusted'.[11] Knowing everyone and being so numerous they acted as a kind of voluntary vigilante corps. They were also occasionally entrusted by the local authority with executing a council order—as in 1738, when they caught and killed every dog in town following an outbreak of rabies.

Riots were another matter. The town guard certainly had no stomach to face a mob while the caddies were likely to be first among the crowd if they thought popular justice was to be meted out. The composition of the town mob no doubt varied from time to time according to its objectives, but it often contained artisans and mechanics of a more middle-class than working-class character, while in 1736 there were well-grounded suspicions that quite prominent citizens as well as apprentices and journeymen took part in the capture and lynching of Captain Porteous. After 1750 the acknowledged leader of the Edinburgh mob appears to have been a shoemaker in the Cowgate named Joseph Smith. He led demonstrations against the English radical John Wilkes (who was violently anti-Scottish), and against the judges of the Court of Session during the Douglas Cause, as well as being the ringleader in several grain riots. In 1767 he sacked the home of a landlord whose eviction of a tenant had led to the poor man committing suicide. Chambers said that the town council itself, 'rather from fear than from respect', used to send for him in emergencies 'with a promise of amendment and a hogshead of good ale'.[12] Thomas Brown in 1791 listed eight major riots in the town since 1740: four of them were aimed at millers, meal-mongers and distillers accused of hording or misusing grain in time of scarcity; one was a riot against bodysnatchers, one a riot against papists, and one a riot of footmen against a play on at the theatre called 'High Life below Stairs' which they considered insulted and misrepresented their calling.[13]

All this may make the Old Town sound like a dangerous residence for men of property and gentility. Yet in reality the riot was an institution with its own conventions used by a variety of citizens (seldom the very poorest) to rectify what they regarded as the grossest injustices of their rulers. It had, as Chambers said, 'a part in the state'. The mob never rampaged out of control through the streets: on the contrary, it picked targets for destruction with care, and kept to them remarkably scrupulously. Few lives were ever lost: apart from the lynched Captain Porteous, there appear to be only two people who died in all this eighteenth-century disorder, and they were both rioters shot by the defenders of property. With this we may contrast a military incident in Leith in 1779, when a Highland regiment refused orders to embark: at least twelve mutineers, two loyal soldiers and an officer died when they shot it out on the quayside; thirty more were shot and wounded.[14] In a sense, too, as we have argued in a previous chapter (pages 226–8 above) the Edinburgh mob was a declining institution in the eighteenth century at least as far as political influence was concerned. In the sixteenth and seventeenth centuries the crowd had often played an important role, for example in various sixteenth-century palace revolutions, at the Reformation, in the dispute over the new prayer book before the National Covenant, and later at the trial of the crew of the *Worcester* and at the Union. But certainly after the Porteous Riot in 1736 it never again seriously swayed or threatened the government.

Before the building of the New Town, English visitors found that one of the most remarkable things about life in Edinburgh was the way different social classes inhabited the same buildings. In their own cities there were rich areas and poor areas, the slums of Wapping and Shoreditch, for instance lying at a distance from the splendid quarters of Bedford Square and Bloomsbury. Edinburgh had nothing like this. There were, admittedly, some ruinous tenements occupied by Highland 'chairmen' (the men who carried the sedan chairs through the city) and unskilled porters: in the Canongate there were a number of seventeenth- and eighteenth-century mansions that belonged (or had belonged until recently) to the highest nobles in the land—Moray House, Huntly House and Queensberry House, for instance. But much more typical were the tall tenements along the High Street, the Pleasance, the Cowgate, and the West Bow, and in the wynds and closes that led off them. Here the social division was denoted not vertically, by fashionable and unfashionable streets and areas, but horizontally, according to which floor one lived on. The most respectable floors were generally the second and third, presumably because one thereby lived above the worst of the smell but had not so many steps to climb as if one lived in the fourth or higher. In 1773 for instance, one tenement in the High Street had a fishmonger's house on the ground floor, a respectable lodging house on the second floor, the rooms of the dowager Countess of Balcarres on the third floor, Mrs. Buchan of Kelly living above that, the 'misses Elliots, milliners and mantuamakers' above that, and the garrets occupied by 'a great variety of tailors and other tradesmen'.[15] These were in a sense almost all 'middle-class' inhabitants of one kind or another, but nobody would ever have found an English dowager sandwiching herself between a fishmonger and a crowd of tailors and milliners.

The New Town of course, was built on different principles, for a new and quite different mode of middle-class living. Laid out in classical squares and long straight streets with splendid houses and spacious gardens and with circuses and crescents added later as it spread out of the original grid to the north and the north-east, it was the cold, clear and beautiful expression of the rational confidence of the eighteenth-century middle class. James Craig engraved these lines at the edge of his original drawing:

August, around what PUBLIC WORKS I see
Lo! Stately streets, Lo! Squares that court the breeze

See! Long canals and deepened rivers join
Each part with each, and with the encircling Main
The whole enlivened Isle.

These words (with a faint echo about them of Caliban's dream in the *Tempest*) were a vision for a metropolis that would break with the chaotic past and testify in stones and mortar to an ordered and harmonious world. The mob, the caddy, and the chamber-pot emptied out of the top-floor had no place in Anne Street or Charlotte Square. Heaven forbid!

The movement into the New Town of the richer members of the middle class, along with those of gentry and nobility who had town quarters in Edinburgh, began slowly. In 1774 an observer said that the new houses seemed too English, and were not very popular.[16] In the next two decades, however, the trickle became a flood, and the transfer began to affect the social mixture in the Old Town. William Creech, who still lived there, wrote that already by 1783 a French teacher was living in Lord Justice Clerk Tinwald's old house, Lord President Craigie's house was occupied by a saleswoman of old furniture, Lord Drummore's house had been abandoned by a chairman because it was too pokey, and after 1787 an iron-monger was using the late President Dundas's house for a store.[17] As the change accelerated—and the number of houses in the New Town rose from about two thousand in 1815 to about five thousand in 1830—so the social gulf widened between the two towns. Chambers in 1833 showed how completely the building of the New Town had caused a redistribution of the population according to class:

> The fine gentlemen who daily exhibit their foreign dresses and manners on Princes St have no idea of a race of people who roost in the tall houses of the Lawnmarket and the West Bow, and retain about them many of the primitive modes of life and habits of thought that flourished among their grandfathers . . . Edinburgh is in fact two towns more ways than one. It contains an upper and an under town—the one a sort of thoroughfare for the children of business and fashion, the other a den of retreat for the poor, the diseased and the ignorant.[18]

It had become like London. It is worth observing, however, that the shake-out was not simply into a working-class town and a middle-class town, for only the most wealthy of the middle class could afford the move. The tradesmen, and what the French would call the 'petit bourgeoisie', mainly stayed behind in the increasingly overcrowded closes of the Old Town. This was often the case in other British cities, and as the nineteenth century wore on it helped to establish the solidarity of many who were not strictly labourers with the working-class movement as a whole—as, for instance, in the Chartist agitation of the 1840s.

Which were those groups in the middle classes whose activities contributed most to the prosperity and lively intellectual life of the late eighteenth-century city? Edinburgh was not primarily a business town, but business thrived as a result of the growing affluence of the inhabitants, and (as elsewhere in Scotland) the strict old guild rules began to loosen in the ranks of the merchants and tradesmen. As early as 1729 the council began to permit retailers in a long list of wares to sell at will in Edinburgh for payment of an annual licence instead of obliging them to become members of the Merchant Company: by 1817, the Lord Provost was saying that the only advantage burgesses and guild brethren now received was to obtain their imports into Leith at a slightly lower rate, and to be able to guarantee their children an education at Heriots' Hospital, George Watsons' College or the Merchants' Maiden School even if they should subsequently become bankrupt in the course of their trade.[19] Meanwhile, in the incorporated trades apprenticeships tended to become progressively shorter, and new occupations grew up which fell completely outside the scope of the traditional guilds. These were often extremely prosperous, and brought into being a consumer goods industry that added to Edinburgh's attractiveness as a social centre:

In 1763 there was one Glass-house at Leith for the manufacture of green bottles: in 1783 there were three Glass-houses; in 1790 there were six; and as fine chrystal and window-glass is made at Leith as anywhere in Europe . . . In 1763 there were six printing houses in Edinburgh; in 1790 there were sixteen . . . In 1763 few coaches or chaises were made in Edinburgh. The nobility and gentry in general bought their carriages in London . . . in 1783 coaches and chaises were constructed as elegantly in Edinburgh as anywhere in Europe and it may be added, stronger and cheaper.[20]

While the business interests of the merchants and tradesmen thus changed and unfolded in new ways, the political institutions of the same class remained exactly as before. The Town Council consisted of a narrow group of thirty-three merchants and members of the incorporated trades, who could only be elected by the retiring council. This self-perpetuating oligarchy had an unsavoury reputation for political toadyism, for inefficiency, and for feathering the nests of its own members in the award of building contracts. Henry Cockburn thus described it in the 1820s in words which the citizens of Edinburgh have from time to time continued to regard as apposite:

> Within this Pandemonium sat the town-council, omnipotent, corrupt, impenetrable. Nothing was beyond its grasp: no variety of opinion disturbed its unanimity for the pleasure of Dundas was the sole rule for every one of them . . . Silent, powerful, submissive, mysterious and irresponsible, they might have been sitting in Venice.[21]

It is not surprising that some important functions of local government such as lighting, cleansing and police should have been progressively taken from the Council and invested in separate bodies of Commissioners (at least partially elected by the ratepayers) from 1772 onwards—nor that the confusion of municipal affairs should have ended in 1833 in the town having to declare itself bankrupt. What is astonishing is that from this petty clique came those who conceived the New Town, laid out the rules for its construction, and with a lavish hand constructed the great public works, like the bridges, the Mound and the new churches. Thus, in a list of those who contributed much to the well-being of the town, the Council must, surprisingly enough, be given a place.

The real leaders of Edinburgh society, however, were not to be found among merchants and tradesmen (either in their business capacity or as local politicians) but among professional men: and among the professions there were none, in numbers, wealth or prestige, to equal the lawyers. When Williamson was constructing his first street directories to Edinburgh in the 1770s he found it natural to list the citizens by putting the advocates first, then their clerks, then the writers to the signet and their clerks—and then the nobility and gentry with town houses, and finally the remainder of the middle class without much further distinction.

The lawyers' closest links, indeed, were with the country gentry of the Lothians rather than with the 'mercantile interest' of their own city. Every advocate or writer who made a success of his calling sought an estate in East Lothian or Midlothian, or even further afield: it was an excellent investment, and it conferred upon his family the political privilege and social prestige that all landowners relished. Conversely, landowners overburdened with children found themselves mulling over the advantages of a career at the Scottish bar for a younger son, or of a lawyer as a husband for a favourite daughter. So general was intermarriage and exchange of personnel between lawyers and gentlemen that they came to treat one another as perfect equals. The social season at Edinburgh in the last half of the eighteenth and early nineteenth centuries gained much of its character from its sense of reunion. The country cousins, the gentry and the lesser nobility who owned land in the provinces came in to throng the assembly halls and the dinner tables, and the town cousins, the judges, the advocates and the writers received them with enthusiasm and a pride in their urban and 'metropolitan' culture.

At such times the intimacy of the two classes had more than polite significance. The lawyers included many who were among the most intelligent and enthusiastic intellects in Scotland. They were highly trained, some having attended a continental university as well as one in their own country. They were broadly read: many strove to make a place for themselves by writing works of philosophy or *belles lettres*. They were politically well-connected: the greatest Scottish statesmen in London used great lawyers (like Lord Milton or Duncan Forbes of Culloden) as their agents in their homeland. They were involved in making and executing economic policy, as members of the Board of Trustees for Manufactures and Commissioners of the Forfeited Estates. Above all they were avidly sociable. They were the backbone of the city's innumerable clubs and societies which existed for every possible purpose from drinking one another under the table to awarding premiums to virtuous manufacturers. In short, they formed a cultural eilte.

For a country gentleman from one of the remoter Lowland districts to come to Edinburgh and mingle with the legal intelligentsia on equal terms must have been an exciting and invigorating experience: who knows what ideas he carried home as a result of his encounters? For instance, almost all the judges developed an overpowering interest in agricultural improvement. Lord Kames, with an estate in Stirlingshire, was the author of *The Gentleman Farmer*, the most influential of all

Scottish handbooks before the 1790s: Lord Hailes was renowned for the long leases he gave his East Lothian tenants; Lord Monboddo had a model estate in Kincardineshire; Lord Gardenstone became so obsessed by plans for his new village at Laurencekirk that he abandoned every other interest in life; Lord Milton's enthusiasm for rural industries made him a founder of the British Linen Company; Lord Tinwald put his money into the exploitation of an antimony mine in the south-west. Conversation among the lawyers, contemporaries noted, was as likely to turn on a new strain of turnips or a new breed of cattle as on new ideas in philosophy or literature. Edinburgh could thus act as a power-house from which ideas on improvement, instead of being the monopoly of isolated eccentrics, became widely diffused through the country.

The composition of the legal profession widened slightly during the eighteenth century: the table below shows the results of analysing three hundred Writers to the Signet according to the occupation of their fathers.

FATHER'S STANDING	Period in which Writers qualified		
	1690–1749	1750–1789	1790–1829
Legal profession	22	20	30
Landowner	49	41	25
Minister	9	10	3
Army officer, colonial adventurer or civil office-holder	3	1	10
Physician, teacher or architect	2	10	8
Tenant-farmer	1	3	9
Merchant	12	13	13
Tradesman	2	1	2
Unskilled labourer	—	1	—

Source: *The Society of Writers to His Majesty's Signet*, Edinburgh 1936.

The fall in the percentage of those whose parents were landowners and ministers is counterbalanced by a rise in those whose parents belonged to the expanding professions (doctors, colonial adventurers, soldiers, and so on) or to the newly affluent Lothian farmer class. This represents no decline in the importance of the gentry: since the numbers of writers increased rapidly towards 1800, the absolute number of recruits from the landowning class probably did not fall at all. Rather it shows the success of those who exploited the new openings for the middle class in the period following the Union.

It is also worth noticing some of the constant features in the table. One half or more of the new writers to the signet always came from legal or gentry families: mercantile families failed to increase their share above one recruit in eight: the children of middle-class tradesmen had only a very slim chance of becoming lawyers, and those of unskilled labourers virtually none. In these ways the legal profession remained something of a caste that did not readily open itself to talent from every quarter.

The Edinburgh lawyer of the 1820s was a much more affluent man than his predecessors. Chambers in 1833 compared the kind of lodging that an eminent lawyer of the eighteenth century had enjoyed in the Old Town with what his successors were used to in the New. Lord Kennet 'a most respectable judge and landed gentleman', had lived with his family in a flat in Forrester's Wynd by the Lawnmarket, which he rented for £15 a year: it consisted of three rooms and a kitchen, and the family was waited on by three servants—a nurse, who slept with the children in the lawyer's study, a servant-maid, who slept under the kitchen dresser, and a man servant, who slept out of the house. A gentleman of comparable rank half a century later:

> Finds it necessary to have a self-contained house in Moray Place or some equally splendid district for which he pays a rent of about £160 . . . and which consists of four flats containing the following apartments: on the sunk floor, a complete suite of culinary apartments with accommodation for servants: on a second floor, dining-room in front, business room or library, and a bed-room behind; on third floor, drawing room occupying the whole front of the house with two large apartments behind, generally occupied as bedroom and dressing room . . . fourth flat, a nursery and a number of good bed-rooms, besides which there is perhaps a suite of small rooms immediately under the slates. The furniture of such a house would not cost less than fifteen hundred pounds, but more generally is purchased at the rate of two thousand.[22]

Scores of elegant houses of this type remain in the New Town. Many of them have since been rendered down again to the kind of accommodation Lord Kennet had had in the Old Town. The fall in the numbers of domestic servants and the rise in urban site values has forced those of the middle class who wish to go on living in the New Town to lower once more their grander expectations of accommodation.

After the lawyers, the profession which contributed most to the life of eighteenth-century Edinburgh was undoubtedly that of teacher. The description of course, covers many different kinds of people, from Principal William Robertson of the University, who in the 1770s kept his own carriage a fact 'unequalled in any former period of the history of the Church or of the University'[23], to humble inhabitants of the Old Town like Miss Marcoucci who kept a dancing-school in James's Court, and Mrs. M'Ever who had a pastry-school in Peebles Wynd. But education in all its forms was a growth industry in eighteenth-century Edinburgh, and all those who lived by it had a fair chance of prospering.

The University, first, reached the height of its reputation between 1760 and 1820. The intellectual achievements of its professors (see also below chapter XIX) were a magnet to students. William Cullen and Joseph Black, for instance, filled the chair of Chemistry from 1755 to 1795: their combined labours transformed the sciences of chemistry and physics, and they were followed by men no less skilled in teaching. The Medical School of the University, founded in 1726, had immense prestige due in no small measure to the professional dynasty of the Monros, three generations of whom, each called Alexander Monro, held the Chair of Anatomy in unbroken succession from 1720 to 1846. In the Faculty of Arts, William Robertson was the most famous historian in Europe after Edward Gibbon. Adam Ferguson is regarded as one of the fathers of sociology: his successor in the Chair of Moral Philosophy, Dugald Stewart, was one of the most influential teachers of his age. It was a characteristic of these men that most were as brilliant at teaching as they were at scholarship. Perhaps the system of paying them no salary except student's fees spurred them on. Oxbridge professors had a steady salary irrespective of whether they lectured or not, so they seldom taught; Edinburgh professors were paid according to the number of students who attended their classes, and they had a great reputation as lecturers. Herman Boerhaave of Leyden University was heard to wish that God would send Edinburgh professors larger salaries, and thereby render them less dangerous rivals.[24]

The University of Edinburgh was also popular because it offered a very wide range of subjects: 'every age and rank (of student) have a liberty of choosing such lectures as are most suited to their inclinations, pleasures or pursuits in life', explained Edward Topham. Furthermore, the professors themselves were an object lesson in genteel behaviour, 'an example of civility and good manners as of morality and virtue . . . though all of them are men of letters and skilled in the sciences they profess, they are not less acquainted with the world, and with polite behaviour, than with polite literature'.[25] The Town Council (who had sole patronage in all appointments to university chairs) did not hesitate to attract men from other universities (like Cullen and Black from Glasgow) to be an ornament to their own. They showed remarkable aptitude in choosing those who were not merely polite, but also scholars and good teachers: in a way it is as surprising an attribute of that body as their patronage of the New Town.

The number of students attending Edinburgh University increased many times during the period: at the start of the eighteenth century there were about 400, by 1780 about 1000, and by 1815 about 2000. They came from many different places. An important (and until 1815 an increasing) proportion came from England, Ireland or the colonies, most frequently from 'solid, middle-class homes . . . the sons of English squires, prosperous merchants and well-to-do clergymen'.[26] English dissenters found Scottish universities useful as they were barred by the Test Act from attending Oxford and Cambridge. Englishmen were particularly numerous in the medical faculty, and as they often attended Edinburgh for a final year after studies elsewhere they were a markedly older group in the student body than the Scots, who first came in their early teens. Some of the Scots came from provincial districts within Scotland, and either took lodgings, preferably at the homes of the professors, or stayed with their parents in a New Town house. Many of the gentry took such a home for the whole year while their children were at school or college. Yet others were the children of Edinburgh parents, of lawyers, and of merchants and 'tradesmen' in the eighteenth-century sense of the term) but seldom of children of proletarian origins. They too, of course, returned home each day after attending lectures.

Edinburgh was famous for many educational establishments apart from the University. There was the Royal High School, which more than doubled its size from about 200 pupils in 1760 to about 500 by 1783, and by 1790 was believed to be the largest school in Britain. Heriot's Hospital at the same date educated over 100 boys, and George

Watson's about sixty; for girls, the Merchants' Maiden Hospital and the Trades' Maiden Hospital were of similar size to Watsons.' These were only the most famous and popular schools from a wide variety of public and private establishments, for quite suddenly around 1760 there had occurred a surge forward in educational provision, the council founding four supplementary 'English schools' in 1759, and private enterprise following up to provide fashionable boarding schools for each sex and a multitude of specialised teachers offering subjects especially suitable to the middle class.[27] It was one of the attractions of the city in the later years of the century that boys could get an education from private teachers in almost every subject under the sun, from fortification, gunnery and gauging to modern languages, book-keeping and Greek (see also chapter XVIII below). For girls, the situation was best expressed by Elizabeth Grant, seventeen years old in 1814 and the daughter of a Highland laird who also practised at the Edinburgh bar.

> Six masters were engaged for us girls, three every day; Mr Penson for the pianoforte, M. Elouis for the harp, M. L'Espinasse for French, Signor something for Italian and Mr I forget who for drawing, Mr Scott for writing and ciphering and oh! I was near forgetting a seventh, the most important of all, Mr Smart for dancing.[28]

Edinburgh, indeed, was what Hugo Arnot described it as in 1779, a city dependent for its support 'chiefly upon the college of justice, the seminaries of education and the inducement which as a capital it affords to genteel people to reside in it'.[29] As such it was the main centre of the cultural 'golden age' which we shall discuss at greater length in the final chapter. But Edinburgh's Athenian society was not the only achievement of the middle class, nor the cultural enlightenment (narrowly defined) necessarily its most significant expression. On the other side of Scotland a different section of the middle class was busy with other things.

3. GLASGOW AND THE BUSINESS CLASSES

Even before the Industrial Revolution, Glasgow was a city of markedly different character from Edinburgh. At the start of the period, when Edinburgh was invariably criticised for its squalid tenements and obscene sanitation, Glasgow won nothing but garlands of praise from visiting foreigners. Daniel Defoe's description (published in 1727, but relating to his visit twenty years earlier) is typical:

> It is a large stately and well-built city, standing on a plain in a manner four-square, and the five principal streets are the fairest for breadth, and the finest built I have ever seen in one city together. The houses are all of stone, and generally uniform in height as well as in front. The lower stories (of those near the Cross) for the most part, stand on vast square Doric columns with arches which open into the shops, adding to the strength as well as beauty of the building. In a word, 'tis one of the cleanliest, most beautiful and best built cities in Great Britain.[30]

The seventeenth-century town described by Defoe was elegant despite its substantial growth: it had doubled in size between the Union of Crowns in 1603 and the Union of Parliaments in 1707, and by the latter date was already among the ten largest and most successful towns in Great Britain. Its reputation for graciousness was not lightly given up even under the much great pressure of expansion in the eighteenth century. Population grew from about 13,000 in 1707 to about 40,000 in 1780: in the 1780s and 1790s new streets and squares for middle-class residence were still being laid out as near the modern centre as George Square, the area where the richest of the new industrialists lived, and at the 'New Town' of Blythswood. At Laurieston on the south of the Clyde the scheme was no less ambitious, and fashionable streets were laid out with suitably grand names such as Carlton Place, Cavendish Street and Marlborough Street. Unfortunately the unplanned sprawl of industry and the unchecked rise of population overwhelmed this district, and Laurieston became the core of the Gorbals slums early in the nineteenth century. It was the fantastic growth associated with the industrial revolution—from 40,000 inhabitants in 1780 to no less than 200,000 in 1830 which finally put paid to the reputation of Glasgow as a beautiful city. Since, however, the appalling problems which arose from the deterioration of housing and public health affected the working poor rather than the middle class, who continued to move to new quarters further and further from the slummy centre, they need not be considered here. It is sufficient to say that the government of the city charged with responsibility of solving these problems did not differ materially either in constitution or in ineptitude from that of Edinburgh.

The Town Council, self-seeking and corrupt, was an oligarchy of merchants and tradesmen from the old guilds. A 'police statute' providing elected bodies with special powers over such things as cleansing, lighting and water supply in some parts of the town, was obtained for Glasgow in 1800. They kept at bay some of the worst horrors of total neglect, but usually only in those areas of middle-class residence where the richest of the ratepayers lived.

The structure of the middle class in Glasgow was very different from that of Edinburgh. Any analysis is beset with pit-falls, but in the table below we have attempted to compare the middle class of the two cities at the point when it first becomes possible with the publication of the first street directories, for Edinburgh in 1773-4, and for Glasgow ten years later. For each city one thousand entries taken at random were examined.

OCCUPATION	Edinburgh 1773/4	Glasgow 1783/4
Nobles and gentry	5.4	1.0
Professional men	28.8	12.3
Merchants and Manufacturers	12.5	30.0
Small tradesmen, artisans, craftsmen, 'mechanics', etc.	30.5	42.1
Retailers of food and drink	12.3	11.7
Ship-masters and boatmen	3.1	1.0
Room-setters	4.2	0.4
Miscellaneous	3.2	1.5

Edinburgh attracted five times as many noblemen and gentry as Glasgow even in 1773, and the proportion would be much larger fifty years later when the New Town in the capital was completed. There were in fact no nobles living in Glasgow (several dukes and earls had property in Edinburgh) and many of the 'gentry' living there could probably be more aptly described as merchants with estates. Again, the occupation of 'room-setter' in Edinburgh (usually carried on by a widow or maiden lady) had no real counterpart in Glasgow: it also reflected the capital's prestige as a social centre in which to spend the season, as a tourist centre, and as a centre for education with a large student population needing lodgings. Shipmasters lived at Leith (in the area covered by the Edinburgh directory) but not in the environs of Glasgow at that date, when the Clyde was still only fifteen inches deep at low water: they lived down the water at Port Glasgow and Greenock.

and the only nautical men at Glasgow were boatmen who took travellers and goods in barges along or across the Clyde. Against these contrasts, it is interesting that sellers of food and drink were equally numerous in both cities: most of them were sellers of drink—Hugo Arnot calculated in 1779 that there were somewhere between 1600 and 2000 ale sellers in Edinburgh, and they were at least as numerous in the west. One of the problems of analysing the Glasgow Directory was deciding in which pigeon hole to put some of the sellers of drink, as it was obviously a part-time occupation of many tradesmen: where is one to place Walter McAdam, vinter and horse-setter, or John Elder, cordiner and spirit dealer? Even barbers in Glasgow sometimes combined cutting hair and letting blood with selling restorative alcohol.

More significant differences were revealed in the remaining categories. Glasgow had an appreciable professional class—with a university and several noted schools, and with the need for locally-based lawyers and notaries to oil the wheels of trade: but it was less than half as important as that of Edinburgh in proportion to the size of the two cities. Similarly, Edinburgh had a significant business class, composed partly of traditional merchants who imported and exported through Leith and partly of newer men such as the bankers and the masters of sugar houses or printing works: she had a still larger class of tradesmen and artisans who ministered in innumerable ways to the needs of middle-class residents and visiting gentry. But in Glasgow the business class was more than twice as large, and the artisan class was half as large again even though only the most 'middle-class' artisans would have found an entry in such a directory. The expression 'manufacturer', which occurs repeatedly in the Glasgow directory, is not known at all in the Edinburgh one. It is interesting that in Edinburgh nearly one in three of all the entrants in the directory was a professional man, and one in eight a 'businessman': in Glasgow one in eight was a professional man, and one in three a businessman—exactly the reverse proportions if the source is an accurate guide.

The greatness of Glasgow was built upon the entrepreneurial skill of her businessmen, whether merchants or manufacturers. Enterprise and resilience had been their noted attributes over a long period. Even in the seventeenth century, when Scottish merchants generally had a bad reputation of unadventurousness, those of Glasgow were pressing forward horizons to the West Indies and America when this meant smuggling ships and goods past the English administrators of the

Navigation Acts; they were also establishing sugar refineries, cloth manufactories, soapworks, distilleries and so on, indicative of a precocious willingness to adventure with novel industrial techniques. In the eighteenth century, especially after 1740 when economic expansion was much more rapid, observers noted again and again the initiative of the Glasgow man, his 'spirit of industry' and catholic interest in novelty. Thus Alexander Carlyle, looking back at the town as it was on the verge of its great success in the tobacco trade, in his student days in 1743, described it in these terms:

> The city of Glasgow at this time, though very industrious, wealthy and commercial, was far inferior to what it afterwards became, both before and after the failure of the Virginia trade. The modes of life, too, and manners, were different from what they are at present . . . But the merchants had industry and stock, and the habits of business, and were ready to seize with eagerness and prosecute with vigour every new object in commerce or manufactures that promised success.[31]

Thirty years later the community ran into its first great commercial storm when the War of American Independence left her with no obvious staple. From this test the business class of the city emerged triumphant, having replaced the Virginia trade by traffic with the West Indies and Europe, and simultaneously commenced building up a new kind of industrial system based on the manufacture of cotton textiles. By the 1790s the industrial revolution was beginning to work its transformation. The reporter in the *Statistical Account* spoke of its first material results:

> Riches in Glasgow were formerly the portion of a few merchants. These, from the influence of the manufactures are now diffusing themselves widely among a great number of manufacturers, mechanics and artisans. This has made an alteration in the houses, dress, furniture, education and amusements of the people of Glasgow within a few years which is astonishing to the older inhabitants . . . and as many of the merchants have of late years been engaging in manufactures and trade, the distance in point of rank and consequence between merchants and tradesmen has now become less conspicuous than it was before the American War.[32]

The pioneer industrialists of these years not only carried the burden of developing the economy of Glasgow. They were also laying the foundations of a new Scottish economic order, and in so doing, affected the lives of all who lived since. There has never been any small band of Scots who by their initiative and enterprise made so great an impact on the history of their nation. Where did they come from?

The origins of the early industrialists are as various as their achievements. One important group were substantial merchants trading overseas whose industrial interests were an extension of their exporting activities—if you had to fill a boat with cargo for sale in the stores of Virginia, you may as well set up a manufactory as buy the goods from Manchester. Thus John Glassford, the greatest of all the merchants of the tobacco trade before the American War, had interests in breweries, tanworks, dyeworks, the vitriol works at Prestonpans, the iron works at Carron, printfields and a ribbon manufacture. In the last two he was closely associated with his sister's husband, Archibald Ingram, the Provost of Glasgow who 'ended with a large and profitable business throughout Great Britain, Virginia, Maryland and the West Indies'.[33] The extensive textile printing industry in the Vale of Leven was begun in 1770 solely on the initiative of William Stirling, who came of a dynasty of Glasgow merchants but evidently took little part in foreign trade himself. In the next generation he was parallelled by James Dunlop of Garnkirk and Carmyle, son of a tobacco merchant who had, after the habit of his kind, bought land with his profits: James switched the family resources to exploiting the coal-measures of this estate on a massive scale, and he also had interests in the Clyde iron works and Dumbarton glass works when his business empire crashed in bankruptcy in the depression of 1793. One of his associates was Andrew Houston, the son of yet another famous father on the trans-Atlantic trade, who, like Stirling and Dunlop, was turning towards industry.

The contribution of the mercantile families also extended to banking. The elder Dunlop and the elder Houston had been, in 1750, the leading projectors of the Glasgow Ship Bank, the first bank in the West of Scotland. The Glasgow Arms Bank founded in the same year was likewise dependent on leading merchants (seven of its original partners eventually became Lord Provosts of the city). The Thistle Bank of 1761 had the same origin: in this case John Glassford was the leading projector. The merchants thus did an enormous amount to ensure that Glasgow had a reputation as an industrial and financial centre before

Workers at Leadhills, c.1780. David Allan's watercolours show (bottom) the washer boys breaking lumps of lead ore before it was fed to the furnace, and (top) the furnace being tapped. The Earl of Hopetoun, who owned the lead-mines in the village, can be seen entering the washing shed with his Countess in the bottom picture

Margaret Suttie, an Edinburgh salt hawker, 1799. Note how the size and weight of her burden compares with that of a coal mining girl below

Janet Cumming, eleven years old: "I carry the large bits of coal from the wall-face to the pit bottom . . . the weight is usually a hundredweight"

the cotton boom started. The experience and 'spirit for manufacturing' which they had already stimulated was itself a large part of the explanation for the success of the city in the years that followed.

When the cotton boom began, however, the great merchant houses played little direct part in it. For one thing, their affairs were at this point in some confusion, and they were too busy extracting themselves from North America and searching for alternative openings in the West Indies and elsewhere to bother about secondary considerations of a speculative nature. Secondly, proper appreciation of 'Arkwright's happy invention of machinery, so easily constructed and so judiciously planned that with one great water wheel above four thousand threads of cotton yarn are spun at once' came to other business channels than those involved in transatlantic trade.[34] It was the linen drapers, the cloth and yarn merchants who had long bought and sold textiles in Lancashire as part of their trade, who first heard of the English inventions, saw their potential and began to put them into practice.

The linen drapers concerned were seldom men of established family or great wealth: the occupation, often in Glasgow called an 'English merchant', was traditionally one in which a man of small means could start on a peddling trade, and raise himself by degrees to wealth and status. David Dale, who probably did more to bring the technology of the textile factory into Scotland than any other man, was described as:

> Originally a herd boy at Stewarton, and afterwards a weaver at Paisley, Hamilton and Cambuslang. He came here as a young man, and became a dealer in linen yarn, tramping the country and buying in pickles from farmers' wives. From this small beginning he developed a large trade in importing yarn from the Low Countries.[35]

Arkwright's first Scottish agent, John Buchanan, was the son of such an 'English merchant', and related to a family of Lanarkshire bonnet-lairds: he sent his brother Archibald to be apprentice at the inventor's famous mill at Cromford in Derbyshire, and when he returned they set up the early Scottish concerns at Deanston and Catrine. Kirkman Finlay, their cousin and partner, stretched his activities from manufacturing into trade, where he became the leader among those who burst the trammelling monopoly of the London East India Company in trade to India and China. He was the son of a 'merchant and manufacturer', and the grandson of a small laird who had been Buchanan's neighbour. In the 1820s the firm of James and William Campbell was beginning to make the reputation which sustained it as one of the leading millowners in the Victorian city: they were two sons of a small farmer in Lowland Perthshire who in the 1790s had immigrated to the city and set themselves to the draper's trade. Henry Houldsworth was an immigrant of a different character, a factory manager coming from Nottingham in the early days of the Industrial Revolution, 'to teach them how to spin fine numbers in the Woodside Cotton Mill'. By 1831 he was himself the second largest spinner in the city.

Some of the themes in this pattern are repeated again and again, and not only among the cotton-masters. A great many industrial pioneers of all kinds were the sons of farmers or small lairds in the West of Scotland. Thus William and James Baird, who by first applying on a large scale Neilson's hot-blast to the blackband ore deposits became the greatest of the ironmasters of the 1830s, were the sons of a small farmer in Monkland. Charles Tennant, founder of the largest chemical works in the world at St. Rollox, was the son of an Ayrshire farmer who had been a friend and neighbour of Robert Burns. John and Arthur Pollock were the younger sons of a laird of ancient lineage and small estate: they made a fortune by pioneering the import of Canadian timber, and their descendants largely dissipated it buying immense territories in Renfrew, Argyll, Fife and the west of Ireland. Not that one needed to have originated on the land to feel the urge to return to it: a very large number of all the pioneers ultimately bought land and built country houses upon it, just as their predecessors the merchants had invested in estates and gracious houses in the tobacco age and before. It was regarded as the natural culmination of a successful career in business: very often it still is.

After the farmers and small lairds, the group that provided probably the largest number of significant pioneers was the tradesmen. This, not unnaturally, was particularly true of those whose bent was towards invention. James Watt was the son of a Clydeside merchant and shipwright; J. B. Neilson's father was an enginewright at Govan colliery; Robert Napier was the son and grandson of master-smiths of Dumbarton and Glasgow. Tradesmen also provided sons who became entrepreneurial leaders. The link is obvious in the case of Henry Tennent, whose father was a maltman and who was himself a great brewer. In the case of a man like David Hutcheson, founder of a shipping-line, whose father was a cooper of Inverkeithing in Fife, it is less so. John Leadbeatter, one of the pioneers of the factory system in linens, was the son of a Penicuik wright who moved to Lanark. His career might have been a blue-print for success:

> having developed a taste for study and books rather than handicraft (he) was sent . . . to push his way in the then rising city of Glasgow. There he succeeded in obtaining a situation as a clerk, and was not content with mastering the duties of his situation but in his spare time . . . he assiduously cultivated his intellect by attending evening classes, studying French and taking an active part in debating societies and writing essays on various social and scientific subjects.[36]

The English, too, provided more men for Scottish business than Henry Houldsworth alone. William Dixon, from Northumberland, coal owner and ironmaster of Govan in the busy decades from 1771 to 1822 was the other outstanding southerner in Glasgow's business. In an earlier generation and a different district there had been Samuel Garbett and John Roebuck, the Birmingham metal worker and Birmingham doctor who with William Caddell the Cockenzie merchant founded Carron iron-works. Later on Robert Owen, though a Welshman and not an Englishman, came to replace David Dale as the presiding genius of New Lanark. One hears much of the stream of Scots who went south to enrich the business life of England, but the significance of the movement in the opposite direction both of workers and managers is often overlooked. The former were welcome in the south because of their drive and their high standard of education. The latter were needed in the north because they knew how to do a particular job still unfamiliar in the less developed Scottish economy—how to plough by the latest methods, how to operate new paper-making machinery, how to manage a new textile process, and so on. In some industries— for instance in eighteenth-century lead mining and iron manufacture, their contribution both in management and skilled manpower was a most important one.

All this may lead to the conclusion that one of Glasgow's main sources of strength was her acceptance into business of all men of ability, irrespective of where they came from, who their fathers were, or how they had been trained. Even in the days when the guilds were strong, there is evidence that it was exceptionally easy for an outsider or a man of humble parentage to advance in Glasgow.[37] The substance of guild restrictionism in the trades and crafts of the city had in any case vanished by 1740, which was earlier even than in London and left the burgh, despite her ancient charter, as free on the eve of the industrial revolution as upstart English towns like Birmingham or Bradford. This must have been an advantage.

On the other hand, there were wide sectors of Scottish society who still sent no recruits to the Glasgow business class. None of the pioneers were the sons of a nobleman, a baronet or a knight: the aristocracy and the upper echelons of the landed gentry put their children elsewhere. Though they did play their part in industrialisation in other parts of Scotland it was usually as mine-owners, as investors in transport improvements and as sympathetic landlords rather than as entrepreneurs. The children of professional men, too, were surprisingly rare among Glasgow pioneers. There appear to be none from the families either of lawyers or of teachers, though there were some who were sons of the manse, like John Burns the pioneer steamship owner, and Robert Carrick, who began as a clerk in the Ship Bank, worked his way up to be leading partner, and died in 1815 leaving a fortune in land and securities worth about £500,000—'it was certainly the biggest pile that a Glasgow man had as yet scraped together'.[38] Returned colonial adventurers and the inheritors of their fortunes were another group who did not make the contribution one might perhaps have expected, though before 1740 Colonel William MacDowell had come home from St. Kitts to invest part of his wife's inheritance developing the sugar house, and his son invested more as a founder of the Ship Bank in 1750. Lastly, apart from David Dale, little was seen of men from the humblest walks of life, the landless agricultural worker, the unskilled labourer, the poor Highlander, and so forth. They found a career in commerce above their reach. The other missing groups presumably disdained it, and looked to a career in Edinburgh, or in the army or the church, if they could not immediately fulfill their ambition of becoming landowners themselves.

It would be interesting to know as much about the religious affiliations and the childhood upbringing of the great entrepreneurs as we do about their parentage. There is, however, too little information to let us generalise, though we know revealing details about isolated figures. David Dale, for instance, felt his religious convictions so powerfully that he left the Church of Scotland to become a founder member of a new sect, and for thirty-seven years preached as their pastor to a congregation of Independents in Greyfriars Wynd. The Presbyterian mob occasionally taunted him for being unordained. As for the Bairds of Gartsherrie, they were reared by a pious mother in a manner that might have been calculated to maximise their urge to succeed. In her son's words:

She was married in comparative poverty while her husband was sub-tenant of the small and not very productive farm of Woodhead. By her sagacity and indomitable energy she contributed largely to her husband's prosperity and to form in her children those habits of diligence and integrity by which they became distinguished. When they were old enough to go to school she always found time among the many and onerous duties of the farm, to assist them at their lessons, and she was careful in imparting to them the best religious instruction. The children were all early instructed in farm labour, and all of them, as they grew up, had a task assigned to them commensurate with their strength; but nothing, however pressing, was allowed to interrupt their lessons or interfere with their school hours. Thus was her family imbued with the best principles and trained to the practice of industry and economy: and the lessons then acquired they never forgot.[39]

How far these were common experiences of other pioneers we cannot say but, whatever else, the Glasgow middle class was not the society of illiterate boors which business tycoons are sometimes assumed to be. Many of the parents of the pioneers held formal education in the same respect as Mrs. Baird, and even when their children left school with little more than a smattering of elementary education they could, like young J. B. Neilson 'employ their leisure learning grammar, drawing and mathematics', and like John Leadbetter 'assiduously cultivate their intellect by attending evening classes'.[40] Jupiter Carlyle in the 1740s said of the merchants that 'few of them could be called learned'; yet he described a society founded by Provost Andrew Cochrane, the professed object of which was 'to inquire into the nature and principles of trade in all its branches, and communicate their knowledge and views on that subject to each other'. Adam Smith was among its members, and had a great respect for Cochrane:

Dr. Smith acknowledged his obligation to this gentleman's information when he was collecting materials for his *Wealth of Nations*; and the junior merchants who have flourished since his time, and extended their commerce far beyond what was then dreamt of, confess with respectful remembrance that it was Andrew Cochrane who first opened and enlarged their views.[41]

There were many other clubs in Glasgow after this time, some of them convivial, some social, some intellectual, several of them the meeting place of the town and university. Adam Smith was also a member of the Literary Society of Glasgow College, founded in 1752; it included most of the professors and many distinguished citizens, and the minutes of the Chamber of Commerce from 1783 onwards testify to the respect in which Smith, in turn, was held by the leading citizens when they came to formulate policy. David Dale, for instance, was one of his acknowledged admirers and disciples.

It was also to the Literary Society that Joseph Black, when a lecturer at the college, communicated his discovery of latent heat. Black's greatest work, however, was surely his patronage and encouragement of the young James Watt which led to the discovery by the latter of the principle of the separate condenser (see page 483 below). There is something altogether symbolic of the intellectual atmosphere of eighteenth-century Scotland that one of the most epoch-making inventions of the industrial revolution should have come about through the meeting of an instrument-maker from Greenock with a chemistry lecturer from Belfast over a collection of astronomical instruments given to the college by a Glasgow merchant who had made his fortune in the West Indies. It was in such an atmosphere at once intimate and intellectual, but in no sense exclusive, that the seed of eighteenth-century genius was most readily able to take root and to grow.

CHAPTER XVI

The Industrial Labour Force - I

1. THE STRUCTURE OF THE WORK FORCE

Although one of the most important social consequences of the industrial revolution was the creation of a large class of industrial wage-earners, industrial workers were not in themselves new. One needs only to recall the seventeenth-century colliers and salters whose degradation into serfdom we followed in the first part of this book, or the masons, carters and general labourers who worked for wages in the burghs in the late medieval and early modern period. We have also pointed out how wide is the spectrum covered by the Scottish term 'tradesman'. A baker of 1700 who baked bread in his own ovens and sold it over the counter to his own customers was a middle-class figure: his apprentice and his journeymen who assisted him in return for their keep and a weekly wage, but who had every hope of being able one day to afford their own ovens and shops were only temporarily working-class. On the other hand, even at an early date, some journeymen could never reasonably have expected to achieve any measure of economic independence, and would go on to their dying day making up materials for some external employer. Then there were women and children in peasants' families who worked by knitting and spinning on piece-work for a merchant who came round to their homes to supply the fibre and uplift the yarn, and cottars who split the year between cultivating the fields and carrying on some industrial occupation such as weaving or shoemaking in their own homes. Sometimes these men sold their produce on their own account, but often they simply worked for an employer in a nearby town. In all these ways Scotland for centuries had had some kind of industrial work force. Long before the industrial

391

revolution its numbers had probably been slowly on the increase as the market served by industry gradually widened.

What was unprecedented about the situation at the end of the eighteenth century was the speed with which the work force was being added to. There was an explosive increase in the number of industrial jobs available, especially for women and adolescents. There was a hardly less explosive increase in the number of people who had little alternative but to seek industrial employment, as population in the Lowlands, the Highlands, and Ireland in varying degrees grew faster than employment could be found for it on the land. Industrialisation brought the workers together in adventure and misfortune in great urban slums, destroying for ever the ethics and contacts of the trades-men guilds, and severing at a stroke the paternal reins of rural life. Consequently, the new workers, infinitely more numerous than the old, developed attitudes that were different from or explicitly hostile to the interests and social customs of the rest of society. Most of their effective concerted political action, however, took place long after 1830.

Although in its early stages the industrial revolution was partly a rural phenomenon, it was always in the towns that it made the most dramatic and most lasting impact. The table below shows how six burghs of predominantly industrial and proletarian character, grew—though all for slightly different reasons and in slightly different ways (the figure for Glasgow differs from that on page 261 above because a slightly different area is included). They are worth regarding in detail.

	Glasgow	Paisley	Dundee	Arbroath	Kilmarnock	Greenock
c. 1695–1707	13,000	4,500	?	2,000	?	2,000
1755	23,000	7,000	12,500	2,000	4,500	4,000
1801	77,000	31,000	27,000	5,000	8,000	17,500
1831	202,000	57,000	45,000	6,500	18,000	27,500

Paisley is perhaps the prime example of a town where the growth of an industrial work force depended almost solely on new textiles. Before the Union she was an indifferent centre for coarse linens; she then developed expertise in the manufacture of white thread (imitated from Holland), of fine lawns and cambrics (imitated from France) and of silk gauze (imitated from London). In the half century after 1790 all this was eclipsed when she became the leading town in the world for the manufacture of certain classes of high-grade cottons, especially Paisley shawls. By 1831, when she was the fourth burgh in Scotland and larger than any town in Scotland had been a century earlier, possibly nearly half the occupied population worked at the looms[1]— a degree of concentration and uniformity in one occupation that must have been unusual even at that date, and which was certainly a source of instability and weakness to her in the decades that followed.

This is an extreme case, but it is worth pausing to stress the enormous number of people involved throughout the Lowlands of Scotland in the manufacture of cotton in all its branches. In 1826 Sir John Sinclair supposed that 154,000 hands found work in this trade, compared to 76,000 in linen and hemp, 24,800 in woollens and a mere 13,000 in the iron trade. For all the other manufacturing industries of Scotland lumped together he would only allow 19,000.[2] We should, perhaps, treat this as only a series of guesses: but it was made by a man who, though no statistician in the modern sense of the word, had spent more time gathering information about Scottish society than anyone else in his lifetime. We should also remember that his figures refer to individual workers, not to heads of families, and a large majority of those in most branches of the cotton industry were women and children. Tambouring, for instance, the embroidery by hand of pieces of high quality cotton goods such as Paisley shawls, employed many tens of thousands of female outworkers in the countryside, almost all of them the wives and daughters of agricultural workers or unskilled labourers doing it at home to make a small supplementary addition to the household budget. Even allowing for this, however, and even allowing for very substantial margins of error in the original calculation, the orders of magnitude leave no doubt of the great dominance of cotton over all other textiles, or of the overwhelming primacy of textiles over everything else. Before the hot-blast discovery of 1828, the industrial revolution in Scotland even more than in England was little else than this revolution in textiles.

Of the other towns on our table, Dundee and Arbroath were both burghs where the old national staple, linen, had been transformed by the mechanisation of flax-spinning, though Dundee was always an important commercial and retail centre as well. Kilmarnock is slightly more complex: her growth rested partly on the shoe industry, and partly on the diversified woollen trade manufacturing carpets, bonnets and worsted shawls. Greenock was more complex still. She became among the six most populous towns in Scotland without being distinguished for any textile and without developing any one overwhelmingly important single staple trade. By 1830 her largest industry was shipbuilding along with iron-founding and forging, sugar-refining, rope-spinning, sail-making, paper-making, leather-working, the manufacture of earthenware, brewing, distilling and so forth. The town was probably oversupplied with labour through becoming the main port of entry and exit for Irishmen and Highlanders, many of whom gravitated into her unskilled trades and stayed there for relatively short periods before moving in search of better jobs in the hinterland or overseas.

Much the largest and most important of all the Scottish industrial cities, however, was Glasgow, by 1831 the third city of the United Kingdom exceeded only by London and Manchester. Thanks to the labours of James Cleland, her local statistician, we are better informed about her social structure than about that of any other town in Scotland. The gist of an enquiry he made into the distribution of the occupied population in 1831 is given in a table opposite: though no doubt an imperfect survey, and certainly in places an ambiguous one in terms of the categories used, it has considerable intrinsic interest.

There are several remarkable features in all this, even if the precise meaning of all the categories is by no means always clear. Firstly, not less than a third of the occupied population of Glasgow was involved in manufacturing cotton textiles (virtually the only fibre processed in the city); but those who attended the factory spindles and powerlooms were still possibly outnumbered by handloom weavers and others who worked at home. Even in its leading sector the Industrial Revolution had thus not yet fully converted the workforce into a race of machine minders.

Again, the very considerable number of people grouped under 'trades' suggests something of the abiding vitality and strength of the traditional occupations of the city, though not by any means all were carried on in a perfectly traditional way. For example, many of the 2900 people in the drink trade were wage earners in the city's distilleries and breweries, and no longer merely publicans and home-brewers as their ancestors would have been. Hardly any of the 3100 milliners and seamstresses were tradespeople in the old sense: they were out-workers making up hats and clothes at very low piece-rates for small independent capitalists. The same must have been true of many

TABLE I

Occupied Population of Glasgow, 1831 (000s)

1. *Professional mercantile and clerical*

    Professional (clergy, professors, teachers, students and literary persons, 2.7; writers and others connected with the law, 0.6; surgeons, druggists and chemists, 0.5) 3.8

    Mercantile (merchants and bankers, 1.7; agents, factors and accountants 0.5) 2.2

    Clerical (clerks and commercial travellers) 1.8

    Total: 7.8

2. *Textile Manufacture*

    Weavers, warpers and winders 15.2

    Cotton spinners and steam-loom weavers 9.9

    Tambourers, darners and clippers 1.2

    Muslin manufacturers and calenderers 1.3

    Dyers, calico printers, bleachers, etc. 1.7

    Engravers, block and print cutters 0.4

    Machinists, engineers and mill-wrights 0.9

    Total: 30.6

3. *Trades*

    Clothing trades (tailors, clothiers and hatters, 2.1; haberdashers mercers, drapers, hosiers, glovers, 0.3; milliners, straw-hat makers and seamstresses, 3.1; tanners and shoemakers 2.7) 8.2

    Metal trades (brass, iron and type founders and moulders, 0.9; smiths, braziers and pewterers, 1.9; ironmongers and nailors, 0.5) 3.3

    Construction trades (masons, bricklayers, etc., 1.5; upholsterers, sawyers, etc., 3.0; slaters and plasterers, 0.6; painters, plumbers, glaziers, etc., 0.8) 5.9

    Food and drink, etc. trades (grocers and victuallers, 1.1; greengrocers, etc., 0.4; bakers, cooks and confectioners, 1.1; fleshers and fishmongers, 0.5; distillers, brewers and others employed in the spirit trade, 2.9; tobacconists, drysalters, soap and candlemakers, 0.4) 6.4

    Other miscellaneous trades (booksellers and binders, 0.5; compositors and printers, 0.6; jewellers, clockmakers, etc.; 0.3; barbers and hairdressers, 0.2; potters, glass-cutters, etc., 0.5; coachmakers and wheelwrights, 0.3; coopers and turners, 0.5; flaxdressers and rope makers, etc., 0.3; brush, basket, comb and spoon makers, 0.3) 3.5

    Total: 27.3

4. *Servants, unskilled, labouring and casual employment*

Servants	9.0
Waiters, postboys, hostlers and grooms	0.7
Porters and watchmen	1.3
Warehousemen and supernumeraries	1.1
Colliers, quarrymen and labourers	6.6
Cow keepers, carters and carriers	1.5
Washers, dressmakers and manglers	0.6
Hawkers and dealers in small wares	1.3
Furniture brokers and dealers in old clothes	0.3
Total:	22.4
5. Numerous miscellaneous occupations (unspecified)	6.4
Grand total	94.5

Source: See footnote 15.

of the tailors and shoemakers, working under conditions more akin to the sweatshop than the guild. Cleland counted only 2900 retailing shops apart from pawnbrokers and druggists. Eliminating the construction trades, this would suggest there was only about one shop to every seven or eight 'tradesmen'. Fewer and fewer could any longer have enjoyed a reasonable hope that the day would come when they could own their own business, and the bare term tradesman began to lose almost all the middle-class overtones it had once had. The expression 'shopkeeper' was beginning to be used instead to denote the minority that would come to own a shop.

Then there were the unskilled. Those classified here as 'servants, or in unskilled, labouring or casual employments' amounted to nearly one in four of the occupied population. A few, like the city's colliers, were not really unskilled at all, but on the other hand many who were genuinely unskilled were not included within this particular group. Many of the 6400 in 'numerous unspecified occupations' must have belonged to the same bracket, and, making a more significant difference, many of those involved in textile manufacture or in such trades as millinery, brewing and tanning, and even construction labourers, must also have been able to step into their jobs and reach the top of their earning power (such as it was) within a few weeks with virtually no training at all. If we define the unskilled in this way it would almost certainly be more correct to put the proportion of such workers in

Glasgow at one in two or one in three rather than the one in four suggested by a superficial reading of the table.

Some details here suggest the degree to which Glasgow, like Greenock, was oversupplied with labour in spite of the tremendous vitality of her industries. There were, for instance, more people described as 'hawkers, dealers in small wares, furniture brokers and dealers in old clothes' than there were masons, bricklayers and their assistants, and as many 'porters, and watchmen' as slaters, plasterers, painters, plumbers and glaziers. Such figures give a hint of the pathetic difficulties that many experienced in getting a job at all in the city, and perhaps also of the relative unresponsiveness of the construction trades to the problem of providing homes for a population increasing at a rate of over 5000 a year between 1811 and 1831. No-one acquainted with the city today will be unaware that the growth of Glasgow became the growth of the largest slum problem this country has ever known.

2. THE STANDARD OF LIVING

Was the working class better or worse off as the result of industrialisation? The question, which has been much debated among British historians in recent decades, looks simple; but it is impossible to answer in any simple or straightforward way. Much depends on exactly how the problem is framed. Should we, for example, try to compare the lot of such people as weavers or masons in the preindustrial towns of 1750 or 1770 with the lot of workers in the same trades in 1820 or 1830 when industrialisation was well under way? Or should we compare the lot of a 'peasant' in the preindustrial world with that of a 'worker' in industrial society, since most industrial workers in 1830 were immediately descended from those who had lived on the land? If so which peasants and which workers do we choose? One might compare the existence of a Highland crofter in the late eighteenth century with that of his descendants who became skilled workers in a cotton factory after 1820, and demonstrate that for some families industrialisation brought the blessings of comparative affluence and escape from the stagnation of life on a potato plot in the rainy glens. Equally one might follow the career of a Stirlingshire tenant who lost his farm in the agricultural revolution and ended up as a tubercular weaver trying to keep body and soul together on five shillings a week and a gill of whisky: for him, industrialisation was a disaster. Perhaps the question should be whether or not those for whom the Industrial Revolution came as a blessing outnumbered those to whom it brought deterioration. This, however, is unanswerable: we do not know enough about the composition, origins and real earnings of the work force to construct any satisfactory quantitative basis for the enquiry. Is it helpful, in any case, to be told that two cases of abject misery and two cases of roaring success average no material change in the condition of the four people concerned? The half-century from 1780 to 1830 was a period in which the fortunes of different groups within the work force varied so widely that generalisations which treat the 'working class' as if it was a homogeneous entity usually obscure more than they reveal.

This does not mean that nothing at all can be said by way of generalisation. It is, for instance, demonstrable that the great majority of industrial workers were exposed to a greater risk of an early death for themselves and their families through urbanisation. The transfer from agriculture to industry usually meant a move from country to town, and the towns had always been much more dangerous to live in than the countryside owing to the overcrowding and lack of sanitation within them. Furthermore, the towns were growing even more dangerous towards the end of the period—at least if Glasgow is typical, for here, according to contemporary medical experts, the death-rate rose through the 1820s and 1830s thanks to the return of typhus and other diseases intimately connected with urban filth.[3] It is also true that by going into the towns the workers deprived their children of many of their opportunities for a good primary education, though this would represent deterioration only for those from the rural Lowlands since Highland and Irish children had never had the same chances even in the countryside (see pages 461–72 below). Similarly they were largely deprived of the guidance and help of the church, whose ministry and building completely failed to expand in working-class areas of the towns in anything like proportion to the rise in the number of souls to be cared for. Though the Church of Scotland failed most obviously, even the secession churches fell to the temptation of concentrating their ministry upon middle-class and lower middle-class residential areas. As a consequence of this and of many other factors the incidence of alcoholism and intemperance rose. Sheriff

Alison was not considered either facetious or alarmist when he told a Royal Commission of 1838 that 'there are 10,000 men in Glasgow who get drunk on Saturday night, who are drunk all Sunday, and are in a state of intoxication or half-intoxication all Monday and go to work on Tuesday'.[4]

Those aspects of the standard of living that concern levels of consumption rather than the general condition of the environment are mainly dependent on the movement of wages and prices, since whether or not the worker was better off depended primarily on what he could buy with his earnings. The table overleaf illustrates some complexities and main trends of this question in respect of certain traditional groups in the industrial labour force of two towns, but not, note, in respect of those groups most intimately affected by the industrial revolution itself, the factory workers, the weavers and the colliers. These are dealt with separately in the following sections.

The first column in this table, relating to the 1790s, represents the culmination of three or four decades during which things had been generally improving. Henry Hamilton's verdict on this period before the end of the century seems approximately correct: between 1750 and 1790 the price of oatmeal, the staple food of the Scots, rose by little more than fifty per cent, the prices of most other provisions roughly doubled and the wages of labour rose by two-and-a-half or three times.[5] The *Statistical Account* testifies repeatedly to the abundant coal in the artisans' grates, the new furniture in their houses, the linen and cotton textiles on their backs, and to their increasing consumption of wheat bread, cheese, butter, bacon, mutton, beef, sugar and tea. Even unskilled labourers who still only ate mutton, beef and wheat bread irregularly or in very small quantities, were comforted as the margin widened between themselves and the dreadful brink of subsistence.

The forty years after 1790 were nothing like so uniformly prosperous as the previous thirty had been. The second column represents the peak of twenty years of inflation which had accompanied the wars against France: the prices of most foods except oatmeal then stood at almost double what they had been in 1790, but only the luckiest and most skilled of the journeymen (the sawyers, for instance, on our table) also increased their wages by one hundred per cent. The wages of the rest of these workers lagged, increasing by twenty-five to fifty per cent, which was less even than the rise of the price of oatmeal;

TABLE II

1. *Wages*	1790[1]	1812	1819	1831-3[2]
Mason (Glasgow) per day	2/–	3/–	2/6	2/4
Mason (Arbroath) per day	1/8	2/1½	1/6	1/8½
Carpenter (Glasgow) per day	2/–	3/–	2/4	2/4
Carpenter (Arbroath) per day	1/4	?	2/4	2/–
Blacksmith (Glasgow) per day	?	2/6	2/10	2/10
Blacksmith (Arbroath) per day	?	2/8	3/4	2/6
Sawyer (Glasgow) per day	2/–	4/–	1/3	1/6
Labourer (Glasgow) per day	1/4	1/10	1/3	1/6

2. *Prices*[3]	1790-2	1812	1819	1831-3
Oatmeal (peck) Glasgow	1/0½	1/9	1/3	1/2
Oatmeal (peck) Arbroath	1/1	?	1/4	1/–
Wheatbread (quartern loaf) Glasgow	?	1/4	0/11½	0/8
Wheatbread (quartern loaf) Arbroath	?	1/6	0/11	0/8
Cheese (lb.) Glasgow	0/4½	1/0	0/8½	0/6
Cheese (lb.) Arbroath	0/3½	?	0/4	0/4
Beef (lb.) Glasgow	0/3½	0/6	0/5	0/5
Beef (lb.) Arbroath	0/4½	0/8	0/7	0/5
Houserent (2 aparts. per ann.) Glasgow	?	100/–	90/–	85/–
Houserent per ann. Arbroath	?	60/–	55/–	55/–

(1) In this column Glasgow wages and Arbroath wages and prices relate to 1790 and 1791. Glasgow prices are actually those for Cambuslang, 5 miles S.E. of the centre of Glasgow, for 1790.
(2) Glasgow wages and prices relate to 1831, Arbroath for 1833.
(3) All quantities have, so far as possible, been reduced to a uniform standard.

Source: *Statistical Account, New Statistical Account,* James Cleland, *Enumeration.*

they therefore inevitably sacrificed some of the gains made in the good years before 1790 while the wars lasted. In some years—for instance in 1799 and 1800—the price of grain suddenly doubled over what it had been the two years previously. Though these disruptions were caused by bad harvests and were of short duration, while they lasted they must have driven many even among the artisans into the most desperate penury. The near-starvation conditions described by Younger at St. Boswells (see page 318 above) applies to a family of shoemakers.

The remaining columns represent what happened after the war. As early as 1813 the all-round price-fall began, though meal and bread fell more than most other foods and both fell much more than house rent. Money wages came down too after 1812, but it does not look as if they fell faster than the average cost of living for any of the groups on our table except the sawyers. Journeymen in the other skilled trades who had held their 1790 standard of living in all but the worst years of the war probably held it again over the two ensuing decades but did not (except perhaps in one or two exceptional cases like the smiths) markedly improve upon it. The less skilled who had lost ground in the war regained some of it in the 1820s. For both types of worker the period as a whole represented not an absolute prolonged or catastrophic deterioration in the level of real wages but rather a sharp setback to the expectations of the previous generation that things would go on getting better and better.

The picture we have drawn here is limited in regard to the callings involved, and the story for large vital groups, the factory workers, the weavers and the miners, is in many respects a different one, as we shall see. The question of unemployment also needs to be taken into account, and is doubly vexed by the absence of any statistics at all. It is, however, fairly safe to assert that as long as the French wars lasted, with their big demand for human cannon-fodder, there was no serious problem at home except when some extraneous circumstances—like the slump of 1812 brought about by the dislocations of war in the markets of Europe and America—caused a widespread short-term commercial crisis. After 1815, however, demobilisation of the armed services followed by an accelerating stream of immigrants from Ireland and the Highlands and a continuing high rate of natural increase among the Lowland Scots, began to pour labour on to the urban market faster than the expanding economy could mop it up. Nor did the economy expand evenly. Some of the worst depressions of the nineteenth century occurred when the chronic problem of oversupply of labour was exacerbated by periodic nation-wide shocks to trade, like those of 1816, 1819 and 1826, when mills stopped work, ships lay idle and banks were besieged by anxious creditors. It is impossible to understand the social atmosphere of the years after 1815 without appreciating how misery and tension were heightened by this endemic and epidemic unemployment. The experience of it plunged into beggary all those who were directly affected, and the fear of it rocked to their foundations the security and solidarity of the remainder. Unemployment must also have operated to drive down the wages of those who remained at work, and this may in particular affect our column for 1819. Some of the other peculiarities of the figures for this year—for instance that masons' wages were evidently much lower in Arbroath than in Glasgow, but blacksmiths' wages were rather higher—are probably explicable in terms of a very imperfect labour market. In a society in which the workers were largely unorganised and in which information about the rate or wages prevailing in another town could usually come only by word of mouth by someone who had tramped to it, it was only to be expected that there would be wide and persistent differentials from place to place. To produce a full and satisfactory account of the course of real wages over these years we shall need a series of painstaking regional studies by local historians.

Among the casualties of urban unemployment was the old Scottish poor law. The traditional methods of poor relief, obliging the able-bodied poor to fend for themselves or rely on the generosity of their own families, and only giving where it was quite unavoidable a pittance of supplementary help out of the church collections to the elderly, the sickly, the widowed and the orphan, had barely served even in country parishes. It would not and could not serve in the great towns. For one thing the church authorities were not acquainted with a tithe of the old, the ill and the bereaved, many of whom had no families at all in the town to whom they could turn for relief: for another, there was no provision at all for dealing with periodic mass-unemployment of the able-bodied in an industrial slump. By Scottish law they were not entitled to poor relief in any form.

Different authorities tried to cope in different ways, some by raising occasional relief-funds by subscription from the well-to-do when a slump struck, some by adopting a form of compulsory poor-rate levied on all taxable householders (as was done in England) and applying this to the relief of the helpless, and some by desperate and sincere efforts, like those which Thomas Chalmers initiated in his poverty-stricken Glasgow parish of St. Johns, to make the old volun-tary system work through inquisitorial visitation by the kirk elders. The matter came to a head in the great debates of the 1830s, culminating in the Scottish Poor Law Reform Act of 1845 which introduced the principles of mandatory rating, central supervision, and legal relief for the able-bodied to the Scottish statute book. That, however, is a subject we need not go into here. It is enough to note that the problems of pauperism within our period were considerably increased by the failure of the state to respond to them by modernising or extending even the vestigial welfare machinery it had established in the seventeenth century.

To carry our discussion of the industrial work force beyond a broad outline we must now discuss three groups within it who were themselves central figures in the transformation brought about by industrialisation: the factory workers in the textile mills, the weavers, and the colliers. Together they came to comprise a high percentage of the work force. Individually their fortunes and their particular conditions of work differed so widely as to render meaningless any further generalisations that fail to take full account of each. To them we must devote the remainder of this chapter and the whole of the next.

3. THE COUNTRY TEXTILE MILLS

The first processes to be transformed by the technological revolution of the eighteenth century were in spinning. There were three major steps in this direction. The first merely improved the efficiency of domestic spinners without requiring either a new labour force or a new place for them to work in. Traditionally the spinning both of woollen and linen yarn in Scotland had been the work of women and girls in their homes at odd hours during the day, either on a distaff (in the most backward parts) or on a simple spinning wheel. About 1770 a two-handed wheel with double spindles came into use, though it was not widely distributed until towards the end of the century. Even this simple improvement doubled the productivity of the domestic spinner: in some linen districts by the 1790s women were making eightpence a day on the two-handed wheel, at least twopence more than they could have got as field labourers or farm servants. More sophisticated was the invention of the spinning jenny of James Hargreaves of Blackburn in 1764, which, although for a long time it could only spin soft and fragile cotton wefts, revolutionised that branch of textile manufacture by multiplying the spinner's productivity initially by eight times, and later by as much as sixteen, twenty or thirty times. The jenny, like the two-handed wheel, could still easily be used at home by a woman or child, although the larger ones were gathered into workshops in the 1780s and operated by men. Spinningdale in Sutherland founded by David Dale and a group of local proprietors was an early jenny factory.

The second step brought most of the early large-scale factories. In 1768 Richard Arkwright invented waterframe spinning, by which hard cotton warps of considerable strength were made on large machines driven by waterpower. They could be attended by women and children since no muscular force was required. The first great cotton mills housing machines of this type in Scotland, such as those at Catrine, New Lanark, Deanston, Balfron and Stanley founded between 1784 and 1786, were placed on fast-running streams in the countryside. By the early nineteenth century their prosperity was threatened by developments in mule-spinning in the towns, but the advent of the powerloom requiring an extremely tough warp, combined with further refinements to the waterframe through throstle gearing which increased its velocity, gave these rural mills an unexpected new lease of life. Flax was being spun on a type of waterframe by the 1790s, and this technique swept through the linen industry in the next few years.

The third step, in many ways the most important of all, was initiated by Samuel Crompton in 1779 when he invented a machine which he named the mule because it combined many of the advantages of the jenny with those of the waterframe. It was able to produce fine, regular and fairly strong cotton yarn suitable for both warp and weft. At first, like the largest types of jenny, it required a man's strength to move it, but it was still suitable both for the home and the small workshop. It was integrated into the factory system by the application of Watt's steam-engine to drive it, and mule factories became general between 1790 and 1812. This was followed by improvements in the 1820s to make the mules 'self-acting', which doubled the number of spindles that one operative could look after. Nevertheless adult males remained indispensable in the processes of mule-spinning in the factory even when the machinery became self-acting, though they were increasingly outnumbered by the children and adolescents who served as their assistants. Mule-spinning mills were the characteristic factories of the sprawling towns on the coal-fields: they were not often country mills and most yarn in Scotland was consequently produced in the towns by the end of the period.

The other processes that were easily taken into the factories were concerned with the preparation of fibres before spinning, such as heckling, carding and the manufacture of rovings (thick spirals of cotton wool fed into the spinning machines). Printing cottons and linens on revolving cylinders operated by steam power began in Scotland about 1785: this was largely a male job. Almost all the other occupations, as well as reeling (putting the yarn on bobbins or in warps after spinning) and calendering (hot-pressing and packing) were usually done by women and children or adolescents.

Weaving came into the factory much more slowly. Edward Cartwright made a powerloom in England in 1784, which, famous though it was, turned out to be little more than a crude demonstration model. Robert Millar of Glasgow deserves perhaps equal credit for bringing a powerloom into successful production for the first time in 1798. Even this was very imperfect, and some of the problems (such as stopping the loom when the weft broke or the shuttle caught without damaging the fabric by shock) were not solved for decades. The 1820s saw the start of the breakthrough. At the beginning of that decade there were still only 2000 powerlooms in Scotland, by the end there were 10,000. These, however, were still almost all in cotton, only a few hundred were in linen and none at all were in woollens. The vast majority of powerloom hands were women and girls, and the factories (not numerous even by 1830) were usually located near the mule-spinning works in the towns. On the other hand some very large integrated powerloom and waterframe concerns often combined with a certain amount of rural mule-spinning were developed at some of the older rural sites such as Catrine in Ayrshire.

At first sight it seems remarkable that in this involved and headlong series of technical changes relatively little new employment should have emerged for adult males. One reason was the nature of the work, which did not require muscular strength except for the spinners in a mule factory. Edward Baines explained in 1835:

> The greater number of operatives are employed in clearing the cotton from the cards, shifting the cans at the drawing frames, removing and replacing bobbins at the roving frames, throstles and mules, piecing the threads which break at those machines, sweeping up the cotton waste, adjusting the cloth in the powerlooms, winding, warping and dressing the warp.[6]

All this could be done by women and children. Employers found there were special advantages in using children small enough to crawl under the machinery to sweep away fluff during spinning, and many believed that only those caught below the age of twelve could ever develop sufficient manual dexterity to become first-class piecers in their teens.

There was more to it than this, however. In the earliest stages of the country waterframe mills the most pressing reason why so few men were employed within the factories was because so few were willing to come. Factory work demanded submission to a work-discipline of a wholly new and unfamiliar kind. The employers had built expensive mills and installed within them sophisticated machinery that was kept in motion by unflagging automatic power: to operate efficiently it was essential to have a labour force of several hundred working together and geared to the rhythm of the machine. The employees must turn up early on Monday morning when the water-frames were put in motion, work their twelve or fourteen hour day without interruptions except at predetermined breaks to allow for meals, and repeat the process with unfailing fidelity to the overseer each day until Saturday evening—week after week, month after month, year after year, with Sundays off and perhaps two other days holiday in the whole twelvemonth.

These demands, which would strain the patience of even the most dedicated overtime worker of today, were completely alien to the work traditions of the eighteenth-century Scot. The peasant was accustomed to spending the day in the fields, labouring at his own pace on a variety of different tasks according to the season, the weather and the dictates of his own judgement. Even a farm-hand working for a wage was (and is) swayed more by these things than by his employer's instructions. A domestic craftsman, such as a weaver, would spend the day at home, working on his web for fully as long as the factory operative, yet able to stop the loom just when he chose in order to speak to a neighbour, to send his child assistant out to play, or to order his wife to make him a cup of tea and a bannock. If he wished, he could work all night on Friday to take his ease on Saturday, Sunday and Monday—a course that many in fact chose in preference to higher and more regular earnings. There was no master to tell him when to work and when to stop working except himself. There was so little experience in Scotland of work that called for mass toil under an overseer outside the house that people at first regarded factory work as semi-servile, on a par with what went on in the charity workhouses of some large burghs where paupers were driven from dawn to dusk to make them industrious and moral, or with conditions in the collieries and salt-works where many workers were still until 1799 the heritable property of their masters.

It was therefore most unlikely that anything but the most pressing economic needs would have got large numbers of males into these first factories. In the 1780s and 1790s moreover, the supply of agricultural labour in the Lowlands was still not greatly exceeding the demand, and rural wage packets were still getting fatter. Domestic weaving too was at that period exceedingly prosperous, and much more likely to attract ambitious and stable recruits from the land than the factories were. Such men as did come to the factory gates looking for jobs—Highlanders, for example, in desperate straits, or casual labourers who had drifted out of low grade jobs in the towns—were often the least suitable. Employers found they proved restless, refractory and un-reliable, more trouble than they were worth. At Catrine it was said of the Highland recruit: 'he never sits at ease at a loom, it is like putting a deer in the plough', and Henry Houldsworth in Glasgow had a similar experience when he tried to recruit his first machine spinners.[7]

The employers, therefore, had doubly good reasons for seeking to build up their work force primarily from women and children. They could do almost all the jobs (for less pay, too), and since they were the traditional dependents in the Scottish family, used to doing what they were told at home, they were more amenable to strict discipline at work. Children, especially, were attractive. If caught young they could be bent like saplings to the new ways, trained up to perform speedily, exactly and without question whatever was required at work, and (with any luck) they would eventually become themselves the parents of a new generation of operatives to whom the factory was neither an alien nor a particularly unpleasant environment.

The pioneers had still to face the problem of drawing together and keeping sufficiently large numbers of women and children. This was especially difficult for these earliest waterframe mills, which were both placed in deep rural areas and of unprecedented size. Within ten years New Lanark, Catrine, Deanston, Balfron, Blantyre and Stanley were each employing between 300 and 1500 hands, which represented a chain of industrial units each considerably larger than anything seen before. Only the iron-works at Carron and the lead mines at Leadhills and Wanlockhead were of comparable magnitude before 1800.

To solve the physical problem of accommodation the great textile factories were therefore obliged to begin by building a village round the mill, taking as their models the communities that improving landlords so often established on their estates in Scotland as an integral part of agricultural change. The houses were neat, well-built, low-rented, provided with gardens and generally superior to the traditional cottages of the poorest peasantry. On the other hand the houses were seldom built with quite so much space, or the villages endowed with quite so many amenities as those of the improving lairds. The factory masters, for disciplinary reasons, deplored both the establishment of inns and the creation of machinery for community self-government, things which often appealed to at least the more genial landowners.

For the employers, seeking a population of women and children, the ideal inhabitant for every house in their village would have been a poor widow with numerous healthy infants. New Lanark had thirty-four widows in the community in 1793 and Catrine forty-four in 1819, and they were not the only mills to state publicly how warmly they would welcome more. Inevitably, however, supply fell short of demand. In order to attract women it was first necessary to attract their husbands, and most houses contained a man who was something of a burden to the factory owner. There were various ways of disposing of him. With luck he might find employment outside the firm—on a farm or in the nearest burgh. Within the concern it might be possible to employ him in construction or maintenance where discipline need not be too tight or too humiliating. New Lanark in 1795 had had ninety masons, carpenters and labourers busy extending the works for seven years, and eighty-seven mechanics making and repairing the machinery. Or he might be employed as a handloom weaver, working up some of the company's yarn at home. On the factory floor relatively few males objected to the life of an overseer, and if there was still a superfluity the firm might inaugurate a smaller spinning department that utilised large jennies or mules at which a man's strength was needed. In most of these cases there had to be at least a partial acceptance by the men involved of the demands of factory discipline, and high wages in comparison to what could be earned in alternative occupations remained necessary to sugar the pill, and to keep them and their dependents within the community.

Some of the rural mills also employed numbers of orphan children, though in Scotland this was less usual than in England, and New Lanark may have been the only important concern to do so on a large scale. Here David Dale had built barracks capable of housing 500 children by 1797. Visitors came to see both the mills and the no less famous squad of clean and obedient orphans. They described it all in great detail. The children slept in 'well-aired rooms, three in a bed', on a straw mattress with sheets and blankets, the dormitories being scrubbed weekly and lime-washed twice a year. They were given cotton clothes in summer (washed fortnightly) with woollen suits or linen dresses in winter; they rose at 6.00 a.m. and left work thirteen hours later, having had an hour and a half off for meals, and then attended the factory school for two hours; many of the children kept books in the boxes by their beds; they ate oatmeal porridge with milk twice a day, soup for lunch, with barley bread and potatoes, bread and cheese alternating with seven ounces of beef per child on different days, and occasionally herrings; finally, the visitors were always impressed by how well-behaved the children were, how their moral and religious education was attended to, and how healthy they were. Thomas Garnett wrote about the establishment:

> What ground for exultation must this afford to the worthy owner! What a number of people are here made happy and comfortable who would, many of them, have been cut off by disease, or, wallowing in dirt, been ruined by indolence . . . If I was tempted to envy any of my fellow-creatures it would be such men as . . . Mr Dale for the good they have done to mankind.[8]

To us it must seem extraordinary that any firm that permitted children to work a thirteen hour day should merit such extravagant praise, and self-evident that David Dale was not in business just to be a disinterested philanthropist. Yet by the standards of his day his factory, like the majority of these rural waterframe works, was well-run. Another such was Deanston up in Stirlingshire where James Smith was manager; here a fairly critical government factory commissioner in 1833 commented that 'it is impossible not to see an air of parental kindness on one side and of industry and its attendant comforts on the other'.[9] David Dale, James Smith and many of their contemporaries approached the problem of management in a thoroughly eighteenth-century spirit of benevolent absolutism. They worked their labour long hours, they kept a tight reign over behaviour on the factory floor and in the village and they emphasised above all else the virtues of obedience, industriousness and cleanliness, but they also generally provided reasonable houses, paid for a schoolmaster who at least taught the children to read, and tried to keep a paternal, personal and friendly element in labour relations. They were much more like improving lairds than tycoons.

David Dale, of course, was ultimately replaced at New Lanark by his son-in-law the protosocialist Robert Owen, whose long regime of a quarter of a century of management ended in 1825. Yet most of the changes Owen made were of degree rather than kind: he made the regulations against drunkenness and theft more efficient, he inaugurated a proper cleansing service for the village, he reduced the working hours in 1816 from thirteen to twelve (they had been fourteen hours for a time, but that was against his own wishes and in deference to those of his partners). Slightly more radical was the introduction of an incentive system for workers with good production records (most employers preferred to fine workers who did badly rather than reward those who did well). His factory school was extraordinarily enlightened; no children worked under the age of ten, but instead attended the day school; those over ten attended an evening school for an hour and a half. The curriculum included reading, writing, arithmetic, music, dancing, with sewing for the girls and military exercises for the boys: to this was ultimately added classes in geography, history and the natural sciences. But Robert Owen consistently remained at New Lanark the great paternalist, no less master on the factory floor than David Dale had been before him.[9]

His theories of co-operative socialism, which earned him so much notoriety in his day and such celebrity after his death, were strictly for extramural use. After 1815 Owen produced a series of proposals for 'villages of co-operation' in which the poor and the unemployed could be set to work at productive units owned and organised by themselves. In 1825, when Owen was away in the United States, a group of Owenities did attempt to build such a community at Orbiston in Lanarkshire: 290 people joined it, and it made a brave attempt at communist living with farmers, foundrymen, printers, weavers, tailors and shoemakers each contributing their share to co-operative production. It fell, however, due to internal quarrels among the organisers and to insufficient finance. It was wound up within two years. Owen's personal interest in the scheme seems to have been minimal, and it is impossible to escape a slight suspicion that he was happier when his Utopias were on paper or in a far continent than when he was faced with working men building them on his doorstep.[10]

4. THE URBAN SPINNERS

In the industrial towns where most yarn came to be spun after 1800 things were inevitably rather different from what they had been in early rural factories. The employers found it both less necessary and more difficult to act in the manner of squires. It was needless to build a community round the town factory when workers could find accommodation in the tenements thrown up and subdivided by speculative builders: nor did women and children have to be specially attracted to the site when they could be drawn from the families of the wider proletariat of the city, the weavers, journeymen and labourers already concentrated in the vicinity. It was also impossible for a single employer to make a moral impression on a town. In order to do so he had to combine with other employers—either for benevolent purposes, such as endowing a church or an institution, or for industrial purposes, such as to enforce some aspect of discipline and to alter the rate of wages. The workers, in turn, suspected such common action by an employing class much more than if it was done by a solitary individual. While rural factory workers had identified themselves closely with their locality, their factory and their master, urban factory workers identified themselves much more with one another whichever firm they worked for. The materials for class warfare in the towns were therefore much more combustible than they were in the villages.

After about 1800 there were other very important ways in which the labour force in the urban factories differed from that in the first country concerns. Factory employment was losing its initial unfamiliarity. Especially after the Napoleonic Wars, when demobilisation and the accelerated influx of Highlanders and Irishman to the cities threw a strain on the capacity of the economy to absorb all the excess labour, factory jobs were sought after with an enthusiasm that would have seemed unbelievable twenty years before. This itself was enough to give trained factory hands a new assurance and prestige in the proletariat. It was very much reinforced by the fact that these town factories used mules, and the mule, unlike the waterframe, needed the strength and skill of an adult man to operate it. Skilled, trained male spinners who had been in the factories since boyhood were much preferred to casual incomers from other trades who had neither the understanding of what was required nor the stamina to carry it out to the rhythm of the machines. The factory masters were ready to make substantial concessions to retain them. The spinners were allowed to choose their own assistants: it was therefore their own children and kin and not those of strangers from outside who got the jobs as piecers and cleaners directly under the spinner's supervision, or jobs as reelers and carders in other departments of the mill. Spinners were even allowed in some mills to pay another worker to take their place at the mules on a Friday or a Saturday in order to increase the length of their own weekends.

The Glasgow spinners developed one of the first effective Scottish trade unions. In shadowy form it can be traced back to 1805, though it was not until 1816 that it showed much life: thereafter it maintained continuous existence for more than twenty years despite being badly winded by a lock-out of 1824 which kept it quiet for four or five years afterwards. Its membership in the early 1820s and again in the 1830s was estimated at around 800—not a majority even of the adult males, but enough to exercise direct control over several thousand of their dependent kin in the factories, and certainly enough to paralyse a wide section of the cotton trade if they came out on strike.

The main aims of the union were to resist reductions of wages and to maintain their trade against dilution. Both were threats to their standards of living in the deflation and unemployment that followed the end of the Napoleonic Wars, and both were sharpened in the 1820s when self-acting mules demanding both less strength and less experience from the operatives began to be introduced. In these circumstances the union found itself fighting its fellow workers as much as the employers. Sheriff Alison was obviously a hostile commentator, but his remarks in 1838 were substantially borne out by what had been repeatedly said on earlier occasions both by Factory Commissions and by handloom weavers who wanted to get their own children into the mills:

Every trade he was referring to, cotton-spinning, iron-moulding and mining round Glasgow is fenced round by prohibitions which render it impossible for a person to get into it, except a son or a brother or some new relation of an already existing member; in short, it is the old spirit of monopoly revived in the persons of the skilled labourers, with this difference, that it is not a few merchants but a few hundred or thousand workmen who exclude a hundred thousand of unskilled workmen . . . it is just a system of the aristocracy of skilled labour against the general mass of unskilled labour; and I think the question is far more between one class of workmen and other than between workmen and masters.[11]

Such statements may have exaggerated the degree to which such action was effective, but they do not appear to misrepresent its aims.

Industrial disputes in the Glasgow cotton trade in the 1820s and 1830s were of a violence that has seldom been approached even in that city's bitter history. The masters brought in blackleg labour to break the power of the union and paraded it in front of the organised spinners, apparently in a deliberate attempt to provoke violence. If this was their intention they succeeded. Several non-union workers were killed, blinded or maimed by having vitriol poured into their faces in ambush attacks, like the miserable Mary M'Shaffrey who was mistaken for another girl who had taken a job as a female spinner in a mule-spinning mill where the men were trying to keep a monopoly of the self-acting machines: 'they came up to her and asked "What is your name?" and she made some evasive answer. I suppose she thought they wanted her for some improper purposes; they asked her again, "What is your name?" and she still did not give an answer; and then they threw a cup of vitriol in her face; they never heard her name'.[12]

How well off were these urban cotton factory workers? For a spinner's family a lot depended on a set of more or less fortuitous circumstances—whether trade was booming and employment regular, whether the man's health had yet given way ('all the adult male spinners are pale and thin' said a medical report of 1833[13]), and whether the children were old enough to work themselves, or still so young as to be a burden on the family economy. A spinner in a prosperous Glasgow mule factory especially if he had two or three children in their teens was very well off in the 1820s and early 1830s compared to most of the city's labour force. Such a man might earn £1 a week or more himself, with his children each contributing up to seven or eight shillings a week extra to the family budget. His rented house might be only a 'good room and kitchen' in a tenement with a 'wash-house below' but it would be full of respectable furniture, such as a chest of drawers, a table, chairs, a mahogany bedstead, a well-stocked china-cabinet, and books. A grandfather clock was perhaps the characteristic status symbol of an operative family, having the advantage that the case looked magnificent even if the works were in the pawnshop. The diet of a prosperous Glasgow spinner's family included sugar, tea, coffee, white bread and butter, and good fresh meat three or four days a week. Much less well off were the East of Scotland flax-spinning workers. Many of those at Kirkcaldy, for example, lived 'entirely upon potatoes with a little herring or fat', and others again 'have porridge and milk or beer generally for breakfast and supper, potatoes, oats or barley cake, or broth, or kail for dinner'.[14]

According to James Cleland in 1831 'the wages of cotton spinners did not vary during the ten years preceding 1820, and very little since that period':[15] this would bear out a general impression that British cotton factory operatives as a whole (except in the very worst years of unemployment) improved their lot substantially in the years after 1813 when prices fell and their wages kept more or less to their wartime level. The Glasgow men were inclined to attribute their good fortune to the efforts of their union. In the flax-spinning trade of the east of Scotland wages were never so high and labour never so well organised: in 1833 earnings appear to have been approximately twenty-five per cent below those in cotton.[16]

For the spinner's wife work at the factory usually ended with marriage. 'Spinners almost always marry young', said Sir David Barry, 'and select girls from seventeen to twenty-two, who immediately quit the mill on being married'.[17] Of the female labour-force in cotton and flax factories investigated in 1833 two thirds were under twenty-one years of age, a quarter were aged between twenty-one and thirty-one, and a mere eight per cent were over thirty-one. Among the men fifty-seven per cent were minors, seventeen per cent were between twenty-one and thirty-one and a quarter were over thirty-one.[18] Once married, the girls bore many children—seven or eight apiece, according to detailed medical reports from Deanston and Catrine villages, and the situation was no doubt the same in the towns.[19] Many observers thought that factory families were large mainly because wages were high and parents were not afraid to have children when they knew they could contribute relatively early to the family income. Certainly

414

as long as the husband was in good health the wife was likely to be well off, and if through the chronic illnesses that dogged many mule-spinners the women then had to face long years as the wives of invalids and ultimately as widows, a clutch of teenage children could be a precious support.

Nevertheless in many respects the family life of the factory workers must have seemed bizarre to the rest of the labour force, and especially to those accustomed to the traditions of domestic industry. Instead of having their husbands working alongside them in the home, the wives never saw them on weekdays between dawn and dusk. Instead of bringing their children up in their own houses within the fixed frame-work of family relationships and parental discipline, they pushed them off to the factory at the age of ten or eleven (if not before) and never saw them either for the whole day's length. It is true that in mule-spinning factories children often worked directly under their fathers or other close kin, but even where this was the case the relationship was different from that in the home. The child saw the father himself subjected to the overseer's discipline, and discovered that his own earning power was not related primarily to what his father taught him about the mule but to his own endurance and uncritical obedience in doing simple mechanical tasks on the factory floor. This was probably one reason why family ties were looser among textile factory workers than in most occupations, a fact to which the middle classes were in-clined to attribute many moral evils. Sheriff Alison believed that three-quarters of the factory girls lost their virginity before they were twenty; and that his blunt allegations of prostitution and promiscuity among girl factory hands were not groundless is shown by the descriptions of life in a Dundee flax mill by John Myles, accepted as authentic at the time.[20]

It was partly because the middle classes felt that children could not be adequately protected in the mills against vicious conditions and the avarice of unscrupulous employers that the first statutes regulating the hours and conditions of labour related to minors in cotton factories. The Health and Morals of Apprentices' Act of 1802, concerned only with pauper children in the waterframe mills, restricted their hours of work to twelve. The Factory Act of 1819, also applying only to cotton mills, prohibited the work of children under nine and did not permit any child under sixteen to be worked more than twelve hours a day. The major statute, however, was the great Factory Act of 1833, which provided for wholetime paid Government inspectors to go round the factories to enforce the legislation. It also declared that no child under nine should be employed in any textile mill of any description or work there for more than nine hours in a day before they were twelve years old. It is often said that the 1833 Act was the first effective one because for the first time it provided for inspection, but in Scotland the fact that conditions were found by the first factory commissioners to be much better in cotton mills where the earliest acts applied than in flax mills where they did not suggests that the previous legislation had not been wholly without effect.

Just how bad were factory conditions for children on the eve of the reforms of 1833? Much of the evidence that was bandied about in the passionate debates of the period was so slanted as to be almost worthless as historical information, but the testimony of Sir David Barry, who was a doctor appointed by the Royal Commission to report in Scotland, made a real effort to give an impartial answer.

At the time of his enquiry few started before they were ten or eleven—though it might have been different a generation before (the commissioner was introduced to one worker, Alexander Crabbe, who had entered a Dundee flax mill when he was four and a half). In 1834, in the cotton industry, out of a sample of 12,000 factory workers he found five aged eight, ninety-nine aged nine and 450 aged ten; in the flax-spinning mills out of 7000 workers he found nine under nine years, seventy aged nine and 245 aged ten. In the two textiles together only five per cent of the total labour force employed was under eleven, as opposed to thirty per cent between eleven and sixteen and twenty-eight per cent between sixteen and twenty-one. So by the early 1830s it was overwhelmingly an industry employing adolescents rather than one employing infants.[21]

On the other hand, all the children, irrespective of whether they were nine years old or sixteen were working a day of inhuman length. Twelve hours was general, fourteen fairly common in the east of Scotland especially, and there were instances in flax mills of even longer hours worked in a trade rush. John Myles wrote a book purporting to be the autobiography of a Dundee operative. Though it was almost certainly fictitious, the fact that it was tacitly accepted in the town as true seems to show that it was based on working-class experience and that he was not grossly distorting what went on in the flax trade. This is what he said:

Hopetoun House, West Lothian. The central block is William Adam's masterpiece

The interior of Mellerstain House, Berwickshire. There is no finer
example of the art of Robert Adam in Scotland

Dr. Joseph Black lecturing: note the ghost of that smile which "began to form on his countenance when he was about to exhibit or relate anything that he considered particularly interesting"

When I went to a spinning mill I was about seven years of age. I had to get out of bed every morning at five o'clock, commence work at half-past five, stop at nine for breakfast, begin again at half-past nine, work until two, which was the dinner hour, start again at half-past two, and continue until half-past seven at night. Such were the nominal hours: but in reality there were no regular hours, masters and managers did with us as they liked. The clocks at the factories were often put forward in the morning and back at night, and instead of being instruments for the measurement of time they were used as cloaks for cheatery and oppression. Though this was known amongst all hands, all were afraid to speak.[22]

Two breaks in a day were normally allowed to permit the workers to eat (there were, of course, no factory canteens, but they brought food with them and were sometimes allowed to eat it on the premises). A six day week was worked, and there were generally two days holiday in the year apart from Sundays.

For this toil the children were paid better than they would have been in any outside employment at the same age: in the cotton trade a girl of eleven could easily earn 3/8d. a week (twice the cost of the family's house rent), and double it before she was twenty; boys' wages were higher still (girls outnumbered boys by almost two to one in cotton factories and three to one in flax mills). Nor was the work itself onerous, in so far as it demanded little more than simple repetition of physically light tasks. Even the length of the working day could be parallelled in several other occupations, including handloom weaving carried on in the home. What made work in the textile mills so peculiarly grinding was that throughout these long hours the children had no opportunity of sitting down, of breaking off for play or relaxation or of allowing the attention to wander. They had to become extensions of the machine itself: Sir David Barry deplored as the worst feature this 'undeviating necessity of forcing both their mental and bodily exertions to keep exact pace with the motions of machinery propelled by an unceasing, unvarying power . . . their attention is obliged to be as unremitting as the motion of a steam engine.'[23]

But it was John Myles, again, who told from Dundee experience to what misery and suffering this could lead:

One poor boy . . . was carrying an armful of bobbins from one flat to another. When ascending the stair he sat down to rest himself, as his legs were sore and swollen by incessant standing. In a few moments he was fast asleep. Whilst enjoying this stolen repose the master happened to pass. Without the least warning he gave him a violent slap on the side of the head, which stunned and stupified him. In a half-sleeping state of stupefaction he ran to the roving frame, which he sometimes attended, and five minutes had barely elapsed when his left hand got entangled with the machinery and two of his fingers were crushed to a jelly and had to be immediately amputated.[24]

The medical effects of factory employment on children were, of course, Sir David Barry's particular concern. In some ways he was able to report that things were not so bad as some had feared from the alarming stories circulating elsewhere. In Scotland corporal punishment in the mills was, he said, now practically unknown, which was certainly not the case in England in 1833 and had not always been the case in Scotland. Even at paternal Catrine the employers admitted that the children had been beaten a good deal in the early days of the mill to make them attentive. Barry found no conclusive evidence that the long hours of factory labour caused actual malformation of the bones of the leg, or such distortions of the pelvis that factory girls were unable to bear children without exceptional agony in childbirth, as some had alleged. On the other hand he found that both sexes did suffer badly even in their adolescent years from varicose veins in the legs through incessant standing. He also appended long lists of gruesome and pathetic accidents that had been caused by children getting their fingers or limbs caught in unfenced gearing or being dragged by their ragged clothing into other parts of the machinery just as Myles had described. Their exhaustion through overlong hours and deprivation of sleep undermined both their general health and their watchfulness of danger.

If these aspects of factory life were dramatic and aroused a good deal of contemporary comment and sympathy, more suffering and death was probably brought about by lung illnesses. Less attention was drawn to them because the diseases were wide-spread across the whole of the working-class, yet they were certainly made worse both by bad conditions in the factory rooms and by low resistence due to exhaustion after a long factory day. The risk of pneumonia and bronchitis was particularly high in the wet-spinning flax factories. That of James Kirkland in Dunfermline, for example, was staffed with bare-footed little girls aged from ten to fourteen standing on a dirty, wet, flagged floor, in dresses soaked by the spray from the spindles; the atmosphere was described as disagreeable and vapory, there were no sanitary precautions and no rooms for washing, dressing or eating. The children were 'wet, filthy, draggled and miserable'.[25] The risk of tuberculosis and industrial silicosis was greatly increased by dusty work in the scutching and carding rooms, and the heat and close atmosphere of some sorts of cotton spinning. Boys, according to Sir David Barry, were less well able to withstand the rigours of factory work than girls, and rapidly lost 'the rose chubbiness of boyhood and became paler and thinner than boys not so employed', growing up as white-faced cadaverous operatives. Girls who joined the factory below the age of eleven, were he thought, better able to survive in good health than girls who tried to acclimatise themselves to the work in their mid-teens.

The most pathetic case he reported, however, was probably that of Anne Ward an adult worker whom he interviewed in her slum in Dundee at the request of the local flax-workers themselves.

Married. No children. Very hoarse. Aged twenty-five. Employed in carding room. Began mill-work about six years ago. Has felt her chest much oppressed about nine months ago: threw up a tea-cup full of dark blood with thick spittle this day at two o'clock. Breathing much oppressed with wheezing, is really very ill. If any other employment presented, would leave the mill. Was brought up at country service. Obliged to sit up in bed at night from difficulty in breathing. Earns five shillings per week. Cannot write.[26]

The medical report hardly needs to be glossed. If one side of the coin of factory employment is the adult male artisan whom we have described with his grandfather clock and mahogany bed, the other is the multitude of poor casualties of the system dying like this in jobs they dared not leave for fear of becoming totally unemployed. We can be sure the day Anne Ward finally collapsed the factory manager delighted the heart of another girl by taking her on in the carding-room.

CHAPTER XVII

The Industrial Labour Force - II

1. THE HANDLOOM WEAVERS

In many ways the story of the handloom weavers is the opposite of that of the cotton spinners. The latter began the Industrial Revolution as a despised calling and ended up around 1830 as aristocrats of labour. The weavers began in the 1780s as the most confident and affluent of all groups, and ended up in the 1830s appallingly depressed and pauperised. Theirs is the prime example of the decline and fall of a prosperous occupation in the years of industrialisation.

Yet it would be a great mistake to imagine handloom weaving as a traditionally remunerative occupation. Before about 1760 there was nothing notable about it: the trade in woollens had been stagnant for eighty years, linens had begun gently to expand in the previous decade or two, and weavers enjoyed only a modest way of life. It was the early phases of industrialisation itself that began to give them wealth. The demand for linens accelerated sharply; silks were introduced at Paisley about 1760 and proved an immediate local success; and then came cottons, whose growth so quickly eclipsed all that had gone before. The spinning inventions—waterframes, jennies and mules—produced a surplus of yarns of all kinds at such low cost that employers could afford to pay high piece-rates to the weavers to get it speedily manufactured and on to the market as cloth. Thirdly, the productivity of weavers was greatly increased by the invention of the flying shuttle, which began to be fitted to Scottish handlooms in the 1770s and which immediately doubled the output of cloth per weaver. Further improvements increased this again, and the Jacquard loom which was applicable

420

to certain classes of weaving in linen after 1801 represented another major advance in productivity.

The effects of this new-found prosperity became obvious about 1780. Some weavers still lived a traditional life, like those of Drum-lithie near Stonehaven where John Duncan (later a noted amateur botanist) served his apprenticeship: here every householder in the village had a workshop and a loom, rented a large garden and a croft of land from two to four acres, and kept a cow which was taken out to the common by the village cowherd every morning.[1] The father and sons of the family would weave, the mother and daughter still make linen yarn on the wheel, and everyone take turns at cultivating the croft and cutting peats from the moor in the summer. In the fast-growing weaving towns like Paisley, however, or in suburban weaving villages like Calton outside Glasgow, weavers abandoned all traces of agricultural work and became full-time servants of the loom, obtaining their yarn from factories and not from their womenfolk, but still employing their families about the handloom in the various side jobs that enabled it to be utilised as efficiently as possible. While country weavers maintained their place for several years, it was these town weavers who multiplied many times over as the industrial revolution began. Cotton weaving was almost exclusively a full-time occupation. Andrew Brown calculated as early as 1795 that 39,000 weavers and their apprentices were engaged in this industry, along with another 13,000 women and girls in their families who helped them dress the looms.[2] The numbers certainly increased again fast after that.

Growth on this scale led to an influx of migrants. It is not clear where they all came from; the Irish and the Highlanders, so prominent later, seem to have played only a small part before 1800 and the bulk of recruits at this time must have come from the surplus of the rural Lowlands. Prosperity may also have led to early marriages and large families among established weavers who found both that they could now afford to marry young and that their children could help them at the loom from the age of nine or ten. A youth could know all that there was to know even about fine weaving by the time he was sixteen or seventeen, and the fear of marriage and of children as a burden must, as a consequence, have been diminished.

Viewed over the watershed of the long decline that began after-wards the years of the late eighteenth century seemed like a lost paradise. This was how one handloom weaver put it in 1845:

Then was the daisy portion of weaving, the bright and mid-day period of all who pitched a shuttle, and of the happy one whose luck it was to win a weaver's smile. Four days did the weaver work, for then four days was a week, as far as working went and such a week to a skilled workman brought forty shillings. Sunday Monday and Tuesday were of course jubilee. Lawn frills gorged freely from under the wrists of his fine blue, gilt-buttoned coat. He dusted his head with white flour on Sunday, smirked, and wore a cane. Walked in clean slippers on Monday. Tuesday heard him talk war bravado, quote Volney and get drunk. Weaving commenced gradually on Wednesday . . .[3]

The *Statistical Account* bears out much of this impression of relaxed prosperity, if not the flamboyance. The minister of the Abbey Parish of Paisley, for instance, after saying that an industrious weaver could make from twenty-five to thirty shillings a week, adds that a journeyman who was moderately industrious and careful, 'to which character, indeed, there are but too many exceptions', can live with his family in a manner well above that of 'very decent farmers' in the surrounding countryside.[4] At Coupar Angus, a linen-weaving centre equidistant from Perth and Dundee, the minister commented on the striking contrast between the condition of the people in 1793 to what it had been forty years before:

At present, few servant lads are to be seen in church without their coats of English cloth, hats on their heads and watches in their pockets. At the period just referred to a watch, an eight day clock or a tea kettle were scarcely to be met with. At present there are few houses without one or another of these articles; perhaps one half of the families in the parish are possessed of all of them.[5]

The weavers' life, though doubtless not for all by any means as rosy as the quotations imply, supported a culture of great interest. This was particularly true of Paisley, the focus of the skilled trade where incomes were highest and the opportunities for leisure greatest. Here the weavers joined clubs for playing golf, for curling, fishing and hunting, and formed literary, debating and political societies. They were notorious radicals in politics, many supporting the Friends of the People and the United Scotsmen in the 1790s, though some people thought them too fond of argument ever to take effective action to gain their ends. In religion they were enthusiastic sectaries: 'intensely theological, often religious, well-versed in all the intricacies of Calvinism, severest critics of the ministers' discourses and keenest of heresy hunters, scenting it from afar in phrase or simile, herein only being strong conservatives'.[6] Each weaving town had its own religious bent. Paisley was a centre of anti-burgers and later of baptists, and also had congregations of methodists and unitarians, otherwise rare kirks in Scotland. Dunfermline, originator of the linen damask trade, was also nursing mother of Gillespie's relief church. In Glasgow the seceders were exceedingly strong. Independent congregations of varying degrees of eccentricity were perhaps more liable to spring up in weaving centres than anywhere else in Scotland. Books were fuel for the flames of intellectual contentiousness 'scattered over every available spot in the large kitchen and in great demand after the day's labour'.[7] They read avidly everything from Tom Paine to Thomas Boston, and there was a surprising hunger for the English classics, such as Shakespeare, Milton, Bunyan and Addison, as well as for modern Scottish writers such as Burns, Galt and Scott. In Paisley the arrival of the newspapers was a signal for work to stop until the leading articles had been discussed in the streets.

The weavers produced men who excelled in many walks of life, but most readily, it seems, in such gentle pursuits as botany, ornithology, engraving and acting. Above all the weavers of Paisley excelled as poets: 'it was a common saying at that time that in Paisley every third man you met was a poet'.[8] In the 1790s these included Robert Tannahill, song-writer, Gavin Turnbull, a gifted lyric poet, Alexander Wilson, a writer of ballads and satires who emigrated to America and became the first great ornithologist of the United States, James Scadlock, who became an engraver, and James Paterson and William Maclaren, who like Wilson, were suspected by the Government of being rabble rousers. Their verse was not subtle: it was composed at work and meant to be sung to the strong rhythms of the loom. Surprisingly little of it dealt with weaving, apart from a few well-known fine anonymous ballads and some pieces by Alexander Wilson. Most of it was strongly influenced by Burns and dwelt on conventional poetic subjects. At its best it had, like the verse of Tannahill, considerable direct appeal:

Naw naething is heard but the wind whistling drearie
And naething is seen but the wide spreading snaw
The trees are a' bare and the birds mute and dowie
They shake the cauld drift frae their wings as they flee
And chirp out their plaints, seeming wae for my Johnnie
'Tis winter wi' them and 'tis winter wi' me.

The weavers were not a group among whom one would readily expect to meet successful trades unionism. Working at their own pace in their own homes, it was difficult for them to unite and remain together for sustained industrial action. Nevertheless, their prosperity, independence and strong feeling for radicalism to some extent offset these disadvantages. In Paisley, for example, the weavers in 1773 resisted a cut in wages by systematically picketing and intimidating workers who made up silk and linen for less than the traditional piece-rates, and threatening manufacturers who tried to carry the webs to blackleg labour in surrounding villages. In 1779 a mob of Glasgow weavers demonstrated so effectively against a bill to allow French cambric into the country that the proposed legislation was dropped. In 1787 the Calton weavers in Glasgow rioted again, apparently in an effort to increase their wages. Their methods were more extreme than those of the Paisley men: they smashed the looms and cut the webs of blacklegs, and broke into the warehouses of recalcitrant employers in order to drag out their stock and burn it before their doors. The magistrates, having been routed in the streets with their officers, called in the military. Three weavers were shot dead before order was restored.[9]

All this, however, was desultory and disorganised in comparison to the events which led up to the great weavers' strike of 1812. Twice in the first decade of the nineteenth century the Scottish weavers, along with the English, had petitioned Parliament to regulate some aspects of their trade and especially to fix a minimum wage for labour. In 1803 Parliament partially responded with two arbitration acts that regulated the methods of giving out work and required all disputes to be decided by summary processes before the justices; but they refused the main request to fix a minimum statutory wage. The second petition, made over the years 1809–11, also fell on stony ground. By this time there was a feeling of impending crisis in the trade. Wage increases had not been keeping pace with war-time inflation, largely because the

Edinburgh New Town. The view from No. 20 Nelson Street in the New
Town: gracious living for the eighteenth-century middle class

Leith Harbour in 1822. The middle-class loungers appear to be awaiting the arrival of the passenger boat, perhaps a ferry from across the Forth.

ranks of the weavers were becoming flooded with hopeful outsiders who wished to share their prosperity but who were ready to take lower wages to get work.

On meeting rebuff from Parliament in 1811, the weavers in both Scotland and England made plans to form a union. The Scots took the lead, not because their weavers were the more numerous but most probably because they were the better educated, the more articulate and the more skilled. A federation of affiliated societies embracing the main weaving districts was established. Central committees, composed of representatives from smaller local committees, were formed in Scotland at Glasgow, Paisley and Perth, in England at Manchester, Bolton, Preston and Carlisle, and in Ireland at Belfast. Weekly meetings of delegates were held at union headquarters in Glasgow. The aims of the association were to prevent dilution. They aimed to restrict entry into the trade by not allowing persons to enter without a seven-year apprenticeship, by limiting the number of apprentices any one weaver could have, and by regulating the transfer of journeymen. They also called upon magistrates to use their authority to fix a reasonable rate of wages in the cotton manufacture. Glasgow was chosen as the first local authority in which to fight this matter out, and the men drew up a table of prices for weavers' work. The employers, however, contested the jurisdiction of the magistrate in this matter, and in *Fulton* versus *Mutrie*, a famous leading case before the Court of Session, the judges found that even if they did exercise their power to fix wages, these would be the 'ordinary' and not a 'minimum' rate, so employers could not be compelled to abide by any figure arrived at. The manufacturers rightly took this as a green light to do what they liked, and ignored the weavers' list.

It was this that triggered off the great strike of 1812. The weavers came out from Aberdeen to Carlisle, while Glasgow 'exhibited the appearance of one continued Sunday', and for nine weeks they held out in an attempt to enforce their table of prices.[10] There was little violence, no attempts made to call on English or Irish weavers for sympathetic strike action, and the efforts of English Luddites to spur the Scots into systematic machine breaking were spurned. The strike was finally broken by the unexpected arrest of the Glasgow committee in February 1813: its leaders were put on trial before the High Court of Justiciary, found guilty, and sentenced to terms of imprisonment varying from four to eighteen months. Their crime was taking part in a combination to raise wages—though some serious doubt exists as to whether this could be fairly called a crime under the existing law of Scotland.[11] As a result of this severity, the weavers' union was totally extinguished.

The strike of 1812 was looked upon by later generations of hand-loom weavers as the turning point in the history of their trade. From thenceforth they began to go into a prolonged, agonising and scarcely interrupted decline until by the 1830s enormous numbers were living on the edge of destitution. Witnesses before Royal Commissions of that decade illuminated again and again the degradation into which they had fallen, in standards of nutrition as in everything else:

> I remember in former times that the weaver could sit down to a tea-breakfast, and have his butter and ham like an ordinary furnished table: but the general breakfast now is porridge and buttermilk, and the dinner potatoes and possibly a herring, or any cheap article; as for broth or flesh meat, it is a very rare thing that is in a weaver's house.[12]

Sugar and tea consumption was rising, but it was 'used rather as a substitute, a cheaper substitute for more substantial things, such as meat and things of that kind which they are unable to afford'. Beer consumption fell while that of spirits rose steeply. Weavers had never been abstemious, but a note of desperation crept into their drinking: 'in a great many cases ardent spirits are resorted to, to allay the anxiety and care which poverty produces, especially among females, I believe.' Standards of clothing went the same way. Rags became common-place: 'I have known the situation of a weaver such that he was obliged to borrow his neighbours shoes before he could go to the warehouse'.[13] Weavers gave up owning their own houses, a thing which many had done at Paisley in the good days, and became among the poorest of tenants, crowded into cellars and attics in the most squalid areas of the town. They ceased attending church because their clothes were too bad for them to appear in a respectable congregation. They played a declining part in political activities after 1820, and in literary and cultural life. The education that they could give to their children suffered from the need to save every penny; this was, said some witnesses, a source of more bitter regret to the weavers than any other aspect of their plight. Children in the handloom weavers household were indeed much worse off in almost every way than those in the cotton factories, at least in the opinion of the Government reporter on child labour in 1833.

> The occupation of draw-boys and girls to harness-loom weavers in their own shops is by far the lowest and least sought after of any connected with the manufacture of cotton. They are poor neglected, ragged, dirty children, they are seldom taught any thing and they work as long as the weavers, that is, as long as they can see; standing on the same spot, always barefooted, on an earthen, cold, damp floor, in a close damp cellar, for thirteen or fourteen hours a day. They earn two shillings per week, and eat porridge if their parents can afford it, if not potatoes and salt.[14]

It was no wonder that the children took factory employment when they could escape, for they earned more than twice the wages in better conditions with shorter hours. Nor was it surprising that, when the young adolescents discovered they could easily outstrip their fathers' earnings, parental authority was quickly undermined: 'they threaten to leave the house and take up other lodgings; they consider that they are able to maintain themselves'.[15]

The question as to how far handloom weavers earnings actually did fall between their wartime peak and the depths of the 1830s is not capable of an easy answer. For one thing, incomes fell very unevenly between different branches of weaving. In sections of the woollen manufacture, for instance in broad-loom carpet weaving, wages of fifteen to eighteen shillings a week were still being earned in the 1830s: likewise the damask linen weavers of Dunfermline were only just beginning to go into a decline in the late 1820s. The local historian in 1828 noticed that Dunfermline was one of the few places where artisans still faithfully attended the churches.[16] Again, those who wove elaborately patterned fine muslins and shawls which demanded a high degree of skill and attention were for a long time much better off than those who wove plain coarse cottons and linens. According to evidence before the Handloom Weavers' Commission of 1839 the average earnings of the adult Paisley shawl weaver fell from twenty-five shillings a week between 1810 and 1816, to 21/9 between 1816 and 1820: then to 18/6 between 1821 and 1825, and 11/7 between 1826 and 1830. For the Glasgow gingham and pullicate weaver average weekly earnings fell from 20/9 between 1810 to 1816 right down to 11/9 from 1816 to 1820, then from 10/9 from 1821 to 1825 and 7/6 between

1826 and 1830.[17] Other weavers earned still less: there were plenty struggling on family incomes of five shillings a week in the 1830s who in 1815 would have earned a full pound for the same work. Even though the price of meal fell by about a third between 1814 and 1832, and the price of butter by almost half, the decline in real wages was still enormous.

What was the cause of this collapse? It cannot have been primarily due to the introduction of power-driven machinery, which was not an important competitor of handlooms at all until after about 1825. Even as late as 1829 there was still a much greater capacity in handlooms than in powerlooms, and they were still almost exclusively concentrated in the manufacture of plain cottons. Indeed, far from the powerloom having driven out the handloom, the cheapness of handloom operations due to low wages held back the introduction of the powerloom. If old methods could do the job at such small cost where was the incentive to perfect the new?

The main trouble was gross oversupply of labour. It is not difficult to see why in the first place the trade was popular with incomers. It was so prosperous around 1790 or 1800 that everyone envied the weaver: 'a country lad who could get a loom . . . could, after first web-weaving of two months' labour, earn as much as a well-paid mason, the highest out-door workmen I remember'.[18] But why, as wages fell, did the numbers in handloom weaving go on increasing? Though remote country weaving villages fell by the wayside, all the great weaving towns went on growing in size and squalor without in any way diversifying their economy: the most careful calculations put the number of handlooms in operation in Scotland at the end of the 1830s at about 84,000 (one half in cotton), and all the indications were that this was a considerably greater number than there had been in 1815.[19] Not until after 1840 did the total employed in handloom weaving start to drop.

This continued inrush into a collapsing trade was a symptom of the plight of an adult male immigrating into the towns after the Napoleonic Wars. It was all the same whether he came from the Lowlands, or, as more and more were doing, from the Highlands and from over-populated Ireland. He arrived unused to urban life, undisciplined in factory ways, and too old to be of interest to the factory employer who wanted hands young and deft to train. He was also without other industrial skills: to train him for a craft was out of the question, because at the age of twenty or thirty he would have had to begin on the same level as an eager apprentice of twelve. Besides, the power of the unions was enough in many places to slam the door on his chances of even being considered: 'Every trade finds it has a redundancy and a combination is formed to shut out anyone who is not connected with their own families, and it requires great interest to get in'.[20]

Handloom weaving, however, was very easy to enter. There were no effective apprenticeship requirements, after the failure of the campaign in 1811–12, except in a few areas such as within the bounds of the burgh of Dunfermline where as late as 1828 the workers had managed to hold the restrictions of their ancient guild intact. There were no effective trade unions to oppose dilution, though once again specialised workers could sometimes take action. Galashiels woollen weavers, for example, earning from twelve to seventeen shillings a week in 1839 would not allow the employment in their trade of cotton weavers from Peebles who were used to earning only six shillings. Then again, the art of weaving plain types of cotton and linen fabrics was extremely easy to learn: after a few weeks' practise the whole family could make cloth of a sort, the man using his strength to operate a loom making a plain wide cloth and his wife or young adolescent child moving a second smaller loom producing a narrow fabric. As prosperity fell such two loom families became more and more numerous as attempts were made to stop the collapse of the household budget. Finally, handloom weaving appealed to the immigrant because he could keep his family working around him. For those who feared the factory and its influence on their children, or who felt themselves on the quaking sands of urban insecurity, this was a material consideration. Other unskilled workers who were themselves outside the trade sent their children to learn weaving even in its dotage, either because they could not get them into the factories or because they preferred not to try. In fact, if autobiographical evidence is any guide a stranger's boy was more likely to be brutally treated in a weaver's shop than on a factory floor.[21]

Once in the trade, a newly recruited weaver found himself on a fast-descending escalator. Year by year earnings fell as the host of small manufacturers, the 'small corks', used the pool of labour as a weapon in their bitter competition with one another, cutting prices by cutting wage costs. The men were generally unable to stop these systematic reductions though they continued at Paisley to try to keep to a table of prices. Nothing, however, could conceal their basic weakness: 'other trades . . . being concentrated, can defend themselves very well . . .

we being scattered over the whole face of the country cannot communicate with each other and are easily routed by our masters'.[22] Year by year the weaver himself got older, less able to withdraw from the trade, yet from ageing and under-nourishment less able to gain from it even those meagre earnings he had won in the past, until he was at last reduced to winning little more than a child. The periodic slumps and stoppages of trade at the bottom of the trade cycle, when they occurred then, reduced everyone to the same dead level of suffering. The weavers before 1830 had ceased to contribute to those Friendly Societies and Savings Banks by which they had previously tried to put something by against the day of adversity.

An end to this miserable process did not come until the 1840s, when the pool of immigrating labour began to be mopped up by new activity, especially by railway construction, and the boom in iron and coal. Thereafter the handloom trade, exhausted by poverty and then increasingly desiccated by the growing strength and perfection of mechanical weaving, sank rapidly within a couple of decades to oblivion. No one, save the sentimental, the nostalgic, and the arts-and-craft fanatics regretted its actual demise. Even the latter were misguided in their regret. The mechanical loom was ultimately able to produce finer work than the handloom and the cliché about the industrial revolution destroying the quality of design and execution in craft industries is in this instance (as in a good many others) a romantic illusion.

2. THE MINERS

The coal-miners, the third largest group in the working class after the agricultural labourers and the textile workers, were affected by a set of unique social and economic circumstances. In the first place until 1799 most of them were serfs, a status which they shared in Scottish society with none but the salters. Secondly, the work of the miners was unchanged by any advances in technique. Throughout the whole of the industrial revolution period the only important innovation underground was the introduction (after about 1780 in most places) of a steam engine to drain the mines and sometimes to lift the coals; the miners themselves went on hewing in the nineteenth century with exactly the same tools as their ancestors had done two hundred years before. Consequently the only way the coal-owner could expand production was normally by employing more men. It was this, in the end, which tore the bottom out of serfdom.

In an earlier chapter we traced the miners' descent into servility. In 1701 a coping stone was put on a century of repressive legislation by excluding colliers and salters (alone of all the Scottish population) from the Scottish equivalent of Habeas Corpus. Thereafter it only remained for a series of legal decisions to confirm and strengthen its application. Thus in 1708 it was established that colliers who had escaped from their master as long as eight years before could nevertheless be brought back to work for him as serfs. Even running away to serve His Majesty's Royal Navy did not solve the workers' problem, for, as the tutors of the Duke of Hamilton once wrote to a sea captain, asking him to return a boy from the mines, 'it is contrary to the laws of this realm to keep any man's bond-servant without a certificate from his master or a testimonial from a judge'.[23] In 1762 it was established that the coal owner was entitled to move his ascripted colliers to any mine where he had work for them, and they had no right to refuse to go. In 1769 it was found that a lessee, who hired the men with the rest of the equipment to work the mine, could also move them about like pit-ponies. It must have been something like this that lay behind the following letter, struggling with grammar and spelling, which was addressed to Lord Grange about 1750 from six colliers who had taken work in a neighbouring pit while his own was temporarily closed down.

Humbly sheweth—
That we are all your Lordship's servants and is willing to serve your Lordship when that you have work for us but . . . at the tyme is at Pinky under Mr Robertson and . . . at the time John Birel overseman to the Duke of Hametoun is hard upon us in stoping us of bread where we now are be lifting us out of this work to place us in the said Dukes work at Bowerstouness, And now the workmen that is there sweares that up, that we go to that work that they shall be our dead. And now we humbly beg that you out of your clemency and goodness will keep us from goeing to that place where our life will be in so much danger and we your lordships humble petitioners shall ever pray.[24]

The servile tone (it can be matched by a serf of Sir James Wemyss of

Bogie who described himself as 'Sir Jeamses faithfull and most obedient salter and servant whill I am'[25]) was appropriate to a master who had ferocious powers of corporal punishment. The Royal Commission on Mines in 1842 found a very old man of 81 who had begun to work for Lord Grange in 1770:

> Was first yoked to the coal work at Preston Grange when I was nine years of age: we were then all slaves to the Preston Grange laird. Even if we had no work on the colliery in my father's time we could seek none other without a written licence and agreement to return. Even then the laird or the tacksmen selected our place of work, and if we did not do his bidding we were placed by the necks in iron collars called juggs and fastened to the wall, or 'made to go the rown'. The latter I recollect well, the men's hands were tied in face of the horse at the gin and made run round backwards all day'.[26]

It was not literally true that the men were slaves. 'They had' said Adam Smith 'privileges which slaves have not. Their property after maintenance is their own, they cannot be sold but along with the work, they enjoy marriage and religion'.[27] They earned wages, and at Rutherglen in 1747 they even established their right to vote as burgesses in a town council election. It was also the case that, in theory at least, they put themselves into servitude by a voluntary bond, either by working as adults for a year and a day in a colliery or by accepting a present, 'arles', in return for an oath to serve. Another note in the Prestongrange record says:

> 24 December 1748. Then were entered and bound to the coall works William and Helen Taits by giving each of them a pair new shoes on earnest at one shilling nine pence per pair, which was booked in the oncost bill of this date.[28]

Children were drawn into servitude by 'arling' at the christening (a device of doubtful legality) or by their parents signing documents like that by which William Kennedy at Bogie in 1733 obliged 'me and my heirs duely and thankfully to serve the said Sir James Wemyss, heirs and assigneys whatsomever in the station of coallier all the days of our lives'.[29] This last example, if it was really enforcible in law, was tantamount to signing away the liberty of generations unborn. In practice serfdom almost invariably was hereditary, in the sense that sons followed fathers whatever the niceties of the law.

Even in the eighteenth century, however, there was probably never a time when every collier was a serf. High wages are one indication; if the masters had absolute control over the whole labour force earnings would surely have been pared down to subsistence level, whereas in fact hewers' earnings were consistently two or three times as high as farm servants wages and showed a tendency (though they varied very greatly) to increase from about six shillings a week early in the century to eight shillings or more in the middle, then to twelve or thirteen shillings around 1770 and fifteen shillings or more around 1790.[30] Furthermore there is substantial evidence of labour mobility. Serfs ran off to other mines, especially from the East of Scotland to the West, which would be hard to explain if they were simply exchanging one bondage for another. One owner in the Edinburgh area advertised for free colliers in 1743, offering his men liberty to leave on a week's notice, and agents openly recruited colliers for the Newcastle field from around Glasgow in 1755 without any consciousness that they might be thereby breaking the law.[31] It is indeed possible that serfdom was less deeply engrained in the newer coalfields of the west than it was in the east. It is noticeable how many of the worst examples of oppressive conditions consistently come from Fife and the Lothians. The coalfield of the East of Scotland, producing indifferent fuel and geologically difficult to work, was exposed even on its home market to severe competition from the very much better endowed coalfield of Northumberland and Durham. Possibly the only way Forth coalmasters were able to survive was by exploiting their labour to a degree unparallelled elsewhere in the United Kingdom.

The first initiative towards emancipation was taken by the colliers themselves. In 1762 there were reports of disturbances, and of the masters meeting together in Edinburgh to take steps to maintain serfdom. In 1770 a West India negro brought to Fife as a slave by a returned colonial adventurer applied to the Court of Session for his liberty, his case being supported by funds raised by the local colliers, salters and farm-workers. His master died, however, before a decision was reached, and thus ended what had obviously been regarded as a test case applicable not merely to negro slavery in Scotland. In 1772 a decision of the English courts ruled that on English soil no man could be deemed a slave.[32]

All this, of course, made the position of the masters in Scotland increasingly difficult to uphold, and many of them were becoming doubtful even of the economic benefits of serfdom to themselves in view of the need to obtain abundant recruits for an expanding industry. In 1774, therefore, they placed a bill to emancipate the colliers and salters from serfdom before Parliament, declaring that it would both 'remove the reproach of allowing such a state of servitude to exist in a free country' and increase the number of people willing to enter the mines. It made, however, a very imperfect act. Only new recruits were automatically free; all others had to institute proceedings before the Sheriff Courts and even then might have to wait for anything up to ten years before they got their liberty. Relatively few took advantage of the change in the law, the arling of children continued, and masters still prosecuted those who left the work without complying with the statute. It was not until 1799 that an act was passed unconditionally removing the last traces of servitude. Even that was only saved from further qualifying clauses by the representations of some six hundred Lanarkshire miners who paid two shillings each for a lawyer to put their case to Parliament.[33]

To the surprise of the employers, emancipation was followed by no immediate rush of new recruits. On the contrary, wrote Robert Bald nine years afterwards, 'very few solitary instances occur of labourers or mechanics becoming colliers',[34] and many miners seized the opportunity to join the army or take labouring jobs on the surface at less than half the wages. Hewers' wages rose to a peak of about twenty-three shillings for a five day week during the Napoleonic Wars.

With peace and demobilisation after 1815, together with accelerated Irish immigration, the manpower shortage began to ease. Despite rapid expansion within the industry in the 1820s and early 1830s the miners were on the defensive to keep up their real earnings. From 1817 onwards organised unions appear in many places, especially in the western counties of Ayrshire, Lanarkshire, Renfrew and Dunbartonshire fighting wage reductions, limiting output to maintain the price of labour, and in some places trying to operate a closed shop to keep out strangers. The owners freely retaliated by importing Irish blackleg labour, which began a tradition of bitter racial and religious hatred that marred life in the West of Scotland throughout the nineteenth century and is not dead today. In 1824 there was a terrifying incident during a strike in Midlothian in which a party of blacklegs was ambushed underground and had their ears severed.[35] How far the unions succeeded in arresting the fall of wages is another matter: the evidence is contradictory and miners' earnings are always hard to calculate, but it looks as though hewers were not, by 1830, taking home more than between ten and sixteen shillings a week. On the other hand, it was repeatedly said that they did not work much above eight days in the fortnight, which was a shorter week than in the days of serfdom.

At all times, however, the condition of a mining community depended a great deal on other things than personal liberty and the rate of wages. How the wages were paid was one consideration; even before the end of the eighteenth century many Scottish mines were operating a 'sutlery' or truck system, by which workers were allowed to draw what goods they needed from a company store against future payment of wages. Since the credit allowed was at first liberal, and the price of the goods extortionate, the miners rapidly fell into debt to the shop. Then when pay-day came round, the men found that they were given little or no money into their own hands—their old debt was simply paid off by a paper transaction, and permission given to them to live upon tick for another term. They thus found it impossible to attempt to save up money, or to shop around for cheaper goods, or in some cases even to leave their employment. A web of debt held the worker like a fly, and the spiders were only too willing to pump whisky and beer into their customers to keep them in a state of still greater and more supine paralysis.[36]

A lot of the comfort in a miner's family also depended on whether or not the collier's wife was obliged to work below ground. In the West of Scotland the custom, if it had ever been widespread, was certainly abolished before 1800. Any women employed at these collieries were either given surface jobs or work on the farms that some companies maintained to provide for their horses. Consequently the miners' homes were comfortable: the Factory Commission reporter of 1833, for instance, described the colliers' houses he visited in Glasgow as 'usefully and cleanly furnished with deal tables and chairs, box beds, plenty of fuel, and warm food—flesh meat two or three times a week' ready for the man on his return from work.[37] The Earl of Dundonald shortly before 1793 abolished underground labour for women at his mines at Culross and combined this reform with the abolition of truck. He reported startling improvements in the condition and self-respect of his men, many of whom were of course still serfs:

435

They carried the taste for the *elegantiorum* of life farther than may be thought necessary; most of them had silver watches, clocks in all their houses; several of them on a Sunday wore silk stockings, tambour embroidered silk vests, with their hair well dress'd and powdered.[38]

Robert Bald the manager at Alloa, writing in 1808, reported similar social changes when horses were substituted for female labour below the surface. He remarked that 'a chest of mahogany drawers, and an eight-day clock with a mahogany case are the great objects of their ambition', and that 'the desire they have of procuring such articles is a great mean of preventing their money being spent in ale-houses and therefore deserves every praise'.[39]

In the East of Scotland, however, it was very unusual for owners to act with the generosity of Dundonald and Bald. Here, until 1840 and beyond, the bad old traditions of the married women working below ground went on as they had done since the seventeenth century. It was customary for the collier's wife or daughter to drag the coal from the face where her husband worked to the foot of the shaft, and then to carry it up the steep turnpike stair to the pithead. Bald described exactly what happened:

> The mother . . . descends the pit with her older daughters, when each, having a basket of a suitable form, lays it down, and into it the large coals are rolled: and such is the weight that it frequently takes two men to lift the burden upon their backs: the girls are loaded according to their strength. The mother sets out first, carrying a lighted candle in her teeth; the girls follow, and in this manner they proceed to the pit bottom and with weary steps and slow, ascend the stairs, halting occasionally to draw breath, till they arrive at the hill or pit top, where the coals are laid down for sale; and in this manner they go for eight or ten hours almost without resting. It is no uncommon thing to see them when ascending the pit weeping most bitterly from the excessive severity of the labour.[40]

He calculated that a woman normally carried a hundred-weight and a half on each journey, that might be repeated two dozen times a day: this was equivalent to climbing with such a load every day once from the surface of Loch Tay to the summit of Ben Lawers, or four times from Portobello to the top of Arthur's Seat. The effect of this on the women themselves was unspeakable: the Royal Commission on the Mines of 1842 is full of harrowing stories of miscarriages and accidents in the mines, and of pictures of ugly and misshapen girls of eighteen. It was generally admitted that a collier's wife was old at thirty, though her husband suffered much more from actual ill-health. 'Black-spit', silicosis, made most hewers invalids before they were forty.

Women's work below ground had a brutalising effect on the home. The wife had to leave about dawn, depositing her smallest children with some old women in the mining community 'who, for a small gratuity, keeps three or four children at a time and who in their mother's absence feeds them with ale or whisky mixed with water'.[41] She returned at nightfall to a cold house, fearfully exhausted, having to feed the baby and prepare food for the remainder of her family as they, too, returned from the pits. The result was complete squalor even in households where the total earning capacity was high, simply because no woman could possibly cope. Thus at Tranent in 1842 the miners kept pigs, ducks and fowls in their houses, drank spirits hard and ran into debt: 'no working man would marry a collier's daughter, so little do they know of domestic duty'.[42] The commissioners saw a house at Pathhead where the parents and seven children lived in a room not more than ten foot by fourteen, the furniture consisting of two old bedsteads, nearly destitute of covering, and some bits of broken crockery. They did not think it untypical.

To some extent this contrast between miners' homes where the wife stayed behind and those where she worked underground may be affected by drawing examples of the first mainly from the start of the nineteenth century. There are signs that for Scottish coal-miners as a whole the decades between about 1790 and 1810 represented a peak in their standard of living which they did not approach again until after 1850. Colliers in central and eastern Scotland who were over fifty years old when interviewed by the Royal Commission in 1842 almost all said that young miners had then been able to afford more and better food than men of the same age and strength could now. Meal, bacon, flesh-meat and whisky had all been cheaper and more lavishly consumed, and in some places men had been able to keep a cow. Now only cloth was cheaper, but 'what is the use of getting fine clothing cheap if our baggies (bellies) be empty?'[43] Possibly the increasing use of the truck system accounts for the increased real cost of food for the miners. The other thing that all the miners complained of was the destitution with which they were faced as they grew older. They were often granted no more than eightpence or one shilling a week by the kirk session from the poor's funds and thereby reduced to begging from their families, or looking after infants for a pittance while their mothers went down the pits. 'When colliers live as long as I have and the work is out of them, they are left to starve', said Robert Young, aged 63.[44] Some employers allowed them free-house room and coal, but there was no certainty even of this.

The main concern of the Royal Commission of 1842, however, was with the labour of children. There is no reason to believe that the conditions they found were new, or that they had originated in the circumstances of the industrial revolution: as far as we are able to judge children had always been widely used, but it was only with this report that the exact nature of their employment came to light.

In the West of Scotland, again, things were better than elsewhere. Only a quarter of the work force there were under eighteen years old, and a mere ten per cent under thirteen, whereas in the Lothians forty per cent were under eighteen years old and in West Lothian no less than twenty-five per cent were under thirteen—a grim shaft of statistical light. Only boys were allowed down the mines in the west: some started work when they were about eight as 'trappers'—opening and shutting the gates underground for coal or people to pass through; at the age of ten they became 'quarter men', allowed to draw their fathers' coal from the face to the pit-shaft bottom where it was (in this region) brought to the surface by machinery. By age of sixteen or seventeen they had become 'three-quarter men', allowed to use a pick and hew for themselves. The length of the working day underground was normally between eleven and thirteen hours, with nothing allowed for meals: these were snatched cold below ground as and when the work permitted.

In the East of Scotland girls as well as boys worked underground, and commonly began when they were only six or seven to face a day of fourteen hours and even more. The labour they were capable of doing almost defies belief: Margaret Leveston at Fordel colliery carried loads of half a hundred-weight at six years old; Jane Johnson at Sheriffhall could carry two hundred-weight when she was fifteen; Janet Cuming at eleven years old, worked daily from five in the morning to five at night, but on Fridays kept going all night until noon on

438

Saturdays. It was mainly girls who were used to move the coal underground, and carry it up the shafts with the women. Rebecca Simpson
at Falkirk, also eleven years old, described how she and her sister drew
a cart with ropes and chains, one pulling in front and one pushing
behind: 'if it is difficult to draw, brother George, who is fourteen
years old, helps us up the brae'.[45] The cart held seven hundred-weight
and they had to run it two hundred yards fourteen times a day up a
steep slope.

Boys in the east generally helped their fathers as hewers but some
who were too young had jobs as trappers, engine minders or pump-
boys. They were not necessarily better off. Alexander Gray, ten years
old, described his job at New Craighall Colliery.

> I pump out the water in the under-bottom of the pit to keep the
> men's rooms dry. I am obliged to pump fast or the water would
> cover me. I had to run away a few weeks ago, as the water came up
> so fast that I could not pump at all, and the men were obliged to
> gang. The water frequently covers my legs and those of the men
> when they sit to pick.[46]

Accidents of all kinds were as commonplace (both for children and
adults) as inquests upon them were rare:

> Brother Robert was killed on the 21st January last: a piece of roof fell
> upon his head, and he died instantly. He was brought home, coffined
> and buried in Bo'ness kirk-yard. No-one came to enquire how he
> was killed; they never do in this place.[47]

Collier work was extraordinarily brutalising. It was not merely
that children acquired, in the words of a schoolmaster at Tranent,
'hellish dispositions' as soon as they went down the pit, nor that they
were almost as totally ignorant as it is possible for human beings to be.
The Royal Commission found children of twelve years old at Loan-
head who did not know where Edinburgh was, and were almost
wholly destitute of any vestige of religious knowledge in a society that
normally regarded this as the most important form of learning.
According to the commissioners, marriage itself came to be regarded
only as a means of increasing earnings. As long as the colliers were
bachelors they had to pay a girl to be bearer out of their own earnings—
a 'fremed' bearer, as one was called who was neither wife nor kin to
the hewer. When they were married their wives not only carried the

coals for them free: they bore them children who, at the age of five, could begin to contribute their bit to the family income. 'I married early, as the hiring of women to bear my coals took away all my profit', explained one miner who had first gone down the pit in 1791. 'Children were and are property, for they are taken down as soon as they can carry coal', explained another who had himself begun in 1782.[48] Outsiders regarded mining families as brutish, unpredictable, clannish and dangerous: in Fife in the eighteenth century there was a prejudice against allowing them even to be buried in consecrated ground like ordinary folk.

The work traditions of the East of Scotland miners were a means of utilising to the maximum every member of a worker's family. This was itself a reflection of a labour shortage that had initially been caused by the horror in which their serfdom was held by the rest of the community. A vicious circle was thus set up which perpetuated itself even after 1799, since the work traditions themselves had by then become so vile that still no-one would willingly enter the trade. It was eventually broken by the humanitarian reforms imposed by Parliament in the middle of the nineteenth century. These ultimately changed the whole framework of the miners' life, until by the end of the nineteenth century they were playing a major part in the working-class movement and were among the most articulate and thoughtful of all working groups.

3. THE WORKING CLASS AND THE RADICALS

The weavers, in their life, culture, fortunes and traditions, bore little resemblance to the colliers: neither bore much resemblance to the spinners, and they and other factory workers had little in common with such traditional callings as masons and smiths. The diversity of the working class is still greater than we have been able to demonstrate in two short chapters. We could, for example, have discussed the lead-miners, a small but most unusual group largely composed of English immigrants and their descendants who lived in very isolated communities under exceptionally benevolent employers: well-educated, articulate, working short hours for high pay and keeping their wives and children above ground, they resembled the weavers rather than the

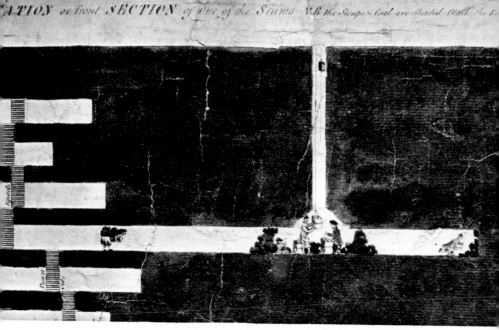

Gilmerton Colliery, Midlothian. The mines in cross-section. Notice the male hewers and the female bearers

Glasgow merchants in the central hall of the Royal Exchange shortly after its opening in the early nineteenth century

Highland Troops in Germany in 1630

Highland Troops in France in 1815

colliers. They resembled them also in the sharp decline of their living standards after 1815.[49] Or we could have discussed the iron-workers at the new foundries, like Carron and Falkirk, where the Royal Commission of 1842 found conditions of child labour not very much better than those in the coalmines: the illiterate boy-moulders of Carron, aged nine and upwards, worked a twelve-hour day (with twenty minutes off for food) at the scorching furnace-mouth: they 'often get burned'.[50] One of the biggest groups in textile manufacture were the women and girls who 'tamboured', (i.e. embroidered by hand) the fine cotton textiles made in Paisley and Glasgow: they were the wives of other labourers, and worked in their own homes at low rates for a putter-out. Then it would be particularly interesting to know more about the great anonymous squad of 'general labourers' who lived in the big towns and used the only saleable gift they had—physical strength—to do any job that offered. How numerous were they? How often were they unemployed? Where did their children find employment? They belonged to the grey underworld of the unskilled who were probably increasing in numbers after about 1810 but of whose life we otherwise know surprisingly little.

To speak of a 'working-class' suggests that all these diverse elements had an underlying unity. The employers appeared to recognise this when they spoke as they did increasingly after about 1780 of the 'labouring classes', or the 'industrious classes'. But did the workers themselves recognise any unity of interest beneath their diversity of form? They did not do so through their trade unions. Those of which we have spoken, the spinners, the weavers and the colliers, like others such as those among the papermakers and the iron-founders were narrowly sectional and aimed as much against their own class as against the employers. They fought mainly to protect a particular trade from invasion by outsiders, which was the ethic of the seventeenth-century guild rather than the ethic of the class war.

Did any unity appear in political form? It was certainly here that the other classes expected it and feared it after 1789, trembling from the example of the French Revolution and its aftermath. Indeed, reading the pamphlets of middle-class writers and the reports of spies, judges and officials in government pay as they debated anxiously whether 'the labouring classes' were 'loyal and peaceful' or 'seditious and disaffected', it is easy to conclude that the urban labour force also saw itself in these unanimous and straightforward terms. But does the history of the radical movement bear out the notion that the workers participated as a class embattled in a common interest?

Before 1830 radicalism in Scotland hit two main peaks—in the years 1792–4, associated with the Scottish Conventions, and around 1820, the year of the so-called 'Radical War'. Of the two, the first was the more important and dramatic. Throughout the 1780s it had been prefaced by a reforming movement of mild character that demanded a measure of electoral change and called for an end to the patronage exercised by political 'managers' through bribery and nepotism in church and state. But these first reformers were drawn mainly from sections of the gentry, with some lawyers and academics, attracted by the campaign of the Yorkshire freeholders in England, together with some merchants and definitely middle-class 'tradesmen' who were primarily interested in burgh reform. Before 1789 it was almost impossible even to suspect anyone below this social level of having any radical political opinions. The populace in Edinburgh and Paisley had demonstrated against John Wilkes, the anti-Scottish radical of London, and rioted against the Catholics in 1779. Neither protest disturbed the philosophy of the establishment.

The first favourable reaction to the French Revolution also came from the middle class: in the summer of 1790, for instance, the Whig Club of Dundee described it in an address to the National Assembly of France as 'the triumph of liberty and reason over despotism, ignorance and superstition'.[51] The following year, however, the reform movement began to take on a new and much more radical tone. In February 1791 Tom Paine published the first part of the Rights of Man: part two followed twelve months later. It was, in effect, a call for universal suffrage, the redistribution of property and the abolition of titles: it was scathing in its attack on the British establishment and enthusiastic in its descriptions of all that had happened in France. There is no doubt that it found ready readers among many in the literate population who had never considered themselves political animals before, and the action of banning it by the Government in May 1792 had the effect of adding to its fame and popularity. 'I know', wrote one Edinburgh journalist, 'that in a small town in the north of Scotland before the proclamation there was just one copy of Paine's pamphlet; and the bookseller of the place declared three weecks ago that he had since then sold seven hundred and fifty'.[52]

Paine had suggested that the road to radical reform was 'by a general convention elected for the purpose'. In July 1792 a reform society was established in Edinburgh calling itself 'The Friends of the People': it was rather less like the English society of the same name (which tended to be Whiggish and have a high subscription) than like Thomas Hardy's London Corresponding Society founded in the English capital the previous year. The Edinburgh society soon had imitators throughout Scotland, and between December 1792 and October 1793 it held three 'general conventions', of which the third and last drew delegates from many areas in England as well as from Scotland. Each convention and its aftermath frightened away more and more of the upper middle class from both the reform movement as a whole and from the ranks of the Friends of the People. The first one was well patronised by a section of the Edinburgh advocates, by Lord Daer (heir of the Earl of Selkirk) and by Lieutenant Colonel Dalrymple of Fordell. Its most ardent literary defender was Colonel Macleod, M.P. for Inverness. The last one was totally deserted by the lawyers, attended by Lord Daer only for a few days and openly renounced by Colonel Macleod. In this sense it might be said that the convention movement became progressively more proletarian as time passed.

Yet the degree to which it can be called a Scottish working-class movement remains very doubtful. The effective leader of the radical wing in the first convention was Thomas Muir, a Glasgow advocate of very great eloquence and power who was sentenced by Lord Braxfield (after a travesty of a trial in 1793) to fourteen years at the Australia convict settlement in Botany Bay. T. F. Palmer, who played a similar role in the second convention and suffered a similar fate, was a unitarian minister from Dundee. The leaders of the third convention, Maurice Margarot and Joseph Gerrard, who were also arrested and transported, were English delegates. The Scottish working class seems to have been conspicuously absent in the leadership. As for the rank and file, they were usually described as 'shopkeepers and artisans'. Undoubtedly the weavers were there in force, and Alexander Wilson the Paisley weaver poet was more enthusiastic in favour of Tom Paine than Burns himself. Otherwise shopkeepers and tradesmen were dominant. Tailors, cobblers, brewers, bakers, tanners, butchers and hairdressers were the Friends of the People. Colliers, spinners, foundrymen, masons, distillery workers, general labourers and agricultural workers were not.

Had the Friends of the People perhaps wider and deeper support from the working classes who stayed outside their ranks ? In the summer and autumn of 1792 there were outbreaks of rioting in many places in the East of Scotland—in Edinburgh itself, in Aberdeen, Perth and Dundee, in Ross-shire, at Peebles and near Duns in Berwickshire; the West of Scotland was relatively quiet apart from a riot in Lanark. All these were officially attributed by government spokesmen to 'an almost universal spirit of reform and opposition to the established government and legal administrators which has wonderfully diffused through the manufacturing towns'.[53] Yet on closer investigation many of these riots turned out not to be about politics at all. In Ross-shire Lord Adam Gordon, Commander-in-Chief in Scotland, wrote privately to the Lord Advocate that the rioters were not in the least disloyal or rebellious: the riots were the result of the peasants' appre-hension, 'too well founded', that the landed proprietors were about to let their lands to sheep farmers and turn their tenants adrift. In Lanark the occasion for the riot was the enclosure by the magistrates of part of the burgh moor which had formerly lain open to the people. In Berwickshire the occasion was unpopular turnpikes. 1792 was also the year of highest corn-price for a decade, and the tumult at Dundee and possibly at other places was related to the scarcity of meal and the unjust working of the corn laws.

Yet, in the towns at least, the political overtones of these riots were not all imagined. Perth, 'a very dangerous place' in Lord Adam Gor-don's estimation, celebrated the entry of the French into Brussels by erecting a Tree of Liberty at the town cross, compelling the churches to ring their bells and the middle-class citizens to illuminate their windows. The hilarious atmosphere was enhanced by other incidents:

> The Duke of Athole went among the mob, and being desired by some of them, his Grace, in a very prudent manner, honoured them and cried out, 'Liberty and Equality'.[54]

At Dundee there were similar scenes, with the same symbol of the Tree of Liberty used and the same slogans shouted. But the Friends of the People, instead of welcoming such demonstrations and providing leadership, unhesitatingly and without exception condemned them. They threatened to expel from their membership anyone joining the rioters. This, combined with the prompt movement of troops and the successes of the Government's programme of repression from 1793, quenched any flicker of revolutionary fire that may momentarily have burned in North Britain.

There were alarms and disturbances on various occasions after 1792, but they all served to illuminate the absence of both unity and political enthusiasm in the Scottish lower classes. In 1794 there was consternation at the discovery of a cache of arms in Edinburgh. At first the government believed they had uncovered a plot by a committee of the third convention to start an armed uprising of the Friends of the People; it turned out to be a one-man plot by Robert Watt, a self-deluded former government spy. He was duly hanged as a traitor, and by a revolting medieval custom his head was cut off and shown to the people. The Militia Riots of 1797 were more serious. At Tranent eleven colliers were killed and twelve more wounded by soldiers firing on a demonstration, and from Ayrshire to Aberdeenshire there were sporadic disturbances which caused much local fright. The cause was a bill to conscript able-bodied males for military service between the ages of nineteen and twenty-three, and the aim of the rioters was usually to burn the parish-registers from which a list of such males could be compiled. The resentment was thus hardly connected with radical politics, let alone with an organised working-class movement. The United Scotsmen, a small and shadowy secret society advocating annual Parliaments and universal suffrage and maintaining contact with the United Irishmen (who had successfully raised rebellion in their own country) operated from 1797 until 1802. As far as can be judged they were a group of genuine proletarian radicals, with strong support among the weavers of Paisley, Perth, Glasgow and Dunfermline. Their ringleader, George Mealmaker who was arrested in November 1797 and received the usual sentence of fourteen years transportation was a weaver of Dundee. Their complete failure to start anything of significance even in the year of the Militia Riots underlined again both the success of the government's repression and the uninflammable character of the Scottish populace as a whole.

A decade and a half of silence followed the extinction of the United Scotsmen. The rise of Napoleon in France was intensely demoralising to British democrats, since it seemed to prove their adversaries' old claim that liberty would lead through anarchy back to tyranny. The war against the Emperor, with the blockade and the invasion scare, rallied practically everyone behind the government on a wave of old-fashioned patriotic enthusiasm. England from time to time in these years was still troubled by quasi-political disturbances, and by machine-breaking Luddites. Scotland was not: the main domestic event of these years, the campaign of the weavers for a regulation of their wages and apprenticeship, culminating in the strike of 1812, studiously avoided either industrial or political help from other sections of the discontented, such as the English Luddites who proffered their services.

After the peace, when it became feasible to relight the torch of political radicalism, it was done from England through two activists, William Cobbett the journalist and old Major Cartwright, who had first begun to agitate for Parliamentary reform in the 1770s and now made a tour of the Scottish manufacturing districts. A network of reform societies sprang up in the towns, much as the Friends of the People had done in the past. History also began to repeat itself when various local radical leaders were charged with seditious activities in 1817—but the courts were no longer as savagely prejudiced as they had been in the days when Lord Braxfield sent Thomas Muir to Botany Bay. One leader, Neil Douglas, a universalist preacher, was acquitted by the jury: 'Among other charges, he was indicted with having drawn a parallel between the Prince Regent and Belshazzar—in many respects only too true'.[55] Two more, Alexander M'Laren, a weaver, and Thomas Baird, a shopkeeper, accused of incendiary speeches in Kilmarnock, were sentenced to six months imprisonment each. The last, Thomas McKinlay, another weaver, was charged with conspiracy, but the case against him collapsed when the principal witness for the prosecution announced in court that he had been bribed by the advocate-depute to testify against the prisoner.

The serious events of 1819–20 marked the second high water in the tide of radicalism. They were prefaced by a grave industrial depression and spreading unemployment, with riots and mass meetings in Glasgow and Paisley that expressed the resentment of many who had fought for their country and returned to find themselves treated as seditious rabble and industrial scrap. At the meeting in Paisley the Cap of Liberty, symbol of French democracy, was placed on the chairman's head. The East of Scotland was less excited: Cockburn reported that 'Edinburgh was as quiet as the grave, or even as Peebles.'[56] A summer of demonstrations in England culminated in August 1819 with the 'massacre of Peterloo', when the Manchester yeomanry charged a peaceful crowd listening to a radical speaker, killing eleven and injuring over 400. The Government, in a panic, passed a code of repressive legislation, the Six Acts, and in February 1820 they arrested twenty-seven members of a Glasgow radical committee on suspicion that they were planning an uprising to take place in Scotland and England simultaneously. Then, on April 1st, a placard appeared on the streets of Glasgow and the surrounding towns, calling for an immediate national strike of all workmen and a rising on April 5th 'to show the world that we are not that lawless, sanguinary rabble which our oppressors would persuade the higher circles we are but a brave and generous people determined to be free'.[57] Nobody knows for certain the origin of this placard: the government asserted it had come from a seditious society, the reformers that it was the work of a government *agent provocateur* intended to spring a trap. On balance it seems as if the government's account is the more likely to have been correct, since Home Office correspondence gives no hint that the proclamation did not take the authorities by surprise. On April 5th the streets of Glasgow were lined with troops: there was a brief encounter in the evening between three hundred radicals and a party of cavalry in which no-one came to harm. Earlier the same day, however, a party of forty or fifty radicals had left the town and marched towards Carron, hoping to rendezvous with a group from Stirlingshire and seize the guns at the iron works: they were halted by a party of yeomanry and hussars at Bonnymuir, and fled after a short fight in which four were wounded. Out of forty-seven prisoners taken in the disturbances, three were executed—one of them James Wilson, yet another weaver, on scandalously slender grounds. Most of the remainder were released largely because of the reluctance of juries in Paisley and elsewhere to find anyone guilty. Agitation subsided throughout the country.

Despite this pathetic outcome several features of the 'Radical War', as the incident was too grandly called, suggest the degree to which the industrial labour force was just starting to recognise a common interest and to respond to a call to act together. The centre of demonstrations had now become the same as the centre of the industrial revolution—Glasgow, Paisley, Greenock and other towns of the west which had generally stood aside in the demonstrations of 1792 and left them to peripheral burghs like Perth and Dundee. Secondly, the response to the strike call seems to have been quite remarkable: contemporaries estimated that 60,000 downed tools, and the stoppage lasted a week. This surely indicates a degree of identification with

447

political radicalism that had been lacking before. Lastly, the leaders appeared to be increasingly proletarian. 'Each successive change of leaders brought forward men of a lower grade, with less of intellect, but still more reckless than their predecessors',[58] was how Alexander Richmond put it, himself an inside witness to what passed. In future crises, such as that which preceded the Great Reform Bill of 1832 and in the Chartist years of 1838–42 and 1848, these features would become gradually more prominent, until at the end of the nineteenth century, with the stiffening ideology of Marxism, the appeal to working-class solidarity began to take on a general social meaning and political significance in ordinary times as well as in crisis.

However, for the period before 1830 it would be wrong to describe the industrial labour-force as 'a working class' unless we are only using the term to describe the fact that they were wage earners and did not own the means of production. Certainly it cannot be used to imply that they normally saw themselves as belonging to a wider or more meaningful group than that of their own particular trade; nor can it be used to conceal the fact that many were struggling to maintain or improve a standard of living in a situation in which they regarded other labouring men to be at least as much a threat as their employers. Similarly it is meaningful to use the expression 'class war' to describe the motives for a great many actions of employers, judges and middle-class writers when faced with the 'labouring classes' whom they regarded as a threat to their own power or property. But it is hardly legitimate to use the term to describe the reaction of the workers to this repression since they simply did not feel the same united hostility towards their social superiors that their superiors felt towards them. This came later: but it is surely reasonable to assert that socialism, when it came, did not so much 'preach the class war' as open the eyes of workers to the extent to which it had already been fought against them for generations. The wonder is they did not see it sooner.

CHAPTER XVIII

Education

1. INTRODUCTION

In 1802 Alexander Christison, a master at Edinburgh High School, published a book entitled *The General Diffusion of Knowledge One Great Cause of the Prosperity of North Britain*. His thesis was that the extraordinary material and cultural progress of Scotland since 1750, while due to a number of causes (he listed the Union treaty, the 'beneficence of patriotic sovereigns, the generous attention of the British parliament and the efforts of enlightened statesmen') was above all attributable to the standards of Scottish education—a system so remarkable in its scope, so liberal in its ideas and so universal in its application that it had become the most precious inheritance which his generation had to hand on to its successors. Christison wrote in support of the contemporary campaign to raise teachers' salaries above the level fixed by the old Scottish statute of 1696: to this extent his work was polemical. An act in 1803 at least partially remedied the original grievance. His opinions, however, were echoed again and again in the next quarter of a century. It is hard to think of any subject on which Scots were so united as this determination to praise and to attribute wonders to the national tradition of education:

> ... the Scots now burst with unrivalled ardour and intelligence into every channel of industry that was laid open to them ... the beneficial change which took place in Scotland in the course of thirty or forty years is such as was never exhibited in the same time in any country on the face of the earth—and on no principle can it be accounted for except that of the superior intelligence of all classes resulting from the instructions for instruction.[1]

The reason for this continuous fervour of feeling was partly that many still felt, despite the act of 1803, that the tradition itself was threatened by inadequate salaries and an insufficient number of schools in the new towns. Many Scots too were inspired to support the campaign of their countryman, Lord Brougham, who was urging upon his fellow Members of Parliament at Westminster the benefits that would accrue to England if she would adopt a system of national education like that already existing in the north. They felt they had good cause to blow a blast on the national trumpet.

The system that gave rise to such self-congratulation had been inherited from the greatest days of church ascendency. Knox holding like Calvin and Luther the realistic view that children were born 'ignorant of godliness', and believing (the words are those of an eighteenth-century presbytery) that the business of education was to prepare children 'for the business of life and the purpose of eternity', had laid down a programme of godly training. There were to be schools in every parish, schools in every burgh 'able at least to teach grammar and the latin tongue', colleges teaching at least logic, rhetoric and languages in every 'notable town'; every child was to be made to attend, and money should be provided so that the poorest who went to the parish schools should if they proved scholars eventually be able to go on to college.[2] The seventeenth century, by proclamations of Privy Council, Acts of Parliament, municipal by-laws and a great deal of energetic effort by the kirk at all levels had brought into being much of what Knox had proposed—periods when episcopalians were in control being scarcely less fruitful than periods of presbyterian ascendency. On parish schools, the relevant statute affecting the eighteenth century was that of 1696, which decreed that a school should be erected in every parish in the kingdom and the salary of its teacher met by a tax on the local heritors and tenants. Should they prove lax, the local presbytery could ask the Commissioners of Supply for the shire to compel the heritors to meet their obligations. Many parishes, we now know, had already achieved this by 1696 (see above p. 88 and below p. 452). As for grammar schools in the burghs, some had been founded before the Reformation and were adapted after 1560 to new educational aims; others were new foundations. By 1700 there were few burghs that did not have some kind of town school where the school-masters' salary was largely met by municipal funds. The five universities too, except Edinburgh and Marischal College Aberdeen, were pre-Reformation foundations that had been reformed after 1560 and were now, immediately after 1690, in the process of being reformed again by ecclesiastical and educational authorities. Education had never become compulsory by law: but it was expected (in the 1690s at any rate) that ministers and kirk-sessions would be able to exert a moral pressure that few parents would be able to resist. Still less had education ever become free: it was left to kirk-sessions to provide the fees for the poorest out of their benevolence, supplemented by a few bursaries and by private or municipal charity.

Indeed, in the eyes of most Scots writing about national education in the 1820s, much of the virtue of the system lay in the financial arrangements. Education was not free: that would have made it like charity, and therefore undervalued by those who received it. On the other hand the fact that it was supported by a tax on heritors in country districts, and out of municipal funds in burghs, meant that it could be cheap, and children could receive at least elementary education for a trifling sum. That the law could be invoked to set up a school and to ensure the continuous payment of a master's salary was reckoned to be Scotland's other great advantage over England, where all schools were either private profit-making concerns or were endowed by the fluctuating streams of private charity, and where no-one could compel a school to be erected or to remain in existence no matter the degree of local need. The benefits that followed for Scotland, according to the apologists, included a love of learning among all classes in the population, opportunity for everyone who had talent to make his way in the world however humble his origin, a relative absence of social tension due to the easy mixing of children of all classes in the schools, and a literate and intelligent working class better equipped both to work productively and to refute the disturbing arguments of the radicals than was the case with its English counterpart.

In fact, by the third decade of the nineteenth century it was doubtful if the national system of education was functioning any longer in the same way as its admirers supposed. *Scotland, a half-educated nation* was the disturbing title of a book published in 1834 by the Rev. George Lewis of Dundee, substantiating its allegations by drawing together and amplifying the evidence of half-a-dozen public and private investigations into the quantity and quality of Scottish education over the previous fifteen years. According to Lewis about one-fifth or one-sixth of the population fell between the ages of six and fourteen, but only one person in twelve was actually enrolled in day schools. As far back as 1818 it had been shown that of 5081 schools involved in elementary teaching only 942 belonged to the publicly-financed national sector: 2479 were fee-paying private schools, 212 were charity day schools and 1448 were charity Sunday schools. Of the children, only 54,000 (a little more than a fifth of those being educated and perhaps a tenth of those needing education) were going to publicly financed schools: 112,000 were in private schools, 10,000 were in charity day schools and 75,000 were in Sunday schools.[3] A still greater blow to Scottish self-respect were the government's returns of 1833/4, showing only a negligible difference in the proportion of the population enrolled in day schools in the two halves of Britain: in England and Wales the figure was nine per cent, in Scotland 9.6 per cent, though it was admitted that there might be statistical imperfections.[4] These hard figures made it very difficult to escape the conclusion that the boasted tradition of the Scottish system had either collapsed over large areas in recent years as the result of industrialisation (the worst records, as one might expect, came from the big towns) or that it had in fact never worked at all in the way its apologists supposed. The task of the historian is to discover which of these two hypotheses is more nearly true. Had there ever been, in any meaningful sense, a national system of education, and if so, had it done what was commonly claimed for it?

2. THE PAROCHIAL SYSTEM IN THE LOWLANDS

One of the striking things about the investigations of the 1820s and 1830s was their exposure of very wide regional differences: the educational experience of the rural Lowlands was very different from that of the rural Highlands, and the experience of the towns was different from both. The story of Scottish elementary schools from 1690 has little meaning unless these distinctions are kept in mind from the start.

In the rural Lowlands the aim of the educators to get one school in every parish, properly financed by a tax on heritors and properly subject to the disciplinary inspections of the kirk, had already been achieved over wide areas before 1696. We know, for example, that at that date sixty-one out of the sixty-five parishes in the three Lothian counties had a school; so had fifty-seven out of the sixty parishes of Fife and forty-two out of the forty-four parishes in Angus. In the north-east similar standards had been achieved in the presbyteries of Aberdeen, Ellon and Turriff before 1702.[5]

Things were not everywhere so satisfactory. It seems, for example, possible that neither in Stirlingshire nor in Ayrshire were there schools in more than half the parishes at the start of the eighteenth century.[6] Returns sent to Glasgow in 1696 from the Presbytery of Middlebie in Dumfriesshire indicated that seven out of the eleven parishes had at that time no settled schoolmaster: 'we are abundantly sensible that the prevailing disorders of these places flow from the want of education as one cause.' The adjacent Presbytery of Lochmaben reported 'very few' teachers, and the Presbytery of Paisley in Renfrewshire was only a little better off.[7] However, by the time of the *Statistical Account* one hundred years later all these gaps had been filled. One school had been set up according to statute in every Lowland country parish. Presumably this work of consolidation went on piecemeal, faster first in one place than in another, with local setbacks and local advances, depending now on the vigour of the presbyteries and now on the resistance of heritors. There is every reason to believe that in those areas where virtually complete coverage had not been achieved by 1700 it had come about by 1760. In other words, the establishment of a net-work of local schools in Lowland rural areas preceded the period of fast economic growth in the countryside, and did not merely happen to coincide in time.

The establishment of parochial schools, however, could not automatically solve all the problems of educational provision. Parishes, even in the Lowlands, were often quite large. In Stirlingshire, for example, the average size was about three or four miles in length by two or three miles in breadth, but Balfron was seven miles long, Falkirk six miles by four, and St Ninians ten miles by five and a half. Even a school in dead centre could mean a long walk for six-year-old legs. Parishes could also be very populous even in 1750. According to Webster's survey, the average population of the twenty-two Stirlingshire parishes (excluding Stirling itself) was about 1600, of whom something like 250 would have been children between the ages of five and twelve; Falkirk, however, had nearly 4000 inhabitants (presumably about 650 children), and St Ninians nearly 6500, of whom over 1000 would have been of school age.[8]

How could the parochial system cope even with these numbers? They would be increased by a half or doubled in most parishes in the eighty years following 1750. One parish school usually contained only one parish schoolmaster, and the law before the nineteenth century made no statutory provision either for the multiplication of publicly-financed schools or for the provision of additional teachers in the face of rising needs. One schoolmaster seems to have coped, on average, with something like fifty or sixty children in a parish school.

The exigencies of this situation meant that, firstly, there was often little pressure brought by the local authority (in this case the minister and the kirk-session) to keep children at school for more than about four years, there was little pressure to keep girls at school even for so long (or to send them at all, sometimes), and great regularity of attendance throughout the year was not insisted upon. Given this degree of departure from the spirit of John Knox's intentions, the average parish school in the rural Lowlands before 1750 probably could, with any luck, get most of the boys through its doors for a short time in their lives. But wherever the parish was above average in extent or in population, and whenever the levels of population began to rise at all rapidly, the shoe-string broke. Other schools then had to be provided, either by charity or by private enterprise, to supplement the national system and maintain even the semblance of provision for all.

The attitudes of authority towards the private school that existed entirely off fees paid by the pupils—'adventure schools', as they were called—was modified by pressure of events. Even in the seventeenth century there had been many places where men and women opened their homes to instruct a few children in reading and writing, and plenty of parents willing to pay a few pence for their services. Inevitably, the kirk-session was suspicious, partly because too many private schools might undermine attendance at the parish school, partly because they feared the teacher might be incompetent or doctrinally unorthodox. They therefore claimed and often exercised the right to shut down any school of which they did not approve. Nevertheless from an early date it was also often recognised that adventure schools might also be able to fill a niche in large parishes where it was impossible for every child to attend one school, and there are even cases (for example at Prestonpans in 1698 and 1699) where a teacher received from the kirk-session the fees for a score or more poor children that had been taught *gratis* in her school.[9] This latter desire to use adventure schools as auxiliaries in the parochial system gradually overcame the itch to shut them down as undesirable rivals, even in kirk circles. In any case, by the middle decades of the century, the kirk-session became virtually powerless to prevent adventure schools appearing when and where their proprietors wished. The last instances of parish schoolmasters complaining that private schools in the area were prejudicial to their interest appear to come in Aberdeenshire about 1748, in Stirlingshire about 1757, and in Ayrshire about 1766: in none of these cases does any action appear to have been taken against the offenders.

Schools and schoolmasters endowed by charity also appeared in the course of the eighteenth century to supplement the work of the parish school. Only in isolated cases in the Lowlands were these the work of the Scottish S.P.C.K., whose great contribution to the transformation of the Highlands we shall discuss later. Many of them were the results of the generosity of landowners, like those of Polmont in 1758 who opened a public subscription in order to provide for a second teacher because 'the number of scholars that for ordinary attend the school of this parish renders the right and careful instruction of these children a task too difficult to be discharged by one man.'[10] Others were directed towards the problems of providing cheap schools for girls, where they could learn to read, but also to spin, sew and knit. Less important than the adventure schools, they were, nevertheless, also locally useful supplements to the parochial system.

Although educational historians have sometimes deplored the advent and multiplication of adventure schools, which almost inevitably had less well-qualified teachers and lower educational standards than the parish schools, they were in one sense a measure of the success of the kirk and the parochial schoolmasters in persuading the peasantry that education was desirable. People increasingly came to want their children to read and write even if the parochial school was too distant or too full to go to, so they were willing to pay for private education nearer at hand. It is difficult to see how the desire for learning, once it had been aroused, could have been continuously met in a situation of rising population without the great expansion of adventure schools. Between them, the parochial schools and the adventure schools of the Lowlands were able to maintain a rural society in which almost everyone seems to have been able to read and write from at least as early as the mid-eighteenth century, despite all the subsequent social demographic and economic changes before 1830. That was a remarkable achievement, certainly not parallelled in England, and probably parallelled in very few societies anywhere in the world, except for Prussia, parts of Switzerland and a few Puritan areas in the United States.

What was education like in an eighteenth-century country school? Inevitably we cannot say as much about the adventure schools as about the rest, since their records have not normally survived. The 1826 returns to Parliament on the state of education in every parish, however, show that virtually all taught writing and arithmetic in addition to English reading, but only exceptionally offered Latin, mathematics, book-keeping or other subjects.[11] This was clearly a narrower curriculum, and one offered by less well-qualified teachers, than that available at the parish schools, but standards were not by any means always negligible. John Murdoch, for example, opened an adventure school in the Ayrshire parish of Alloway in 1765, and taught Robert Burns to read and write, with demonstrably excellent results. James Beattie, an Aberdeenshire cobbler, taught without a fee in the parish of Auchterless for over sixty years and left a host of grateful pupils to keep his memory green. 'If ye dinna think o' the meanin' ', he used to say to his boys, 'hoo can ye be richt?'[12]

The parish schools, of course, taught reading, writing and arithmetic, but they also had a long tradition of teaching at least some of the children Latin. As far back as 1690, forty out of the forty-two schools in Angus, nineteen out of the twenty-one schools in East Lothian and forty-eight out of fifty-five schools in Fife were occupied by masters qualified to teach Latin. The returns of 1826 show that the position was then not very different, and indicated that before 1803 it had also been normal to have facilities to teach Latin.[13] The list of subjects that might be taught in parish schools in the first quarter of the nineteenth century was indeed quite a long one. Many schools were able to teach some kind of applied or theoretical mathematics slightly more advanced than arithmetic. Book-keeping, land-surveying, geometry and, sometimes, algebra, were not unusual, and had sometimes been taught in the schools since 1760 or 1780. Geography, Greek and French were the other three subjects most commonly available, although they were much more often among the master's qualifications rather than among the subjects actually taught. However, the number of children who ever took any subjects apart from reading, writing and arithmetic in a parish school was probably always a very small proportion of the total. The first proper investigation into this question was made in 123 parochial schools in the north-east in 1832. Of 7700 children enrolled, ninety-six per cent were being instructed in primary 'English', fifty-one per cent received additional instruction in writing (composition as well as penmanship) and thirty per cent were taught arithmetic as a special subject—but only five per cent learnt Latin and two per cent learnt geography and 'mathematics'. Of the total number, only thirty-six were learning Greek and only two were learning French.[14] This is probably typical of the traditional rural situation, not representative of decline from some previous high standards.

There was also the matter of religious instruction. In the late eighteenth and early nineteenth centuries moral and religious teaching still formed a crucial part of the life of every parish school. The kirk-session, assisted by the heritors, still carried out inspections, and examined the children in their catechism. The Bible was still part of every child's first reading, and in many schools was almost the only reading book available until well into the nineteenth century. 'The easy and ever-repeated reading of that sacred classic of the whole world, the Bible, for instance, will make any capable person not only "wise unto salvation" but also lettered, cultivated, refined beyond "the guess of folly".'[15] Apologists were anxious to emphasise that the Scottish system of education was beneficial to social order precisely because the masters took such pains to instil into their pupils the basic precepts of Christian morality. Nevertheless, however much the schools might seem to be carrying on an old tradition of Calvinist instruction, the position had really changed basically since the late seventeenth century. For one thing, the kirk-session itself was no longer composed of men obsessed with the niceties of theological belief. They were more likely to express approbation of a child's handwriting than of his explanation of the doctrine of grace. For another, the schoolmasters, themselves under the more liberal influences of the late eighteenth century, had given up various practices on which an earlier age had laid great importance—like ensuring that every child went to church on Sunday in order to be able to open the lessons on Monday morning with a close cross-examination of his class to the meaning and content of the sermon. In 1675 the Synod of Aberdeen had instructed its presbyteries to find out whether each master

. . . caus all his scollers learne the catechisme. If he require them to learne an forme of prayer for morning and evening, and a blessing before and after meals. If he chastise them for cursing, swearing, lying, speaking profanietie; for disobedience to parents and what vices that appeares in them.[16]

It had not bothered to ask any other questions (apart from one about the teacher's salary) concerning the schools under its care. It is not surprising, comments the historian of Aberdeenshire education, 'that when a boy of the seventeenth century got hold of Volume I of Ellon Kirk Session minutes, and indulged his childish urge to scribble, he wrote, "The fear of the Lord is the beginning of wisdom".'[17] The main difference between the late seventeenth century and the late eighteenth is that at the latter period neither the church nor its scholars thought the fear of the Lord was also the sole end of wisdom.

In some other ways parochial schools perhaps changed rather less between 1690 and 1830 than we might suppose. Corporal punishment was widespread at the beginning of the period. Possibly its use diminished: Thomas Somerville, speaking in 1814 about the late 1740s said that school discipline was 'universally more rigorous than it is now' and equated its decline with the general amelioration in the upbringing of children since that date.[18] There were writers at both periods who pleaded for the tawse to be used as sparingly as possible. Complaints about the mechanical methods of teaching, and of children repeating parrot-wise what they could not understand also recurs as a theme. Perhaps the most determined efforts to impart more understanding to the learning process came in the latter half of the period, but it is hard to know if they were any more successful than before.

Fees, at least, rose very little between 1690 and 1803: in the 1790s in Aberdeenshire the usual rate of 1/6d. a quarter for reading and writing and two shillings a quarter for Latin and arithmetic. The *Statistical Account* suggests this was about in line with practice in the rest of the country. After the act of 1803 adjusting schoolmasters' salaries they rose by fifty per cent, or even doubled: it was in any case a time of inflation, but when prices and wages fell again after 1813 school fees stayed where they were, leaving the real cost of a parish school education higher than it had been before the Napoleonic Wars. To judge by the returns of 1826, fees at adventure schools kept very much in step with those in parochial schools, although the teachers in these schools were completely dependent on what they received from the children and did not, like the parish teacher, receive a salary from the heritors. It was, of course, always open to the kirk-session to pay the fees of any poor children whose parents could not afford to send them to school, and it was often done where there were orphans or the children of orphans: but most country parents regarded the acceptance of parish charity in this sense as degrading for the whole family, and would put up with considerable hardship for themselves in order to afford the fees for their children.

Few, however, could afford to allow their children to remain at school when there were opportunities for them to contribute to the family income by working in the fields—attendance at haytime and harvest in particular, was always extremely thin. There was, indeed, a chronic problem of absenteeism: 'there is no disadvantage under which country parochial schools more generally or more grievously labour.'[19] In 1832, for example, it was estimated in the counties of Aberdeen, Banff and Moray, that less than half of the children enrolled actually attended the school for as much as six months of the year, that the average on the roll in winter was fifty per cent higher than it was in summer, and that, although the average age at which a child entered school was $5\frac{1}{2}$ years and the age at which it left was fifteen years, the time actually spent in attendance was highly discontinuous. In one sense the success of the parish school system depended on the under-employment of juvenile labour in the countryside. Had there been more jobs for these age groups there would almost certainly have been fewer children at school.

As for the parish schoolmasters, their standards of living fell compared to that of other members of rural society. There were many complaints that neither their income from salaries nor from fees rose at all in the eighteenth century, despite inflation in the closing decades and even after the state had adjusted the salaries that could legally be paid to them by the act of 1803 their condition was only slightly improved. Many complained that any country craftsman could earn more than they in a year; and more complained of the houses provided for them by the heritors, usually but-and-ben cottages that might have seemed tolerable in the rougher days of the seventeenth century but now appeared as a social insult. A typical comment was one made (during the enquiry of 1826) about the schoolmaster's house at Strachan, Kincardineshire:

It is neither plaster lathed nor coomceiled, is singularly incommodious, insufferably cold, is not dry, and would be deemed uninhabitable by anybody but a schoolmaster.[20]

Many people said that as the relative standard of living of schoolmasters slipped it had become impossible to recruit such good teachers as in the past, and pointed to an act of the General Assembly in 1706 that had recommended that graduates should always be preferred in appointments to vacant schools. It is doubtful if there was much deterioration: the act of 1706 was probably as hopeful an expression of intent as a similar act would have been in 1830, and any falling off in academic quality was probably offset by the fact that fewer teachers in the late eighteenth century and later were impatiently filling in time in the village school while they awaited a call to a parish as minister. Some at both periods found they could not make a living without doing some other job (such as being postmaster or landsurveyor) at the same time. Adventure school teachers almost always had a job—as craftsman or shopkeeper or seamstress—and with them it was often hard to tell whether teaching or this other job was the sideline that kept the wolf from the door.

By any modern standards, of course, the whole system appears to be ramshackle, inadequate and disgraceful, with much of the teaching mechanical, many of the teachers slap-happy with the tawse, with classes much too large, attendance much too irregular and far too little to learn. Yet what was actually achieved by these schools was the construction of a literate peasant society in the Scottish Lowlands that was not merely able to read but apparently loved reading. One writer after another comes out with evidence of this—George Robertson discusses the books the cottar and the farmer kept in his house; Alexander Somerville tells how as a farm worker he was able to borrow or buy the works of Scottish poets, *The Voyages of Anson*, and George Miller's *Book of Nature* (see p. 323 above); the first biographer of Burns tells the traveller not to be surprised when he comes to Scotland because:

However humble their condition the peasantry in the southern districts can all read and are generally more or less skilful in writing and arithmetic, and under the disguise of their uncouth appearance .... they possess a laudable zeal for knowledge ... not generally found among the same class of men in other countries in Europe.[21]

It is difficult not to believe, as so many contemporary commentators obviously did, that the stimulus of education did give the rural population the tools to make the best of the remarkable opportunities that opened in eighteenth-century Scotland, not often by making them bookish, or by encouraging them to go on to higher education, or even often to desert their agricultural calling, but by opening their intellectual horizons and thus breaking the mental cake of irrational custom, so that they could make the very best of the agricultural revolution. It was not without irony that a system of schools originally intended to make the population fit citizens of a Godly Commonwealth came instead to fit them for the role of pioneers in a successful materialist state.

3. CHARITY IN THE HIGHLANDS

For geographical and historical reasons the parochial system operated beyond the Highland line under enormous obstacles that had no counterpart in the Lowlands. Firstly, most of the Highlands had only recently been brought under the curb of the state, and therefore had no older tradition of schooling on which to build. There were very few schools in the Highlands before the last quarter of the seventeenth century, and very few Highlanders who saw the point of attending one. Secondly, Highlanders spoke Gaelic, a language that relatively few ministers and teachers could understand. There were virtually no Gaelic books; though a translation of the Psalms was published in 1690, there was no translation of the New Testament until 1767, and none of the whole Bible until after 1800. It is said, however, that Tom Paine was available in a rough Gaelic translation by 1792.[22] Thirdly, Highland parishes were of immense size. Glenorchy was sixty miles long and twenty-four miles wide. Kilmalie was sixty miles long and thirty miles wide. These were extreme, but Buchanan on the very edge of the Lowlands in Stirlingshire was eighteen miles by nine, and Drymen in the same county, nine miles by seven. Given that parishes were often more or less evenly populated and without any major village concentrations, it was almost impossible for a single fixed conventional parochial school, the minimum that heritors were obliged to finance, to make any impression at all on the massive problem of illiteracy.

The Church of Scotland and the heritors did in fact make considerable efforts to meet their responsibilities. There is reason to believe that
by the middle of the eighteenth century less than a fifth of Highland
parishes were without some kind of school supported by a tax on
landowners and that fifty years later virtually all the parishes had such
a school. Furthermore, some parish authorities realised that to establish
a single school in an enormous parish was indeed of very little practical
use, and modified the rules according to local need. Thus at Inver-
chaolain in Argyll in 1755:

> There is no *parochial* school, nor would such a school if we had one
> be of use to above a fifth of the parish . . . hence it has come about
> that usually we have had five little schools kept about six months in
> the year.[23]

This was a parish with a populous coastline twenty miles long and
the rest of the people in inland glens separated by high mountains. A
solution of this kind—to divide the legal provision among several
institutions, or even to maintain several small schools by persuading
the heritors to pay more than they were strictly obliged in law—was
sensible in its way, though obviously the standards at any one school
were likely to be lower than in the orthodox parochial schools in the
Lowlands. Shortly after the middle of the eighteenth century, however,
it was decided for bureaucratic reasons to make the heritors concentrate
on paying a full salary for one school and to leave the provision of
additional schools in the parish to charity.

By that time the Highlands had become the main objective of the
charity school movement. This had begun in the first decade of the
century through the enthusiasm of a group of gentry, 'men of knowledge, solid piety and estates'[24], who had been moved by the illiteracy,
ignorance and superstition of the Highlanders, concerned by their
abiding Jacobitism, and alarmed by the current success of Catholic
missionaries in winning converts, while the Church of Scotland was
still in disarray throughout the north over the breach between Presbyterians and Episcopalians. In 1700 the Catholics were said to have
six priests on Skye, there had been a 'serious landslide to Rome' along
the Great Glen, and in 1712 a secret seminary had been set up in the
Braes of Glenlivet to teach the sons of the local gentry who could not
go abroad for instruction. At the same time the group was very
impressed by the information they were receiving from London about

the work of the English S.P.C.K., founded in 1699, and of the prevailing belief of English reformers in charity schools as the panacea for social ills.

The upshot was the foundation in 1709 of a Scottish Society for the Propagation of Christian Knowledge, an imitation of the equivalent body in England with whom it remained in close correspondence, but quite separate from it in organisation, and Presbyterian in creed. Its form was that of a non-profit making joint stock company with a patent from the Crown. Its purpose was to found schools 'where religion and virtue might be taught to young and old' in the shape of reading, writing, arithmetic and religious instruction. Since knowledge of Gaelic was reckoned to be one of the roots of the superstition and barbarity they were pledged to fight, its use was forbidden until 1766, when a more realistic policy prevailed: it had been reported that the children were mouthing scriptural passages in English which they could not understand. Nevertheless, almost all the Highland charity schools remained schools for learning English: the Highlanders themselves realising the advantage their children had in the external world if they could speak and read English had little interest in sending their children to schools that did not do most of the teaching in that language.

From the start the General Assembly backed the society with enthusiasm and money. The state gave it legal backing and moral support on the understanding that affection for the Hanoverian succession would form a conspicuous part of its moral teaching. Unfortunately it failed to provide any direct funds. Consequently the Scottish S.P.C.K. remained a poor society, until the last decade of the century never receiving more than £2000 a year for its work. Nevertheless, the number of schools erected multiplied rapidly: there were five by 1711, twenty-five by 1715, and no fewer than 176 by 1758, teaching nearly 6500 pupils. By 1808 there was no great increase over mid-century, only 189 schools, but the number of pupils attending had doubled to 13,000. This was probably about the peak. Not all these schools were in the Highlands, though; there was important work done by the society in Orkney, Lowland Caithness and Banff and eastern Aberdeenshire, for example, and even schools for a time in Fife, Edinburgh and the Borders. Under a second patent obtained in 1738 the S.P.C.K. were also empowered to establish spinning schools, which also taught reading. By the end of the century there were nearly a hundred of these, with an enrolment (mainly girls) of about 2300.

Thereafter the torch of charitable enthusiasm began to pass from the S.P.C.K. to other societies. The Gaelic Society of Edinburgh, alarmed by continuing stories of illiteracy in the remotest parts, was formed in 1811 and began to establish schools in the north, followed within a few years by the Gaelic societies of Glasgow and Inverness. These schools usually tackled the problem by becoming 'ambulatory', moving from place to place round the parish at intervals of six months or so when they had taught some of the children the elements of reading. They were also distinguished for a very earnest moral purpose, grimmer, by all accounts, than that of the S.P.C.K. In 1826 the Gaelic Society of Inverness carried out a survey of the total educational facilities in the Highlands and Islands, including in this definition Orkney, Shetland and all the shores of the Moray Firth as well as more properly Highland parts. They found almost 500 schools in existence, teaching almost 25,000 children. About one third were parochial schools, one quarter S.P.C.K. schools, and the remaining forty per cent or so attached to the three Gaelic societies.[25]

The general picture of Highland education, therefore, appears to be of a steadily increasing number of school places, of which much the largest proportion was consistently provided by charity schools. Against this must be set the fact that population, too, was increasing very fast, especially in the remotest areas where there were still fewest schools. Charity tried hard, but it is doubtful if it did much more than keep abreast of this increase after about 1780.

What did charity do for the children? Contemporaries were inclined to attribute to it a great deal of moral reformation, by which they meant primarily that the Highlanders were losing their distinctive cultural habits. Thus the first historian of Moray wrote in a book published in 1775, but probably written appreciably earlier, about the S.P.C.K.:

The happy effects of this truely pious institution are visible in this Province. Christian Knowledge is increased, heathenish customs are abandoned, the number of Papists is diminished, disaffection to the Government is lessened, and the English language is so diffused that in the remotest glens it is spoken by the young people and in the low country, in Inveravon, Glenlivet, Knockando, Edinkylie, Nairn and Ardersier, where till of late public worship was performed in Irish there is now no occasion for Ministers having this language.[26]

It is much too crude to attribute this erosion of traditional Highland life to the charity schools alone, but reasonable to assume they acted as a lubricant, helping the change to come about more rapidly and possibly making it less painful. It was in any case very much better if when forced to emigrate from the glens the peasants took with them knowledge of the English tongue, an ability to read and a grounding in Lowland values: children with some acquaintance of the southerners' culture did not face the terrible economic and social handicap of those who emigrated knowing only Gaelic and the folklore of their glen.

Many people also attributed to the charity schools the extraordinary Presbyterian revivalist movements that started up in the last quarter of the eighteenth century, and swept like bush fires into several parts of the Highlands that had hitherto been more or less indifferent to religion —Ross-shire, northern Perthshire and, later, Skye were centres of this enthusiasm. It is again too simple to attribute this merely to the S.P.C.K. and its successors, though the emphasis that the charity schools placed on being able to read in order to understand the Bible must have had an effect.

The direct inspiration for the movement, however, came partly from evangelical traditions still existing within the Church of Scotland, partly from the teaching of English evangelicals, and partly from the missionary tours of Robert and James Haldane, whose 'Society for Propagating the Gospel at Home' began in 1798 a campaign of Highland conversion. Though the Gaelic societies, particularly that of Inverness, had some share after 1811 in spreading the movement, it was already alight a generation before they got started. And the psychological harrowing of the soil was done not so much by the schools as by the catastrophic break-up of the material norms of Highland life, from which the people fled towards the compensations of an intense spiritual enthusiasm like leaves before a storm. Consider, for instance, the vision of Hell seen by an early nineteenth-century Ross-shire crofter seer, David Ross:

'There', said the angel 'is a laird who has been driving out his tenants from their farms ... He is now for ever doomed to be alternately bitten by serpents and have his wounds licked over by the fiery tongues of hell-hounds. Poor fellow! Little did he think during his few moments of heartless pleasures and dissipation that he was sowing for himself the seeds of such an eternity of woe!' ...

'This is too terrible a sight for me to look at,' said David, 'Oh! What an empty thing it is to be born to a fortune if, as in this case, he be also born to be an heir of hell! How much better to be born in humble circumstances and not to be trammelled by the accursed weight of riches.'[27]

In Ross-shire, where depopulating sheep clearances began early and were particularly severe, the revival originated chiefly among an illiterate laity and reached an immediate and sustained level of popular fervour. In Argyll, where there were in the period before 1830 few large clearances but at least as many schools there was less evidence of revivalism.

In simpler educational terms what did the charity school movement achieve? The inquiries carried out in the 1820s shows how very incomplete their success had been after more than a century of striving. Out of 400,000 people in the Highlands and Islands only one in sixteen was enrolled in a school: about one-fifth were of school age. In general, only one half of those over the age of eight were able to read, but there were big regional variations. In the Hebrides, Wester Ross and western Inverness-shire only three in ten could read; in Easter Ross, eastern Inverness-shire, the Highland parts of Moray and Cromarty, in Sutherland and in Caithness six in ten could read, and in Argyll and Highland Perthshire as many as seven in ten. In Orkney and Shetland, which were not Highland at all though they had some of the same problems of geographical isolation and diffusion, the figure was nine readers for every ten of population. By contrast, in one Hebridean parish on Harris in the 1790s only one person in twenty had been able to read. Thirty years later the position on the same island had improved —but only to three in twenty. No-one seems to have thought it worthwhile even to ask how many could write or do arithmetic.[28] Their effort had been a brave one, and it had been much better than nothing. But the results fell far below that of the parochial system in the rural Lowlands.

4. BURGH SCHOOLS AND UNIVERSITIES

The Scottish burghs were apparently under exactly the same statutory obligations to provide schools as the countryside: the Act of the Privy

Council of 1616 and the Acts of Parliament of 1633 and 1696 made no distinction at all between urban and rural areas, and stated simply that every parish, wheresoever it might be, had to provide one school and one schoolmaster. In practice, however, burgh schools differed in several important respects from other parochial schools. For one thing, they were almost invariably under the direct control of town council, and supported by the funds of the council, so that the church had little say in how they were run. This was partly because many of the earliest and most admired schools that acted as models for the rest, like those at Edinburgh and Aberdeen, were pre-Reformation foundations that had fallen under secular control during the fifteenth and sixteenth centuries. Other councils were unwilling to have less freedom than they. For another thing, virtually all burgh schools at the start of the eighteenth century were grammar schools, where Latin formed an important part of the teaching: we have seen that at the same period many rural schools were also grammar schools, in the literal sense that they had a master who could teach Latin, but generally speaking the best and most noted of those in every shire were in the towns. The fact that councils were often intensely proud of their grammar schools and wanted to do all they could to boost their reputation over rivals in other towns, combined with the fact that their legal obligation stretched no further than to provide one school for the parish (often conterminous with the town itself) meant that there was a continual temptation to pursue the ideals of educational quality at the expense of the ideal of education for all. Thus a town like Edinburgh could become nationally famous for its educational facilities while perhaps a third of its citizens remained more or less totally illiterate.

In small burghs, however, educational provision compared favourably with that obtaining in Lowland country parishes. Here the grammar school taught reading, writing and arithmetic as primary subjects (probably competing in this with one or more private adventure schools), but also took more boys on to a Latin curriculum than most schools in the countryside. Indeed, boys would often come on to the burgh grammar school from parish schools in order to take advantage of more advanced teaching. In the course of the eighteenth century other subjects were often added: geography was sometimes taught, and Greek; book-keeping became fairly general, and navigation too, if the burgh was on the coast. All these subjects were taught at Dunbar, for instance, in the course of the eighteenth century, and all but Greek were taught at Kinghorn. Wigtown, much more exceptionally, taught French.[29] The population of all these places increased in the course of the eighteenth and early nineteenth centuries, but even in 1830 they were still little more than large villages. Perhaps it was here that Scottish education approached most nearly to its ideals both of being available to all and of being able to offer a secondary curriculum to those who wished it. It is difficult to be sure how generous councils were in this type of community with grants to poor scholars, but there is nothing to suggest that their record compared unfavourably with that of the heritors and the church in more strictly rural areas.

In the larger burghs things stood in black contrast. It was difficult to get any affluent, complacent and powerful council, largely immune from church pressure, even to acknowledge that the crowded and populous parishes under their care needed public provision for universal elementary education. Edinburgh was typical. When asked by the local presbytery in 1706 what schools it supported within its immediate jurisdiction (i.e., exclusive of Leith and the Canongate), it could only instance the High School, where children did not attend until they could already read and write, Heriot's Hospital, with over a hundred places all reserved for the sons of poor merchants, the Merchants' Maiden and Trades' Maiden Hospitals, with about fifty places reserved for the daughters of poor merchants or poor members of the craft guilds, and a single charity school, attached to the Tolbooth Kirk with about sixty places provided free to the less illustrious poor.[30] Yet there were at the time already several thousand children in the area who would either have to remain illiterate or to pay adventure teachers operating outside public control. There were large numbers of these, but it is doubtful if even then they could adequately fill the gap left by the absence of proper municipal elementary schools.

As the city grew and its provision for popular education became more and more glaringly deficient, its conscience was intermittently prodded. In 1758 the S.P.C.K. and the presbytery for once found a sympathetic Lord Provost, George Drummond (the same who helped to found the New Town), and together drew up a memorandum on the state of elementary teaching in the capital. There were, declared their joint report, twenty-four 'English schools', two being charity schools and the rest adventure schools. In the last group, four or five charged fees in excess of 12/6d a quarter, about twelve charged five shillings, four charged four shillings and one charged only three shillings—even the last figure was double the normal charge in a country school for teaching reading and writing. There were also five or six additional schools taught by women, for unspecified charges. The average attendance at the schools taught by men was thirty, with half as many in the others. The conclusion was that only 800 children in the city were being taught to read out of a total of some 3000 'fit to go to school'—probably in this context 'fit to go to school' only meant all the children between 6 and 9 years old.[31]

Edinburgh prepared to take action on this report. The S.P.C.K. agreed to open three additional 'charity working schools', providing reading, writing, arithmetic, spinning and knitting, if the corporation would establish four 'English schools' to teach reading, writing and arithmetic at modest rates, originally agreed at two shillings a quarter and comparable with those of a country parochial school. It is difficult to see how even these seven extra schools could have done more than teach a fraction of the 2200 children still needing places, but it was at least a purposeful start. The scheme, however, was suddenly torpedoed. The town council, before their four schools had even opened, put up the fees to three shillings a quarter for reading, plus 2/6d a quarter each for writing and arithmetic. These schools were thus made to turn their backs on the poor, whom the S.P.C.K. and the presbytery had tried to help, and they began to compete with the more expensive adventure schools for middle-class children. The council was not even ashamed about it, and published a notice in the local papers in 1761 stating that:

> The greater part of the scholars are children of reputable burgesses and others of considerable rank both in town and country, and not of the lowest class of inhabitants only, as hath been industriously propagated to the prejudice of the said schools.[32]

By 1773 their fees were standing at five shillings a quarter for reading. It is not altogether surprising that the S.P.C.K. washed its hands of Edinburgh, and closed all its own schools in the city within ten years.

Meanwhile, of course, the city grew and grew: even without Leith it had a population of 48,000 in 1750, of 66,000 in 1801, and of 136,000 by 1831, but the city fathers rested quietly upon their imaginary laurels. Christian charity managed to endow a few new charity day schools and establish something like a net-work of Sunday schools (after 1800) at which the children of the poor could get a crumb of teaching in reading and writing on one day in seven. The most intelligent effort here came in 1813, when Sheriff John Wood began to urge upon local congregations the need for them to establish and support well-run day schools for their own immediate neighbourhood—the so-called sessional or local schools at which scholars would pay for elementary instruction sums that really were like those in rural parochial schools. Very little had been achieved in this direction, however, before 1830, and even in 1843, after a decade of most intensive charitable effort, the first detailed studies of literacy in the city showed that, for example, only half the children in Canongate parish attended as much as a Sunday school, and round the West Port two-thirds of the children could not read at all.[33] It was a terrible record for the boasted 'democratic intellect' of the Athens of the North.

If this was the record of the capital, it was perhaps not to be expected that the situation would be any better in the industrial west, where the aggregate population of the three burghs of Glasgow, Greenock and Paisley rose from 42,000 in 1750, to 125,000 in 1801, to 287,000 in 1831. Here the problems of councils unwilling and unable to face the challenge squarely, were compounded by parents who were reluctant to send their children to school at all. Part of the trouble was the mass of Irish who came from a society that laid no premium on education, and who were at first puzzled by and indifferent to the native enthusiasm for school attendance. Even when they began to catch this enthusiasm they found their Catholicism an almost insuperable obstacle; all the parish and burgh schools, all the S.P.C.K. schools, all the charity schools and all the Sunday schools were run by Protestants who were only too anxious to teach Papists the error of their ways. If they wanted education without indoctrination by heretics, therefore, they would have to open their own schools—as, indeed, they began to do in a small way in the last two or three decades of the period. But their faith most effectively shut them off from the whole of the national system.

A still bigger problem was the temptation of factory employment. The textile industry needed child labour from the age of seven or eight onwards, and though the wages paid were small it often seemed to parents wiser to send them to a factory where they could earn money than to a school which demanded fees for their attendance. Writer after writer at the end of the eighteenth century complains of this attitude as something novel and totally deplorable in Scottish society.

A few voices were also raised by the representatives of manufacturers to say that education was indeed wasted on the poor, that it gave them ideas above the menial station in life to which they were called, and even in the words of the Rev. Nathaniel Paterson of Galashiels, that 'there can be no training of the volatile minds of youth equal to that which is maintained at the factories.'[34] Such notions were novel to Scotland, where in the seventeenth century a minister had been arraigned before the presbytery just for saying 'it is not needful for the common people to learn to read . . . it was never good for the land since there were so many scholars in it.'[35] They had, however, for a long time had wide currency in England, and English ideas were popular and fashionable in late eighteenth-century Scotland. It is, therefore, to the credit of the Church of Scotland and of the Scottish intelligentsia as a whole that they stuck to their guns and continued to struggle at least for the ideal that education, consisting at the minimum of reading, writing and arithmetic, ought to be for all. Through the advocacy of Lord Brougham they even began to influence English society towards its first grudging acceptance of the same view.

Unfortunately, the Scottish idealists had an uphill struggle in their own cities in the early nineteenth century. The figures that George Lewis published in 1834 indicated the national failure to cope with the problem. One-fifth or one-sixth of the population fell between the ages of five and fourteen and ought to have been at school. At Old Machar parish in Aberdeen one in twenty-five was in fact at school; at Dundee one in thirteen; at Paisley at most one in fifteen; at Greenock one in twelve—and many of these attended only in the evening. Glasgow had about two hundred educational establishments, almost all adventure schools or church schools of one description or another, but only a third of the children of school age attended them. In some parts of the town the ignorance was literally unfathomable. Barony parish with a population of 78,000 could only be examined by sampling, but in the area looked at only one in twenty-six was at day school, and one in seventeen attended either day or evening school.[36] In this parish in the 1790s it had still been possible to claim that virtually all those bred in the parish could read, and most could write and understand arithmetic: 'They often cheerfully deny themselves many of the comforts of life to give their children education.'[37]

Yet even forty years later it would be an exaggeration to say that educational traditions had totally collapsed. One investigation undertaken among Scottish mill-workers in 1833 indicated that the ability to read was still all but universal: ninety-six per cent out of a sample of 28,000 possessed it, as opposed to eighty-six per cent in England. Reading, on the other hand, was something that could be picked up at odd times and in odd places, perhaps at a Sunday school, and the returns from the factories gave no hint as to the extent of reading knowledge. The ability to write was a better test of educational standards, and here the factory workers were not nearly so well off: only fifty-three per cent were literate in this sense, varying regionally from forty-six per cent in Aberdeenshire to sixty-eight per cent in Ayrshire (excluding the smallest samples). The English average was forty-three per cent.[38]

On the whole, therefore, it is difficult to avoid the conclusion that provision for elementary education deteriorated for most members of Scottish society in the half-century beginning around 1780, and that was primarily due to the shift in the distribution of population away from a rural environment where knowledge of reading and writing was still universal and the parochial system still provided the major channel of education towards an urban environment where illiteracy, or semi-literacy, was widespread and the public authorities chose to ignore the evil. The Achilles heel of the national system of education had been its failure to provide means for making town councils provide the good cheap schools like those that still determined the general character of the countryside.

George Lewis ended his comments on this condition of urban education in Scotland with these remarks:

> The voluntary system . . . gives to those whom Providence has blessed with abundance a monopoly of the best schoolmasters for the education of their children; and leaves the poor man nothing but the dregs. It cheats the poor man by giving him the worst article without even the poor consolation of only paying for it the worst price; dissociates the different classes of society in early life; and by separating at school those who are too apt to be altogether separated in manhood, breaks society into discordant parts, so that we look in vain in the large towns of Scotland for those kindly feelings between all classes which arose in the parish schools of Scotland.'[39]

When we come to consider secondary and university education in the larger towns, the manner in which it was reserved for middle-class and upper-class Scots becomes almost self-evident. Sir John Sinclair, for instance, unselfconsciously divided the section on education in his *Analysis of the Statistical Account* of 1826 into two halves. Part One deals with the Parochial System. Part Two is 'on the Education of the Higher Orders of Society', and begins succinctly: 'the education of boys belonging to the higher ranks is carried on: 1, at home; 2, at private schools; 3, at great public-schools; 4, at public seminaries known under the name of academies, and 5, at universities.'[40] When he and his contemporaries referred with approval to social mixing in great town schools like the High School of Edinburgh they did not mean the mixing of the sons of the rich with the sons of the poor: they meant the mixing of the sons of the gentry (and occasionally of the aristocracy) with the sons of middle-class merchants and 'tradesmen'. Admittedly the social spectrum covered by these terms in a Scottish burgh was a broad one, and it was something to have a school where the future Marquis of Tweeddale sat down in the same class-room as the son of a shop-keeper. But they did not sit down with the sons of labourers, chair-men, coal-heavers, journeymen shoemakers, ale-house waiters, tan-house workers and caddies—the men who comprised the backbone of the capital's working class.

Given the premise that in the burghs secondary education was for the middle class, it must be admitted that the large and middling burghs devised a network of educational institutions admirably suited to this end. There were, in the first place, the traditional grammar schools, designed primarily to teach Latin and often doing so with a fresh and commendable liveliness. English scholars, like Dr. Johnson, were liable to condemn Scottish classical teaching as insufficiently rigorous, but what it lacked in emphasis on grammatical formality it certainly made up in attempting to understand the purpose and inspiration of classical authorship. Many schools, for example, added the study of Roman antiquities and geography to the study of Latin texts. The High School of Edinburgh at one time possessed a model prepared in 1738:

A very beautiful and nice model of Caesar's Bridge over the Rhine (done from the famous Palladio's Copperplate Design) of Wainscot; which being presented before the Honourable Magistrates, one of the scholars, a gentleman of an admirable lively genius, read to them Caesar's description of the bridge, which he explained very distinctly, and thereafter demonstrated to them the structure and several parts thereof to the great satisfaction, and to the approbation of all present.[41]

Sometimes the grammar schools offered no more in their curriculum than Latin, with or without elementary Greek—but such subjects, while admirable for those intending to go into the church or law, and suitable for the elegant accomplishments of the landed gentry, were inadequate for those who wanted either to participate in the modern culture of the west or to follow a commercial career. The gaps were filled in various ways. Sometimes the grammar schools themselves came to offer a more varied curriculum in school hours, including (as at Dundee or Ayr) mathematics, book-keeping, drawing, French and even German. Sometimes the teachers at the grammar school, while keeping school hours for the classics, took classes in other subjects privately. More often the gaps were filled by independent tutors and private schools. Thus Walter Scott, while he was a pupil at Edinburgh High School learning Latin and Greek, also learnt French, German, geography, fortification, drawing and painting from private tutors. At the same time he could have attended in the city classes in several branches of mathematics, in elocution, art, dancing, fencing, instrumental music and church music, in book-keeping and in experimental science. 'It is unlikely', writes the historian of Edinburgh's eighteenth-century education, 'that there was such a variety and scope of private schools in any other city in the United Kingdom, apart from London.'[42] But many other Scottish burghs, including several of the second rank such as Dumfries, Ayr and Montrose, also prided themselves on the scope and variety of the private schools that were attracted to the town. (See above, p. 365.)

It was from England, however, that the inspiration came for the most radical attempts to provide for the middle class a comprehensive modern education in a new kind of school—the academies. The first of these had been founded in England in the second half of the seventeenth century by dissenters, who wished to withdraw their children from anglican schools and give them a thorough grounding in practical subjects that would fit them for their everyday occupations in trade or industry. Such was the reputation they gained in a short while that anglican or non-sectarian academies began to be erected in imitation of those of the dissenters throughout England, and these also began to attract the attention of the Scots. Perth Town Council in 1760 heard a report from their adviser, the Rev. James Bonnar:

> In times long past, all learning was made to consist in the grammatical knowledge of dead languages ... but Providence has cast our lot in happier times, when things begin to be valued according to their use, and men of the greatest abilities have employed their skill in making the sciences contribute ... to the improvement of the merchant, mechanic and farmer, in their respective arts. ... The people of England have ... private academies established in almost every great town where not only the languages but those sciences which are of the greatest use in life are taught in a compendious and practical manner.[43]

Perth subsequently became the first burgh in Scotland to erect an academy. Its great success led to the eventual establishment of similar academies at Dundee in 1786, at Inverness in 1787, at Elgin and Fortrose in 1791, at Ayr in 1794, at Annan in 1801, at Dumfries in 1802 and at Tain in 1810. No academies were established in university burghs, unless the Andersonian Institute at Glasgow is regarded as one. (Edinburgh Academy was founded in 1824 as a classical school to rival the High School by teaching Latin and Greek in the English manner, not as an ordinary academy.) They regarded themselves, indeed, as providing in the smaller provincial centres what the universities provided in the large burghs, but at a cheaper rate, on a smaller scale, and of course, without specialised training for physicians, lawyers, or ministers.

The curriculum in these new schools excluded classics and concentrated on such subjects as mathematics, natural science, astronomy, physics, history, chemistry, drawing, painting, and sometimes geography and French. Only at Perth was the academy controlled and financed by the council in the same manner as the grammar school; the more usual arrangement was for the school to be erected by public subscription and for the council to share control with a committee of management. They thus provided effective and relevant semi-technical education in a period which urgently needed a middle class with such a background.

In 1796 the Andersonian Institute was founded in Glasgow with the evident intention of supplementing the traditional curricula of the burgh's older schools without venturing into direct competition either with them or with Glasgow University. It was, said one of its first professors:

> undoubtedly well adapted to the education of young gentlemen
> designed for manufacture or commerce who are too often sent from
> the grammar school to the counting house without acquiring that
> knowledge which will enable them to fill up in a rational manner the
> many vacant hours . . . or which will enable him to make those
> improvements in his business he would do if acquainted with the
> principles on which his different operations depend.[44]

Its main business was the provision of a 'complete scientific course
on physics and chemistry with their application to the arts and manufactures', but it also ran courses on mathematics, botany and agriculture. Since between 500 and 1000 students attended the courses in a
year it must have met some demand in Scotland's commercial capital.
About half the number, rather surprisingly, were women. Thomas
Garnett said it was 'the first regular institution in which the fair sex
have been admitted to the temple of knowledge on the same footing
as men.' On the other hand it is impossible not to exclude a suspicion
that many of these students were not serious: two out of the three
physics and chemistry courses offered were described as 'popular' and
consisted of 'pleasing and interesting experiments' in which the professor
played to the gallery. The Andersonian Institute is now the University
of Strathclyde.

The five Scottish universities themselves embarked upon a period
of remarkable growth and change during the eighteenth century.
Something of this has already been described in an earlier chapter:
something must be left for discussion in a later chapter on cultural
achievement, but certain points are relevant here before we leave the
general subject of Scottish education. One is the extraordinary expansion in what was taught at the universities. In the seventeenth
century this had been restricted to little more than theology, ancient
languages, philosophy and mathematics. In the eighteenth century,
Edinburgh (which was throughout the pacemaker) added four chairs
in law between 1707 and 1722, a Faculty of Medicine in 1726 that had
eleven constituent chairs by 1831, a chair in Rhetoric in 1760, and four
chairs in science—Chemistry, Natural History, Astronomy and
Agriculture. The other universities, after a lag, followed the same
general lines of development. This was another facet of the phenome-

non that produced the academies and the Andersonian Institute—a decline of interest in abstract speculation, and an expansion of those concrete and utilitarian studies that would help men to deal with the world as they found it.

No less sweeping was the revolution in the way in which students were taught, or learnt to teach themselves. At the end of the seventeenth century all teaching had been carried on by 'regents' who were responsible for taking their class through all subjects in a four-year degree irrespective of their own particular bent or specialisation. In the interests of more competent instruction this was given up in Edinburgh in 1708, and everywhere else (except at Marischal College, Aberdeen) by 1735. Similarly, all lectures had traditionally been dictated in Latin, until in 1729 Francis Hutcheson of the Philosophy chair at Glasgow began a course of lectures in English, which changed and electrified the academic climate of his day (though not everywhere: as late as 1776 a student who had been reading Church History at St Andrews remarked that he had not heard a word from his professor except in Latin for three years.[45]) By the end of the eighteenth century Scotland was famous for the succession of great lecturers who could keep an audience gripped and attentive, like Joseph Black, William Cullen or Thomas Hope teaching chemistry, Adam Smith on political economy, Dugald Stewart on moral philosophy and John Millar on law.

In some ways, however, the most interesting development of all was the rise of student societies where young men involved in a particular subject gathered to discuss and debate the implications of what they heard in the lecture room, supplying the elements of argumentative stimulation and speculation that would be given today by a good tutor. Edinburgh, especially under Principal Robertson in the thirty years after 1762, once more led the way. Some societies became so rich and powerful that they could obtain charters from the crown and build their own halls—like the Royal Medical Society and the Royal Physical Society. The Speculative Society was allowed its own rooms in the university building. Many other societies, more humble but not less serious-minded, met in taverns. 'What had been in the seventeenth century a prosperous Arts College with a small but respected Divinity school attached to it', writes Professor Horn, 'became in the middle of the eighteenth century one of the leading universities of Europe.' And elsewhere he continues:

Judging by what students so diverse as Brougham, Benjamin Constant and Necker de Sausure wrote in after life of their student days at Edinburgh, it is quite clear that they learned as much from these student societies as from the professors in the classrooms. If the University of Edinburgh continued to be *par excellence* the university which prepared young men for active and useful careers, this was no longer due solely to the width of its curriculum and the manner in which the component subjects were taught by the professor.[46]

The number of university places available increased over the period —Edinburgh grew from about 400 in the late seventeenth century to about 1300 in the last decade of the eighteenth, and then to 2300 by 1824. At the latter date Glasgow had 1240 students, the two colleges at Aberdeen together about 550, and St Andrews still under 300, though all reported an increase since 1790. This gives a total of about 4400 places in 1824, many of them, particularly in Edinburgh, occupied by English or foreign students.[47] If every place had been occupied by a Scot, this would have represented about one in five hundred of the total population. The average age of entry of a Scottish student to the university was still only about fourteen years as late as 1830; most students stayed three or four years, and the proportion of the population between the age groups of fourteen and eighteen was at least eight per cent—thus the proportion of children of what was then considered university age who actually attended a university cannot have exceeded one in forty and was probably much smaller.

We must also consider that the minimum cost of attending Edinburgh university for one year about 1820 was £30—not much, perhaps, by English standards, but far too much for a weaver or a farm-worker when their wages hovered around £15 to £25 a year; bursaries were few and far between, and not likely to go to the children of the labouring classes. The plain fact of the matter was that throughout the eighteenth and early nineteenth centuries Scottish universities were well outside the pocket of the majority of the Scottish people. Like the burgh schools, they managed to reach a considerable distance down the middle class but the 'lad o' pairts', the poor man's son who was educated at the parish school and subsequently made a great name for himself in the world, though not entirely a figment of the sentimental imagination, was seldom found at a Scottish university. Robert Burns, Thomas Telford, Alexander Somerville and Hugh

Miller are representatives of famous children of very poor parents: none of them went either to a grammar school or to a university. On the other hand Thomas Carlyle, son of a struggling Dumfriesshire mason with his own small building business, and James Rennie, son of a middling East Lothian farmer, both advanced from the local parish school to a grammar school (in Annan and Dunbar respectively) and then on to Edinburgh University. They are representative of a group perhaps best described as lower middle class who did find in Scotland educational opportunities which would almost certainly have been denied to their equivalents in England.

In conclusion, what is left of the idea that the Scots had a uniquely good system of education during and immediately after the eighteenth century? Obviously it was not all that it was sometimes supposed to be: the parochial system of schools subsidised by the tax-payer did not provide an adequate basis even for universal literacy in the countryside unless it was supplemented by charity on the one hand and adventure schools on the other; education in the towns was of very shabby standards for the poor; the grammar schools and the universities were largely the preserves of the middle class and effectively closed to the children of labourers for financial reasons.

On the other hand there were two great achievements. The first was the almost universal and intelligent literacy of the Lowlands, which must have reached its height at some point about the middle of the eighteenth century, and then slowly declined as a higher proportion of Scots came to live in the ill-provided towns. The second was the really splendid education which became available to the middle class for professional and commercial training through the grammar schools, the academies and the universities and which effectively kept abreast of the demands of the times from 1760 to 1830. It is therefore difficult not to conclude that Alexander Christison was basically correct: the 'general diffusion of knowledge' was indeed 'one great cause of prosperity' among the Scots, even if the manner in which it was diffused was not quite as simple, as satisfactory or as universal as he was inclined to suggest.

CHAPTER XIX

The Golden Age of Scottish Culture

1. ACADEMICS AND ARTISTS

The cultural achievements of Scotland between the middle of the eighteenth century and the years around 1830 make a fitting conclusion to our study of 270 years of Scottish social history. However genius be measured, the galaxy of great and original-minded men that came together within the space of seventy or eighty years is comparable in brilliance with that of any other such intellectual constellation in a small country in the history of Europe. It is a large claim, but the stars were numerous, and shed their luminance upon many different aspects of human knowledge and experience.

Take philosophy for example. Thanks largely to the cramping suspicion of all novelty by the kirk the seventeenth century had been a black age for speculative minds, and little had been taught in the universities except a rudimentary Aristotelianism. But the eighteenth century was full of notable Scottish philosophers. The greatest, of course, was the incomparable David Hume (1711–1776) whose *Treatise of Human Nature* was inspired by the desire to do for philosophy what Newton had done for physics: it seemed at the time mainly destructive, and to uproot 'all traditional certainties: matter, the soul, God, Nature, causation, miracles'[1]; only later did philosophers begin to value the essentially constructive elements which lay on the other side of the coin from his scepticism, and to see him as probably the most original thinker the British Isles have ever produced. But Hume had already been preceded by a noted philosopher, Francis Hutcheson, father of the moral sense theory, whose greatest service to Scotland was to introduce lectures in English (at Glasgow University where he

480

became professor in 1729) and to propagate the teaching of the great European and English philosophers of whom the north had been kept in ignorance so long. Similarly Hume was succeeded by a string of notable men. Of his would-be refuters Thomas Reid (1710–1796) was the most penetrating and impressive, and from him sprang the school of Scottish 'common-sense' philosophy carried further by his immediate successors George Campbell and Dugald Stewart.

Other men in chairs of moral philosophy worked at other problems. Adam Smith, Hutcheson's successor in the Glasgow chair and Hume's own close friend and only rival to intellectual pre-eminence laid the foundations of all subsequent economics in the limpid paragraphs of the *Wealth of Nations*. Simultaneously, Adam Ferguson, at Edinburgh, and John Millar, in the chair of civil law at Glasgow, though neither the quality of their thought nor their influence upon contemporaries was of the same order as that of Smith and Hume, can fairly be regarded as the fathers of modern sociology. Their work was a bridge towards that of William Robertson, the principal of Edinburgh University, whose work as a historian had a strong bent towards the social sciences. It has been said of him that if Gibbon had not been his contemporary he would have been beyond question the greatest historian of his age.[2]

There are perhaps three things that are most striking about Scottish philosophy in the eighteenth century. The first is the speed of its growth from nothing. The seventeenth century was blank; the eighteenth century got off to a fair start with Hutcheson, experienced Hume like a blazing comet, and then had a number of concerned and competent native philosophers to take something from Hume and to carry on a sensible and informed discussion among themselves. There could so easily have been Hutcheson, then Hume as a brilliant accident, and then silence. But thanks, partly at least, to reform and development within the Scottish universities, a tradition was built up after Hutcheson which involved academics in philosophical disquisition without the possibility of interference from theologians. A good deal of Scottish higher education came to be focused upon it.

Again, Scottish philosophy came to be distinctly slanted towards moral problems, and therefore towards the affairs of society. No doubt it got this from Hutcheson, and Hutcheson got it from his Calvinism: it was demonstrated not only in Hume's fascination with ethics, but also in Reid's immediate appreciation of crisis if Hume was allowed to get away with it. If Hume was right the foundations of moral behaviour were rocked: the 'common sense school' seemed to appeal back to a consensus of society to affirm that Hume was wrong, and thereby to rebuild what he was destroying. Lastly, Scottish philosophers were avidly interested in other disciplines than their own. This followed to some extent from the second point: if philosophy was about morals, and morals affected the whole of society, then all the social sciences could legitimately become the philosopher's field. It led Hume into an active interest in both history and economics. For several years he was actually better known as an historian than as a philosopher. It led Adam Smith right out of philosophy and into economics. It led Adam Ferguson and John Millar towards sociology and William Robertson into history.

It also led to brilliant teaching, for the philosophers felt it their duty to educate the future leaders of other disciplines in a rational approach to moral and social problems. Francis Hutcheson, Adam Smith and John Millar were outstanding teachers in their day, but Dugald Stewart was the most excellent of all. His pupils included a whole generation of intellectuals who came to Edinburgh University at the start of the nineteenth century like Henry Cockburn who wrote: 'to me his lectures were like the opening of the heavens.' A compulsive involvement in the world and a compulsive curiosity about the social sciences were perhaps, in the end, the very best thing that the Scottish philosophers gave to the world.

Among the scientists the stars shone with scarcely less luminescence than they did among philosophers. James Hutton a student of Edinburgh though not a teacher there, was the founder of modern geology. At the same university Isaac Newton's friend David Gregory, and his successor in the mathematics chair Colin Maclaurin, were teaching the Newtonian system long before the master's own university of Cambridge accepted it. The medical men at Edinburgh and Glasgow were a Pleiades of talent, and if no single one of them could outshine Herman Boerhaave of Leyden, the collective reputation of the teaching and practice of their new faculties outshone in the end even that of the Dutch universities.

The chemists were another outstanding group. William Cullen held a place in the development of the subject resembling that of Hutcheson twenty years earlier in the development of philosophy. Joseph Black, who succeeded him first in 1756 at the lectureship in

Glasgow and then in 1766 in the chair at Edinburgh, was one of the great *savants* of Europe. The experiments that led up to his discovery of carbon dioxide, announced to the world in an M.D. thesis ('there is perhaps no other instance of a graduation thesis so weighted with significant novelty'[3]), set a new standard in measurement and profundity of thought, and opened chemistry up for the subsequent discoveries of Priestley, Scheele, Cavendish and Lavoisier. His second great research breakthrough was in physics, the discovery of latent heat and its corollary, the theory of specific heat. It was while engaged in this particular research that Black met James Watt. The story is well-known: how Watt came to Glasgow University to take care of certain scientific instruments; how Black befriended, inspired and financed him in his early attempts to improve Newcomen's pump; and how the discovery of latent heat helped Watt towards the idea of a separate condenser. Watt later moved away from Scotland and Black, finding in Birmingham and his partnership with Boulton the capital and business expertise necessary to develop his invention so crucial in the history of the industrial revolution. But if it had not been for his earlier friendship with Black it is more than possible that his engine would never have seen the light of day.

Black's successors contained no one of the same calibre as himself, but there were men of distinction among them. The best original research was done by Black's pupils: Daniel Rutherford's discovery of nitrogen in 1772 and Thomas Hope's discovery of strontium in 1791 were both substantial. The tradition of great teaching was no less marked in chemistry than in philosophy. Cullen had been a popular lecturer, endeavouring to make the science 'a study for every man of good education'. Black, in his tenure of the chair at Edinburgh, had been one of the most inspiring in the university, and his classes were attended by many outsiders who were not students at all. He had 'many from the workshop', said his first biographer, 'and he saw that the number of such hearers must increase with the increasing activity and prosperity of the country: and these appeared to him as by no means the least important part of his auditory'.[4] Hope, in the half century from 1798 over which he held Black's old chair, issued nearly 17,000 class tickets and he was the first man in Britain to give an exposition of Lavoisier's chemical theories. Similarly at Glasgow another of Black's successors, Thomas Thomson, was the first man to give a public account of the atomic theory of the Irish chemist Dalton.

Just how far the academic tradition directly enriched technology in the industrial revolution is, however, apart from the single instance of Watt and Black, somewhat doubtful. In industrial chemistry the leading advances were certainly made by men who had attended chemistry classes at Glasgow or Edinburgh, and who generally maintained some kind of correspondence with the professors. Yet in the end they found little of the research done at the universities helpful to themselves. One of the first innovations in textile chemistry, for instance, was turkey-red dyeing, but George Mackintosh who established its manufacture in Scotland did so with the help of a French expert, P. J. Papillion. Again, despite the direct research into textile bleaching by Cullen, Black and several other Scottish academics, the crucial invention of bleaching powder came when the industrialist Charles Tennant developed an idea from another French chemist, Claude-Louis Berthollet, which had been communicated to him from Watt at Birmingham. The Earl of Dundonald's extraction and distillation of tar from coal and Charles Mackintosh's use of naphtha to waterproof cloth (hence 'mackintoshes') were two other industrial applications of chemistry which owed neither their inception nor their development to the academics, though the latter were very interested in both when they occurred. Thus for all the sympathy and broad interests of the university chemists from Cullen onwards, they seemed in practice to do little compared to what industry could do for itself. Probably the methods of chemistry before Dalton's atomic theory were still too hit-or-miss for a systematic or well-directed application to industry to occur.

On the other hand there is an imponderable factor in the indirect contribution of student teaching. It is hard to know how many people who would otherwise have remained untouched by and uninterested in the processes of chemistry were inspired by the exciting instruction of Cullen, Black and Hope, or by the classes at the Andersonian Institute, and later adapted some of the ideas they had imbibed in the lecture halls to the problems of production as they met them in their everyday jobs. It is harder still to evaluate the atmosphere of sheer intellectual quest transmitted by these great chemists. A student did not have to be a budding industrialist or even a scientist to be moved by Joseph Black as, with a slight smile playing at the corners of his mouth, he reproduced on a bench for an audience his own classic experiments in isolating carbon dioxide or demonstrating latent heat. As a vision of how much one restless mind could discover it could not fail to stir all other minds who beheld it. One of a university teacher's main functions is to inspire people with curiosity: if eighteenth-century Scotland had curiosity in such good measure it was surely due in no small degree to men like Joseph Black.

If we turn from academics to artists, the achievement, though more patchy, is hardly less striking. It is true that Lowland musical achievements were inconsiderable—has there been a Scottish composer of outstanding merit in any generation? Nor did the Scots produce playwrights, despite the cry from the stalls, 'Whaur's your Wullie Shakespeare noo?', when John Home's melodrama *Douglas* was first performed in Edinburgh. In painting it was another story. As masters of portraiture, Allan Ramsay junior (son of the poet) and Henry Raeburn have no peers in eighteenth-century Britain save Hogarth and Gainsborough. William Aikman at the beginning of the century and David Allan, the Nasmyths and Wilkie later were all notable men—and this in a field where Scotland had almost no seventeenth-century tradition to build on. In the lesser art of printing fine books the work of Robert Foulis of Glasgow was, in mid-century, quite outstanding.

Architecture, however, was the one art in eighteenth-century Britain where the Scots provided a large proportion, if not an absolute majority, of the most brilliant creative minds in the kingdom. At the start of the century Colen Campbell was the leading exponent of Palladianism, and James Gibbs the finest champion of Baroque. After 1760 the innovators were Robert Adam and his brothers, proclaiming neo-Classicism. They were rivalled only by James Stuart, the London-born son of a Scottish mariner, who pioneered the Greek revival, and Sir William Chambers, scion of a Scoto-Swedish family, whose best-known work is Somerset House. In civil engineering, architecture's new half-brother created in the transport revolution of the eighteenth century, the world was dominated by Thomas Telford, son of an Eskdale shepherd. Of his notable contemporaries, John Rennie, John Smeaton, and Robert and Alan Stevenson (of the light-houses) were all Scots.

Not all these men worked in Scotland. Colen Campbell and James Stuart never did. James Gibbs is represented only by one church and Sir William Chambers only by two houses. Even the most famous of the Scottish-born did their most spectacular work outside Scotland:

the most elaborately decorated Adam country houses are in Derbyshire and Middlesex, and the most comprehensive urban architecture from his hand the now-demolished Adelphi in London. Although Telford built over a thousand bridges in Scotland, mainly while engaged on the 730 miles of Highland road constructed under his supervision, the finest ones are in Wales. His cast-iron bridge at Craigellachie over the Spey, the seven spans over the Tay at Dunkeld and the high Dean Bridge over the Water of Leith at Edinburgh, fine as they are, do not compare with the breath-taking crossing of the Menai Straits to Anglesey or the Pont Cysyllte aqueduct carrying the Ellesmere canal over a gorge.

In the first decades of the eighteenth century the most noted builders working within Scotland were all followers of Sir William Bruce. William Adam, inspired by Gibbs and Vanbrugh, was the first to carry the classical tradition in the north further. Of the score or so country mansions that he built, Duff House, in Banff, a four-square baroque tower-house ('its rich texture and towering bulk convey a memorable impression of seignorial pomp'5), and Hopetoun in West Lothian are unquestionably the finest. The latter is a Versailles among Scottish homes, swallowing within itself a complete mansion built by Bruce for the family a generation before. The design is not entirely his own; it owes some of its originality to the fact that the portico which he planned as a conventional central focal point was never built, and his sons, completing the building thirty years after their father had begun it in 1723 altered details of the domed pavilions so that the eye tends to rest upon them—or rather to switch from one to the other along the line of the colonnades and the main block, thus emphasising more effectively than anything else could the great sweep and size of the house. But the main conception is his, and if he had built nothing else Hopetoun should stamp William Adam as worthy of much more than the patronising line he usually receives in histories of British architecture.

Hopetoun, however, has additional importance in the story of his great son, Robert Adam (1728–1792). The first significant commission that Robert and his brother John obtained was the completion of the house after their father's death. Their work, and their friendship with the Earl, led to other commissions from the Scottish nobility, and, still more important, to a Grand Tour for Robert which spanned the years 1754–8. Seldom has a foreign visit by a British architect been more momentous. He returned from a tour of archeological sites in Italy and Yugoslavia convinced that he had discovered exactly how the Romans had built and decorated their houses and public buildings, and determined to create in Britain a new and purer classicism. The result is what all the world now calls the 'Adam style'.

It was not, of course, really Roman at all. We have little idea even now of how the Romans decorated their buildings. What he produced was ornament based on an amalgamation of many elements, Roman, Greek, Renaissance, but all so transformed by his vision that it had a unity, a freshness and an elegance all its own. It created an international upheaval in interior design. Architects working on buildings as far apart as the palace of Catherine the Great in St Petersburg and the State House at Boston in New England tried to copy Robert Adam's great masterpieces in England, Kedleston, Kenwood, Syon and Osterley. Within Britain 'everything was Adamatic'.[6] His style was taken up by almost all who worked in the decorative arts—by silver-smiths, by furniture-makers, by potters (like the great Wedgwood), by ornamental masons, by iron-founders and even by book-binders. This was partly the effect of fashion, and partly because Adam patterns, though elegant and original, were not hard to imitate. It was also because a great many Adam motifs were readily translatable to an object of small scale, which enabled the middle classes to participate in the *beau monde* and to identify themselves with the tastes of the great. Very few Englishmen (or Scots) could afford a private palace like Syon, but an Adam fireplace would go into any prosperous lawyer's house and any farmer could eat muffins from an Adam muffin-dish. Even today so-called 'Adam' electric fires in suburban houses owe their popularity not to any intrinsic beauty but to the unmistakable echoes of a stately home conveyed by two urns and a row of beading in shallow relief on either side of the glowing bar.

The exteriors of Robert Adam's houses are much less distinctive than their interiors, since, despite his claims to have done so, he never developed a style for the elevations that marked a clean break with his predecessors. On the other hand he could show here a great deal of variety and ingenuity. Edinburgh has some fine examples; Register House, in a Palladian manner, the portico of the Old College of the university, in a Roman manner (the dome is a later addition), and the northern side of Charlotte Square. Now that the Adelphi in London is destroyed the last named is perhaps the best surviving example of his skill as an urban architect in fusing a row of terraced houses into a single rich and sensitive composition. 'He could make several frontages look like a single palace'.[7] Lastly he devised an original castle style, sometimes referred to as Georgian Gothic, but apparently owing more to his study of Roman Spalato than to anything from the Middle Ages. Culzean in Ayrshire, is the best known, but Seton in East Lothian is the purest, a castle deliberately purged of Gothic features, 'a neo-classical building, albeit of a highly original kind, unique in Britain and indeed in Europe'.[8] The interiors of these houses were invariably classical, and Culzean provides as splendid an example of Adam decoration within a house as any in Scotland, Mellerstain excepted.

The New Town of Edinburgh was, of course, a major architectural achievement in itself—and one of European significance. It was the work of many hands besides Adam's. Craig's original conception of an oblong grid joined to the old town by the Mound and the North Bridge had been realised by 1800 and, in addition to Adam's contributions it already contained several individual buildings of excellence. Of these Sir William Chambers' town house for Sir Lawrence Dundas is the most impertinent, since it usurped the site in St Andrew's Square intended for St Andrew's Church, which now has to sit, most inappropriately, half-way along George Street. After 1800 the New Town expanded again: to the north, in the grid beyond Heriot Row associated primarily with Robert Reid (1776–1856); to the east, in the mounting terraces of Calton Hill, by William Playfair (1789–1857); to the north-west, in the elegant circuses and crescents of the feu of the Earl of Moray, by Gillespie Graham (1777–1855). There is more variety of prospect and design in the later developments than there was in the first plan, and the individual public buildings are every bit as good, especially Playfair's National Gallery and the Royal Scottish Academy that stand together on the south side of Princes Street, and Thomas Hamilton's Athenian *tour de force*, the Royal High School on Calton Hill.

There is indeed something about Edinburgh in this period that made architects build better than they knew. Other Scottish towns were capable of fine development: small towns like Cupar in Fife or Banff and large towns like Aberdeen and sections of Glasgow and Perth had elegant new terraced quarters constructed in the same period as Edinburgh's New Town. The architects associated with Edinburgh, too, could sometimes build well outside the city: Playfair's Dollar

Academy, for instance, is an excellent building by any standard. But it was only when these men were working within the capital that their talents seemed to fuse into a scheme of genius. It is hard to say why. No doubt the competition between them brought out the best in each. No doubt they found clients willing to indulge them, as the town council in particular did until its generosity brought it to bankruptcy in the 1830s. No doubt the plan had a momentum of its own which called for the finest work and therefore received it: they knew what they were doing, they were building an Athens of the North, and they had the taste and the resources to do so with magnificent conviction. The citizens need something of the same conviction now to save the New Town from the vandalism of neglect and development carried on today with the consent of the present council, whose crocodile tears and pretty exhibitions do nothing at all to stop the builders' rape of the capital.

2. POETRY AND NOVELS

So far our account of the cultural achievement has inevitably been little more than a catalogue of names and buildings—there is so much to describe it is difficult to linger. We may, however, perhaps pause when we come to consider Scottish imaginative literature, since it faces us with a very curious paradox. The achievement of these years is unsurpassed both in quality and concentration. Burns, in his greatest verse, stands at the apogee of our poetry, but he does not stand alone; he is preceded by Allan Ramsay, senior, and Robert Fergusson to say nothing of a small galaxy of minor poets. Scott, too, stands at the apogee of our achievement in the novel and he, too, does not stand alone; apart from James Hogg, his times are associated with Tobias Smollett, John Galt, Henry Mackenzie, Susan Ferrier and J. B. Lockhart. Yet in poetry almost instantaneously on Burns's death, and in prose very soon after Scott stopped writing, Scottish imaginative literature dropped in its tracks. Of course it did not die for ever; but it died as a continuous tradition. As David Craig has said:

Odd works by George Macdonald and Stevenson, *The House with the Green Shutters*, Gibbon's *Scots Quair*, Hugh MacDiarmid's poetry from *Sangschaw* to *Stony Limits*—certainly these amount to

489

as fine a body of work as that of the ages of Burns and Scott. But, considered for its continuity as a tradition, Scottish culture during the past century has only in isolated phases afforded us the experience of minds of a fine quality working in creative literature.[9]

Why should Scottish imaginative literature of the eighteenth century thus beat up to a crescendo of achievement and then break off into a silence broken only by staccato outbursts? This is a problem to which there is perhaps no simple answer, but traditions in poetry and fiction both appeared to lead into a cul-de-sac from which it was difficult to make further meaningful advance.

In poetry the cul-de-sac was a linguistic one. In the early sixteenth century practically the only medium for any kind of serious expression in prose or in poetry was the Scottish language, which was, in its vocabulary, its constructions and its rhythms plainly distinct from English, though allied to it closely enough for a Scotsman and an Englishman to converse without an interpreter. Sixteenth-century Scottish was rather more distinct from English than modern Danish is from Norwegian, but not so distinct as those two languages are from Swedish. From the Reformation onwards, however, there were more and more pressures to replace Scottish by English. The Reformer's Bible was in English, for the Scots from the start used translations prepared in the south and eventually adopted the Authorised Version of James VI and I. Politicians and civil servants after the Union of the Crowns in 1603 began to use standard English for official documents. The National Covenant itself was written in English, and at the end of the century the two greatest exponents of Scottish nationalism, Andrew Fletcher of Saltoun and Lord Belhaven, even if they spoke with a Scottish accent, wrote and published their speeches against the Union of Parliaments in beautifully measured English. It would not have occurred to anyone to do otherwise who wished to receive attention from the political public. The courtly poets of the mid-century, like Drummond of Hawthornden and Montrose, wrote their polished and melancholy verse in English just as their forebears a hundred years earlier would have written in Scottish. The only Scottish verse of any vigour after about 1630 was found in the bucolic celebrations of the Sempills, like Robert Sempill's 'Piper of Kilbarchan':

> Now who shall play, the Day it Daws
> Or Hunts Up, when the cock he craws

Or who can for our Kirk-town-cause
Stand us in stead?
On bagpipes now no body blaws
Sen Habbie's dead.

By the opening of the eighteenth century, therefore, Scottish had become merely the language of the poor, the uncouth and the humorous, and even in its common usage it was being constantly modified and diluted by English. The landed classes and the middle-class intelligentsia wrote English, and increasingly after the Union sought the most perfect English forms. To speak with a Scottish inflexion was to betray one's provincial origins, and all who aspired to polite society tried to get rid of their dialect in both written and spoken form. Lord Monboddo said of David Hume that he died confessing not his sins but his Scotticisms. One of the most popular books of the third quarter of the century was James Beattie's *Scotticisms, arranged in Alphabetical Order designed to correct Improprieties of Speech and Writing*, written 'to put young writers and speakers on their guard against some of those Scottish idioms which, in this country, are liable to be mistaken for English.' Some of the most popular lectures in the same period were those of Thomas Sheridan who 'lectured in his Irish brogue to entranced members of the Select Society of Edinburgh on the proper pronunciation of English.'[10]

Scottish, nevertheless, survived as an acceptable language for poetry, or at least, for certain types of poetry. This was partly because of tradition: some Scots poems, for example John Barbour's *Brus*, Blind Harry's *Wallace* and some of Sir David Lindsay's, remained as part of the normal national cultural background which even peasants' children heard recited by their elders. Songs in the vernacular also had a grip on all classes of society, both as ballads and lyrical folksong: they were handed on within the household, and the fact that they were written in the vernacular did not make them unacceptable even to the genteel. The work of Allan Ramsay (1686–1758), too, went a long way towards ensuring the survival of Scottish as a vehicle for poetry; not only was the best of his own verse vigorous and unaffected, in the Sempill tradition, but his two collections of older Scottish poetry, *The Ever Green* (1724) and the *Tea-Table Miscellany* (1724–1737), deliberately tried to recall intellectual Scotsmen to a recollection of the past poetic achievements of their language. On the other hand, Ramsay was so apologetic about reprinting old vernacular verse that he appeared to imply it really was suitable only for the archaic, the rollicking and the sentimental; a vehicle for song and humour but not for 'serious' modern expression.

Nevertheless, narrowed though it was to this particular constricting channel, Scottish poetry could draw for its life upon the expressive language that was still spoken in the farmtouns and taverns of eighteenth-century Scotland, and that was still written in prose or verse in bawdy and trivial chapbooks which church and gentry so much objected to, but which found a ready sale from hawkers' packs throughout the land. Undoubtedly its most original voice before Burns's was Robert Fergusson, the dissipated son of an Edinburgh clerk, who died in 1774 at the understandably early age of twenty-four. Poems like 'Tron-Kirk Bell' showed the peculiar suppleness and glow of the vernacular:

> Wanwordy, crazy, dinsome thing,
> As e'er was fram'd to jow or ring . . .

But nothing more serious than the celebration of food and drink was ever his business. Alcohol is the greatest good of the greatest number:

> The tinker billies i' the Bow
> Are now less eidant clinking,
> As lang's their pith or siller dow,
> They're daffin', and they're drinking.
> Bedown Leith-walk what burrochs reel
> Of ilka trade and station
> That gar their wives an' childer feel
> Toom weyms for their libation
> O' drink thir days.

With Robert Burns (1759–1796) Scottish poetry reached a peak that it had not approached for two hundred years, and which it was hardly to approach again in the following two hundred years. There was, of course, a great deal of the traditional explosive joy in eating, drinking and wenching. It can be boring, but at best it lifts his lyrical verse high above conventional levels of insipid sentiment. There is, for instance, much happiness but no false chastity in 'Rigs o' barley':

I hae been blythe wi' comrades dear;
I hae been merry drinking;
I hae been joyfu' gath'rin gear;
I hae been happy thinking:
But a' the pleasures e'er I saw
Tho' three times doubl'd fairly
That happy night was worth them a',
Among the rigs o' barley.

In Burns there was more than mere rustic celebration. There was his ability, unequalled among either Scottish or English poets, to write marvellous songs. There was his one epic ballad, 'Tam o' Shanter', that would have made his reputation if he had written nothing else. There was his ability to take a pedestrian observation—the unearthing of a mouse's nest, the sight of a louse on a lady's bonnet—and make it memorable. There was his brilliant gift of satire, at its sharpest impaling the religiosity of his fellow men of Ayrshire in 'Holy Willie's Prayer' or 'The Holy Fair'. Whenever he is successful it is the virtuosity of his use of the Scottish language that makes him so. Sometimes it pours out of him, lavish, yet exact and expressive, as in his address to the louse:

Swith, in some beggar's hasset squattle
There ye creep, and sprawl and sprattle
Wi' ither kindred, jumping cattle . . .

Sometimes it is used with spare cunning to exploit the double meaning of religious language in the two-faced talk of a hypocrite:

O L . . d yestreen, Thou kens, wi' Meg—
Thy pardon I sincerely beg—
O! may't ne'er be a livin' plague
    To my dishonour,
An' I'll ne'er lift a lawless leg
    Again upon her.

In Burns the Scottish tongue was always unforced and natural. Even if it was no longer quite the same as it had been in the sixteenth century, one cannot escape the knowledge that it was the language of the Ayrshire peasant society into which he was born and in which he remained for the greater part of his life. That society, however, was

493

changing rapidly at the end of the century. Rich peasants were becoming capitalist farmers, members of a genteel class that spoke English. Poor peasants were becoming farm-workers. Everyone was exposed to purer English from their employers, from the church and from the schools.

Consequently, at about the time of Burns's death there occurred a triple crisis in Scottish poetry. Firstly, nobody could excel Burns in the particular use to which he had put his language, for his genius was impossible to outshine. There were many imitators mesmerised by his achievements who dug their own poetic graves trying to do what he did. Also, poets were increasingly cut off from the linguistic base of a Scottish tongue. Only twenty years after the agricultural revolution the vernacular had become something largely remembered from the past, quaint: and the poet's use of it was increasingly derivative, forced and folksy.

On the other hand, Scottish poets of this twilight time simply could not use English properly, and thus could not investigate at all those realms of poetry that lay beyond the song, the rural celebration and the satire. Burns himself usually went along with the eighteenth-century conviction that Scottish was unsuitable for a serious poem, and when he wanted to write solemnly he wrote in English. Sometimes the result was insipid, sometimes it was absurd. Thus in 'The Cottar's Saturday Night';

> But now the Supper crowns their simple board,
> The healsome *Porritch*, chief of SCOTIA's food . . .

Almost all his contemporaries and successors also found themselves tongue-tied in a language that even yet did not seem to come naturally from their own hearts. The only eighteenth-century Scot who did not was James Thomson (1700–1748) author of that fine English classical poem *The Seasons*, which had considerable influence upon Wordsworth. He was the son of a Roxburghshire minister, and lived entirely in England from the age of twenty-five.

It is right at least to mention that the eighteenth century also saw the greatest achievements of Gaelic poetry. It is difficult for one who is not a Gaelic speaker to judge how great these were, but those who know are inclined to rank Alexander Macdonald (?1700–1768), Duncan Ban MacIntyre (1724–1812), Rob Donn (1714–1778) and Dugald Buchanan (1716–1768) among the finest poets Scotland has produced writing in any tongue at any time. Macdonald was the poet of war and love, moved by the landing of Prince Charles to splendid martial verse, and moved by many different loves in a way that makes all translators timorous. 'His amorous language, indeed,' one has remarked 'needs frequent asterisks at the hands of publishers.'[11] MacIntyre was above all a poet of nature, of sweet love-songs and satires. Donn was strongly influenced by the verse of Pope, which he had heard in Gaelic translation from his local minister. Buchanan was a writer of hymns and religious poetry of great power. If in this diversity there was anything common to all of them it was perhaps their ability to describe nature. Macdonald did it by creaming his noun with adjectives that no doubt sound even better in the Gaelic original than they do in English. That other Celt, Dylan Thomas, would have seen the point and envied the power[12]:

It is most lovely to hear from the fold the faint low of the calf,
vigorous, piebald, handsome, white-backed, short-haired, merry,
white-headed, keen-eyed, red-eared, white-bellied, lively, young,
shaggy, soft-hoofed, well-grown, as it leaps to the lowing of the cows.

All the time this ferment of genuine poetry was taking place in the Highlands, the Lowlands remained oblivious to it. The S.P.C.K. charged Macdonald, who was one of their schoolmasters, with 'composing and singing indecent songs.' Ironically enough, however, Lowland society was simultaneously very excited about bogus Gaelic poetry. James Macpherson of Kingussie had produced what purported to be a translation of an ancient Highland manuscript dealing with the mythical Celtic heroes Fingal and Ossian, but which was in fact a very inferior epic of his own in which echoes of Highland tradition were interlarded with slabs of mock-Milton and mock-Homer. Dr. Johnson made himself unpopular by calling it a fraud: Britain as a whole took it very seriously, and it passed from thence into the bloodstream of European romanticism to become the inspiration of countless poets and composers from William Blake to Mendelssohn. The latter's overture 'Fingal's Cave' is today the best-known memorial to one of the most successful forgeries in the history of literature.

In the development of the novel the question of a linguistic tradition being exhausted and breaking down as a result of social change never arose in the same form as it did for poetry. The first novelists, who were middle-class figures several rungs in the social ladder above the strata from which the poets mainly emerged, used English. Tobias Smollett (1721–1771), who may be considered as the prose-writing equivalent to James Thomson, set off for England at the age of eighteen, and wrote in England after the manner of Fielding and Sterne. There is nothing particularly Scottish about his art apart from the use of some settings and a certain amount of autobiography in *Roderick Random* and *Humphrey Clinker*. Henry Mackenzie (1745–1831) also wrote in English and although he did so from Edinburgh set his novel in England. *The Man of Feeling*, defiantly unreadable though it is to modern taste, greatly moved Burns and started a British fashion for the 'sentimental novel'.

With Sir Walter Scott (1771–1832), however, fiction takes a new beginning that extinguishes all that went before it. Scott's literary debut was in poetry; the *Border Minstrelsy* of 1802 was a collection of ballads gathered by himself and his friends in the Border counties. He followed it with the 'Lay of the Last Minstrel', 'Marmion' and 'The Lady of the Lake', three antiquarian poetic narratives somewhat forced and stilted in their style and language, which enjoyed wide contemporary popularity—'novels in verse' one critic has called them.[13] Then in 1814 he published, anonymously, *Waverley*, a novel based on the Jacobite rising. It was an instantaneous success, and in the next ten years he poured out book after book of historical fiction upon an apparently insatiable public. Between 1814 and 1826 he wrote twenty-two novels.

The best of these deal with Scotland's past in the century before he wrote. *Ivanhoe* and *Quentin Durward*, popular though they were, have no real understanding of England or France or of the Middle Ages in which they were set. By contrast, *Waverley*, *Heart of Midlothian* and *Guy Mannering* move with deftness and understanding among the people and the period they are attempting to portray. *Rob Roy* and *Old Mortality* are slightly less successful, perhaps because they deal with the late seventeenth century in which Scott was not instinctively at home.

Scott's stories are nearly always based on the extraordinary sympathy he is able to create for all his main characters, however diverse or irreconcilable they may appear. There are few villains. In *Waverley*, for example, the heroes are an inexperienced Hanoverian officer who ultimately fights for Prince Charlie; a loyal Hanoverian officer who fights against him; a very old-fashioned Lowland baron, who is by tradition a pedantic Jacobite; and a hot-blooded Highland chief, who also is a Jacobite but who steals the Lowlander's cows. Even the Cameronian officer-preacher who takes Waverley prisoner and falls into an ambush of Highlanders is drawn with a humorous sympathy which forestalls the reader's condemnation of his fanaticism. Scott avoids making serious moral judgements by tucking his characters romantically into the past and then dazzling the reader by the skill of his characterisation. The Scottish dialogue that he puts into the mouths of many of his most memorable characters—like Bailie Jarvie in *Rob Roy* or Cuddie Headrigg in *Old Mortality*—is rendered with superb force and accuracy. (It is, incidentally, remarkable that Scott, who could use Scottish so well in reported speech, could never use it in narrative or poetry.) The geographical scenes in which his action takes place are delineated with splendid economy. The history is sometimes brilliant. The description of the Porteous riots in the first seven chapters of *Heart of Midlothian* is drawn with such care that the reader becomes totally absorbed. But in the end Scott treats his characters not as if they were real people but as if they were actors moving in a beautifully-directed film. His realism is only a tool in his search for a romantic effect: for he is not and does not want to be a realist dealing with living people in the Scotland of his day. There is, underlying all his art, a nostalgia for the Scottish past that seems to say that that which is Scottish and that which is past must therefore be admirable.

Scott's achievement mesmerised his contemporaries as thoroughly as Burns mesmerised his. In his own lifetime, however, Scott had better followers than Burns. John Gibson Lockhart (1794–1854) in *Adam Blair*, and John Galt (1779–1839) in *Annals of the Parish* and *The Provost*, while both concerned with the immediate past, had an independence of mind and art that carried them above the level of mere imitation. It was only after his death that the Scottish novel sank up to its axles in the mud of the kailyard. Scott had, in fact, stumbled upon a very limited vein of literary material and it needed a very special genius to extract anything out of it except lachrymose slush. His successors, after Lockhart, had none of his qualities, and their attempts to write historical novels about the rural past became more and more irrelevant to nineteenth-century Scotland as it turned into an industrial country whose problems did not once engage either the pens or the minds of her main writers.

Why did no one come out of the circle and try to break new

ground? The answer probably lies in the nature of popular taste. The public liked Scott and they liked the kailyard school, and they did not much like anything that came nearer the bone. The experience of James Hogg (1770–1835), the 'Ettrick Shepherd' who was illiterate until he was eighteen, shows something of this. After feeding the market with various nostalgic works he wrote *The Confessions of a Justified Sinner* (1824), a novel about a Calvinist who, believing himself to be justified by faith, concluded that whatever action he did could not be evil or endanger his salvation: driven by the other half of his schizophrenic personality (personified as the devil) he put his theory to the test by committing assassination, fratricide, rape and finally, suicide. It is an astonishing work, powerful, memorable and penetrating. Many modern readers find it the most interesting Scottish novel ever written, but when it was published it met with a uniformly hostile and indifferent reception. Hogg did not persist: except in an occasional short story, like 'The Brownie of Bodsbeck', he wrote no more in this vein. Perhaps if he had lived in a larger society he could have done so, for if the public is big enough an artist can afford to ignore the hostility of ninety-eight per cent and live off the plaudits and patronage of the remaining two per cent. But Scottish society was small and intimate, and if it disliked the work of a novelist there was nothing much he could do to compensate for it except to start writing a different kind of novel or turn his hand to another trade.

Why was the Scottish public so addicted to harmless historical fiction? To some extent it was a traditional taste—the ballads, Barbour's *Brus* and Blind Harry's *Wallace*, all part of the staple literary fare of the peasantry, had been versified forms of history or fiction like Scott's own first popular poems. But it persisted and increased perhaps because it satisfied an emotional need in a time of social change. By the early nineteenth century the economic revolution was uprooting all old ways in agriculture and industry after centuries in which alteration had been so gradual from generation to generation as to be almost imperceptible. People felt their anchors go, and though most were much better off in material terms, they became nostalgic for the old certainties.

There was also a cultural change beginning to come over Edinburgh's own society at the end of the first quarter of the nineteenth century. James Boswell's only rival in the private art of autobiography, Henry Cockburn (1779–1854), sensed it and expressed it in his *Journals* and *Memorials of His Own Time*. He saw many things that were purely Scottish in the capital's society passing away, and manners and fashions becoming increasingly assimilated to those of polite society throughout the United Kingdom. He believed too that it was largely inevitable. The world was getting smaller, and people were more easily drawn to London. Economic change, by affecting England and Scotland simultaneously and in the same way, was bound to make the societies of the two countries more alike. But he also regretted that Scottish national characteristics should be thrown into this rough melting-pot after so many centuries of proud differentiation. He spoke for many when he wrote in his *Journal*:

> The prolongation of Scotch peculiarities, especially of our language and habits, I do earnestly desire. An exact knowledge and feeling of what these have been since 1707 till now would be more curious five hundred years hence than a similar knowledge and feeling of the old Greeks. But the features and expression of a people cannot be perpetuated by legislative engraving. Nothing can prevent the gradual disappearance of local manners under the absorption and assimilation of a far larger, richer and more powerful kindred adjoining kingdom. Burns and Scott have done more for the preservation of proper Scotland than could ever be accomplished by law, statesmen or associations.[14]

Scott deliberately, and Burns unwittingly, thus provided the public with the nostalgic stability and sense of nationhood in the past that it sensed it was losing in the present. The result, however, was catastrophic to literature, as it twisted its head back to front—its poetry looking always to Burns and a dead language, in prose to Scott and a past society. In this frozen posture it was obliged to walk on into the nineteenth century seeing nothing of the real world about it.

It was, incidentally, hardly less catastrophic to the study of Scottish history which became, in the popular mind only an extension of imaginative literature, bound up with myth and a sately remote and anti-English past. It was not, indeed, Scott's fault that his later followers were much less competent historians than he. The start that had been made in the eighteenth century with such professionals as William Robertson to see history as connected with explaining the development of society up to the point of contemporary existence was lost. By common consent the Victorians placed history beneath a rose-coloured

glass, and everyone who beheld Scotland's Romantic Story was expected to exclaim 'here's tae us, wha's like us'.

Alas, the answer to those most mindless words may change over
the centuries.

3. SOCIAL CHANGE AND CULTURAL ACHIEVEMENT

A final chapter is a good place to ask a difficult question. How can we
account for the unprecedented cultural achievements of the Scots in
the century after 1740? Certainly no previous age in Scottish history
had ever approached this concentration of intellectual greatness in so
many different fields. The Middle Ages, though not without distinguished vernacular building and poetry, had produced few figures of
international stature: we may not count Duns Scotus. The sixteenth
century had had George Buchanan, a series of marvellous court poets
known only within Scotland, and some beautiful architecture. The
seventeenth century, relatively sparse in artistic work of the first rank,
had at least produced Napier as a mathematician of major international
reputation, and a number of savants of more limited importance, like
Gregory and Sibbald. Thus, though the achievement before 1700 is
not by any means negligible, it was not of the same order as what
followed. With men like Hume, Smith, Burns, Scott, Black, Watt,
Telford, Robert Adam and Hutton in the first rank, with Ferguson,
Millar, Reid, Robertson, Allan Ramsay junior, Raeburn, William
Adam, Rennie, Boswell and Hogg in the second rank, and a third rank
crowded with talent as diverse as that of William Symington, who
invented steam navigation, and Francis Jeffrey, who founded the
Edinburgh Review, the cultural performance of Scotland between 1740
and 1830 was of dazzling virtuosity. Few people would claim these
standards have been maintained, either, for although many Scotsmen
have distinguished themselves in many parts of the world in the past
hundred and fifty years, there has never again been the same concentration of genius working together within Scotland at the same time.
The age of Hume and Scott was also the age of economic take-off, and
as Scotland's material enrichment was due in no small degree to the
human response to the opportunities that suddenly opened in front of

her, it is possible that any light we can throw on the reasons for the cultural achievements would reflect some truth about the entrepreneurial as well as the intellectual triumphs of the age.

But how can the social historian hope to explain such phenomena? There are many who would say that it is absurd for him even to try, since genius presumably occurs in society at random, and galaxies of genius must be a rare statistical accident. Therefore it must be as fruitless for an historian to try to explain a cultural golden age, whether manifested in Socratic Greece, Elizabethan England or Georgian Scotland, as it would be for him to try to explain the incidence of a shower of meteorites from outer space. Certainly it would be a rash man who believed that he could discover from the study of the past the recipe to bring a new Hume into the world. But it would equally be an incurious man who believed so implicitly that genius was a random accident that he would not wish to examine the historical background in which works of genius saw the light of day. Maybe the social historian cannot fully explain what happened. That is no reason for him not to try.

What were the characteristics common to the majority of cultural pathfinders? In the first place, almost without exception, those who contributed to the mainstream were Lowlanders. The Highlanders had, of course, the Gaelic poets but these made no contribution to the culture of the rest of Scotland, where contemporary Highland poetry and music was neither known nor regarded as worth knowing. Virtually the only Highlanders to make an impression on the outside world were James Macpherson of the Ossianic forgeries, and Adam Ferguson the philosopher who was the son of a Perthshire minister. Yet there is nothing very surprising in the failure of the Highlands before 1800 to contribute to a common culture; they scarcely belonged to one. English was to many of them an alien tongue, educational provision was quite inadequate, and by the last quarter of the century their society was being so rocked by catastrophic social and economic changes as to provide little stable ground even for the further development of Gaelic culture. Nevertheless, since somewhere between a third and a quarter of the Scottish population of 1,250,000 lived in the Highlands around 1750 the failure of this region to play its part throws into sharper relief the great achievement of the Lowlanders.

The great majority of those Lowlanders who made any notable contribution to the cultural golden age came from the middle class.

This is perhaps less expected, since the story of the 'lad o' pairts' is deeply rooted in Scottish tradition. It was certainly not unknown for the son of a manual labourer or a peasant to progress from poverty to riches, though those who did so were generally not the very poorest. The commonest case was the rise of the affluent capitalist farmers from among the peasants in the agrarian revolution, but they tended to come from tenants with large or middling holdings, not from the cottars or servants. In cultural matters it was rather rare for any in those groups to follow the same paths from obscurity to fame except among the poets, who had a rather special advantage in that only the poor spoke Scottish. Burns is the obvious example of a peasant poet. The weaver poets were indisputably proletarian. Hogg came from a family similar to that of Burns but which had lost its farm in the previous generation and been forced into the labouring class. Thomas Carlyle's parents, on the other hand, had already fought their way out of the working class. James Mill the philosopher was the son of a country shoe-maker, but in his family the driving force came from the mother who had married below her status and was determined to drive her son back up the social scale. Outside the literary group, Thomas Telford, the son of a shepherd, fits the stereotype perfectly; but Rennie was the son of a capitalist farmer rather than a peasant, and the inventors Symington, Neilson and the Meikles were sons of independent tradesmen and millwrights rather than wage labourers. Presumably the day-to-day business of keeping alive was still too demanding for most labouring families to leave much time or inclination in any of their members to develop other interests, and if they did, they were more likely to be economic interests to help the individual out of the slough of penury than cultural ones with less immediately obvious practical use.

Within the middle class, however, many people of relatively humble origins played an important part in cultural achievement—especially in the towns. The minor urban bureaucracy produced such men as Adam Smith, son of a customs officer at Kirkcaldy, David Allan the painter, son of the shoremaster at Alloa, and Alexander Wilson the astronomer who discovered sun-spots, son of the town-clerk at St Andrews. Architects like the Adams, or like James Smith and Robert Mylne generally arose from dynasties of master masons. So did some of the better painters, like Alexander and Patrick Nasmyth, while two more artists, Robert Foulis and Allan Ramsay junior, came from the book trade. The children of merchants made their mark as variously as James Hutton, Hugh Blair (the rhetorician) and Charles Mackintosh. Patrick Miller who developed the steamboat with Symington was the son of a banker, Sir Henry Raeburn the son of a mill owner, Allan Ramsay senior the son of a mine manager, John Galt the son of a sea captain. It was from the same strata, and especially from the tradesmen and merchants, that Scotland also mainly drew her business talent at the time of the industrial revolution. She was better placed than most eighteenth-century societies to mobilise the genius of these urban groups because her grammar schools and universities were well fitted to provide higher education for any family with some slight resources which was also willing to make a financial sacrifice to help their children realise their talents.

The learned professions also made a great contribution to Scottish culture in the eighteenth century, proportionately bigger, indeed, than they did to business—as one would expect from the more literary and less commercial callings of the fathers. The record of some of the academic dynasties, like that of the Munros in medicine and Gregories in mathematics and medicine, rivals that of the Adams in building. Sons succeeded fathers in the same, or an allied, university chair, and like the Munros often filled them with a distinction that seems to justify the apparent nepotism. The children of Church of Scotland ministers also make a remarkably distinguished list, including Adam Ferguson, John Millar, Thomas Reid and Dugald Stewart among philosophers, William Robertson the historian and his friend Alexander Carlyle the autobiographer, James Thomson the poet and Sir David Wilkie the painter. The legal profession gave a great literary phalanx headed by Sir Walter Scott, Francis Jeffrey and Henry Cockburn. We should perhaps also include within this group such distinguished *literati* as Lord Kames and Lord Monboddo, who were the sons of minor landowners but made their fortune and reputation at the bar.

Apart from these, however, surprisingly few sons of the landed classes made any original or personal intellectual contributions to the cultural golden age. David Hume is one exception, the second son of a laird of relatively modest estate. Tobias Smollett was another younger son of a similar family. James Boswell, J. L. Macadam of the roads, Sir John Sinclair of the *Statistical Account* and William Ogilvie, whose ideas on the common ownership of land anticipated Henry George, were all from gentry stock, but the only peers with original personal contributions were James Maitland, Earl of Lauderdale, in political economy and Archibald Cochrane, Earl of Dundonald, in industrial chemistry. The list is surprisingly short considering the enormous importance of the landed classes as social and political leaders, and considering that every kind of leisure, educational opportunity and affluence lay at their feet to emancipate them from the drudgery of earning their living. Their relative failure therefore cannot be explained in material terms like that of the manual workers. It can, however, probably be explained in psychological terms. A landowner's family was so secure, and its niche in society so comfortable and so respected, that there was no need for its members to drive for social recognition in the same way as there was for a member of the middle classes, who had to live by his pen, his teaching or his inventive talents, and saw rungs in the ladder above him waiting to be climbed. Even younger sons who would never themselves inherit the broad acres could hope to get a commission in the services, a position in the colonies or an entry into the legal profession without very much effort on their own part. Should a landowner happen to have cultural interests, it always seemed to be sufficient for him to take an amateur's or a patron's part. There was nothing to jerk him out of a very natural and gentlemanly indolence. But works of genius do not ripen like plums in the summer; they have to be quarried out of the mind by the sweat of mental effort. It is doubtful if even the Earl of Dundonald would have become an industrial chemist if the finances of his estate had not been so precarious that he was driven to find a means of saving it from his creditors.

On the other hand, it was surely one of the necessary preconditions for the cultural golden age that the landed classes should be its friendly patrons, even if they could not be its finest participants. The arts, especially, were directly dependent on their patronage. Architects would have had a poor living in the eighteenth century without commissions for country houses and elegant town homes for the gentry; Robert Adam's particular and personal debt to the Earl of Hopetoun was already noted. The painters, similarly, depended largely on the aristocracy and gentry to buy their first pictures and spread the fashion for their art: David Allan, indeed, owed a similar debt to the Earl of Hopetoun as Adam had. The relationship with the poets is less easy to define. Burns was lionised in Edinburgh, paraded before Lord Daer and given unsolicited bad advice on how to write poems by the Earl of Buchan and Lord Woodhouselee. This advice did not spoil his art; but the notice of the gentry was essential to give his poetry social acceptance and this acceptance was in turn probably essential if Burns was to continue to give his best. Much earlier, Allan Ramsay senior betrayed his own need to be socially accepted when he gave his collection of vernacular poetry the very genteel title of a *Tea-Table Miscellany*. James Hogg and James Thomson both owed a lot to the direct encouragement and help of intelligent lairds who had recognised their talent when they were still in their teens. Philosophers, too, often found noble patrons: David Hume and Adam Ferguson lived for a time in the families of English peers, and Adam Smith gave up his chair at Glasgow to become tutor and travelling companion to the heir of the Duke of Buccleuch. John Millar was first discovered by Lord Kames. William Cullen owed a great deal to the patronage of the Dukes of Hamilton and Argyll.

It is easy to see that such connections were in many cases not only financially rewarding but also fed some deep-seated need among intellectuals for approval by and association with the great. Sometimes this took the form of accepting tutorships, sometimes of claiming kinship. Hume earnestly affirmed his relationship to the Earl of Home, and Ramsay proclaimed the noble blood of Douglas ran in his veins. Sometimes it took the form of buying an estate and establishing a private landed dynasty in imitation of the lairds. William Adam thus purchased land in Fife and gave the house he built upon it the pretentious name of Blairadam, and Sir Walter Scott built at Abbotsford a castle in which to live like the barons of his fancy.

This identification with the landed classes was accompanied by a lack of social and political iconoclasm. David Hume, for instance, was ready enough to attack the creeds of the church and Adam Smith to destroy the basis of mercantilist economics, but no one ventured to do the same for property and social privilege. The intellectual critics of the administration in the early nineteenth century, led by Francis Jeffrey and Henry Cockburn, were orthodox Whigs involved in no more than a minor disagreement with other gentlemen in power. Burns, so often lauded as a democrat, never permitted himself more than a little bitter sarcasm about the gentry in times when it was safe to do so, and he was quicker to denounce the French Revolution than either Wordsworth or Coleridge. The nearest thing to a Scottish radical thinker was William Ogilvie, who, being himself the son of a landowner had a less awed view of the rights of property. But Ogilvie is a very small footnote in the history of political thought.

There was thus in Scotland no equivalent to the French revolutionary philosophers like Voltaire and Rousseau, to England's Tom Paine, or even to John Wilkes, John Cartwright, Thomas Spence and William Cobbett. Indeed, any of those Englishmen who fought with their pens and minds for what we now regard as the basic democratic rights of all British subjects would have raised an eyebrow to hear latter-day Scottish historians boasting of the 'democratic intellect' of the north. William Cobbett was more realistic when he called upon heaven to protect him from the 'Scotch feelosophers'.

In other ways, however, Scottish intellectual life probably gained from the association with the landed classes. In particular the nobles and gentry were as cosmopolitan as they could afford to be. They wanted to see England, to keep a London house and to go on the Grand Tour of France and Italy if it were within their pocket. The tastes they acquired and which they helped to form in the artists and thinkers they took with them saved Scottish culture from becoming over-folksy and insular. But in regard to historical causation the main point is that Scottish intellectuals were so emotionally dependent upon the approval and support of the landed classes that it is scarcely conceivable that the cultural golden age could have taken place if the gentry and nobility had been unwilling to become its patrons.

A second precondition for the golden age was the character of national education. Very few of the cultural pathfinders were self-taught; the great majority not only attended either an adventure school or a parish school, but also went on afterwards to the nearest grammar school. No doubt the genius of some would have broken through even without a formal education as did, for example, that of James Hogg, who was still illiterate at eighteen. But it can hardly be denied that the relatively wide social coverage of the schools over the whole of the middle class combined with the relatively enlightened character of their curricula helped the country to maximise its talents.

It is hard, in particular, to imagine the golden age without the universities, who educated so many of the leaders and later harboured a high proportion of the most distinguished intellectuals in their chairs. The character of the eighteenth-century Scottish university depended much on reforms that had been instigated after the Revolution and carried forward with great vigour in Edinburgh particularly during the principalship of William Carstares between 1703 and 1716, and in Glasgow particularly in the days of Francis Hutcheson between 1730 and 1746. The aim of the reform movement had been to increase the number of university places, to modernise the teaching and to add to the variety and scope of courses offered by establishing new chairs. The abolition of the regent system at Edinburgh in 1708, of lecturing on all subjects in Latin at Glasgow about 1730, and the creation of medical schools at Edinburgh and Glasgow were all milestones on this road. By the time William Robertson became principal of Edinburgh in 1762, a post he filled illustriously for thirty years, Scottish universities were famous throughout Britain and Europe for the breadth of their intake from the middle class, for the relative cheapness of their fees, for the excellence and relevance of their instruction, and for the toleration by the university authorities of diverse opinions among the lecturers. It is true that David Hume was never given a chair, but he made an open avowal of his atheism in an age that still expected all universities to be formally devoted to Christian orthodoxy. In defence of those who declined to appoint him at Edinburgh University in 1745 it should be recalled that the professor was formally required to teach 'Pneumatics, i.e., the Being and perfections of the one true God, the nature of the angels and of the soul of man, and the duties of natural religion.'[15] It would have needed some cynicism to appoint Hume! The universities certainly tolerated many other men like Adam Smith, whose religious views were perhaps not very different from Hume's but which were not so openly flaunted.

It is difficult to differentiate between the attractions of the universities and those of the eighteenth-century Scottish towns in which they were situated. David Hume in his correspondence with Adam Smith more than once returned to the problem of where to settle:

> Paris is the most agreeable town in Europe, and suits me best, but it is a foreign country. London is the capital of my own country (sic); but it never pleased me much. Letters are held there in no honour; Scotsmen are hated, superstition and ignorance gain ground daily. Edinburgh has many objections and many allurements . . .[16]

In the end both Hume and Smith and many like them spent much of their lives in Edinburgh. It is a fair guess that what Hume in another letter called 'good company' was the greatest allurement. Alexander Carlyle described how he and his friends, the cream of the university, the clergy, the lawyers and the visiting gentry, met in a city large enough to be diverse and small enough to be intimate:

Robertson and John Home and Bannatine and I lived all in the country and came only periodically to the town. Blair and Jardine both lived in it, and suppers being the only fashionable meal at that time, we dined where best we could, and by cadies assembled our friends to meet us in a tavern by nine o'clock; and a fine time it was when we could collect David Hume, Adam Smith, Adam Ferguson, Lord Elibank and Drs. Blair and Jardine, on an hour's warning. I remembered one night that David Hume, who, having dined abroad, came rather late to us, and directly pulled a large key from his pocket which he laid on the table. This he said was given him by his maid Peggy (much more like a man than a woman) that she might not sit up for him, for she said when the honest fellows came in from the country he never returned home till after one o'clock.[17]

There was more in all this than jollification and the passing of the claret bottle. There was listening. The mutual debt of James Watt and Joseph Black is famous; so is the deep friendship of Adam Smith and David Hume; but the circles joined, for Joseph Black was one of Adam Smith's most esteemed friends ('no man has less nonsense in his head than Dr. Black') and was, with James Hutton, his literary executor. The *Wealth of Nations* reflects the spirit of these friendships. Smith's extraordinary ability to recall precise details from a very wide range of human experience and to fit them into a carefully constructed logical argument combines something of the scientific exactness of Black's observations with the philosophical limpidity of Hume. It is at once the work of a highly original mind and of a man who attended carefully while others were speaking. For many besides Adam Smith the warm sociability of the eighteenth-century town must have formed the ideal environment for the cross-fertilisation of minds. A colder, larger, more formal or more compartmentalised society could never have been as stimulating.

Why was there no comparable flowing of Scottish culture before the middle of the eighteenth century? In several material ways conditions were not earlier so propitious. There was a Lowland middle class in the seventeenth century no less than in the eighteenth, but it was neither so large nor so prosperous as it became in the fifty years before 1800. Merchants, tradesmen and many in the learned professions lived on much smaller incomes than their successors; the struggle to make ends meet was greater, physical comforts were fewer, and the need to devote all the energies of all the sons to breadwinning as soon as possible was more pressing. Though too much comfort and too assumed a place in society is perhaps discouraging to the achievement of individual genius, too little may also blight it. Similarly, despite the cultural interests of landowners like Montrose and Drummond of Hawthornden, themselves poets, or of the architect Sir William Bruce and his clients, fewer members of the landed classes had then the inclination to be patrons. This was partly because, like the middle classes, they were not as prosperous as they later became. It was also because they were not as secure. In the eighteenth century a combination of rising rents, the operation of the law of entail and firm Hanoverian rule gave Lowland landowners an exceptionally strong base from which to dabble in the arts, but in the seventeenth century none of these factors operated. When the fortunes of the family were eroded by debt, its position assailed by changes in political regimes, and the house itself perhaps in some danger of physical attack, the cultural interests that a landed gentleman felt able to develop were necessarily limited.

Educational institutions, also, were not so well developed in the seventeenth century. It was true that the parish school network was well established by the end of the century and that many of these were apparently grammar schools providing more than elementary instruction in reading and writing. The universities, however, were much smaller and more restricted. Glasgow, for example, had only 250 students as late as 1696 and Edinburgh only 300 or 400 for most of the seventeenth century. It is doubtful if either were large enough in membership or broad enough in teaching to bring about the kind of intellectual ferment so characteristic of Edinburgh and Glasgow in the eighteenth century.

Lastly, there was the question of religion. Whatever the material condition of the middle and upper classes, and of the universities, it is hard to imagine that a cultural golden age could have come into being in the chilling religious atmosphere of the seventeenth century. Its inhibiting effect worked in several ways. Firstly, it was the largest single factor in political insecurity: most of the years between 1638 and 1660 were in uproar, the following three decades were niggled by covenanter troubles, with a final *coup d'état* in 1689. Then there was the spread of puritanism, rooted before the Union of the Crowns, held in check for a time thereafter, but becoming rampant after 1638. The Restoration saw only a partial return to the freer attitudes of an earlier age, but the Revolution was followed by a further campaign of puritan repression only a little less marked than that of the 1640s. Thereafter it withered slowly. It had lost a good deal of impetus even by the 1720s, and was obviously dying in most places after the mid-century. Where and when it was strong it was fatal to artistic expression. Thanks to the very strict control that the presbyterian system of church courts from the kirk-session to the General Assembly exercised over the minutiae of national and parish life before 1712 it either destroyed or came near to destroying the Scottish tradition in poetry, painting, music and drama. Even architecture produced little that was worthwhile in the severest periods.

At least as damaging as puritanism, however, was the kirk's intolerance of deviant belief, an intolerance shared by episcopalian and presbyterian alike, but, as far as intellectuals were concerned, generally worse among presbyterians. The most notorious case, the more shocking because it came at a time when most European countries were moving towards greater toleration, was the trial and execution for blasphemy in 1696 of an Edinburgh student, Thomas Aikenhead, for allegedly denying the divinity of Christ. He died on the testimony of a single witness. Hume, half a century later, used sometimes to complain of the hostility of the elder ministers, but in practice he was given the greatest freedom to write and speak as he chose. It is not hard to imagine what would have happened to him in Aikenhead's day.

The kirk, however, had more subtle and perhaps more persuasive ways than the dramatic heresy trial of enforcing orthodoxy. It was able, through the kirk-session, to call any miscreants and non-attenders before it. It appointed the parish schoolmaster and rigorously inspected his school. It had great influence in the universities, where, even if the town council and not the church appointed the professors, the whole code of discipline, teaching and religious observation was designed to ensure conformity. The emphasis in every home and school on repeating and understanding the catechism impressed on every child the importance of holding the right belief. Since justification was by faith and faith must be orthodox, orthodoxy was a prerequisite to salvation. On the other hand, by believing in the priesthood of all believers the Calvinist also stressed that every man must find his own way to God in his innermost thoughts and prayers. But this required the individual to become a reflective and intellectual being, with all the dangers that he might reach an independent and unorthodox conclusion about God. To guard against this it was doubly necessary for the church courts to detect and call to heel a deviant before he imperilled his own soul and began to infect those of the rest of the flock.

Lastly, the domination of the church was responsible for a large deflection of effort and talent away from the enrichment of secular life. The middle class in particular gave many of its best brains to the ministry which would, in later times, have been spread more widely in other callings. While there still seemed to be a chance of achieving the Godly Commonwealth on earth there was no shortage of sacrifice of human effort, and what was not poured out to this end was regarded in some sense as profitless waste.

Perhaps, then, the decay of the old kirk in the or five six decades after 1700 did more than anything else to produce the golden age of cultural achievement that followed. Several factors accounted for its fall. The settlement of 1690, though it established presbyterianism and restored the General Assembly, denied the church the unquestioning support of civil law. Excommunication thus lost its material terrors. This so weakened the church courts that they were unable to keep control over orthodoxy to the degree that they had in the past and the tendency of Calvinism to fly apart in sectarian disputes now began to be its leading characteristic. As the splits developed these not only destroyed the kirk's monolithic character and presented men with a variety of possible beliefs, but it had the important psychological effect of encouraging individuals to think that their opinion might very well be as good as the next man's.

Again, over much of Europe public opinion turned increasingly to the view that a degree of religious toleration was preferable to endless war. The seventeenth century had seen intensely cruel struggles waged between Catholic and Protestant ideologies on the Continent, and between Anglican and Puritan or Presbyterian and Episcopalian in these islands; in the end society had sickened, the hot disputes of the fathers had become sterile to the sons, and governments began to agree to religious compromises. Scotland was certainly not in the van of the movement towards toleration, but she could not be untouched by it. The Union of 1707 was a religious compromise of a sort, soldering a Presbyterian and an Anglican state into one joint kingdom. Although little freedom was given to Catholics in the eighteenth century other churches in Scotland got a certain degree of elbow room they would never have had before. Lastly, the Patronage Act of 1712 ultimately modified the character of the ministry by making the ministers the creatures of the landed classes. They became increasingly imbued with the characteristic upper-class values of Anglophilia, politeness, toleration and moderation, rather than those popular ones of Anglophobia, conservatism and fanaticism.

Of course, all this did not happen at once, nor did it happen simply, or at the same pace in every part of the Lowlands. But it is important to notice that the decay of the old kirk for the most part predated the cultural golden age. It was not the scepticism of Hume or the satire of Burns that blew away the clerical narrowness of the past. It was because the power of the old clerics was already waning that Hume got the chance to be sceptical and Burns to be satirical with impunity.

It would, however, be very naïve to suppose that the only link between religious belief and the cultural golden age was the negative one, that the less there was of religious belief the more golden would be the culture of the age. For one thing the national educational institutions on which so much depended had not only been formed in the past by the kirk but were now mainly reformed and modernised by the leaders of the kirk. This was true at school level: the Scottish S.P.C.K. was a religious body of educational pioneers, and the founders of Perth Academy were influenced principally by a report of the Rev. James Bonnar. It was still more true of the universities, which were first set on their programme of enlargement and change by a church commission of the 1690s. William Carstares, the principal who did so much to transform Edinburgh University in the opening years of the eighteenth century was more famous still as Scotland's leading ecclesiastic after the Revolution; William Robertson, who guided the University for three of the finest decades in her history after 1762 was simultaneously the great leader of the Moderates in the Church of Scotland and a distinguished Moderator of the General Assembly. Many of the ordinary professors were also ministers; many of the ministers outside the universities were also close colleagues and friends of those within. It is true that few of these academic clergy any longer resembled the formidable old Calvinists of tradition. William Robertson in his *History*, for instance, referred to John Knox as a barbarian. But the Moderate clergy were neither lukewarm nor hypocritical in their beliefs; they simply held the reasonable view that the virtues of being moderate were more truly Christian than the habit of being fanatical.

We have also noted earlier how many of the leaders of the intellectual movement were the sons of ministers, like Adam Ferguson and Thomas Reid, and how many more were the sons of deeply religious fathers outside the ministry, often of a rather old-fashioned kind, like Robert Burns and Thomas Carlyle. The second half of the eighteenth century in Scotland was not, in other words, by any means an irreligious age, in the sense that people either generally disbelieved or were uninterested in the tenets of formal religion. On the other hand, in contrast to the previous century, the church now sought neither to force its own view of ecclesiastical polity upon every citizen nor to direct all social effort to the single end of building the City of God upon earth. Through the Moderate leadership of the established church it lent its own great prestige to the achievement of diffuse secular aims, both cultural and economic. This surely made the social climate more propitious for attaining them than if the church had simply dug itself in and obliged all intellectuals to deny their faith before they could get the freedom to think for themselves.

In a more general way, moreover, it is impossible not to suspect that the remarkable drive that so characterises eighteenth-century Scotland in both intellectual and economic affairs is not connected with Calvinist habits of reflection and seriousness of individual purpose first imbibed in the seventeenth century and now carried forward into the eighteenth. Some of the ways in which this might have come about have already been discussed at length in chapter III (see pp. 94–100 above) and there is no need to reiterate them in detail here. It is possible that the nation gained a particular stimulus from adopting in the seventeenth century an ideology with one over-riding and narrowly religious aim and then, finding this intrinsically impossible to achieve, from being catapulted into an eighteenth-century world where the legitimate objects of aspiration were suddenly felt to be wider and more diverse. The energy generated towards the achievement of the original objective was continued in the race for the new ones, and society for a time got the best of both worlds. The aftermath of Protestant religious enthusiasm seems often to bring such material benefits: as well as the example of Scotland it could be argued that something like this happened, for instance, in the seventeenth-century Netherlands after the war against Spain, in eighteenth-century Colonial America after the failure of puritan ideals and in nineteenth-century Denmark in the wake of Lutheran revival. In most of these instances economic adventurousness was at least as evident as intellectual stir, as it certainly was in Scotland in the agrarian and industrial revolutions.

To conclude and summarise our argument, the golden age of Scottish culture was achieved largely by the Lowland middle class with the approval and patronage (but not the initiative) of the landed classes, against a complex background of historical change—of economic change enabling Scotland better to afford her culture, of educational change in her universities and schools, and of psychological change in the attitude of society towards its own aspirations. To stress any one factor to the exclusion of the others would distort what happened; to weigh one nicely against the other would be a fruitless attempt to balance what cannot be quantified. Yet, though we cannot see clearly all the links in the chain of historical causation we can see clearly enough that there is a chain. Though genius may occur in the human race as a random accident, the conditions under which genius can come to fruition are not in the least accidental, for man in his achievements is shaped by the past even as he endeavours in his own generation to fashion the future.

Postscript

Scotland in 1830 had come over a watershed. The social and economic stagnation of a peasant society was banished; the industrial and agrarian revolution since 1780 had committed her not merely to being an industrialised society but also to becoming a society where rapid and accelerating social change was the normal condition of life. Already people found it hard to remember how their fathers had lived, and unnerving that their world moved at so great a pace. They welcomed the novels of Scott and the poetry of Burns, partly because they recalled the past and gave them a reassuring sense of continuity. At the same time the Church of Scotland began to undergo a further change as the Evangelicals, who stood tor conservative presbyterian and puritan values, waxed in power. Their triumph in the 1830s resulted in a marked revival of puritanism even within the established church; in the 1840s it led to the disruption and to the setting up of a Free Church dedicated to religious conservatism. Such things were perhaps the first symptoms of general doubt (as yet unacknowledged and unconscious) as to whether all economic growth and all social change was really progress. Hitherto nobody except a few sour Calvinists had seriously doubted that the world was getting better and better, more polite, more civilised and more perfect. This self-confidence among eighteenth-century intellectuals in the greatness of contemporary achievement is one of the things that makes that age so refreshing a contrast to our own.

Since Pandora had opened her box, however, neither the creeping nostalgia nor the reviving puritanism of 1830 could slow or halt the processes of economic change. In 1828 J. B. Neilson's application of the hot-blast process to smelting the blackband ironstone of the Central Belt gave the Scottish economy the cue for its next major advance.

Taken in conjunction with the experiments going on mainly in England
to perfect a railway to carry passengers and goods behind a steam
locomotive, and the development in Scotland of Symington and Miller's
iron-clad steamboats, it led to the birth of Scottish heavy industry with
the swelling boom in iron towns and engineering in the 1830s and
1840s and the gigantic construction of shipyards on Clydeside in the
last quarter of the century. All this, of course, greatly increased the
national income even over what it had been in 1830, and it led to a
more general prosperity for the working class by the end of the Victorian era than could have been dreamed of in any previous age.

But it also led to social problems of unbelievable complexity.
Already in 1830 many of the traditional institutions in Scottish society
were dangerously out of date. Burgh constitutions designed for the
minute towns of the sixteenth century were hopelessly inefficient to
cope with the problems of cities of up to 200,000 people. Sanitation,
over-crowding, dereliction, the housing problems that had been
growing unchecked since the start of the industrial revolution, became
in the decades after 1830 of monstrous proportions. So, too, in the
continuous industrial development, did the problems of poor-relief
and primary education; the machinery in 1830 had not been altered
since the seventeenth century, but it could not continue unaltered for
long if social catastrophe was to be averted.

In some ways the biggest change in the decades before 1830 had
been Scotland's tendency to become more British and less specifically
Scottish. The glories of her cultural golden age were passing away in
art, literature and philosophy, though not yet in science or technology.
The end of significant building in the New Town of Edinburgh and
the decline in the international reputation of her universities and reviews
were all symptomatic of this. More talent than before was drawn to
London: with the coming of the railway and the telegraph later in the
nineteenth century more companies could be run from London and
more government directed from London. Scots very frequently
emigrated to London in order to participate in both activities. On the
other hand, since the main social problems affecting Britain in the
nineteenth century were the outcome of similar economic changes in all
her component parts it did not much matter to Scotland that the
solutions to her difficulties were British in character. It was the English
civil servant Edwin Chadwick who did most to determine how Edinburgh and Glasgow should solve their sanitary problems, and it was

appropriate that it should be so, since they were of the same type as the problems of London and Leeds, and machinery fit to sweep one set of Augean stables could be used to sweep the other. It was the same with the factory acts. Even in poor law and education, where more elaborate account was taken by Westminster of distinctive Scottish conditions, the ideas that were ultimately applied to Scotland were very similar to those applied to England for the excellent reason that, despite different traditions at an earlier date, the nineteenth-century problems that had to be solved were common to both countries.

Scotland, however, in 1830 also stood on the brink of a political change—and one at least as pregnant for the future as any other aspect of the shifting world. Within two years the Great Reform Bill would have become law, and the first step gingerly taken towards giving political representation to the middle classes. From this would spring in time further Reform Bills giving the franchise to a wider and wider spectrum of the Scottish people until, by the end of the nineteenth century, adult male suffrage had almost arrived, and after the First World War, adult female suffrage as well. With the coming of democracy the Scottish people for the first time attained the freedom to decide for themselves what form of government most suited their social needs. From the end of the nineteenth century until after the middle of the twentieth century it never seriously crossed their minds that anything other than government from Westminster was appropriate for Scotland. Whether they will keep to the same course in the next half century remains to be seen; it is in no way fitting for an historian to set himself up as a prophet.

All the historical considerations of the period since 1830, however, raise themes and problems that ought to form the matter, not for a postcript, but for another volume that, in due course, must be written.

Notes, References and Further Reading

Notes, References and Further Reading

CHAPTER I

1. G. W. S. Barrow, *Feudal Britain* (London 1956), p. 124
2. The only attempt to discuss Scottish medieval population is in a rather unsatisfactory article by T. M. Cooper, 'The numbers and distribution of the population of medieval Scotland', *Scottish Historical Review* XXVI (1926) 1–9
3. Quoted in I. F. Grant, *The Social and Economic Development of Scotland before 1603* (Edinburgh 1930), p. 21
4. Quoted *ibid* p. 23
5. *Ibid* p. 52
6. W. M. Mackenzie, *The Scottish Burghs* (Edinburgh 1949), p. 138
7. *Ibid* p. 36
8. *A Source Book of Scottish History*, ed. W. Croft Dickinson *et. al.* (London, 1952–3), II p. 132. Spelling modernised
9. Quoted in W. Croft Dickinson, *Scotland from the Earliest Times to 1603* (London 1961), p. 71

10. Quoted in Grant *op. cit.* p. 73
11. Quoted in L. A. Barbé, *Sidelights on the History, Industries and Social Life of Scotland* (Glasgow 1919), p. 289
12. *Scotland before 1700 from Contemporary Documents*, ed. P. Hume Brown (Edinburgh 1893), pp. 58–9
13. For more about Scottish agriculture in its backward phase, see Chapters V and VI
14. *Scotland before 1700*, pp. 11–12
15. Quoted in J. S. Richardson and H. B. Mackintosh, *Elgin Cathedral* (Ministry of Works guide, H.M.S.O. 1950), p. 24
16. W. F. Skene, *The Highlanders of Scotland* (Stirling, ed. 1902), p. 181
17. *Scotland before 1700*, pp. 12, 60–1, 160–73
18. W. Croft Dickinson, *op. cit.*, p. 244
19. For more about burgh life, see Chapter VII

Further Reading

W. Croft Dickinson's narrative text-book, *Scotland from the earliest times to 1603* (London, 1961) is a very readable introduction and has a good bibliography. For the early middle ages it should be supplemented by G. W. S. Barrow, *Feudal Britain*

(London, 1956). I. F. Grant, *The Social and Economic Development of Scotland before 1603* (Edinburgh, 1930) is the only attempt at a medieval Scottish social or economic history: it is hard to read through but illuminating to dip into. Rural society is discussed in T. B. Franklin, *A History of Scottish Farming* (Edinburgh, 1952) and the burghs in W. M. Mackenzie, *The Scottish Burghs* (Edinburgh, 1949). J. Davidson and A. Gray, *The Scottish Staple at Veere* (London, 1909) discusses best the foreign trade of the burghs. W. C. Mackenzie, *The Highlands and Isles of Scotland: A Historical Survey* is the most convenient account of the Highland history.

CHAPTER II

1. David Patrick, in his introduction to *Statuta Ecclesiae Scoticanae 1225-1559* (Scottish History Society 1907), p. xcii. For details of what was involved see *Concilia Scotiae* (ed. Joseph Robertson, Bannatyne Club 1866) II, pp. 301-2. But you will need to understand Latin

2. Gordon Donaldson, *The Scottish Reformation* (Cambridge 1960), p. 15-16. The first chapter of this book is an excellent summary of the plight of the church before 1560

3. *Ibid* p. 24

4. John Knox, *History of the Reformation in Scotland* (ed. W. Croft Dickinson, Edinburgh 1949), I, p. 25

5. Donaldson, *op. cit.*, p. 75

6. *Ibid* chapter V

7. G. Donaldson, *Scotland: Church and Nation through sixteen centuries* (SCM Press, London 1960), p. 63

8. W. Croft Dickinson, *Scotland from*

the Earliest Times to 1603 (Edinburgh 1961), p. 354

9. The quotations are all from S. A. Burrell, 'The Apocalyptic vision of the Early Covenanters', *Scottish Historical Review*, Vol. XLIII (1964), pp. 1-24

10. *Ibid* p. 2. The writer was the poet William Drummond of Hawthornden

11. W. Notestein, *The Scot in History* (New Haven 1946), p. 144

12. For the social structure of the south-west see on page 137 below. But note also the long tradition in this area of religious radicalism of one kind and another described in G. Donaldson, 'Scotland's Conservative North in the Sixteenth and Seventeenth Centuries' *Transactions of the Royal Historical Society*, fifth series, Vol. XVI (1966), pp. 65-79

Further Reading

Church history of the sixteenth and seventeenth centuries is the special province of Professor Gordon Donaldson, whose *Reformation in Scotland* (Cambridge 1960) is a scholarly, lucid and original account of what happened between 1550 and 1600. His text-book *Scotland James V to James VII* (Edinburgh 1965) covers a wider period and is particularly good on political and ecclesiastical matters. His brief *Scotland, Church and Nation through Sixteen Centuries* (London 1960) is the most readable and useful short history of the church.

Other historians have written a great deal on these centuries: the difficulty is to be selective. David Hay Fleming in *The Reformation in Scotland* (London 1910) rooted out the lapses of the Catholic clergy with almost unhealthy zeal. Jasper Ridley's *John Knox* (London 1968) is the best biography of that complicated man. Duncan Shaw *The General Assemblies of the Church of Scotland 1560-1600* (Edinburgh 1964) traces the early history of that institution. Catholic historians have recently contributed a notable volume entitled *Essays on the Scottish Reformation 1513-1625* (ed. D. Mc-Roberts, Glasgow 1962), and there is a useful review article by Maurice Lee 'The Scottish Reformation after 400 Years' in *Scottish Historical Review* Vol. XLIV (1965).

The seventeenth century is less-well served on religious matters, except by Donaldson's textbook, but S. A. Burrell, 'The Apocalyptic Vision of the Early Covenanters', *Scottish Historial Review*, Vol. XLIII (1964) is exceptionally stimulating and G. D. Henderson, *Religious Life in Seventeenth Century Scotland* (Cambridge 1937) is worthwhile. See also I. B. Cowan, 'The Covenanters: a revision article' in *Scottish Historical Review* Vol. XLVII (1968).

CHAPTER III

1. The Book of Discipline is printed by W. Croft Dickinson in his edition of John Knox's *History of the Reformation in Scotland* (London 1949), II Appendix VIII
2. *Ibid* p. 306
3. *Ibid* p. 309
4. *Ibid* p. 295
5. *Ibid* pp. 290, 303
6. *Ibid* p. 29
7. G. Donaldson, 'The Parish Clergy and the Reformation' in *Essays on the Scottish Reformation 1513-1625*, ed. D. McRoberts (Glasgow 1962) p. 135
8. A. Ross, 'Reformation and Repression' in *ibid*, p. 403
9. *The Records of the Commissions of the General Assembly, 1646-1647* (ed. A. F. Mitchell and J. Christie, Scottish History Society, 1892) p. 252
10. *Minutes of the Synod of Argyll, 1639-1651* (ed. D. C. Mactavish, Scottish History Society, 1943), I, p. 68
11. *Records of the Presbyteries of Inverness and Dingwall, 1643-1688* (ed.

William Mackay, Scottish History Society 1896), pp. xxi, xxiv, xxv
12. *Ibid* p. xvii
13. *Ibid* pp. 279 ff
14. G. D. Henderson, *The Scottish Ruling Elder* (London 1935), p. 123.
15. *Register of the Kirk Session of St. Andrews 1559-1600* (ed. D. Hay Fleming, Scottish History Society 1889), I, p. 107
16. *Selections from the Records of the Kirk Session . . . of Aberdeen* (ed. John Stuart, Spalding Club 1846), pp. 24, 46, 61, 66, 67
17. Sir George Mackenzie, quoted in Donaldson *Scotland: James V–James VII*, p. 366
18. *The Booke of the Universall Kirk*, ed. A. Peterkin (Edinburgh 1839), p. 435
19. W. C. Mackenzie, *Andrew Fletcher of Saltoun* (Edinburgh 1935), Chapter VIII
20. *Register of the Kirk Session of St. Andrews; The Buik of the Kirk of the Canagait 1564-1567* (ed. A. B. Calderwood, Scottish Record Society 1961); G. Lorimer, *Leaves*

from the *Buik of the West Kirke* (Edinburgh 1885)

21. P. Hume Brown, *Early Travellers in Scotland* (Edinburgh 1891), p. 101
22. Henderson *op. cit.* p. 116
23. R. Chambers, *Domestic Annals of Scotland* (Edinburgh 1859), II, p. 243
24. Knox, *op. cit.* II, p. 64
25. *The Booke of the Universall Kirk*, p. 160
26. *A Source Book of Scottish History* (ed. W. Croft Dickinson *et. al.*, London 1954), III, 395
27. Henderson, *op. cit.*, pp. 109, 120
28. *Acts of the General Assembly, 1638–1842* (Church Law Society, Edinburgh, 1843), p. 229
29. John Durkan, 'Education in the Century of the Reformation' in *Essays on the Scottish Reformation*, pp. 145–68
30. *A Source Book of Scottish History*, III, p. 401
31. *Acts of the General Assembly, 1638–1842*, p. 63
32. *Scotland: James V–James VII*, p. 264
33. These remarkable regulations are printed in William Boyd, *Education in Ayrshire through Seven Centuries* (London 1961), pp. 26–30
34. I. J. Simpson, *Education in Aberdeenshire before 1872* (London 1947), p. 23
35. *Ibid* p. 22
36. Quoted by Ross, 'Reformation and Repression', in *Essays on the Scottish Reformation*, p. 385
37. *Booke of the Universall Kirk*, p. 435
38. *Register of the Kirk Session of St. Andrews*, passim.

39. *Register of the Privy Council of Scotland*, XIII, pp. 834–6
40. *Selections from the Records of the Kirk Session . . . of Aberdeen*, p. 97
41. A. A. Cormack, *Poor Relief in Scotland* (Aberdeen 1923) chapter XVI
42. Max Weber, *The Protestant Ethic and the Spirit of Capitalism*. There is a convenient paper-back edition by Unwin University Books (London 1967). See also R. H. Tawney, *Religion and the Rise of Capitalism* (various editions)
43. *Booke of the Universall Kirk*, p. 436, Henderson, *ibid.* pp. 113, T. C. Smout, *Scottish Trade on the Eve of Union* (Edinburgh 1963), p. 77
44. Scottish Record Office. Andrew Russell Papers, box 5
45. Quoted in Henry Hamilton, *Economic History of Scotland in the Eighteenth Century* (Oxford 1963), p. xiv
46. Weber, *op. cit.* p. 117
47. D. C. McClelland, *The Achieving Society* (Princeton 1961), briefly summarised in M. W. Flinn, *Origins of the Industrial Revolution* (London 1966), pp. 87–9, from which this quotation is drawn
48. M. W. Flinn, 'Social Theory and the Industrial Revolution', in *Social Theory and Economic Change*, ed. T. Burns and S. B. Saul (Edinburgh 1965)
49. Marjorie Plant, *The Domestic Life of Scotland in the Eighteenth Century* (Edinburgh 1952), pp. 3–7

Further Reading

Relatively few secondary studies have been made in these fields: for this reason I have footnoted the text much more than in most chapters, and the curious will find a great deal of interest among the printed kirk-session and presbytery records, etc., cited there. He only has to look up his own local church records to find a great deal more. The best account of kirk-discipline is undoubtedly that by G. D. Henderson, *The Scottish Ruling Elder* (London, 1935). A. Ross, 'Reformation and Repression' in *Essays on the Scottish Reformation 1513-1625* gives a useful account of how it was used against Catholics. There are other relevant essays in that collection to the topics touched on here. A. Cormack, *Poor Relief in Scotland* (Aberdeen 1923) is the only book on that subject: it urgently needs full modern academic treatment. Books on education abound, mostly repeating errors from one another. The best and freshest account is in an unpublished Edinburgh Ph.D. thesis by J. M. Beale, 'A History of the Burgh and Parochial Schools of Fife from the Reformation to 1872'. The various local studies published for the Scottish Council of Research in Education are of varying merit, but that by W. Boyd, *Education in Ayrshire through Seven Centuries* (London 1961) has a lot of interesting seventeenth-century information.

The whole problem of religion and the rise of capitalism has not, to my mind, ever been properly studied for Scotland. The interested student should read the works cited in footnotes 42, 47 and 48, and reflect. But for a view in some ways opposed to the one given here, see S. A. Burrell, 'Calvinism, Capitalism and the Middle Classes: Some Afterthoughts on an Old Problem', *Journal of Modern History* Vol. XXXII (1960).

CHAPTER IV

1. Quoted in J. Warrack, *Domestic Life in Scotland 1488-1688* (London 1920), p. 3
2. James I, *Basilikon Doron* (ed. James Craigie, Scottish Text Society 1942), p. 83
3. D. W. L. Tough, *The Last Years of a Frontier* (Oxford 1928), p. 183
4. See, for instance, William Robertson, *Ayrshire, its History and Historic Families* (Kilmarnock 1908), I, pp. 130-95
5. James Fergusson, *Lowland Lairds* (London 1949), Chapter 2
6. Quoted in I. F. Grant, *The Macleods, the History of a Clan 1200-1956* (London 1959), p. 139
7. Quoted *ibid*, p. 139
8. P. Hume Brown, *Early Travellers in Scotland* (Edinburgh 1891), pp. 88-9
9. *Basilikon Doron*, pp. 85-6

10. Quoted in D. H. Willson, *King James VI and I* (London 1956), p. 313
11. D. Mathew, *Scotland Under Charles I* (London 1955), p. 119
12. Quoted in T. A. Fischer, *The Scots in Sweden* (Edinburgh 1907), p. 77
13. Quoted in S. G. E. Lythe, *The Economy of Scotland in its European Setting* (Edinburgh 1960), p. 199
14. *Basilikon Doron* p. 71
15. W. C. Mackenzie, *The Highlands and Isles of Scotland: a Historical Survey* (Edinburgh, 2nd ed. 1949), p. 210
16. Quoted in I. F. Grant, *The Social and Economic Development of Scotland before 1603* (Edinburgh 1930), p. 528
17. J. Irvine Smith, 'The Rise of Modern Scots Law' in *An Introduction to Scottish Legal History* (Stair Society, 1958), p. 45

18. *The Glamis Book of Record* (ed. A. H. Millar, Scottish History Society 1890), p. 33
19. *Records of the Kirk Session . . .*

of Aberdeen (Spalding Club 1866), p. 290
20. I. F. Grant, *The Economic History of Scotland* (London 1934), p. 161

Further Reading

G. Donaldson's *Scotland: James V–James VII* is again very valuable here. There is a good biography of James VI by D. H.Willson, *King James VI and I* (London 1956) and another by D. Mathew, *James I* (London 1967) less well informed on the Scottish background. D. Mathew, however, had written a study of *Scotland under Charles I* which, while marred by a number of misconceptions, is refreshing in its examination of the political and economic behaviour of old and new men among the nobility. Seventeenth-century Highland affairs are well dealt with by Audrey Cunningham, *The Loyal Clans* (Cambridge 1932): see also Walter Scott, *Legend of Montrose*, W. C. Mackenzie, *The Highlands and Isles of Scotland* and Donald Gregory, *The History of the Western Highlands* (London 1881). The sixteenth-century border administration has been admirably described by T. I. Rae, *The Administration of the Scottish Frontier 1513–1603* (Edinburgh 1966): see also D. L. W. Tough, *The Last Years of a Frontier* (Oxford 1928). Professor H. R. Trevor-Roper has a chapter on what Cromwell tried to do in Scotland in *Religion, the Reformation and Social Change* (London 1967).

For economic affairs see S. G. E. Lythe, *The Economy of Scotland in its European Setting, 1550–1625* (Edinburgh 1960). and T. C. Smout, *Scottish Trade on the Eve of Union 1660–1707* (Edinburgh 1963). The chronological gap between is partially filled by Theodora Keith, 'The Economic Condition of Scotland under the Commonwealth and the Protectorate,' *Scottish Historical Review*, Vol. X (1918) pp. 273–84. Another article, T. C. Smout and A. Fenton, 'Scottish Agriculture before the Improvers: an Exploration', *Agricultural History Review*, Vol. XIII (1965) deals with aspects of the rural economy of the seventeenth century and its relationship to political change.

CHAPTER V

1. *Scotland and Scotsmen in the Eighteenth Century*, ed. Alexander Allardyce, Edinburgh 1888, II, p. 192
2. Scottish Record Office, Dalhousie Muniments
3. *Macfarlane's Geographical Collections* (ed. A. Mitchell and J. T. Clark, Scottish History Society 1908), III, p. 143
4. The Baron Court book is printed in *The Black Book of Taymouth* (ed. C. Innes, Bannatyne Club 1855)
5. This is printed in *Records of the Baron*

Court of Stitchill 1655–1807. (ed. C. B. Gunn, Scottish History Society 1905)
6. *The Court Book of the Barony of Urie 1604–1747* (ed. D. G. Barron, Scottish History Society 1892)
7. 'The Forbes Baron Court Book 1659–1678' edited J. M. Thomson in *Miscellany of the Scottish History Society*, Vol. III (1919)
8. The 'Boorlaw Book of Yester and Gifford' ed. The Marquis of Tweeddale is printed in *Transac-*

tions of the East Lothian Antiquarian and Field Naturalists' Society, Vol. VII (1958)

9. E. Burt, Letters from a Gentleman in the North of Scotland (London 1754), II, p. 155

10. Macfarlane's Geographical Collections II, pp. 69, 73, 102

11. Ibid, II, p. 66

12. Ibid III, p. 225

13. Scotland and the Protectorate (ed. C. H. Firth, Scottish History Society 1899), pp. 405-11

14. List of Pollable Persons within the Shire of Aberdeen (ed. John Stuart, Spalding Club 1844)

Further Reading

The early chapters of J. E. Handley, *Scottish Farming in the Eighteenth Century* (London 1953) and Malcolm Gray, *The Highland Economy 1750-1850* (Edinburgh 1957) give an idea of peasant farms on the eve of the great transformation, though what is true of the early eighteenth century is by no means automatically true of the seventeenth. J. A. Symon, *Scottish Farming Past and Present* (Edinburgh 1959) has a chapter VI directly on the seventeenth century, and a local study with good economic material is Andrew Mackerral, *Kintyre in the Seventeenth Century* (Edinburgh 1948). The printed baron court books, and the 'Boorlaw Book of Yester and Gifford', for all of which see the footnotes to this chapter, are also interesting. The only extended 'agricultural report' on any part of the kingdom was that by Andrew Symson on Galloway, printed as *A Large description of Galloway* (Edinburgh 1923) and also in *Macfarlane's Geographical Collections* (edited A. Mitchell and J. T. Clark, Scottish History Society 1908) Volume II. See also an interesting document printed by Alexander Fenton, 'Skene of Hallyard's manuscript of Husbandrie', *Agricultural Historical Review*, Vol. XI (1963), pp. 65-81, and Mr Fenton's article 'The Rural Economy of East Lothian in the seventeenth and eighteenth century' in *Transactions of the East Lothian Antiquarian and Field Naturalists' Society*, Vol. IX (1963).

CHAPTER VI

1. Scottish Record Office: Dalhousie Muniments

2. Quoted by B. R. S. Megaw 'Goat-Keeping in the Old Highland Economy', *Scottish Studies* Vol. VII (1963), p. 207

3. Scottish Record Office: Dalhousie Muniments. In the seventeenth century £12 Scots — £1 sterling

4. Quoted in I. F. Grant, *The Macleods, the History of a Clan 1200-1956* (London 1959), p. 244

5. R. Chambers, *Domestic Annals of Scotland* (Edinburgh 1858), I, p. 209

6. *Early Travellers in Scotland*, ed. P Hume Brown (Edinburgh 1891) pp. 121-2

7. J. Warrack, *Domestic Life in Scotland 1488-1688* (London 1920)

8. Stewart Cruden, *Castle Campbell* (Ministry of Works, H.M.S.O. 1953), p. 13

9. D. Mathew, *Scotland Under Charles I* (London 1955), pp. 121-2

10. *Ibid*, p. 113

11. W. Macgill, *Old Ross-shire Scotland* (Inverness 1909), p. 124

12. *Scotland and the Protectorate* (ed. C. H.

Firth, Scottish History Society,
1899), pp. 405-11
13. *List of Pollable Persons within the Shire
of Aberdeen* (ed. John Stuart,
Spalding Club 1844)
14. *Trans. of the East Lothian Antiq. and
Field Nat. Soc.*, Vol. VII (1958)
15. Quoted in I. F. Grant, *Social and
Economic Development of Scotland
before 1603* (Edinburgh 1930), pp.
248-9
16. C. Lowther, *Our Journall into
Scotland* (ed. 'W.D.', Edinburgh
1894), pp. 11-12
17. *Early Travellers*, p. 275
18. *Black Book of Taymouth* (Bannatyne
Club 1855) p. 418
19. Macgill, *op. cit.*, p. 131
20. *Early Travellers*, p. 260

21. Scottish Record Office: Dalhousie
Muniments
22. *Early Travellers*, p. 270
23. *Ibid*, p. 232
24. *Macfarlane's Geographical Collections*,
II, p. 102
25. T. C. Smout and A. Fenton, 'Scottish
Agriculture before the Improvers:
an Exploration', *Agricultural History
Review*, Vol. XIII (1965)
26. *Black Book of Taymouth*, p. 379
27. *Statistical Account of Scotland*, VIII,
p. 452
28. Sir Robert Sibbald, *Provision for the
Poor in time of Dearth and Scarcity*
(Edinburgh 1699), p. 3
29. *Statistical Account of Scotland*, VI,
132n

Further Reading

Much of the reading for the previous chapter is relevant also to this. The Stair Society
Volume for 1958, *An Introduction to Scottish Legal History* explains much about
tenures. I. F. Grant, *The Social and Economic Development of Scotland before 1603*
(Edinburgh 1930) and T. B. Franklin, *A History of Scottish Farming* (Edinburgh 1952)
both give some account of the feuing movement. The life of the seventeenth-century
magnates is considered in I. F. Grant, *The Macleods, the History of a Clan 1200-1956*
(London 1959) and in David Mathew, *Scotland under Charles I* (London 1955). The
humbler lairds get more attention in W. MacGill, *Old Ross-Shire and Scotland*
(Inverness, 1909). See also E. Dunbar-Dunbar, *Social Life in Former Days* (Edinburgh
1865). Furniture and household plenishings is the main subject of J. Warrack, *Domestic
Life in Scotland 1488-1688* (London 1920). Costume is described in several books:
Stuart Maxwell and Robin Hutchison, *Scottish Costume 1550-1850* (London 1598),
J. T. Dunbar, *History of Highland Dress* (Edinburgh 1962) and R. M. D. Grange, *A
Short History of the Scottish Dress* (London 1966) and H. F. McClintock, *Old Highland
Dress* (Dundalk 1949) are all useful. The everyday life of the peasants before the
eighteenth century has never attracted the same attention, but anyone who reads
P. Hume Brown, *Early Travellers in Scotland* (Edinburgh 1891) with attention may
learn a good deal. See also A. Fenton, 'Farm Servant life in the 17th-19th Centuries'
in *Scottish Agriculture*, 1965. Those interested in the structure of rural society should
certainly peruse the *List of Pollable Persons within the Shire of Aberdeen* (ed. John
Stuart, Spalding Club 1844), full of interest for those with good digestions.

CHAPTER VII

1. National Library of Scotland, M.S. 33.5.16, 'Discourse anent the improvements may be made in Scotland for advancing the wealth of the Kingdom'
2. J. D. Marwick, *Edinburgh Guilds and Crafts* (Scottish Burgh Record Society 1849), p. 142
3. W. Croft Dickinson, *Scotland from the earliest times to 1603* (Edinburgh 1961), p. 236
4. T. C. Smout, 'The Glasgow merchant community in the seventeenth century', *Scottish Historical Review* Vol. XLVII (1968), pp. 53-71
5. Quoted in L. A. Barbé, *Sidelights on the History Industries and Social Life of Scotland* (London 1919), pp. 296-7. The date of Skene's book is wrongly given in Barbé
6. C. Creighton, *A History of Epidemics in Britain* (new edition, London 1965), I, p. 235
7. D. Calderwood, *Historie of the Kirk of Scotland* (Wodrow Society 1843) IV, p. 377
8. *Ibid*, VI, p. 591
9. A. Lassen, 'The Population of Denmark in 1660', *Scandinavian Economic History Review*, Vol. XIII (1965), pp. 1-30
10. A. McKerral, *Kintyre in the Seventeenth Century* (Edinburgh 1948), Chapter IX
11. T. C. Smout, *Scottish Trade on the Eve of Union 1660-1707* (Edinburgh 1963), p. 77
12. Dundee Town Council Archives: M.S. Shipping lists

13. T. C. Smout, *Scottish Trade*, p. 85
14. R. Chambers, *Domestic Annals of Scotland* (Edinburgh 1858), II, p. 238
15. Gordon Donaldson, *Scotland: James V to James VII* (Edinburgh 1965), p. 252
16. W. Macgill, *Old Ross-shire and Scotland* (Inverness 1909), pp. 124-5
17. H. Lumsden and P. H. Aitken, *History of the Hammermen of Glasgow* (Paisley 1912)
18. I. F. Grant, *Social and Economic Development of Scotland before 1603* (Edinburgh 1930), pp. 413-14
19. Lumsden and Aitken, *op. cit.*
20. *The Register of Apprentices of the City of Edinburgh 1583-1666* (ed. F. J. Grant, Scottish Record Society 1906) and *Register of Edinburgh Apprentices 1666-1700* (ed. C. B. B. Watson, Scottish Record Society 1929)
21. M. Wood, 'Edinburgh Poll Tax Returns', *Book of the Old Edinburgh Club*, Vol. XXV (1945), pp. 90-126
22. *Ibid.*
23. Calderwood, *op. cit.*, VI, p. 27
24. Chambers, *Domestic Annals*, II, pp. 437-8
25. *The Court Book of the Burgh of Kirkintilloch 1658-1694* (ed. G. S. Pryde, Scottish History Society 1963), p. lxx
26. *Ibid*, p. lxix
27. Chambers, *Domestic Annals*, III, p. 247
28. T. S. Ashton and J. Sykes, *The Coal Industry of the Eighteenth Century* (Manchester 1929), p. 74

Further Reading

There is no shortage of things to read. A. Ballard, 'The Theory of the Scottish Burgh' in *Scottish Historical Review*, Vol. XIII (1916) makes a good starting point. W. M. Mackenzie, *The Scottish Burghs* (Edinburgh 1949) has much to say about the sixteenth and seventeenth centuries as well as about the earlier period; T. Pagan, *The Convention of the Royal Burghs of Scotland* (Glasgow 1926) is a study of the burghs' relations with one another and with the state; David Murray, *Early Burgh Organisation in Scotland* (Glasgow 1924) contains much about Glasgow and some other towns of the west. A great deal of source material has been published by the Scottish Burgh Records Society, and some by the Scottish Records Society: a glance at the open shelves in any large library will show the range of what is available.

Brief and useful accounts of the social life of the burghs are to be found in both W. Croft Dickinson, *Scotland from the earliest times to 1603* (Edinburgh 1961) and I. F. Grant, *Social and Economic Development of Scotland before 1603* (Edinburgh 1930). For epidemics see C. Creighton, *A History of Epidemics in Britain* (new edition, London 1965): this and several other topics touched on in this chapter are discussed in L. A. Barbé, *Sidelights on the History, Industries and Social Life of Scotland* (London 1919).

Mercantile life is dealt with by S. G. E. Lythe, *The Economy of Scotland in its European Setting 1550–1625* (Edinburgh 1960) and T. C. Smout, *Scottish Trade on the Eve of Union 1660–1707* (Edinburgh 1963). The latter also has an article more specifically on the social structure of the merchants, 'The Glasgow Merchant community in the seventeenth century', in *Scottish Historical Review*, Vol. XLVII (1968).

There are a number of books published on the craft guilds, mainly before 1914: any local bibliography will give full details of what is available for a given town. Among the best are H. Lumsden and P. H. Aitken, *History of the Hammermen of Glasgow* (Paisley 1912), J. D. Marwick, *Edinburgh Guilds and Crafts* (Scottish Burgh Records Society 1909) and J. H. Macadam, *The Baxters Book of St. Andrews* (Leith 1903). M. Wood 'Edinburgh Poll Tax Returns', *Book of the Old Edinburgh Club*, Vol. XXV (1945) gives a view of the structure of urban society not easy to arrive at elsewhere. G. S. Pryde's introduction to *The Court Book of Kirkintilloch 1658–1694* (Scottish History Society 1963) is an admirable summary of the institutions and life of the smallest burghs. Of several accounts of the coal-mining serfs the best and most convenient is probably that of an anonymous writer, 'Slavery in Scotland' *Edinburgh Review*, Vol. CLXXXIX (1899). *A Source Book of Scottish History*, ed. W. C. Dickinson and G. Donaldson, Vol. III (1954) is useful for several aspects of this chapter, not least for the problem of servitude.

CHAPTER VIII

1. Quoted in *Dictionary of National Biography*, III (1908), p. 191
2. Quoted in H. R. Trevor-Roper,

Religion, the Reformation and Social Change (London 1967), p. 426
3. Geoffrey Grigson, *The Shell Coun-*

try Alphabet (London 1966), pp. 204-5

4. G. Donaldson, *Scotland James V-James VII* (Edinburgh 1965), p. 268

5. T. C. Smout, *Scottish Trade on the Eve of Union 1660-1707* (Edinburgh 1963), p. 102

6. Stewart Cruden, *The Scottish Castle* (Edinburgh 1960), chapter VII

7. *Ibid*, pp. 173-4

8. J. G. Dunbar, *The Historic Architecture of Scotland* (London 1966), p. 98

9. Ian Finlay, *Scottish Gold and Silver Work* (London 1956), p. 73

10. Quoted in H. R. Trevor-Roper, *op. cit.*, p. 137

11. D. Mathew, *Scotland Under Charles I* (London 1956), pp. 54-5

12. E. Dunbar-Dunbar, *Social Life in*

Former Days (Edinburgh 1866), II, p. 144

13. R. Chambers, *Domestic Annals*, I, pp. 203-6

14. Mathew, *op. cit.*, p. 55

15. For these details and much else in this section see G. F. Black, *A Calendar of Cases of Witchcraft in Scotland 1510-1727* (New York 1938), p. 30

16. W. Stephen, *History of the Scottish Church* (Edinburgh 1896), II, p. 282

17. Mathew, *op. cit.*, p. 55

18. See, for example, J. G. Campbell, *Superstitions of the Highlands* (Glasgow 1900)

19. R. Chambers, *Domestic Annals*, II. pp. 285-91

20. Quoted in G. F. Black, *op. cit.*

Further Reading

For biography, see the *Dictionary of National Biography*, and also R. Chambers, *Biographical Dictionary of Eminent Scotsmen* (revised and edited by T. Thomson, London 1875) and Joseph Irving, *The Book of Scotsmen* (Paisley 1881); P. Hume Brown, *George Buchanan* (Edinburgh 1890); E. W. Hobson, *John Napier and the Invention of Logarithms* (Cambridge 1914) and the *Napier Tercentenary Memorial Volume* (ed. C. G. Knott for Royal Society of Edinburgh, London 1915) are useful. The works of the major poets have been published at length by the Scottish Text Society (for the Lowlanders) and by the Scottish Gaelic Text Society (for the Highlanders). The Ballads are printed in F. J. Child, *The English and Scottish Popular Ballads* (Cambridge 1882-1898). Selections of all types of poetry are given in the *Oxford Book of Scottish Verse* (ed. J. MacQueen and T. Scott, Oxford 1966), *Golden Treasury of Scottish Verse* (ed. Hugh MacDiarmid, London 1946), *A Scots Anthology* (ed. J. W. Oliver and J. C. Smith, Edinburgh 1949) and Kenneth H. Jackson, *A Celtic Miscellany* (London, 1951). Urquhart's *Works* were published by the Maitland Club in 1834.

For other branches of culture see, H. G. Farmer, *A History of Music in Scotland* (1947) and (for the piobaireachd) Archibald of Kilberry's article in *Piping Times*, 1953. I. F. Grant, *The MacLeods: The History of a Clan* (London 1959) has a lot on the cultural life at Dunvegan. Ian Finlay, *Art in Scotland* (London 1948), *Scottish Crafts* (London 1948) and *Scottish Gold and Silver Work* (London 1956) are useful.

Architecture is well served by large surveys and small. Among the monumental are D. Macgibbon and T. Ross, *Castellated and Domestic Architecture in Scotland* (Edinburgh 1887-1892) and the fine inventories of ancient monuments published by the Royal

NOTES TO PP 211-236

Commission on the Ancient and Historical Monuments of Scotland. The most recent volumes are the best: *Stirlingshire* (1963) and *Peeblesshire* (1967). Somewhat more easily managed are Oliver Hill, *Scottish Castles of the Sixteenth and Seventeenth Centuries* (London 1943), which is beautifully illustrated, and Nigel Tranter, *The Fortified House in Scotland* (Edinburgh 1962-1966). The latter has some inaccuracies. Best of all are Stewart Cruden, *The Scottish Castle* (Edinburgh 1960), George Hay, *The Architecture of Scottish post-Reformation Churches* (Oxford 1957) and J. G. Dunbar, *The Historic Architecture of Scotland* (London 1966).

For witch-craft the only good full account is G. F. Black, *A Calendar of Cases of Witchcraft in Scotland, 1510-1727*: the pages spared to it in D. Mathew, *Scotland Under Charles I* (London 1955) and the cases given in R. Chambers, *Domestic Annals of Scotland* (Edinburgh 1858-1861) are well worth reading. No-one should ignore H. R. Trevor-Roper's brilliant essay on the 'European Witch-Craze' in *Religion, Reformation and Social Change* (London 1967), though it only marginally draws upon Scottish evidence and not all its generalisations seem to be applicable to the Scottish experience.

CHAPTER IX

1. See T. C. Smout, 'The Road to Union' in Geoffrey Holmes, *Britain after the Glorious Revolution 1689-1714* (London 1969) for a discussion of this complicated question and of the conflicting historians' views

2. The best accounts are G. P. Insh, *The Company of Scotland* (London 1932) and John Prebble, *The Darien Disaster* (London 1968)

3. Both quoted in W. L. Mathieson, *Church and Reform in Scotland, 1797-1843* (Glasgow 1916), pp. 107-8

4. *Early Travellers in Scotland*, ed. P. Hume Brown (Edinburgh 1891), p. 271

5. Quoted in R. Chambers, *Domestic Annals of Scotland* (Edinburgh 1861), III, p. 218

6. *Ibid*, III, pp. 234-6

7. Quoted in A. R. B. Haldane, *The Drove Roads of Scotland* (London 1952), p. 26

8. See for example Scottish Record Office, Forfeited Estates papers, E. 783.68

9. Sir Walter Scott's *Heart of Midlothian* gives the best account. There has probably never been so brilliant a piece of historical research so brilliantly disguised as fiction

10. *Readings in Economic and Social History*, ed. M. W. Flinn (London 1964) p. 119

11. *Acts of the General Assembly of the Church of Scotland* (Church Law Society 1843), p. 241

12. *Ibid*, pp. 387, 442

13. A. Carlyle, *Autobiography* (Edinburgh 1860), p. 561

14. G. D. Henderson, *The Scottish Ruling Elder* (London 1935), p. 140

15. Carlyle, *op. cit.*, p. 84

16. Quoted in W. Ferguson, *Scotland 1689 to the present* (Edinburgh 1968), p. 123

17. *Ibid* p. 227

18. John Mitchell 'Memories of Ayrshire' in *Miscellany of the Scottish History Society* Vol. *VI* (1939) p. 302

19. G. D. Henderson, *op. cit.*, p. 138
20. Hugo Arnot, *The History of Edinburgh* (1779), pp. 366-7
21. *Acts of the General Assembly*, p. 729
22. John Mitchell, *op. cit.*, pp. 302-3

Further Reading

W. Ferguson, *Scotland 1689 to the Present* (Edinburgh 1968) is an important book, especially good on eighteenth century political and ecclesiastical affairs: it effectively replaces G. S. Pryde, *Scotland from 1603 to the Present Day* (Edinburgh 1962), but the latter's pamphlet for the Historical Association, *Central and Local Government in Scotland since 1707* (1960) is a good brief account of administration. The best full-length study of the Union is still James Mackinnon, *The Union of England and Scotland* (London 1896) but there is a fairly large modern literature on the subject surveyed in T. C. Smout, 'The Road to Union', in *Britain after the Glorious Revolution 1689-1714*, ed. G. K. Holmes (London 1969). P. W. J. Riley, *The English Ministers and Scotland* (London 1964) is a detailed study of the period from the Union to 1727. These older books of W. L. Mathieson mainly on Scottish political and ecclesiastical history are still useful, *Scotland and the Union, 1695 to 1747* (Glasgow 1905), *The Awakening of Scotland 1747-1797* (Glasgow 1910) and *Church and Reform in Scotland* (Glasgow 1916). H. W. Meikle, *Scotland and the French Revolution* (Glasgow 1912) is an exceptionally good account of the radicals to which nothing of importance was added until Ferguson's text book (see above).

On ecclesiastical history there are many books but few good ones. John Cunningham, *The Church History of Scotland*, Vol. II (Edinburgh 1882) and George Grub, *The Ecclesiastical History of Scotland*, Vols. III and IV (Edinburgh 1861) are probably still the most useful for the eighteenth century.

For the Highlands, Audrey Cunningham, *The Loyal Clans* (Cambridge 1932) is still helpful in this period; see also C. Petrie, *The Jacobite Movement* (3rd edition London 1959); John Prebble, *Culloden* (London 1961), is a very good popular account, in some ways more satisfactory than his *Glencoe* (London 1966).

Finally, no-one should miss reading Sir Walter Scott on the Porteous Riots in *Heart of Midlothian* and on the Jacobites of the '45 in *Waverley*, both of which exist in many editions.

CHAPTER X

1. Sir John Clerk, 'Observations on the present circumstances of Scotland', printed in *Miscellany of the Scottish History Society*, Vol. X (1965), p. 191
2. Daniel Defoe, *Advantages of Scotland by an Incorporate Union with England* (Edinburgh 1706) and *The Fifth*

Essay at Removing National Prejudices (Edinburgh 1706)
3. The usual assertion that smuggling did not materially assist the Scots to get a foothold in the tobacco trade ignores the evidence marshalled by T. C. Barker, 'Smuggling in the Eighteenth Century:

The Evidence of the Scottish Tobacco Trade', *Virginia Magazine of History and Biography* (1954)

4. The facts of the Russia trade can be gleaned from *Tabeller over Skibsfart og Varetransport gennem Øresund* (ed. N. Bang and K. Korst, Copenhagen and Leipzig, 1909-45). For the other statistics see the sources quoted in the bibliography at the end of this chapter

5. Quoted in H. Hamilton, *An Economic History of Scotland in the Eighteenth Century* (Oxford 1963), p. 323

6. W. W. Rostow, *The Stages of Economic Growth* (Cambridge 1960), p. 31

7. George Robertson, *Rural Recollections* (Irvine 1829), p. 383. The context makes it clear he is not referring to the Lothians alone

8. See the neglected article by G. W. Daniels, 'Early Records of a Great Manchester Cotton-spinning Firm' in *Economic Journal*, Vol. XXV (1915).

9. Sir John Sinclair, *Analysis of the Statistical Account of Scotland* (London 1826), I, 321

10. Alistair G. Thomson, 'The paper industry in Scotland', unpublished Ph.D. thesis, Edinburgh 1965

11. *Statistical Account*, I, pp. 513-14

12. Robertson, *op. cit.*, pp. 24-5

13. G. Unwin, *Samuel Oldknow and the Arkwrights* (Manchester 1924), p. 66

14. G. M. Mitchell, 'The English and Scottish Cotton Industries: a Study in Interrelation', *Scottish Historical Review*, Vol. XXII (1925), p. 105

15. See Charles Singer *et al. A History of Technology*, Vol. IV (Oxford 1958), and *New Statistical Account*, VI, pp. 140-148

16. Quoted by Mitchell, *op. cit.*, pp. 108-9

17. Sir John Sinclair, *ibid*, I, pp. 44-9

18. *Ibid*, I, p. 57

Further Reading

The pathbreaking study in Scottish economic history of the eighteenth century was made by Henry Hamilton, *The Industrial Revolution in Scotland* (Oxford 1932). His subsequent book, *An Economic History of Scotland in the Eighteenth Century* (Oxford 1963), though a revised, rewritten and enlarged version of the first, incorporating a lot of new information particularly on trade and the cotton industry, somehow misses the excitement of it all. His article 'Economic growth in Scotland 1720-1770', *Scottish Journal of Political Economy*, Vol. VI (1959) is also worth reading.

R. H. Campbell is the other leading historian who has contributed his best work to this field. Much of his general text book on Scottish economic history, *Scotland since 1707* (Oxford 1965) is about the eighteenth century, and so is much of his source book written in collaboration with James Dow, *Source Book of Scottish Economic and Social History* (Oxford 1968). In *Carron Company* (Edinburgh 1961) he has examined one of the leading firms in the Scottish eighteenth century. In an important review, 'An Economic History of Scotland in the Eighteenth Century', *Scottish Journal of Political Economy*, Vol. XI (1964), he made some cogent criticisms of Henry Hamilton's last book, and another contribution, 'The Industrial revolution; a revision article' in *Scottish Historical Review*, Vol. XLVI (1967) contains a splendid bibliography of the subject. No-one, however, should attempt to study the Scottish industrial revolution in isolation. M. W. Flinn, *Origins of the Industrial Revolution* (London 1966) and T. S. Ashton, *The Industrial Revolution 1760–1830* (London 1948) provide the best rapid introduction to the British background.

For the background to and impact of the Union of 1707 see a pair of articles by T. C. Smout and R. H. Campbell, 'The Anglo-Scottish Union of 1707' in *Economic History Review* second series, Vol. XVI (1964), and T. C. Smout, *Scottish Trade on the Eve of Union* (Edinburgh 1963). Two articles by Jacob Price, 'The Rise of Glasgow in the Chesapeake Tobacco Trade' conveniently reprinted in *Studies in Scottish Business History*, ed. P. L. Payne (London 1967) and 'The Economic Growth of the Chesapeake and the European Market 1697–1775,' *Journal of Economic History*, Vol. XXIV (1964) shed by far the clearest light upon the tobacco trade. A. R. B. Haldane, *The Drove Roads of Scotland* (Edinburgh 1952) is the standard work on the cattle trade. Rondo Cameron, *Banking in the Early Stages of Industrialisation* (New York 1967), contains the best modern account of Scottish banks in the eighteenth century. Many other works of Scottish economic history are mentioned in the bibliographies for chapters XIII–XVIII.

CHAPTER XI

1. The exact figure quoted was 1,048,000. Sir John Sinclair, *Analysis of the Statistical Account of Scotland* ((Edinburgh 1826), I, pp. 148–9

2. A. J. Youngson, 'Alexander Webster and his "Account of the Number of People in Scotland in the year 1755" ', *Population Studies*, Vol. XV (1961–2); D. J. Withrington, 'The S.P.C.K. and Highland Schools in the Mid-Eighteenth Century', *Scottish Historical Review*, Vol. XLI (1962)

3. I. C. C. Graham, *Colonists from Scotland: Emigration to North America 1707–1783* (Oxford 1956)

4. James Cleland, *Enumeration of the Inhabitants of Glasgow* (Glasgow 1820) p. 6

5. Adam Smith, *Wealth of Nations* (Everyman edition, London 1910), p. 70

6. Sinclair, *op. cit.*, I, pp. 163–4

7. *Statistical Account*, XVII, p. 283

8. *Ibid*, V, p. 22

9. Quoted in R. N. Salaman, *The History and Social Influence of the Potato* (Cambridge 1949), p. 364

10. Sir John Sinclair, *An Account of the Systems of Husbandry of Scotland* (Edinburgh 1812), I, p. 269, II, p 132

11. Quoted in Salaman, *op. cit.*, p. 392

12. *Ibid*, p. 370

13. Sinclair, *Analysis of the Statistical Account*, appendix, p. 40

14. Quoted in Salaman, *op. cit.*, p. 394

15. H. Gille, 'Demographic History of the North European Countries in the Eighteenth Century', *Population Studies*, Vol. III (1949), p. 47

16. C. Creighton, *History of Epidemics in Britain* (new ed. London 1965); J. H. F. Brotherston, *The Early Public Health Movement in Scotland* (London 1952), pp. 25–9

17. R. Chambers, *Domestic Annals of Scotland* (Edinburgh 1858), I, p. 427, II, pp. 85, 140, 347

18. The anonymous author of MS 316 in Edinburgh University Library,

writing c. 1760 on 'The interest of Scotland in the branches of agriculture, population and commerce', folio 81

19. Brotherston, *op. cit.*, p. 29; Alexander Monro, primus, *Works* (1781) p. 485: N.B. the pagination is erratic, and this page follows 684; Robert Watt, *An Inquiry into the Relative Mortality of the Principal Diseases of Children in Glasgow* (reprinted, Glasgow 1888), p. 49

20. Brotherston, *op. cit.*, p. 30

21. *Statistical Account*, II, p. 453

22. *Ibid*, II, p. 571

23. Monro, *op. cit.*, p. 681

24. *Statistical Account*, III, p. 427

25. Watt, *op. cit.*, p. 49; Robert Cowan, *Vital Statistics of Glasgow* (Glasgow 1838), p. 28; Brotherston, *op. cit.*, p. 33

26. M. W. Flinn, introduction to his edition of Edwin Chadwick, *Report on the Sanitary Conditions of the Labouring Population of Great Britain* (Edinburgh 1965), p. 18

27. Hugo Arnot, *History of Edinburgh* (Edinburgh 1779), pp. 549-555; James Cleland, *Annals of Glasgow* (Glasgow 1816) I, p. 231

28. Quoted in J. D. Comrie, *History of Scottish Medicine* (London 1932), II, p. 423

29. William Buchan, *Domestic Medicine* (ed. London 1772), p. 1

30. *Ibid*, p. 126

31. Watt, *op. cit.*, p. 49; Sinclair, *Analysis*, p. 138

32. Watt, *op. cit.*, p. 49; James Cleland, *Enumeration of the Inhabitants of the City of Glasgow* (Glasgow 1832), p. 9

Further Reading

A full history of Scottish population has never been attempted, but J. H. F. Brotherston, *Observations on the Early Public Health Movement in Scotland* (London 1952) gives in his first chapter much the best account of the eighteenth-century situation. Sir John Sinclair's discussion in *Analysis of the Statistical Account of Scotland* (Edinburgh 1826) begins well but tails off sadly: his references back to the *Statistical Account* are well worth pursuing. D. F. Macdonald, *Scotland's Shifting Population 1770–1850* (Glasgow 1937) is rather disappointing and misses some opportunities, but R. N. Salaman, *The History and Social Influence of the Potato* (Cambridge 1939) has excellent chapters on Scotland. Thomas Ferguson, *The Dawn of Scottish Social Welfare* (London 1948) has some bearing on matters discussed in this chapter, as does J. D. Comrie, *History of Scottish Medicine* (London 1932). William Buchan's *Domestic Medicine*, in one or other of its many editions, is well worth browsing through.

Dr. Webster's survey and a digest of some subsequent census material has been printed by J. G. Kyd, in *Scottish Population Statistics* (Scottish History Society 1952). The full census returns for 1801, 1811, 1821 and 1831 are printed in the following *Parliamentary Papers*: 1801, vi; 1801/2, vi, vii; 1812, x, xi; 1822, xxi, xv; 1831, xviii.

CHAPTER XII

1. G. S. Pryde, *The Treaty of Union of 1707* (Edinburgh 1950), p. 27

2. *Scotland and Scotsmen in the Eighteenth Century from the MSS of John*

Ramsay of Ochtertyre, ed. A. Allardyce (Edinburgh 1888), II, p. 557

3. Sir John Sinclair, General Report of the Agricultural State and Political Circumstances of Scotland (Edinburgh 1814), Appendix I, pp. 227-8

4. W. Ferguson, Scotland 1689 to the Present (Edinburgh 1968), p. 156

5. Lord Gardenstone, Letter to the People of Laurencekirk (ed. Edinburgh 1823), p. 47; Letters of John Cockburn of Ormiston to his Gardener 1727-1744 (ed. James Colville, Scottish History Society 1904), p. xxiv; Scotland and Scotsmen, II, p. 385

6. Quoted in James Ferguson, Lowland Lairds (London 1949), p. 121 note

7. Scotland and Scotsmen, II, pp. 216-17; Thomas Somerville, My Own Life and Times 1741-1814 (Edinburgh 1861), pp. 359-60

8. Sinclair, General Report, I, p. 89

9. William Mackintosh, An Essay on Ways and Means for Inclosing (Edinburgh 1729), pp. 229-30

10. Quoted in Marjorie Plant, The Domestic Life of Scotland in the Eighteenth Century (Edinburgh 1952), pp. 28, 30

11. George Robertson, Rural Recollections (Irvine 1829), p. 68

12. Sinclair, General Report, pp. 158-63

13. Plant, Domestic Life, p. 115

14. Quoted, ibid, p. 190

15. Memoirs of the Life of Sir John Clerk of Penicuik 1676-1755 (Edinburgh 1892), p. xi

16. Selections from the Family Papers Preserved at Caldwell (Maitland Club 1954), I, p. 270

17. Letters of John Cockburn, pp. xxxix, 79-80

18. Report on the MSS of the Rt. Hon. Lord Polwarth, Vol. V. (Historical MSS Commission 1961), pp. 146-7

19. Monymusk Papers 1713-1755 (ed. H. Hamilton, Scottish History Society 1945); Life and Labour on an Aberdeenshire Estate (ed. H. Hamilton, Third Spalding Club 1946)

20. Scotland and Scotsmen, II, p. 235, n

21. Statistical Account, VI, p. 129

22. The Gorden's Mill Farming Club 1758-1764, ed. J. H. Smith (Edinburgh 1962)

23. Scotland and Scotsmen, II, p. 236

24. Ibid, II, p. 245

25. Robertson, Rural Recollections, pp. 352-3, 359

26. Scotland and Scotsmen, II, pp. 384-5

Further Reading

The revolution in manners is extremely well conveyed in a number of good books. H. G. Graham, *The Social Life of Scotland in the Eighteenth Century* (various editions, the first London 1899) is a classic, and Marjorie Plant, *The Domestic Life of Scotland in the Eighteenth Century* (Edinburgh 1948) is rather slighter. Of contemporary autobiographical studies, Thomas Somerville, *My Own Life and Times 1741-1814* (Edinburgh 1861) and *Scotland and Scotsmen in the Eighteenth Century from the MSS of John Ramsay of Ochtertyre*, ed. A. Allardyce (Edinburgh 1888) are both tremendous value.

To understand the dynamics of improvement there is, indeed, still no substitute for reading the relevant chapters in the second volume of *Scotland and Scotsmen*. The relevant textbooks, though adequate in other ways somehow fail to convey how or why improvement took place: but see J. E. Handley, *Scottish Farming in the Eighteenth*

Century (London 1953), J. A. Symon, *Scottish Farming Past and Present* (Edinburgh 1959) and Henry Hamilton, *An Economic History of Scotland in the Eighteenth Century* (Oxford 1963). The papers of two of the improvers are published, with good introductions by their editors, in *Letters of John Cockburn of Ormiston to his Gardener 1727–1744* (ed. J. Colville, Scottish History Society 1904) and *Monymusk Papers 1713–1755* (ed. H. Hamilton, Scottish History Society 1945). Those interested in the details of the later and more significant period, however, might consult Sir John Sinclair's *General Report of the Agricultural State and Political Circumstances of Scotland* (Edinburgh 1814) or one of the local county reports of which a list is given in Symon, *Scottish Farming*. George Robertson, *Rural Recollections* (Irvine 1829) is a mine of information for the later period.

The interrelationship between landownership and industrial development is discussed in T. C. Smout, 'Scottish Landowners and Economic Growth, 1650–1850' in *Scottish Journal of Political Economy*, Vol. XI (1964). The best account of village development so far is in J. M. Houston 'Village Planning in Scotland 1745–1845', *The Advancement of Science* Vol. V (1948), but a critical visit to Ormiston, Cuminestown, Callendar or Crieff, for example, can be instructive and enjoyable in itself.

CHAPTER XIII

1. George Robertson, *Rural Recollections* (Irvine 1829), pp. 98–9
2. *Ibid*, p. 99
3. Samuel Robinson, *Reminiscences of Wigtonshire* (Hamilton 1872), p. 43
4. *Monymusk Papers 1713–1755* (ed. H. Hamilton, Scottish History Society 1945), p. xvii
5. *The Travel Diaries of Thomas Robert Malthus*, ed. Patricia James (Cambridge 1966), p. 223
6. G. Robertson, *op. cit.*, p. 352
7. Thomas Robertson, *Outline of the General Report upon the Size of Farms* (Edinburgh 1796), p. 43
8. *Ibid*, p. 56
9. Robert Wilson, *An Enquiry into the Causes of the High Prices of Corn and Labour* (Edinburgh 1815), pp. 47–9
10. Robertson, *op. cit.*, p. 57
11. Sinclair, *General Report of the Agricultural State and Political Circumstances of Scotland* (Edinburgh 1814), I, pp. 179–81

12. *Ibid*, Appendix, I, p. 300
13. G. Robertson, *op. cit.*, p. 105
14. Sinclair, *op. cit.*, I, pp. 131–8, Appendix, pp. 286–92
15. *Brougham and his Early Friends*, ed. R. H. M. B. Atkinson and G. A. Jackson (London 1908), II, pp. 102–3. I am indebted to Dr. R. W. Sturgess for this reference
16. G. Robertson, *op. cit.*, p. 106
17. *Scotland and Scotsmen in the Eighteenth Century from the MSS of John Ramsay of Ochtertyre*, ed. A. Allardyce (Edinburgh 1888), II, pp. 233–5
18. L. J. Saunders, *Scottish Democracy 1815–1840* (Edinburgh 1950), pp. 50–1
19. Quoted in H. G. Graham, *The Social Life of Scotland in the Eighteenth Century* (ed. Edinburgh 1937), p. 214
20. John Younger, *Autobiography* (Kelso 1881), p. 128
21. A. J. Youngson, *The Making of*

Classical Edinburgh 1750–1840 (Edinburgh 1966), p. 37

22. Vide B. R. Mitchell and P. Deane, *Abstract of British Historical Statistics* (Cambridge 1962), pp. 348–9

23. Alexander Somerville, *The Autobiography of a Working Man* (London 1848), p. 10

24. *Ibid*, p. 71

25. Hugh Miller, *My School and Schoolmasters* (Edinburgh 1856), p. 177

26. *Ibid*, pp. 215–16

27. W. Cobbett, *Rural Rides . . . together with Tours of Scotland . . . and Letters from Ireland*, ed. G. D. H. and M. Cole (London 1930), III, p. 783

28. Cobbett, *op. cit.*, III, pp. 784–5. Miller, *op. cit.*, pp. 228–31

29. Somerville, *op. cit.*, pp. 17–18, 38–42, 85–96

30. Cobbett, *op. cit.*, III, p. 765

31. *Caledonian Mercury*, 21 April 1724. The following account is based largely on this paper, together with the information in R. Chambers, *Domestic Annals of Scotland* (Edin-

burgh 1858), III, pp. 492–3, and in Robert Wodrow, *Analecta* (Maitland Club 1843), III, p. 152, and *The Correspondence of the Rev. Robert Wodrow* (Wodrow Society 1843), III, pp. 125, 127

32. H. Hamilton, *An Economic History of Scotland in the Eighteenth Century* (Oxford 1963), p. 82

33. William Mackintosh, *An Essay on Ways and Means for Inclosing* (Edinburgh 1729), pp. 160–3

34. *Ibid*, pp. 160–1

35. James Robertson, *General View of the Agriculture in the Southern Districts of the County of Perth* (London 1794), p. 64

36. (Anon.) *Humble Pleadings for the Good Old-Way* (n.p. 1712), appendix, p. 7

37. *Scotland and Scotsmen*, II, pp. 546–7

38. Thomas Boston, *Human Nature in the Fourfold State* (ninth edition, Edinburgh 1752), p. 253

39. Ralph Erskine, *Works* (Glasgow 1765), II, pp. 541–2

40. *Ibid*, II, p. 558

Further Reading

L. J. Saunders, *Scottish Democracy 1815–1840* (Edinburgh 1950) contains much the best modern account of social change in the agricultural revolution, though most of the modern books on Scottish farming and on eighteenth-century social and economic history mentioned previously are useful again here. George Robertson, *Rural Recollections* (Irvine 1829) remains a major source, but his account, and those of such upper-class observers as John Ramsay and Thomas Somerville (see bibliography for Chapter XII) can be supplemented by several autobiographical descriptions from the rural workers themselves. The two best (both very readable) are Alexander Somerville, *The Autobiography of a Working Man* (London 1848 and subsequent editions) and Samuel Robinson, *Reminiscences of Wigtonshire* (Hamilton 1872); Hugh Miller, *My Schools and Schoolmasters* (2nd ed. Edinburgh 1854 and subsequent editions) writes as a country mason, and John Younger, *Autobiography* (Kelso 1881) as a country shoemaker, but both throw a bright light on rural change.

Anyone wishing to trace the agricultural revolution on the local scene should begin by reading the entries for his or her area in the *Statistical Account* and the *New Statistical Account*. The latter has the parishes conveniently arranged under counties, but in the former they were entered haphazardly: there is an index in volume XX. There are also two series of *Agricultural Reports* carried out under the auspices of Sir John Sinclair's Board of Agriculture between 1793 and 1816. Each county was covered at least twice; there is a convenient list in J. A. Symon, *Scottish Farming Past and Present* (Edinburgh 1959), pp. 445-447. Sinclair's *General Report of the Agriculture State and Political Circumstances of Scotland* (Edinburgh 1814), three volumes and two volumes of appendices, is a summary of the foregoing with additional new material.

CHAPTER XIV

1. M. Martin, *A Description of the Western Isles* (ed. Glasgow 1884), pp. 77–8
2. John Prebble, 'Religion and the Massacre of Glencoe', *Scottish Historical Review*, Vol. XLVI (1967), pp. 185–8
3. E. Burt, *Letters from a Gentleman in the North of Scotland* (ed. London 1815), II, p. 84
4. Martin, *op. cit.*, p. 100
5. Quoted in (Thomas Douglas) Earl of Selkirk, *Observations on the Present State of the Highlands of Scotland* (London 1805) Appendix p. 1
6. E. Dunbar Dunbar, *Social Life in Former Days* (Edinburgh 1866), pp. 144–5
7. Martin, *op. cit.*, p. 97
8. I. F. Grant, *The Macleods: the history of a clan 1200–1956* (London 1959), p. 330
9. Martin, *op. cit.*, p. 106
10. Burt, *op. cit.*, I, p. 148
11. *Ibid*, II, pp. 88–9
12. *Ibid*, II, p. 180
13. *Ibid*, II, p. 109
14. Martin, *op. cit.*, pp. 267–8
15. *The Letter-book of Bailie John Steuart of Inverness 1715–1752* (ed. W. Mackay, Scottish History Society, 1915)
16. Martin, *op. cit.*, pp. 101–2, Burt, *op. cit.*, II, pp. 102–3

17. For an effective dialogue, see the Earl of Selkirk's pamphlet cited in footnote 5 and [Robert Brown] *Remarks on the Earl of Selkirk's Observations* (Edinburgh 1806)
18. Burt, *op. cit.*, II, pp. 208–14. See also page 224 above
19. Thomas Pennant, *A Tour in Scotland and Voyage to the Hebrides 1772* (ed. London 1790), I, pp. 404–5
20. Samuel Johnson, *Works* (London 1787–9), VIII, p. 334
21. *Statistical Account*, VIII, 359n
22. *Argyll Estate Instructions 1771–1805* (ed. E. R. Cregeen, Scottish History Society 1964), pp. xviii–xix
23. For Ullapool see Jean Dunlop 'The British Fisheries Society 1786–1893', Edinburgh Ph.D., 1951; for Tomintoul see V. Gaffney, *The Lordship of Strathavon* (Third Spalding Club 1960). The quotations relating to Beauly are from *Scottish Forfeited Estates Papers 1715: 1745* (ed. A. H. Millar, Scottish History Society 1909), p. 62
24. Malcolm Gray, *The Highland Economy 1750–1850* (Edinburgh 1957), pp. 134–5
25. Pennant, *op. cit.*, I, p. 353
26. John L. Buchanan, *Travels in the Western Hebrides* (London 1793), p. 6
27. *Statistical Account*, X, pp. 369–70
28. Select Committee on Emigration,

third report. *Parliamentary Papers 1826-7*, V, p. 291

29. J. Prebble, *The Highland Clearances* (London 1963), p. 100

30. His best-known book is *Gloomy Memories in the Highlands of Scotland* of which there are numerous editions

31. Pennant, *op. cit.*, I, p. 366

32. Sir John Sinclair, *General View of the Agriculture of the Northern Counties and Islands of Scotland* (London 1795) pp. 126-168, appendix pp. 41-5

33. John Henderson, *General View of the Agriculture of the County of Sutherland* (London 1812), pp. 143-4

34. James Loch, *An Account of the Improvements on the Estates of the Marquess of Stafford* (London 1820)

35. John Walker, *Economical History of the Hebrides and Highlands of Scotland* (London 1812), II, p. 404

36. Quoted in Prebble, *op. cit.*, p. 145

37. Sinclair, *op. cit.*, p. iii

38. E.g. John Gray, *Reflections intended to Promote the Success of the Scotch Fishing Company* (London 1788)

Further Reading

The only scholarly, dispassionate and comprehensive study of economic and social change is Malcolm Gray, *The Highland Economy 1750-1850* (Edinburgh 1957). Two articles by the same author are also useful—'The Kelp Industry in the Highlands and Islands', *Economic History Review* second series No. IV (1951) and 'Consolidation of the Crofting System', in *Agricultural History Review*, Vol. V (1956). See also I. F. Grant, *Every-day Life on an Old Highland Farm* (London 1924), and two books by A. R. B. Haldane, *The Drove Roads of Scotland* (Edinburgh 1952) and *New Ways through the Glens* (Edinburgh 1962). The last of these deals with the revolution in road communications associated with the work of Thomas Telford. Three successive articles by M. I. Adam, on the causes of Highland emigration before 1803 in *Scottish Historical Review*, Vols. XVI-XIX (1919-22) are worth consulting.

Not surprisingly much Highland history of the period has been heavily charged with emotion. John Prebble, *Culloden* (London 1961) is not free from this, and his *Highland Clearances* (London 1963) is marred by taking Donald Macleod too much at face value—though both books also contain much interesting material. Ian Grimble, *The Trial of Patrick Sellar* (London 1962) is thick with passion but thin on research. Philip Gaskell, *Morvern Transformed* (Cambridge 1968) is a valuable local study of clearance and social change in one area of the west, favourable to the local lairds but documented and cool-headed.

Of older books, a brief account by Lord Colin Campbell published under the pen-name of Dalriad, *The Crofter in History* (Edinburgh 1885) certainly deserves to be better known. It is in some ways a more informed book than the oft-quoted work of the Earl of Selkirk, *Observations on the Present State of the Highlands of Scotland* (London 1805). William Mackenzie, *A History of the Highland Clearances* (Inverness 1883 and subsequent editions) is a polemic, putting the case of the dispossessed: but it is a splendid source book. The earliest editions are best.

After Martin Martin, *A Description of the Western Isles* (London 1703 and subsequent editions) and Edward Burt, *Letters from a Gentleman in the North of Scotland* (the best edition for informative footnotes is London 1815) there was a fine crop of contemporary descriptions of the Highlands. Among the best for intrinsic interest and literary merit are Thomas Pennant, *A Tour in Scotland and Voyage to the Hebrides* (1772), B. Faujes de St. Fond, *A Journey through England and Scotland to the Hebrides in 1784* and Samuel Johnson, *Journey to the Western Islands of Scotland* (1773) complemented, of course, by the account of the same trip by his alter ego, James Boswell, *Journal of a Tour to the Hebrides*. John L. Buchanan, *Travels in the Western Hebrides* (London 1793) is informative but not elegant. Being a retired missionary he could be franker than the parish incumbents of the *Statistical Account* and *New Statistical Account*. See also John Walker, *Economical History of the Hebrides and Highlands of Scotland* (Edinburgh 1808). Dorothy Wordsworth's *Recollections of a Tour made in Scotland in A.D. 1803* is immortal. Several of the tours are available in various editions.

Finally, the Scottish History Society has published a number of volumes based on Highland landowners' papers. See *Survey of Lochtayside* (ed. M. M. MacArthur 1936), *John Home's Survey of Assynt* (ed. R. J. Adam 1960) and *Argyll Estate Instructions 1771-(1805* ed. E. R. Cregeen, 1964).

CHAPTER XV

1. Elizabeth Grant, *Memoirs of a Highland Lady 1797-1827* (London 1950), p. 2
2. *Statistical Account*, II, p. 88, V, p. 136
3. Signet Library, Edinburgh: Process 62. 39
4. *Statistical Account*, V, pp. 127, 143-4
5. *Ibid*, V, p. 49
6. Scottish Record Office: Forfeited Estates Papers E/729
7. G. Chalmers, *Caledonia* (ed. Paisley 1887), II, p. 881
8. *Coltness Collections* (ed. James Dennistoun, Maitland Club 1842), II, pp. 48-9
9. Joseph Taylor, *A Journey to Edenborough* (Edinburgh 1903), pp. 134-5
10. Edward Topham, *Letters from Edinburgh* (London 1776), pp. 14-15
11. E. Burt, *Letters from a Gentleman in the North of Scotland* (ed. London 1815), I, pp. 21-2
12. Robert Chambers, *Traditions of Edinburgh* (Edinburgh 1825), II, p. 146
13. Thomas Brown, *A New Guide to the City of Edinburgh* (Edinburgh 1792), pp. 30-3
14. *Scots Magazine*, Vol. XLI (1779), pp. 219-20
15. R. Chambers, *Reekiana or Minor Antiquities of Edinburgh* (Edinburgh 1833), pp. 227-8
16. Topham, *op. cit.*, pp. 13-14
17. William Creech, *Letters respecting the Trade, Manners etc of Edinburgh* (Edinburgh 1793), p. 7
18. R. Chambers, *Reekiana*, pp. 90-1
19. James D. Marwick, *Edinburgh Guilds and Crafts* (Scottish Burgh Record Society, 1909), pp. 201-2, 214-15
20. Creech, *op. cit.*, pp. 16-17, 19
21. Henry Cockburn, *Memorials* (ed. Edinburgh 1910), p. 87
22. R. Chambers, *Reekiana*, pp. xxviii
23. Creech, *op. cit.*, p. 11
24. D. B. Horn, *A Short History of the University of Edinburgh* (Edinburgh 1967), p. 61
25. Topham, *op. cit.*, p. 205
26. D. B. Horn, *op. cit.*, p. 65

27. Alexander Law, *Education in Edinburgh in the Eighteenth Century* (Edinburgh 1965)
28. Elizabeth Grant, *op. cit.*, p. 211
29. Hugo Arnot, *History of Edinburgh* (Edinburgh 1779), p. 337
30. Daniel Defoe, *A Tour thro' the whole island of Great Britain*, ed. G. D. H. Cole (London 1927), II, p. 748 ff
31. Alexander Carlyle, *Autobiography* (Edinburgh 1860), pp. 72-3
32. *Statistical Account*, V, pp. 534-5
33. J. O. Mitchell, *Old Glasgow Essays* (Glasgow 1905), p. 123

34. Andrew Brown, *History of Glasgow* (Glasgow 1795), p. 223
35. Mitchell, *op. cit.*, p. 41
36. *Memoirs and Portraits of One Hundred Glasgow Men* (Glasgow 1883)
37. T. C. Smout, 'The Glasgow Merchant Community in the Seventeenth Century' *Scottish Historical Review*, Vol. XLVII (1968)
38. Mitchell, *op. cit.*, p. 170
39. A. M. Macgeorge, *The Bairds of Gartsherrie* (Glasgow 1875)
40. *Memoirs and Portraits of One Hundred Glasgow Men*
41. Carlyle, *op. cit.*, p. 73

Further Reading

C. R. Fay, *Adam Smith and the Scotland of his Day* (Cambridge 1956) succeeds in conveying better than most the exciting atmosphere of the urban middle-class intellectual milieu in both Edinburgh and Glasgow. For Edinburgh, two books by Robert Chambers, *Traditions of Edinburgh* (Edinburgh 1825) and *Reekiana or Minor Antiquities of Edinburgh* (Edinburgh 1833) are full of nuggets among a fair amount of antiquarian dross. A. J. Youngson, *The Making of Classical Edinburgh* (Edinburgh 1966) is excellent both as social history and as an account of eighteenth-century architectural activity. D. B. Horn, *A Short History of the University of Edinburgh* (Edinburgh 1967) and Alexander Law, *Education in Edinburgh in the Eighteenth Century* (Edinburgh 1965) deal well with the college and schools. See also Douglas Young, *Edinburgh in the Age of Sir Walter Scott* (Oklahoma 1965) and J. Grant, *Old and New Edinburgh* (London 1882). Hugo Arnot, *History of Edinburgh* (Edinburgh 1779) is an admirable contemporary history. Alexander Carlyle, *Autobiography* (Edinburgh 1860) and Henry Cockburn, *Memorials* (ed. Edinburgh 1910) convey the atmosphere of their Athenian age at successive periods in masterly prose.

For Glasgow the standard history is George Eyre-Todd, *History of Glasgow* (Glasgow 1934), Vol. III, but it is often evasive where the social historian wants to know most. Three older histories, John Gibson, *History of Glasgow* (Glasgow 1777), Andrew Brown, *History of Glasgow* (Glasgow 1795) and James Cleland, *Annals of Glasgow* (Glasgow 1816) are useful supplementary accounts of contemporary developments. See also J. R. Kellet, *Glasgow, a Concise History* (n.p., n.d.). For the entrepreneurs something can be gleaned from J. O. Mitchell, *Old Glasgow Essays* (Glasgow 1905), *Memoirs and Portraits of One Hundred Glasgow Men* (Glasgow 1883), *The Old Country Houses of the Old Glasgow Gentry* (Glasgow 1870), and such biographies as A. M. MacGeorge, *The Bairds of Gartsherrie* (Glasgow 1875) and James Napier, *Life of Robert Napier* (Edinburgh 1904), but there is no good study of the business class.

CHAPTER XVI

1. *New Statistical Account*, VII, pp. 254, 268
2. Sir John Sinclair, *Analysis of the Statistical Account* (London 1826), I, p. 321
3. Robert Cowan, *Vital Statistics of Glasgow* (Glasgow 1838), p. 46
4. Report of Select Committee on Combinations, *Parliamentary Papers* 1837/8, Vol. VIII, p. 186
5. Henry Hamilton, *An Economic History of Scotland in the Eighteenth Century* (Oxford 1963), p. 377
6. Edward Baines, *History of the Cotton Manufacture in Great Britain* (London 1835), p. 456
7. Sidney Pollard, *The Genesis of Modern Management* (London 1965), p. 161
8. Thomas Garnett, *Observations on a Tour through the Highlands* (London 1800), ii, p. 236
9. Frank Podmore, *Robert Owen: a biography* (London 1923) is still the best account.
10. W. H. G. Armytage, *Heaven's Below* (London 1961) gives a detailed account of Orbiston
11. *Parliamentary Papers* 1837/8 Vol. VIII, p. 130
12. *Ibid*, p. 183
13. Medical Reports by Sir David Barry

to Commissioners inquiring into the Employment of Children in Factories, *Parliamentary Papers* 1833, Vol. XXI, p. 72
14. *Ibid*, pp. 9, 41-3
15. James Cleland, *Enumeration of the Inhabitants of the City of Glasgow* (Glasgow 1832), p. 231
16. Supplementary Report of Factories Inquiry, *Parliamentary Papers* 1834, Vol. XX, pp. 33, 35
17. *Parliamentary Papers* 1833, Vol. XXI, p. 73
18. *Parliamentary Papers* 1834, Vol. XX, pp. 33, 35
19. *Ibid*, pp. 44, 47
20. *Parliamentary Papers* 1837/8, Vol. VIII, p. 167; J. Myles, *Chapters in the Life of a Dundee Factory Boy* (ed. Dundee 1951). I am indebted to Dr Bruce Lenman for a critical appraisal of the latter.
21. *Parliamentary Papers*, 1834, Vol. XX, pp. 33, 35
22. Myles, *op. cit.*, p. 11
23. *Parliamentary Papers* 1833, Vol. XXI, pp. 10, 72
24. Myles, *op. cit.*, pp. 12-13
25. *Parliamentary Papers* 1833, Vol. XXI, p. 3. See also p. 72
26. *Ibid*, p. 12

Further Reading

Remarkably little has been written on the wages and conditions of Scottish craftsmen or factory workers. For the eighteenth century Henry Hamilton, *An Economic History of Scotland in the Eighteenth Century* (Oxford 1963) has some useful chapters. Two relevant and important books by English historians deal with the impact of the factory system on management and on the family; the first has extensive Scottish material: Sidney Pollard, *The Genesis of Modern Management* (London 1965) and Neil J. Smelser, *Social Change in the Industrial Revolution* (London 1959). The only full study of how an industrialist treated his workers is Frank Podmore, *Robert Owen: a biography*

(London 1923), supplemented by M. Cole, *Robert Owen of New Lanark* (London 1953) —but Owen was highly exceptional in any case.

On the other hand there is a wealth of Parliamentary Papers of which only a small number have been cited in this chapter. See Report of Select Committee on Children in Manufactories, *Parliamentary Papers* 1816, Vol. III; Report of Select Committee on Children in Mills, *Parliamentary Papers* 1831-2, Vol. XV; Factory Inquiry Commission Reports, *Parliamentary Papers* 1833, Vols. XX, XXI, 1834, Vols. XIX, XX; Reports of Select Committees on Combinations, *Parliamentary Papers* 1825, Vol. IV; *Parliamentary Papers* 1837-8, Vol. VIII. See also J. Myles, *Chapters in the Life of a Dundee Factory Boy*, first published in 1850, and reprinted in Dundee in 1951.

The *Statistical Account* and *New Statistical Account* give a good deal of information on wage rates, but are guarded about conditions.

CHAPTER XVII

1. William Jolly, *The Life of John Duncan, Scotch Weaver and Botanist* (London 1883), pp. 23 ff
2. Andrew Brown, *History of Glasgow* (Glasgow 1795), p. 243
3. William Thom, *Rhymes and Recollections of a Handloom Weaver* (London 1845), p. 9
4. *Statistical Account*, VII, p. 90
5. *Ibid*, XVII, p. 12
6. Jolly, *ibid*, p. 23-4
7. David Gilmour, *Reminiscences of the 'Pen' Folk* (Paisley 1871), p. 21
8. M. Blair, *The Paisley Shawl* (Paisley 1904), p. 50
9. W. Hector, *Selections from the Judicial Records of Renfrewshire* (Paisley 1878) II, pp. 196-204; H. W. Meikle, *Scotland and the French Revolution* (Glasgow 1912), pp. 64-5
10. A. B. Richmond, *Condition of the Manufacturing Population* (London 1825), p. 29
11. J. L. Gray, 'The Law of Combination in Scotland', *Economica*, Vol. VIII (1928)
12. Report from Select Committee on

Handloom Weavers, *Parliamentary Papers* 1834 Vol. X, p. 53
13. *Ibid*, pp. 53, 89
14. Medical Reports by Sir David Barry, *Parliamentary Papers* 1833 Vol. XXI, p. 43
15. *Parliamentary Papers* 1834 Vol. X, p. 41
16. A. Mercer, *History of Dunfermline* (Dunfermline 1828), pp. 192-3
17. Reports from Assistant Handloom Weavers Commissioners, *Parliamentary Papers* 1839, Vol. XLII, p. 15
18. *Ibid* p. 54
19. Brenda Gaskin 'The decline of the hand-loom weaving industry in Scotland during the years 1815–1845' Edinburgh Ph.D. Thesis (1955) Chapter I
20. *Parliamentary Papers* 1834, Vol. X, p. 77
21. See, for example, William Jolly, *op. cit.*, William Thom, *op. cit.*, D. Gilmour, *Paisley Weavers of Other Days* (Paisley 1876)
22. *Parliamentary Papers* 1834, Vol. X, p. 73
23. J. Barrowman, 'Slavery in the Coal-

Mines of Scotland', *Transactions of the Federated Institution of Mining Engineers*, Vol. XIV (1897-8), pp. 272-3

24. National Library of Scotland MSS: Prestongrange Colliery Books

25. National Library of Scotland MSS: Wemyss of Bogie papers Ch. 651

26. Children's Employment (Mines) Commission, Appendix to First Report, *Parliamentary Papers* 1842, Vol. XVI, p. 450

27. Quoted in T. S. Ashton and J. Sykes, *The Coal Industry of the Eighteenth Century* (Manchester 1929), p. 75

28. National Library of Scotland MSS: Prestongrange Colliery Books

29. National Library of Scotland MSS: Wemyss of Bogie Papers Ch. 652

30. Henry Hamilton, *An Economic History of Scotland in the Eighteenth Century* (Oxford 1963), pp. 369-71; Ashton and Sykes, *op. cit.*, pp. 77-8; *Statistical Account*, XIII, p. 477. But see evidence for much higher wages in mid-century in B. R. Duckham 'Life and Labour in a Scottish colliery 1698-1775', *Scottish Historical Review* Vol. XLVII (1968)

31. Ashton and Sykes, *op. cit.*, p. 77; Sidney Pollard, *The Genesis of Modern Management* (London 1965), p. 171

32. W. Ferguson, *Scotland: 1689 to the Present* (Edinburgh 1968), pp. 188-9

33. H. Hamilton, *op. cit.*, p. 371

34. Robert Bald, *A General View of the*

Coal Trade of Scotland (Edinburgh 1812) p. 78

35. 'Minutes of Evidence before Select Committee on Combination Laws', *Parliamentary Papers* 1825, Vol. IV, pp. 64-87, 332-5

36. [Archibald Cochrane] *Description of the Estate and Abbey at Culross* (Edinburgh 1793), pp. 69-71

37. *Parliamentary Papers* 1833, Vol. XXI, p. 51

38. [Archibald Cochrane] *op. cit.*, pp. 66-7

39. Bald, *op. cit.*, p. 140

40. *Ibid*, 131-2

41. *Ibid*, p. 131

42. *Parliamentary Papers*, 1842, Vol. XVI, p. 469

43. *Ibid*, p. 487

44. *Ibid*, p. 460

45. *Ibid*, p. 484

46. *Ibid*, p. 449

47. *Ibid*, pp. 476-7

48. *Ibid*, pp. 467, 452

49. T. C. Smout, 'Lead-mining in Scotland 1650-1850', in *Studies in Scottish Business History*, ed. P. L. Payne (London 1967)

50. *Parliamentary Papers* 1842, Vol. XVI, pp. 481-3

51. Meikle, (see facing page), pp. 44-6

52. *Ibid*, p. 80

53. *Ibid*, p. 82

54. *Ibid*, p. 96n, quoting the *Caledonian Mercury*, Nov. 12, 1792

55. *Ibid*, p. 223

56. Quoted in Ferguson, *op. cit.*, p. 283n

57. Meikle, *op. cit.*, p. 228

58. Richmond, *op. cit.*, p. 185

Further Reading

The only full-length account of the handloom weavers is an excellent thesis which should have been published years ago: Brenda Gaskin, 'The Decline of the Hand-Loom Weaving Industry in Scotland during the years 1815-1845', Edinburgh Ph.D. 1955. Two reports on the handloom weavers from the 1830s are vivid: see *Parlia-*

mentary Papers 1934, Vol. X, *Parliamentary Papers* 1839, Vol. XLII. For biographies of weavers see William Thom, *Rhymes and Recollections of a Handloom Weaver* (London 1845), William Jolly, *The Life of John Duncan, Scotch Weaver and Botanist* (London 1883), David Gilmour, *Paisley Weavers of Other Days* (Paisley 1876), and R. Cantwell, *Alexander Wilson* (Philadelphia 1961). The strike of 1812 is a main topic in A. B. Richmond, *Condition of the Manufacturing Population* (London 1825) and J. L. Gray's important article 'The Law of Combination in Scotland', *Economica*, Vol. VIII (1928).

Coalminers under serfdom are dealt with by T. S. Ashton and J. Sykes, *The Coal Industry of the Eighteenth Century* (Manchester 1929). See also a good recent article by B. F. Duckham, 'Life and labour in a Scottish colliery 1698-1755', *Scottish Historical Review*, Vol. XLVII (1968) and two older pieces, J. Barrowman, 'Slavery in Coalmines of Scotland', *Transactions of the Fed. Inst. of Mining Engineers* Vol. XIV (1897-8) and (Anon.) 'Slavery in Scotland' *Edinburgh Review*, Vol. clxxxix (1899). For the turn of the nineteenth century there are admirable contemporary accounts by Robert Bald, *A General View of the Coal Trade of Scotland* (Edinburgh 1812) and (Archibald Cochrane) *Description of the Estate and Abbey of Culross* (Edinburgh 1793), and an article by P. L. Payne, 'The Govan Collieries, 1804-1805', *Business Hist.*, Vol. III (1961). The 'Report of Select Committee on Combination Laws' *Parliamentary Papers* 1825, Vol. IV throws a bright light on early mining unionism, while the Childrens Employment (Mines) Commission, *Parliamentary Papers*, 1842, Vols. XVI-XVII is a famous and moving revelation of traditional working conditions.

The account of radicalism given here relies heavily on H. W. Meikle, *Scotland and the French Revolution* (Glasgow 1912). See also W. Ferguson, *Scotland: 1689 to the Present* (Edinburgh 1968) and Richmond's book cited above. H. Cockburn, *Memorials* (ed. Edinburgh 1910) presents a sympathetic upper-class Whig view of contemporary events.

CHAPTER XVIII

1. Charles Anderson, *A Statement of the Experience of Scotland with regard to the Education of the People* (Dumfries 1825)

2. John Knox, *History of the Reformation in Scotland* (ed. W. Croft Dickinson, London 1949) II, pp. 295-7

3. George Lewis, *Scotland a Half-Educated Nation* (Glasgow 1834) *passim*. Sinclair, *Analysis*, II, 99.

4. 'Abstract of Educational Returns (Scotland) 1834', *Parliamentary Papers*, 1837, Vol. XLVII, p. 743

5. D. J. Withrington, 'Lists of Schoolmasters teaching Latin 1690', *Scottish History Society Miscellany*, Vol. X (1965); I. J. Simpson, *Education in Aberdeenshire* (London 1942)

6. William Boyd, *Education in Ayrshire* (London 1961); Andrew Bain, *Education in Stirlingshire* (London 1965)

7. *Munimenta Alme Universitatis Glasguensis* (Maitland Club 1854), II. pp. 548-51

8. Bain, *op. cit.*, pp. 110-13

9. D. J. Withrington, 'Schools in the Presbytery of Haddington in the seventeenth century', *Transactions of the East Lothian Antiquarian and*

Field Naturalists Society, Vol. XI (1963)

10. Bain, *op. cit.*, p. 120

11. 'Papers Relating to Parochial Education in Scotland', *Parliamentary Papers*, 1826, Vol. XVIII

12. Simpson, *op. cit.*, p. 199

13. Withrington, 'Lists of Schoolmasters', *Parliamentary Papers*, 1826, Vol. XVIII

14. Allan Menzies, *Report of the Trustees of the Bequest of the late James Dick* (Glasgow 1836)

15. Samuel Brown, junior, quoted in A. R. Thompson, 'The use of libraries by the working class in Scotland in the early nineteenth century', *Scottish Historical Review*, Vol. XLII (1963)

16. Simpson, *op. cit.*, p. 22

17. *Ibid*, p. 23

18. Thomas Somerville, *My Own Life and Times* (Edinburgh 1861), p. 347

19. Menzies, *op. cit.*, p. 25

20. *Parliamentary Papers*, 1826, Vol. XVIII, p. 607

21. Quoted (actually slightly misquoted) by Sir John Sinclair, *Analysis of the Statistical Account* (London 1826), II, p. 99

22. W. Ferguson, *Scotland: 1689 to the Present* (Edinburgh 1968), p. 251

23. Quoted in D. J. Withrington, 'The S.P.C.K. and Highland Schools in Mid-Eighteenth Century', *Scottish Historical Review*, Vol. XLI (1962), p. 26

24. M. G. Jones, *The Charity School Movement* (ed. Cambridge 1964), p. 176

25. *Moral Statistics of the Highlands and Islands of Scotland* (Inverness 1826)

26. Lachlan Shaw, *History of the Province*

of Moray (Edinburgh 1775), p. 381

27. John Sinclair, *The Christian Hero of the North* (Edinburgh 1867) pp. 61-2; see also John Mackay, *The Church in the Highlands* (London 1914) pp. 215-52

28. *Moral Statistics of the Highlands and Islands*

29. James Grant, *History of the Burgh Schools of Scotland* (London 1876), Chapter XIII

30. Alexander Law, *Education in Edinburgh in the Eighteenth Century* (London 1965), p. 30

31. *Ibid*, pp. 49-52

32. *Ibid*, p. 52

33. L. J. Saunders, *Scottish Democracy 1815-1840* (Edinburgh 1950) pp. 275-6

34. *New Statistical Account*, III, Selkirkshire, p. 23

35. Bain, *op. cit.*, p. 83

36. Lewis, *op. cit.*, p. 39

37. *Statistical Account*, XII, p. 123

38. Supplementary report from Factory Inquiry Commissioners, *Parliamentary Papers*, 1834, Vol. XX, p. 42

39. Lewis, *op. cit.*, p. 43

40. Sir John Sinclair, *op. cit.*, II, pp. 99-100

41. Law, *ibid*, pp. 75-6

42. *Ibid*, p. 145

43. Quoted in Law, *ibid*, p. 227

44. T. Garnett, *Observations on a Tour through the Highlands* (London 1800) II, pp. 193-202

45. S. J. Curtis, *History of Education in Great Britain* (London 1948), p. 231

46. D. B. Horn, *A Short History of the University of Edinburgh* (Edinburgh 1967), pp. 40, 93

47. Sinclair, *op. cit.*, II, pp. 108-23

Further Reading

The classic account of educational change in the later part of this period is L. J. Saunders, *Scottish Democracy 1815–1840* which cannot be too highly recommended. R. K. Webb, 'Literacy among the Working Classes in Nineteenth Century Scotland', *Scottish Historical Review*, Vol. XXXIII (1954) is good but draws largely on evidence after 1830. See also A. R. Thompson, 'The Use of Libraries by the Working Class in Scotland in the early Nineteenth Century', *Scottish Historical Review*, Vol. XLII (1963).

For schools, especially in the eighteenth century, there is a series of regional studies of uneven merit published by the Scottish Council for Research in Education at London. The best are W. Boyd, *Education in Ayrshire* (1961), A. Bain, *Education in Stirlingshire* (1965), I. J. Simpson, *Education in Aberdeenshire* (1942) ˉnd A. Law, *Education in Edinburgh in the Eighteenth Century* (1965). See also J. M. Beale, 'A History of the Burgh and Parochial Schools of Fife', Edinburgh Ph.D. thesis 1953. No one should overlook D. J. Withrington's important contribution, 'Lists of Schoolmasters teaching Latin, 1690' in *Scottish History Society Miscellany*, Vol. X (1965). Here, as elsewhere, *Parliamentary Papers* are a valuable source. Volume XVIII for 1826 and Volume XLVII for 1837 give returns for individual schools in considerable detail. See also James Grant, *History of the Burgh Schools of Scotland* (London, 1876).

The Scottish S.P.C.K. is discussed in M. G. Jones, *The Charity School Movement* (ed. Cambridge, 1964), and J. Mason, *A History of Scottish Experiments in Rural Education* (London, 1935). See also D. J. Withrington, 'The S.P.C.K. and Highland Schools in Mid-Eighteenth Century', *Scottish Historical Review*, Vol. XLI (1962).

For the universities see especially J. D. Mackie, *The University of Glasgow: a Short History* (Glasgow, 1954); R. S. Rait, *The Universities of Aberdeen* (Aberdeen 1895); D. B. Horn, *A Short History of the University of Edinburgh* (Edinburgh 1967) and R. G. Cant, *The University of St Andrews; a Short History* (Edinburgh 1946).

Finally, several of the contemporary works cited in the text or footnotes give the feel of Scottish opinion and attitudes to their own educational system, none more revealingly than Sir John Sinclair, *Analysis of the Statistical Account* (London 1826).

CHAPTER XIX

1. Basil Willey, *The Eighteenth Century Background* (London 1940), p. 110
2. Richard Pares, *The Historian's Business and other essays* (Oxford 1961), p. 94
3. *An Eighteenth Century Lectureship in Chemistry* (ed. A. Kent, Glasgow 1950), p. 80
4. *Ibid*, p. 84
5. J. G. Dunbar, *The Historic architecture of Scotland* (London 1966), p. 110
6. James Lees-Milne, *The Age of Adam* (London 1947), p. 155
7. A. E. Richardson, *An Introduction to Georgian Architecture* (London 1949), p. 86
8. John Fleming, 'Robert Adam's Castle Style', *Country Life*, Vol. CXLIII, Nos. 3716–7. May 23, 30, 1968

9. David Craig, *Scottish Literature and the Scottish People, 1680–1830* (London 1961), p. 231

10. David Daiches, *The Paradox of Scottish Culture: the Eighteenth Century Experience* (London 1964), p. 21

11. Magnus Maclean, *The Literature of the Highlands* (London 1926), p. 28

12. The quotation is from Kenneth H. Jackson, *Celtic Miscellany* (London 1951), p. 200

13. *Dictionary of National Biography,* XVII (1909), 1026

14. Quoted in David Craig, *op. cit.,* pp. 151–2

15. M. S. Kuypers, *Studies in the Eighteenth Century Background of Hume's Empiricism* (Minneapolis 1930), p. 9

16. Quoted in C. R. Fay, *Adam Smith and the Scotland of his day* (Cambridge 1956), p. 76

17. A. Carlyle, *Autobiography* (Edinburgh 1860), p. 275

Further Reading

The general cultural background is discussed in a work on the philosophy of the enlightenment, Gladys Bryson, *Man and Society: the Scottish Inquiry of the Eighteenth Century* (Princeton 1945), and in Clive and Bailyn, 'England's Cultural Provinces: Scotland and America', *William and Mary Quarterly*, Third Series, Vol. XI, 1954. For the philosophers see also H. Laurie, *Scottish Philosophy in its National Development* (Glasgow 1902); E. C. Mossner, *Life of David Hume* (Edinburgh 1954); W. R. Scott, *Francis Hutcheson* (Cambridge 1900) and *Adam Smith as Student and Professor* (Glasgow 1937); W. C. Lehmann, *John Millar of Glasgow* (Cambridge 1960) and *Adam Ferguson and the Beginning of Modern Sociology* (New York 1930).

There is no single work on Scottish science, but see A. G. Clement and R. H. S. Robertson, *Scotland's Scientific Heritage* (Edinburgh 1961) for some suggestions and notes; for Hutton and his contribution to geology, see E. B. Bailey, *James Hutton, the Founder of Modern Geology* (Amsterdam 1967). The Scottish contribution to medical science is dealt with in J. D. Comrie, *History of Scottish Medicine* (London 1932) and Douglas Guthrie, *The Medical School of Edinburgh* (Edinburgh 1959).

Scottish literature is served by two controversial introductions from very different pens: David Daiches, *The Paradox of Scottish Culture: the Eighteenth Century Experience* (London 1964), and David Craig, *Scottish Literature and the Scottish People* (London 1961). There are, of course, innumerable editions of Burns, the most recent and definitive is *The Poems and Songs of Robert Burns*, ed. J. Kinsley (Oxford 1968). Nor is it hard to find editions of Fergusson or Allan Ramsay. Both have received exhaustive scholarly publication by the Scottish Text Society since 1945. For Gaelic poetry see the volumes of the Scottish Gaelic Text Society and Magnus Maclean, *The Literature of the Highlands* (ed. Glasgow 1925); also J. L. Campbell, *Highland Songs of the Forty-Five* (Edinburgh 1933). Scott and Galt are easily accessible, though some of the works of Scott can only be obtained in cheap editions at second hand. Heron books, however, are republishing the novels. For a recent sympathetic reassessment of Scott, see A. O. J. Cockshut *The Achievement of Walter Scott* (London 1969). James Hogg, *Confessions of a Justified Sinner* was republished as recently as 1959 (London, Evergreen Books).

For Scottish painting, see Stanley Curtiser, *Scottish Art* (London 1949) and two older books: W. D. McKay, *The Scottish School of Painting* (London 1906) and J. L. Caw, *Scottish Painting Past and Present* (London 1908). See also T. Crouther Gordon, *David Allan* (Alva 1951) and P. A. M. Smart, *The Life and Art of Allan Ramsay* (London 1952). For ceramic arts, see J. Arnold Fleming, *Scottish Pottery* (Glasgow 1923) and for metalwork, Ian Finlay, *Scottish Gold and Silver Work* (London 1956).

For music, see H. G. Farmer, *A History of Music in Scotland* (London 1947). Two more recent books are less systematically historical but illustrate the scope of traditional art: Francis Collinson, *The Traditional and National Music of Scotland* (London 1966) and J. F. and T. M. Flett, *Traditional Dancing in Scotland* (London 1964).

Scottish architecture in the eighteenth century is well covered by J. G. Dunbar, *The Historic Architecture of Scotland* (London 1966); John Fleming, *Robert Adam and His Circle* (London 1962); J. Lees-Milne, *The Age of Adam* (London 1947); A. J. Youngson, *The Making of Classical Edinburgh* (Edinburgh 1966) deal well with the great classic architects. The work of the engineers is best described in L. T. C. Rolt, *Thomas Telford* (London 1958); C. T. G. Boucher, *John Rennie* (Oxford 1960) and A. R. B. Haldane, *New Ways Through the Glens* (Edinburgh 1962). Comprehensive surveys of old buildings on a county basis have been begun for the period after 1707 only since 1951; those so far published by the Royal Commission on Ancient and Historical Monuments (Scotland) are the *Inventories* for the City of Edinburgh (1951) and Stirlingshire (1953), Roxburghshire (1956), Selkirkshire (1957) and Peeblesshire (1967). As far as country houses are concerned, the files of *Country Life* provide a remarkably comprehensive coverage of scholarly articles.

MEDIEVAL SCOTLAND

+ Main Monastic Houses
● Main Burghs

10 0 10 20 30 40 50 60
MILES

ELGIN
PLUSCARDEN
BEAULY
INVERNESS
DEER
Highland Line
ABERDEEN
MONTROSE
COUPAR
ARBROATH
SCONE
DUNDEE
PERTH
BALMERINO
St ANDREWS
CAMBUSKENNETH
STIRLING
DUNFERMLINE
INCHCOLM
HOLYROOD
DUMBARTON
HADDINGTON
GLASGOW
LINLITHGOW
EDINBURGH
COLDINGHAM
PAISLEY
NEWBATTLE
BERWICK
DRYBURGH
KELSO
MELROSE
ROXBURGH
JEDBURGH
IONA
AYR
DUMFRIES
SWEETHEART
KIRCUDBRIGHT
GLENLUCE
DUNDRENNAN

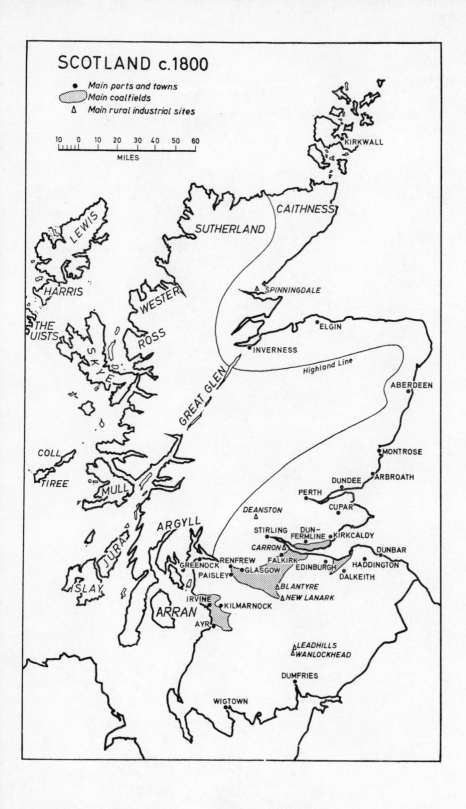

SCOTLAND c.1800

- Main ports and towns
- Main coalfields
- △ Main rural industrial sites

10 0 10 20 30 40 50 60
MILES

KIRKWALL

CAITHNESS

SUTHERLAND

LEWIS

HARRIS

WESTER

THE
UISTS

ROSS

SKYE

△ SPINNINGDALE

ELGIN

INVERNESS

Highland Line

GREAT GLEN

ABERDEEN

COLL

TIREE

MULL

ARGYLL

MONTROSE

DUNDEE
ARBROATH

PERTH

CUPAR

DEANSTON
△

JURA

STIRLING DUN-
FERMLINE KIRKCALDY

CARRON △

ISLAY

GREENOCK

RENFREW FALKIRK
PAISLEY GLASGOW

DUNBAR

EDINBURGH HADDINGTON

DALKEITH

△BLANTYRE
△NEW LANARK

ARRAN

IRVINE

KILMARNOCK

AYR

△LEADHILLS
△WANLOCKHEAD

DUMFRIES

WIGTOWN

INDEXES

INDEXES

Index of Persons

Index of Places and Topics